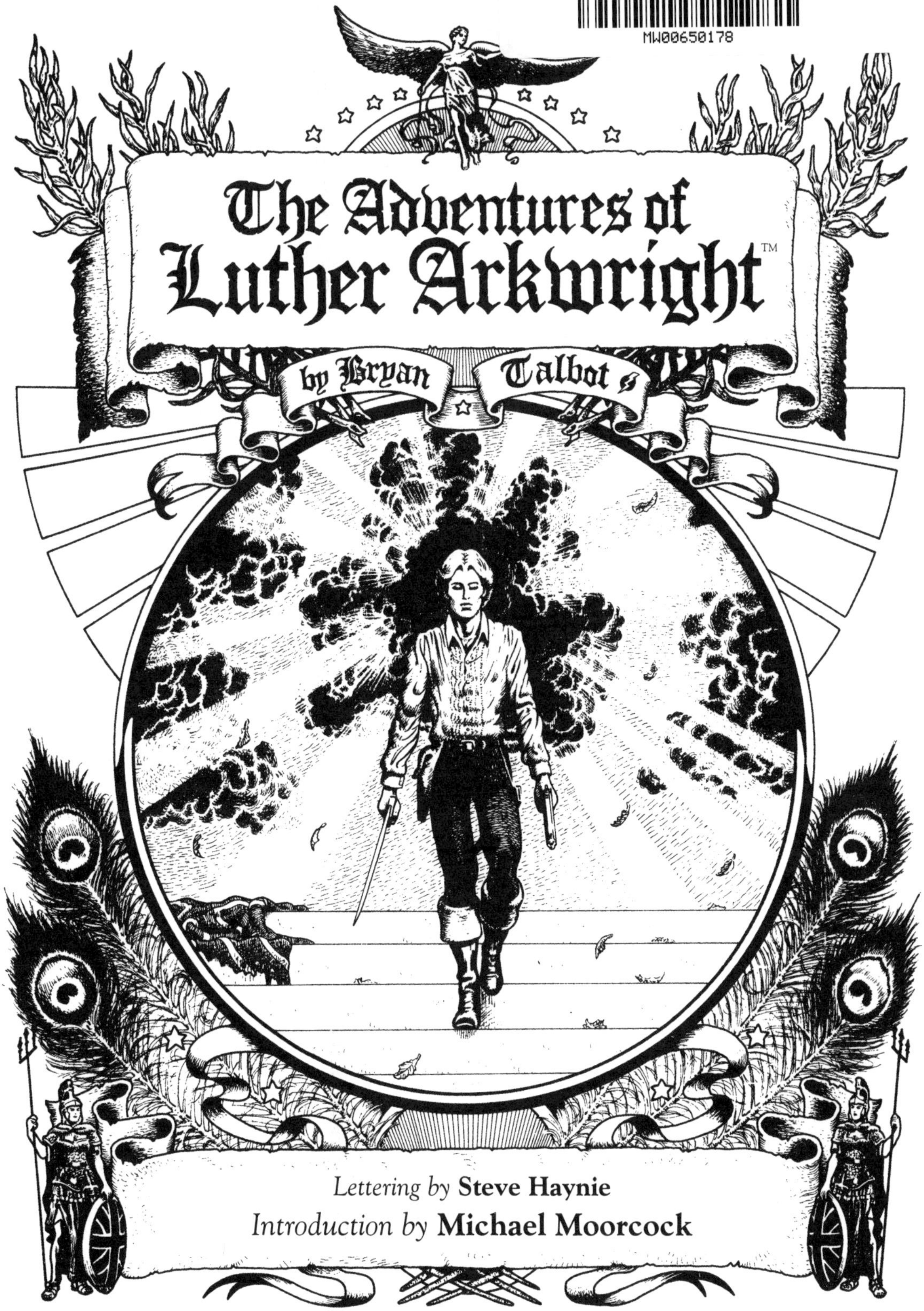
The Adventures of Luther Arkwright™
by Bryan Talbot
Lettering by Steve Haynie
Introduction by Michael Moorcock

There's something solid and Northern English about a name like Arkwright.

It suggests a man with his feet on the ground, prepared to look facts in the face and to do something about them if he has to. Luther, on the other hand, suggests a foreign quality, even an exotic, slightly visionary tinge which would once have been a little disturbing to the average inhabitant of the Lancashire mill towns.

Nowadays, of course, those old weaving towns, which gave the Northern industrial landscape its character, no longer have the same stereotypical image. Be-shawled and be-clogged, shuffling at dawn over the hard cobbles to the factory gates, the workers were the epitome of ground-down wage-slaves. They took the brunt of the "Hungry Thirties."

Nowadays, when they have jobs at all, the workers are much more exotic. They may well still be the epitome of wage slavery, but they wear saris and turbans, and many speak Bengali as their first language. Even Mr. Gradgrind the mill owner is probably now called Mrs. Patel. The average inhabitant of the mill towns is as likely to worship at a mosque or a Hindu temple and still think of the Indian sub-continent as the motherland. The British Empire, in miniature, came home. Britain went from being the hub of the largest and most widespread imperium the world had ever known to a small, crowded nation that had become, almost overnight, multi-ethnic. It was a bit of a shock to the average native.

The conscious and often principled dismantling of the Empire which happened rapidly after 1946, with the coming to Parliament of the first great socialist government, was accompanied by a shortage of manpower caused by the Second World War. Citizens of the British Commonwealth, mostly from the West and East Indies, were encouraged to emigrate to the United Kingdom to fill the thousands of jobs — most of them low-paid — which were urgently available.

After South Africa left the Commonwealth over the issue of apartheid, many South Africans also arrived, together with Nigerians and Ghanians. Frequently idealistic about the "mother country," they found prejudice, wretched exploitation, poverty, and a climate which, if you weren't born to it, can suck the soul from your eyes.

The absorption of these new cultures into the host culture was not as dramatic as some predicted (Enoch Powell, the "intellectual fascist" of the Tory Party warned that racial conflict would bring "rivers of blood" to Britain) and from the beginning there were people dedicated to the cause of social justice who, myself amongst them, eventually saw some of their idealism formalised in the Race Relations Act which made active prejudice, racial slurs and the like, illegal.

Alone, no such act ever changes society, and it did nothing to convince the skinheads and crypto-Nazis, but it does set the standard to which that society aspires. It says that the active expression of racial prejudice is unacceptable in a civilised world. Framed when memories of the Goebbels years were much fresher, the act certainly had respect for words and pictures. It admitted that they could kill.

In England, it did not stop the sentiently challenged from abusing and attacking Pakistani women and children or beating up old black men or kicking a boy to death, but it did give the victims some means of restitution, and it told them that they had specific recourse to the law. Of course it didn't stop racist policemen ignoring complaints (or indeed compounding them!), it didn't stop real life, with all its shades and variations, happening. It didn't stop many people being humiliated, insulted, and attacked. But it did set a standard. A goal.

Britain needed goals. She needed, in fact, a whole new future. As she tried to re-invent herself from her self-image as the burdened mother of a thousand lands to become the European nation she had never accepted she was, many other social upheavals occurred. The imperial ghosts continued to haunt her. The problem of Ireland, whose Protestant population wished to remain within the United Kingdom and whose Catholics did not, was acerbated, originally by "Reverend" Paisley, the Unionist adventurer. The Falklands folly, which need never have been resolved in violence and cheap flag-waving, seemed to say it all. If ever two politicians were deeply grateful for the chance to go to war and make cheap capital of human life, Margaret Thatcher and George Bush

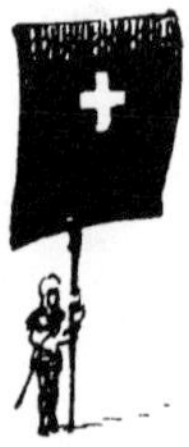

were. Now, one goes raving mad and travels about America pretending to be the Queen, while the other looks enviously at his predecessor who stands strong chance, in the trials of history, of getting off on medical grounds. But one thing's certain, they'll always have the blood of the dead on their hands. The ambitions of these greedy brutes permeates the pages of Luther Arkwright. His quests are quests for alternatives, for a better way.

In those golden years, which were not really an illusion, before the rich organised their attack on us, general prosperity increased significantly and, for a while, so did civic power (the poor were getting richer and the rich were not quite so rich as they had been). 1960s Britain was "swinging" as far as the international community was concerned, and the extraordinary vital mix of cultures had made the country probably the most creatively productive in the world. Ireland, as well as African America and Lancashire, gave us The Beatles and all the other extraordinarily talented musicians who changed the aspirations and capacities of popular music forever. All the arts thrived.

The spread of wealth resulted in a consequent spread of social justice. Macmillan's Tory party neither dared to nor cared to dismantle the social programmes introduced by their predecessors, and when Labour was re-elected in the 1960s, further enlightened legislation gave us for a while probably the best universally available health and education systems, free recourse to the legal system, and much else. Although there was still a lot to fix, and we were beginning to understand the drawbacks of any orthodoxy, liberal or otherwise, it looked like we were getting to Utopia in the fast lane. We began to discuss what we were all going to do with so much leisure and wealth and equity . . .

Thatcher and Reagan represented very different interests to ours. They were in some ways the figureheads, following the direction of Big Business, who offered rhetorical legitimacy for an extraordinary grab-back of power by private capital from the public. They'd been planning it for years. I used to hear them, when I worked in Fleet Street in the early 1960s, talking about "expanding into the public sector." The old edicts of our common law — that that which concerns all, shall be determined by all — were ignored, even mocked. This powerful minority, which owned most of everything already, had no respect for us. The public institutions and utilities, designed to create a fairer society, were their chief targets. They corrupted the rhetoric of public debate, they claimed publicly owned services didn't "work" — i.e. they provided a service, not a profit.

Representing the interests of big business and preaching a free-market philosophy of world deregulation even crazier than the communism it sought to defeat — a universal panacea somehow based on total internal competition which made a nightmare of most ordinary lives — they gave us a set of old-fashioned shoddy "solutions" which got their friends and clients very rich indeed and the rest of us quite a bit poorer. They made virtues of greed and disharmony. The lie became a standard instrument of social intercourse, in government, in business, and, eventually, throughout society. It also inevitably introduced uncertainties and miseries into our world which soon translated into violence and cynicism, eroded the quality of life of millions, and continues to destroy it to this day. It was quite a radical change — more so in Britain, perhaps, than in America — and it was quite a lot for the average thinking person to cope with.

In the face of all this rapidly gained experience and change, just on the cusp of the radical shift when we stopped being a community of citizens and instead were encouraged to become a loose confederation of independent consumers, creative artists were having a hard time.

The British cultural explosion which was first exemplified by the phenomenal success of The Beatles and other rock bands, as well as movies, comics, and literature, occurred as a result of all these various experiences and social tensions. Faced with turning their experience and concerns into concrete work, many talented creative people looked to the conventional forms — the legitimate, respectable forms — and found them incapable of describing these daily realities. Indeed, if you tried to use them, they tended to distort what you needed to say. I had earned the large part of my living writing commercial comics in the '50s and early '60s, and the techniques I had learned were very useful to me when I came to start writing the Jerry Cornelius stories, my first real attempt to match my writing to my observations and experience of my own world — the rapidly changing world of the '60s, the early years of the computer age. I was trying to describe, if you like, a "post-modern" as well as a post-war world, using techniques which somehow achieved that better than more orthodox writing. Most science fiction and popular music of the time was crap, but it did offer us very useful methods and images.

Much of the talent which in an earlier world would have gone into conventional forms was now seeking better ways of expressing itself. The first "pop" artists — Paolozzi and Hamilton in England, Kitai, Warhol, and Co. in the U.S. — drew on comics and science fiction for their images and for a while gave a certain intellectual respectability to those genres. But in a way, this was still the response of "high" artists desperate for subject matter, something to rejuvenate the existing forms. The people who in my view were making genuine innovations were doing it mostly unrecognised and unheralded by the establishment (almost a credential) and they were doing it within the culture.

Out of this general movement, which gave us a vast range of different expressions, came *New Worlds*, the magazine I edited, together with the so-called science-fiction New Wave when people like Ballard, Ellison, and Sladek started throwing some effective literary hand grenades about. In England this movement coincided and married with the experimental rock music movement as well as movements in poetry, painting, and film-making.

From this same vibrant mix surfaced the new comics writers and artists like Alan Moore, Neil Gaiman, and Bryan Talbot

who were inspired by the dynamics of American comics exemplified by the likes of Jack Kirby and Stan Lee, by earlier artists like Mac Raboy and Bob Kane, by the high standards of people like Frank Hampson, Don Lawrence, and the Embleton brothers, by the products of the infamous and legendary Mick Anglo studio (which I had worked with), and by the new science fiction. They had the same impatience with genre as the 'New Wave' science-fiction writers. They wanted the form to do more. They wanted it to say something. They wanted it to express their experience.

Amongst all this fine and impatient talent, Bryan Talbot soon began to stand out. By the late 1970s he had established a reputation as an original storyteller — one of a handful of graphic artists (Moebius, Chaykin, and Simonson are others) who can tell a tale as well as they can draw one. He was marked by the ambition of his stories, as well as their skill. Here was something far more original and idiosyncratic than anyone had attempted before — essentially a way of describing not only what was happening to England but also to the larger world, whose problems the U.K. frequently mirrored. An alternative history of modern times. And, of course, because Talbot was using a popular form to do this, it was also a very good, romantic, inventive, fast-paced yarn.

The Pop artists who had borrowed so much from comics and science fiction a few years earlier were still essentially taking surface elements, isolating them, and introducing them into what was often highly academic art (Warhol is a good example) in some ways similar to the decadent academic art of 19th century France, where ideas of aesthetics and refinements of those aesthetics become more important and often more interesting than the subject.

Popular artists, on the other hand, are not allowed such luxuries. Substance, story, and astonishment is what the audience demands. It can't be talked into buying what it doesn't like. Your living doesn't depend on convincing an establishment that you are worth millions at auction. It depends on entertaining an audience — and keeping it entertained. The popular artist is called upon to master fundamental techniques which the Pop artist might imitate but rarely understand (in terms of their real narrative function, for instance). Narrative is very important in comics. In fact, dynamics of all kinds have to be considered as well as aesthetics. The superb black-and-white pages of Dudley Watkins, for instance, which are masterpieces of counterbalance and clever, unostentatious, internal design, almost certainly borrowing from Beardsley and the Robinsons, inspired many British artists, as did the classically good drawing and meticulous colour work of Hampson, Lawrence, and Ron and Gerry Embleton (all of whom I was privileged to work with). In a graphic illustrator, aesthetics are the hidden bones, sinew, and life-stuff of the drawing, rarely advertised and never the subject. What is more, a kind of social consciousness frequently prevails in the work of the ambitious popular artist, perhaps in the tradition of Gilray and Hogarth, whose very directness of approach can make a very effective attack on the status quo and its evils.

Where this goes wrong is when the graphic artists become successful and self-indulgent, demanding that the public enjoy their skills rather than the story. We have all seen the unfortunate results. Other writer/artists have the good instincts and sense to make greater self-demands and teach themselves new techniques which rise to that ambition, so they are always trying — always straining for something extra — and it is this which gives their work at least part of its vitality. This is what is great about Talbot, and it explains his steadily growing reputation. He clearly follows the Stephen King maxim that if you have the good fortune to be successful at something, it is your duty to try to get better and widen your ambition, to improve the climate for everyone.

I think Luther Arkwright — a kind of alternate history of the British Empire and its ongoing effects — improves all the time. He remains one of my own personal favourites and one of the best examples of what a talented writer/artist can do with a form. I believe that the reason the story remains so fresh and interesting is because under all the glorious invention and wild adventure, glamorous characters and exotic machinery, Talbot deals

in fundamental realities and makes stern self-demands.

He is interested in reality. He is curious about reality. He isn't, thank God, afraid of reality. His dialogue with the real world continues. His attempts to frame and communicate his real experience become increasingly complex and sophisticated. Certain proof of this came with the publication of *The Tale of One Bad Rat*, an admirably original use of the medium and one of the most coherent graphic novels ever published, which demonstrated not only how far Talbot had come from his early successes, but how far the genre itself could be taken.

There is nothing light or academic about the subject Talbot is prepared to tackle! His taste for reality is as strong as his talent for fantasy. He comes from an area of England which, while often wild and beautiful, has a longer history of industrial exploitation and mass poverty than of widespread wealth, and he can see the unpleasant results of the loony Right's appalling, self-serving, financial and social policies. But he is neither pessimistic nor especially cynical. His visionary instincts tell him of a better world, perhaps a slightly more exotic world, which we might even achieve one day. Rather as Luther Arkwright's name suggests to me — his Northern feet are firmly on the ground, but his visionary head is up there peering around, reporting from the clouds.

And what great reports they are! I'm looking forward to the next Luther Arkwright. It gets better all the time. And so does Bryan Talbot.

Enjoy this wonderful story however you choose. There are plenty of levels you can experience it on. I know you'll get at least as much out of it as I do. If you're reading it for the first time, I envy you!

Michael Moorcock
Port Sabatini, Texas
January 1997

“Myth may best be described as the gossamer cloak of folk memory overlaying the bare bones of pre-history. In attempting to understand it, consideration should be given to the possibility that the primitive narrator in telling these stories was not guilty of deliberate misrepresentation but rather that owing to his inability to perceive the relationship between cause and effect, or to distinguish between fact and prejudice, we are presented in them with a series of glimpses of history as seen through a distorting lens.

“The archaeologist must diligently strive by logical means to sift the evidence, pierce the veil, and thus approach the truth.”

J.R. Montpellier
Collected Essays, 1897

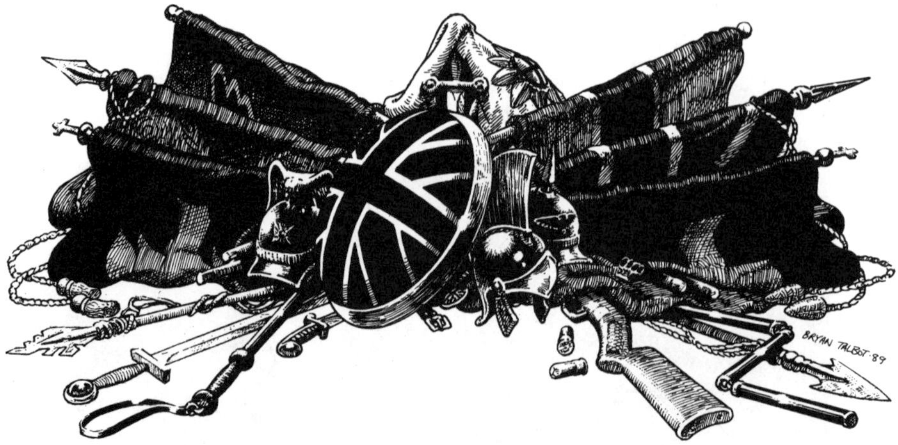
BRYAN TALBOT '89

The Adventures of LUTHER ARKWRIGHT

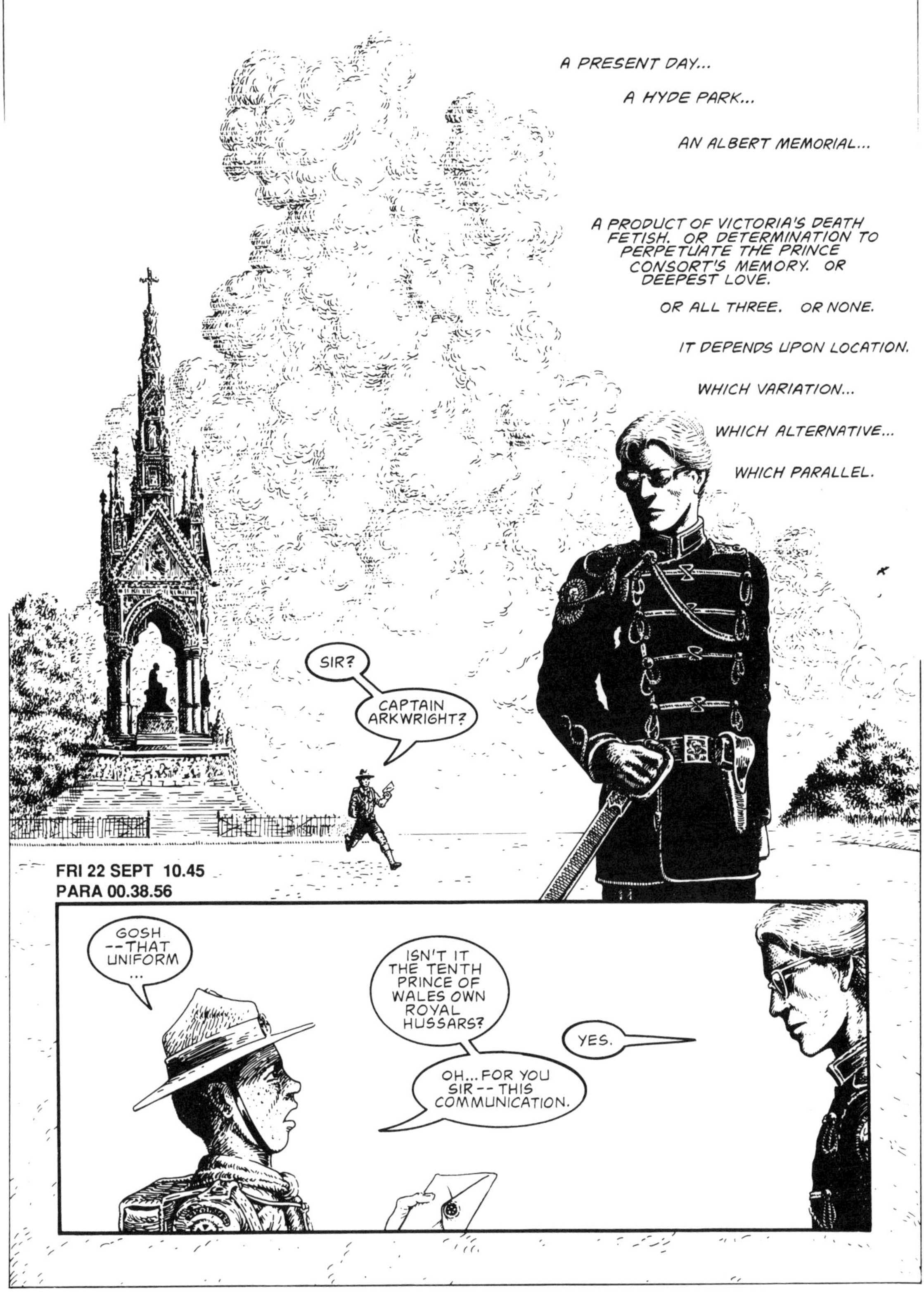
A PRESENT DAY...
A HYDE PARK...
AN ALBERT MEMORIAL...
A PRODUCT OF VICTORIA'S DEATH FETISH. OR DETERMINATION TO PERPETUATE THE PRINCE CONSORT'S MEMORY. OR DEEPEST LOVE.
OR ALL THREE. OR NONE.
IT DEPENDS UPON LOCATION.
WHICH VARIATION...
WHICH ALTERNATIVE...
WHICH PARALLEL.
SIR?
CAPTAIN ARKWRIGHT?
FRI 22 SEPT 10.45
PARA 00.38.56
GOSH --THAT UNIFORM ...
ISN'T IT THE TENTH PRINCE OF WALES OWN ROYAL HUSSARS?
YES.
OH...FOR YOU SIR--THIS COMMUNICATION.

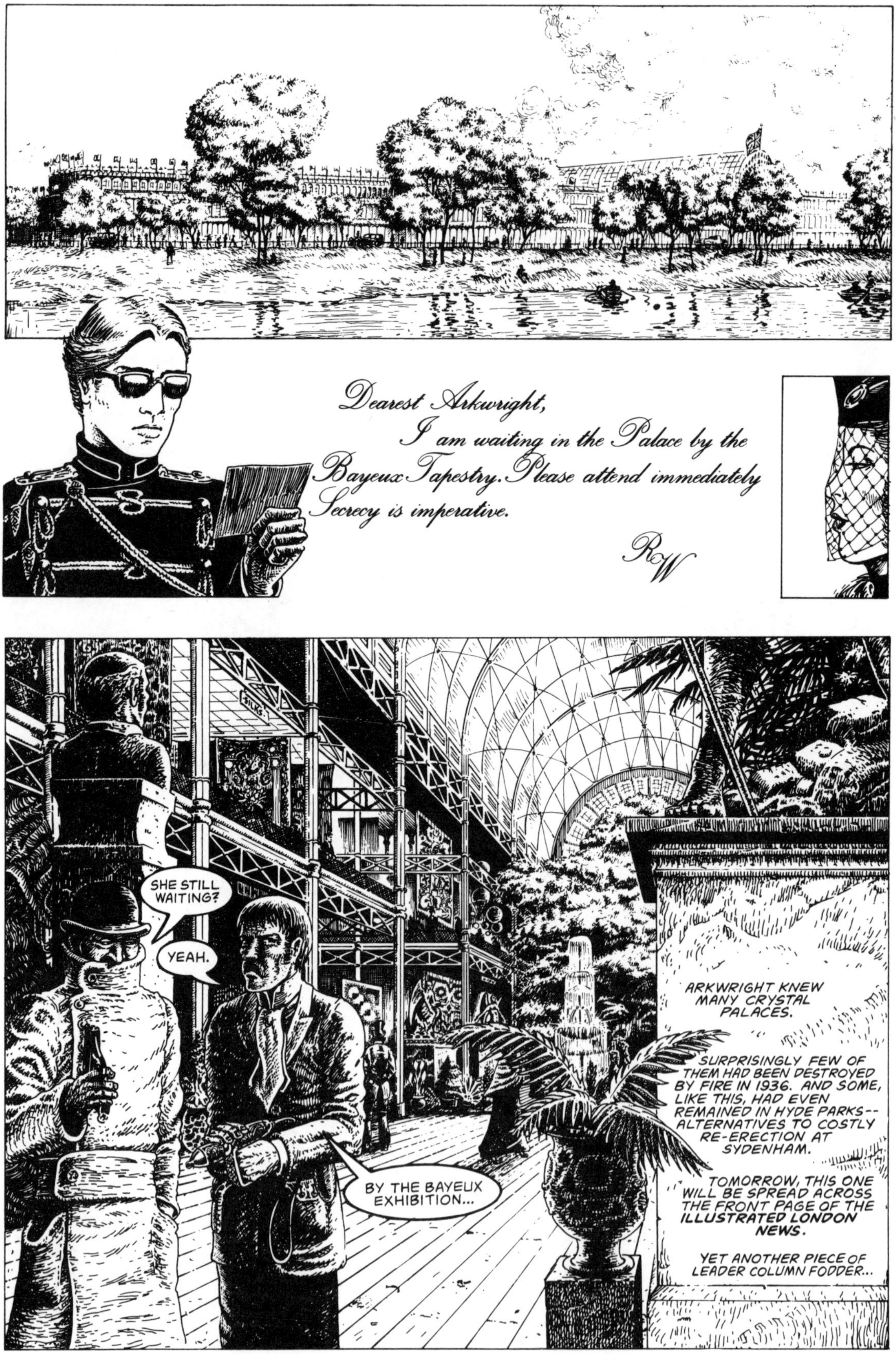
Dearest Arkwright,
I am waiting in the Palace by the Bayeux Tapestry. Please attend immediately
Secrecy is imperative.
RW
SILKS
SHE STILL WAITING?
YEAH.
BY THE BAYEUX EXHIBITION...
ARKWRIGHT KNEW MANY CRYSTAL PALACES.
SURPRISINGLY FEW OF THEM HAD BEEN DESTROYED BY FIRE IN 1936. AND SOME, LIKE THIS, HAD EVEN REMAINED IN HYDE PARKS-- ALTERNATIVES TO COSTLY RE-ERECTION AT SYDENHAM.
TOMORROW, THIS ONE WILL BE SPREAD ACROSS THE FRONT PAGE OF THE ILLUSTRATED LONDON NEWS.
YET ANOTHER PIECE OF LEADER COLUMN FODDER...

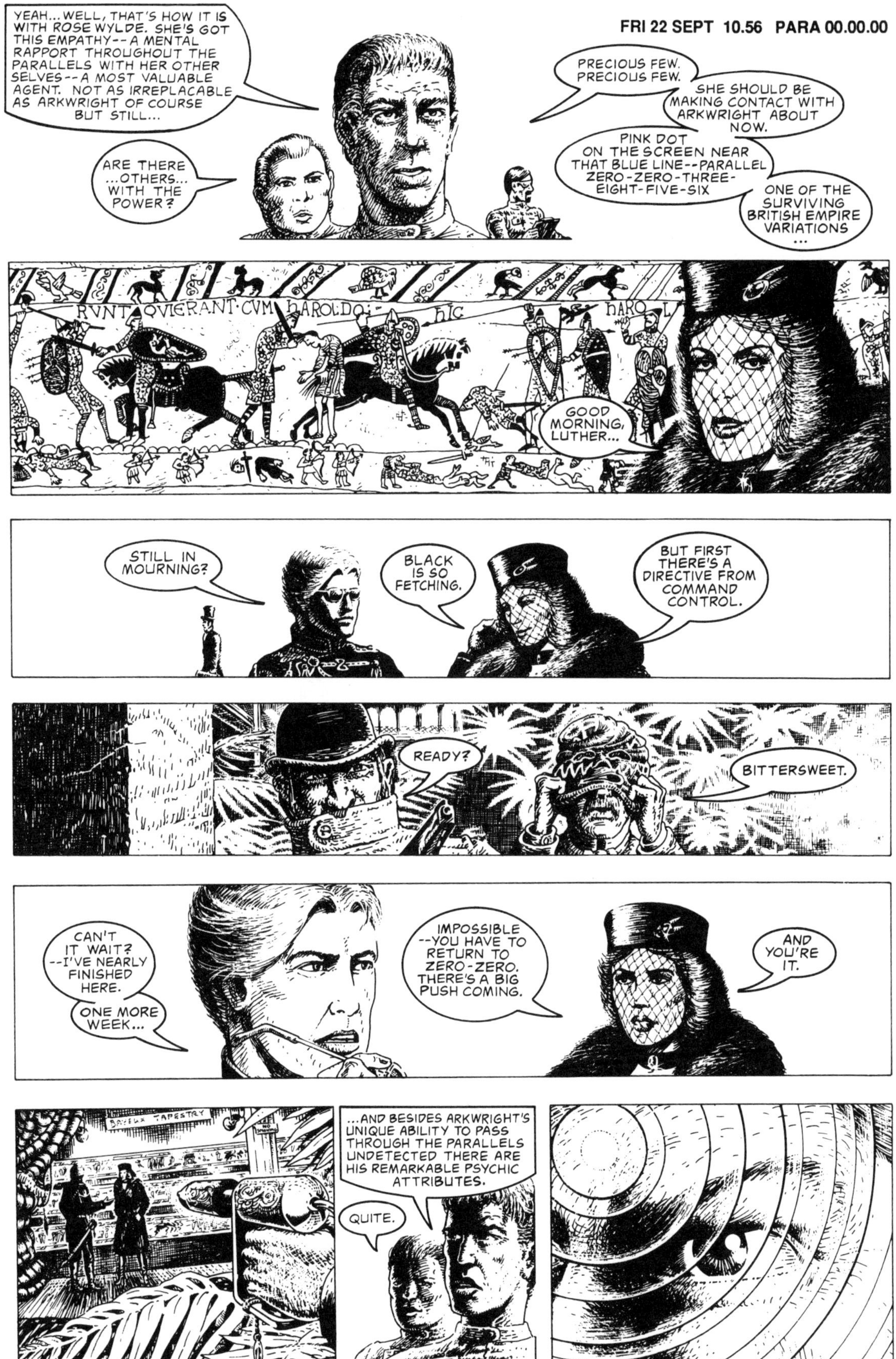
FRI 22 SEPT 10.56 PARA 00.00.00
YEAH... WELL, THAT'S HOW IT IS WITH ROSE WYLDE. SHE'S GOT THIS EMPATHY--A MENTAL RAPPORT THROUGHOUT THE PARALLELS WITH HER OTHER SELVES--A MOST VALUABLE AGENT. NOT AS IRREPLACABLE AS ARKWRIGHT OF COURSE BUT STILL...
ARE THERE ...OTHERS... WITH THE POWER?
PRECIOUS FEW. PRECIOUS FEW.
SHE SHOULD BE MAKING CONTACT WITH ARKWRIGHT ABOUT NOW.
PINK DOT ON THE SCREEN NEAR THAT BLUE LINE--PARALLEL ZERO-ZERO-THREE-EIGHT-FIVE-SIX
ONE OF THE SURVIVING BRITISH EMPIRE VARIATIONS ...
RVNT QVIERANT·CVM HAROLDO: HIC HARO L
GOOD MORNING, LUTHER...
STILL IN MOURNING?
BLACK IS SO FETCHING.
BUT FIRST THERE'S A DIRECTIVE FROM COMMAND CONTROL.
READY?
BITTERSWEET.
CAN'T IT WAIT? --I'VE NEARLY FINISHED HERE.
ONE MORE WEEK...
IMPOSSIBLE --YOU HAVE TO RETURN TO ZERO-ZERO. THERE'S A BIG PUSH COMING.
AND YOU'RE IT.
...AND BESIDES ARKWRIGHT'S UNIQUE ABILITY TO PASS THROUGH THE PARALLELS UNDETECTED THERE ARE HIS REMARKABLE PSYCHIC ATTRIBUTES.
QUITE.
C/U; THOMPSON 'SPITFIRE' Mk II NAPALM PISTOL

TUNIC ALIGHT: SHUT DOWN PAIN: HOW MANY ASSASSINS?: TWO DISRUPTOR AGENTS: RECOMMENCING ATTACK: LOCK ON: FOCUS...

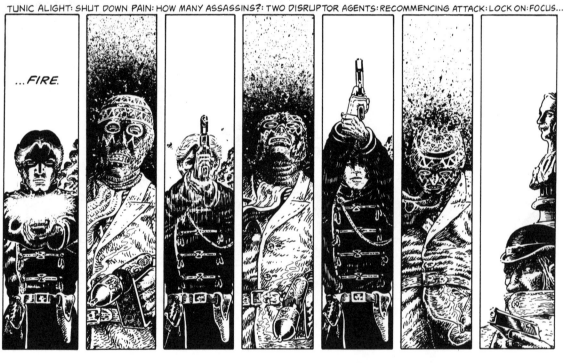

...*FIRE.*

"...AND POLICE HAD TO BE CALLED IN TO FORCIBLY REMOVE THE SUFFRAGATES FROM THE COMMONS. FIREMEN HAVE STILL BEEN UNABLE TO CONTROL THE BLAZE AT THE CRYSTAL PALACE. TEN PEOPLE WERE KILLED AND THIRTY-FOUR INJURED THIS MORNING AS FLAMES ENGULFED THE EXHIBITION CENTRE. THE NIHILIST REVOLUTIONARIES WHO STARTED THE FIRE WERE SHOT BY CAPTAIN LUTHER ARKWRIGHT, V.C. AND BAR, WHO IS MISSING--PRESUMED KILLED IN THE INFERNO... INFORMATION RELEASED BY THE FOREIGN OFFICE THIS AFTERNOON SUGGESTS CAPTAIN ARKWRIGHT WAS INVOLVED IN THE COMMONWEALTH INTELLIGENCE AGENCY..."

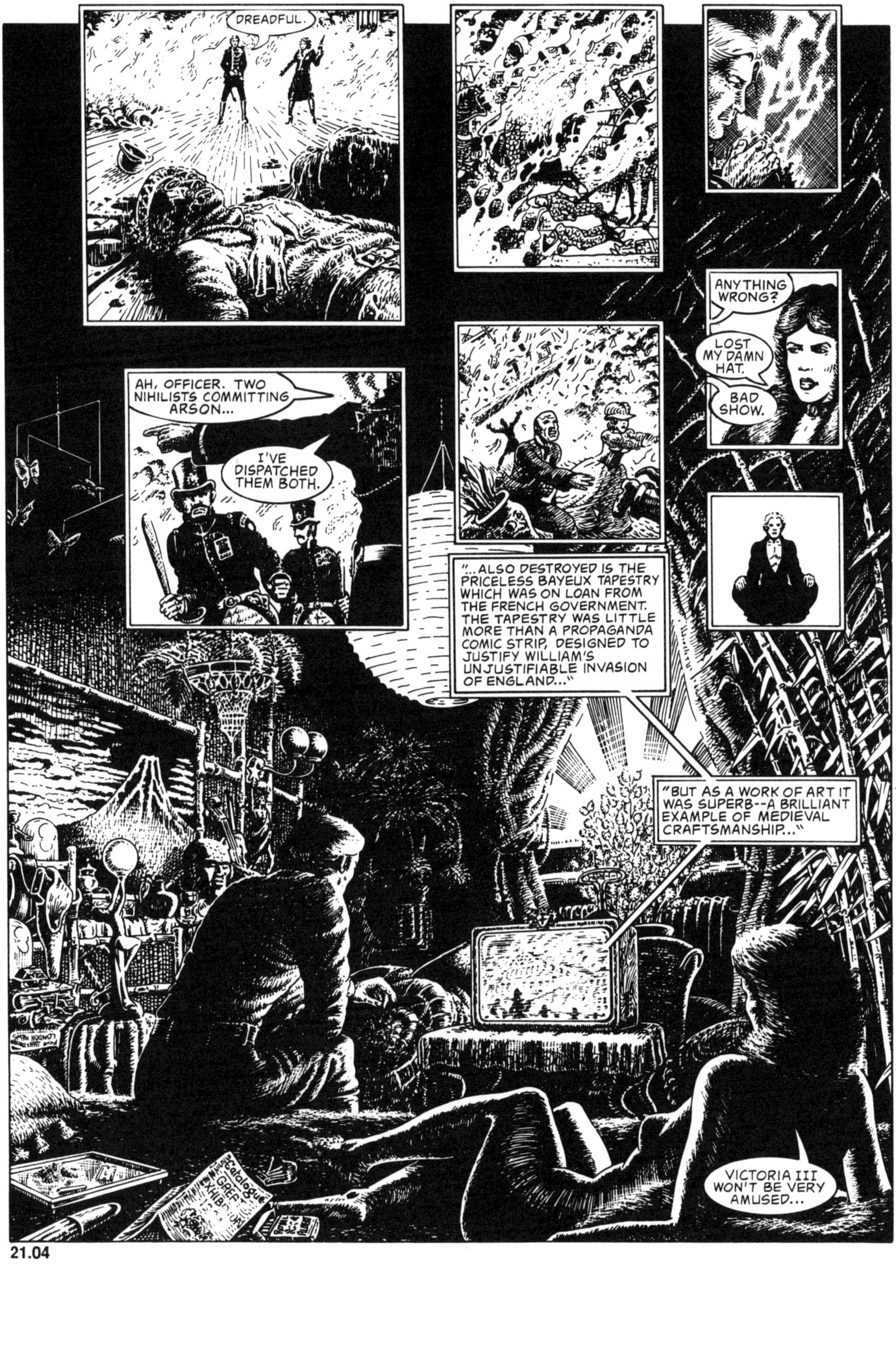

DREADFUL.
ANYTHING WRONG?
LOST MY DAMN HAT.
BAD SHOW.
AH, OFFICER. TWO NIHILISTS COMMITTING ARSON...
I'VE DISPATCHED THEM BOTH.
"...ALSO DESTROYED IS THE PRICELESS BAYEUX TAPESTRY WHICH WAS ON LOAN FROM THE FRENCH GOVERNMENT. THE TAPESTRY WAS LITTLE MORE THAN A PROPAGANDA COMIC STRIP, DESIGNED TO JUSTIFY WILLIAM'S UNJUSTIFIABLE INVASION OF ENGLAND..."
"BUT AS A WORK OF ART IT WAS SUPERB--A BRILLIANT EXAMPLE OF MEDIEVAL CRAFTSMANSHIP..."
VICTORIA III WON'T BE VERY AMUSED...

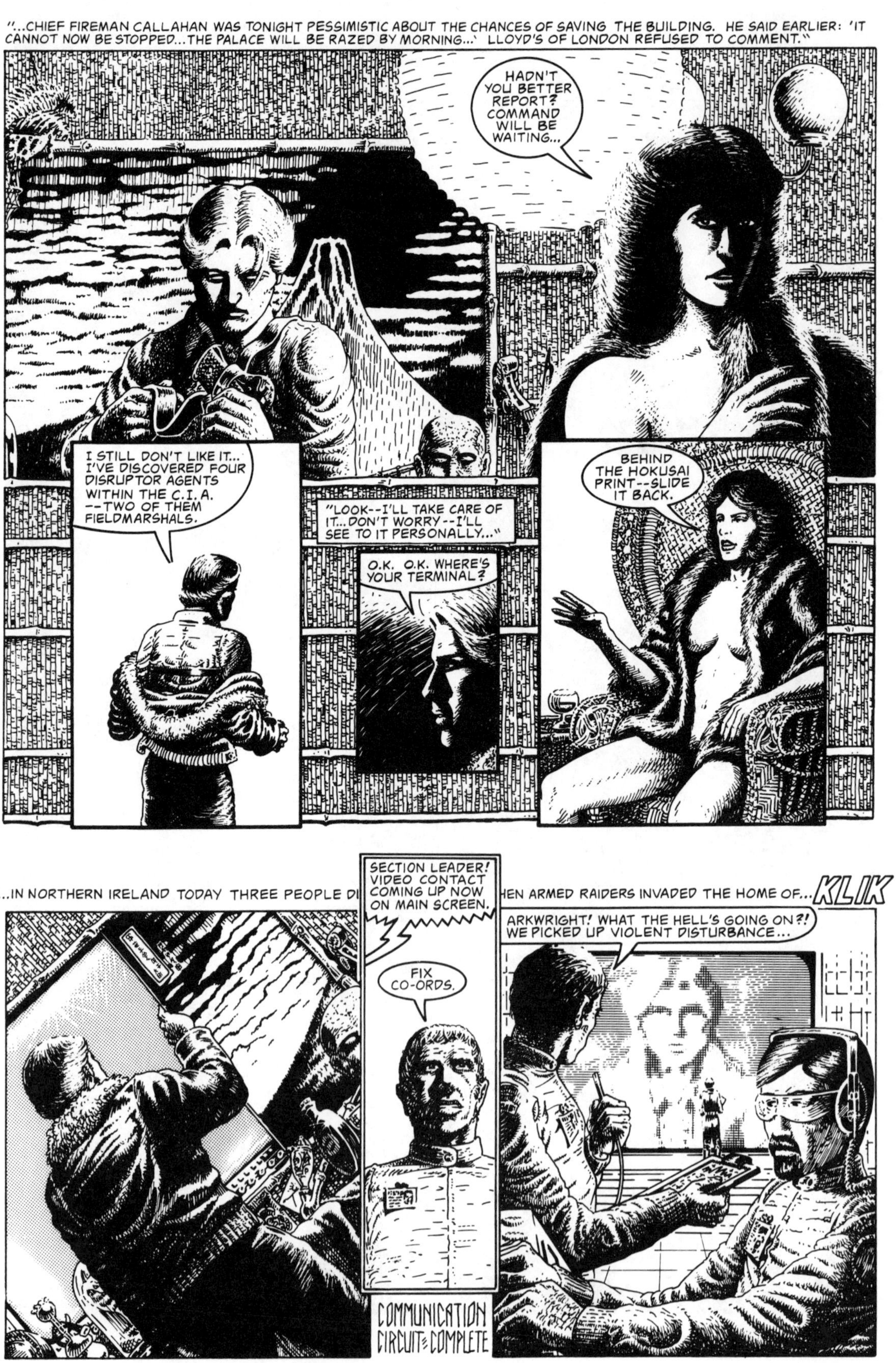
"...CHIEF FIREMAN CALLAHAN WAS TONIGHT PESSIMISTIC ABOUT THE CHANCES OF SAVING THE BUILDING. HE SAID EARLIER: 'IT CANNOT NOW BE STOPPED... THE PALACE WILL BE RAZED BY MORNING...' LLOYD'S OF LONDON REFUSED TO COMMENT."
HADN'T YOU BETTER REPORT? COMMAND WILL BE WAITING...
I STILL DON'T LIKE IT... I'VE DISCOVERED FOUR DISRUPTOR AGENTS WITHIN THE C.I.A. --TWO OF THEM FIELDMARSHALS.
"LOOK--I'LL TAKE CARE OF IT...DON'T WORRY--I'LL SEE TO IT PERSONALLY..."
O.K. O.K. WHERE'S YOUR TERMINAL?
BEHIND THE HOKUSAI PRINT--SLIDE IT BACK.
"...IN NORTHERN IRELAND TODAY THREE PEOPLE DI
HEN ARMED RAIDERS INVADED THE HOME OF...
KLIK
SECTION LEADER! VIDEO CONTACT COMING UP NOW ON MAIN SCREEN.
FIX CO-ORDS.
ARKWRIGHT! WHAT THE HELL'S GOING ON?! WE PICKED UP VIOLENT DISTURBANCE...
COMMUNICATION CIRCUIT COMPLETE

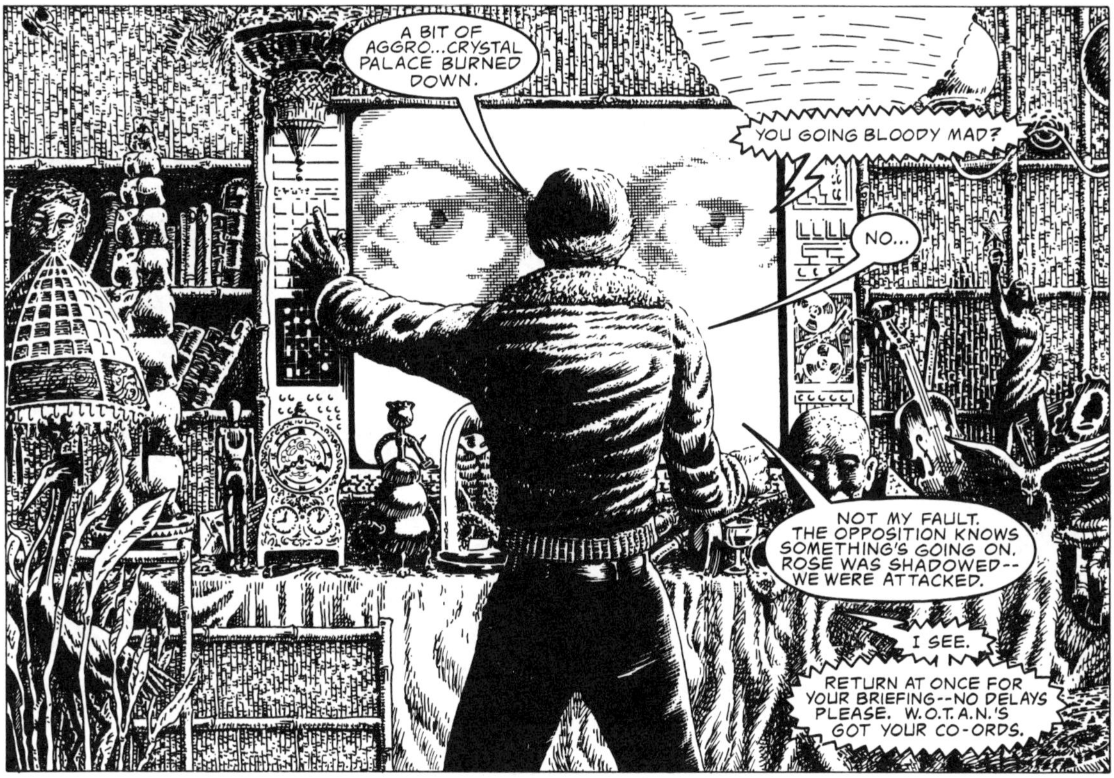
A BIT OF AGGRO...CRYSTAL PALACE BURNED DOWN.
YOU GOING BLOODY MAD?
NO...
NOT MY FAULT. THE OPPOSITION KNOWS SOMETHING'S GOING ON. ROSE WAS SHADOWED-- WE WERE ATTACKED.
I SEE.
RETURN AT ONCE FOR YOUR BRIEFING--NO DELAYS PLEASE. W.O.T.A.N.'S GOT YOUR CO-ORDS.

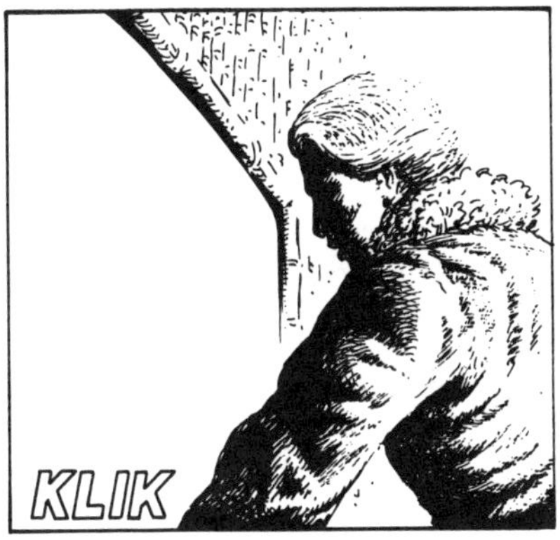
KLIK

"MUST I RETURN IMMEDIATELY?" "NOW."

A SUDDEN REALIZATION: THEY'VE ACTIVATED THE FIRE OPAL! FLASHBACK TO 1913: THE DISCOVERY OF THE FIREFROST CODEX... THEN A DUEL... 1981 AND OCTOBRIANA IN THE SHADE OF THE SPHINX ...TEN MINUTES AGO...TANTRIC LOVEMAKING ...HOT ON THE FURS... FUTURE GLIMPSE OF SELF...FACE UP...BLEEDING...DEAD...ROSE IS TALKING...

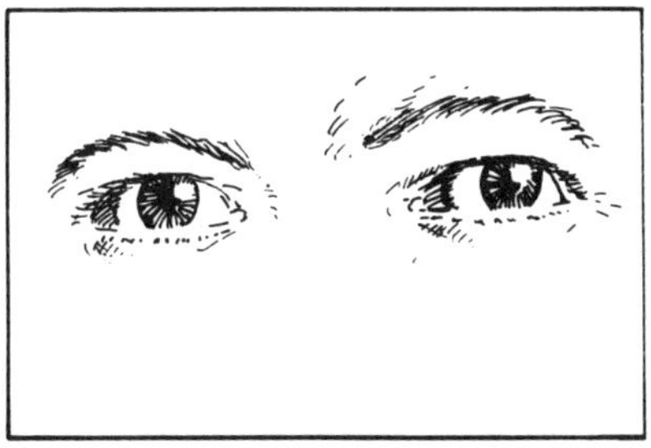

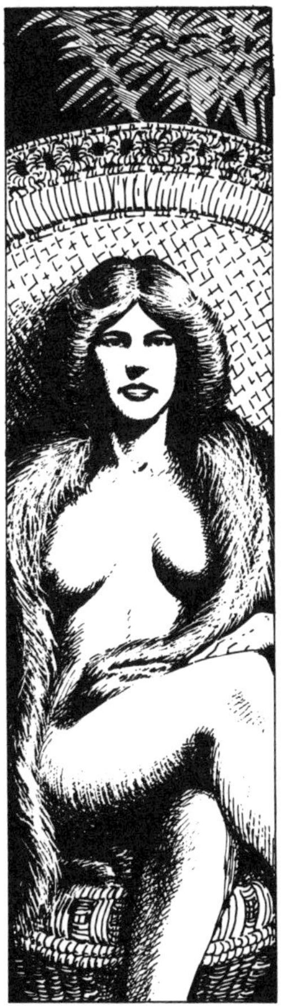

"DESTINY CALLS, LUTHER. NEVER MIND. YOU'LL SEE ONE OF ME SOON. TAKE CARE..."

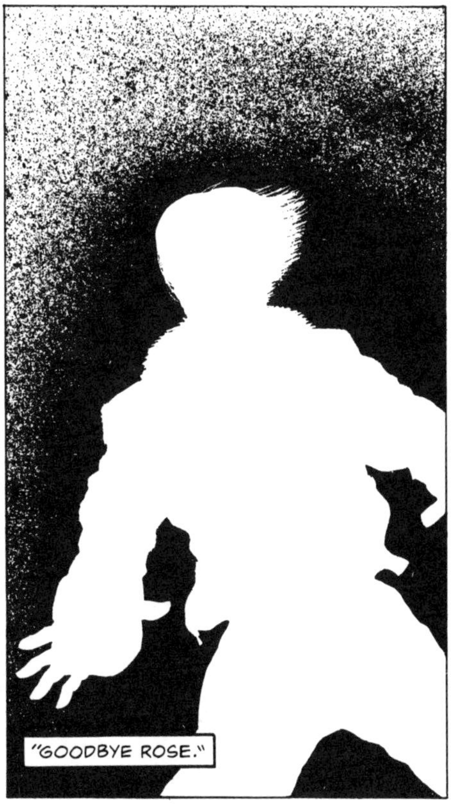
"GOODBYE ROSE."

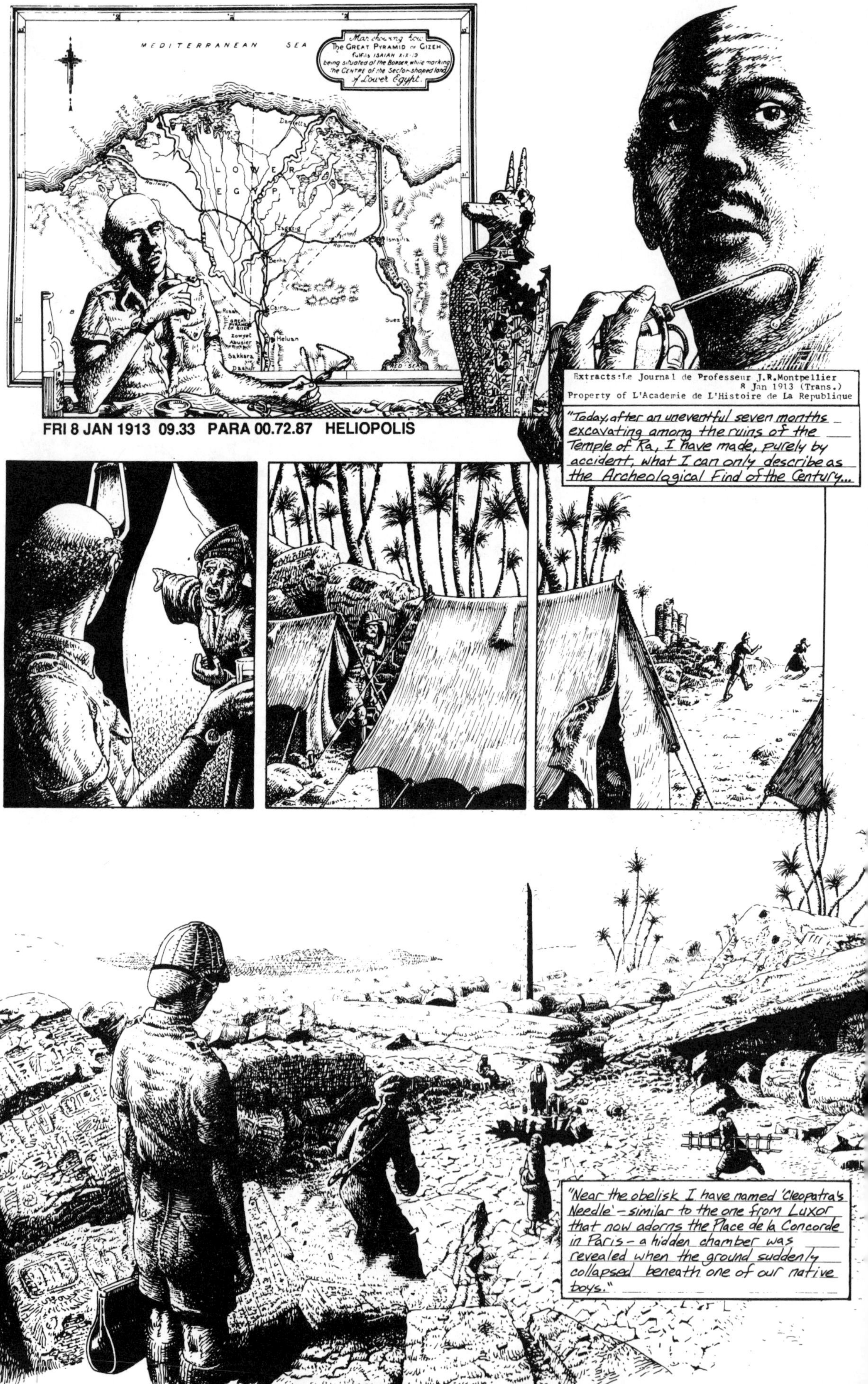
MEDITERRANEAN SEA
The GREAT PYRAMID of GIZEH
fulfils ISAIAH XIX:19
being situated at the BORDER, while marking
the CENTRE of the Sector-shaped land
of Lower Egypt.
LOWER EGYPT
Damietta
Port Said
Railway
Zagazig
Ismailia
Benha
Cairo
Suez
Heluan
Zowyet
Abusier
Sakkara
Dashur
FRI 8 JAN 1913 09.33 PARA 00.72.87 HELIOPOLIS
Extracts: Le Journal de Professeur J.R.Montpellier
8 Jan 1913 (Trans.)
Property of L'Academie de L'Histoire de La Republique
"Today, after an uneventful seven months excavating among the ruins of the Temple of Ra, I have made, purely by accident, what I can only describe as the Archeological Find of the Century...
"Near the obelisk I have named 'Cleopatra's Needle' – similar to the one from Luxor that now adorns the Place de la Concorde in Paris – a hidden chamber was revealed when the ground suddenly collapsed beneath one of our native boys."

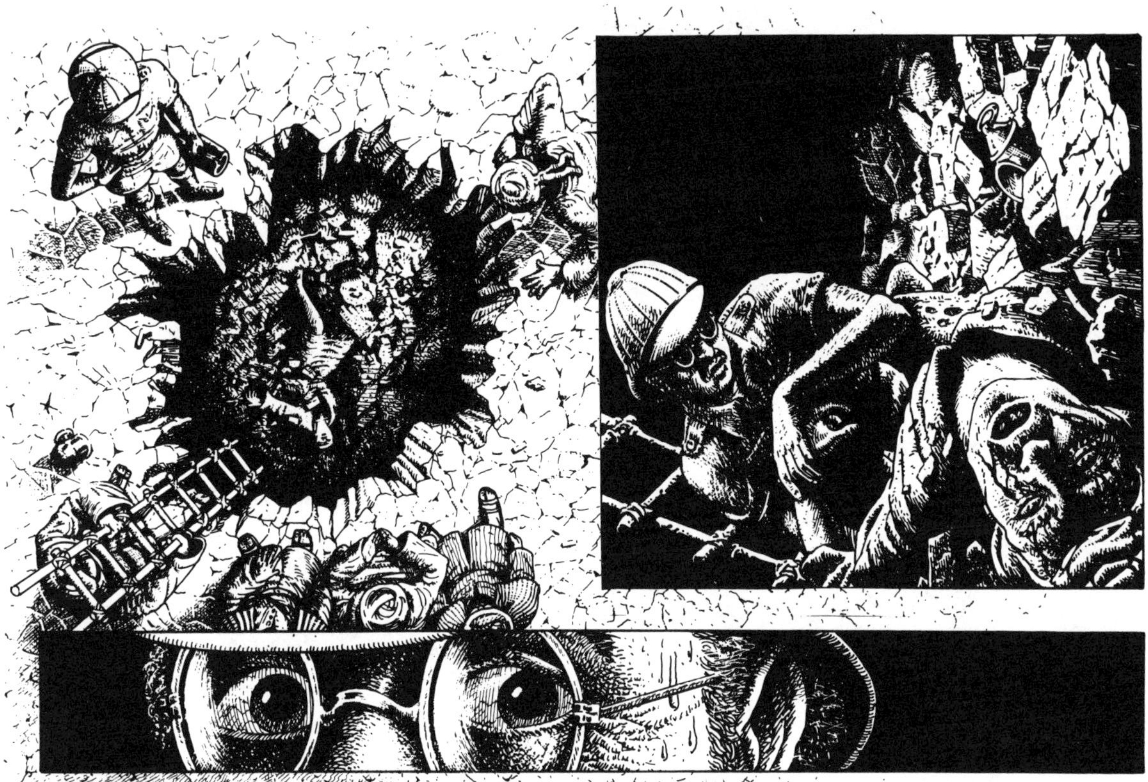

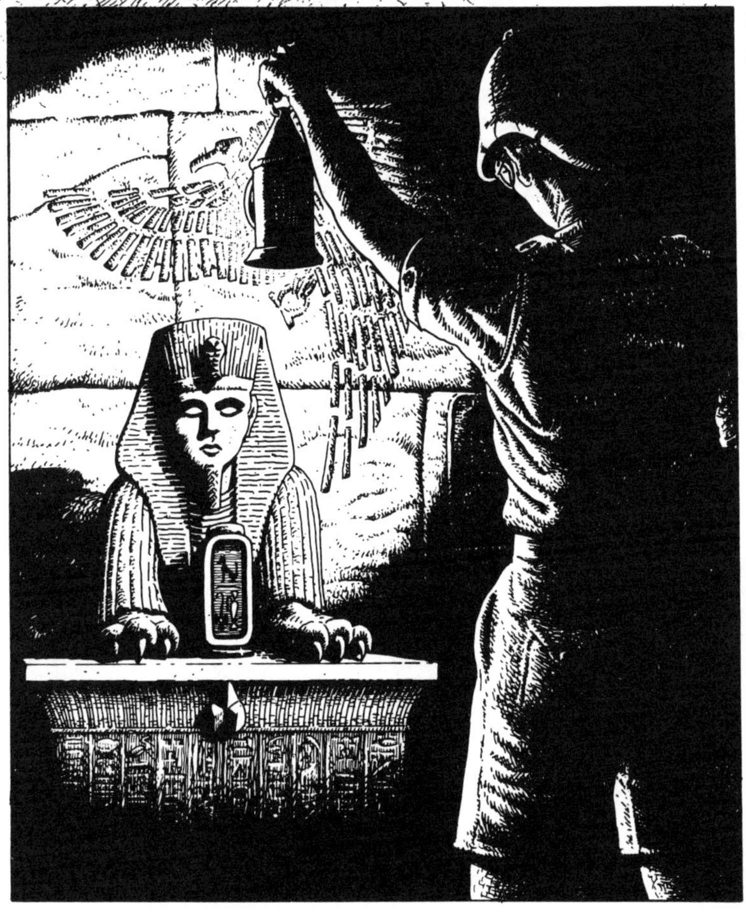

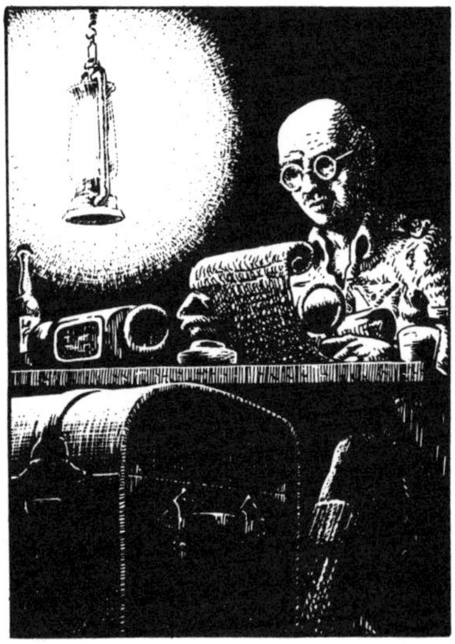

MYSTERIOUS ACCIDENT TO ICONOCLAST.

"Professor J.R. Montpellier, the uninspired but meticulous archaeologist who rose to fame last year by his discovery of the legendary Firefrost Codex, was found dead yesterday morning in his Ypres home. After apparently falling down his stairs, the professor suffered a fractured skull and several other broken bones. Clutched in his left hand was an object described by experts as a Rosicrucian amulet.

"This coincides with the recent theft of the Codex itself from the Musee National de Paris.

"Police are anxious to interview two mysterious men in black who were seen talking to the professor earlier in the day.

"On a lighter note, the monolith 'Cleopatra's Needle' that Professor Montpellier had shipped to France, is to be presented as a gift to our Allies, the people of England. Two magnificent Sphinxes are being cast in bronze to accompany the obelisk, which is to be erected on the Thames Embankment in London."

Le Républicain

23 Sept 1914 (Trans.)

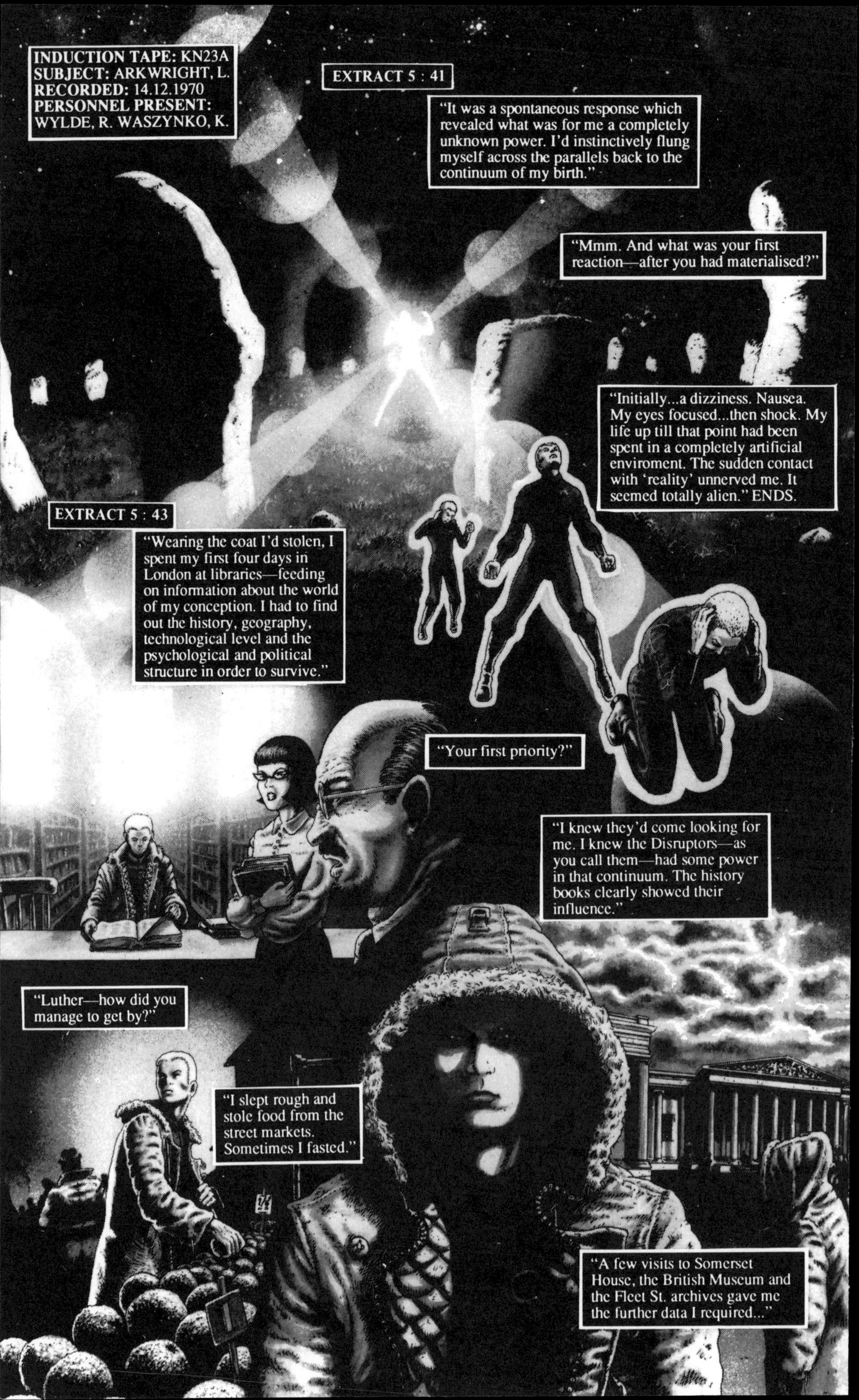
INDUCTION TAPE: KN23A
SUBJECT: ARKWRIGHT, L.
RECORDED: 14.12.1970
PERSONNEL PRESENT:
WYLDE, R. WASZYNKO, K.
EXTRACT 5 : 41
"It was a spontaneous response which revealed what was for me a completely unknown power. I'd instinctively flung myself across the parallels back to the continuum of my birth."
"Mmm. And what was your first reaction—after you had materialised?"
"Initially...a dizziness. Nausea. My eyes focused...then shock. My life up till that point had been spent in a completely artificial enviroment. The sudden contact with 'reality' unnerved me. It seemed totally alien." ENDS.
EXTRACT 5 : 43
"Wearing the coat I'd stolen, I spent my first four days in London at libraries—feeding on information about the world of my conception. I had to find out the history, geography, technological level and the psychological and political structure in order to survive."
"Your first priority?"
"I knew they'd come looking for me. I knew the Disruptors—as you call them—had some power in that continuum. The history books clearly showed their influence."
"Luther—how did you manage to get by?"
"I slept rough and stole food from the street markets. Sometimes I fasted."
"A few visits to Somerset House, the British Museum and the Fleet St. archives gave me the further data I required..."

Daily Mirror

THURS FEB 16 1950

ONE PENNY

FORWARD WITH THE PEOPLE

No. 14,765

Registered at G.P.O. as a Newspaper.

AIR ACE I HOSPITAL TRAGEDY BLAZ

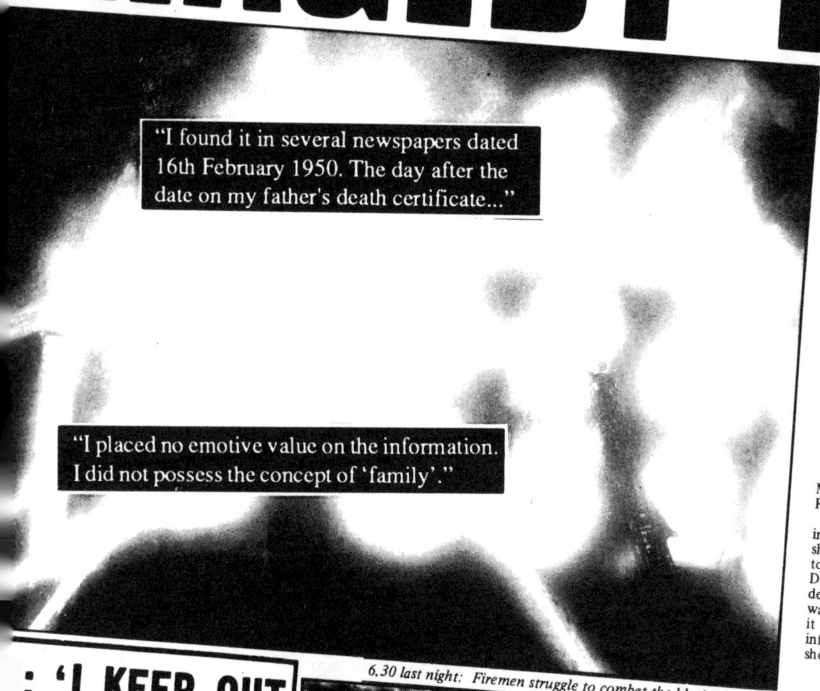

"I found it in several newspapers dated 16th February 1950. The day after the date on my father's death certificate..."
"I placed no emotive value on the information. I did not possess the concept of 'family'."

6.30 last night: Firemen struggle to combat the blazing inferno.

FOUR DEA

Londoners were stunned yesterday as fire swept through St. Mary's Hospital, Paddington. One of the victims was Battle of Britain hero Captain Gavin Arkwright V.C.

Firemen battled the blaze for ten hours and were just getting it under control late last night. Nurses and Doctors acted quickly and efficiently in evacuating patients as soon as the alarm bell rang and no one was injured apart from the four fatal casualties. Capt. Arkwright's wife, Sarah, Dr. David Richardson and Ward Sister Sita Williamson were also killed in the conflagration which began in the very room occupied by Mrs. Arkwright.

The causes of the fire are shrouded in mystery and will be until experts can piece together the events that lead up to the blaze.

Shock

The alarm was sounded by Staff Nurse Vanessa Morgan who, although still shaken, spoke to our Reporter shortly after the outbreak.

"I can't understand it," she sobbed, "I'd been in Mrs. Arkwright's room only ten minutes earlier – she was in the second stage of labour and was about to give birth. Capt. Arkwright was by her side and Dr. Richardson and Sister Williams were handling the delivery. Later I walked past the room and smoke was pouring out from beneath the door. I opened it – the handle burned my hand – it was a white-hot inferno in there!" Nurse Morgan is being treated for shock.

Death of a hero

All Britons will be saddened by the news of the death of Capt. Arkwright who won fame in the last war after newspaper reports of his heroic exploits as a fighter pilot in the R.A.F. Shot down by the Luftwaffe three times and credited with downing more than fifty enemy aircraft, during the War Years Captain Arkwright and his Spitfire stood as a symbol for the courage and determination of our beleagured country. Both the King and Winston Churchill have expressed their sympathy at this most tragic occasion.

Capt. Arkwright's father was also awarded a V.C. in the Great War shortly before he was killed in action.

C.I.D. are anxious to contact the Nurse who earlier reported that three men, dressed entirely in black, had been enquiring about the whereabouts of Mrs. Arkwright's Private Room.

FULL REPORT ON FIRE — P5

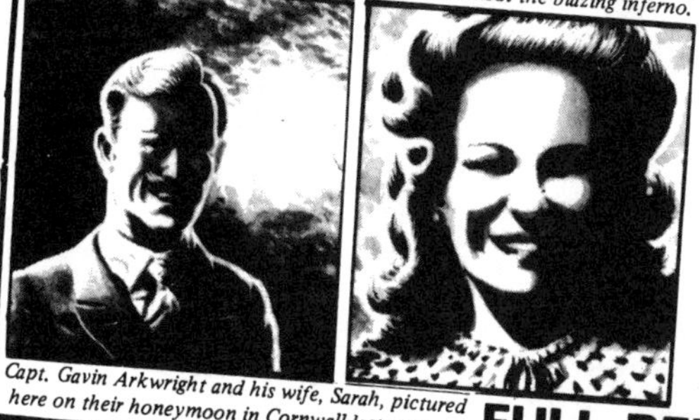

Capt. Gavin Arkwright and his wife, Sarah, pictured here on their honeymoon in Cornwall last year.

: 'I KEEP OUT OIL DISPUTE'

ning the oil tion Bill Shah of the British ir Francis e Shah is ve told Sir not wish to situation.

says British United Press (American).

Mr. Herbert Morrison, Foreign Secretary, saw the Persian Ambassador, Mr. Soheily, yesterday

The British cruiser Gambia (8,000 tons) has arrived in the Persian Gulf.

SRAEL IN NEW CLASH

vernment last night claimed that their driven back Syrian Army units which, d the frontier west of the demilitarised two countries.

said the Syrian forces were engaged by there had been heavy fighting. y complained to the Security Council have confirmed in a report to Lake ting has taken place and said three d been killed and one wounded. 100 Israel soldiers had attacked Arabs ed zone.

en the two countries, which began in weeks ago, is at present before the

VALKER

esday.

r Depu-

rence

on the

In a

'This is our

Labour M.P.s storm: Govt ma

By BILL GREIG

"I realised that the next step was to go into hiding in the certainty I was being hunted down. I fled to Europe..." ENDS.

...ge

...cruiting ... "law and order" ... yesterday to join the ... force.

The first had stepped forward before Premier Holland had finished his broadcast appeal for a volunteer army to combat trouble-makers out to "overthrow orderly government by force."

The Prime Minister issued his call following attempt by saboteurs to ...

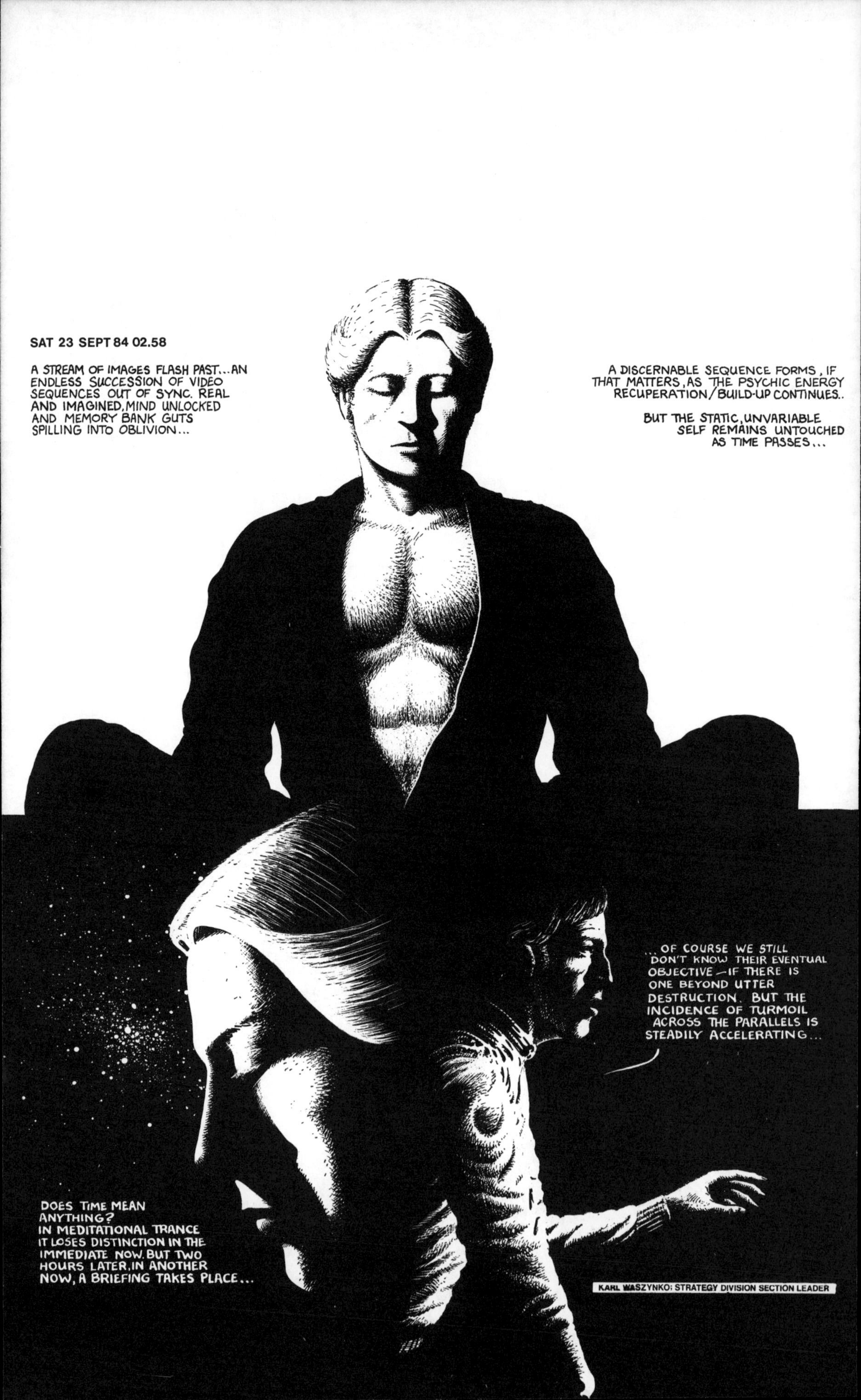
SAT 23 SEPT 84 02.58
A STREAM OF IMAGES FLASH PAST...AN ENDLESS SUCCESSION OF VIDEO SEQUENCES OUT OF SYNC. REAL AND IMAGINED, MIND UNLOCKED AND MEMORY BANK GUTS SPILLING INTO OBLIVION...
A DISCERNABLE SEQUENCE FORMS, IF THAT MATTERS, AS THE PSYCHIC ENERGY RECUPERATION/BUILD-UP CONTINUES..
BUT THE STATIC, UNVARIABLE SELF REMAINS UNTOUCHED AS TIME PASSES...
...OF COURSE WE STILL DON'T KNOW THEIR EVENTUAL OBJECTIVE — IF THERE IS ONE BEYOND UTTER DESTRUCTION. BUT THE INCIDENCE OF TURMOIL ACROSS THE PARALLELS IS STEADILY ACCELERATING...
DOES TIME MEAN ANYTHING? IN MEDITATIONAL TRANCE IT LOSES DISTINCTION IN THE IMMEDIATE NOW. BUT TWO HOURS LATER, IN ANOTHER NOW, A BRIEFING TAKES PLACE...
KARL WASZYNKO: STRATEGY DIVISION SECTION LEADER

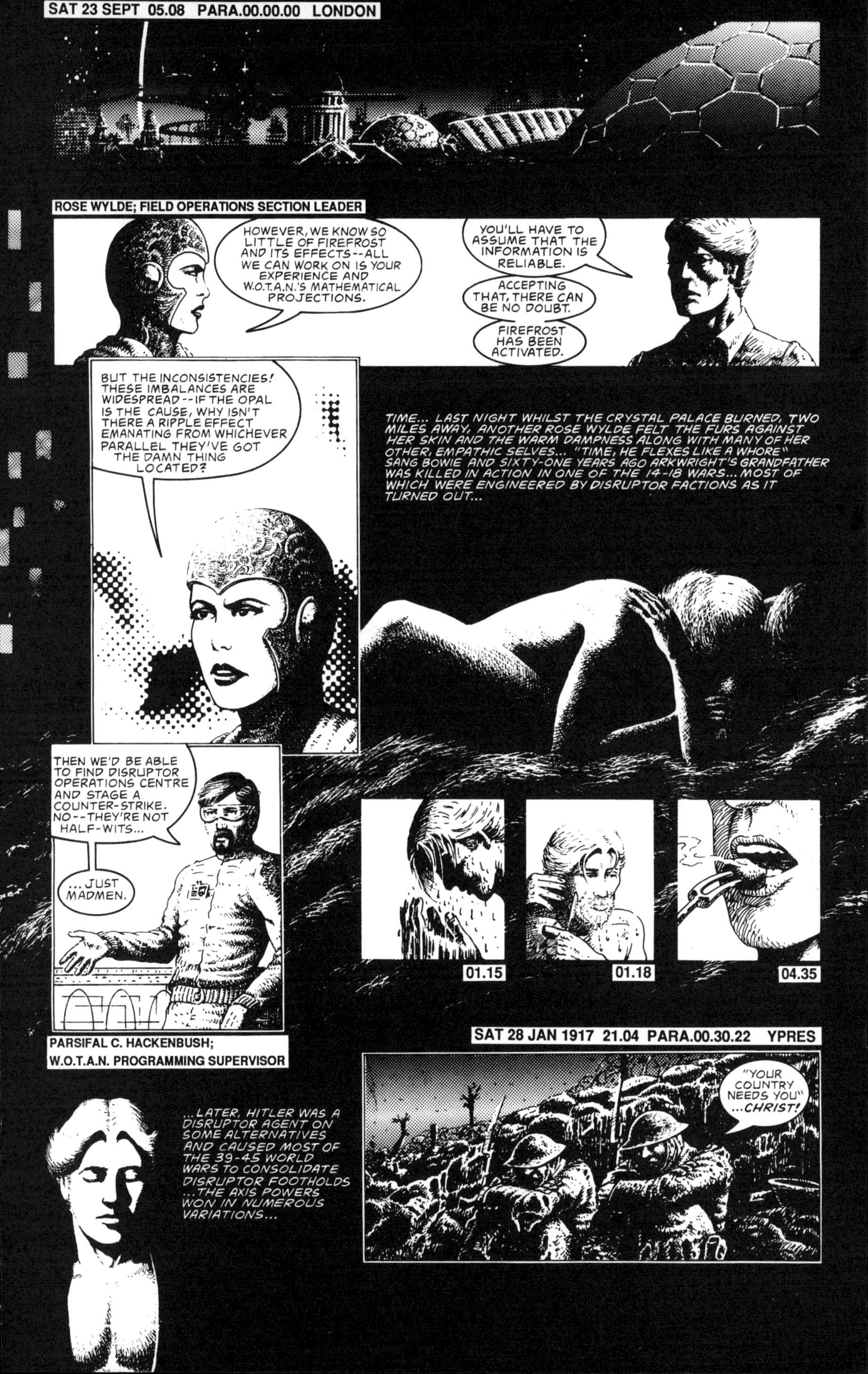

SAT 23 SEPT 05.08 PARA.00.00.00 LONDON
ROSE WYLDE; FIELD OPERATIONS SECTION LEADER
HOWEVER, WE KNOW SO LITTLE OF FIREFROST AND ITS EFFECTS--ALL WE CAN WORK ON IS YOUR EXPERIENCE AND W.O.T.A.N.'S MATHEMATICAL PROJECTIONS.
YOU'LL HAVE TO ASSUME THAT THE INFORMATION IS RELIABLE.
ACCEPTING THAT, THERE CAN BE NO DOUBT.
FIREFROST HAS BEEN ACTIVATED.
BUT THE INCONSISTENCIES! THESE IMBALANCES ARE WIDESPREAD--IF THE OPAL IS THE CAUSE, WHY ISN'T THERE A RIPPLE EFFECT EMANATING FROM WHICHEVER PARALLEL THEY'VE GOT THE DAMN THING LOCATED?
TIME... LAST NIGHT WHILST THE CRYSTAL PALACE BURNED, TWO MILES AWAY, ANOTHER ROSE WYLDE FELT THE FURS AGAINST HER SKIN AND THE WARM DAMPNESS ALONG WITH MANY OF HER OTHER, EMPATHIC SELVES... "TIME, HE FLEXES LIKE A WHORE" SANG BOWIE AND SIXTY-ONE YEARS AGO ARKWRIGHT'S GRANDFATHER WAS KILLED IN ACTION IN ONE OF THE 14-18 WARS... MOST OF WHICH WERE ENGINEERED BY DISRUPTOR FACTIONS AS IT TURNED OUT...
THEN WE'D BE ABLE TO FIND DISRUPTOR OPERATIONS CENTRE AND STAGE A COUNTER-STRIKE. NO--THEY'RE NOT HALF-WITS...
...JUST MADMEN.
PARSIFAL C. HACKENBUSH; W.O.T.A.N. PROGRAMMING SUPERVISOR
01.15
01.18
04.35
SAT 28 JAN 1917 21.04 PARA.00.30.22 YPRES
...LATER, HITLER WAS A DISRUPTOR AGENT ON SOME ALTERNATIVES AND CAUSED MOST OF THE 39-45 WORLD WARS TO CONSOLIDATE DISRUPTOR FOOTHOLDS ...THE AXIS POWERS WON IN NUMEROUS VARIATIONS...
"YOUR COUNTRY NEEDS YOU" ...CHRIST!

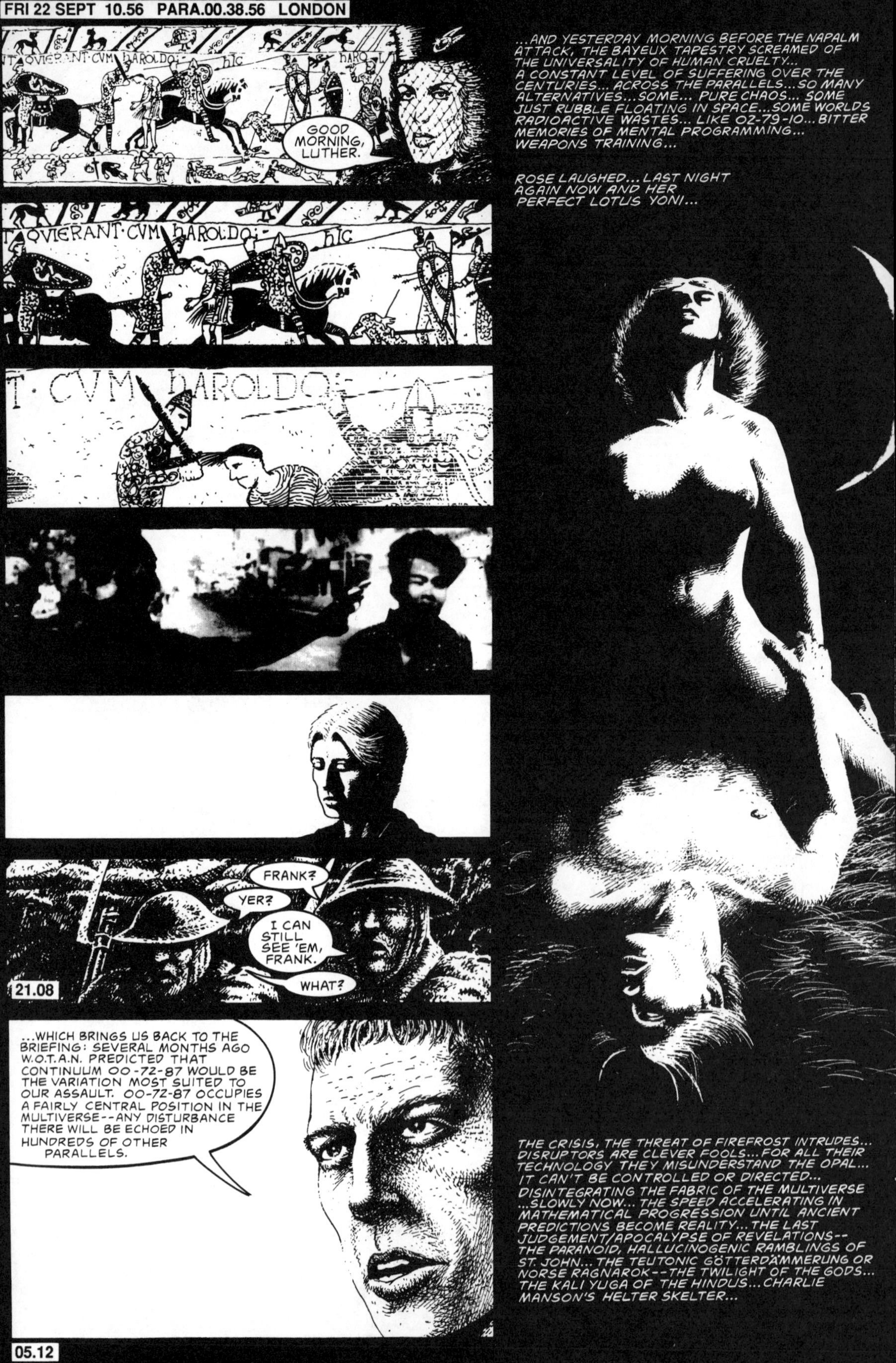
FRI 22 SEPT 10.56 PARA.00.38.56 LONDON
...AND YESTERDAY MORNING BEFORE THE NAPALM ATTACK, THE BAYEUX TAPESTRY SCREAMED OF THE UNIVERSALITY OF HUMAN CRUELTY... A CONSTANT LEVEL OF SUFFERING OVER THE CENTURIES... ACROSS THE PARALLELS... SO MANY ALTERNATIVES... SOME... PURE CHAOS... SOME JUST RUBBLE FLOATING IN SPACE... SOME WORLDS RADIOACTIVE WASTES... LIKE 02-79-10... BITTER MEMORIES OF MENTAL PROGRAMMING... WEAPONS TRAINING...
ROSE LAUGHED... LAST NIGHT AGAIN NOW AND HER PERFECT LOTUS YONI...
GOOD MORNING, LUTHER.
FRANK?
YER?
I CAN STILL SEE 'EM, FRANK.
WHAT?
21.08
...WHICH BRINGS US BACK TO THE BRIEFING: SEVERAL MONTHS AGO W.O.T.A.N. PREDICTED THAT CONTINUUM 00-72-87 WOULD BE THE VARIATION MOST SUITED TO OUR ASSAULT. 00-72-87 OCCUPIES A FAIRLY CENTRAL POSITION IN THE MULTIVERSE--ANY DISTURBANCE THERE WILL BE ECHOED IN HUNDREDS OF OTHER PARALLELS.
THE CRISIS, THE THREAT OF FIREFROST INTRUDES... DISRUPTORS ARE CLEVER FOOLS... FOR ALL THEIR TECHNOLOGY THEY MISUNDERSTAND THE OPAL... IT CAN'T BE CONTROLLED OR DIRECTED... DISINTEGRATING THE FABRIC OF THE MULTIVERSE ...SLOWLY NOW... THE SPEED ACCELERATING IN MATHEMATICAL PROGRESSION UNTIL ANCIENT PREDICTIONS BECOME REALITY... THE LAST JUDGEMENT/APOCALYPSE OF REVELATIONS-- THE PARANOID, HALLUCINOGENIC RAMBLINGS OF ST. JOHN... THE TEUTONIC GÖTTERDÄMMERUNG OR NORSE RAGNAROK--THE TWILIGHT OF THE GODS... THE KALI YUGA OF THE HINDUS... CHARLIE MANSON'S HELTER SKELTER...
05.12

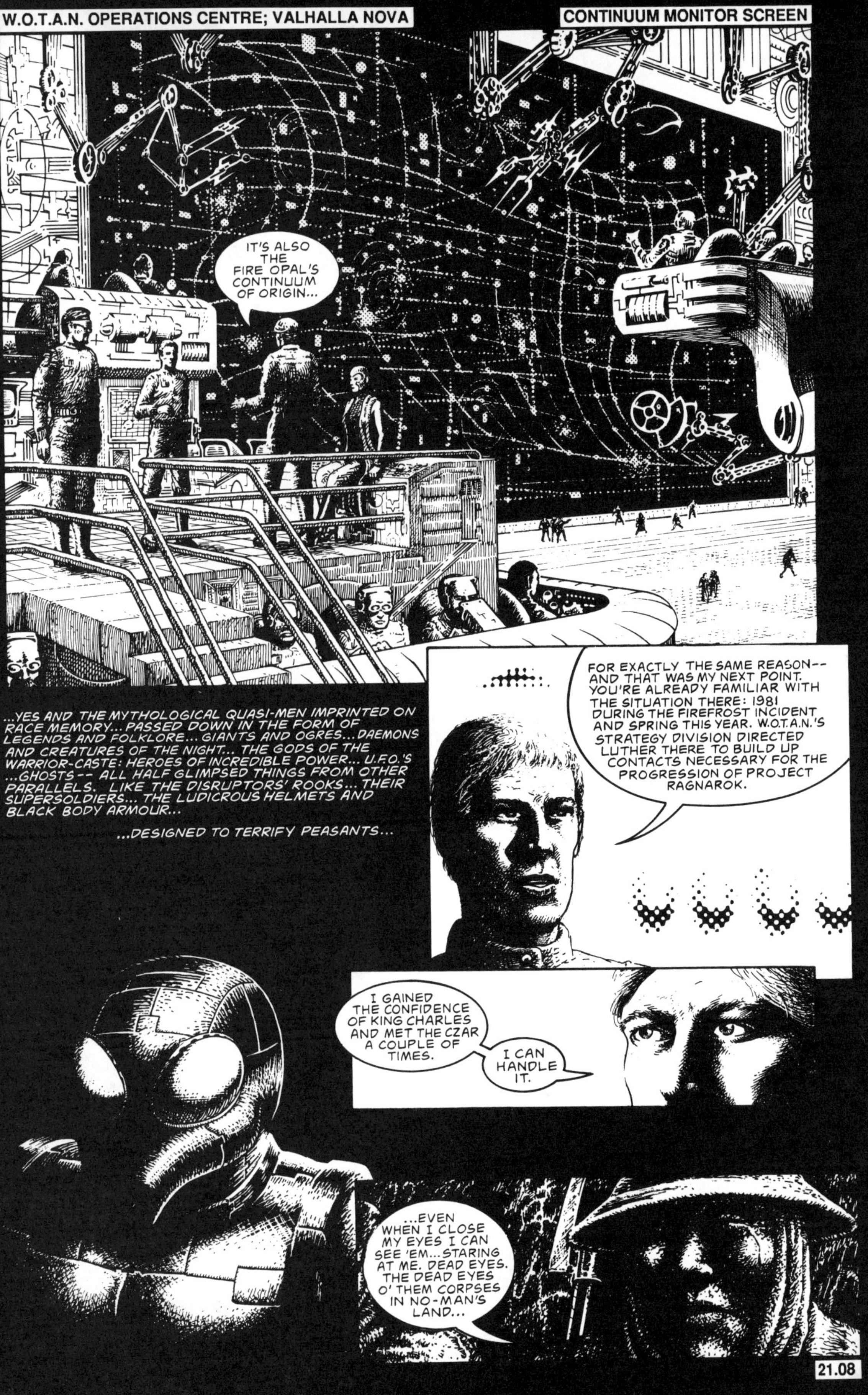
W.O.T.A.N. OPERATIONS CENTRE; VALHALLA NOVA
CONTINUUM MONITOR SCREEN
IT'S ALSO THE FIRE OPAL'S CONTINUUM OF ORIGIN...
...YES AND THE MYTHOLOGICAL QUASI-MEN IMPRINTED ON RACE MEMORY... PASSED DOWN IN THE FORM OF LEGENDS AND FOLKLORE... GIANTS AND OGRES... DAEMONS AND CREATURES OF THE NIGHT... THE GODS OF THE WARRIOR-CASTE: HEROES OF INCREDIBLE POWER... U.F.O.'S ...GHOSTS-- ALL HALF GLIMPSED THINGS FROM OTHER PARALLELS. LIKE THE DISRUPTORS' ROOKS... THEIR SUPERSOLDIERS... THE LUDICROUS HELMETS AND BLACK BODY ARMOUR...
...DESIGNED TO TERRIFY PEASANTS...
FOR EXACTLY THE SAME REASON-- AND THAT WAS MY NEXT POINT. YOU'RE ALREADY FAMILIAR WITH THE SITUATION THERE: 1981 DURING THE FIREFROST INCIDENT AND SPRING THIS YEAR. W.O.T.A.N.'S STRATEGY DIVISION DIRECTED LUTHER THERE TO BUILD UP CONTACTS NECESSARY FOR THE PROGRESSION OF PROJECT RAGNAROK.
I GAINED THE CONFIDENCE OF KING CHARLES AND MET THE CZAR A COUPLE OF TIMES.
I CAN HANDLE IT.
...EVEN WHEN I CLOSE MY EYES I CAN SEE 'EM... STARING AT ME. DEAD EYES. THE DEAD EYES O' THEM CORPSES IN NO-MAN'S LAND...

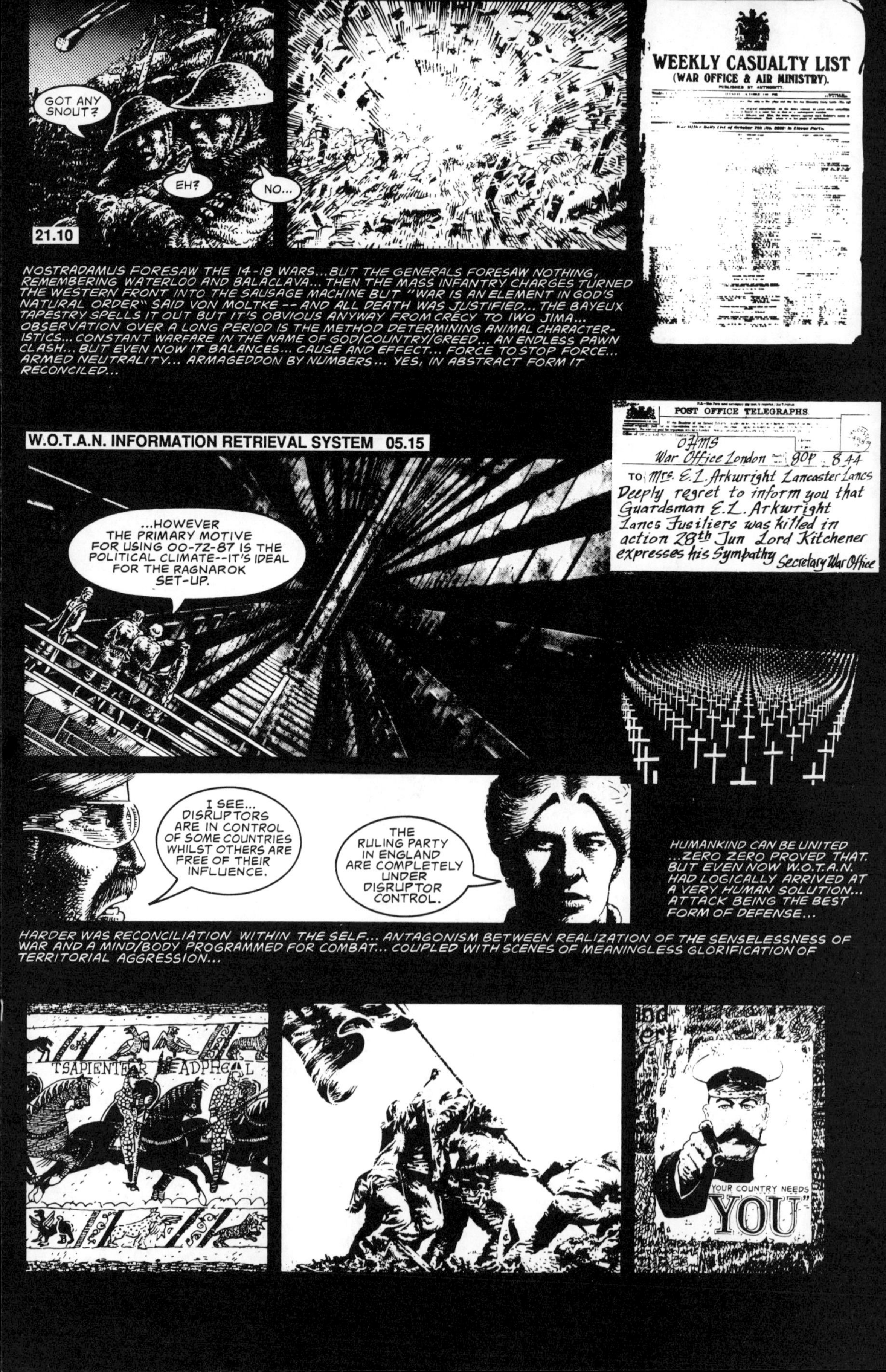
GOT ANY SNOUT?
EH?
NO...
21.10
WEEKLY CASUALTY LIST
(WAR OFFICE & AIR MINISTRY).
NOSTRADAMUS FORESAW THE 14-18 WARS... BUT THE GENERALS FORESAW NOTHING, REMEMBERING WATERLOO AND BALACLAVA... THEN THE MASS INFANTRY CHARGES TURNED THE WESTERN FRONT INTO THE SAUSAGE MACHINE BUT "WAR IS AN ELEMENT IN GOD'S NATURAL ORDER" SAID VON MOLTKE -- AND ALL DEATH WAS JUSTIFIED... THE BAYEUX TAPESTRY SPELLS IT OUT BUT IT'S OBVIOUS ANYWAY FROM CRÉCY TO IWO JIMA... OBSERVATION OVER A LONG PERIOD IS THE METHOD DETERMINING ANIMAL CHARACTERISTICS... CONSTANT WARFARE IN THE NAME OF GOD/COUNTRY/GREED... AN ENDLESS PAWN CLASH... BUT EVEN NOW IT BALANCES... CAUSE AND EFFECT... FORCE TO STOP FORCE... ARMED NEUTRALITY... ARMAGEDDON BY NUMBERS... YES, IN ABSTRACT FORM IT RECONCILED...
POST OFFICE TELEGRAPHS
OHMS
War Office London 9OP 8.44
TO: Mrs. E.L. Arkwright Lancaster Lancs
Deeply regret to inform you that Guardsman E.L. Arkwright Lancs Fusiliers was killed in action 28th Jun Lord Kitchener expresses his Symbathy Secretary War Office
W.O.T.A.N. INFORMATION RETRIEVAL SYSTEM 05.15
...HOWEVER THE PRIMARY MOTIVE FOR USING 00-72-87 IS THE POLITICAL CLIMATE--IT'S IDEAL FOR THE RAGNAROK SET-UP.
I SEE... DISRUPTORS ARE IN CONTROL OF SOME COUNTRIES WHILST OTHERS ARE FREE OF THEIR INFLUENCE.
THE RULING PARTY IN ENGLAND ARE COMPLETELY UNDER DISRUPTOR CONTROL.
HUMANKIND CAN BE UNITED ...ZERO ZERO PROVED THAT. BUT EVEN NOW W.O.T.A.N. HAD LOGICALLY ARRIVED AT A VERY HUMAN SOLUTION... ATTACK BEING THE BEST FORM OF DEFENSE...
HARDER WAS RECONCILIATION WITHIN THE SELF... ANTAGONISM BETWEEN REALIZATION OF THE SENSELESSNESS OF WAR AND A MIND/BODY PROGRAMMED FOR COMBAT... COUPLED WITH SCENES OF MEANINGLESS GLORIFICATION OF TERRITORIAL AGGRESSION...
YOUR COUNTRY NEEDS YOU

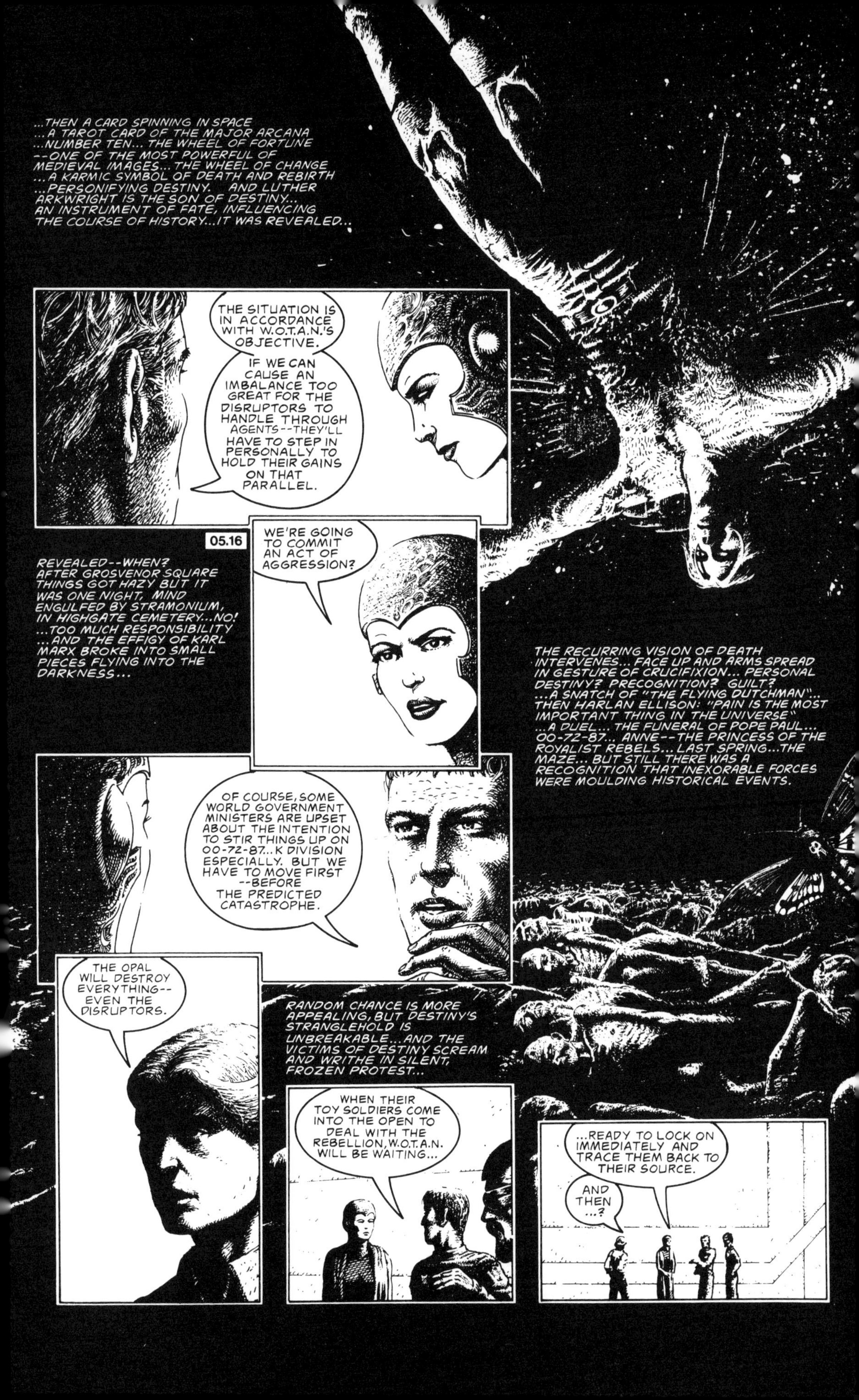
...THEN A CARD SPINNING IN SPACE ...A TAROT CARD OF THE MAJOR ARCANA ...NUMBER TEN... THE WHEEL OF FORTUNE --ONE OF THE MOST POWERFUL OF MEDIEVAL IMAGES... THE WHEEL OF CHANGE ...A KARMIC SYMBOL OF DEATH AND REBIRTH ...PERSONIFYING DESTINY. AND LUTHER ARKWRIGHT IS THE SON OF DESTINY... AN INSTRUMENT OF FATE, INFLUENCING THE COURSE OF HISTORY...IT WAS REVEALED...
THE SITUATION IS IN ACCORDANCE WITH W.O.T.A.N.'S OBJECTIVE.
IF WE CAN CAUSE AN IMBALANCE TOO GREAT FOR THE DISRUPTORS TO HANDLE THROUGH AGENTS--THEY'LL HAVE TO STEP IN PERSONALLY TO HOLD THEIR GAINS ON THAT PARALLEL.
05.16
REVEALED--WHEN? AFTER GROSVENOR SQUARE THINGS GOT HAZY BUT IT WAS ONE NIGHT, MIND ENGULFED BY STRAMONIUM, IN HIGHGATE CEMETERY...NO! ...TOO MUCH RESPONSIBILITY ...AND THE EFFIGY OF KARL MARX BROKE INTO SMALL PIECES FLYING INTO THE DARKNESS...
WE'RE GOING TO COMMIT AN ACT OF AGGRESSION?
THE RECURRING VISION OF DEATH INTERVENES... FACE UP AND ARMS SPREAD IN GESTURE OF CRUCIFIXION... PERSONAL DESTINY? PRECOGNITION? GUILT? ...A SNATCH OF "THE FLYING DUTCHMAN"... THEN HARLAN ELLISON: "PAIN IS THE MOST IMPORTANT THING IN THE UNIVERSE" ...A DUEL... THE FUNERAL OF POPE PAUL... 00-72-87... ANNE--THE PRINCESS OF THE ROYALIST REBELS... LAST SPRING...THE MAZE... BUT STILL THERE WAS A RECOGNITION THAT INEXORABLE FORCES WERE MOULDING HISTORICAL EVENTS.
OF COURSE, SOME WORLD GOVERNMENT MINISTERS ARE UPSET ABOUT THE INTENTION TO STIR THINGS UP ON 00-72-87...K DIVISION ESPECIALLY. BUT WE HAVE TO MOVE FIRST --BEFORE THE PREDICTED CATASTROPHE.
THE OPAL WILL DESTROY EVERYTHING-- EVEN THE DISRUPTORS.
RANDOM CHANCE IS MORE APPEALING, BUT DESTINY'S STRANGLEHOLD IS UNBREAKABLE...AND THE VICTIMS OF DESTINY SCREAM AND WRITHE IN SILENT, FROZEN PROTEST...
WHEN THEIR TOY SOLDIERS COME INTO THE OPEN TO DEAL WITH THE REBELLION, W.O.T.A.N. WILL BE WAITING...
...READY TO LOCK ON IMMEDIATELY AND TRACE THEM BACK TO THEIR SOURCE.
AND THEN ...?

SAT 23 SEPT 02.58

RECONCILIATION COMES AMIDST IMAGES OF MASS DESTRUCTION... CHEMICAL, GERM AND ATOMIC WARFARE PALE BEFORE THE POWER OF FIREFROST AND IT'S LAST NIGHT AGAIN WITH ROSE IN THE THROES OF ORGASM... GASPS AND MOANS AND PULSING FLESH ...AN EASY ONE TO INTERPRET... SEX AND DEATH.

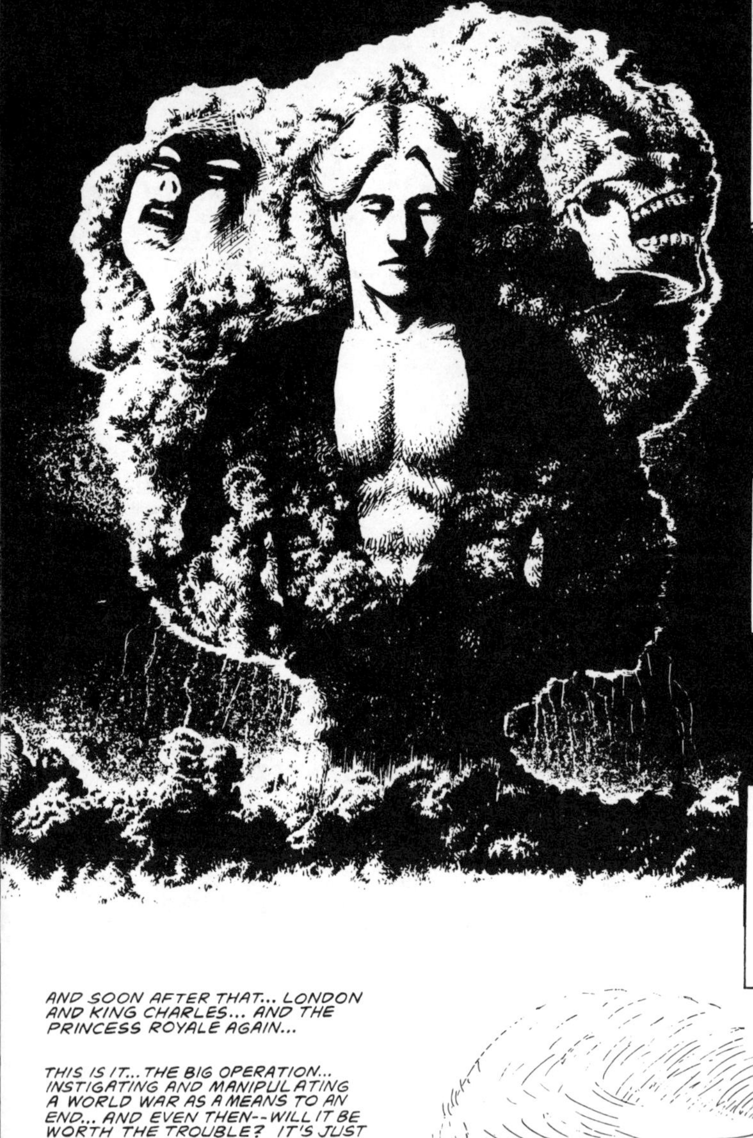

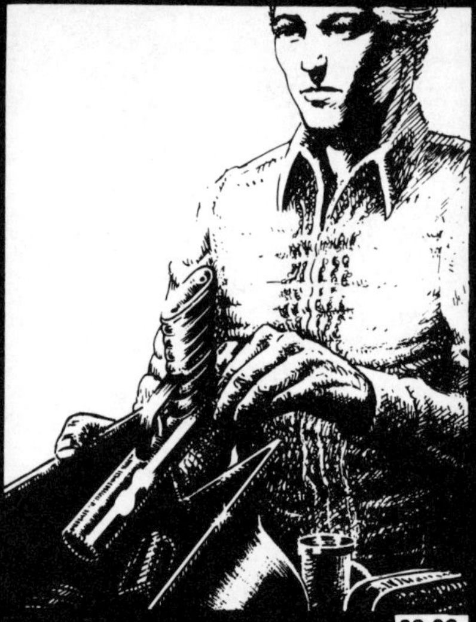

08.26

...AND THE THOUGHT WOULD RECUR LATER, WHILST PACKING. PREPARATION FOR 00-72-87... A "WESSEX" HIGH POWER FLARE GUN... AMPHETAMINE SULPHATE... SUITABLE CURRENCY... THE ARMSTRONG-SIDDLEY ROYAL ALBERT VIBRO BEAMER.

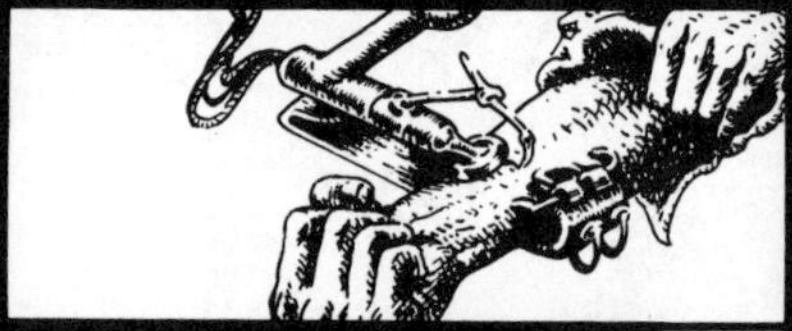

08.38

...THEN THE ANTI-RABIES AND OTHER SHOTS OVER AT MEDICAL AND A QUICK SCAN THROUGH THE TREATY BEFORE LEAVING FOR ST. PETERSBURG...

08.40

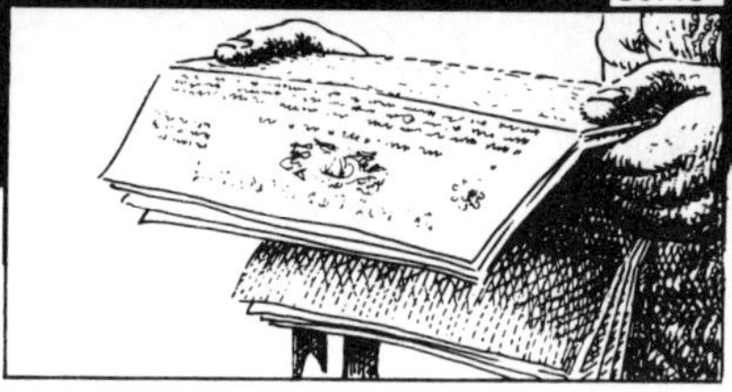

AND SOON AFTER THAT... LONDON AND KING CHARLES... AND THE PRINCESS ROYALE AGAIN...

THIS IS IT... THE BIG OPERATION... INSTIGATING AND MANIPULATING A WORLD WAR AS A MEANS TO AN END... AND EVEN THEN--WILL IT BE WORTH THE TROUBLE? IT'S JUST A LAST DITCH ATTEMPT TO FIND THE OPAL.

AND WHEN/IF THE DOOMSDAY MACHINE IS FOUND, IS THERE ANY CHANCE OF DEACTIVATING IT?

BUT NOW THE QUESTION IS THEORETICAL... THE PLAN OF ACTION MAPPED OUT... IT WILL BE FOLLOWED THROUGH TO ITS CONCLUSION... BY A GENETIC WARRIOR... UNDER D.N.A. DICTATION.

TODAY'S DATE -- 23RD OF SEPTEMBER... THE AUTUMNAL EQUINOX... AND REPLENISHING BURNT-OUT PSYCHIC ENERGY RESERVES, THE MEDITATION CONTINUES...

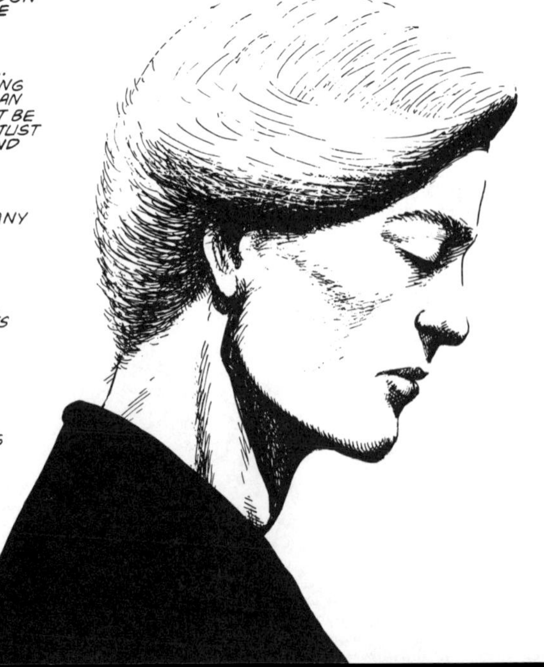

SAT 23 SEPT 02.58

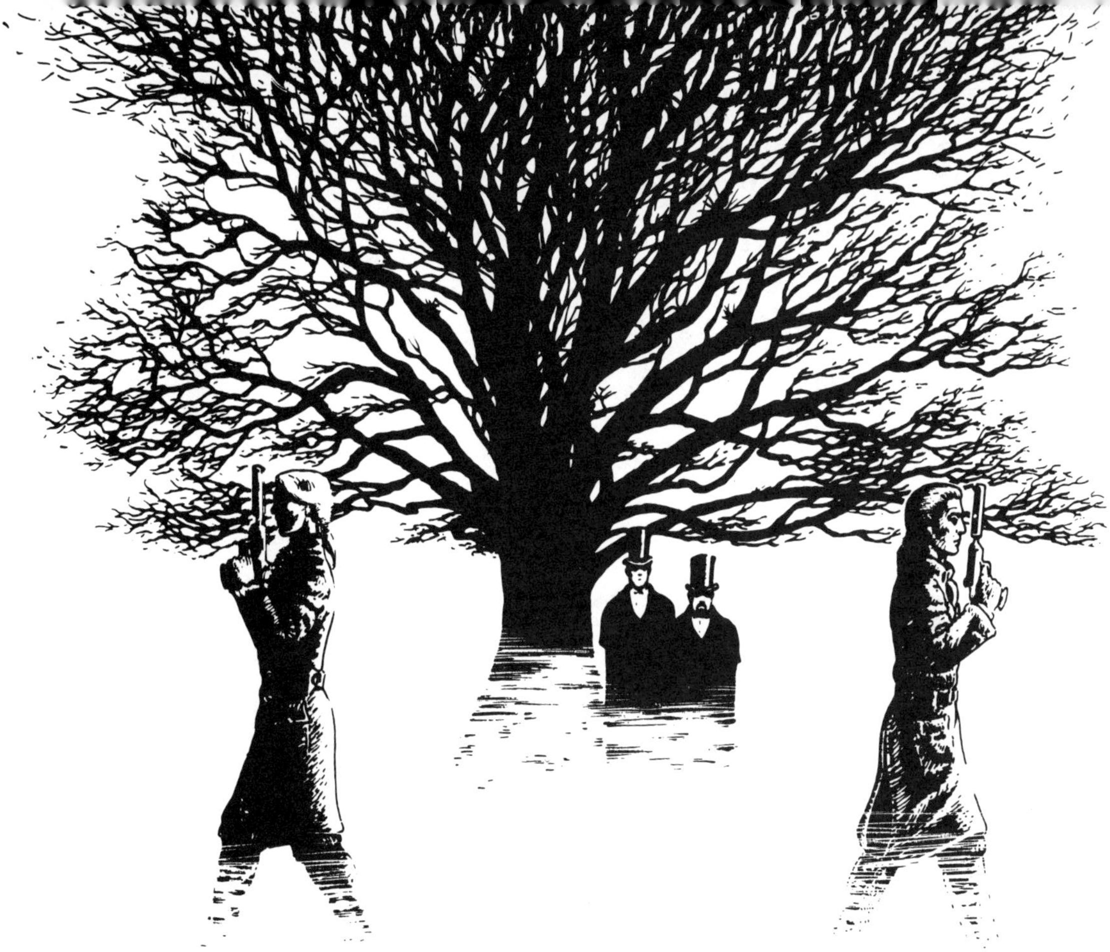

SUN 22 MAY 1981 07.00 PARA 00.39.21 HYDE PARK, LONDON

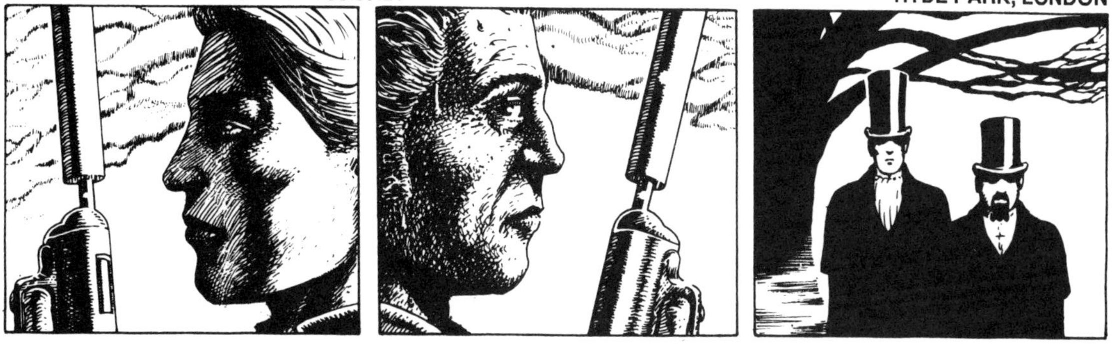

WEAPON; ARMSTRONG-SIDDLEY 'ROYAL ALBERT' VIBRO BEAMER

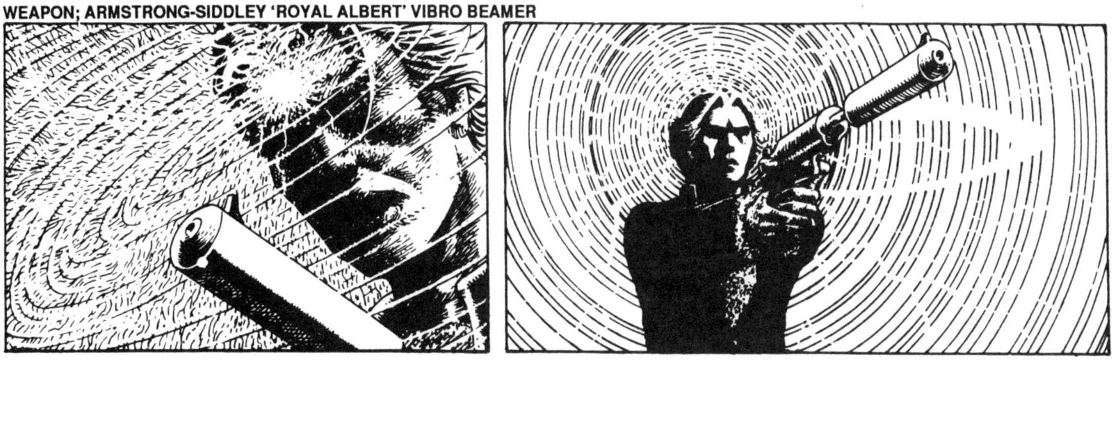

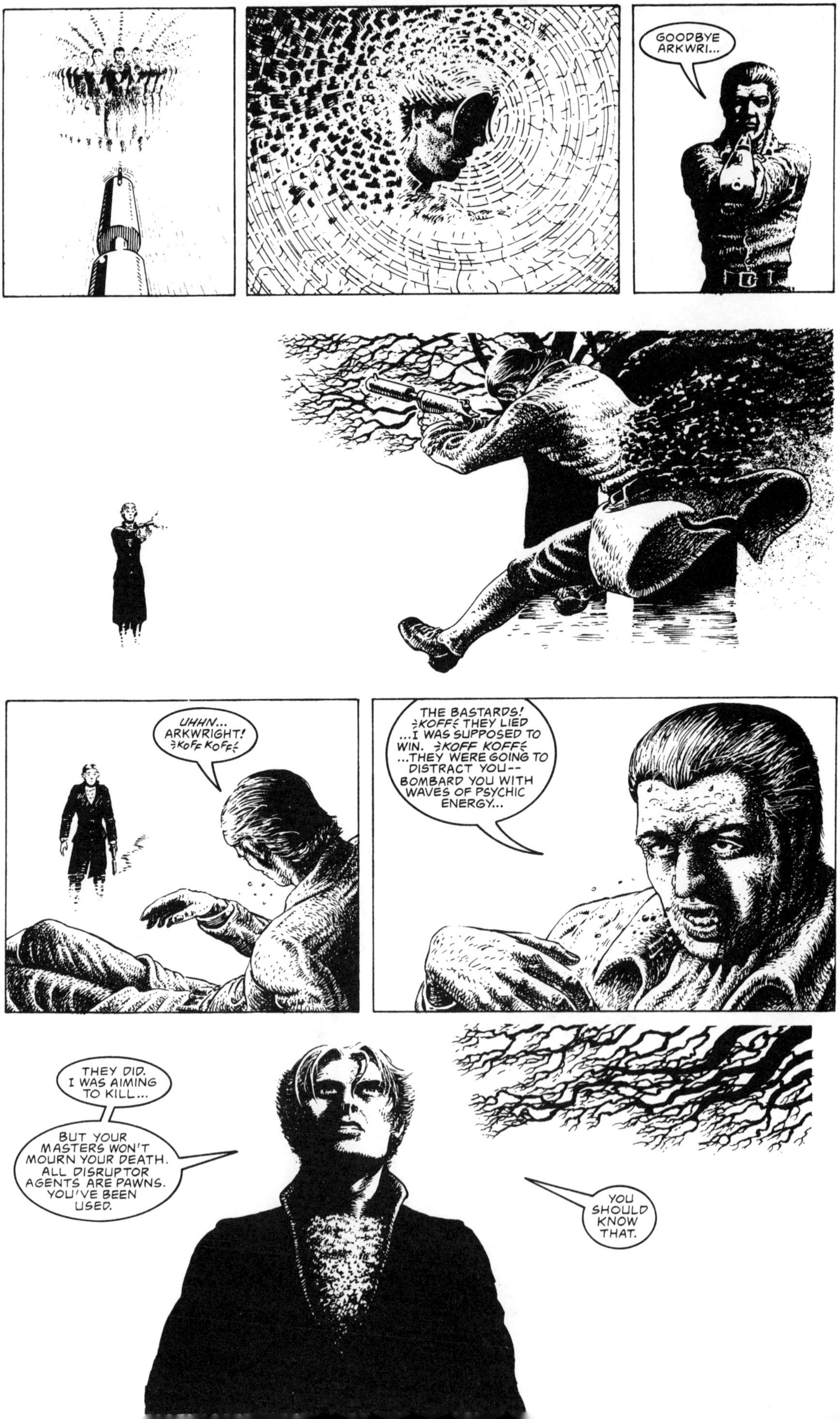
GOODBYE ARKWRI...
UHHN... ARKWRIGHT! KOFF KOFF
THE BASTARDS! KOFF THEY LIED ...I WAS SUPPOSED TO WIN. KOFF KOFF ...THEY WERE GOING TO DISTRACT YOU-- BOMBARD YOU WITH WAVES OF PSYCHIC ENERGY...
THEY DID. I WAS AIMING TO KILL...
BUT YOUR MASTERS WON'T MOURN YOUR DEATH. ALL DISRUPTOR AGENTS ARE PAWNS. YOU'VE BEEN USED.
YOU SHOULD KNOW THAT.

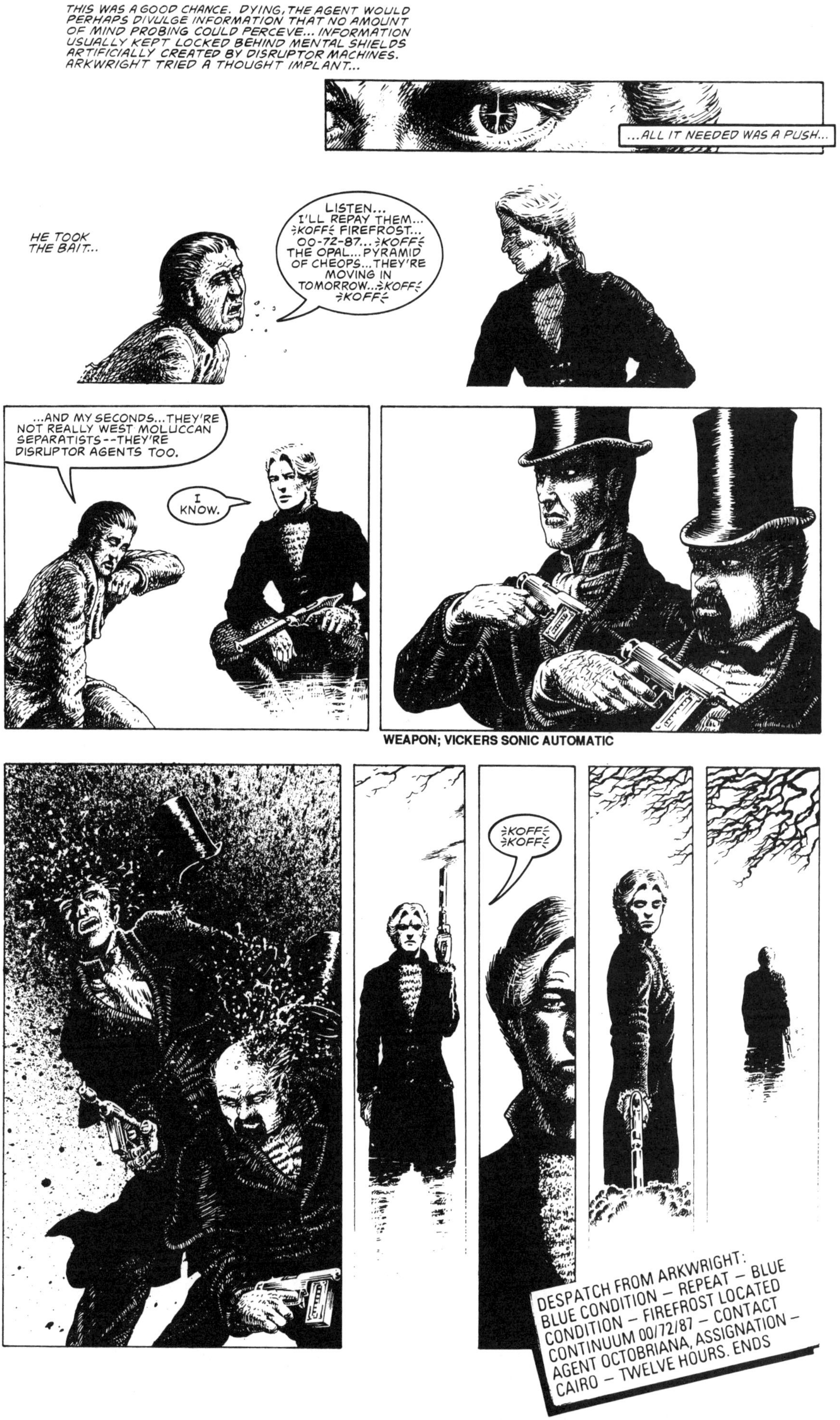
THIS WAS A GOOD CHANCE. DYING, THE AGENT WOULD PERHAPS DIVULGE INFORMATION THAT NO AMOUNT OF MIND PROBING COULD PERCEVE... INFORMATION USUALLY KEPT LOCKED BEHIND MENTAL SHIELDS ARTIFICIALLY CREATED BY DISRUPTOR MACHINES. ARKWRIGHT TRIED A THOUGHT IMPLANT...
...ALL IT NEEDED WAS A PUSH...
HE TOOK THE BAIT...
LISTEN... I'LL REPAY THEM... ≯KOFF≮ FIREFROST... 00-72-87... ≯KOFF≮ THE OPAL... PYRAMID OF CHEOPS... THEY'RE MOVING IN TOMORROW... ≯KOFF≮ ≯KOFF≮
...AND MY SECONDS... THEY'RE NOT REALLY WEST MOLUCCAN SEPARATISTS--THEY'RE DISRUPTOR AGENTS TOO.
I KNOW.
WEAPON; VICKERS SONIC AUTOMATIC
≯KOFF≮ ≯KOFF≮
DESPATCH FROM ARKWRIGHT: BLUE CONDITION — REPEAT — BLUE CONDITION — FIREFROST LOCATED CONTINUUM 00/72/87 — CONTACT AGENT OCTOBRIANA, ASSIGNATION — CAIRO — TWELVE HOURS. ENDS

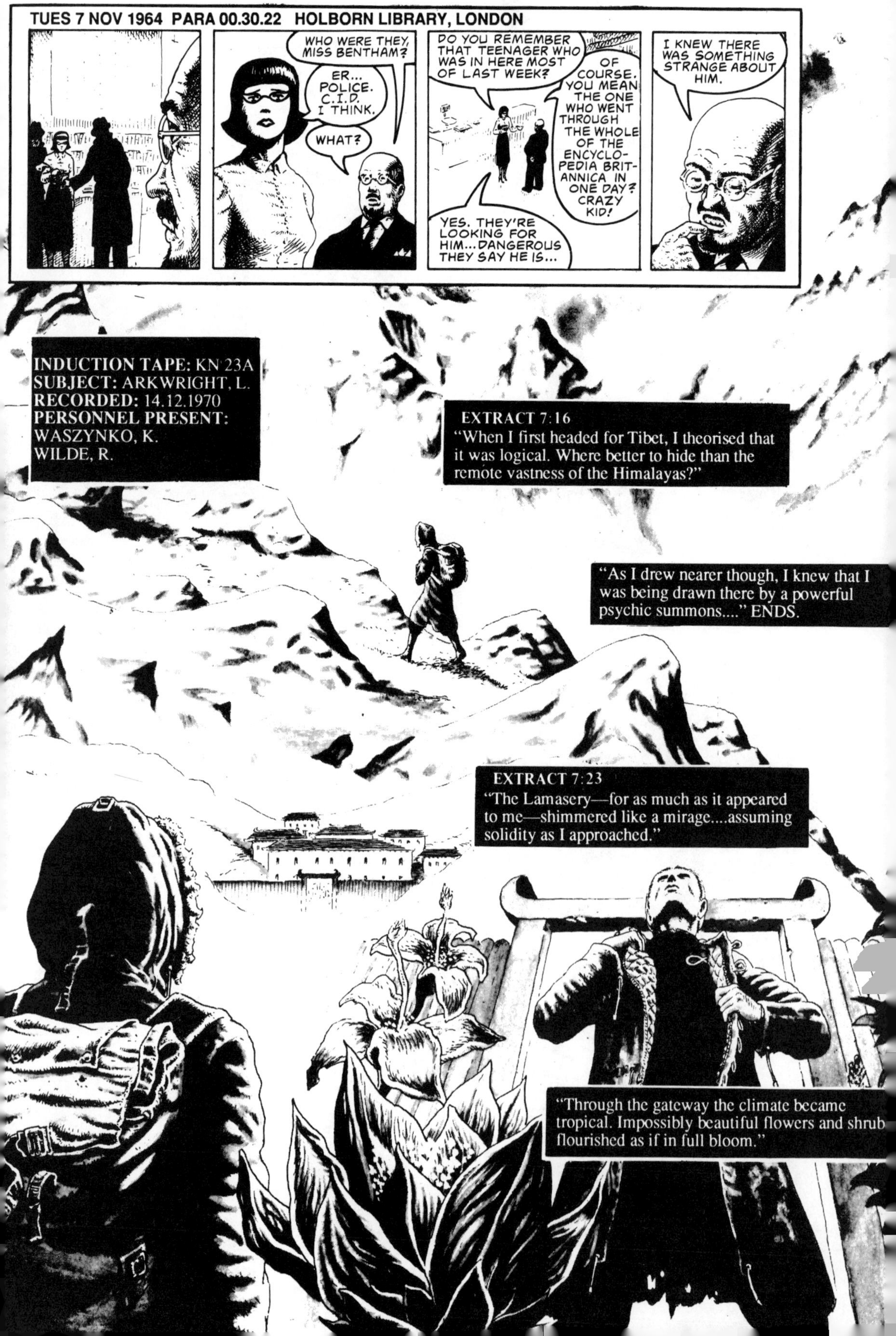
TUES 7 NOV 1964 PARA 00.30.22 HOLBORN LIBRARY, LONDON
WHO WERE THEY, MISS BENTHAM?
ER... POLICE. C.I.D. I THINK.
WHAT?
DO YOU REMEMBER THAT TEENAGER WHO WAS IN HERE MOST OF LAST WEEK?
OF COURSE. YOU MEAN THE ONE WHO WENT THROUGH THE WHOLE OF THE ENCYCLOPEDIA BRITANNICA IN ONE DAY? CRAZY KID!
YES. THEY'RE LOOKING FOR HIM...DANGEROUS THEY SAY HE IS...
I KNEW THERE WAS SOMETHING STRANGE ABOUT HIM.
INDUCTION TAPE: KN 23A
SUBJECT: ARKWRIGHT, L.
RECORDED: 14.12.1970
PERSONNEL PRESENT:
WASZYNKO, K.
WILDE, R.
EXTRACT 7:16
"When I first headed for Tibet, I theorised that it was logical. Where better to hide than the remote vastness of the Himalayas?"
"As I drew nearer though, I knew that I was being drawn there by a powerful psychic summons...." ENDS.
EXTRACT 7:23
"The Lamasery—for as much as it appeared to me—shimmered like a mirage....assuming solidity as I approached."
"Through the gateway the climate became tropical. Impossibly beautiful flowers and shrub flourished as if in full bloom."

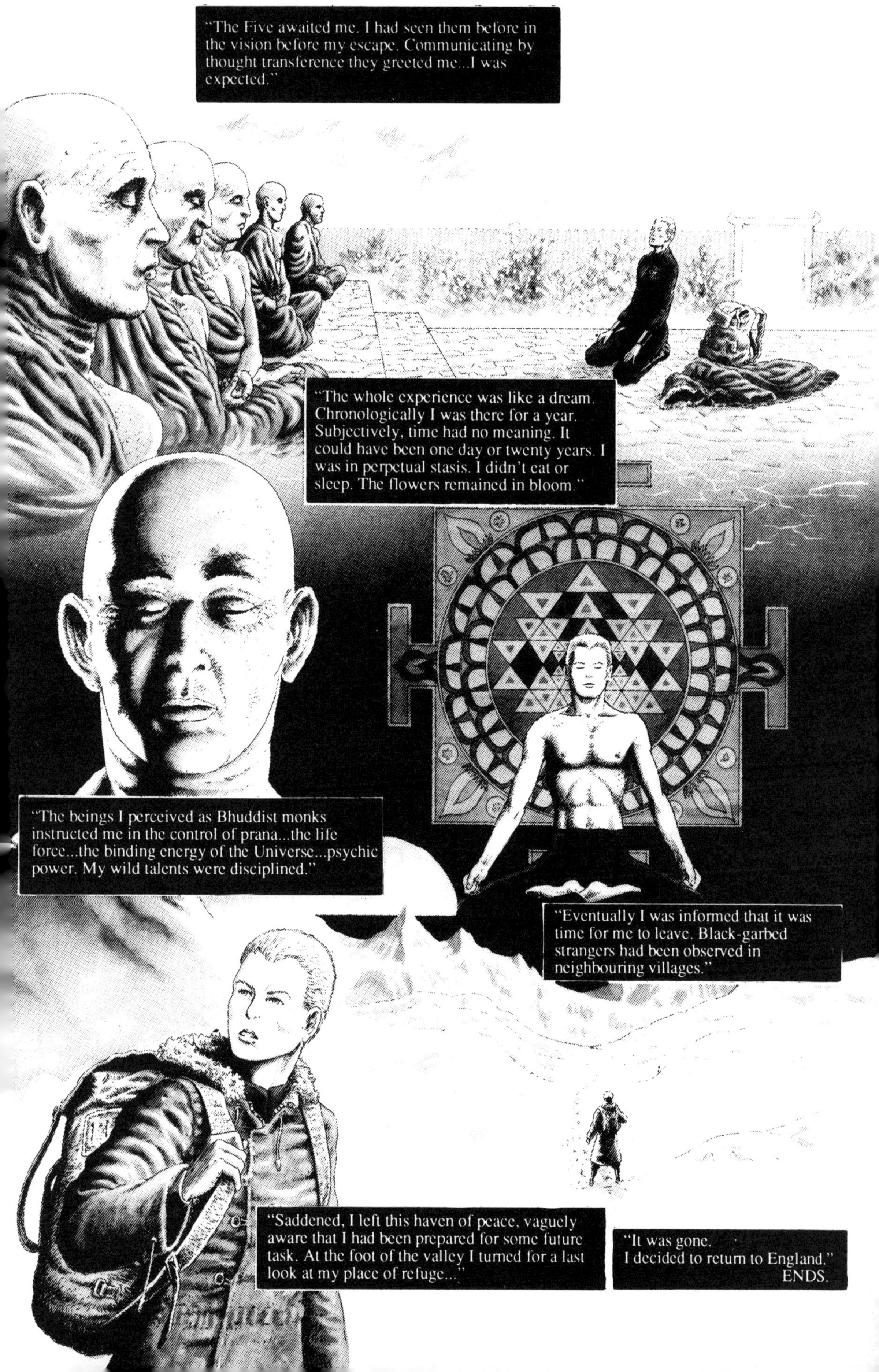
"The Five awaited me. I had seen them before in the vision before my escape. Communicating by thought transference they greeted me...I was expected."
"The whole experience was like a dream. Chronologically I was there for a year. Subjectively, time had no meaning. It could have been one day or twenty years. I was in perpetual stasis. I didn't eat or sleep. The flowers remained in bloom."
"The beings I perceived as Bhuddist monks instructed me in the control of prana...the life force...the binding energy of the Universe...psychic power. My wild talents were disciplined."
"Eventually I was informed that it was time for me to leave. Black-garbed strangers had been observed in neighbouring villages."
"Saddened, I left this haven of peace, vaguely aware that I had been prepared for some future task. At the foot of the valley I turned for a last look at my place of refuge..."
"It was gone.
I decided to return to England."
ENDS.

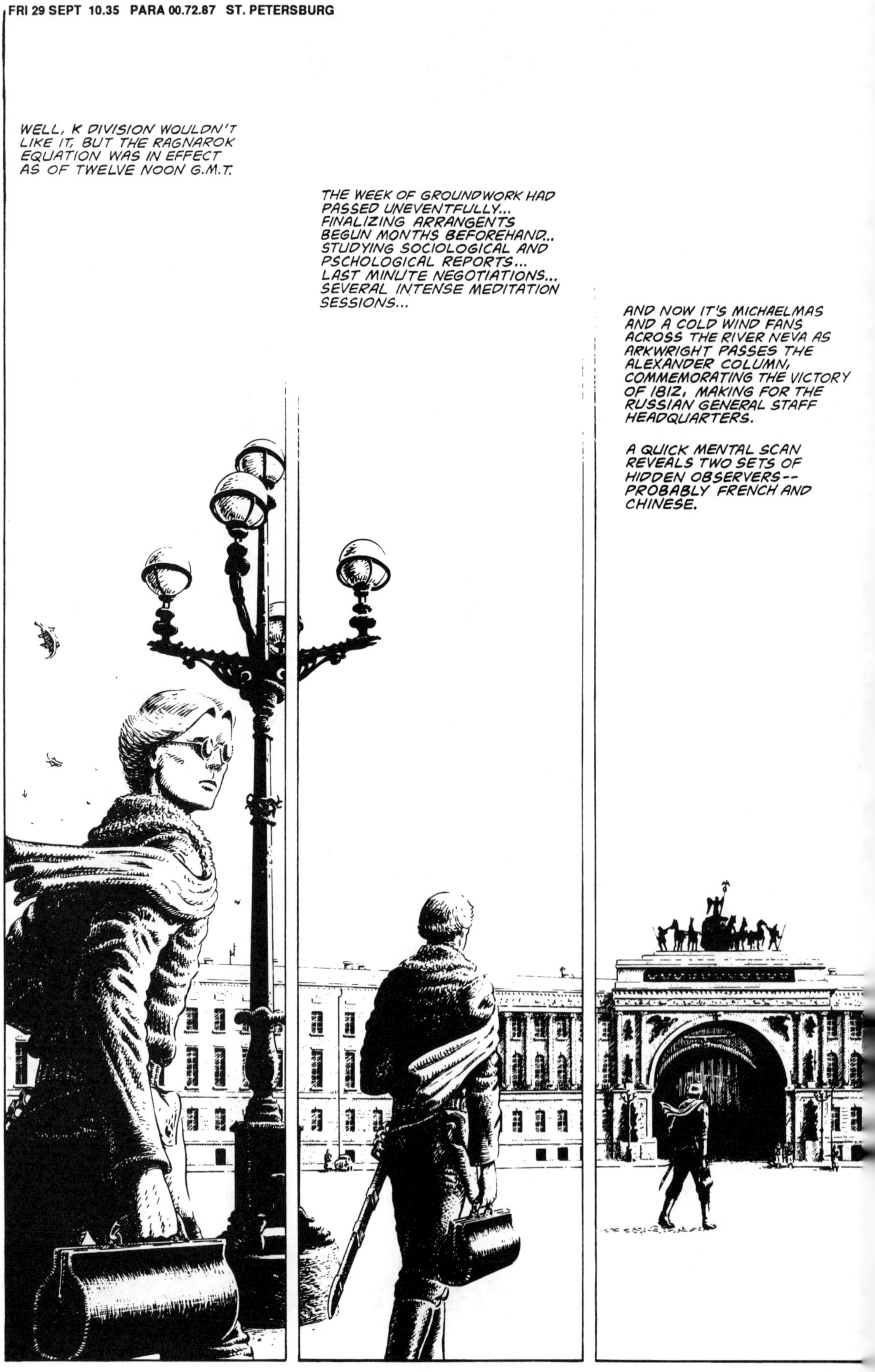
FRI 29 SEPT 10.35 PARA 00.72.87 ST. PETERSBURG
WELL, K DIVISION WOULDN'T LIKE IT, BUT THE RAGNAROK EQUATION WAS IN EFFECT AS OF TWELVE NOON G.M.T.
THE WEEK OF GROUNDWORK HAD PASSED UNEVENTFULLY... FINALIZING ARRANGENTS BEGUN MONTHS BEFOREHAND... STUDYING SOCIOLOGICAL AND PSCHOLOGICAL REPORTS... LAST MINUTE NEGOTIATIONS... SEVERAL INTENSE MEDITATION SESSIONS...
AND NOW IT'S MICHAELMAS AND A COLD WIND FANS ACROSS THE RIVER NEVA AS ARKWRIGHT PASSES THE ALEXANDER COLUMN, COMMEMORATING THE VICTORY OF 1812, MAKING FOR THE RUSSIAN GENERAL STAFF HEADQUARTERS.
A QUICK MENTAL SCAN REVEALS TWO SETS OF HIDDEN OBSERVERS-- PROBABLY FRENCH AND CHINESE.

GULF OF FINLAND 11.13

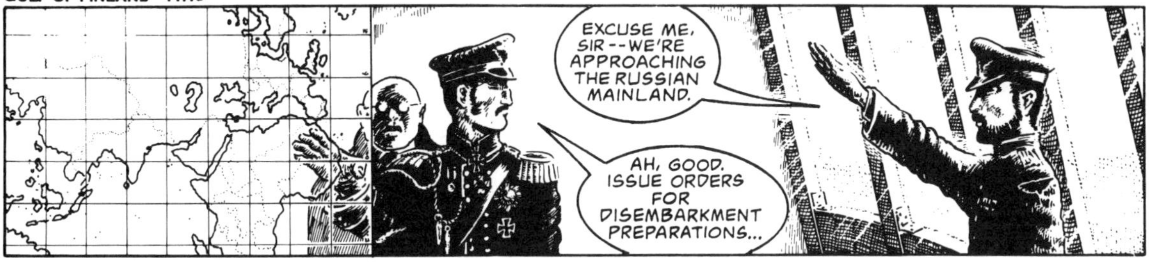
EXCUSE ME, SIR--WE'RE APPROACHING THE RUSSIAN MAINLAND.
AH, GOOD. ISSUE ORDERS FOR DISEMBARKMENT PREPARATIONS...

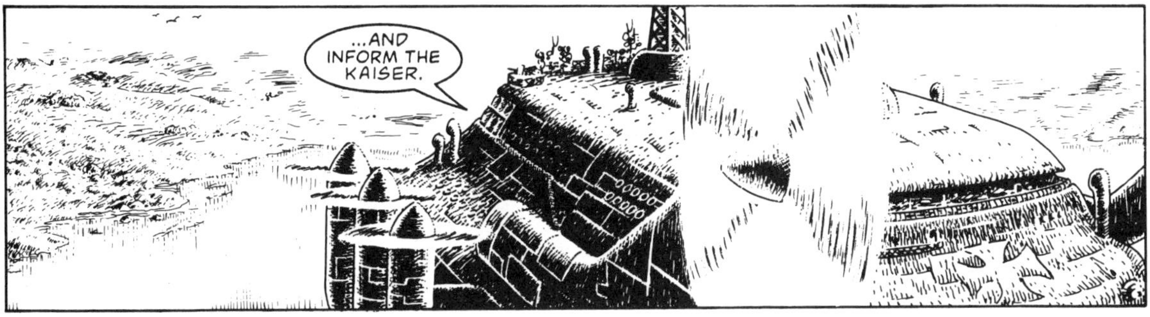
...AND INFORM THE KAISER.

PARA 00.00.00 LONDON 11.00 (9.00 GMT)

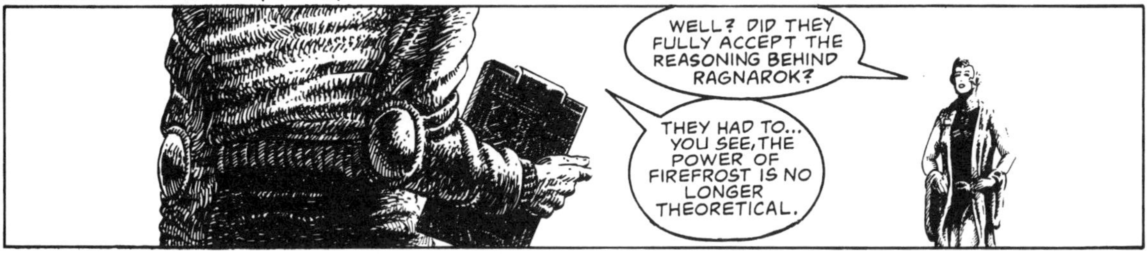
WELL? DID THEY FULLY ACCEPT THE REASONING BEHIND RAGNAROK?
THEY HAD TO... YOU SEE, THE POWER OF FIREFROST IS NO LONGER THEORETICAL.

PARA 00.72.87 LONDON 9.00 GMT

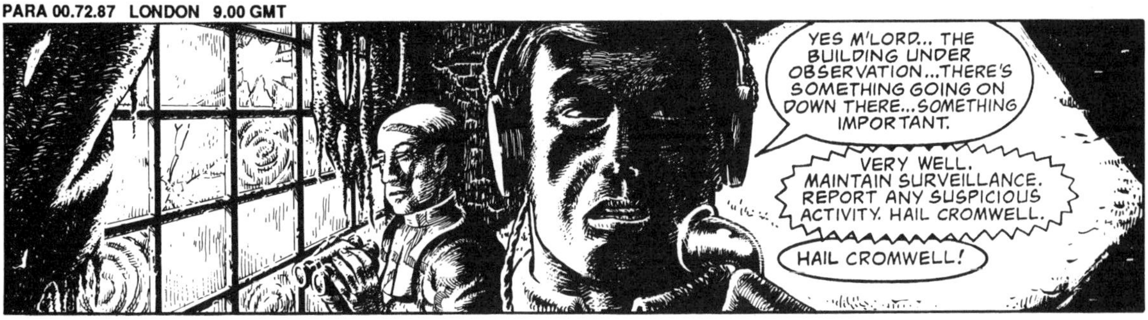
YES M'LORD... THE BUILDING UNDER OBSERVATION...THERE'S SOMETHING GOING ON DOWN THERE...SOMETHING IMPORTANT.
VERY WELL. MAINTAIN SURVEILLANCE. REPORT ANY SUSPICIOUS ACTIVITY. HAIL CROMWELL.
HAIL CROMWELL!

ST. PETERSBURG 11.03

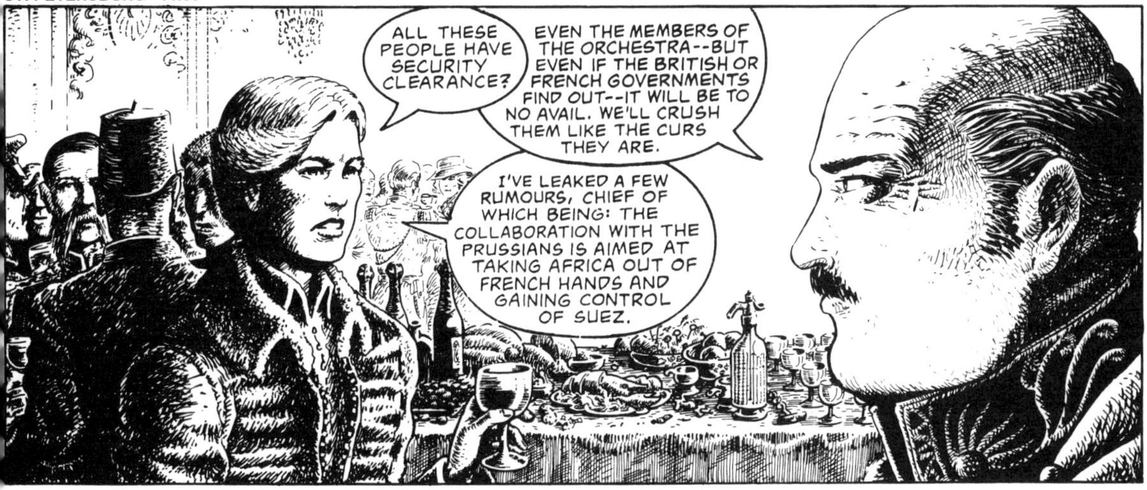
ALL THESE PEOPLE HAVE SECURITY CLEARANCE?
EVEN THE MEMBERS OF THE ORCHESTRA--BUT EVEN IF THE BRITISH OR FRENCH GOVERNMENTS FIND OUT--IT WILL BE TO NO AVAIL. WE'LL CRUSH THEM LIKE THE CURS THEY ARE.
I'VE LEAKED A FEW RUMOURS, CHIEF OF WHICH BEING: THE COLLABORATION WITH THE PRUSSIANS IS AIMED AT TAKING AFRICA OUT OF FRENCH HANDS AND GAINING CONTROL OF SUEZ.

MMM...YES. WE THINK IT WILL PROCEED WITH SMOOTHNESS AND ALACRITY. OF COURSE, THE SUBSTANTIAL LOAN TO THE ENGLISH CROWN AS LAID OUT IN THE TREATY, WILL AID YOUR SIDE CONSIDERABLY.

THE ROYALIST GUERRILLAS ARE BADLY EQUIPPED IT'S TRUE, CZAR NICHOLAS.

WE HAVE BEEN WAITING FOR A CHANCE SUCH AS THIS TO PURGE THE BLASPHEMY OF THE PROTECTORS' DICTATORSHIP. UNTIL THE ENGLISH CIVIL WAR, MONARCHY WAS RECOGNISED AS THE NATURAL SYSTEM OF GOVERNMENT BY EVERY CIVILIZED COUNTRY IN THE WORLD. THEN FRANCE... AND THE U.C.A. ... ITALY... ⸮PFAH!�

I AM A VEHICLE INTENDED TO FULFIL THE WILL OF GOD! I SHALL CLEANSE THE WORLD OF...

WHAT? THAT NOISE... GETTING CLOSER...

OUR ALLIES APPROACH.

ХАСТ!

DEFYING ALL THE LAWS OF AERODYNAMICS, THE IMPERIAL PRUSSIAN COMMAND SHIP, "SIEGFRIED," DESCENDS INTO THE HEART OF ST. PETERSBURG. [LANDMARK REFERENCE EK35: THE CHURCH OF THE SAVIOUR-ON-THE-SPILLED BLOOD.] "THE VERY SPOT WHERE ALEXANDER II WAS MORTALLY WOUNDED BY NIHILIST BOMBS ON THE VERY DAY (MARCH 13TH, 1881) ON WHICH HE HAD SIGNED A DECREE OF REFORM." A.T.Z.

ONLY THE PRUSSIANS COULD AFFORD TO BUILD THAT CONTRAPTION-- WORTH ITS WEIGHT IN GOLD...

THE SIGHT ALONE KEEPS THE SERBS AND POLES IN SUBJUGATION.

PREPARE FOR LANDING! UNDERCARRIAGE DOWN!

MOVE!

WATCH ARCHDUKE WILHELM WHEN HE ENTERS...STRAIGHT INTO HIS OLD BROTHER-IN-LAW ROUTINE--NOT SEEN HIM FOR TWO YEARS.

KLIK

DOWN! DOWN! NOW DUMMKOPF!

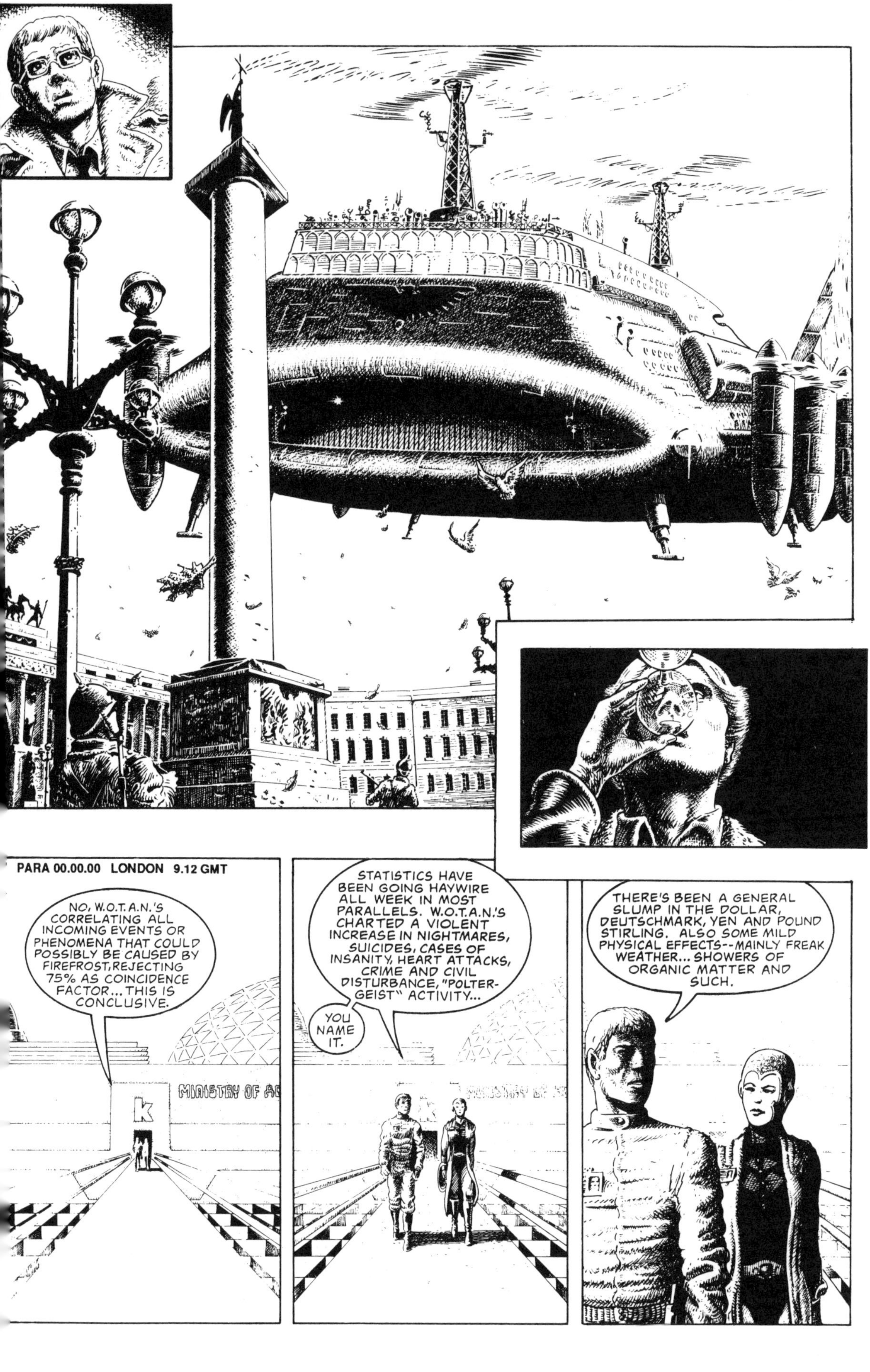
PARA 00.00.00 LONDON 9.12 GMT
NO, W.O.T.A.N.'S CORRELATING ALL INCOMING EVENTS OR PHENOMENA THAT COULD POSSIBLY BE CAUSED BY FIREFROST, REJECTING 75% AS COINCIDENCE FACTOR... THIS IS CONCLUSIVE.
MINISTRY OF A
K
STATISTICS HAVE BEEN GOING HAYWIRE ALL WEEK IN MOST PARALLELS. W.O.T.A.N.'S CHARTED A VIOLENT INCREASE IN NIGHTMARES, SUICIDES, CASES OF INSANITY, HEART ATTACKS, CRIME AND CIVIL DISTURBANCE, "POLTER-GEIST" ACTIVITY...
YOU NAME IT.
THERE'S BEEN A GENERAL SLUMP IN THE DOLLAR, DEUTSCHMARK, YEN AND POUND STIRLING. ALSO SOME MILD PHYSICAL EFFECTS--MAINLY FREAK WEATHER... SHOWERS OF ORGANIC MATTER AND SUCH.

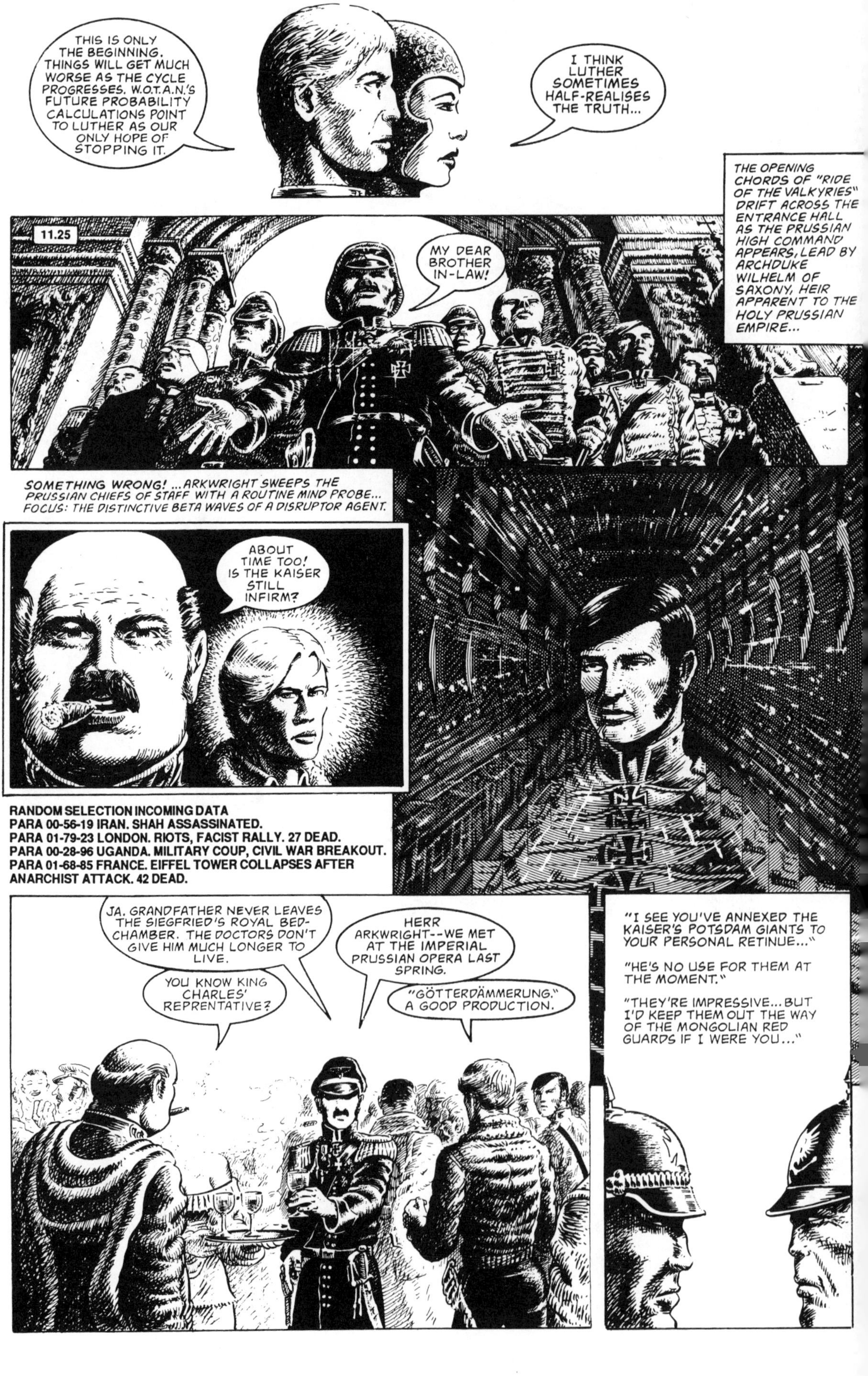
THIS IS ONLY THE BEGINNING. THINGS WILL GET MUCH WORSE AS THE CYCLE PROGRESSES. W.O.T.A.N.'S FUTURE PROBABILITY CALCULATIONS POINT TO LUTHER AS OUR ONLY HOPE OF STOPPING IT.
I THINK LUTHER SOMETIMES HALF-REALISES THE TRUTH...
THE OPENING CHORDS OF "RIDE OF THE VALKYRIES" DRIFT ACROSS THE ENTRANCE HALL AS THE PRUSSIAN HIGH COMMAND APPEARS, LEAD BY ARCHDUKE WILHELM OF SAXONY, HEIR APPARENT TO THE HOLY PRUSSIAN EMPIRE...
11.25
MY DEAR BROTHER IN-LAW!
SOMETHING WRONG! ...ARKWRIGHT SWEEPS THE PRUSSIAN CHIEFS OF STAFF WITH A ROUTINE MIND PROBE... FOCUS: THE DISTINCTIVE BETA WAVES OF A DISRUPTOR AGENT.
ABOUT TIME TOO! IS THE KAISER STILL INFIRM?
RANDOM SELECTION INCOMING DATA
PARA 00-56-19 IRAN. SHAH ASSASSINATED.
PARA 01-79-23 LONDON. RIOTS, FACIST RALLY. 27 DEAD.
PARA 00-28-96 UGANDA. MILITARY COUP, CIVIL WAR BREAKOUT.
PARA 01-68-85 FRANCE. EIFFEL TOWER COLLAPSES AFTER ANARCHIST ATTACK. 42 DEAD.
JA. GRANDFATHER NEVER LEAVES THE SIEGFRIED'S ROYAL BED-CHAMBER. THE DOCTORS DON'T GIVE HIM MUCH LONGER TO LIVE.
YOU KNOW KING CHARLES' REPRENTATIVE?
HERR ARKWRIGHT--WE MET AT THE IMPERIAL PRUSSIAN OPERA LAST SPRING.
"GÖTTERDÄMMERUNG." A GOOD PRODUCTION.
"I SEE YOU'VE ANNEXED THE KAISER'S POTSDAM GIANTS TO YOUR PERSONAL RETINUE..."
"HE'S NO USE FOR THEM AT THE MOMENT."
"THEY'RE IMPRESSIVE... BUT I'D KEEP THEM OUT THE WAY OF THE MONGOLIAN RED GUARDS IF I WERE YOU..."

"AND NOW, IF YOU WILL EXCUSE ME GENTLEMEN, I'LL ORDER PREPARATIONS FOR THE CEREMONY. THIS IS A HISTORIC OCCASION."

AND THE GUESTS ASSEMBLE TO OBSERVE THE SIGNING OF AN ALLIANCE AND A DECLARATION OF WAR...

"NEVER WERE LIVES SO LIGHTLY SIGNED AWAY." KROPOTKIN.

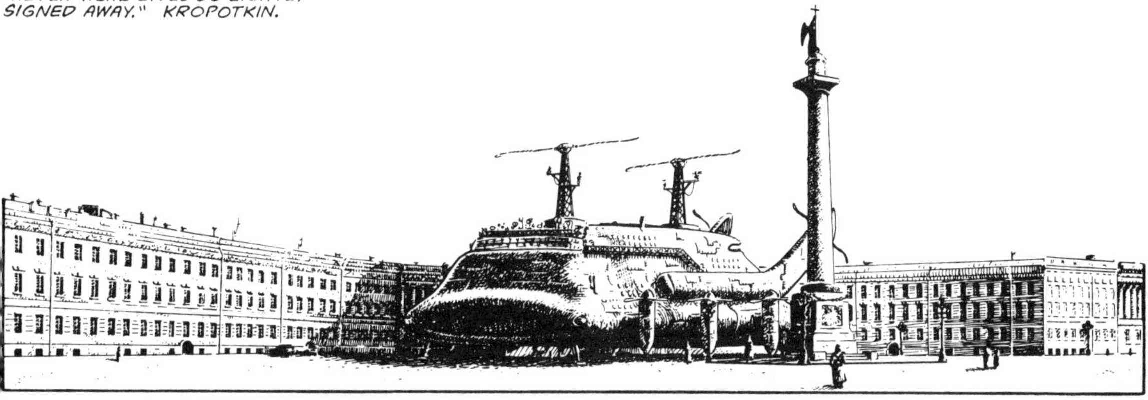

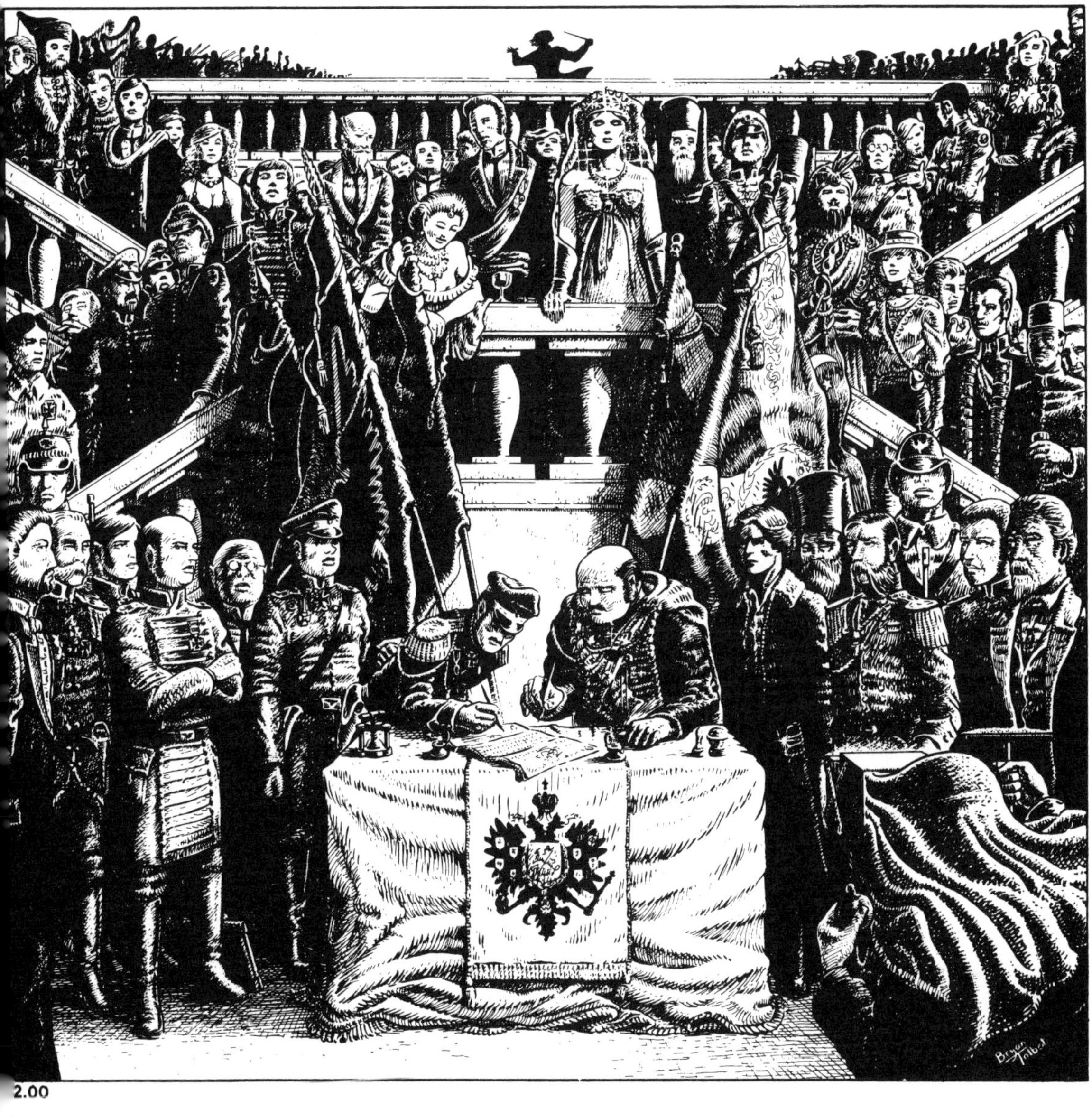
Bryan Talbot

2.00

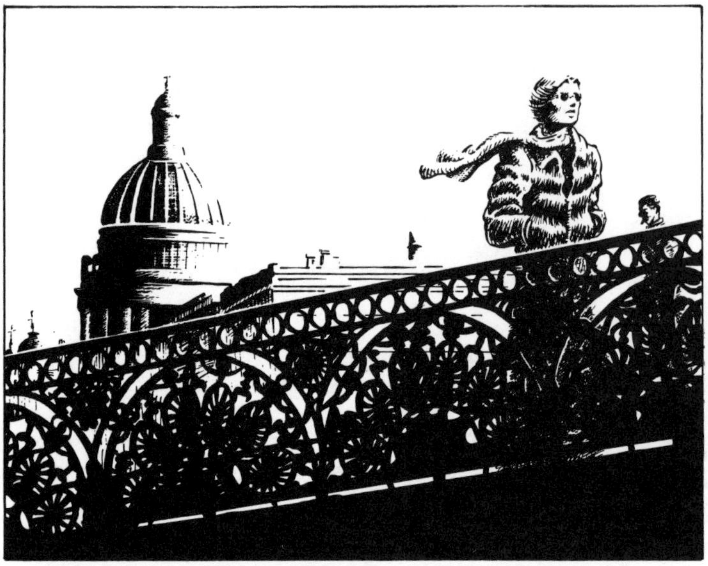

12.24. NOW: BEING TAILED PAST THE CATHEDRALS. THE SHADOW, AMERICAN JUDGING FROM VIBRATIONS, IS EASY ENOUGH TO LOSE IN THE OLD HAYMARKET EN ROUTE TO THE JEWISH QUARTER. AND THERE: A BRIEF EXCHANGE WITH A CONTACT: A WHISPERED LOCATION...

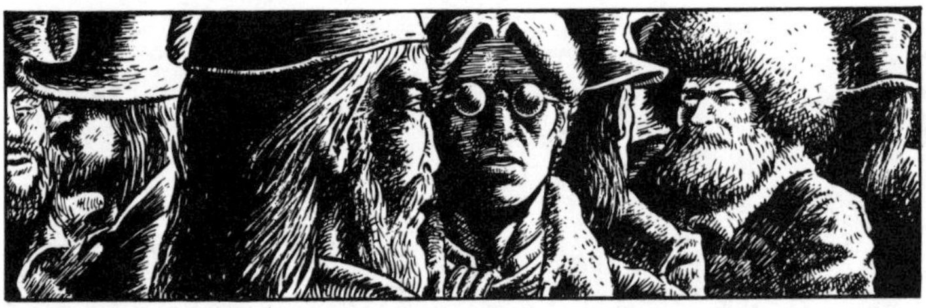

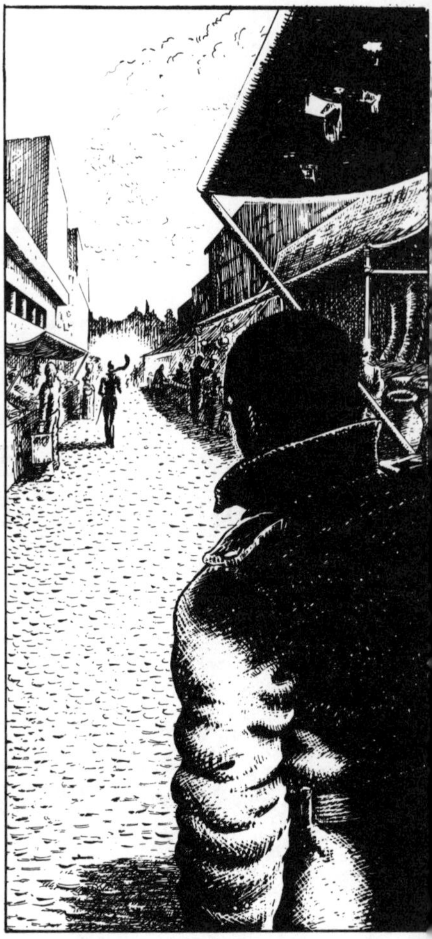

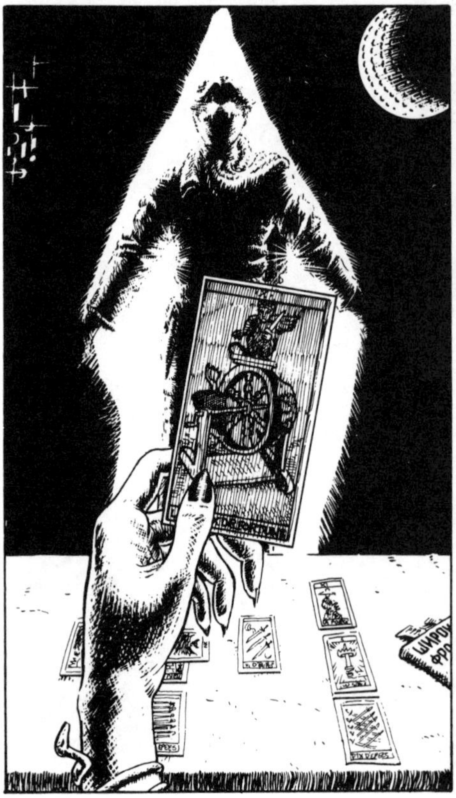

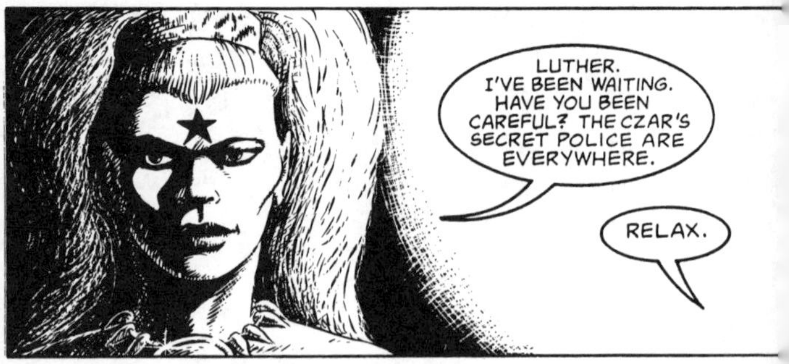
LUTHER. I'VE BEEN WAITING. HAVE YOU BEEN CAREFUL? THE CZAR'S SECRET POLICE ARE EVERYWHERE.
RELAX.

PARA 01-32-69 NORTH AMERICA. VIOLENT TREMORS SAN ANDREAS FAULT.

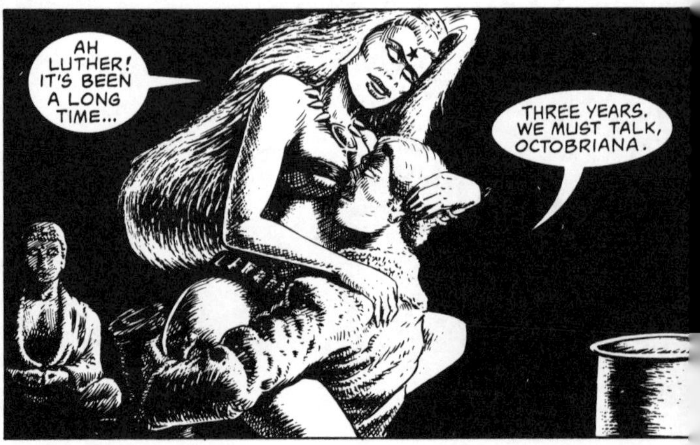
AH LUTHER! IT'S BEEN A LONG TIME...
THREE YEARS. WE MUST TALK, OCTOBRIANA.

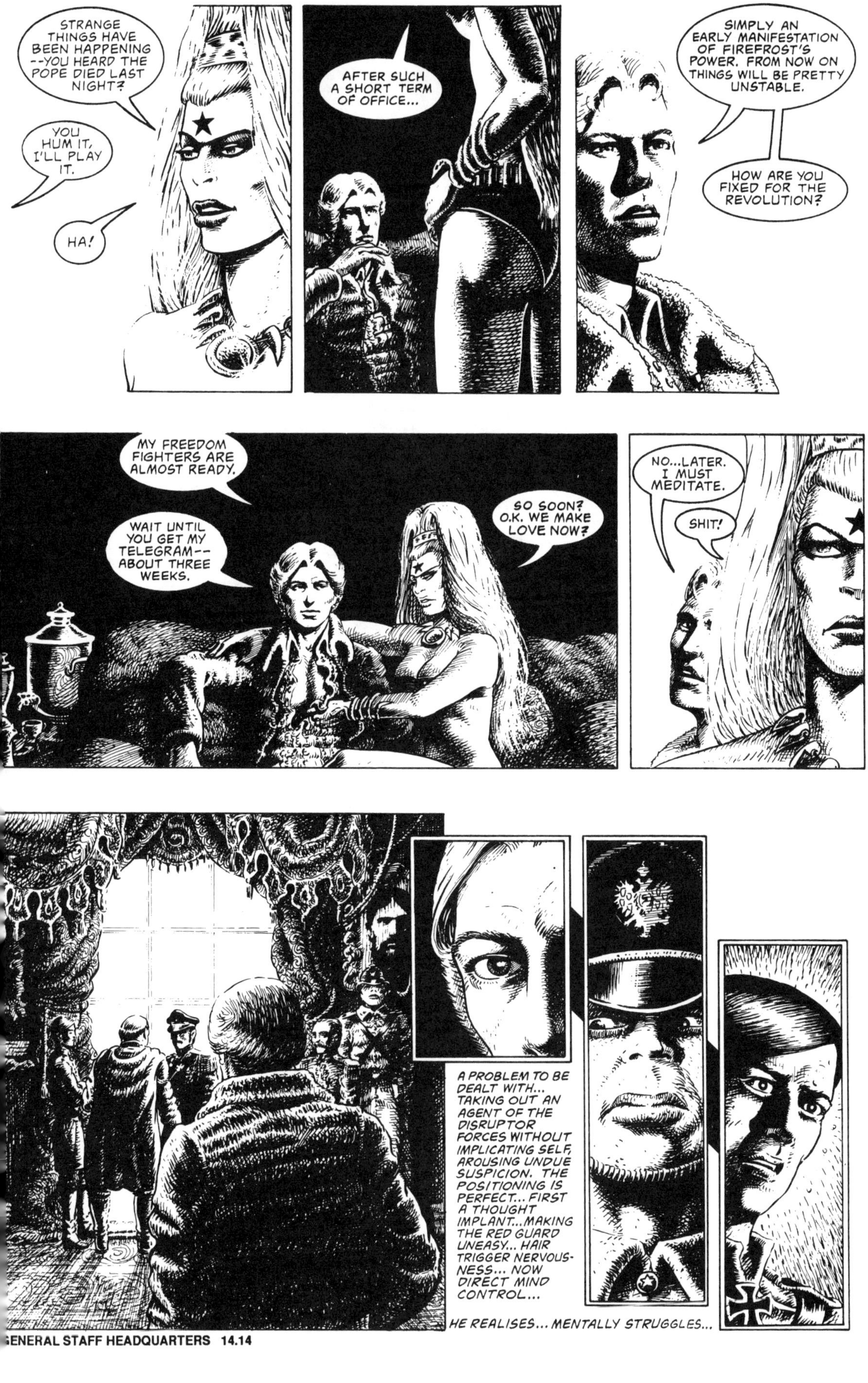
STRANGE THINGS HAVE BEEN HAPPENING --YOU HEARD THE POPE DIED LAST NIGHT?
YOU HUM IT, I'LL PLAY IT.
HA!
AFTER SUCH A SHORT TERM OF OFFICE...
SIMPLY AN EARLY MANIFESTATION OF FIREFROST'S POWER. FROM NOW ON THINGS WILL BE PRETTY UNSTABLE.
HOW ARE YOU FIXED FOR THE REVOLUTION?
MY FREEDOM FIGHTERS ARE ALMOST READY.
WAIT UNTIL YOU GET MY TELEGRAM-- ABOUT THREE WEEKS.
SO SOON? O.K. WE MAKE LOVE NOW?
NO...LATER. I MUST MEDITATE.
SHIT!
A PROBLEM TO BE DEALT WITH... TAKING OUT AN AGENT OF THE DISRUPTOR FORCES WITHOUT IMPLICATING SELF, AROUSING UNDUE SUSPICION. THE POSITIONING IS PERFECT... FIRST A THOUGHT IMPLANT...MAKING THE RED GUARD UNEASY... HAIR TRIGGER NERVOUSNESS... NOW DIRECT MIND CONTROL...
HE REALISES... MENTALLY STRUGGLES...
GENERAL STAFF HEADQUARTERS 14.14

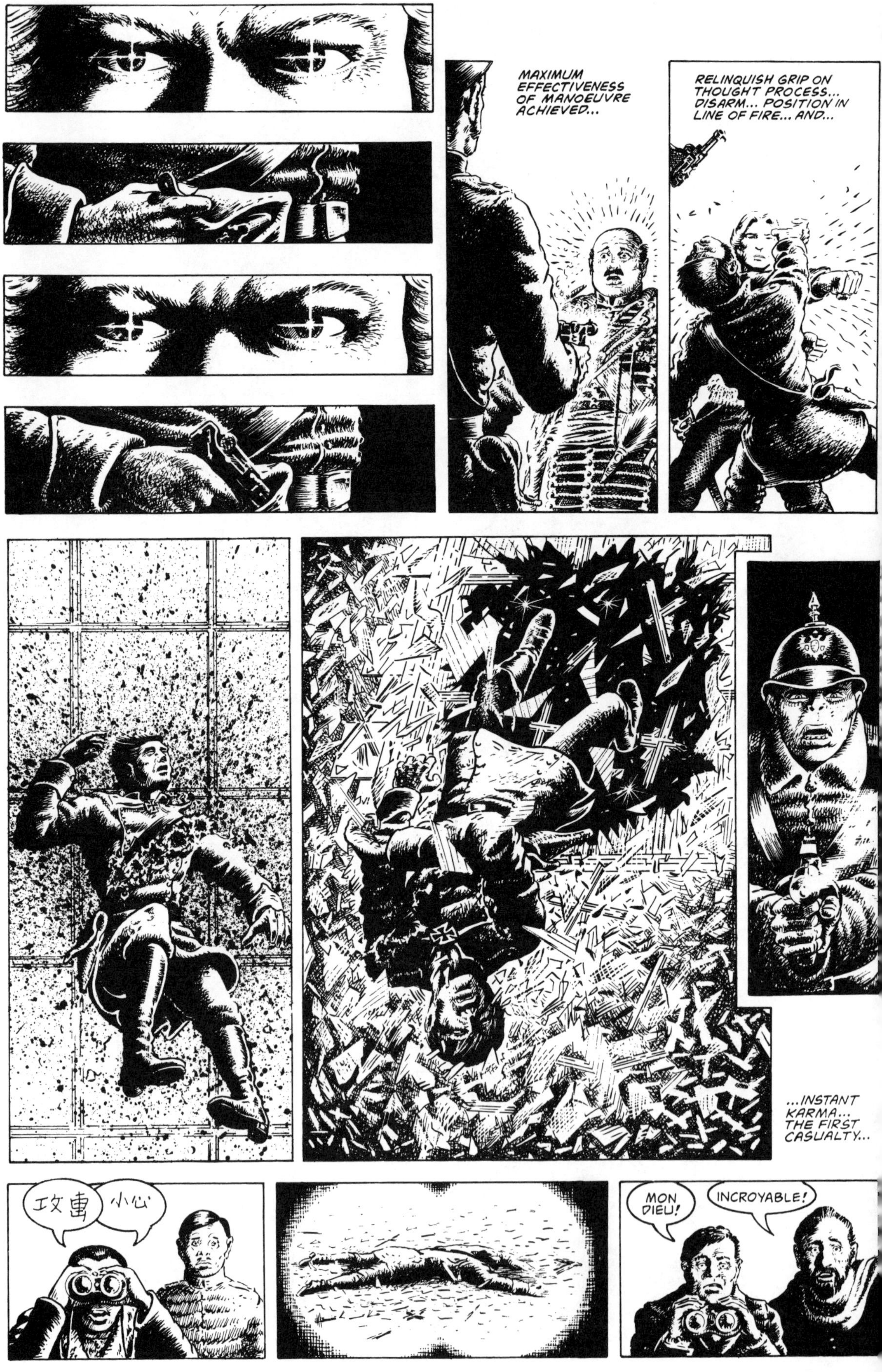

MAXIMUM EFFECTIVENESS OF MANOEUVRE ACHIEVED...
RELINQUISH GRIP ON THOUGHT PROCESS... DISARM... POSITION IN LINE OF FIRE... AND...
...INSTANT KARMA... THE FIRST CASUALTY...
攻車
小心
MON DIEU!
INCROYABLE!

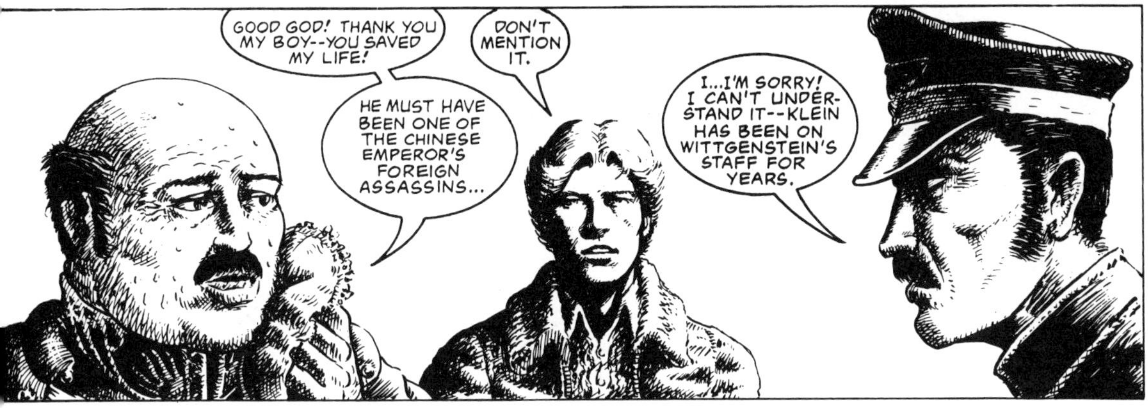
GOOD GOD! THANK YOU MY BOY--YOU SAVED MY LIFE!
DON'T MENTION IT.
HE MUST HAVE BEEN ONE OF THE CHINESE EMPEROR'S FOREIGN ASSASSINS...
I...I'M SORRY! I CAN'T UNDERSTAND IT--KLEIN HAS BEEN ON WITTGENSTEIN'S STAFF FOR YEARS.

20.36

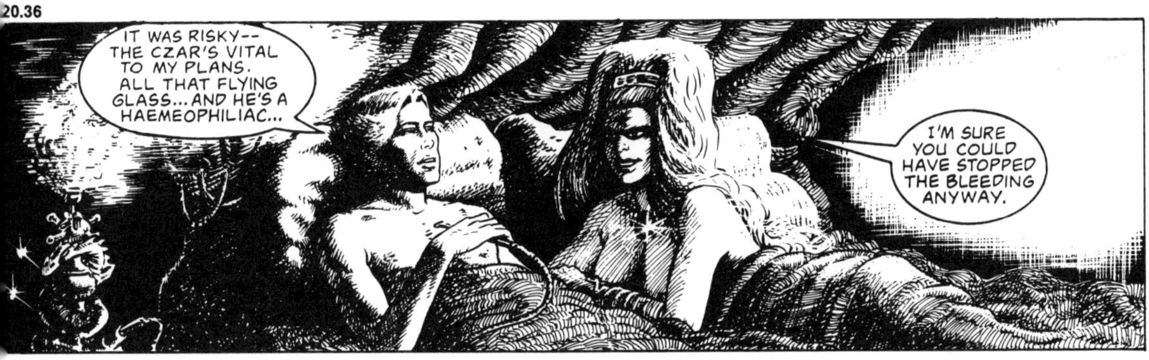
IT WAS RISKY-- THE CZAR'S VITAL TO MY PLANS. ALL THAT FLYING GLASS... AND HE'S A HAEMEOPHILIAC...
I'M SURE YOU COULD HAVE STOPPED THE BLEEDING ANYWAY.

WINTER PALACE 22.48

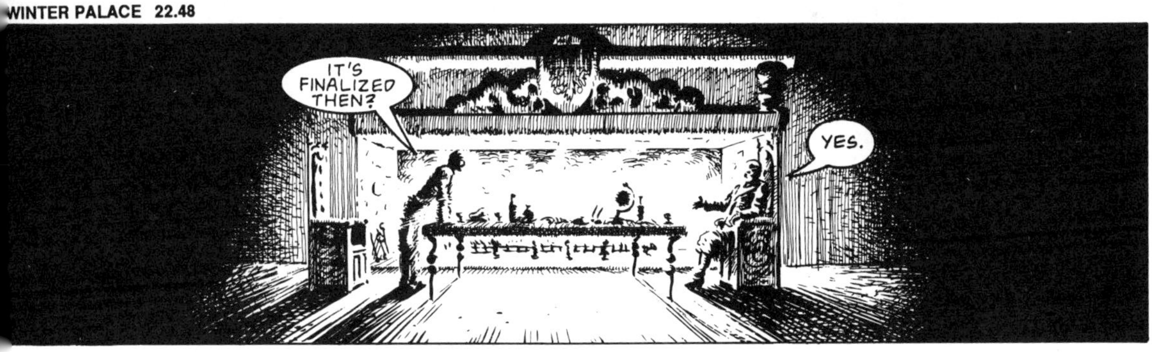
IT'S FINALIZED THEN?
YES.

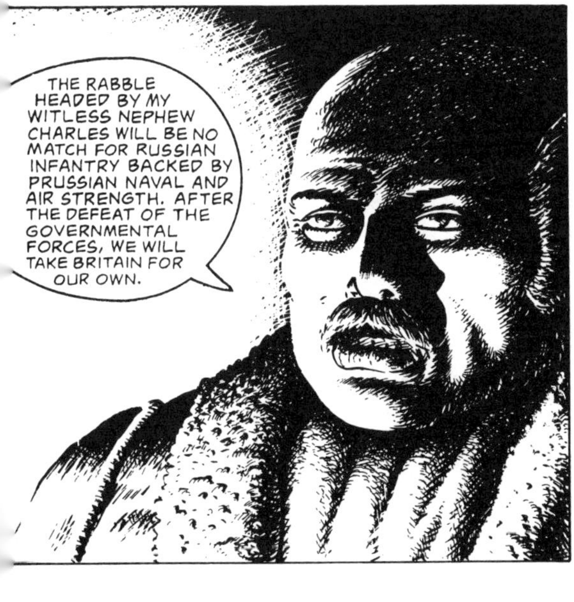
THE RABBLE HEADED BY MY WITLESS NEPHEW CHARLES WILL BE NO MATCH FOR RUSSIAN INFANTRY BACKED BY PRUSSIAN NAVAL AND AIR STRENGTH. AFTER THE DEFEAT OF THE GOVERNMENTAL FORCES, WE WILL TAKE BRITAIN FOR OUR OWN.

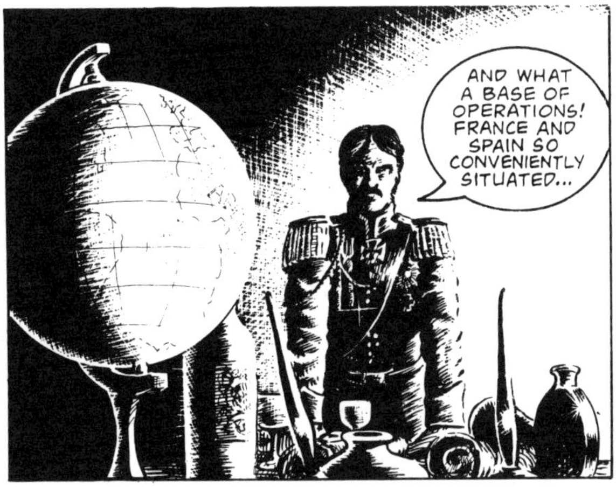
AND WHAT A BASE OF OPERATIONS! FRANCE AND SPAIN SO CONVENIENTLY SITUATED...

PARA 00-84-59 GUYANA. RELIGIOUS SECT MASS SUICIDE. 500 DEAD.
PARA 02-73-71 LONDON. PRIME MINISTER THORPE ASSASSINATED.
PARA 00-81-33 BELFAST. MASS U.F.O. SIGHTINGS AT PROTEST MARCH.

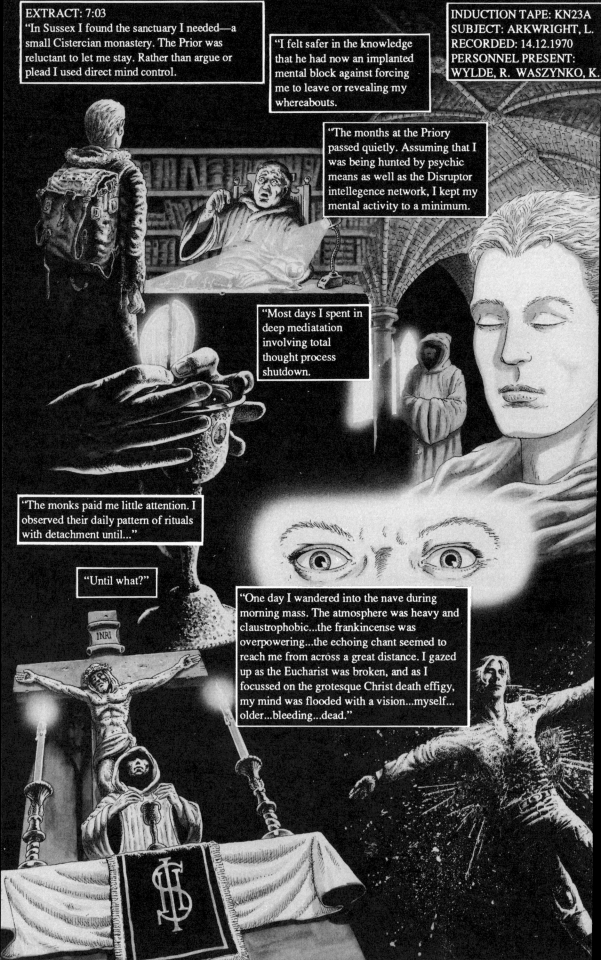

EXTRACT: 7:03
"In Sussex I found the sanctuary I needed—a small Cistercian monastery. The Prior was reluctant to let me stay. Rather than argue or plead I used direct mind control."

"I felt safer in the knowledge that he had now an implanted mental block against forcing me to leave or revealing my whereabouts."

INDUCTION TAPE: KN23A
SUBJECT: ARKWRIGHT, L.
RECORDED: 14.12.1970
PERSONNEL PRESENT:
WYLDE, R. WASZYNKO, K.

"The months at the Priory passed quietly. Assuming that I was being hunted by psychic means as well as the Disruptor intellegence network, I kept my mental activity to a minimum."

"Most days I spent in deep mediatation involving total thought process shutdown."

"The monks paid me little attention. I observed their daily pattern of rituals with detachment until..."

"Until what?"

"One day I wandered into the nave during morning mass. The atmosphere was heavy and claustrophobic...the frankincense was overpowering...the echoing chant seemed to reach me from across a great distance. I gazed up as the Eucharist was broken, and as I focussed on the grotesque Christ death effigy, my mind was flooded with a vision...myself... older...bleeding...dead."

INRI

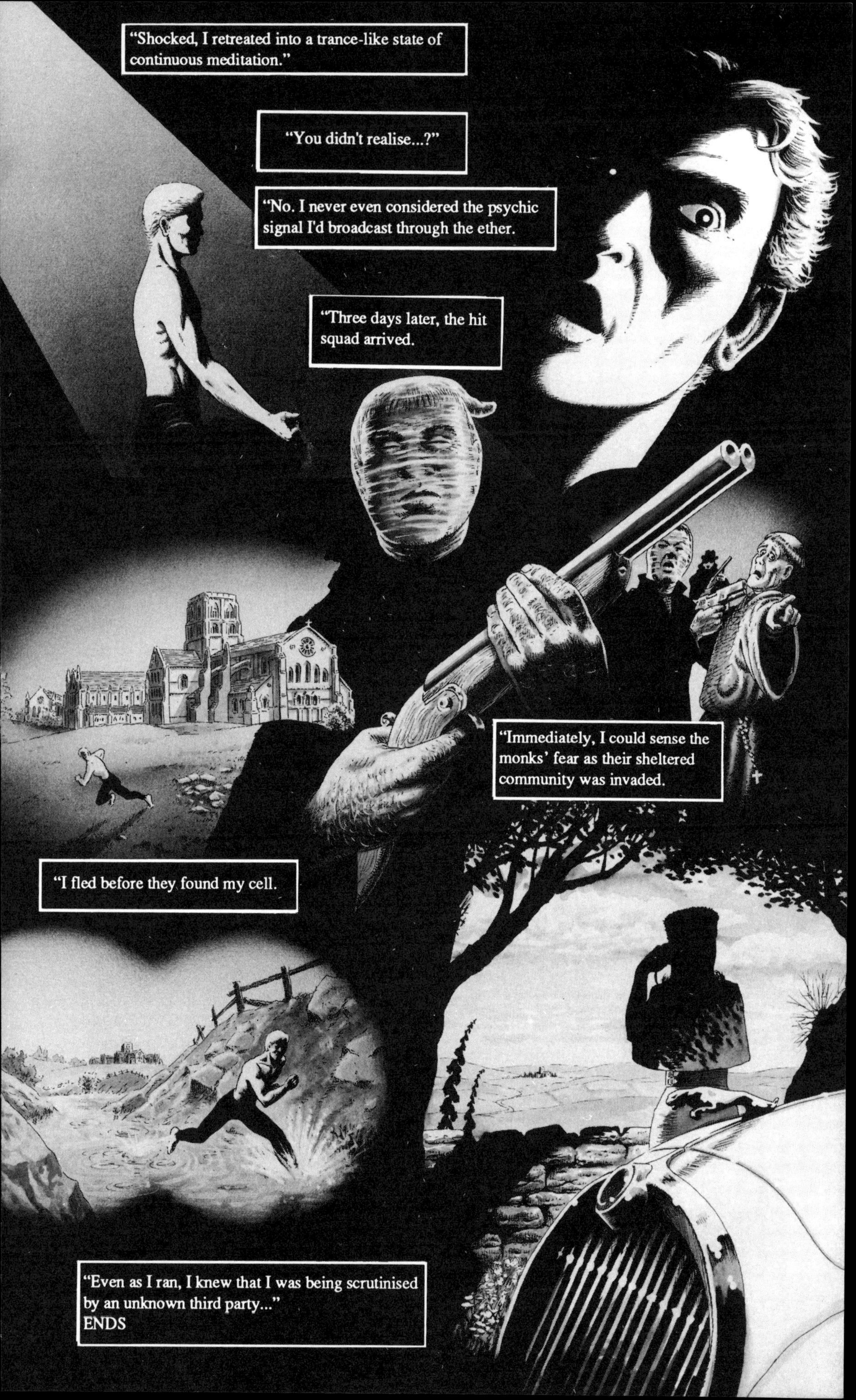

"Shocked, I retreated into a trance-like state of continuous meditation."
"You didn't realise...?"
"No. I never even considered the psychic signal I'd broadcast through the ether.
"Three days later, the hit squad arrived.
"Immediately, I could sense the monks' fear as their sheltered community was invaded.
"I fled before they found my cell.
"Even as I ran, I knew that I was being scrutinised by an unknown third party..."
ENDS

23 JAN 1981 9.05 PARA 00.72.87 GIZA

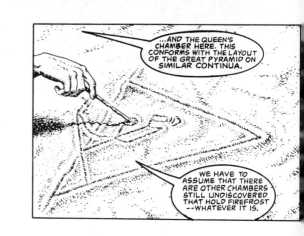

...AND THE QUEEN'S CHAMBER HERE. THIS CONFORMS WITH THE LAYOUT OF THE GREAT PYRAMID ON SIMILAR CONTINUA.

WE HAVE TO ASSUME THAT THERE ARE OTHER CHAMBERS STILL UNDISCOVERED THAT HOLD FIREFROST --WHATEVER IT IS.

WHY TODAY?

I EXPECT THEY CRACKED THE CYPHER CONTAINED IN THE CODEX YEARS AGO-- THEY'VE HAD IT SINCE 1914. THEY KNOW SOMETHING WE DON'T. BUT WHY NOW? IMPOSSIBLE TO SAY.

I WAS JUST FORTUNATE YESTERDAY-- AFTER THE DUEL --TO FIND OUT ABOUT THIS ATTEMPT.

ALL THIS FUSS OVER A SILLY FAIRY STORY!

BUT LIKE YOUR UKRANIAN FOLK-LORE, EGYPTIAN MYTHOLOGY HAS A BASIS OF SOLID FACT... MAINLY STEMMING FROM TRIBAL HISTORY.

THE POINT IS THAT THIS IS THE ONLY PARALLEL THAT HAS COMPLEX LEGENDS IN ITS MYTHOS CONCERNING "THE FIRE OPAL OF SET" ..."THE STONE OF THANATOS" ACCORDING TO THE GREEKS ..."FIREFROST" IN THE TEUTONIC CYCLE.

DA. IT FELL FROM THE SKY AFTER DESTROYING THE OLD GODS. BUT IT'S STILL JUST A STORY.

THE DISRUPTORS DON'T SEEM TO THINK SO.

WE'VE JUST GOT TO WAIT.

WE MAKE LOVE?

"Although the Lord of heaven and earth caused his great stone Witness to be constructed over forty centuries ago, it has pleased him to reserve the understanding of its message to the Millennial Day, which we are now entered upon; as we read: 'In that day there shall be an altar to the Lord in the midst of the land of Egypt, even a pillar at the border thereof to the Lord. And it shall be for [shall serve for] a sign, and for a witness, unto the Lord of hosts in the land of Egypt: for they shall cry unto the Lord because of the oppressors, and he shall send them a saviour, and a great one, and he shall deliver them' (Isaiah 19:19,20).

"It is, of course, the popular belief that the Great Pyramid is a tomb; for there is no doubt that the other pyramids were intended by their builders for this purpose, as mummies have been found in some of them. And yet it is now a well known fact that the accredited builder of the Great Pyramid, Cheops, was not buried inside his great monument.

"His tomb, where he was buried, has been identified by Egyptologists with a deep, and elaborately-cut sepulchral pit, which is situated about a thousand feet away from the Pyramid. Cheops (usually pronouced Keops), therefore, did not intend the Great Pyramid to serve as a tomb; nor, indeed, if we are to believe the reasonable deductions which are based upon historical accounts, did he or his Egyptian subjects know what purpose this immense edifice was intended to serve!"

J.R. Montpellier:
"The Great Pyramid—It's Scientific Features"
1912

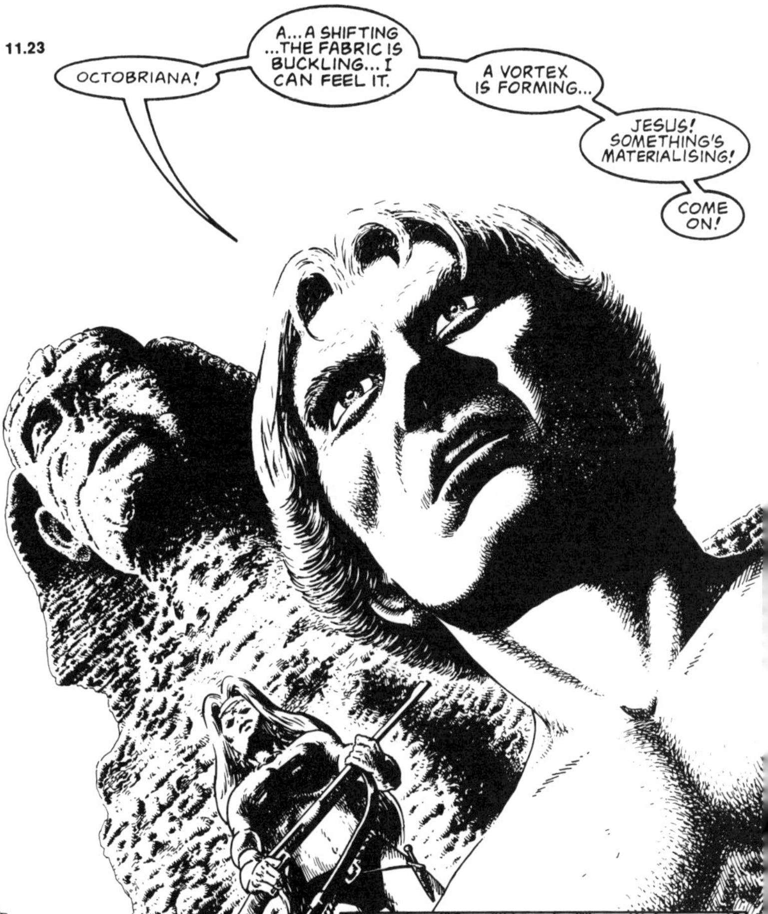
11.23
OCTOBRIANA!
A...A SHIFTING ...THE FABRIC IS BUCKLING... I CAN FEEL IT.
A VORTEX IS FORMING...
JESUS! SOMETHING'S MATERIALISING!
COME ON!

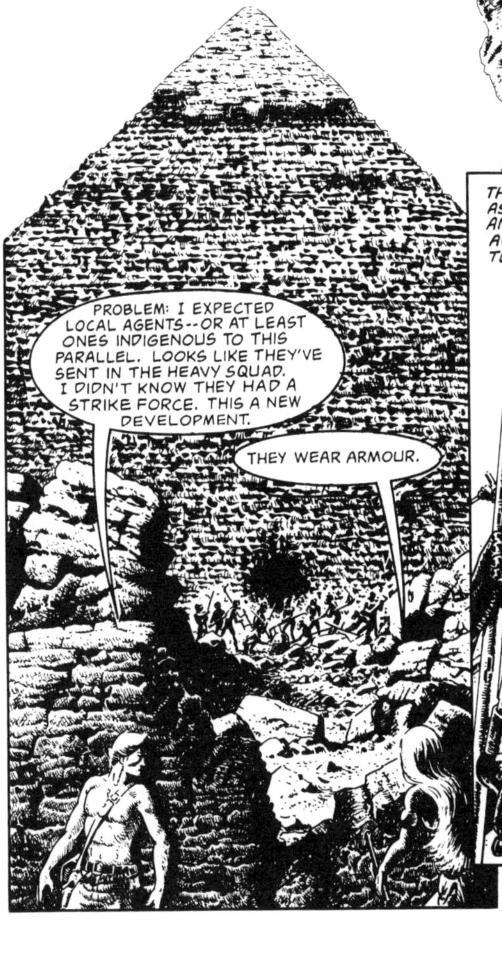
PROBLEM: I EXPECTED LOCAL AGENTS--OR AT LEAST ONES INDIGENOUS TO THIS PARALLEL. LOOKS LIKE THEY'VE SENT IN THE HEAVY SQUAD. I DIDN'T KNOW THEY HAD A STRIKE FORCE. THIS A NEW DEVELOPMENT.
THEY WEAR ARMOUR.

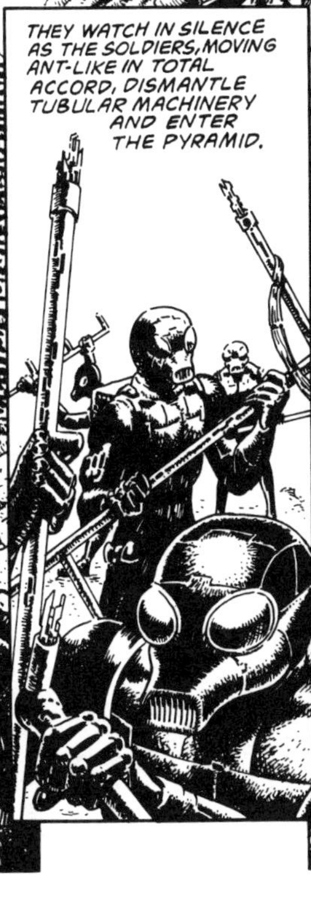
THEY WATCH IN SILENCE AS THE SOLDIERS, MOVING ANT-LIKE IN TOTAL ACCORD, DISMANTLE TUBULAR MACHINERY AND ENTER THE PYRAMID.

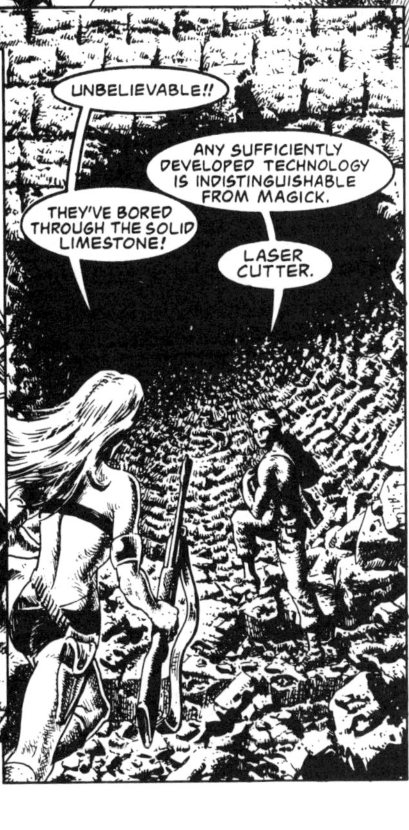
UNBELIEVABLE!!
THEY'VE BORED THROUGH THE SOLID LIMESTONE!
ANY SUFFICIENTLY DEVELOPED TECHNOLOGY IS INDISTINGUISHABLE FROM MAGICK.
LASER CUTTER.

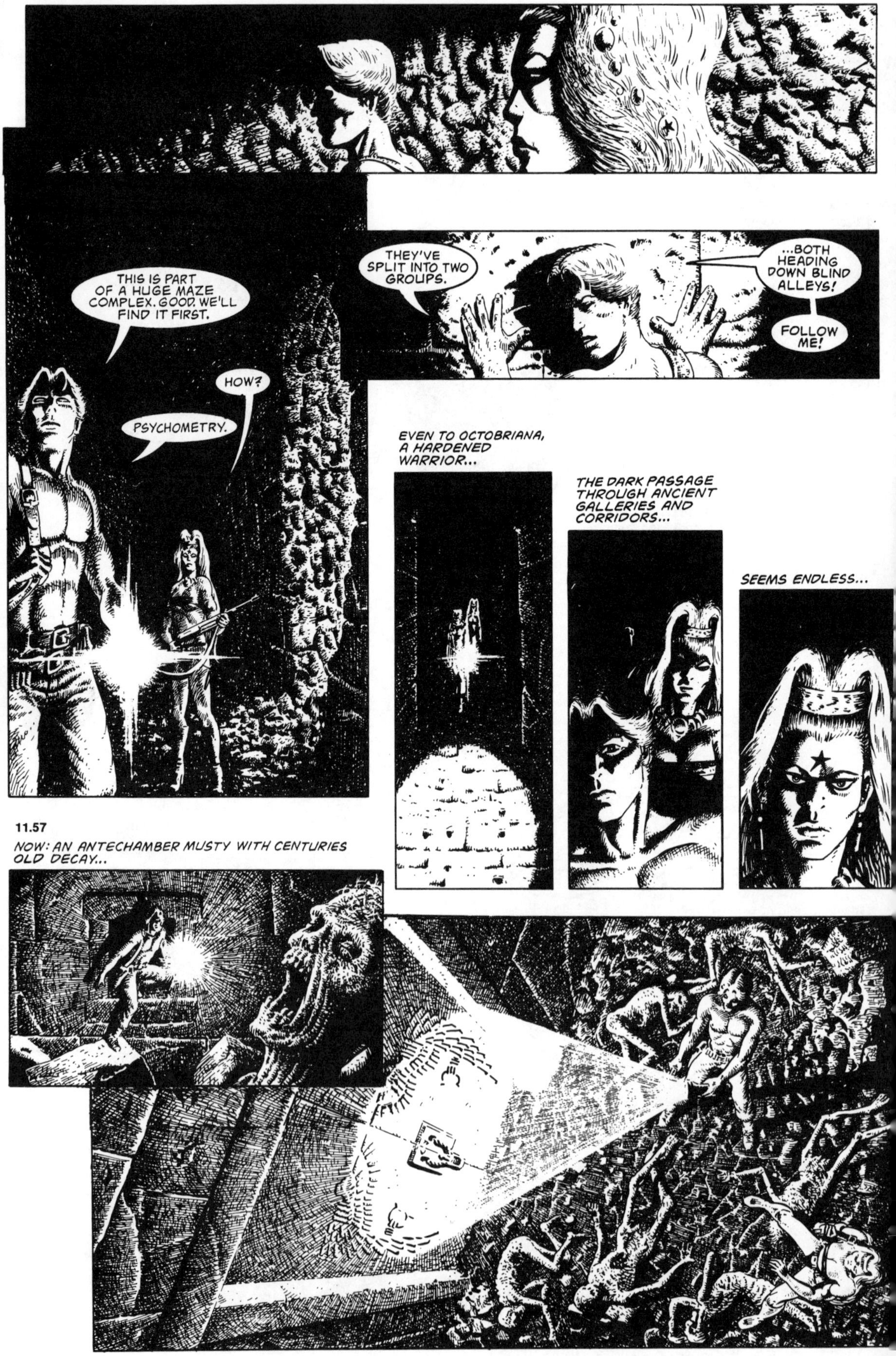
THIS IS PART OF A HUGE MAZE COMPLEX. GOOD. WE'LL FIND IT FIRST.
HOW?
PSYCHOMETRY.
THEY'VE SPLIT INTO TWO GROUPS.
...BOTH HEADING DOWN BLIND ALLEYS!
FOLLOW ME!
EVEN TO OCTOBRIANA, A HARDENED WARRIOR...
THE DARK PASSAGE THROUGH ANCIENT GALLERIES AND CORRIDORS...
SEEMS ENDLESS...
11.57
NOW: AN ANTECHAMBER MUSTY WITH CENTURIES OLD DECAY...

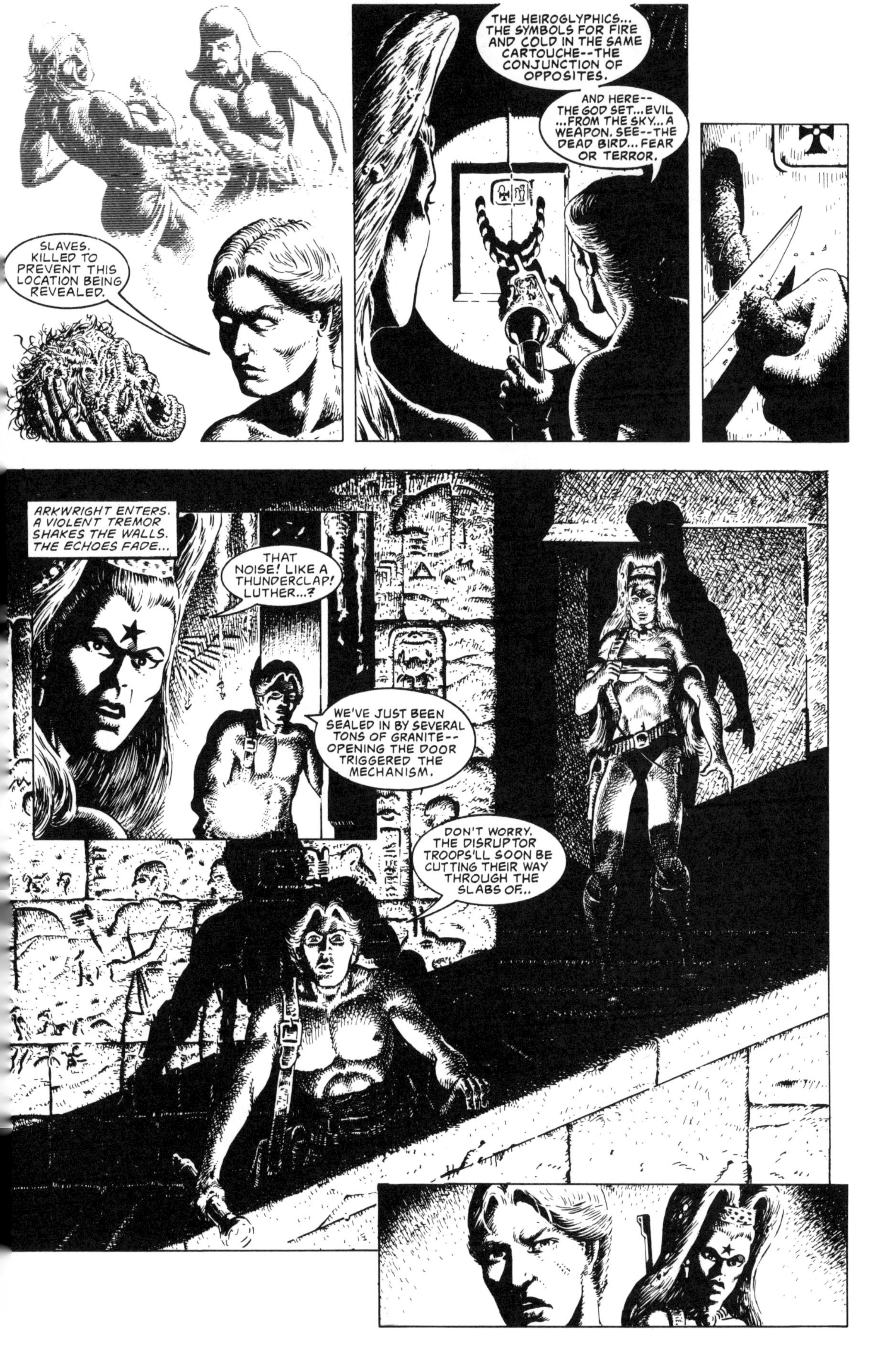
SLAVES. KILLED TO PREVENT THIS LOCATION BEING REVEALED.
THE HEIROGLYPHICS... THE SYMBOLS FOR FIRE AND COLD IN THE SAME CARTOUCHE--THE CONJUNCTION OF OPPOSITES.
AND HERE--THE GOD SET...EVIL ...FROM THE SKY...A WEAPON. SEE--THE DEAD BIRD... FEAR OR TERROR.
ARKWRIGHT ENTERS. A VIOLENT TREMOR SHAKES THE WALLS. THE ECHOES FADE...
THAT NOISE! LIKE A THUNDERCLAP! LUTHER...?
WE'VE JUST BEEN SEALED IN BY SEVERAL TONS OF GRANITE--OPENING THE DOOR TRIGGERED THE MECHANISM.
DON'T WORRY. THE DISRUPTOR TROOPS'LL SOON BE CUTTING THEIR WAY THROUGH THE SLABS OF...

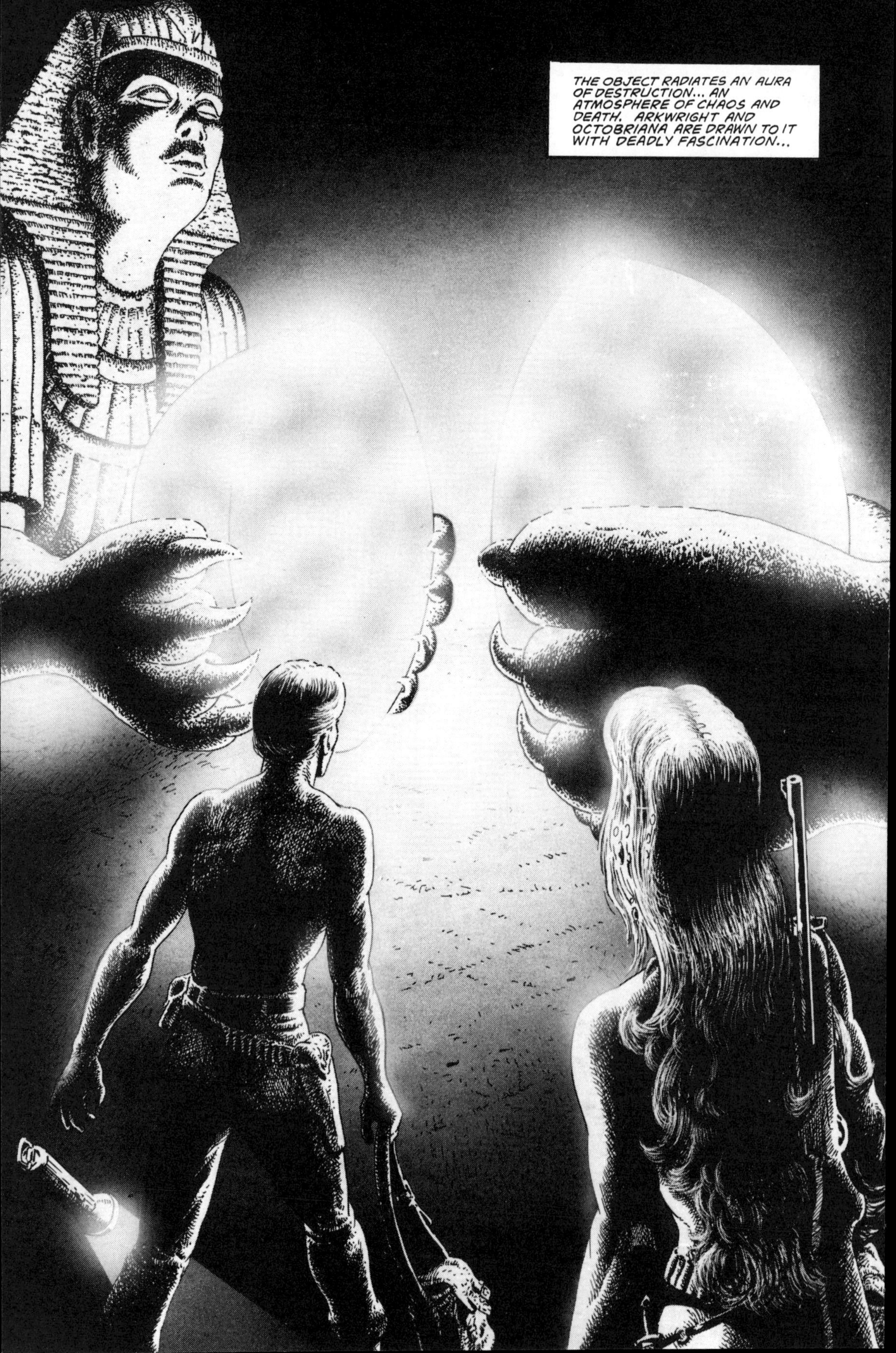
THE OBJECT RADIATES AN AURA OF DESTRUCTION... AN ATMOSPHERE OF CHAOS AND DEATH. ARKWRIGHT AND OCTOBRIANA ARE DRAWN TO IT WITH DEADLY FASCINATION...

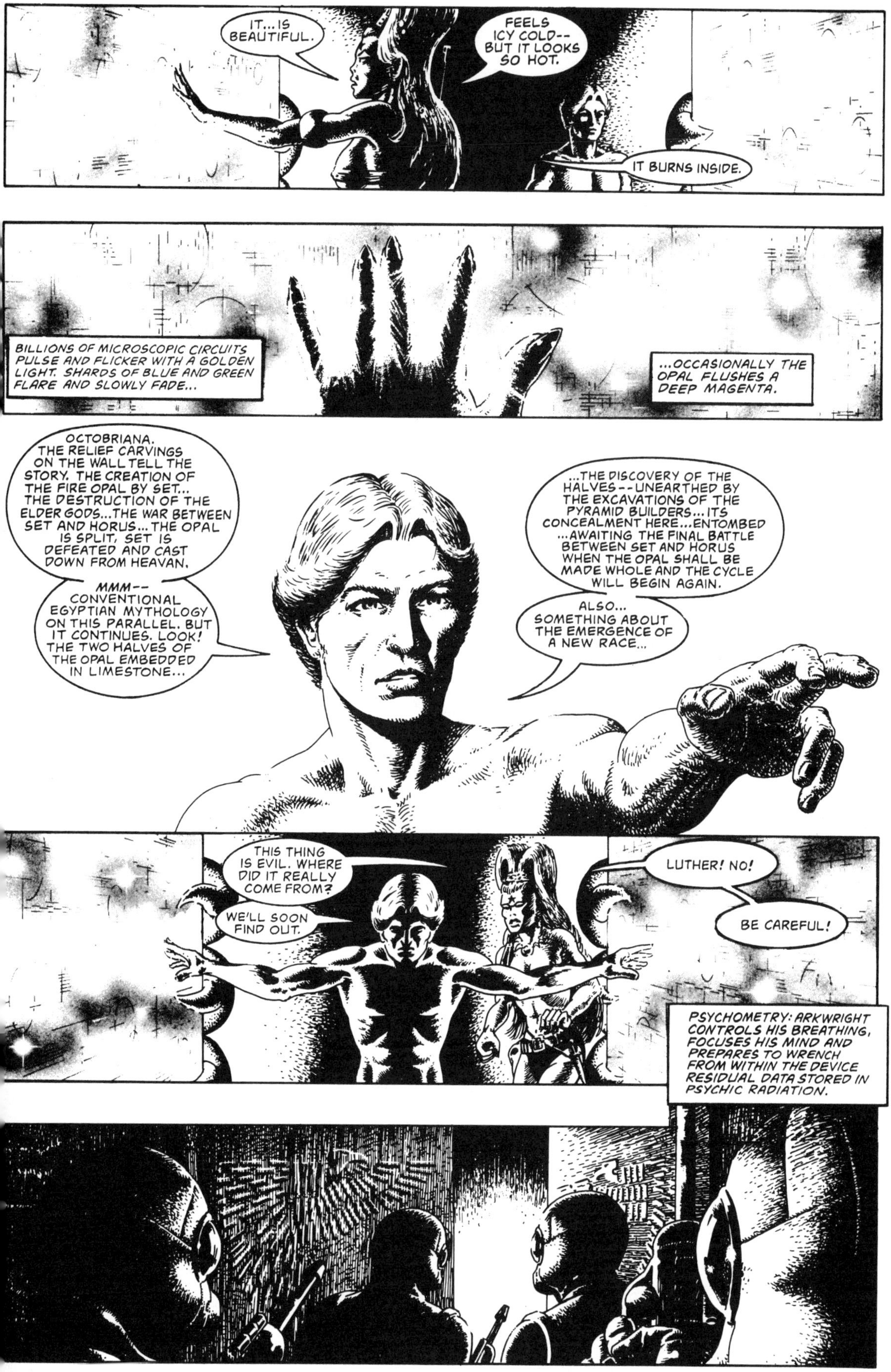
IT... IS BEAUTIFUL.
FEELS ICY COLD-- BUT IT LOOKS SO HOT.
IT BURNS INSIDE.
BILLIONS OF MICROSCOPIC CIRCUITS PULSE AND FLICKER WITH A GOLDEN LIGHT. SHARDS OF BLUE AND GREEN FLARE AND SLOWLY FADE...
...OCCASIONALLY THE OPAL FLUSHES A DEEP MAGENTA.
OCTOBRIANA. THE RELIEF CARVINGS ON THE WALL TELL THE STORY. THE CREATION OF THE FIRE OPAL BY SET... THE DESTRUCTION OF THE ELDER GODS... THE WAR BETWEEN SET AND HORUS... THE OPAL IS SPLIT, SET IS DEFEATED AND CAST DOWN FROM HEAVAN.
MMM-- CONVENTIONAL EGYPTIAN MYTHOLOGY ON THIS PARALLEL. BUT IT CONTINUES. LOOK! THE TWO HALVES OF THE OPAL EMBEDDED IN LIMESTONE...
...THE DISCOVERY OF THE HALVES--UNEARTHED BY THE EXCAVATIONS OF THE PYRAMID BUILDERS... ITS CONCEALMENT HERE... ENTOMBED ...AWAITING THE FINAL BATTLE BETWEEN SET AND HORUS WHEN THE OPAL SHALL BE MADE WHOLE AND THE CYCLE WILL BEGIN AGAIN.
ALSO... SOMETHING ABOUT THE EMERGENCE OF A NEW RACE...
THIS THING IS EVIL. WHERE DID IT REALLY COME FROM?
WE'LL SOON FIND OUT.
LUTHER! NO!
BE CAREFUL!
PSYCHOMETRY: ARKWRIGHT CONTROLS HIS BREATHING, FOCUSES HIS MIND AND PREPARES TO WRENCH FROM WITHIN THE DEVICE RESIDUAL DATA STORED IN PSYCHIC RADIATION.

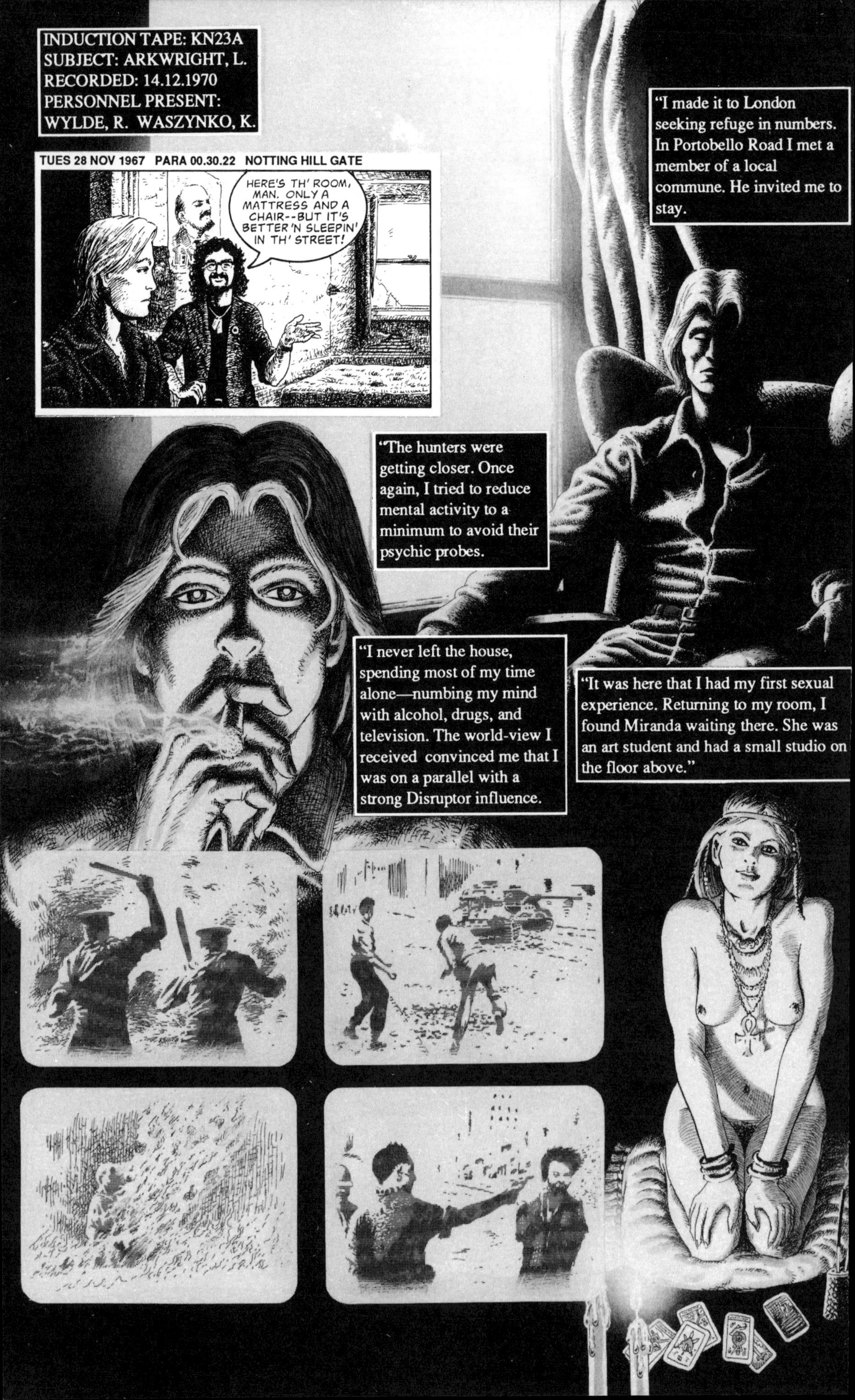
INDUCTION TAPE: KN23A
SUBJECT: ARKWRIGHT, L.
RECORDED: 14.12.1970
PERSONNEL PRESENT:
WYLDE, R. WASZYNKO, K.
"I made it to London seeking refuge in numbers. In Portobello Road I met a member of a local commune. He invited me to stay.
TUES 28 NOV 1967 PARA 00.30.22 NOTTING HILL GATE
HERE'S TH' ROOM, MAN. ONLY A MATTRESS AND A CHAIR--BUT IT'S BETTER'N SLEEPIN' IN TH' STREET!
"The hunters were getting closer. Once again, I tried to reduce mental activity to a minimum to avoid their psychic probes.
"I never left the house, spending most of my time alone—numbing my mind with alcohol, drugs, and television. The world-view I received convinced me that I was on a parallel with a strong Disruptor influence.
"It was here that I had my first sexual experience. Returning to my room, I found Miranda waiting there. She was an art student and had a small studio on the floor above."

FRI 23 FEB 68 03.15

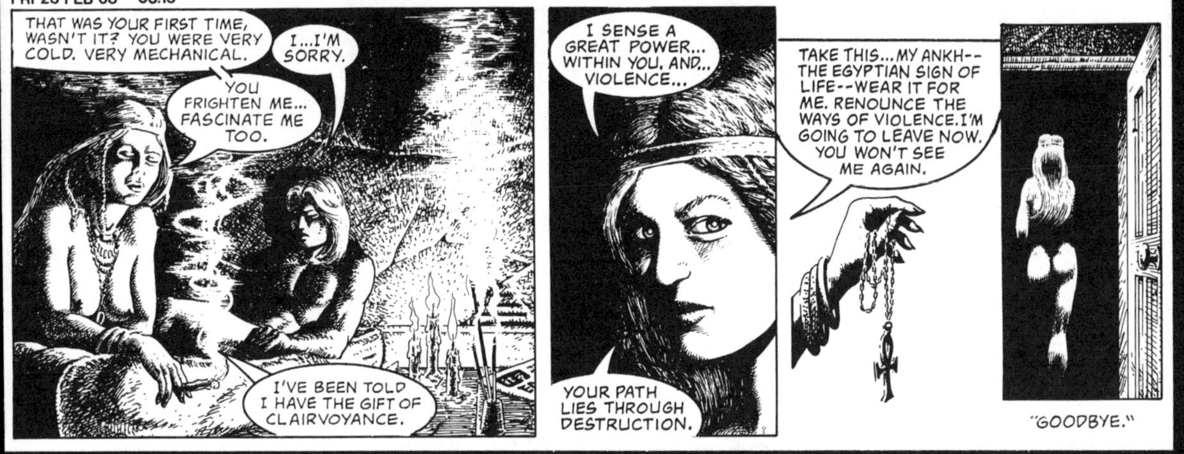

THAT WAS YOUR FIRST TIME, WASN'T IT? YOU WERE VERY COLD. VERY MECHANICAL.
I...I'M SORRY.
YOU FRIGHTEN ME... FASCINATE ME TOO.
I'VE BEEN TOLD I HAVE THE GIFT OF CLAIRVOYANCE.
I SENSE A GREAT POWER... WITHIN YOU, AND... VIOLENCE...
YOUR PATH LIES THROUGH DESTRUCTION.
TAKE THIS...MY ANKH--THE EGYPTIAN SIGN OF LIFE--WEAR IT FOR ME. RENOUNCE THE WAYS OF VIOLENCE. I'M GOING TO LEAVE NOW. YOU WON'T SEE ME AGAIN.
"GOODBYE."

"My lack of involvement in their politics and parasitic reliance upon them for food and drugs soon made the commune members antagonistic. They expressed their hostility at house meeting. I was given an ultimatum to 'join in or get out'.

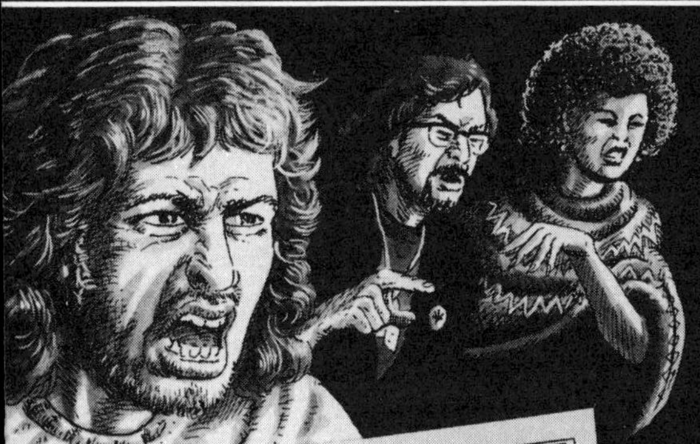

"I went with them to a demostration against American involvement in Vietnam. Naively trying to prove myself, I attacked and injured seven policemen. My detached state of mind dissolved into a frenzy as the pent-up frustration of the last four years was released. It was exhilarating. I enjoyed it. I was fulfilling my programming. Miranda was right.

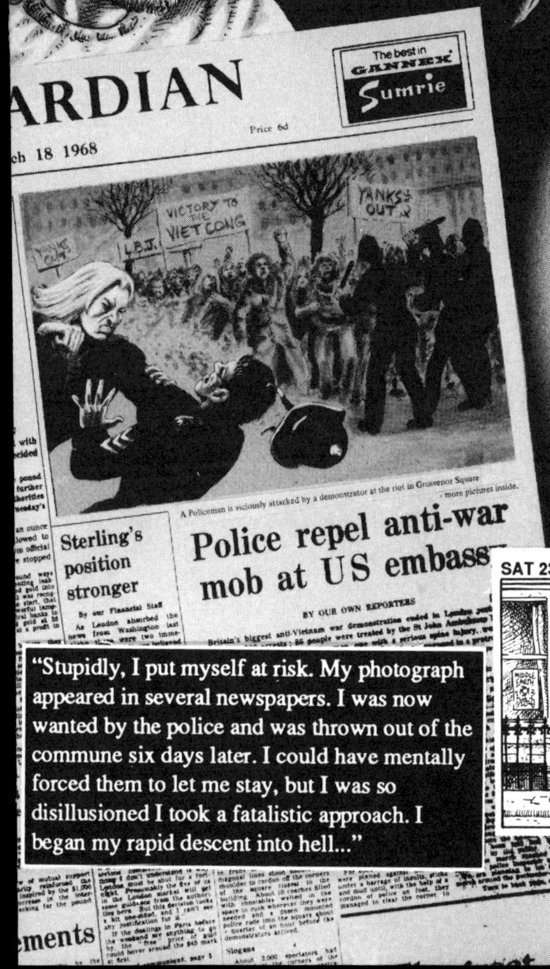

ARDIAN

The best in GANNEX Sumrie

Price 6d

ch 18 1968

VICTORY TO THE VIET CONG
YANKS OUT
L.B.J.

A Policeman is viciously attacked by a demonstrator at the riot in Grosvenor Square - more pictures inside.

Sterling's position stronger

By our Financial Staff

Police repel anti-war mob at US embass

BY OUR OWN REPORTERS

ements

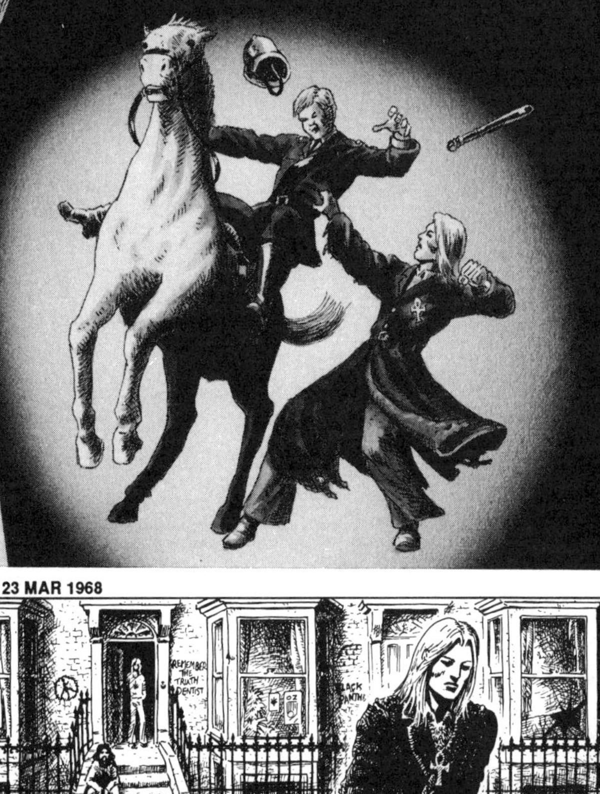

SAT 23 MAR 1968

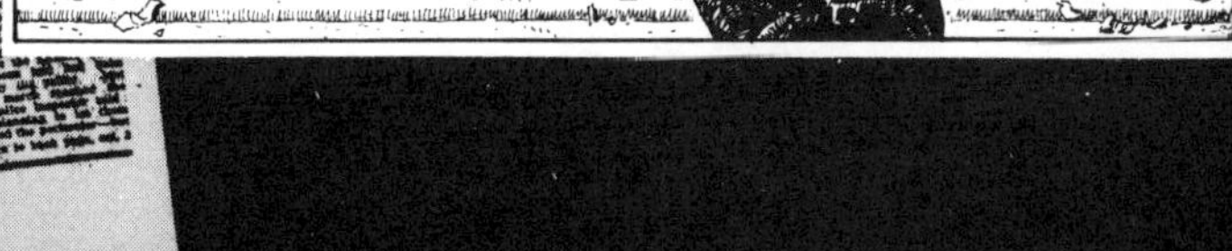

REMEMBER THE TRUTH DENTIST

"Stupidly, I put myself at risk. My photograph appeared in several newspapers. I was now wanted by the police and was thrown out of the commune six days later. I could have mentally forced them to let me stay, but I was so disillusioned I took a fatalistic approach. I began my rapid descent into hell..."

MON 2 OCT 08.35 PARA 00.72.87 LONDON; HAMMERSMITH SLAUGHTERHOUSE

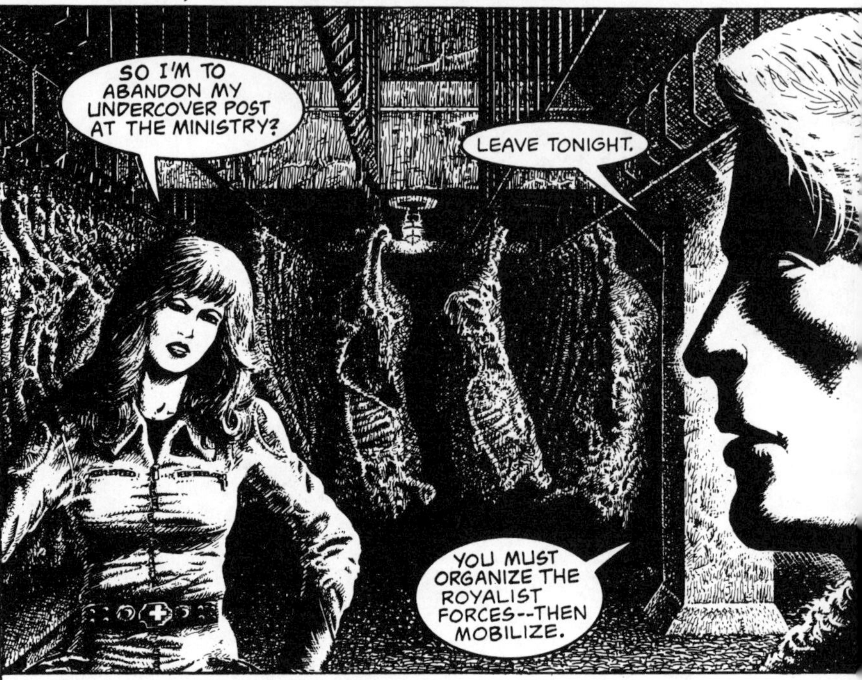

SO I'M TO ABANDON MY UNDERCOVER POST AT THE MINISTRY?
LEAVE TONIGHT.
YOU MUST ORGANIZE THE ROYALIST FORCES--THEN MOBILIZE.

'In London today the atmosphere is tense. A big security clampdown has followed rumours of forthcoming hostilities in both Europe and Africa after the mysterious visit to St. Petersburg last week by the Prussian Heads of Staff.

'Official press hand-outs by the Russian Government announced that this was a goodwill visit, "designed to bring the two World Powers together and further the cause of Peace." I, your reporter, was there in the Russian capital last Friday and the mood was far from peaceful. No pressmen were allowed to be present at the event and the Red Guards were stationed to keep out uninvited onlookers. The hand-outs also mourn the demise of a Prussian officer, Captain Moritz Klein, who "unfortunately fell to his death from an upper story window." It goes on to imply that he was drunk. But it wasn't just me who heard a short burst of machine-gun fire before Klein flew out the stateroom window...'

PARA 01-23-48 BELFAST. REV. IAN PAISLEY KILLED IN MASS BOMBING SPATE.
PARA 00-26-04 INDIA. PRIME MINISTER INDIRA GHANDI ASSASSINATED. CIVIL WAR OUTBREAK.
PARA 01-52-24 LONDON. EPIDEMIC OF SPONTANEOUS HUMAN COMBUSTION. 728 DEAD.
PARA 02-17-69 WASHINGTON. PRESIDENT NIXON ASSASSINATED.
PARA 01-22-09 NORTH ATLANTIC. QEII IN COLLISION WITH ICEBERG.
PARA 01-26-67 GERMANY. RHINE VALLEY SWEPT BY WAVE OF VIOLENT POLTERGEIST ACTIVITY.

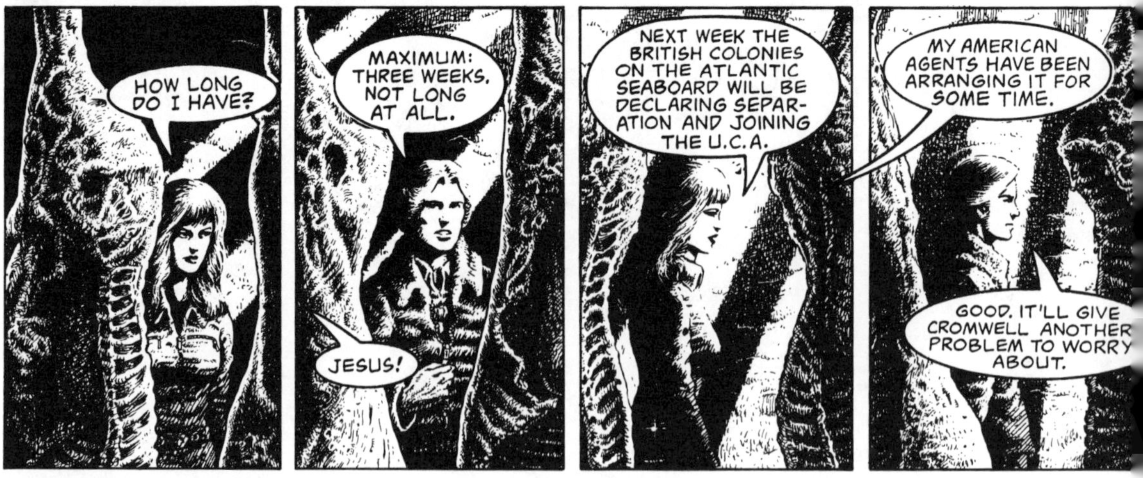

HOW LONG DO I HAVE?
MAXIMUM: THREE WEEKS. NOT LONG AT ALL.
JESUS!
NEXT WEEK THE BRITISH COLONIES ON THE ATLANTIC SEABOARD WILL BE DECLARING SEPARATION AND JOINING THE U.C.A.
MY AMERICAN AGENTS HAVE BEEN ARRANGING IT FOR SOME TIME.
GOOD. IT'LL GIVE CROMWELL ANOTHER PROBLEM TO WORRY ABOUT.

WESMINSTER; LORD PROTECTOR'S PRIVATE QUARTERS 07.15

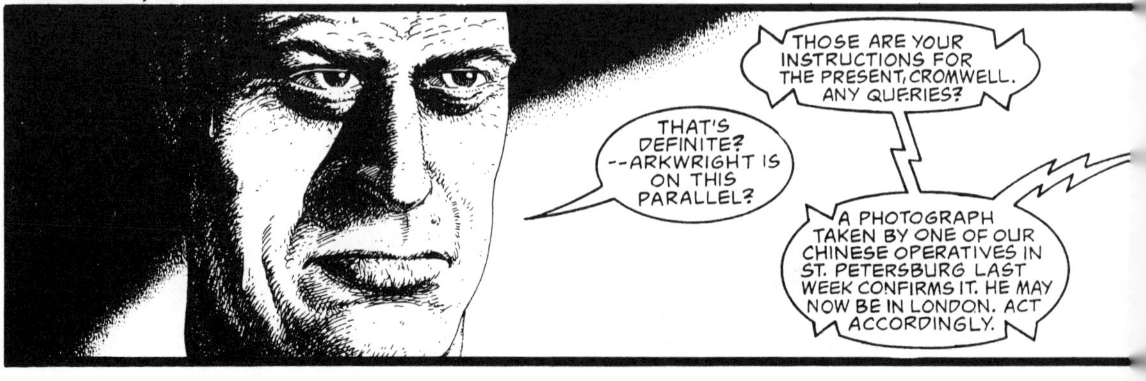

THOSE ARE YOUR INSTRUCTIONS FOR THE PRESENT, CROMWELL. ANY QUERIES?
THAT'S DEFINITE? --ARKWRIGHT IS ON THIS PARALLEL?
A PHOTOGRAPH TAKEN BY ONE OF OUR CHINESE OPERATIVES IN ST. PETERSBURG LAST WEEK CONFIRMS IT. HE MAY NOW BE IN LONDON. ACT ACCORDINGLY.

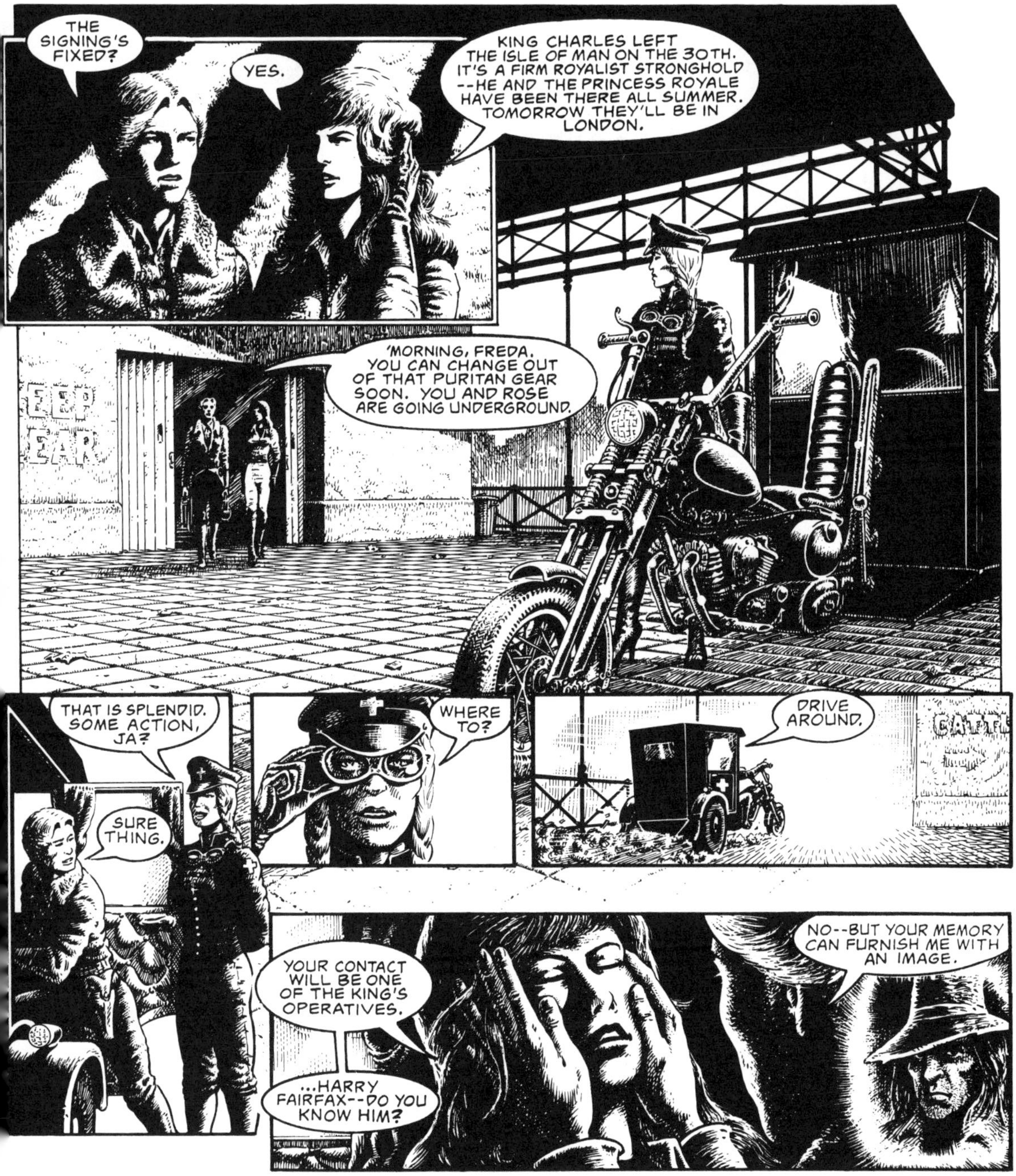
THE SIGNING'S FIXED?
YES.
KING CHARLES LEFT THE ISLE OF MAN ON THE 30TH. IT'S A FIRM ROYALIST STRONGHOLD --HE AND THE PRINCESS ROYALE HAVE BEEN THERE ALL SUMMER. TOMORROW THEY'LL BE IN LONDON.
'MORNING, FREDA. YOU CAN CHANGE OUT OF THAT PURITAN GEAR SOON. YOU AND ROSE ARE GOING UNDERGROUND.
THAT IS SPLENDID. SOME ACTION, JA?
SURE THING.
WHERE TO?
DRIVE AROUND.
YOUR CONTACT WILL BE ONE OF THE KING'S OPERATIVES.
...HARRY FAIRFAX--DO YOU KNOW HIM?
NO--BUT YOUR MEMORY CAN FURNISH ME WITH AN IMAGE.

07.16

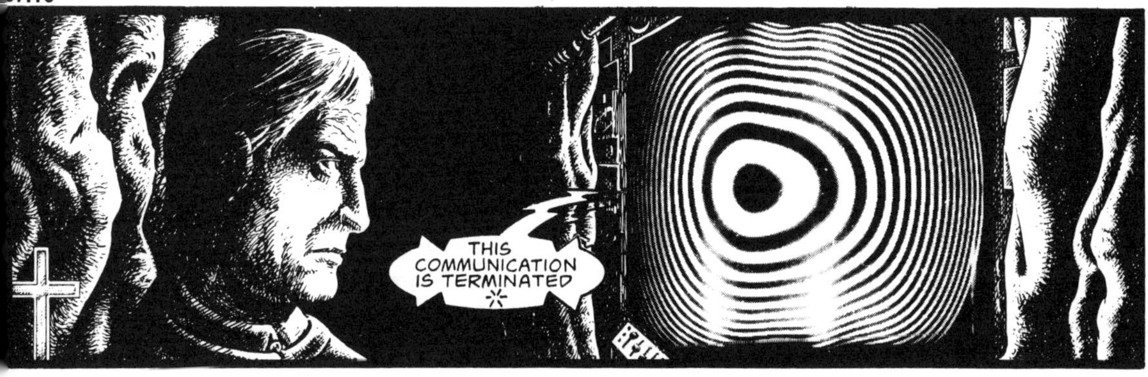
THIS COMMUNICATION IS TERMINATED

SUN 1 OCT 18.43 RUSSIAN TURKEY; CONSTANTINOPLE

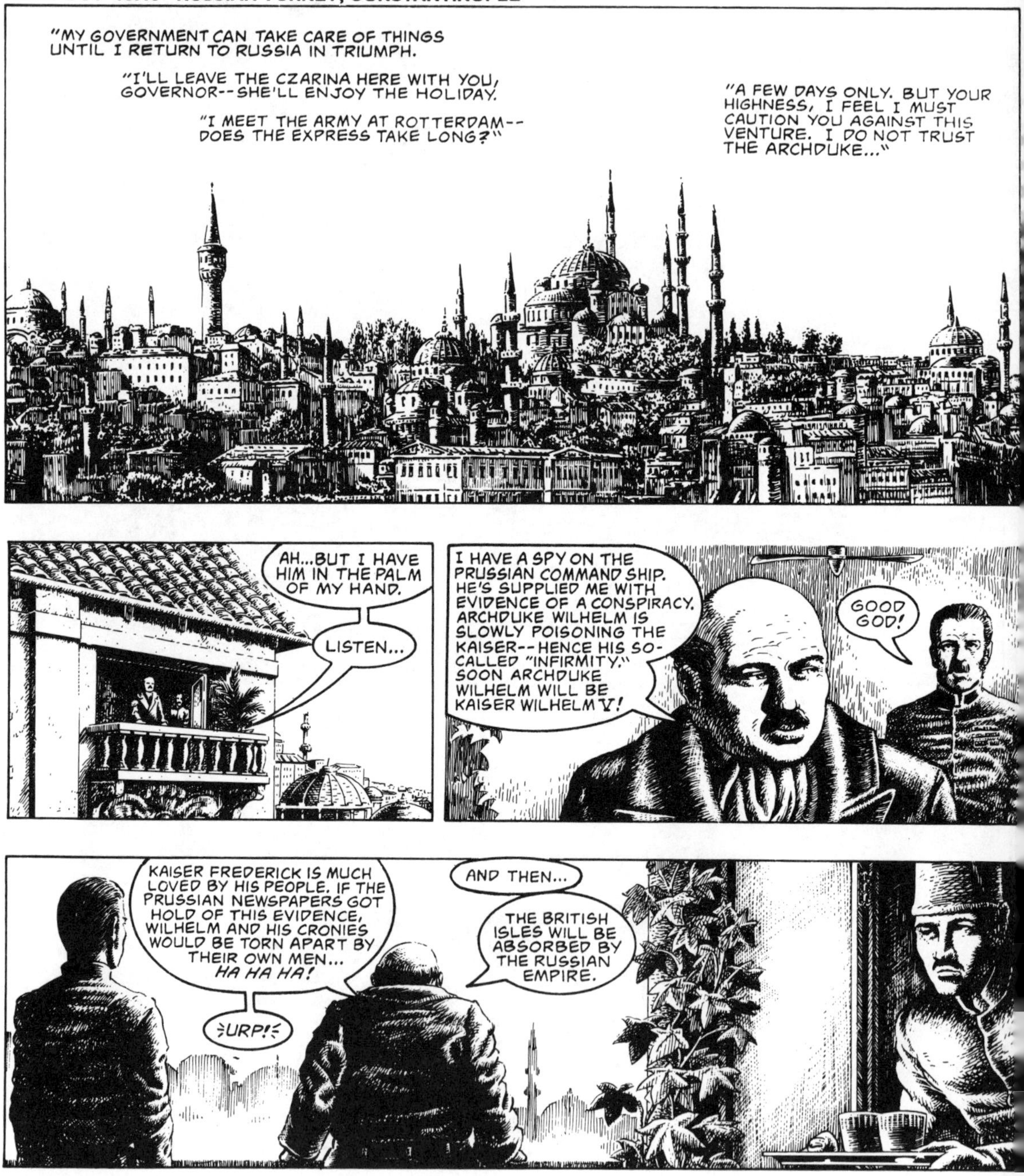
"MY GOVERNMENT CAN TAKE CARE OF THINGS UNTIL I RETURN TO RUSSIA IN TRIUMPH.
"I'LL LEAVE THE CZARINA HERE WITH YOU, GOVERNOR--SHE'LL ENJOY THE HOLIDAY.
"I MEET THE ARMY AT ROTTERDAM--DOES THE EXPRESS TAKE LONG?"
"A FEW DAYS ONLY. BUT YOUR HIGHNESS, I FEEL I MUST CAUTION YOU AGAINST THIS VENTURE. I DO NOT TRUST THE ARCHDUKE..."
AH...BUT I HAVE HIM IN THE PALM OF MY HAND.
LISTEN...
I HAVE A SPY ON THE PRUSSIAN COMMAND SHIP. HE'S SUPPLIED ME WITH EVIDENCE OF A CONSPIRACY. ARCHDUKE WILHELM IS SLOWLY POISONING THE KAISER--HENCE HIS SO-CALLED "INFIRMITY." SOON ARCHDUKE WILHELM WILL BE KAISER WILHELM V!
GOOD GOD!
KAISER FREDERICK IS MUCH LOVED BY HIS PEOPLE. IF THE PRUSSIAN NEWSPAPERS GOT HOLD OF THIS EVIDENCE, WILHELM AND HIS CRONIES WOULD BE TORN APART BY THEIR OWN MEN... HA HA HA!
URP!
AND THEN...
THE BRITISH ISLES WILL BE ABSORBED BY THE RUSSIAN EMPIRE.

WESTMINSTER; INNER CABINET 12.14

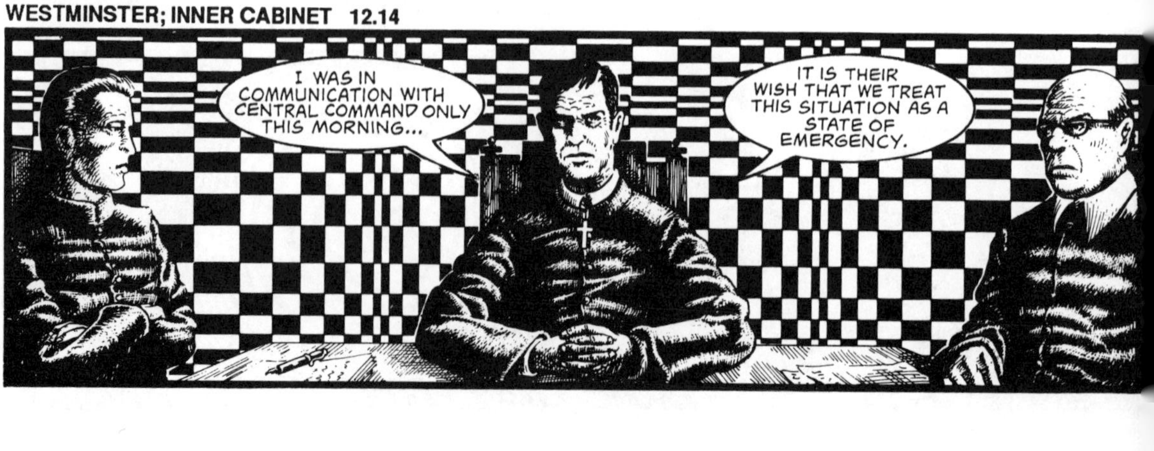
I WAS IN COMMUNICATION WITH CENTRAL COMMAND ONLY THIS MORNING...
IT IS THEIR WISH THAT WE TREAT THIS SITUATION AS A STATE OF EMERGENCY.

PARA 00-98-02 NEW ZEALAND. UFO SIGHTING EPIDEMIC.
PARA 00-89-51 SWITZERLAND. SQUADRON OF LOCKHEED STARFIGHTERS SIMULTANEOUSLY LOSE CONTROL AND CRASH ON GENEVA. 382 DEAD.

BOSWORTH SQUARE 08.55 MIDDLE DISTANCE; CROMWELL'S COLUMN

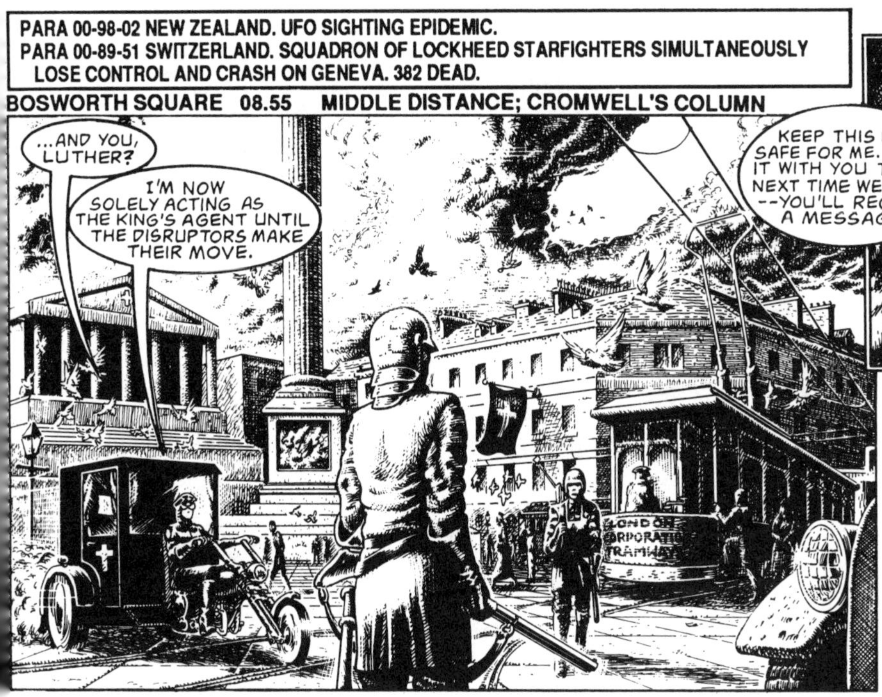

...AND YOU, LUTHER?
I'M NOW SOLELY ACTING AS THE KING'S AGENT UNTIL THE DISRUPTORS MAKE THEIR MOVE.
LONDON CORPORATION TRAMWAYS

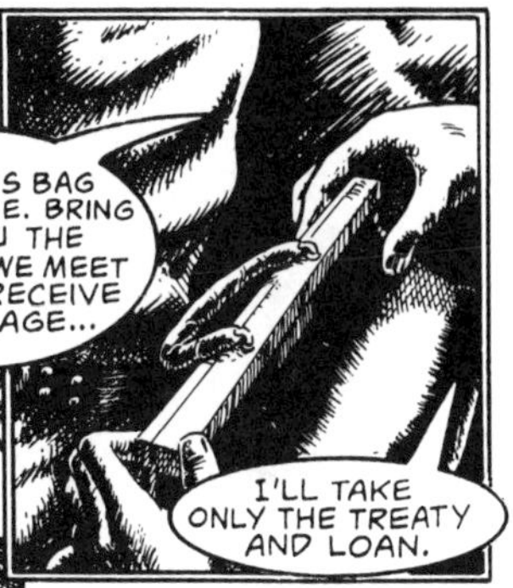

KEEP THIS BAG SAFE FOR ME. BRING IT WITH YOU THE NEXT TIME WE MEET --YOU'LL RECEIVE A MESSAGE...
I'LL TAKE ONLY THE TREATY AND LOAN.

'The architecture in London's centre mirrors the black/white philosophy of the Puritan Regime. In a country whose progress has been impeded by three hundred years of civil war, the Capital remains the focus of Parliamentarian strength. Make no mistake here—the Civil War goes on! Although England has been ruled by a Lord Protector for centuries, the hereditary title always passing to the eldest male in the Cromwell family, the Royalist movement is as strong as ever. The Civil War may have officially ended years ago, but it still goes on "underground"—in the form of countless guerilla attacks and sabotage operations against the fascist Puritan dictatorship.'

Hiram Kowolsky,
Foreign Correspondent,
New Amsterdam Herald

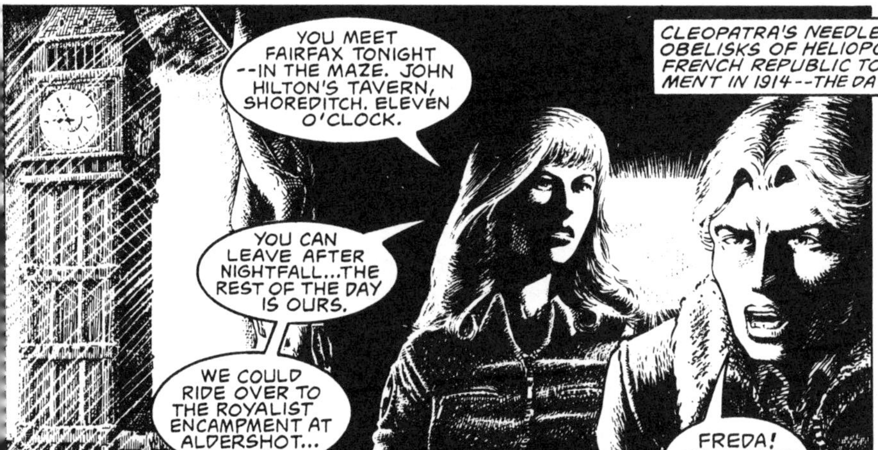

YOU MEET FAIRFAX TONIGHT --IN THE MAZE. JOHN HILTON'S TAVERN, SHOREDITCH. ELEVEN O'CLOCK.
YOU CAN LEAVE AFTER NIGHTFALL...THE REST OF THE DAY IS OURS.
WE COULD RIDE OVER TO THE ROYALIST ENCAMPMENT AT ALDERSHOT...
FREDA! PULL OVER AT THE NEEDLE!
EH?

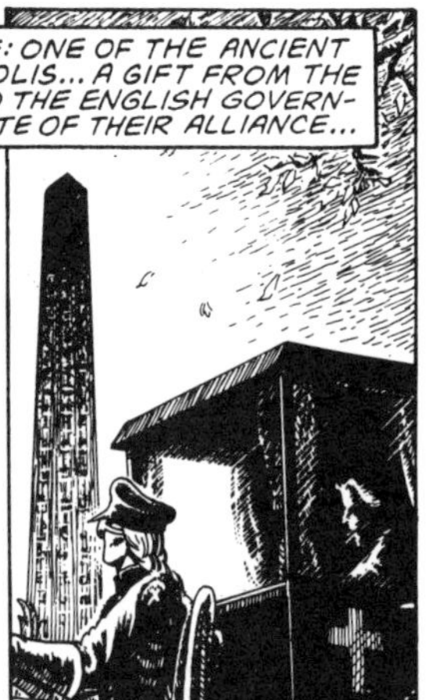

CLEOPATRA'S NEEDLE: ONE OF THE ANCIENT OBELISKS OF HELIOPOLIS... A GIFT FROM THE FRENCH REPUBLIC TO THE ENGLISH GOVERNMENT IN 1914--THE DATE OF THEIR ALLIANCE...

12.14 PARA 00-40-55 BRITAIN. INSANITY RATE SOARING.

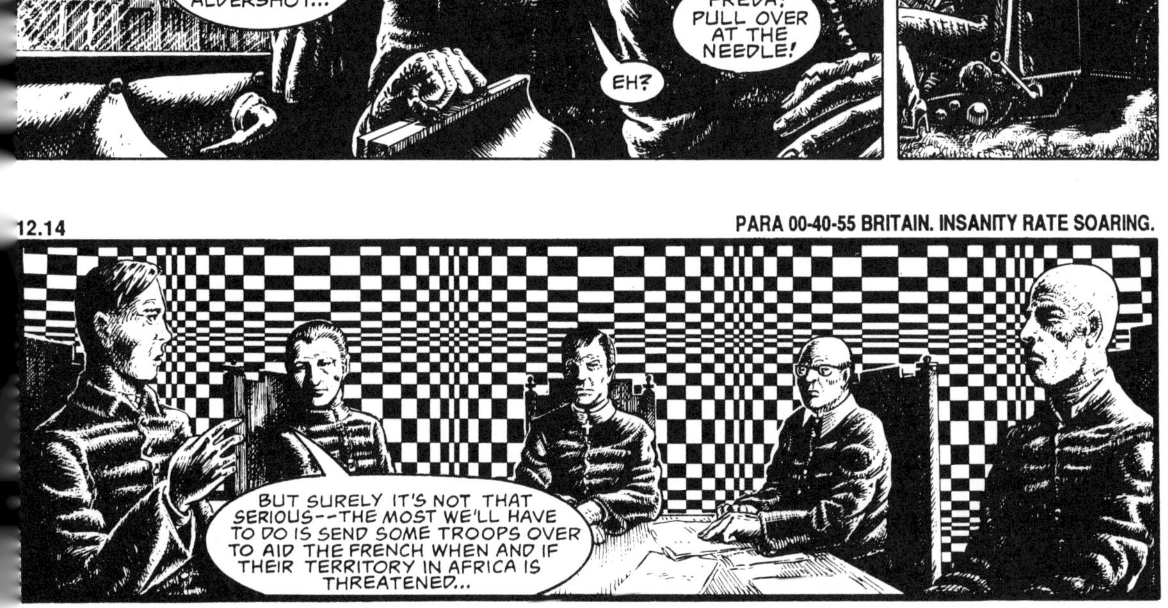

BUT SURELY IT'S NOT THAT SERIOUS--THE MOST WE'LL HAVE TO DO IS SEND SOME TROOPS OVER TO AID THE FRENCH WHEN AND IF THEIR TERRITORY IN AFRICA IS THREATENED...

...ALSO... A TIE-IN WITH FIREFROST... ON THE PARALLEL WHERE FIREFROST WAS CREATED AND, LATER, REDISCOVERED IN EGYPT... IN 1981... OCTOBRIANA IN THE GREAT PYRAMID OF CHEOPS... SCENES OF ALIEN CREATION AND THE DISRUPTORS' SHOCK TROOPS... THEN FUTURE GLIMPSE... THE OBELISK ACTING AS A MADALA IN THE CENTER OF A THEATRE OF WAR... GRIM PRODUCT OF THE RAGNAROK EQUATION... ROSE, DRESSED AS BRITANNIA, SCREAMS AND FALLS--WASTED BY LASER FIRE... NOW 1969 AND A STRANGE FIGURE... ARKWRIGHT... STAGGERS ALONG A DIFFERENT THAMES EMBANKMENT TOWARDS ANOTHER CLEOPATRA'S NEEDLE... THROUGH COLD DECEMBER MORNING... REELING FROM COLD TURKEY AND PSYCHIC ATTACK...

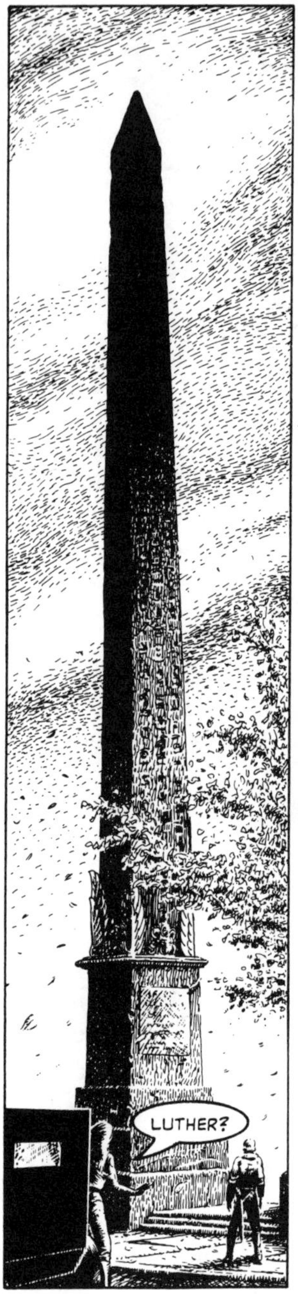
LUTHER?

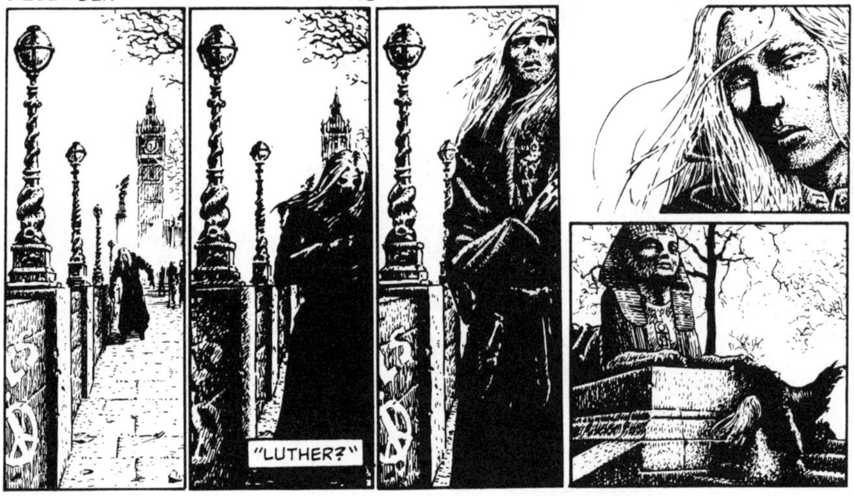
"LUTHER?"

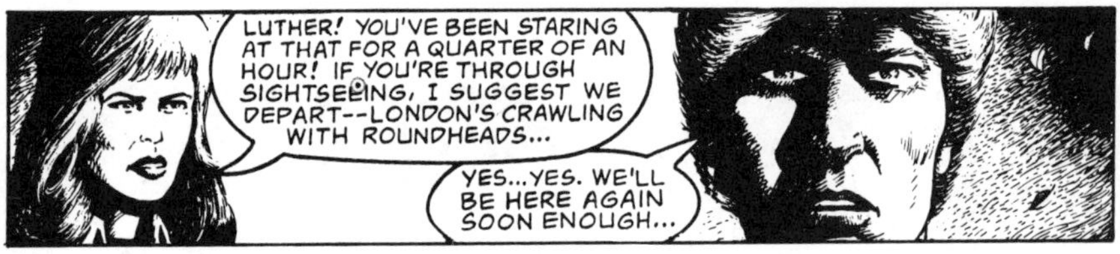
LUTHER! YOU'VE BEEN STARING AT THAT FOR A QUARTER OF AN HOUR! IF YOU'RE THROUGH SIGHTSEEING, I SUGGEST WE DEPART--LONDON'S CRAWLING WITH ROUNDHEADS...
YES...YES. WE'LL BE HERE AGAIN SOON ENOUGH...

WED 4 OCT 15.24 GREATER PRUSSIA; BERLIN

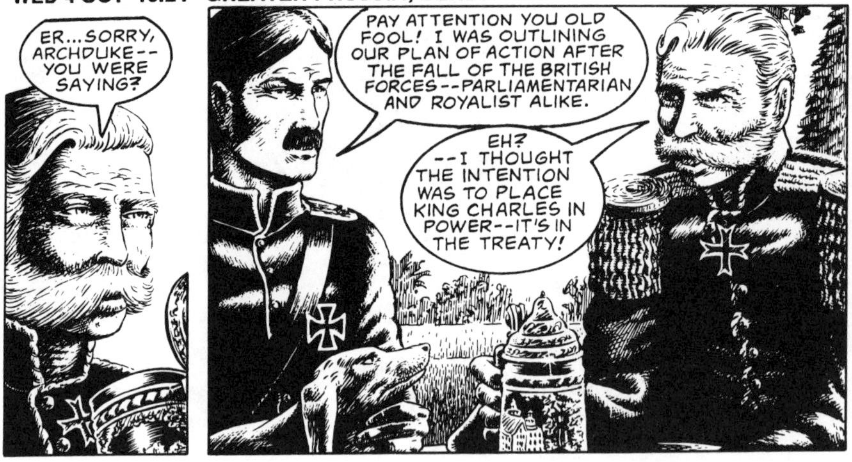
ER...SORRY, ARCHDUKE--YOU WERE SAYING?
PAY ATTENTION YOU OLD FOOL! I WAS OUTLINING OUR PLAN OF ACTION AFTER THE FALL OF THE BRITISH FORCES--PARLIAMENTARIAN AND ROYALIST ALIKE.
EH? --I THOUGHT THE INTENTION WAS TO PLACE KING CHARLES IN POWER--IT'S IN THE TREATY!

12.14 **PARA 02-17-64 WASHINGTON. PRESIDENT NIXON ASSASSINATED.**

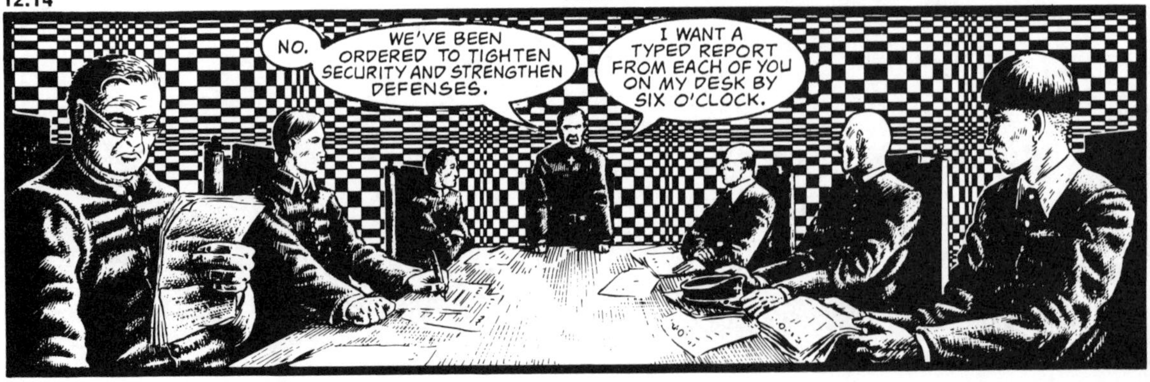
NO.
WE'VE BEEN ORDERED TO TIGHTEN SECURITY AND STRENGTHEN DEFENSES.
I WANT A TYPED REPORT FROM EACH OF YOU ON MY DESK BY SIX O'CLOCK.

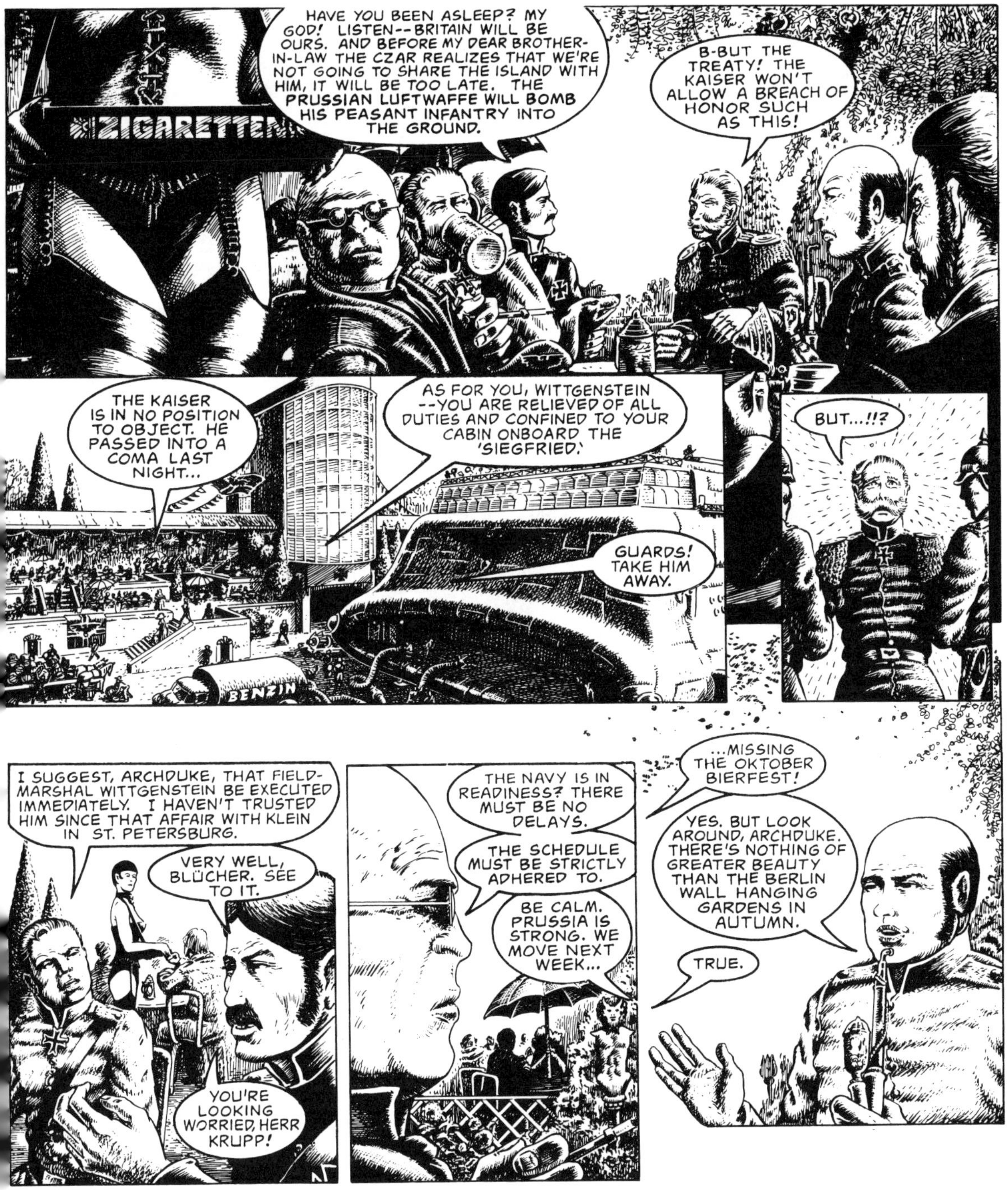
HAVE YOU BEEN ASLEEP? MY GOD! LISTEN--BRITAIN WILL BE OURS. AND BEFORE MY DEAR BROTHER-IN-LAW THE CZAR REALIZES THAT WE'RE NOT GOING TO SHARE THE ISLAND WITH HIM, IT WILL BE TOO LATE. THE PRUSSIAN LUFTWAFFE WILL BOMB HIS PEASANT INFANTRY INTO THE GROUND.
ZIGARETTEN
B-BUT THE TREATY! THE KAISER WON'T ALLOW A BREACH OF HONOR SUCH AS THIS!
THE KAISER IS IN NO POSITION TO OBJECT. HE PASSED INTO A COMA LAST NIGHT...
AS FOR YOU, WITTGENSTEIN --YOU ARE RELIEVED OF ALL DUTIES AND CONFINED TO YOUR CABIN ONBOARD THE 'SIEGFRIED.'
GUARDS! TAKE HIM AWAY.
BENZIN
BUT...!!?
I SUGGEST, ARCHDUKE, THAT FIELD-MARSHAL WITTGENSTEIN BE EXECUTED IMMEDIATELY. I HAVEN'T TRUSTED HIM SINCE THAT AFFAIR WITH KLEIN IN ST. PETERSBURG.
VERY WELL, BLÜCHER. SEE TO IT.
YOU'RE LOOKING WORRIED, HERR KRUPP!
THE NAVY IS IN READINESS? THERE MUST BE NO DELAYS.
THE SCHEDULE MUST BE STRICTLY ADHERED TO.
BE CALM. PRUSSIA IS STRONG. WE MOVE NEXT WEEK...
...MISSING THE OKTOBER BIERFEST!
YES. BUT LOOK AROUND, ARCHDUKE. THERE'S NOTHING OF GREATER BEAUTY THAN THE BERLIN WALL HANGING GARDENS IN AUTUMN.
TRUE.

12.15 **PARA 02-36-72 MIDDLE EAST. EGYPT INVADES ISRAEL. U.S.A. STEPS IN.**

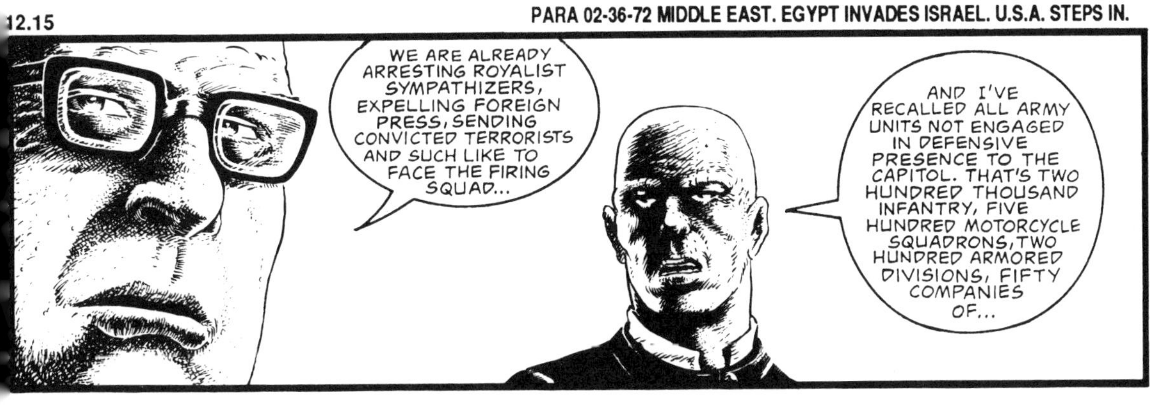
WE ARE ALREADY ARRESTING ROYALIST SYMPATHIZERS, EXPELLING FOREIGN PRESS, SENDING CONVICTED TERRORISTS AND SUCH LIKE TO FACE THE FIRING SQUAD...
AND I'VE RECALLED ALL ARMY UNITS NOT ENGAGED IN DEFENSIVE PRESENCE TO THE CAPITOL. THAT'S TWO HUNDRED THOUSAND INFANTRY, FIVE HUNDRED MOTORCYCLE SQUADRONS, TWO HUNDRED ARMORED DIVISIONS, FIFTY COMPANIES OF...

BLACKFRIARS GATE 22.31

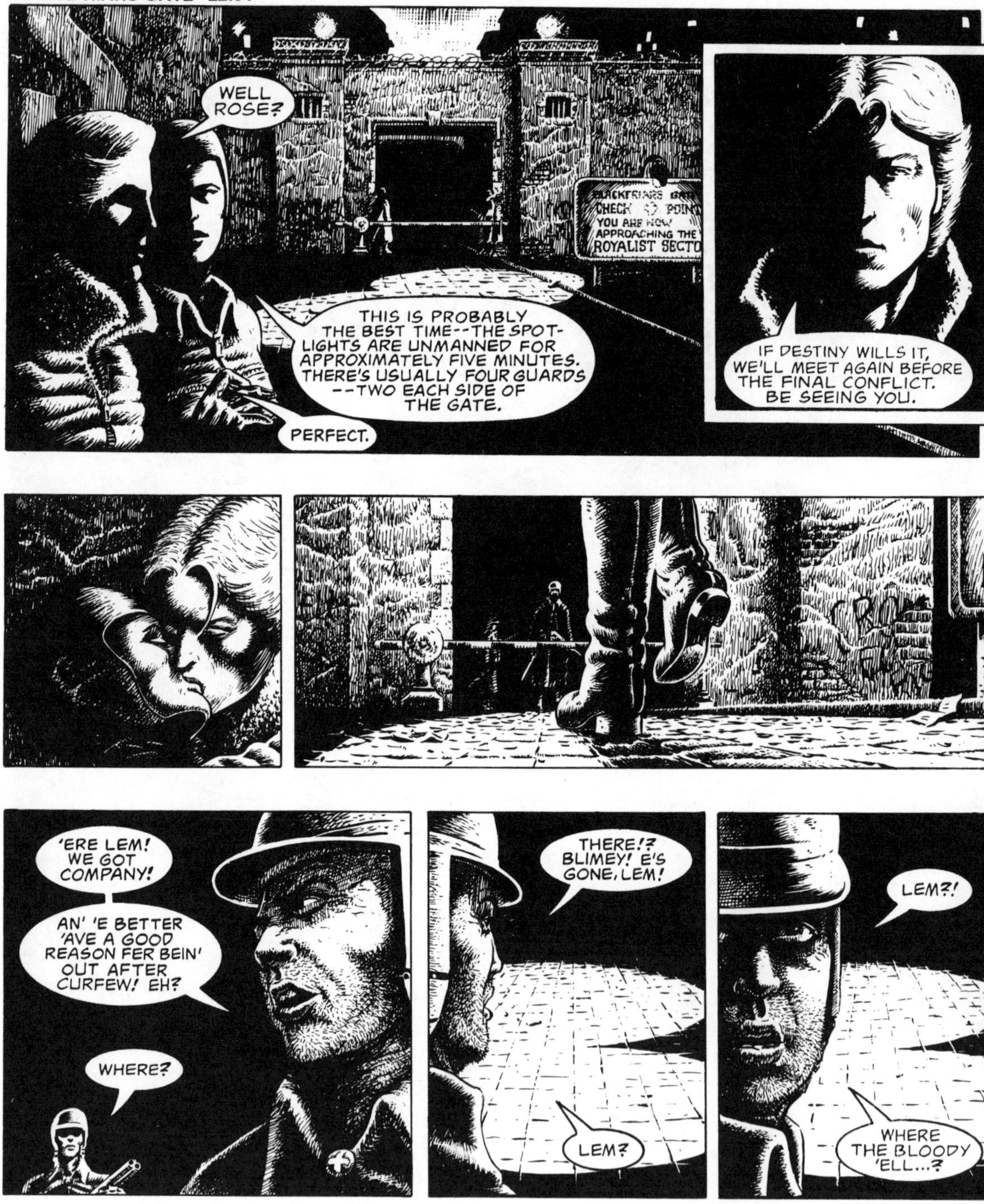
WELL ROSE?
BLACKFRIARS GATE CHECK POINT YOU ARE NOW APPROACHING THE ROYALIST SECTO
THIS IS PROBABLY THE BEST TIME--THE SPOT-LIGHTS ARE UNMANNED FOR APPROXIMATELY FIVE MINUTES. THERE'S USUALLY FOUR GUARDS --TWO EACH SIDE OF THE GATE.
PERFECT.
IF DESTINY WILLS IT, WE'LL MEET AGAIN BEFORE THE FINAL CONFLICT. BE SEEING YOU.
'ERE LEM! WE GOT COMPANY!
AN' 'E BETTER 'AVE A GOOD REASON FER BEIN' OUT AFTER CURFEW! EH?
WHERE?
THERE!? BLIMEY! E'S GONE, LEM!
LEM?
LEM?!
WHERE THE BLOODY 'ELL...?

12.15 PARA 02-85-82 FRANCE. SPECTRAL BATTLE SEEN OVER AGINCOURT FIELD.

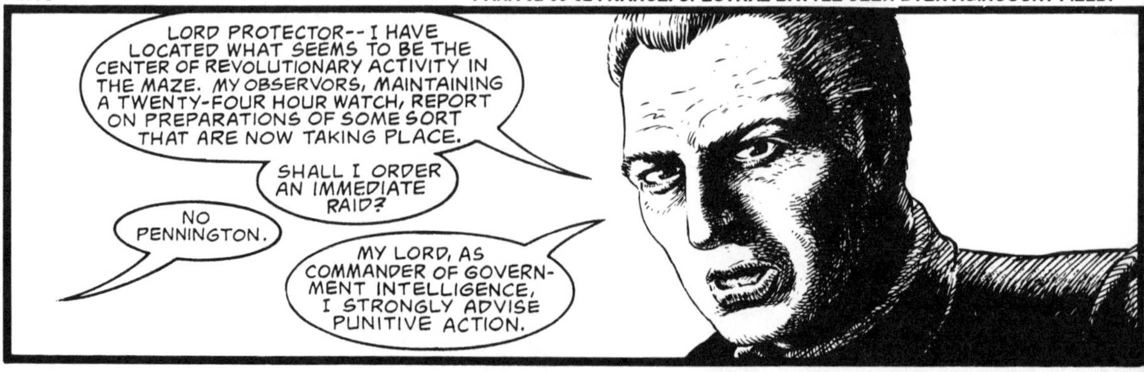
LORD PROTECTOR--I HAVE LOCATED WHAT SEEMS TO BE THE CENTER OF REVOLUTIONARY ACTIVITY IN THE MAZE. MY OBSERVORS, MAINTAINING A TWENTY-FOUR HOUR WATCH, REPORT ON PREPARATIONS OF SOME SORT THAT ARE NOW TAKING PLACE.
SHALL I ORDER AN IMMEDIATE RAID?
NO PENNINGTON.
MY LORD, AS COMMANDER OF GOVERN-MENT INTELLIGENCE, I STRONGLY ADVISE PUNITIVE ACTION.

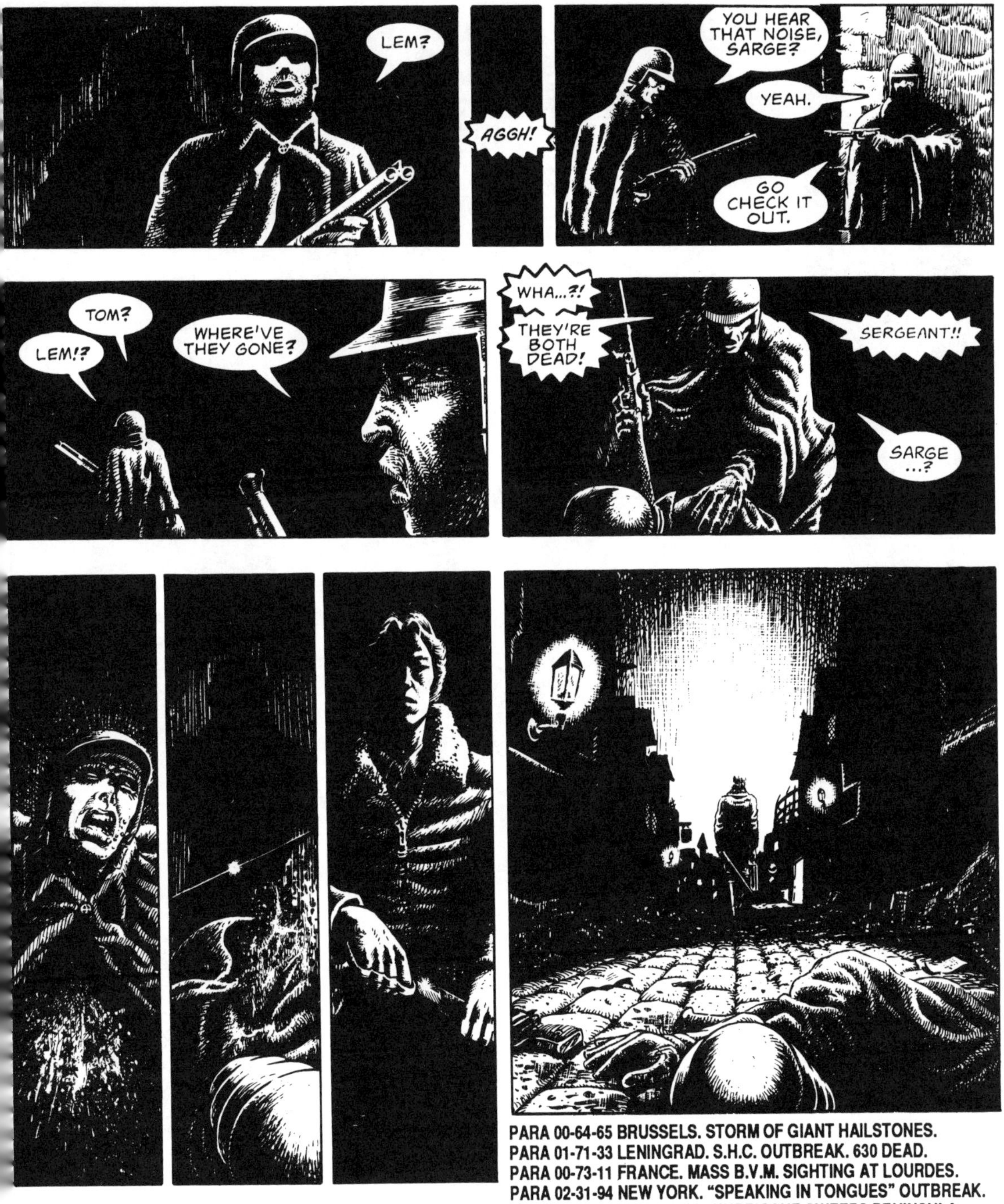
LEM?
AGGH!
YOU HEAR THAT NOISE, SARGE?
YEAH.
GO CHECK IT OUT.
LEM!?
TOM?
WHERE'VE THEY GONE?
WHA...?!
THEY'RE BOTH DEAD!
SERGEANT!!
SARGE ...?
PARA 00-64-65 BRUSSELS. STORM OF GIANT HAILSTONES.
PARA 01-71-33 LENINGRAD. S.H.C. OUTBREAK. 630 DEAD.
PARA 00-73-11 FRANCE. MASS B.V.M. SIGHTING AT LOURDES.
PARA 02-31-94 NEW YORK. "SPEAKING IN TONGUES" OUTBREAK.
PARA 00-66-75 CORNWALL. HURRICANE SWEEPS PENINSULA. DISASTER AREA.

12.15

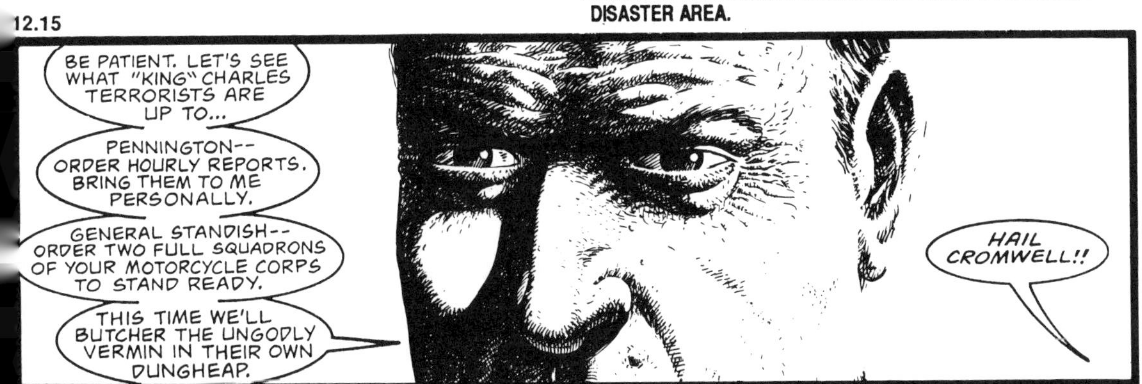
BE PATIENT. LET'S SEE WHAT "KING" CHARLES TERRORISTS ARE UP TO...
PENNINGTON-- ORDER HOURLY REPORTS. BRING THEM TO ME PERSONALLY.
GENERAL STANDISH-- ORDER TWO FULL SQUADRONS OF YOUR MOTORCYCLE CORPS TO STAND READY.
THIS TIME WE'LL BUTCHER THE UNGODLY VERMIN IN THEIR OWN DUNGHEAP.
HAIL CROMWELL!!

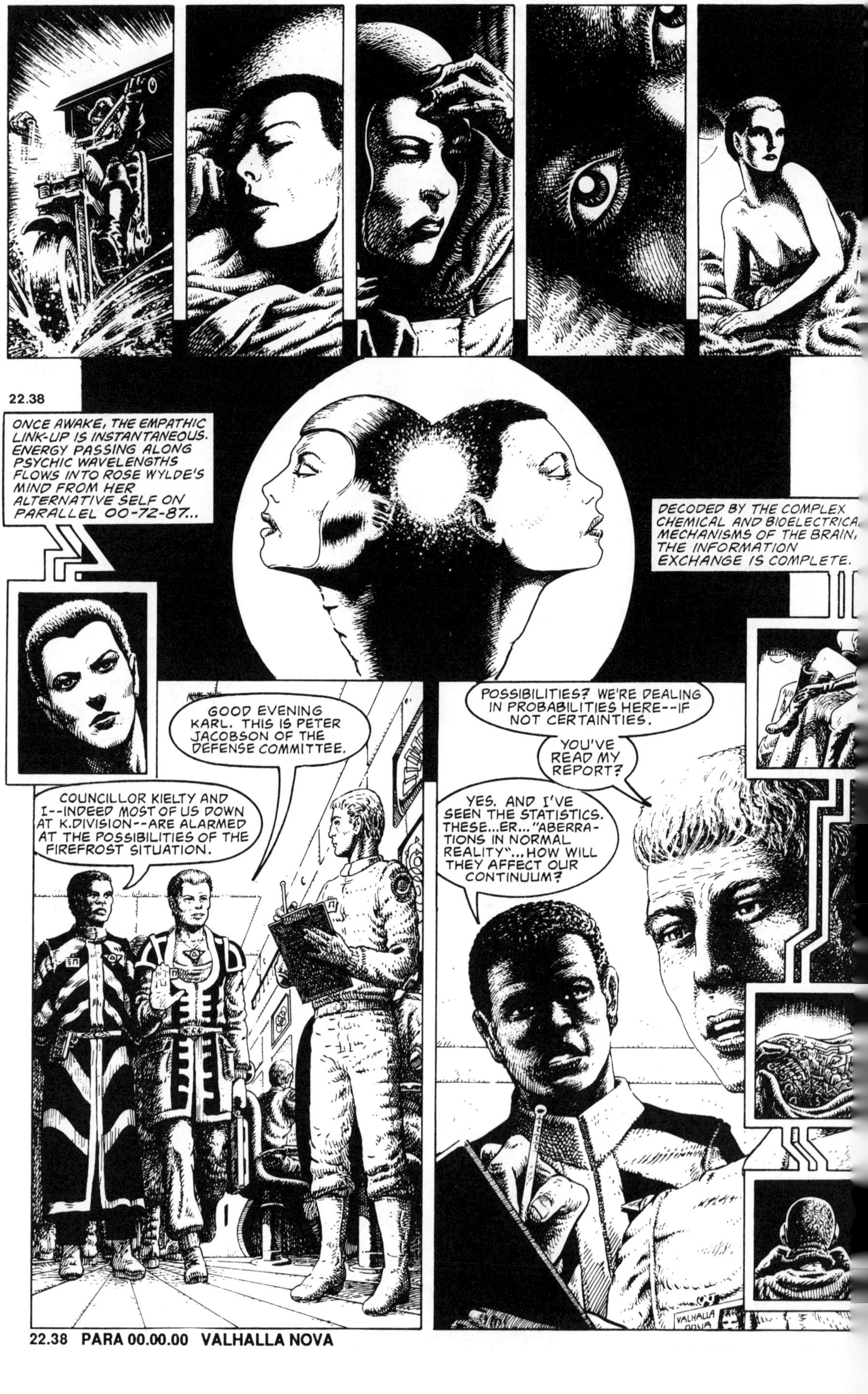

22.38
ONCE AWAKE, THE EMPATHIC LINK-UP IS INSTANTANEOUS. ENERGY PASSING ALONG PSYCHIC WAVELENGTHS FLOWS INTO ROSE WYLDE'S MIND FROM HER ALTERNATIVE SELF ON PARALLEL 00-72-87...
DECODED BY THE COMPLEX CHEMICAL AND BIOELECTRICAL MECHANISMS OF THE BRAIN, THE INFORMATION EXCHANGE IS COMPLETE.
GOOD EVENING KARL. THIS IS PETER JACOBSON OF THE DEFENSE COMMITTEE.
COUNCILLOR KIELTY AND I--INDEED MOST OF US DOWN AT K.DIVISION--ARE ALARMED AT THE POSSIBILITIES OF THE FIREFROST SITUATION.
POSSIBILITIES? WE'RE DEALING IN PROBABILITIES HERE--IF NOT CERTAINTIES.
YOU'VE READ MY REPORT?
YES. AND I'VE SEEN THE STATISTICS. THESE...ER..."ABERRATIONS IN NORMAL REALITY"...HOW WILL THEY AFFECT OUR CONTINUUM?
VALHALLA NOVA
22.38 PARA 00.00.00 VALHALLA NOVA

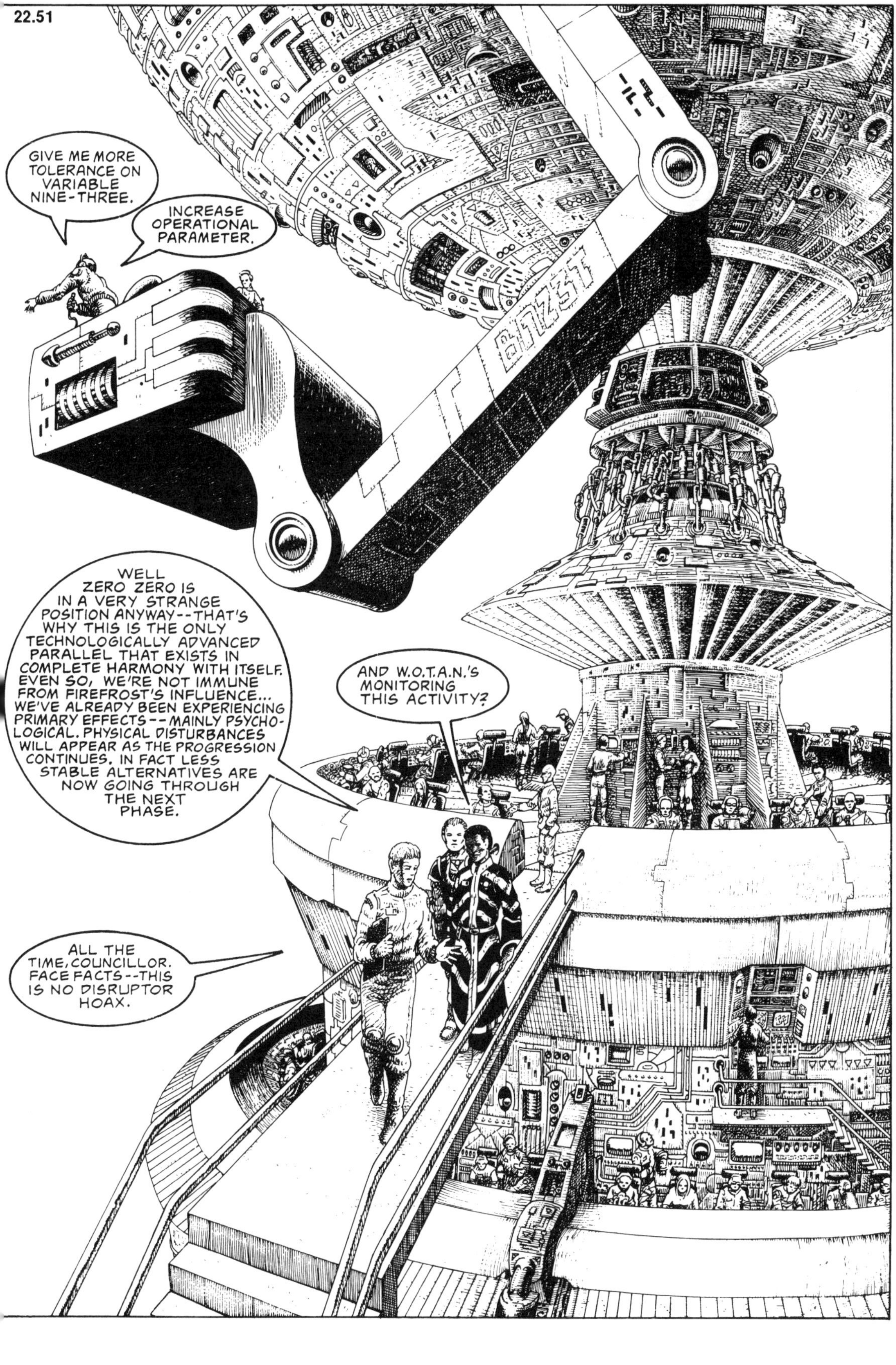
22.51
GIVE ME MORE TOLERANCE ON VARIABLE NINE-THREE.
INCREASE OPERATIONAL PARAMETER.
WELL ZERO ZERO IS IN A VERY STRANGE POSITION ANYWAY--THAT'S WHY THIS IS THE ONLY TECHNOLOGICALLY ADVANCED PARALLEL THAT EXISTS IN COMPLETE HARMONY WITH ITSELF. EVEN SO, WE'RE NOT IMMUNE FROM FIREFROST'S INFLUENCE... WE'VE ALREADY BEEN EXPERIENCING PRIMARY EFFECTS--MAINLY PSYCHOLOGICAL. PHYSICAL DISTURBANCES WILL APPEAR AS THE PROGRESSION CONTINUES. IN FACT LESS STABLE ALTERNATIVES ARE NOW GOING THROUGH THE NEXT PHASE.
AND W.O.T.A.N.'S MONITORING THIS ACTIVITY?
ALL THE TIME, COUNCILLOR. FACE FACTS--THIS IS NO DISRUPTOR HOAX.

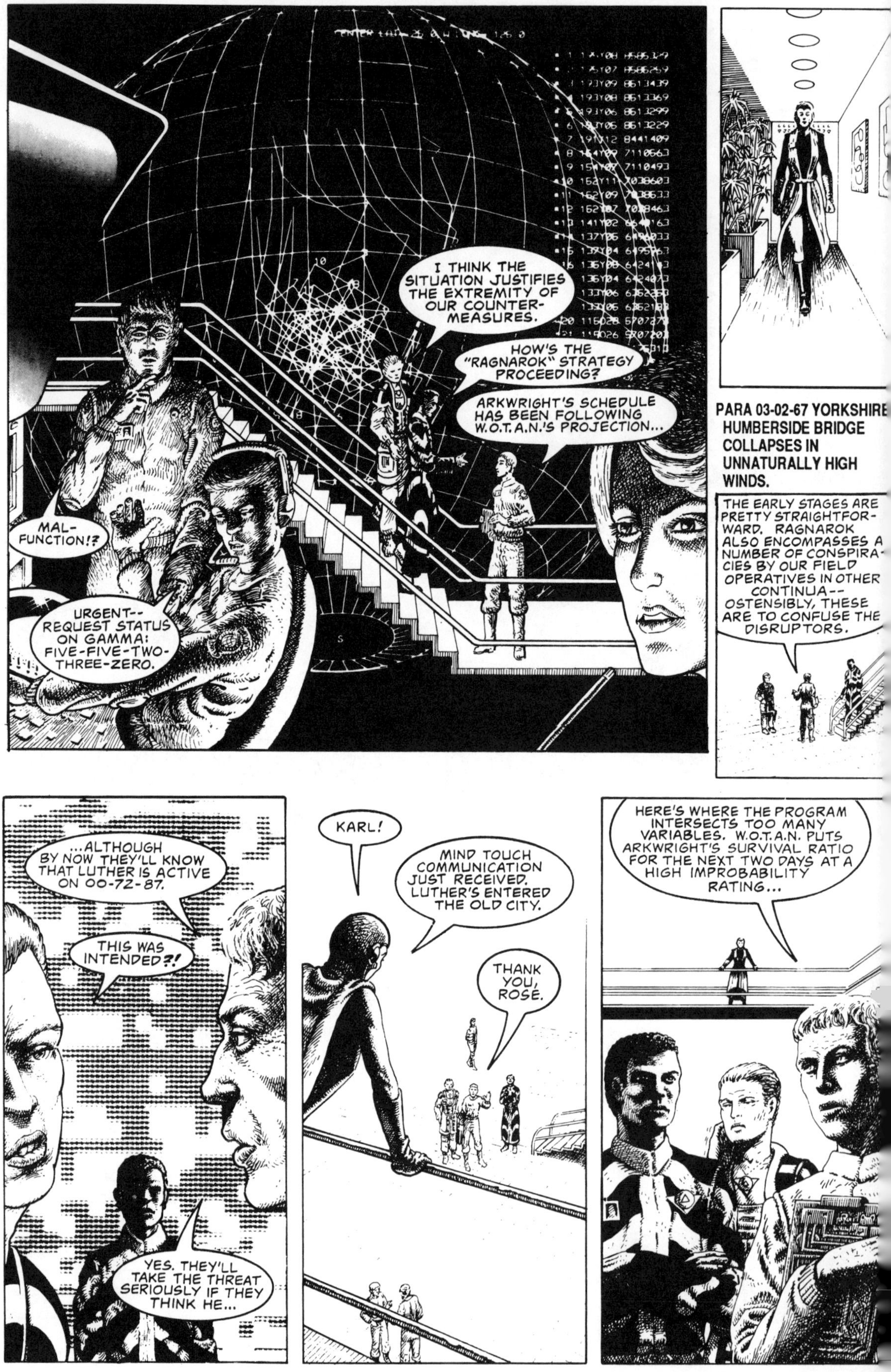
URGENT-- REQUEST STATUS ON GAMMA: FIVE-FIVE-TWO-THREE-ZERO.
MAL-FUNCTION!?
I THINK THE SITUATION JUSTIFIES THE EXTREMITY OF OUR COUNTER-MEASURES.
HOW'S THE "RAGNAROK" STRATEGY PROCEEDING?
ARKWRIGHT'S SCHEDULE HAS BEEN FOLLOWING W.O.T.A.N.'S PROJECTION...
PARA 03-02-67 YORKSHIRE HUMBERSIDE BRIDGE COLLAPSES IN UNNATURALLY HIGH WINDS.
THE EARLY STAGES ARE PRETTY STRAIGHTFORWARD. RAGNAROK ALSO ENCOMPASSES A NUMBER OF CONSPIRACIES BY OUR FIELD OPERATIVES IN OTHER CONTINUA-- OSTENSIBLY, THESE ARE TO CONFUSE THE DISRUPTORS.
...ALTHOUGH BY NOW THEY'LL KNOW THAT LUTHER IS ACTIVE ON 00-72-87.
THIS WAS INTENDED?!
YES. THEY'LL TAKE THE THREAT SERIOUSLY IF THEY THINK HE...
KARL!
MIND TOUCH COMMUNICATION JUST RECEIVED. LUTHER'S ENTERED THE OLD CITY.
THANK YOU, ROSE.
HERE'S WHERE THE PROGRAM INTERSECTS TOO MANY VARIABLES. W.O.T.A.N. PUTS ARKWRIGHT'S SURVIVAL RATIO FOR THE NEXT TWO DAYS AT A HIGH IMPROBABILITY RATING...

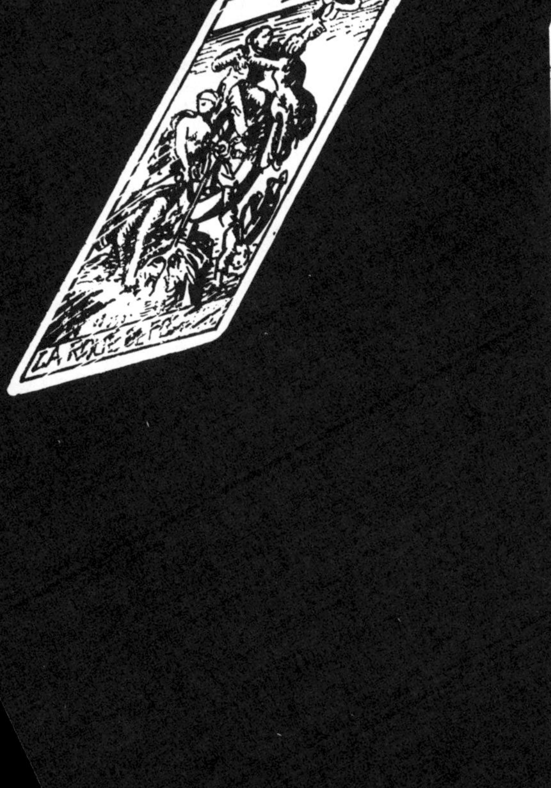

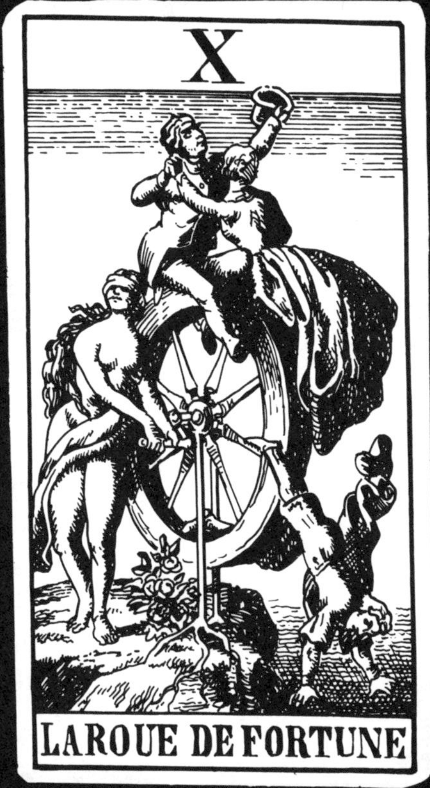
X
LAROUE DE FORTUNE

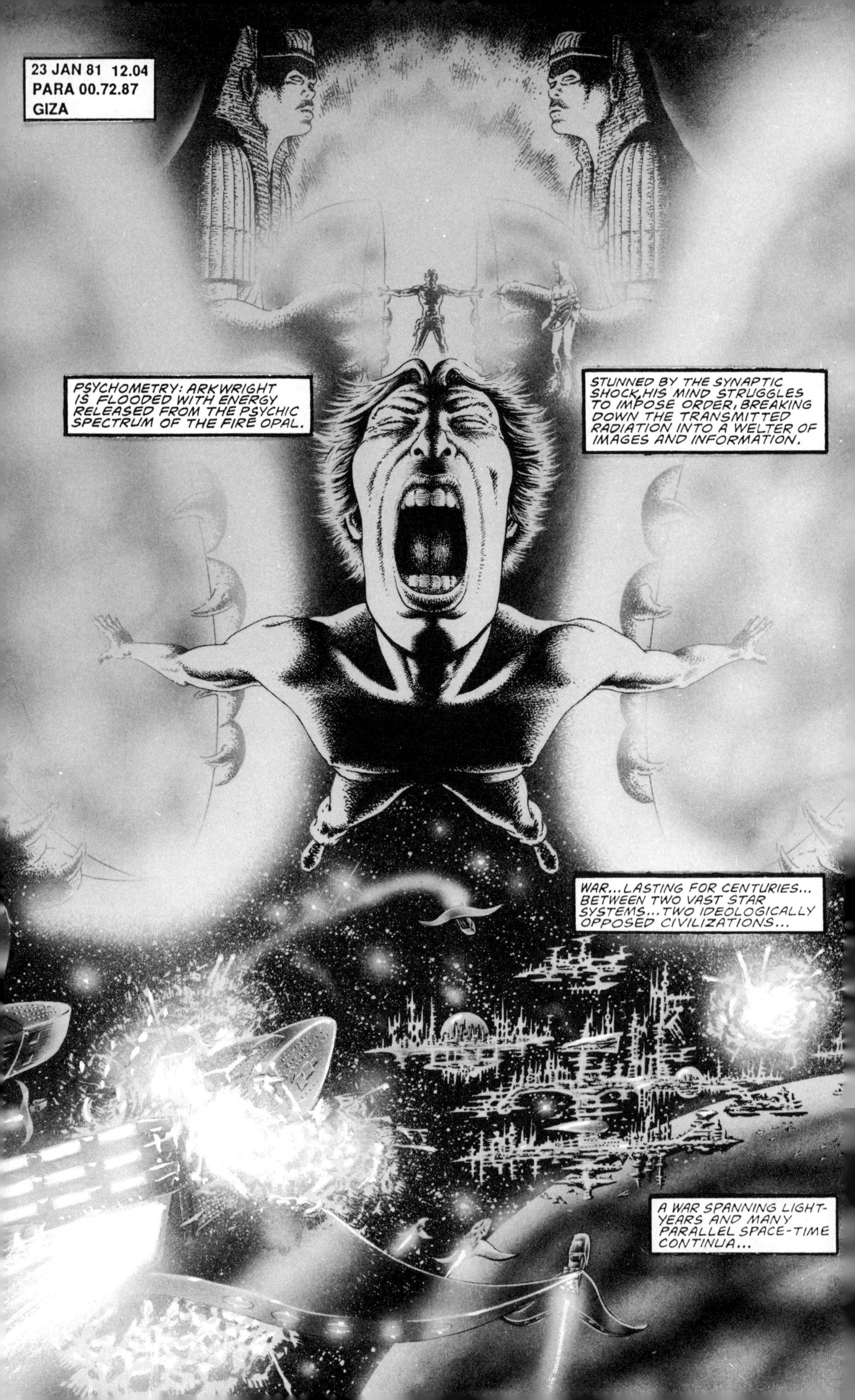
23 JAN 81 12.04
PARA 00.72.87
GIZA
PSYCHOMETRY: ARKWRIGHT IS FLOODED WITH ENERGY RELEASED FROM THE PSYCHIC SPECTRUM OF THE FIRE OPAL.
STUNNED BY THE SYNAPTIC SHOCK, HIS MIND STRUGGLES TO IMPOSE ORDER, BREAKING DOWN THE TRANSMITTED RADIATION INTO A WELTER OF IMAGES AND INFORMATION.
WAR...LASTING FOR CENTURIES... BETWEEN TWO VAST STAR SYSTEMS...TWO IDEOLOGICALLY OPPOSED CIVILIZATIONS...
A WAR SPANNING LIGHT-YEARS AND MANY PARALLEL SPACE-TIME CONTINUA...

HE SEES... WHOLE WORLDS RAVAGED... HUGE ARMIES OF GENETICALLY ENGINEERED TROOPS... MASSIVE WAR MACHINES... INTERMINABLE DESTRUCTION.

THEN FIREFROST: SECRETLY CONSTRUCTED IN AN IMMENSE UNDERGROUND BUNKER BY THE HIGHEST SCIENTISTS OF A PSYCHIC, HUMANOID RACE...

CONSTRUCTED ON ONE PARALLEL ONLY... DRAWING POWER FROM PSIONIC ENERGY --THE BINDING FORCE OF THE UNIVERSE--DESIGNED TO DISRUPT THE ATOMIC STRUCTURE OF THE COSMIC BLUEPRINT... REPLACING ORDER WITH CHAOS... AN APOCALYPSE DEVICE CREATED TO BE THE ULTIMATE DETERRENT.

IT WORKED. UNDER THE DOOMSDAY THREAT OF FIREFROST: FOR DECADES THERE WAS PEACE... NEGO-TIATION... RECONSTRUC-TION... RECOVERY. UNTIL INEVITABLY--AS WITH ANY DETERRENT--IT WAS ACTIVATED...

THROUGHOUT ALL PARALLEL TIMESTREAMS--CHAOS ACCELERATED IN GEOMETRIC PROGRESSION... TIDAL WAVES... EARTH-QUAKES... HURRICANES... FIRESTORMS...

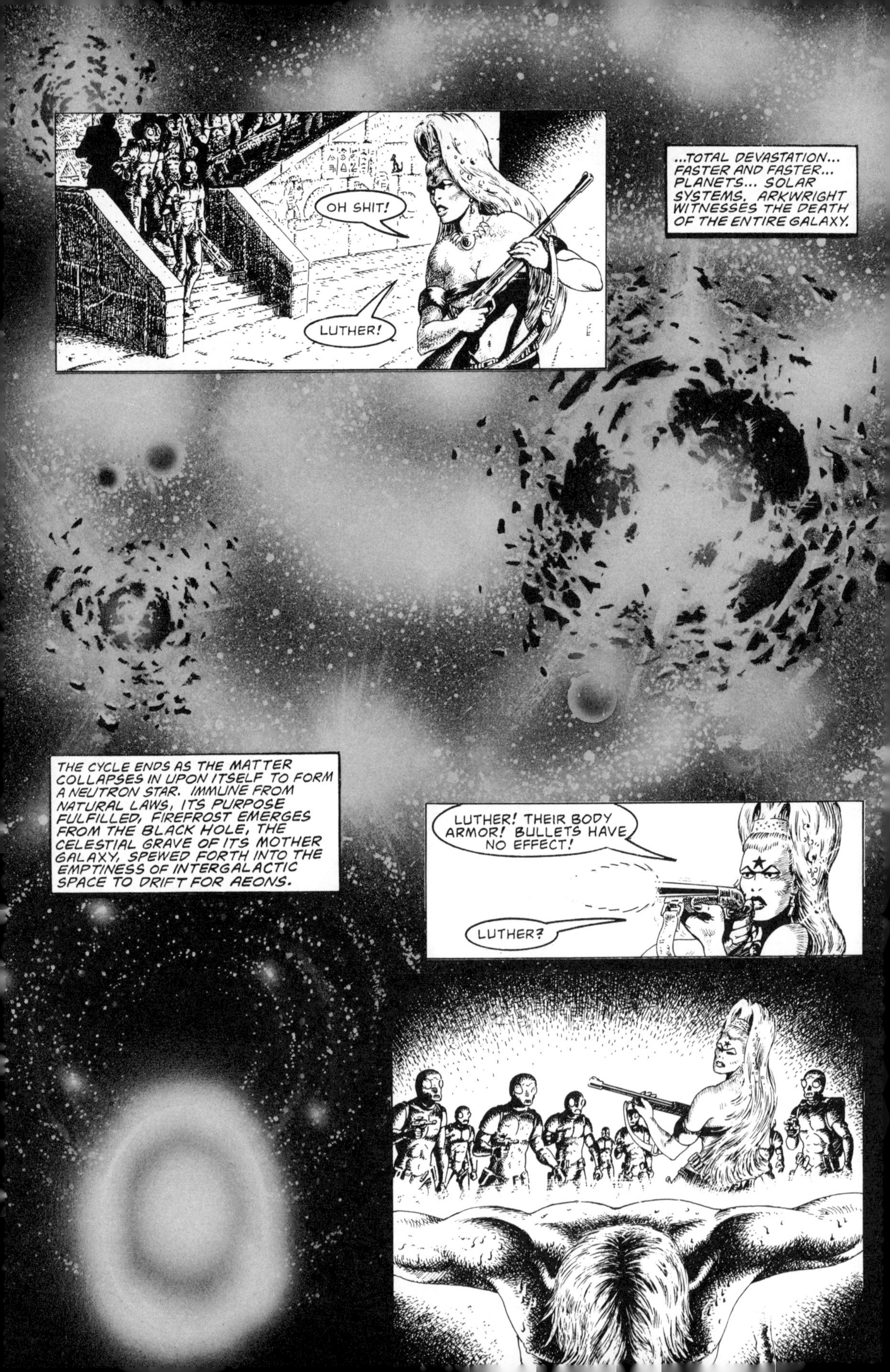
OH SHIT!
LUTHER!
...TOTAL DEVASTATION... FASTER AND FASTER... PLANETS... SOLAR SYSTEMS. ARKWRIGHT WITNESSES THE DEATH OF THE ENTIRE GALAXY.
THE CYCLE ENDS AS THE MATTER COLLAPSES IN UPON ITSELF TO FORM A NEUTRON STAR. IMMUNE FROM NATURAL LAWS, ITS PURPOSE FULFILLED, FIREFROST EMERGES FROM THE BLACK HOLE, THE CELESTIAL GRAVE OF ITS MOTHER GALAXY, SPEWED FORTH INTO THE EMPTINESS OF INTERGALACTIC SPACE TO DRIFT FOR AEONS.
LUTHER! THEIR BODY ARMOR! BULLETS HAVE NO EFFECT!
LUTHER?

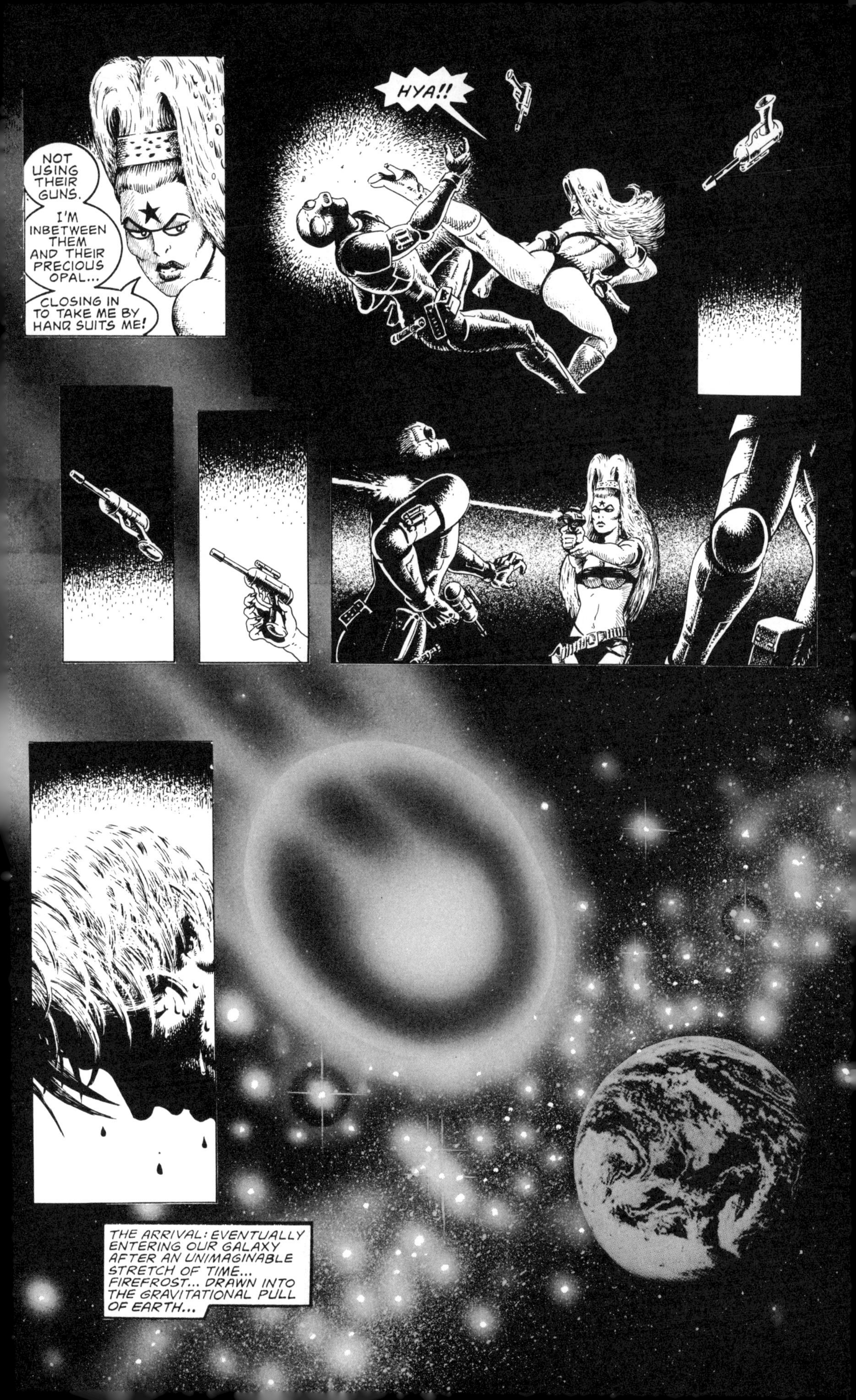
NOT USING THEIR GUNS.
I'M INBETWEEN THEM AND THEIR PRECIOUS OPAL...
CLOSING IN TO TAKE ME BY HAND SUITS ME!
HYA!!
THE ARRIVAL: EVENTUALLY ENTERING OUR GALAXY AFTER AN UNIMAGINABLE STRETCH OF TIME... FIREFROST... DRAWN INTO THE GRAVITATIONAL PULL OF EARTH...

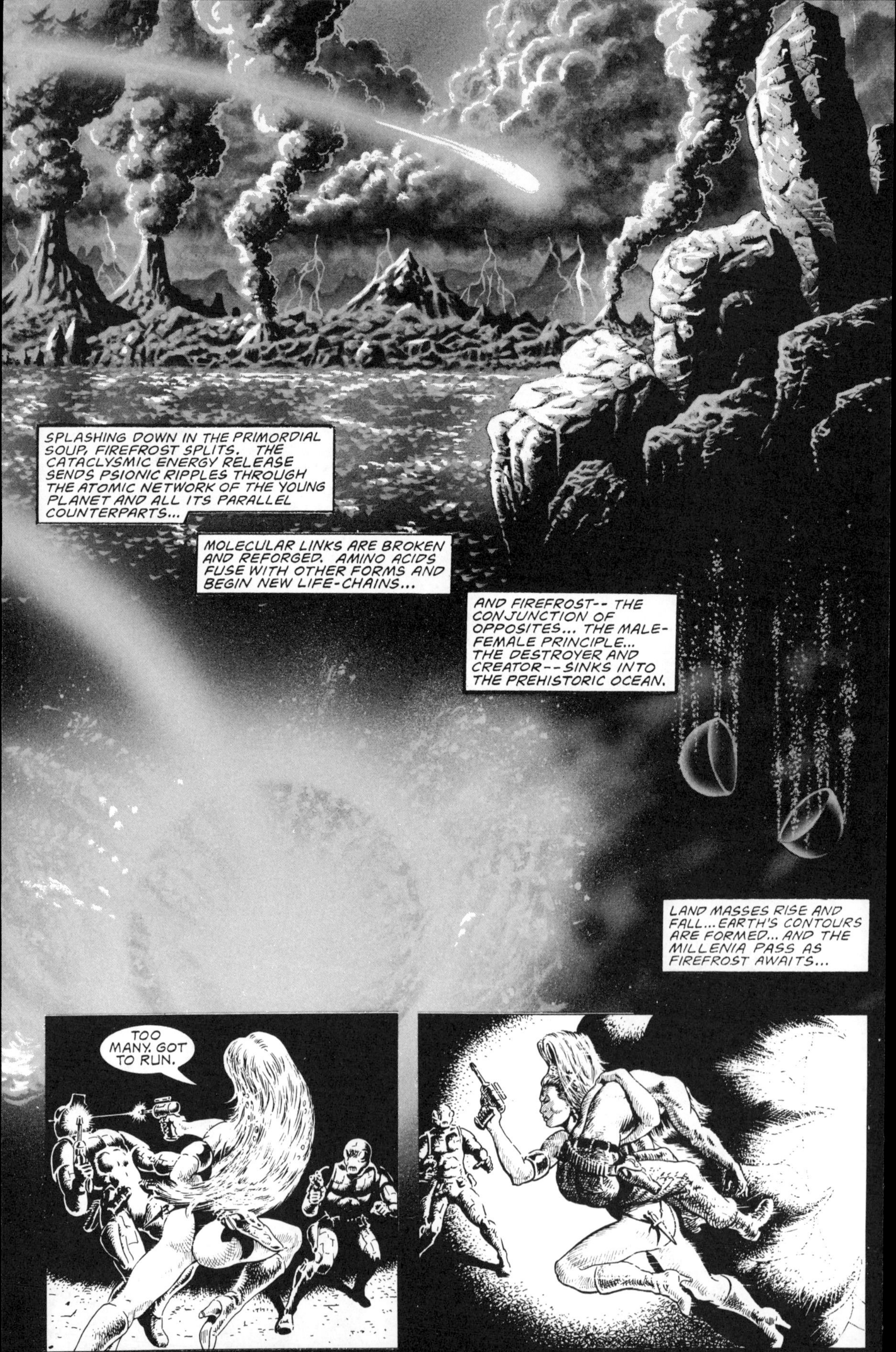
SPLASHING DOWN IN THE PRIMORDIAL SOUP, FIREFROST SPLITS. THE CATACLYSMIC ENERGY RELEASE SENDS PSIONIC RIPPLES THROUGH THE ATOMIC NETWORK OF THE YOUNG PLANET AND ALL ITS PARALLEL COUNTERPARTS...
MOLECULAR LINKS ARE BROKEN AND REFORGED. AMINO ACIDS FUSE WITH OTHER FORMS AND BEGIN NEW LIFE-CHAINS...
AND FIREFROST-- THE CONJUNCTION OF OPPOSITES... THE MALE-FEMALE PRINCIPLE... THE DESTROYER AND CREATOR--SINKS INTO THE PREHISTORIC OCEAN.
LAND MASSES RISE AND FALL... EARTH'S CONTOURS ARE FORMED... AND THE MILLENIA PASS AS FIREFROST AWAITS...
TOO MANY. GOT TO RUN.

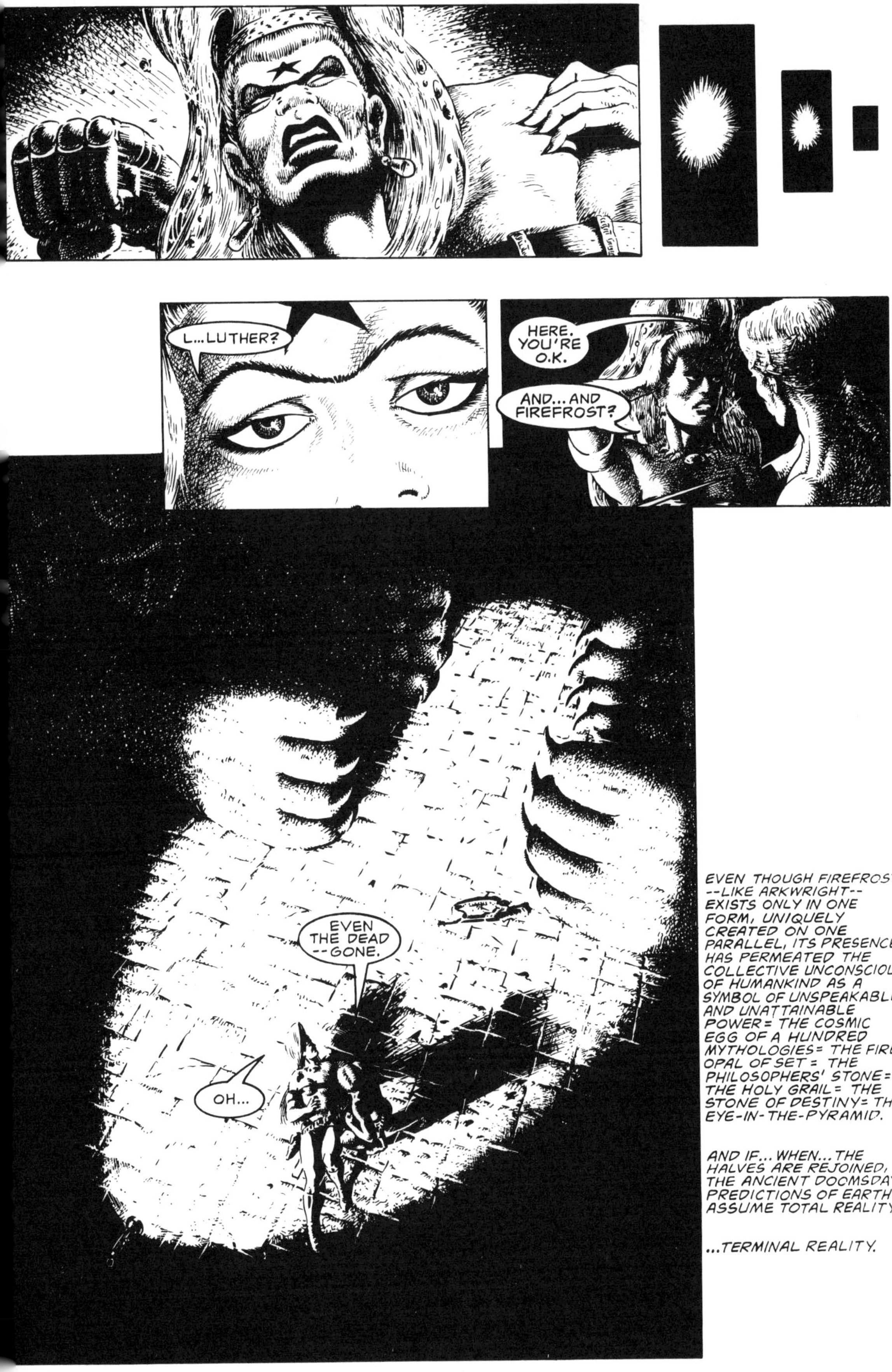
L...LUTHER?
HERE. YOU'RE O.K.
AND... AND FIREFROST?
EVEN THE DEAD --GONE.
OH...

EVEN THOUGH FIREFROST --LIKE ARKWRIGHT-- EXISTS ONLY IN ONE FORM, UNIQUELY CREATED ON ONE PARALLEL, ITS PRESENCE HAS PERMEATED THE COLLECTIVE UNCONSCIOUS OF HUMANKIND AS A SYMBOL OF UNSPEAKABLE AND UNATTAINABLE POWER= THE COSMIC EGG OF A HUNDRED MYTHOLOGIES= THE FIRE OPAL OF SET = THE PHILOSOPHERS' STONE= THE HOLY GRAIL= THE STONE OF DESTINY= THE EYE-IN-THE-PYRAMID.

AND IF... WHEN... THE HALVES ARE REJOINED, THE ANCIENT DOOMSDAY PREDICTIONS OF EARTH ASSUME TOTAL REALITY...

...TERMINAL REALITY.

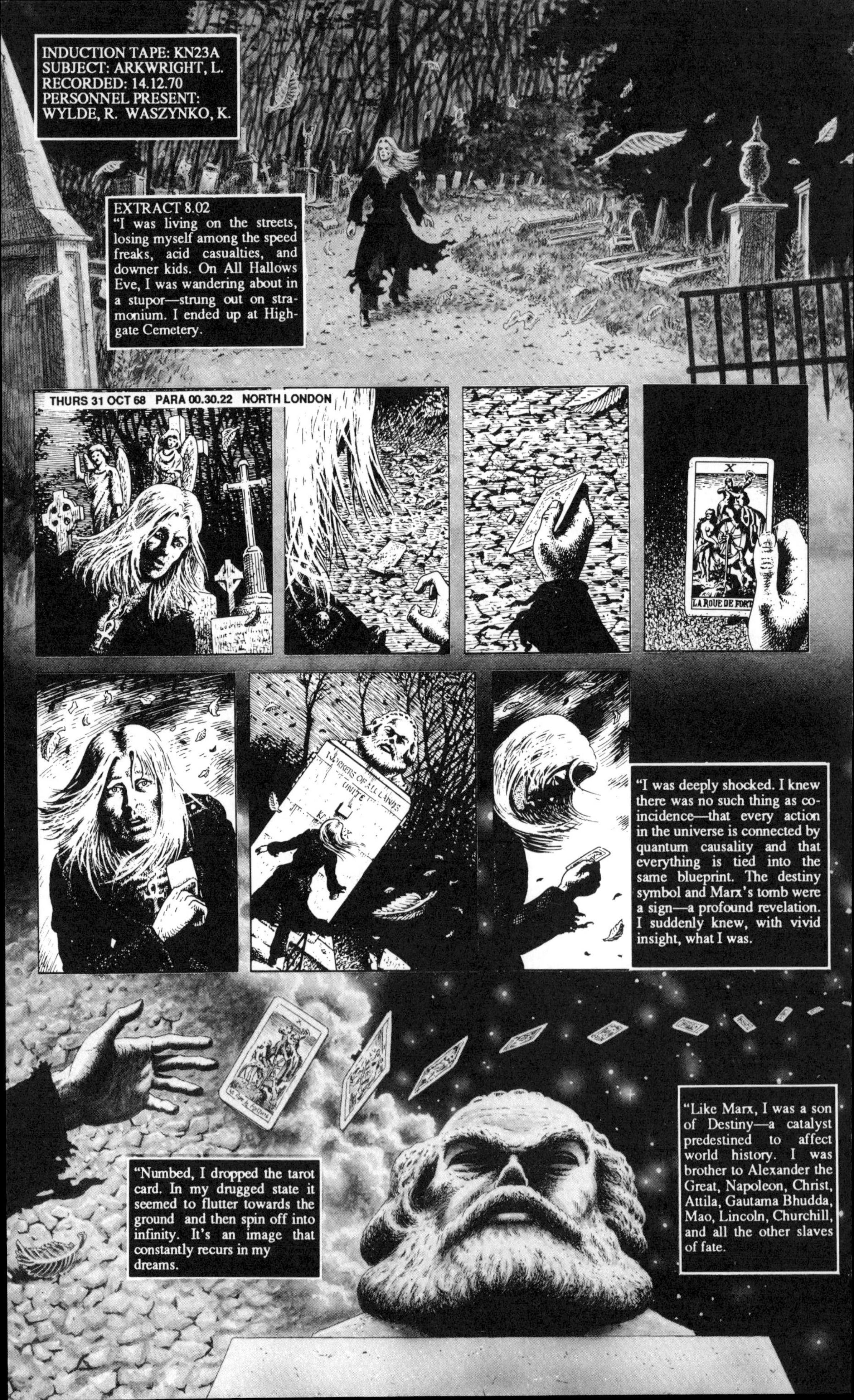
INDUCTION TAPE: KN23A
SUBJECT: ARKWRIGHT, L.
RECORDED: 14.12.70
PERSONNEL PRESENT:
WYLDE, R. WASZYNKO, K.
EXTRACT 8.02
"I was living on the streets, losing myself among the speed freaks, acid casualties, and downer kids. On All Hallows Eve, I was wandering about in a stupor—strung out on stramonium. I ended up at Highgate Cemetery.
THURS 31 OCT 68 PARA 00.30.22 NORTH LONDON
X
LA ROUE DE FORT
WORKERS OF ALL LANDS
UNITE
"I was deeply shocked. I knew there was no such thing as coincidence—that every action in the universe is connected by quantum causality and that everything is tied into the same blueprint. The destiny symbol and Marx's tomb were a sign—a profound revelation. I suddenly knew, with vivid insight, what I was.
"Numbed, I dropped the tarot card. In my drugged state it seemed to flutter towards the ground and then spin off into infinity. It's an image that constantly recurs in my dreams.
"Like Marx, I was a son of Destiny—a catalyst predestined to affect world history. I was brother to Alexander the Great, Napoleon, Christ, Attila, Gautama Bhudda, Mao, Lincoln, Churchill, and all the other slaves of fate.

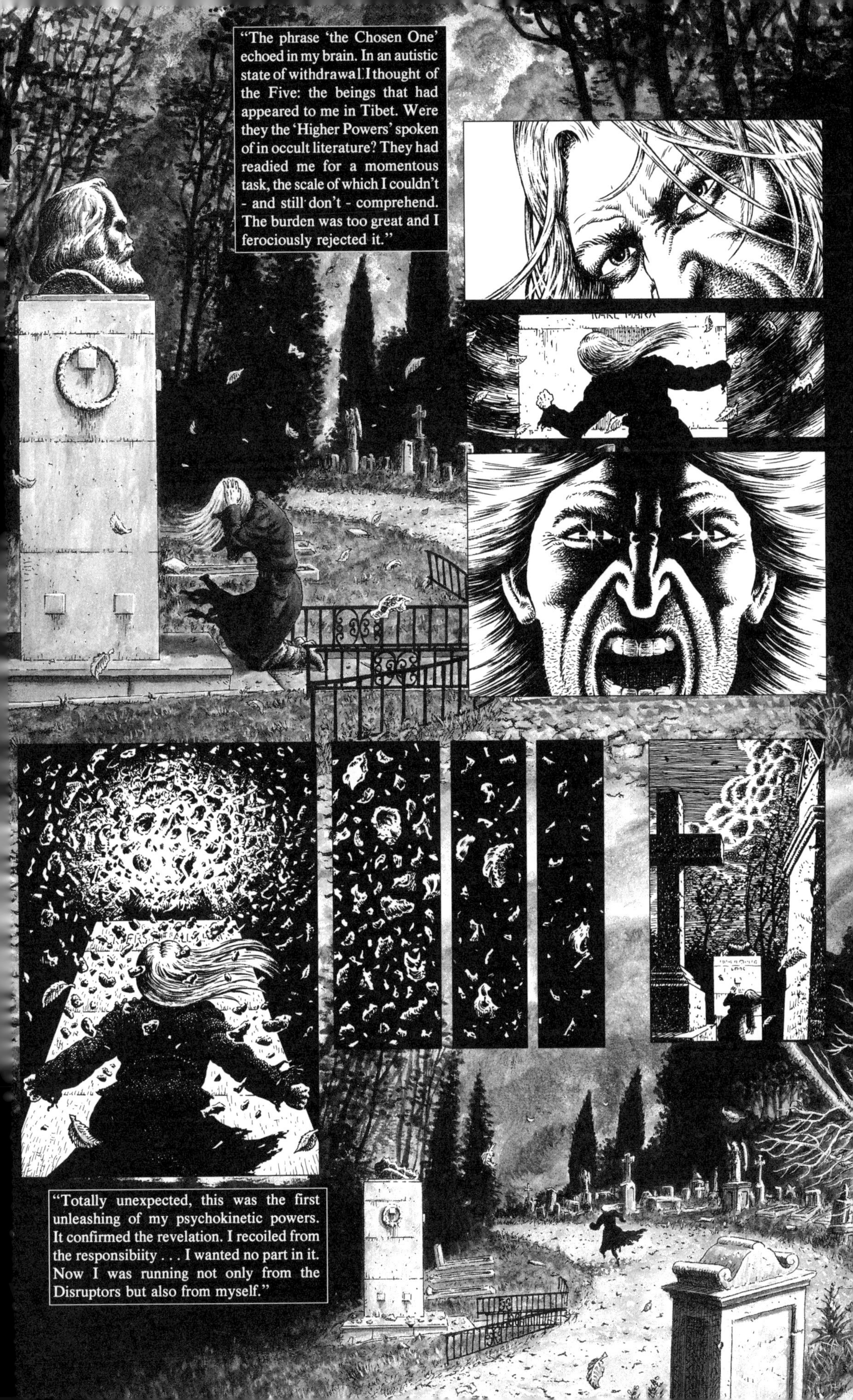
"The phrase 'the Chosen One' echoed in my brain. In an autistic state of withdrawal I thought of the Five: the beings that had appeared to me in Tibet. Were they the 'Higher Powers' spoken of in occult literature? They had readied me for a momentous task, the scale of which I couldn't - and still don't - comprehend. The burden was too great and I ferociously rejected it."
"Totally unexpected, this was the first unleashing of my psychokinetic powers. It confirmed the revelation. I recoiled from the responsibiity . . . I wanted no part in it. Now I was running not only from the Disruptors but also from myself."

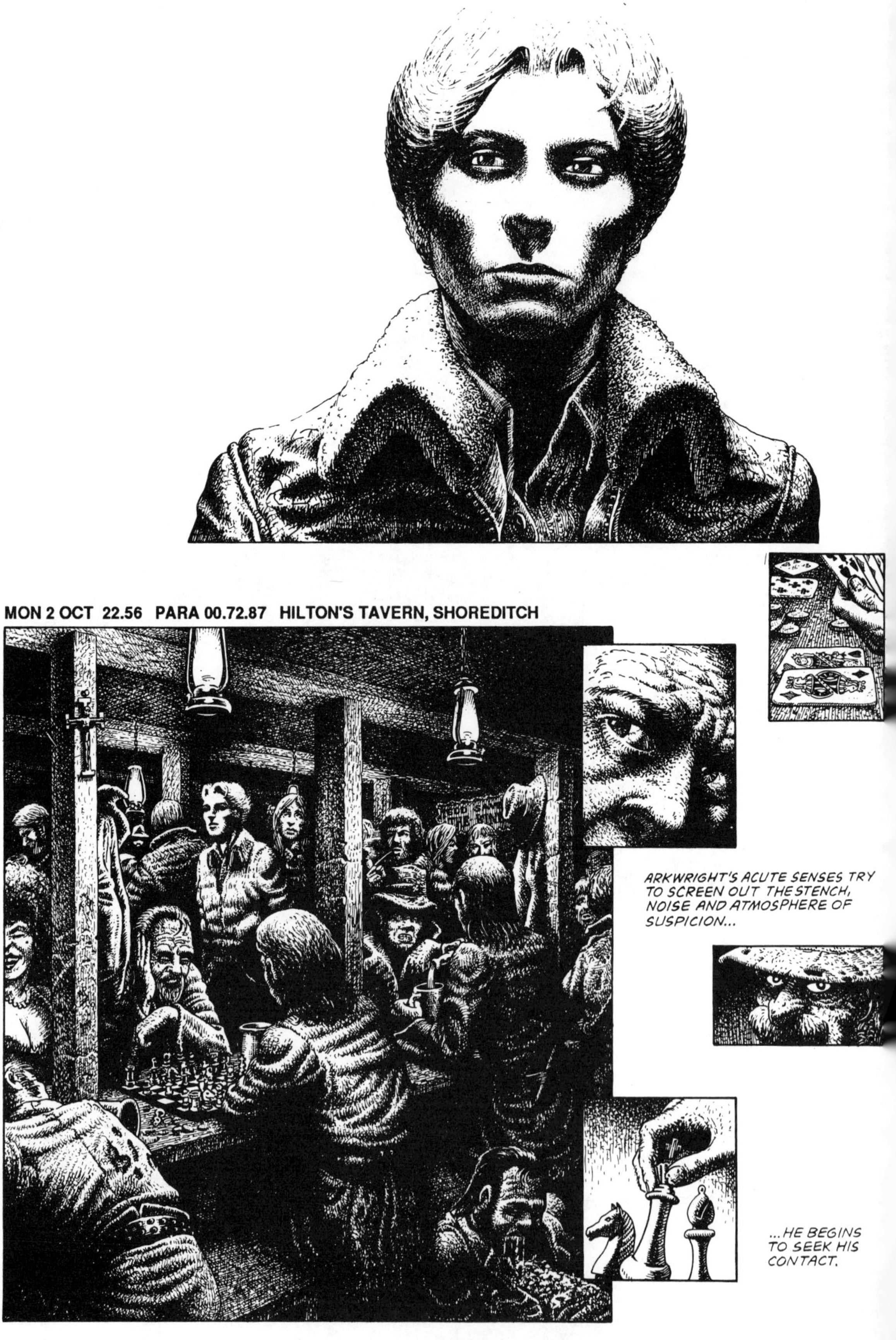
MON 2 OCT 22.56 PARA 00.72.87 HILTON'S TAVERN, SHOREDITCH
ARKWRIGHT'S ACUTE SENSES TRY TO SCREEN OUT THE STENCH, NOISE AND ATMOSPHERE OF SUSPICION...
...HE BEGINS TO SEEK HIS CONTACT.

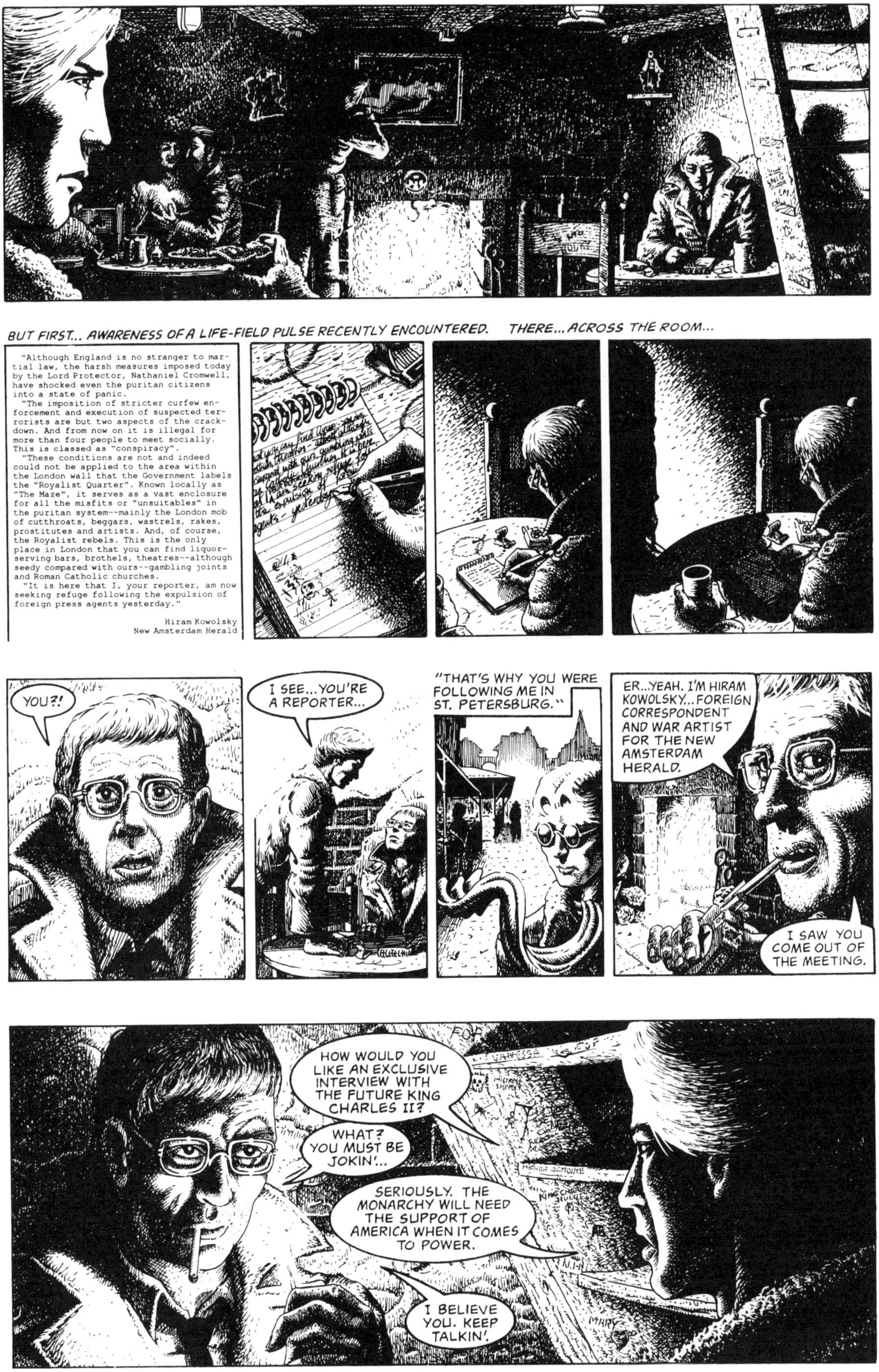
BUT FIRST... AWARENESS OF A LIFE-FIELD PULSE RECENTLY ENCOUNTERED.
THERE... ACROSS THE ROOM...
"Although England is no stranger to martial law, the harsh measures imposed today by the Lord Protector, Nathaniel Cromwell, have shocked even the puritan citizens into a state of panic.
"The imposition of stricter curfew enforcement and execution of suspected terrorists are but two aspects of the crackdown. And from now on it is illegal for more than four people to meet socially. This is classed as "conspiracy".
"These conditions are not and indeed could not be applied to the area within the London wall that the Government labels the "Royalist Quarter". Known locally as "The Maze", it serves as a vast enclosure for all the misfits or "unsuitables" in the puritan system--mainly the London mob of cutthroats, beggars, wastrels, rakes, prostitutes and artists. And, of course, the Royalist rebels. This is the only place in London that you can find liquor-serving bars, brothels, theatres--although seedy compared with ours--gambling joints and Roman Catholic churches.
"It is here that I, your reporter, am now seeking refuge following the expulsion of foreign press agents yesterday."
Hiram Kowolsky
New Amsterdam Herald
YOU?!
I SEE... YOU'RE A REPORTER...
"THAT'S WHY YOU WERE FOLLOWING ME IN ST. PETERSBURG."
ER...YEAH. I'M HIRAM KOWOLSKY... FOREIGN CORRESPONDENT AND WAR ARTIST FOR THE NEW AMSTERDAM HERALD.
I SAW YOU COME OUT OF THE MEETING.
HOW WOULD YOU LIKE AN EXCLUSIVE INTERVIEW WITH THE FUTURE KING CHARLES II?
WHAT? YOU MUST BE JOKIN'...
SERIOUSLY. THE MONARCHY WILL NEED THE SUPPORT OF AMERICA WHEN IT COMES TO POWER.
I BELIEVE YOU. KEEP TALKIN'.

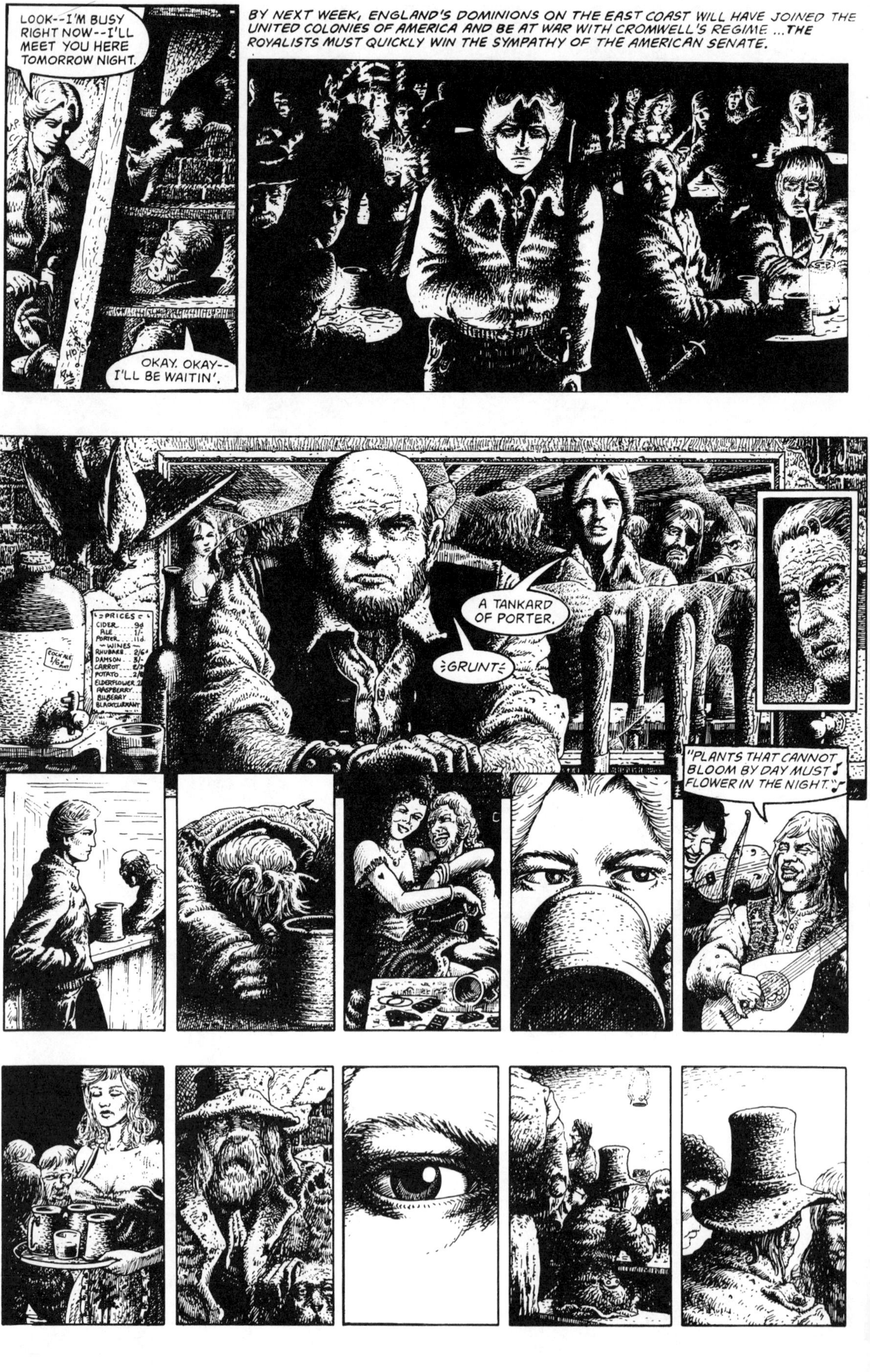
LOOK--I'M BUSY RIGHT NOW--I'LL MEET YOU HERE TOMORROW NIGHT.
OKAY. OKAY-- I'LL BE WAITIN'.
BY NEXT WEEK, ENGLAND'S DOMINIONS ON THE EAST COAST WILL HAVE JOINED THE UNITED COLONIES OF AMERICA AND BE AT WAR WITH CROMWELL'S REGIME ...THE ROYALISTS MUST QUICKLY WIN THE SYMPATHY OF THE AMERICAN SENATE.
PRICES
CIDER 9d
ALE 1/-
PORTER 11d
WINES
RHUBARB 2/6
DAMSON 3/-
CARROT
POTATO
ELDERFLOWER
RASPBERRY
BILBERRY
BLACKCURRANT
A TANKARD OF PORTER.
GRUNT
"PLANTS THAT CANNOT BLOOM BY DAY MUST FLOWER IN THE NIGHT."

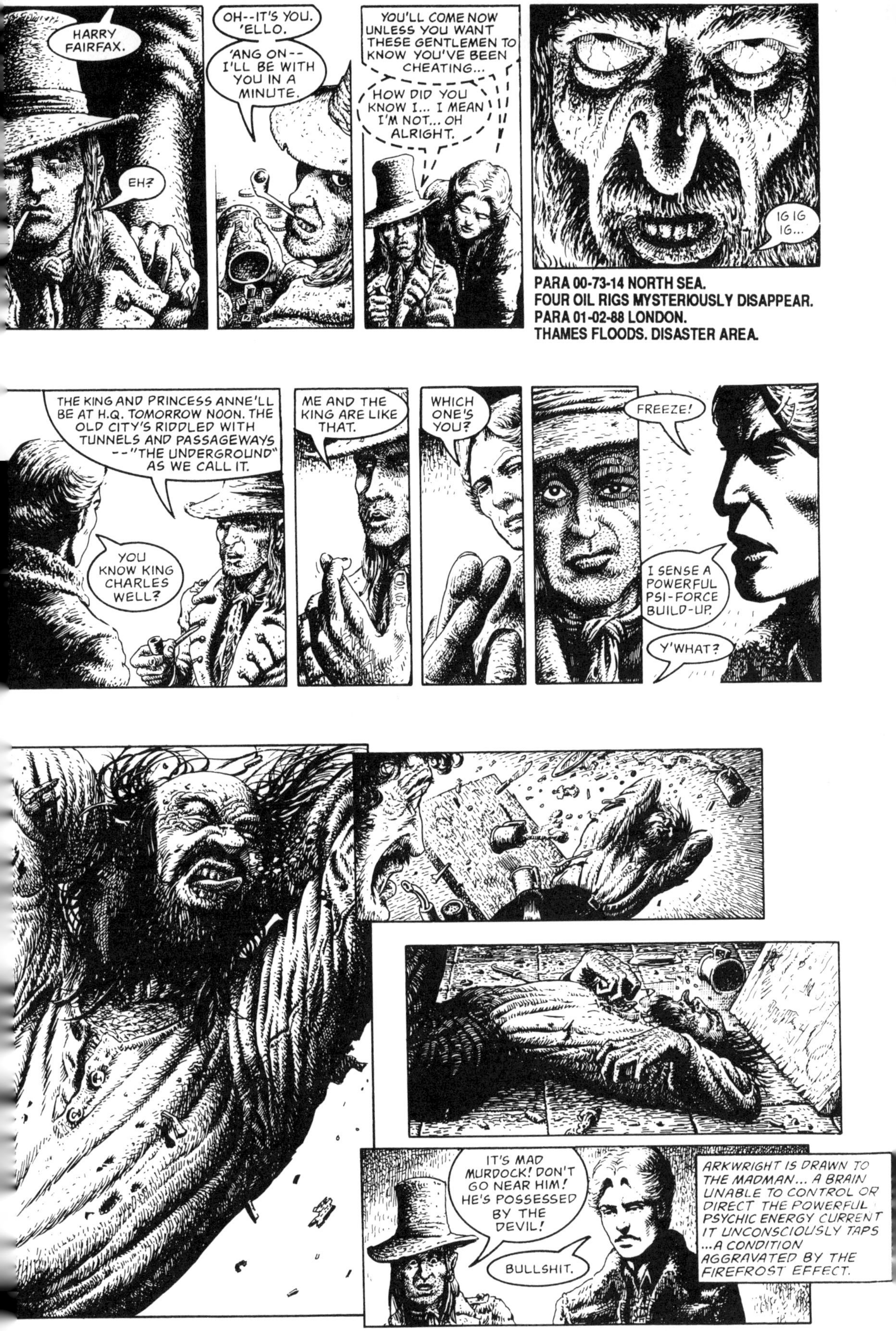
HARRY FAIRFAX.
EH?
OH--IT'S YOU. 'ELLO.
'ANG ON-- I'LL BE WITH YOU IN A MINUTE.
YOU'LL COME NOW UNLESS YOU WANT THESE GENTLEMEN TO KNOW YOU'VE BEEN CHEATING...
HOW DID YOU KNOW I... I MEAN I'M NOT... OH ALRIGHT.
IG IG IG...
PARA 00-73-14 NORTH SEA.
FOUR OIL RIGS MYSTERIOUSLY DISAPPEAR.
PARA 01-02-88 LONDON.
THAMES FLOODS. DISASTER AREA.
THE KING AND PRINCESS ANNE'LL BE AT H.Q. TOMORROW NOON. THE OLD CITY'S RIDDLED WITH TUNNELS AND PASSAGEWAYS --"THE UNDERGROUND" AS WE CALL IT.
YOU KNOW KING CHARLES WELL?
ME AND THE KING ARE LIKE THAT.
WHICH ONE'S YOU?
FREEZE!
I SENSE A POWERFUL PSI-FORCE BUILD-UP.
Y'WHAT?
IT'S MAD MURDOCK! DON'T GO NEAR HIM! HE'S POSSESSED BY THE DEVIL!
BULLSHIT.
ARKWRIGHT IS DRAWN TO THE MADMAN... A BRAIN UNABLE TO CONTROL OR DIRECT THE POWERFUL PSYCHIC ENERGY CURRENT IT UNCONSCIOUSLY TAPS ...A CONDITION AGGRAVATED BY THE FIREFROST EFFECT.

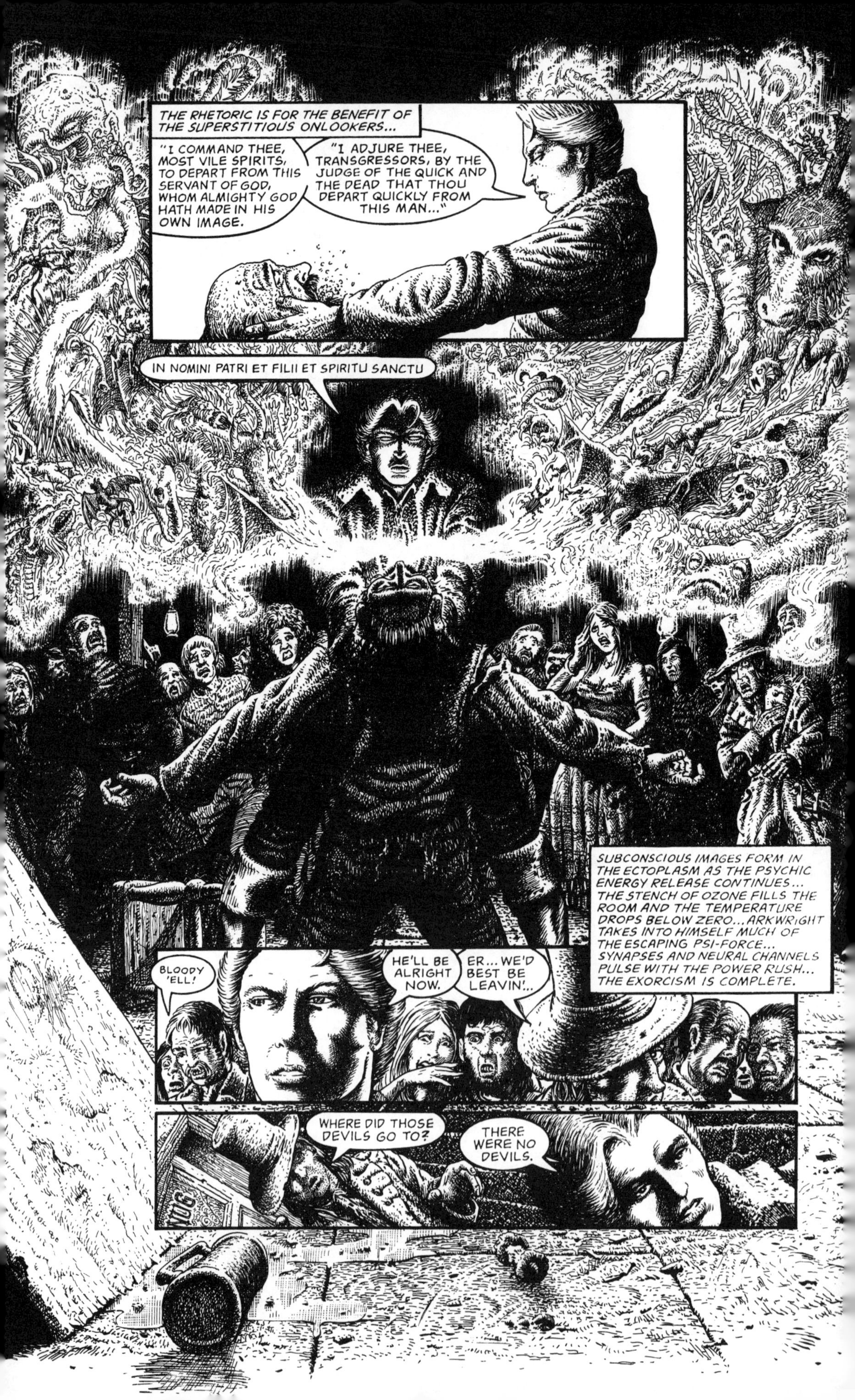

THE RHETORIC IS FOR THE BENEFIT OF THE SUPERSTITIOUS ONLOOKERS...
"I COMMAND THEE, MOST VILE SPIRITS, TO DEPART FROM THIS SERVANT OF GOD, WHOM ALMIGHTY GOD HATH MADE IN HIS OWN IMAGE.
"I ADJURE THEE, TRANSGRESSORS, BY THE JUDGE OF THE QUICK AND THE DEAD THAT THOU DEPART QUICKLY FROM THIS MAN..."
IN NOMINI PATRI ET FILII ET SPIRITU SANCTU
SUBCONSCIOUS IMAGES FORM IN THE ECTOPLASM AS THE PSYCHIC ENERGY RELEASE CONTINUES... THE STENCH OF OZONE FILLS THE ROOM AND THE TEMPERATURE DROPS BELOW ZERO... ARKWRIGHT TAKES INTO HIMSELF MUCH OF THE ESCAPING PSI-FORCE... SYNAPSES AND NEURAL CHANNELS PULSE WITH THE POWER RUSH... THE EXORCISM IS COMPLETE.
BLOODY 'ELL!
HE'LL BE ALRIGHT NOW.
ER... WE'D BEST BE LEAVIN'...
WHERE DID THOSE DEVILS GO TO?
THERE WERE NO DEVILS.

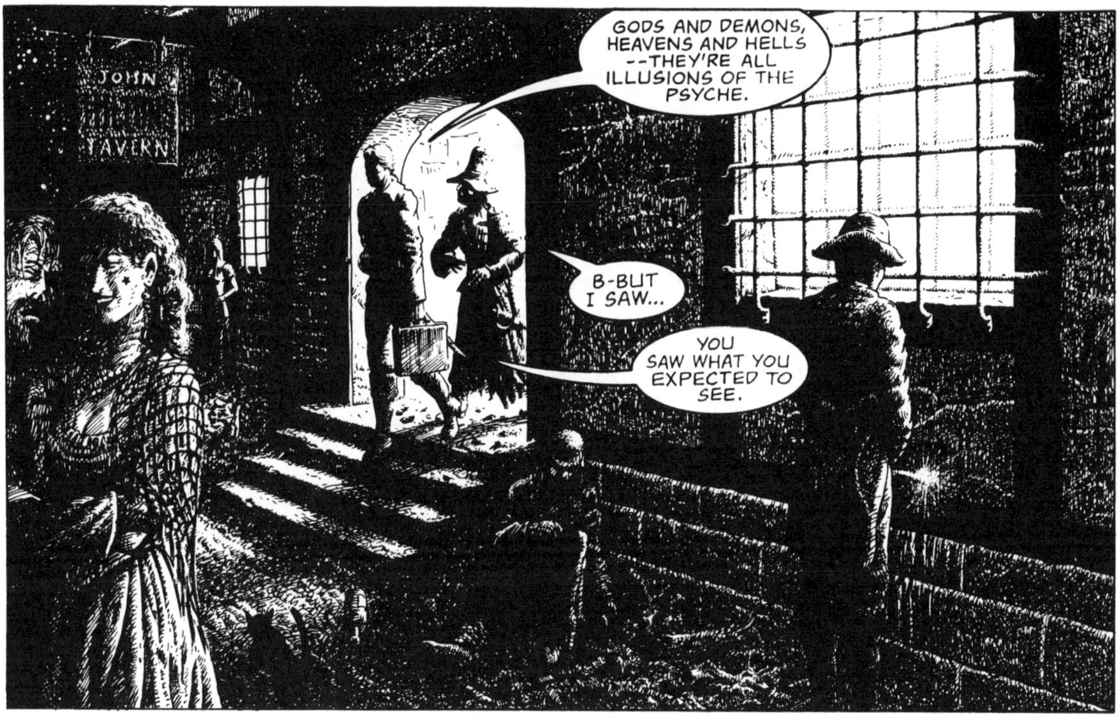
JOHN
TAVERN
GODS AND DEMONS, HEAVENS AND HELLS --THEY'RE ALL ILLUSIONS OF THE PSYCHE.
B-BUT I SAW...
YOU SAW WHAT YOU EXPECTED TO SEE.

PARA 01-53-10 ENGLISH CHANNEL. CHANNEL TUNNEL COLLAPSES.
PARA 00-60-17 SOUTH AMERICA. ARGENTINA DECLARES WAR ON CHILE. CIVIL WAR OUTBREAK IN EL SALVADOR.
PARA 01-82-14 SWITZERLAND. SERIOUS LANDSLIDES IN ALPS.
PARA 00-28-81 CHINA. EMPEROR T'SIANCHI ASSASSINATED DURING COMMUNIST MILITARY COUP.

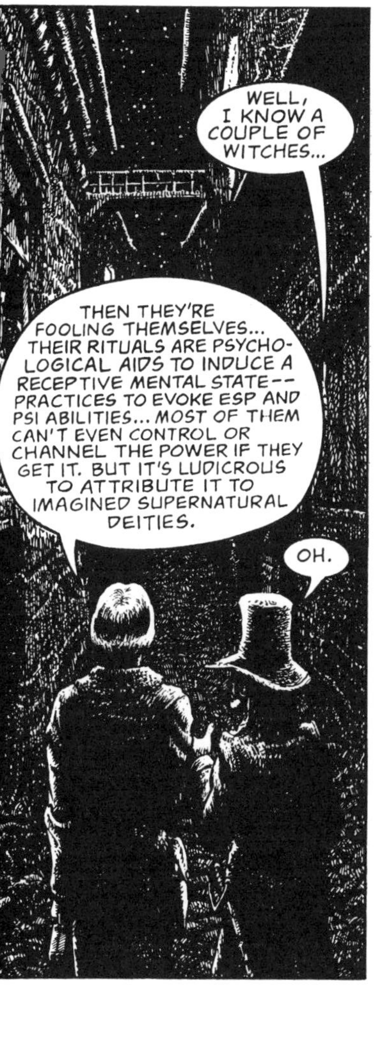
WELL, I KNOW A COUPLE OF WITCHES...
THEN THEY'RE FOOLING THEMSELVES... THEIR RITUALS ARE PSYCHOLOGICAL AIDS TO INDUCE A RECEPTIVE MENTAL STATE--PRACTICES TO EVOKE ESP AND PSI ABILITIES... MOST OF THEM CAN'T EVEN CONTROL OR CHANNEL THE POWER IF THEY GET IT. BUT IT'S LUDICROUS TO ATTRIBUTE IT TO IMAGINED SUPERNATURAL DEITIES.
OH.

WESTMINSTER; LORD PROTECTOR'S PRIVATE QUARTERS 23.54

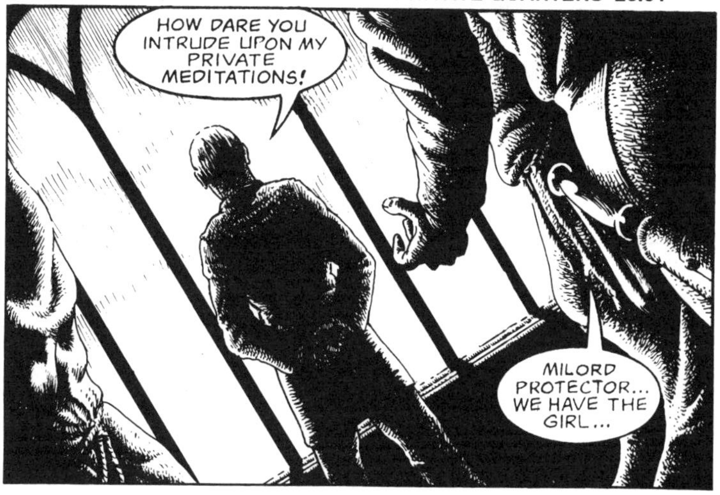
HOW DARE YOU INTRUDE UPON MY PRIVATE MEDITATIONS!
MILORD PROTECTOR... WE HAVE THE GIRL...

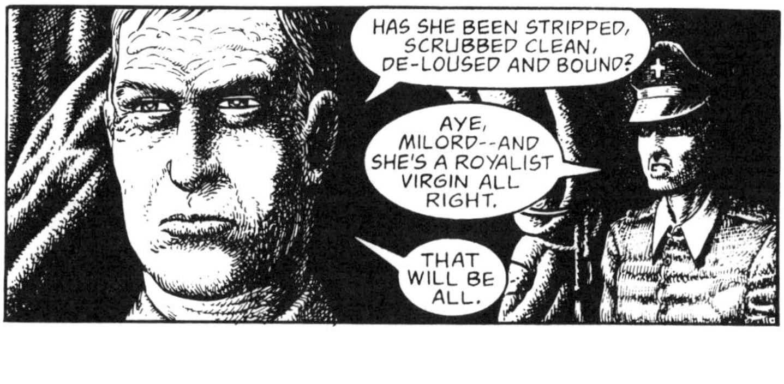
HAS SHE BEEN STRIPPED, SCRUBBED CLEAN, DE-LOUSED AND BOUND?
AYE, MILORD--AND SHE'S A ROYALIST VIRGIN ALL RIGHT.
THAT WILL BE ALL.

CHEAPSIDE 00.04

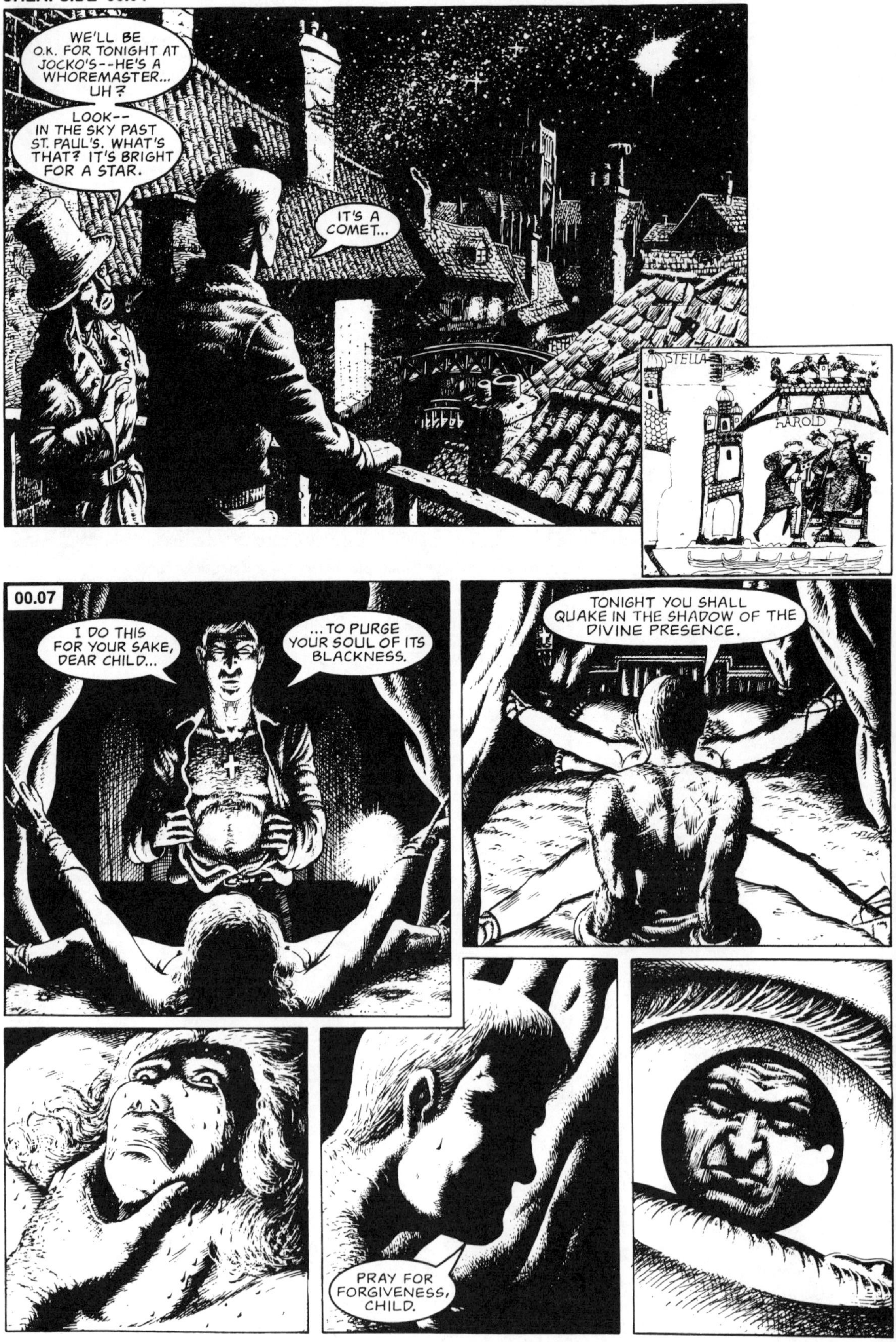
WE'LL BE O.K. FOR TONIGHT AT JOCKO'S--HE'S A WHOREMASTER... UH?
LOOK-- IN THE SKY PAST ST. PAUL'S. WHAT'S THAT? IT'S BRIGHT FOR A STAR.
IT'S A COMET...
STELLA
HAROLD
00.07
I DO THIS FOR YOUR SAKE, DEAR CHILD...
...TO PURGE YOUR SOUL OF ITS BLACKNESS.
TONIGHT YOU SHALL QUAKE IN THE SHADOW OF THE DIVINE PRESENCE.
PRAY FOR FORGIVENESS, CHILD.

"Now is the time for all good citizens to unite in common accord and patriotic spirit against the Imperial threat.

"Never since the end of the Civil War has our National Security been so severely menaced. Bee on your guard against Royalist infiltrators. Report any suspicious behavior at once to your local Watch."

"Your way of life is under attack from Godless, louse-ridden revolutionaries who will stop at nothing to achieve their evil goal—total domination of your country!

"This degenerate scum is well used to anarchy, living as it does in squalid slums, cancerous taverns and damnable whorehouses."

PURITAN MAGAZINE

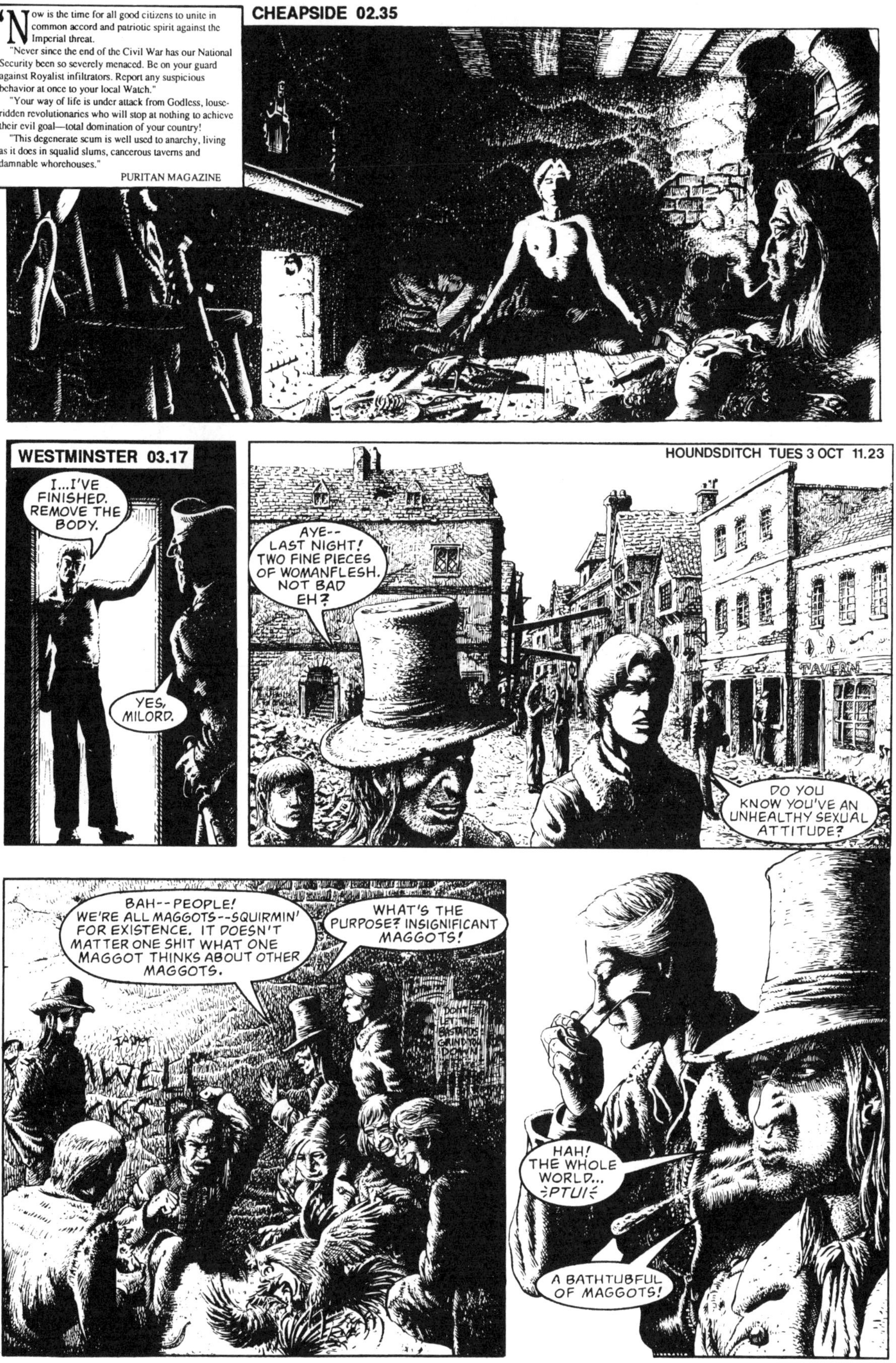
CHEAPSIDE 02.35
WESTMINSTER 03.17
I...I'VE FINISHED. REMOVE THE BODY.
YES, MILORD.
HOUNDSDITCH TUES 3 OCT 11.23
AYE-- LAST NIGHT! TWO FINE PIECES OF WOMANFLESH. NOT BAD EH?
DO YOU KNOW YOU'VE AN UNHEALTHY SEXUAL ATTITUDE?
TAVERN
BAH--PEOPLE! WE'RE ALL MAGGOTS--SQUIRMIN' FOR EXISTENCE. IT DOESN'T MATTER ONE SHIT WHAT ONE MAGGOT THINKS ABOUT OTHER MAGGOTS.
WHAT'S THE PURPOSE? INSIGNIFICANT MAGGOTS!
HAH! THE WHOLE WORLD... PTUI
A BATHTUBFUL OF MAGGOTS!

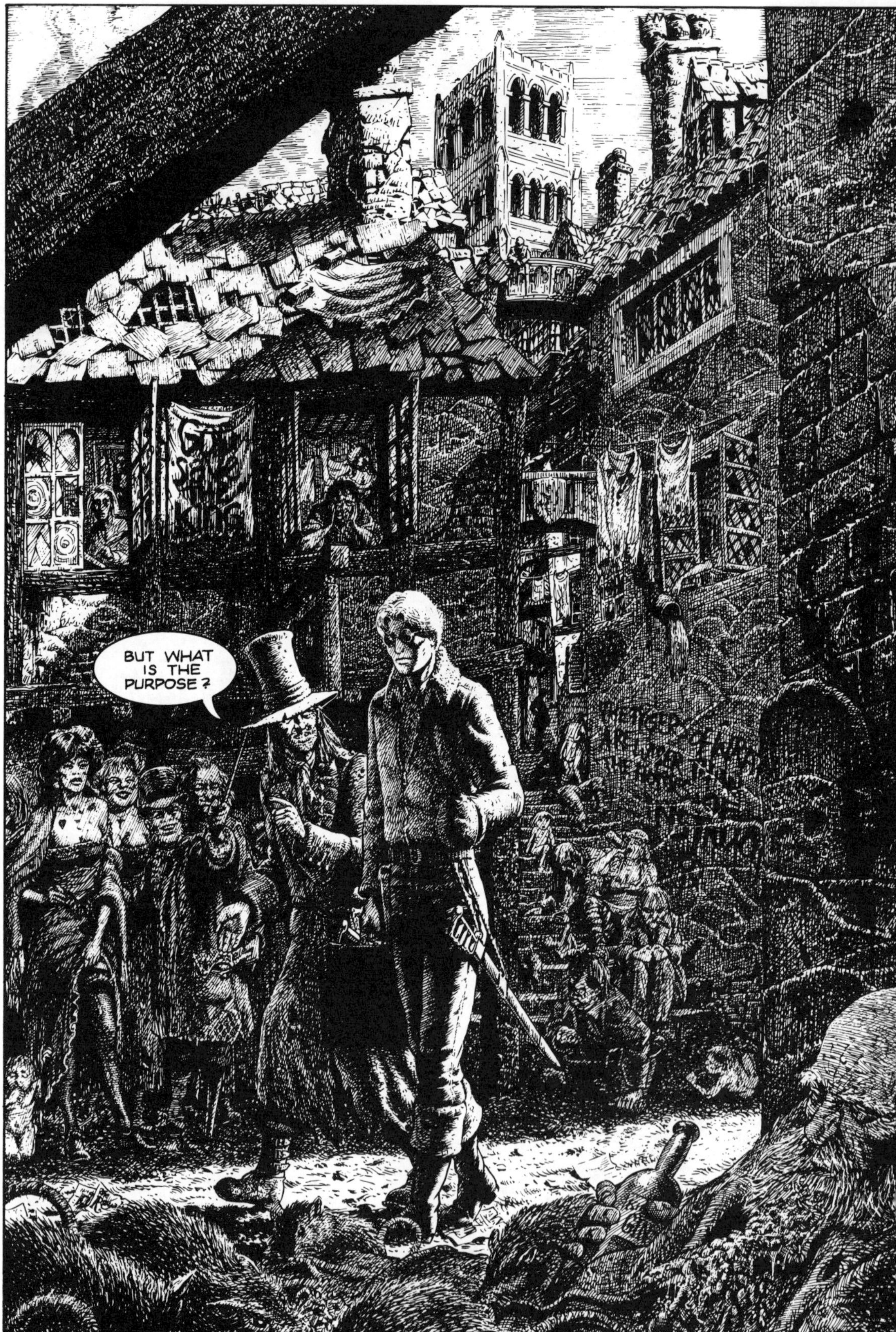
BUT WHAT IS THE PURPOSE?

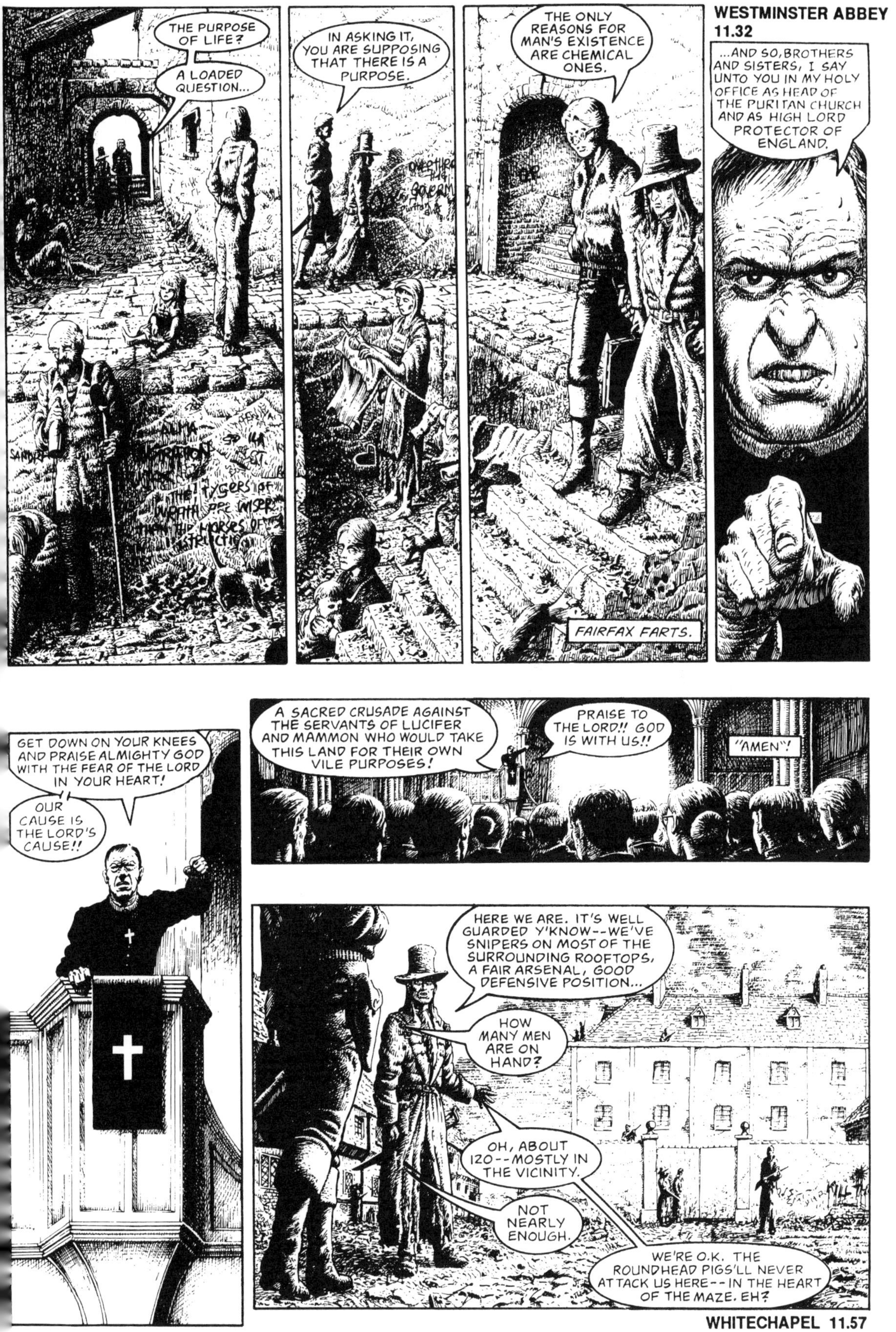
THE PURPOSE OF LIFE?
A LOADED QUESTION...
IN ASKING IT, YOU ARE SUPPOSING THAT THERE IS A PURPOSE.
THE ONLY REASONS FOR MAN'S EXISTENCE ARE CHEMICAL ONES.
FAIRFAX FARTS.
WESTMINSTER ABBEY 11.32
...AND SO, BROTHERS AND SISTERS, I SAY UNTO YOU IN MY HOLY OFFICE AS HEAD OF THE PURITAN CHURCH AND AS HIGH LORD PROTECTOR OF ENGLAND.
GET DOWN ON YOUR KNEES AND PRAISE ALMIGHTY GOD WITH THE FEAR OF THE LORD IN YOUR HEART!
OUR CAUSE IS THE LORD'S CAUSE!!
A SACRED CRUSADE AGAINST THE SERVANTS OF LUCIFER AND MAMMON WHO WOULD TAKE THIS LAND FOR THEIR OWN VILE PURPOSES!
PRAISE TO THE LORD!! GOD IS WITH US!!
"AMEN"!
HERE WE ARE. IT'S WELL GUARDED Y'KNOW--WE'VE SNIPERS ON MOST OF THE SURROUNDING ROOFTOPS, A FAIR ARSENAL, GOOD DEFENSIVE POSITION...
HOW MANY MEN ARE ON HAND?
OH, ABOUT 120--MOSTLY IN THE VICINITY.
NOT NEARLY ENOUGH.
WE'RE O.K. THE ROUNDHEAD PIGS'LL NEVER ATTACK US HERE--IN THE HEART OF THE MAZE. EH?
WHITECHAPEL 11.57

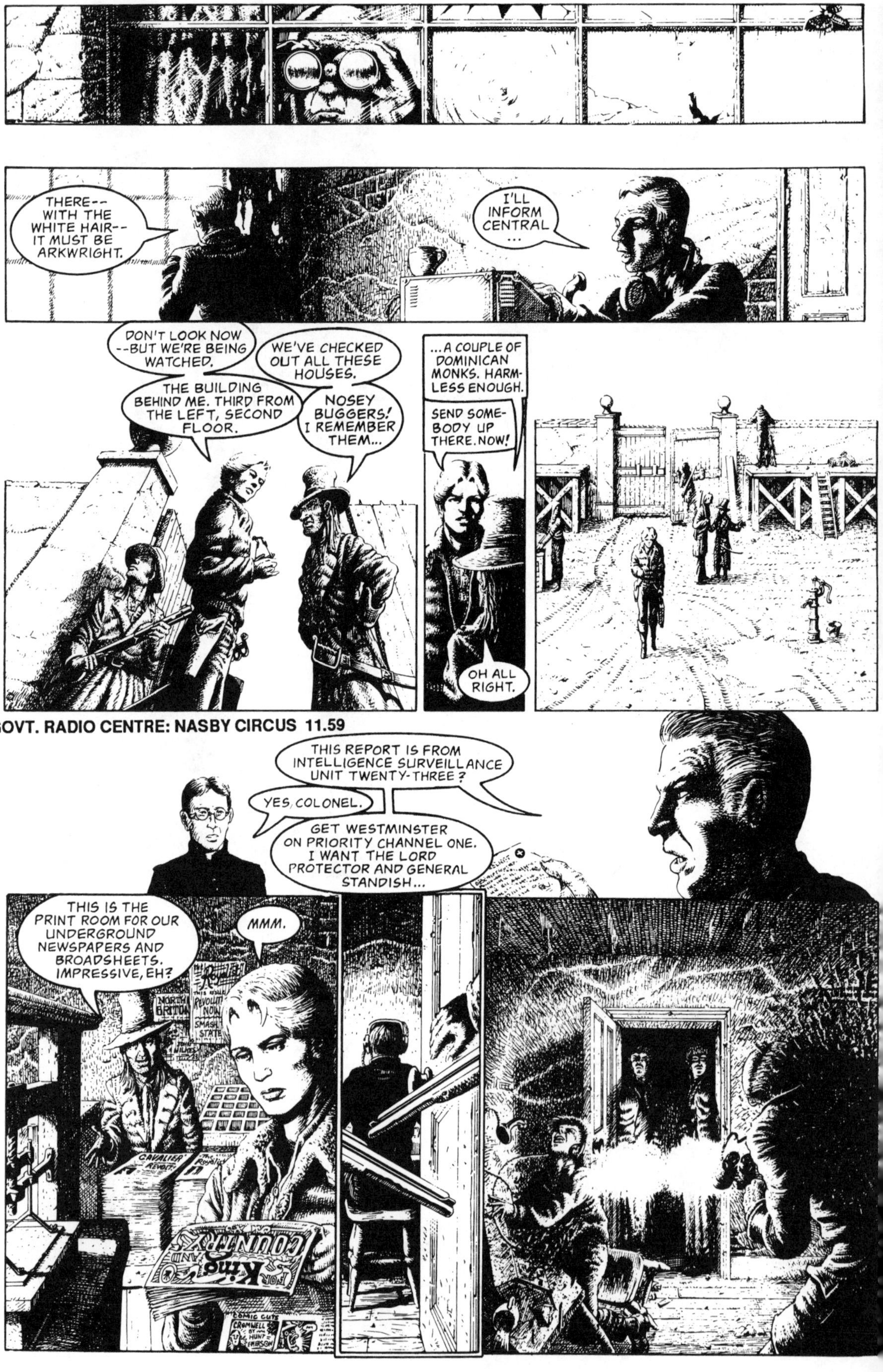
THERE-- WITH THE WHITE HAIR-- IT MUST BE ARKWRIGHT.
I'LL INFORM CENTRAL ...
DON'T LOOK NOW --BUT WE'RE BEING WATCHED.
THE BUILDING BEHIND ME. THIRD FROM THE LEFT, SECOND FLOOR.
WE'VE CHECKED OUT ALL THESE HOUSES.
NOSEY BUGGERS! I REMEMBER THEM...
...A COUPLE OF DOMINICAN MONKS. HARMLESS ENOUGH.
SEND SOMEBODY UP THERE. NOW!
OH ALL RIGHT.
GOVT. RADIO CENTRE: NASBY CIRCUS 11.59
THIS REPORT IS FROM INTELLIGENCE SURVEILLANCE UNIT TWENTY-THREE?
YES, COLONEL.
GET WESTMINSTER ON PRIORITY CHANNEL ONE. I WANT THE LORD PROTECTOR AND GENERAL STANDISH...
THIS IS THE PRINT ROOM FOR OUR UNDERGROUND NEWSPAPERS AND BROADSHEETS. IMPRESSIVE, EH?
MMM.
FOR KING AND COUNTRY
CAVALIER REVOLT!
CROMWELL

HE WAS RIGHT. BUT WAS THAT THE END OF THE THREAT... OR THE BEGINNING?

≈BELCH≈...SOME OF THE KING'S ART TREASURES. HE'S BEEN SELLIN' 'EM OFF IN EUROPE TO RAISE MONEY FOR ARMAMENTS.

C'MON-- THEY'RE WAITIN' FOR US THROUGH HERE.

"Representational Art is banned by the Puritan regime, their religion being iconoclastic by nature. England is the home of non-figurative black and white design or "Optical Art" as it is titled."
ENCYCLOPEDIA AMERICANA

YOUR MAJESTY.

AH--ARKWRIGHT, MY GENERAL! I REMEMBER YOU AS SOMETHING OF A RAKE...

...AND A CHESS HUSTLER. BUT MAJOR WYLDE HAS INFORMED US OF YOUR WORKS ON OUR BEHALF...

HOW WONDERFUL TO SEE YOU AGAIN, LUTHER.

YES SIRE-- MMM-- HERE'S THE WAR LOAN FROM THE KAISER AND YOUR UNCLE, CZAR NICHOLAS.

MY PRINCESS.

HRUMPH. I'LL HAVE A WORD WITH YOU IN PRIVATE ABOUT ANNE'S...ER ...CONDITION.

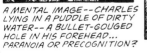
A MENTAL IMAGE--CHARLES LYING IN A PUDDLE OF DIRTY WATER-- A BULLET-GOUGED HOLE IN HIS FOREHEAD... PARANOIA OR PRECOGNITION?

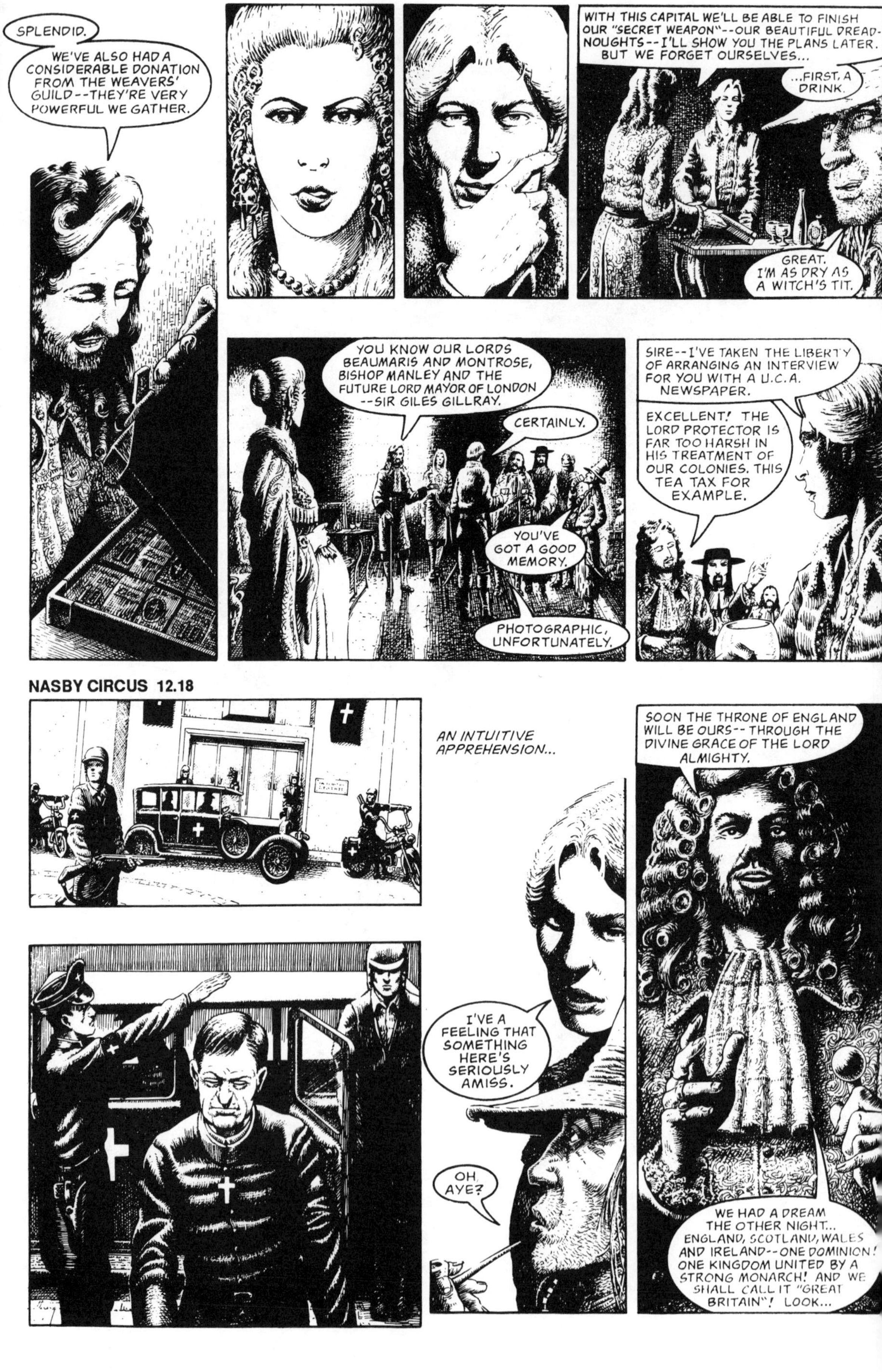
SPLENDID.
WE'VE ALSO HAD A CONSIDERABLE DONATION FROM THE WEAVERS' GUILD--THEY'RE VERY POWERFUL WE GATHER.
WITH THIS CAPITAL WE'LL BE ABLE TO FINISH OUR "SECRET WEAPON"--OUR BEAUTIFUL DREADNOUGHTS--I'LL SHOW YOU THE PLANS LATER. BUT WE FORGET OURSELVES...
...FIRST, A DRINK.
GREAT. I'M AS DRY AS A WITCH'S TIT.
YOU KNOW OUR LORDS BEAUMARIS AND MONTROSE, BISHOP MANLEY AND THE FUTURE LORD MAYOR OF LONDON --SIR GILES GILLRAY.
CERTAINLY.
YOU'VE GOT A GOOD MEMORY.
PHOTOGRAPHIC, UNFORTUNATELY.
SIRE--I'VE TAKEN THE LIBERTY OF ARRANGING AN INTERVIEW FOR YOU WITH A U.C.A. NEWSPAPER.
EXCELLENT! THE LORD PROTECTOR IS FAR TOO HARSH IN HIS TREATMENT OF OUR COLONIES. THIS TEA TAX FOR EXAMPLE.
NASBY CIRCUS 12.18
AN INTUITIVE APPREHENSION...
I'VE A FEELING THAT SOMETHING HERE'S SERIOUSLY AMISS.
OH, AYE?
SOON THE THRONE OF ENGLAND WILL BE OURS--THROUGH THE DIVINE GRACE OF THE LORD ALMIGHTY.
WE HAD A DREAM THE OTHER NIGHT... ENGLAND, SCOTLAND, WALES AND IRELAND--ONE DOMINION! ONE KINGDOM UNITED BY A STRONG MONARCH! AND WE SHALL CALL IT "GREAT BRITAIN"! LOOK...

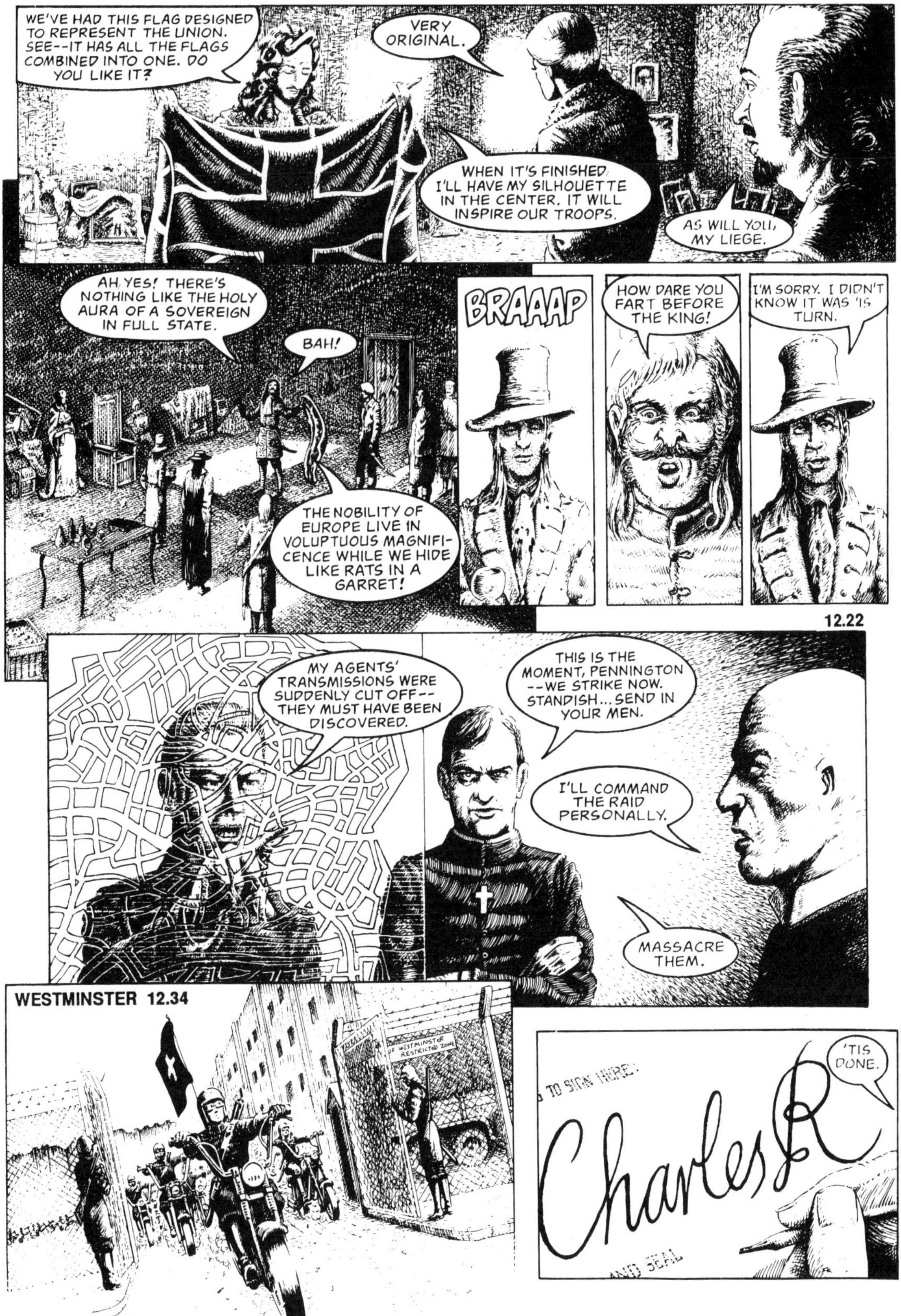
WE'VE HAD THIS FLAG DESIGNED TO REPRESENT THE UNION. SEE--IT HAS ALL THE FLAGS COMBINED INTO ONE. DO YOU LIKE IT?
VERY ORIGINAL.
WHEN IT'S FINISHED, I'LL HAVE MY SILHOUETTE IN THE CENTER. IT WILL INSPIRE OUR TROOPS.
AS WILL YOU, MY LIEGE.
AH, YES! THERE'S NOTHING LIKE THE HOLY AURA OF A SOVEREIGN IN FULL STATE.
BAH!
THE NOBILITY OF EUROPE LIVE IN VOLUPTUOUS MAGNIFICENCE WHILE WE HIDE LIKE RATS IN A GARRET!
BRAAAP
HOW DARE YOU FART BEFORE THE KING!
I'M SORRY. I DIDN'T KNOW IT WAS 'IS TURN.
12.22
MY AGENTS' TRANSMISSIONS WERE SUDDENLY CUT OFF--THEY MUST HAVE BEEN DISCOVERED.
THIS IS THE MOMENT, PENNINGTON--WE STRIKE NOW. STANDISH... SEND IN YOUR MEN.
I'LL COMMAND THE RAID PERSONALLY.
MASSACRE THEM.
WESTMINSTER 12.34
WESTMINSTER RESTRICTED ZONE
TO SIGN HERE:
Charles R
AND SEAL
'TIS DONE.

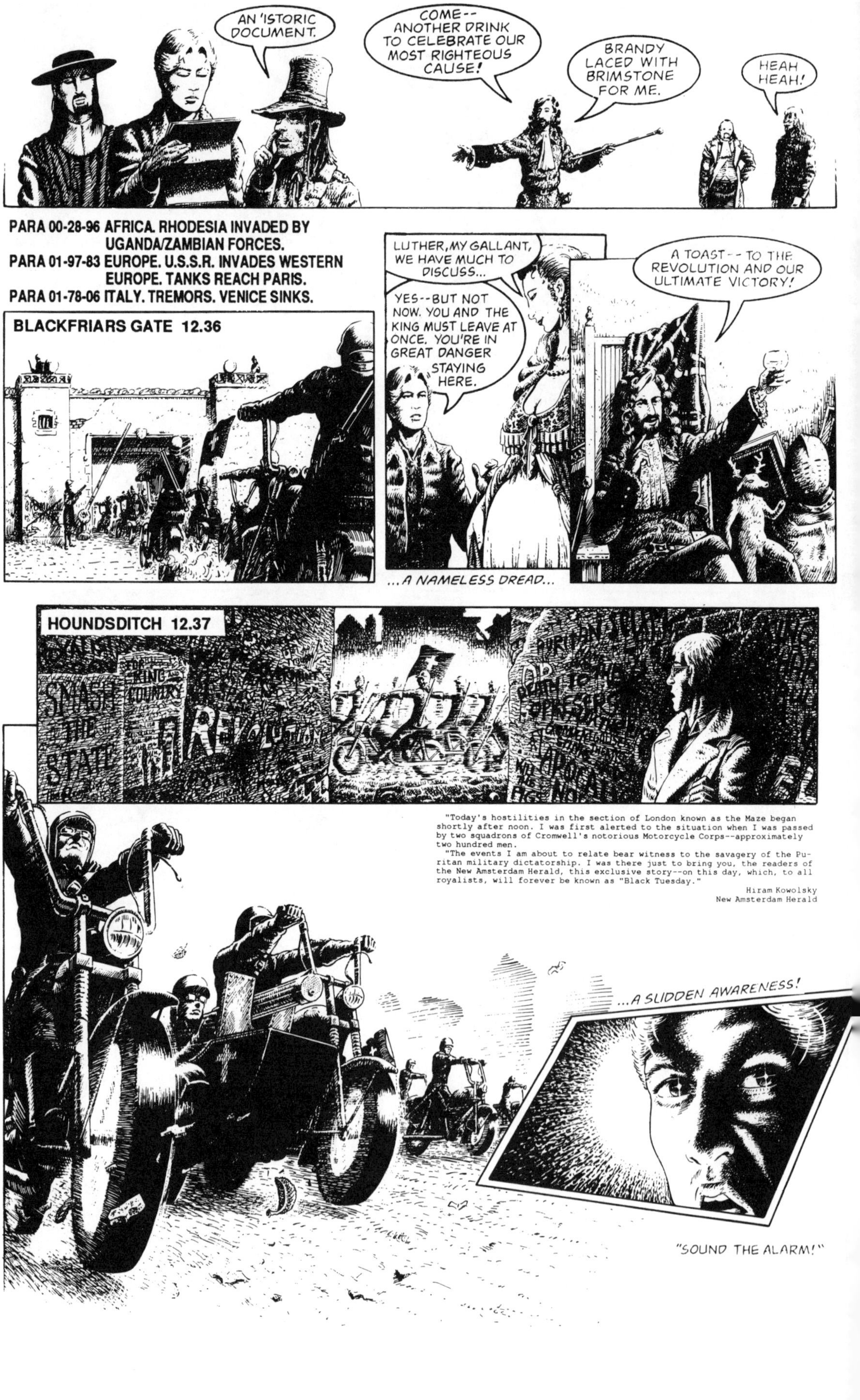

AN 'ISTORIC DOCUMENT.
COME-- ANOTHER DRINK TO CELEBRATE OUR MOST RIGHTEOUS CAUSE!
BRANDY LACED WITH BRIMSTONE FOR ME.
HEAH HEAH!
PARA 00-28-96 AFRICA. RHODESIA INVADED BY UGANDA/ZAMBIAN FORCES.
PARA 01-97-83 EUROPE. U.S.S.R. INVADES WESTERN EUROPE. TANKS REACH PARIS.
PARA 01-78-06 ITALY. TREMORS. VENICE SINKS.
BLACKFRIARS GATE 12.36
LUTHER, MY GALLANT, WE HAVE MUCH TO DISCUSS...
YES--BUT NOT NOW. YOU AND THE KING MUST LEAVE AT ONCE. YOU'RE IN GREAT DANGER STAYING HERE.
A TOAST-- TO THE REVOLUTION AND OUR ULTIMATE VICTORY!
...A NAMELESS DREAD...
HOUNDSDITCH 12.37
SMASH THE STATE
REVOLUTION
"Today's hostilities in the section of London known as the Maze began shortly after noon. I was first alerted to the situation when I was passed by two squadrons of Cromwell's notorious Motorcycle Corps--approximately two hundred men.
"The events I am about to relate bear witness to the savagery of the Puritan military dictatorship. I was there just to bring you, the readers of the New Amsterdam Herald, this exclusive story--on this day, which, to all royalists, will forever be known as "Black Tuesday."
Hiram Kowolsky
New Amsterdam Herald
...A SUDDEN AWARENESS!
"SOUND THE ALARM!"

TUES 3 OCT 12.39 PARA 00.72.87 WHITECHAPEL

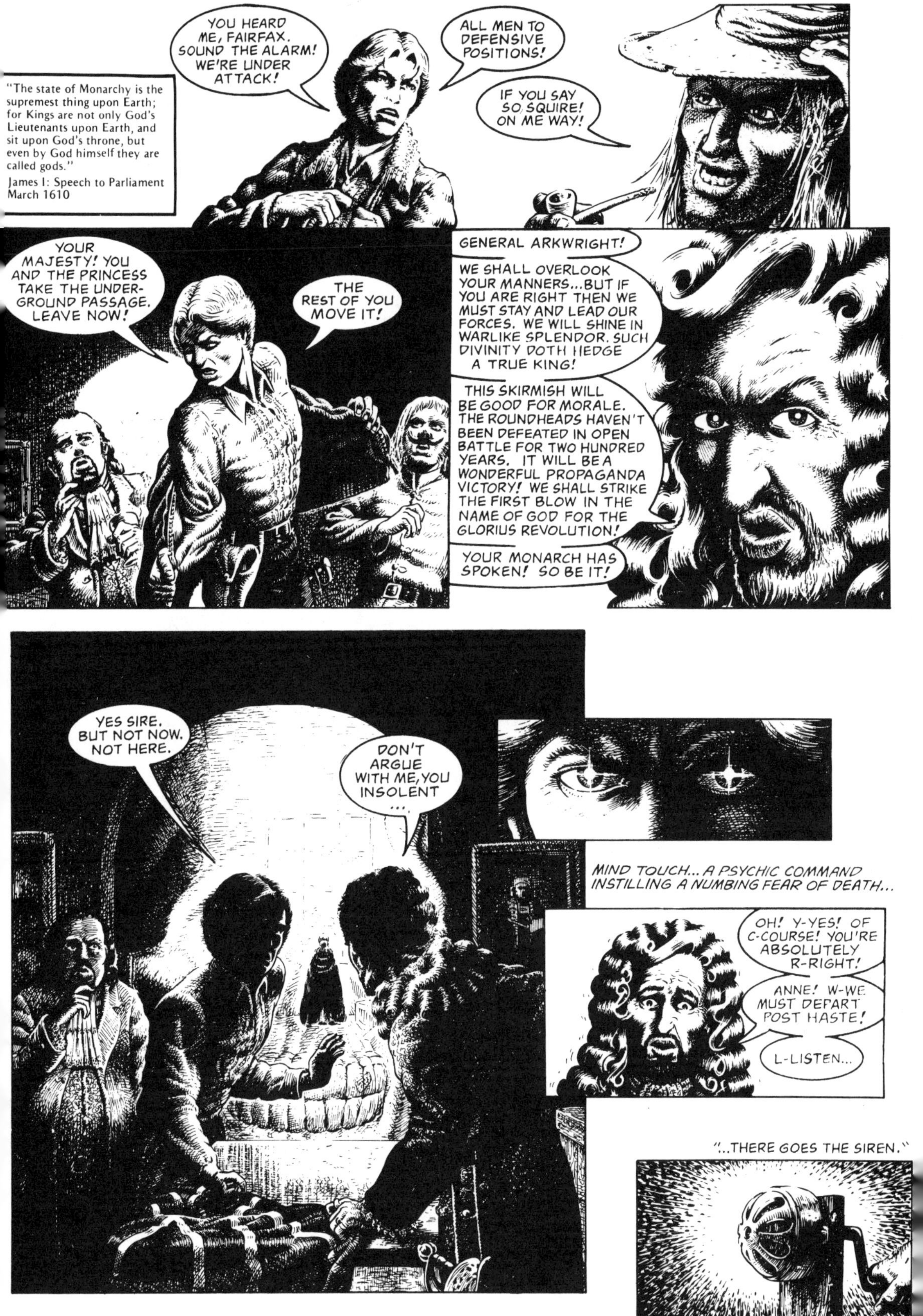

"The state of Monarchy is the supremest thing upon Earth; for Kings are not only God's Lieutenants upon Earth, and sit upon God's throne, but even by God himself they are called gods."
James I: Speech to Parliament March 1610
YOU HEARD ME, FAIRFAX. SOUND THE ALARM! WE'RE UNDER ATTACK!
ALL MEN TO DEFENSIVE POSITIONS!
IF YOU SAY SO, SQUIRE! ON ME WAY!
YOUR MAJESTY! YOU AND THE PRINCESS TAKE THE UNDER-GROUND PASSAGE. LEAVE NOW!
THE REST OF YOU MOVE IT!
GENERAL ARKWRIGHT!
WE SHALL OVERLOOK YOUR MANNERS...BUT IF YOU ARE RIGHT THEN WE MUST STAY AND LEAD OUR FORCES. WE WILL SHINE IN WARLIKE SPLENDOR. SUCH DIVINITY DOTH HEDGE A TRUE KING!
THIS SKIRMISH WILL BE GOOD FOR MORALE. THE ROUNDHEADS HAVEN'T BEEN DEFEATED IN OPEN BATTLE FOR TWO HUNDRED YEARS. IT WILL BE A WONDERFUL PROPAGANDA VICTORY! WE SHALL STRIKE THE FIRST BLOW IN THE NAME OF GOD FOR THE GLORIUS REVOLUTION!
YOUR MONARCH HAS SPOKEN! SO BE IT!
YES SIRE. BUT NOT NOW. NOT HERE.
DON'T ARGUE WITH ME, YOU INSOLENT ...
MIND TOUCH... A PSYCHIC COMMAND INSTILLING A NUMBING FEAR OF DEATH...
OH! Y-YES! OF C-COURSE! YOU'RE ABSOLUTELY R-RIGHT!
ANNE! W-WE MUST DEPART POST HASTE!
L-LISTEN...
"...THERE GOES THE SIREN."

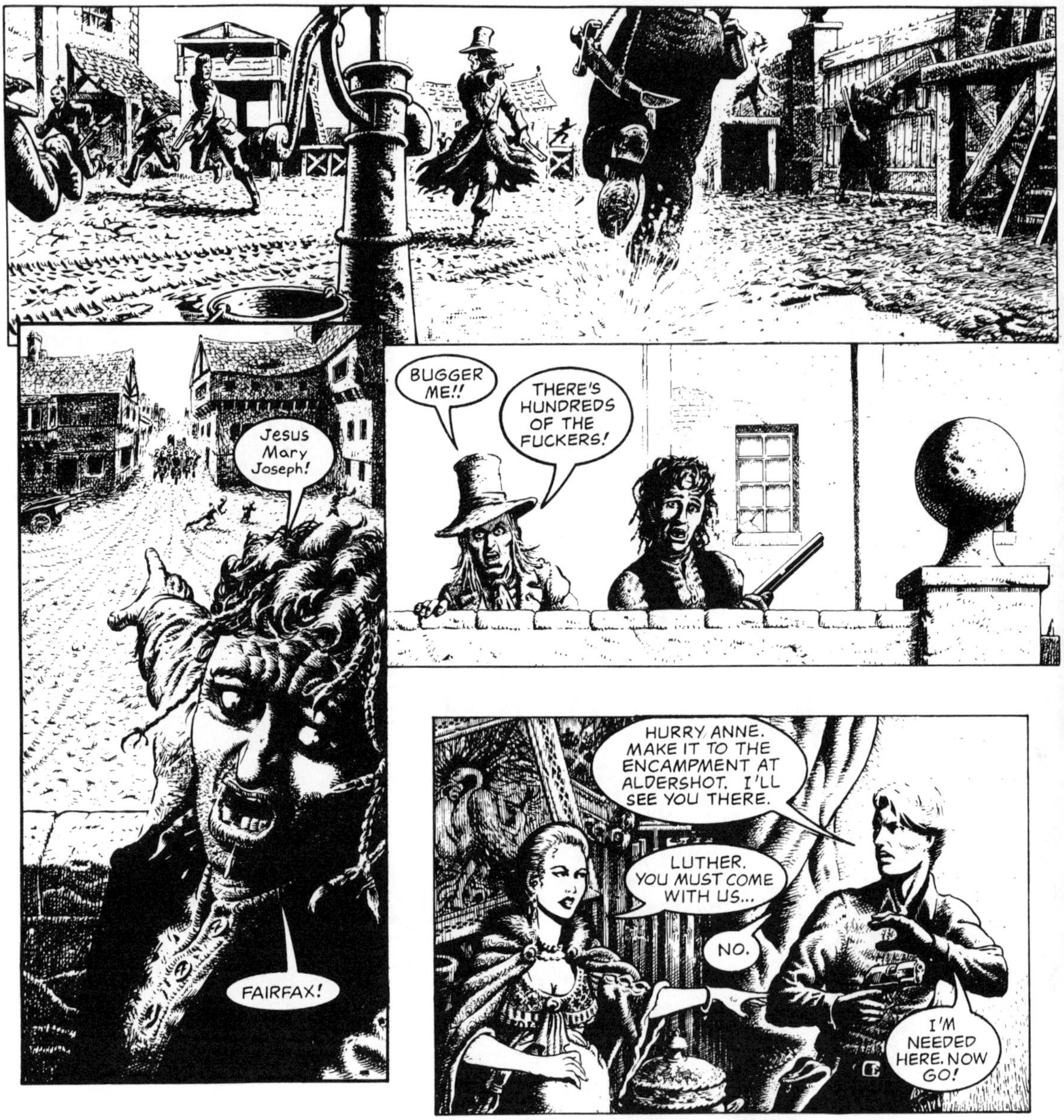
Jesus Mary Joseph!
FAIRFAX!
BUGGER ME!!
THERE'S HUNDREDS OF THE FUCKERS!
HURRY ANNE. MAKE IT TO THE ENCAMPMENT AT ALDERSHOT. I'LL SEE YOU THERE.
LUTHER. YOU MUST COME WITH US...
NO.
I'M NEEDED HERE. NOW GO!

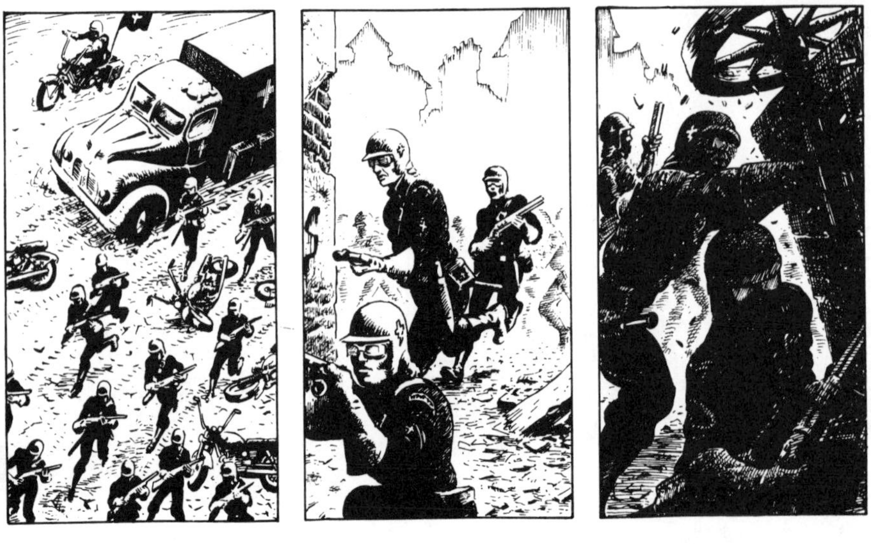

"The English Army was originally formed in 1645 by Oliver Cromwell, (the first Lord Protector and ancestor of Nathaniel Cromwell), as the N.M.A. or "New Model Army". Eve today it is still referred to by th nickname "Oliver's Army". On this fateful day the branch of the Armed Forces employed was the crack strik force the S.P.G.--the "Supreme Puritan Guard". The S.P.G. are the elite Motorcycle Squadrons directly under the command of General Richar Standish or "Dirty Dick" as he is known in the Maze. He and the S.P.G have a reputation for ruthlessness and efficient enforcement of the Commonwealth status quo and are responsible for several atrocities committed in the recent years of th Civil War."

Hiram Kowolsk
New Amsterdam Hera

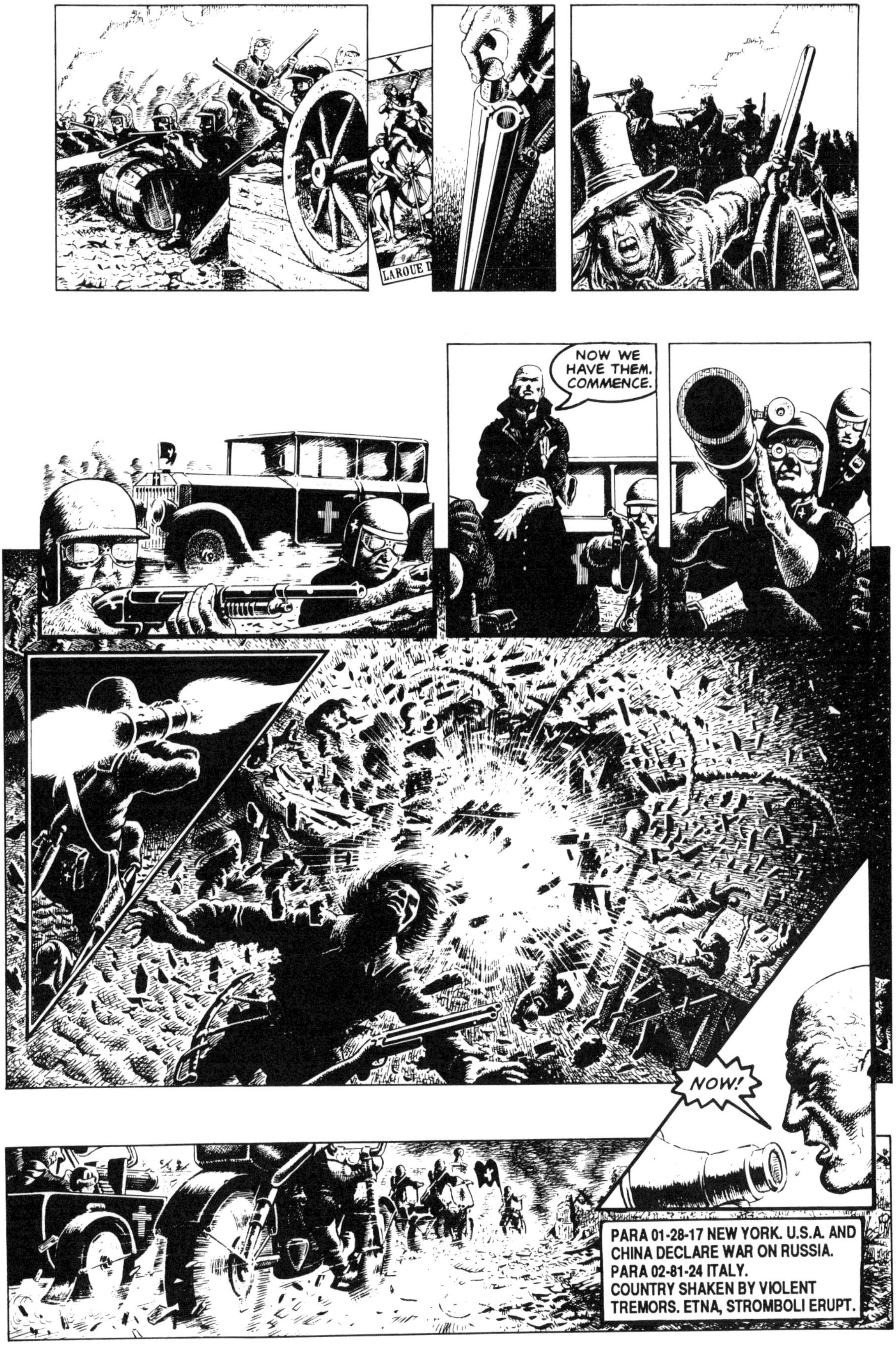
X
LAROUE D
NOW WE HAVE THEM. COMMENCE.
NOW!
PARA 01-28-17 NEW YORK. U.S.A. AND CHINA DECLARE WAR ON RUSSIA.
PARA 02-81-24 ITALY.
COUNTRY SHAKEN BY VIOLENT TREMORS. ETNA, STROMBOLI ERUPT.

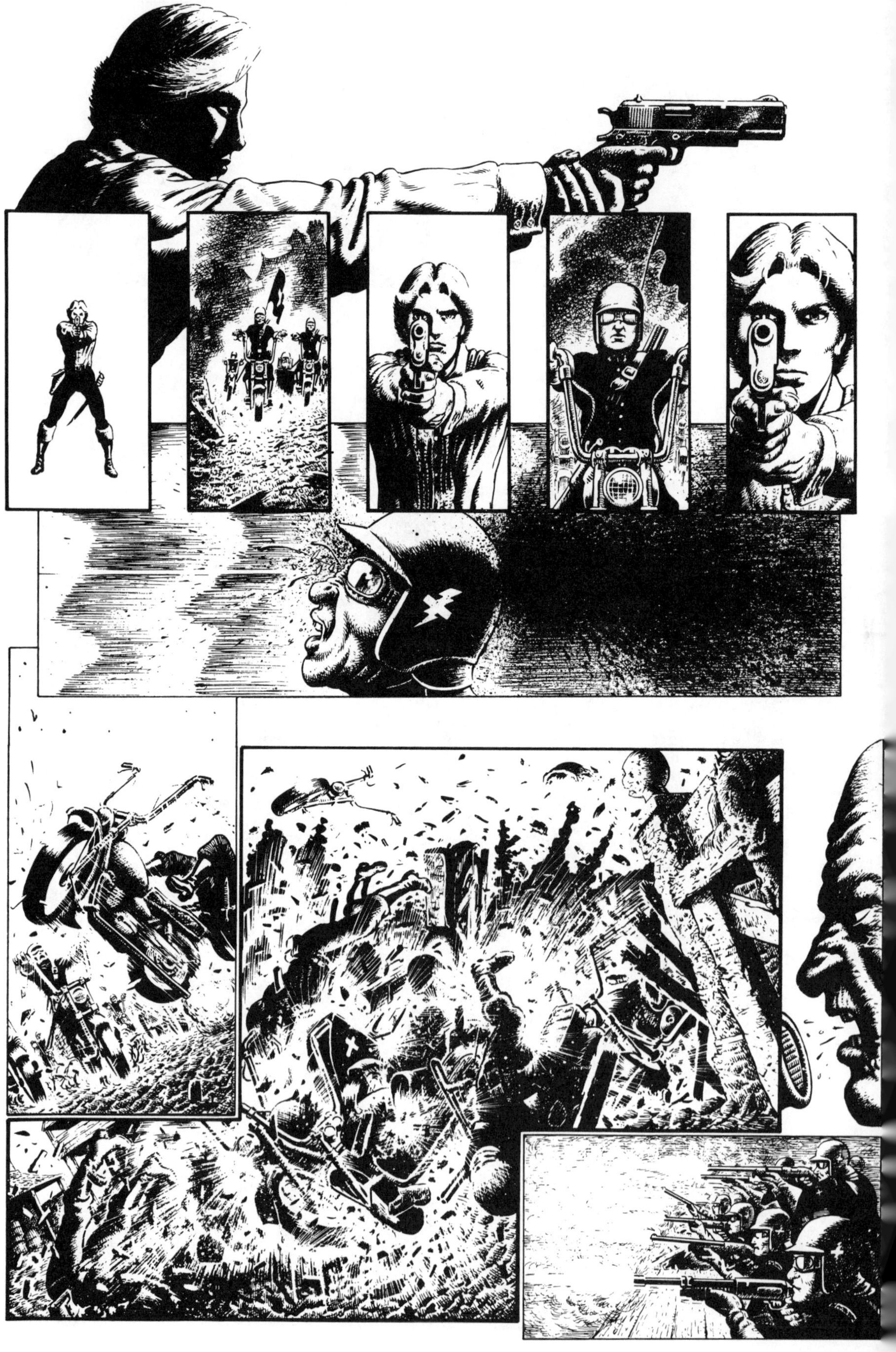

RKWRIGHT CONCENTRATES: PROJECTS CONTAGIOUS HYSTERIA INTO THE MINDS OF THE PARLIAMENTARIANS. THIS BATTLE CAN E WON, DESPITE THE DISRUPTOR-SUPPLIED SUPERIOR TECHNOLOGY. A MATTER OF HOLDING OUT UNTIL THE ROYALIST ORCES LOCATED IN THE MAZE CAN GROUP AND OUTFLANK THE S.P.G. ...

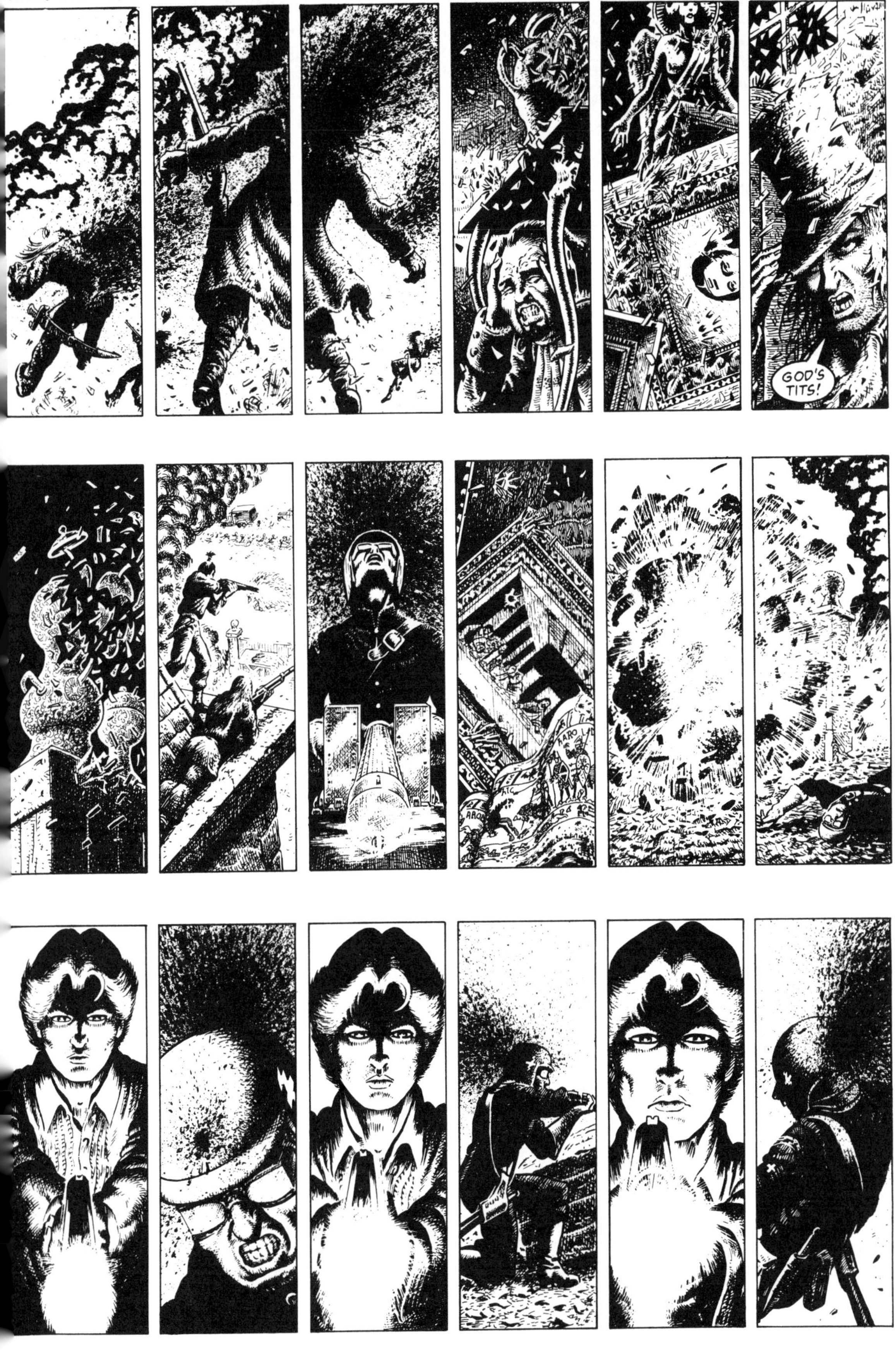
GOD'S TITS!

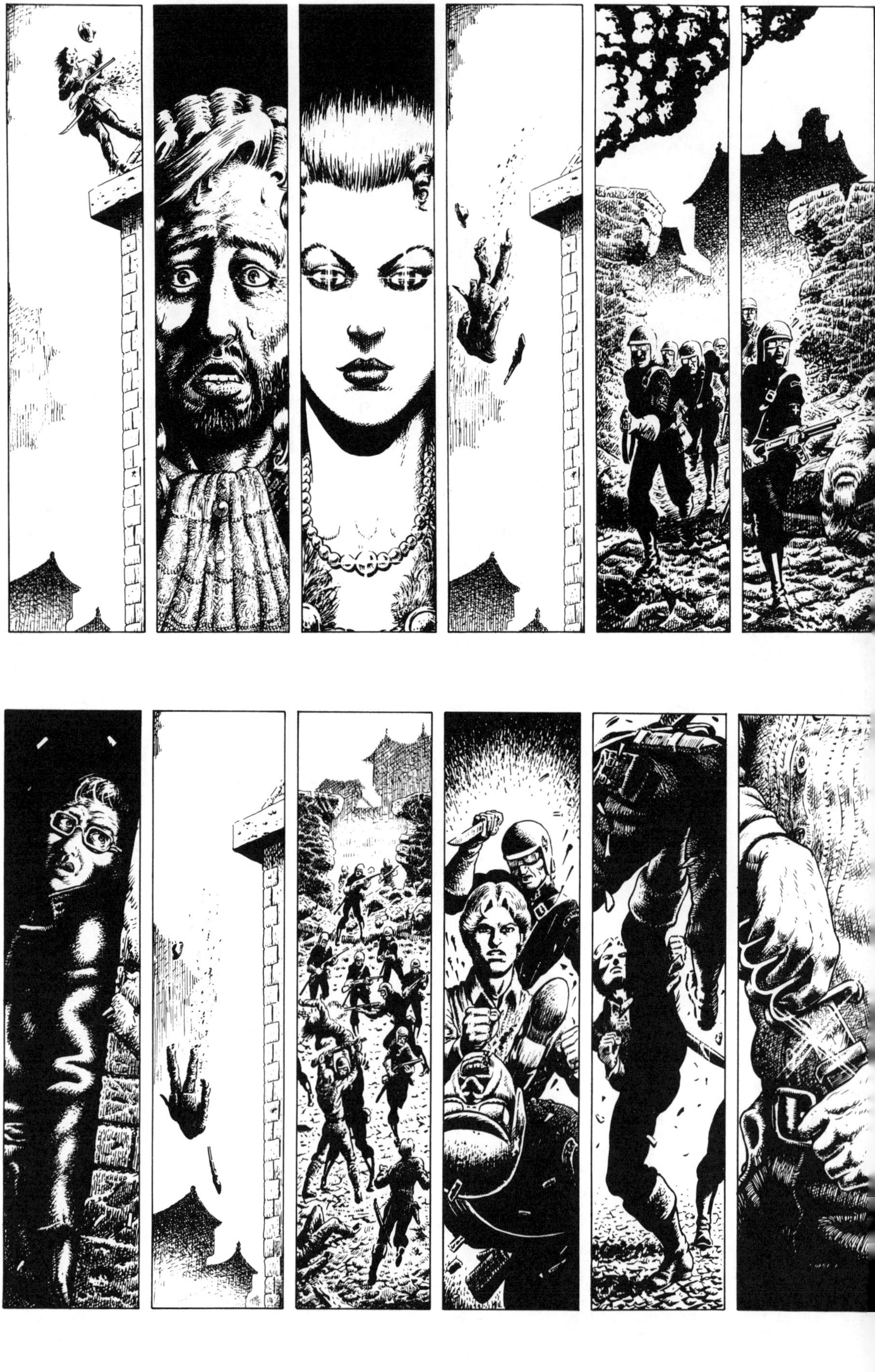

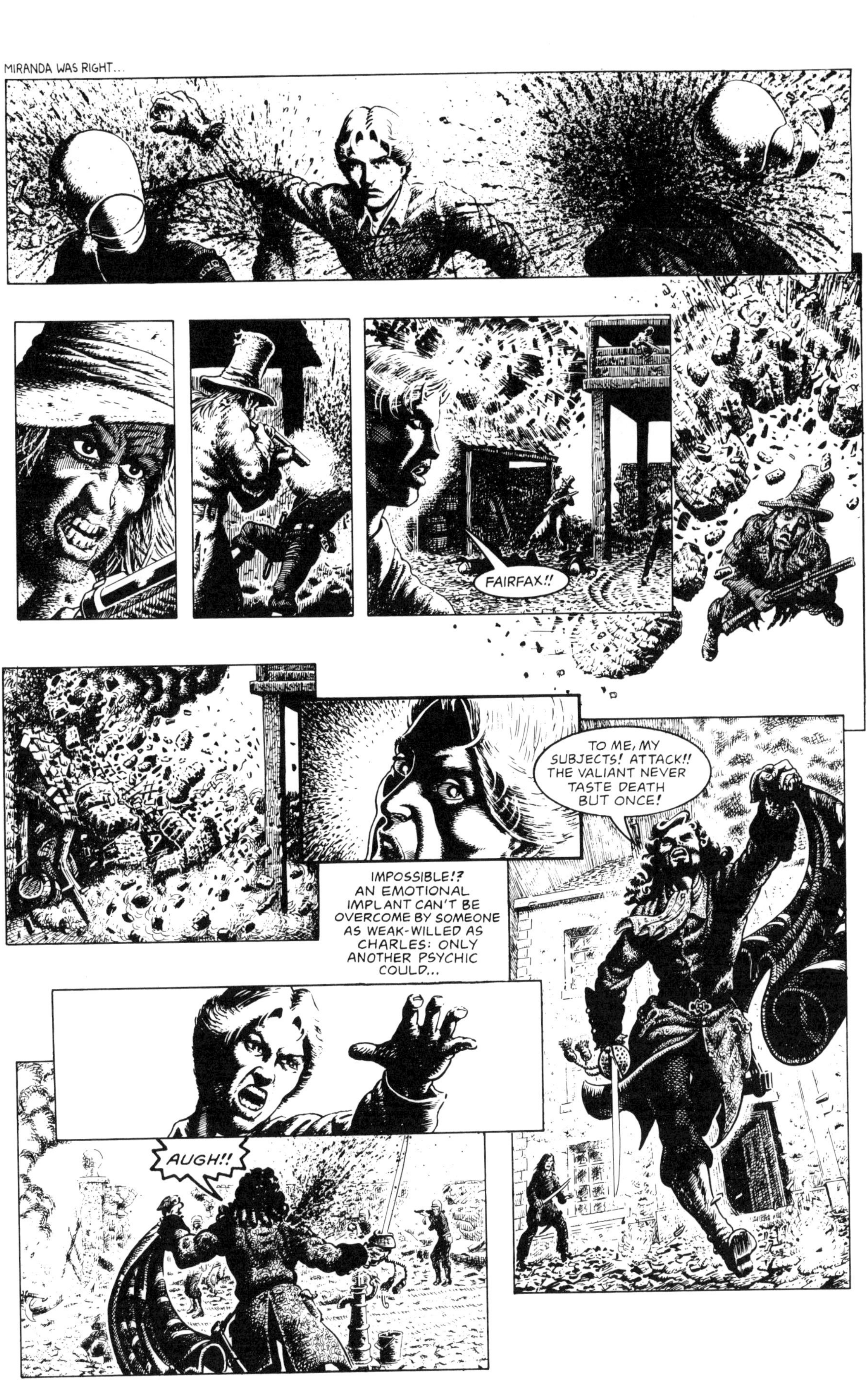
MIRANDA WAS RIGHT...
FAIRFAX!!
TO ME, MY SUBJECTS! ATTACK!! THE VALIANT NEVER TASTE DEATH BUT ONCE!
IMPOSSIBLE!? AN EMOTIONAL IMPLANT CAN'T BE OVERCOME BY SOMEONE AS WEAK-WILLED AS CHARLES: ONLY ANOTHER PSYCHIC COULD...
AUGH!!

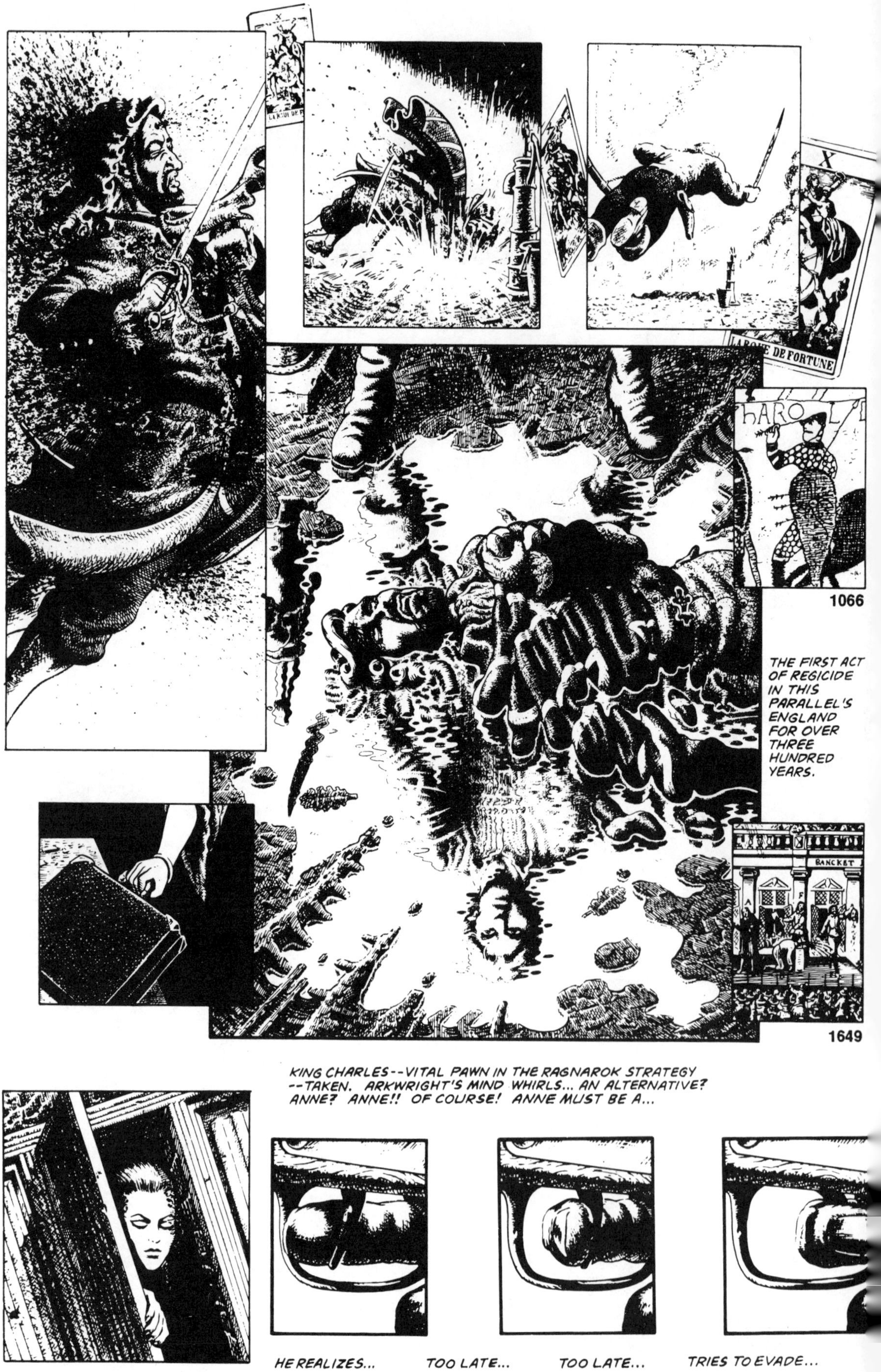

LA ROUE DE FORTUNE
HARO
1066
THE FIRST ACT OF REGICIDE IN THIS PARALLEL'S ENGLAND FOR OVER THREE HUNDRED YEARS.
BANCKET
1649
KING CHARLES--VITAL PAWN IN THE RAGNAROK STRATEGY --TAKEN. ARKWRIGHT'S MIND WHIRLS... AN ALTERNATIVE? ANNE? ANNE!! OF COURSE! ANNE MUST BE A...
HE REALIZES...
TOO LATE...
TOO LATE...
TRIES TO EVADE...

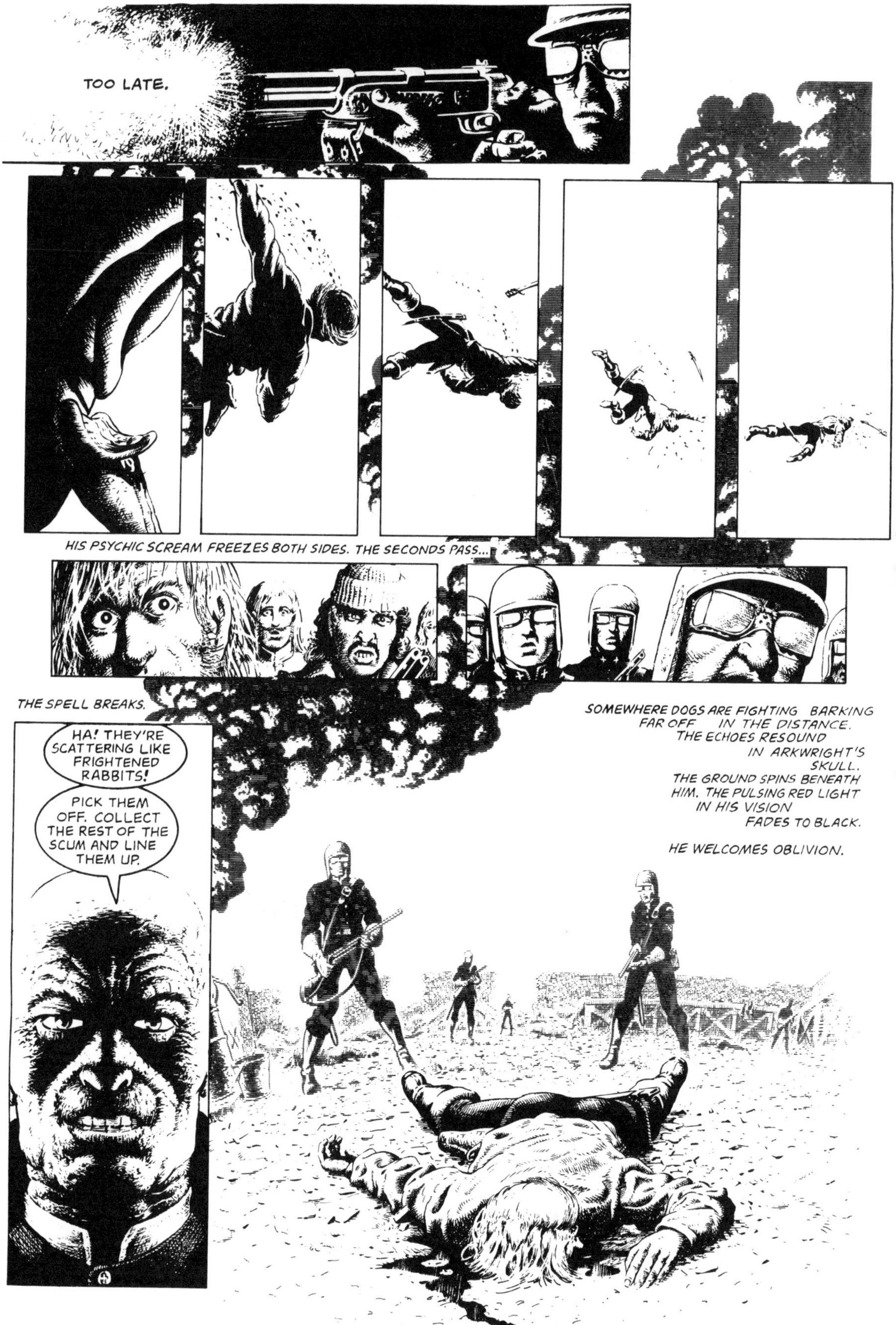
TOO LATE.
HIS PSYCHIC SCREAM FREEZES BOTH SIDES. THE SECONDS PASS...
THE SPELL BREAKS.
HA! THEY'RE SCATTERING LIKE FRIGHTENED RABBITS!
PICK THEM OFF. COLLECT THE REST OF THE SCUM AND LINE THEM UP.
SOMEWHERE DOGS ARE FIGHTING BARKING FAR OFF IN THE DISTANCE. THE ECHOES RESOUND IN ARKWRIGHT'S SKULL. THE GROUND SPINS BENEATH HIM. THE PULSING RED LIGHT IN HIS VISION FADES TO BLACK.
HE WELCOMES OBLIVION.

WED 11 OCT 10.13 PARA OO.72.87 LONDON BRIDGE

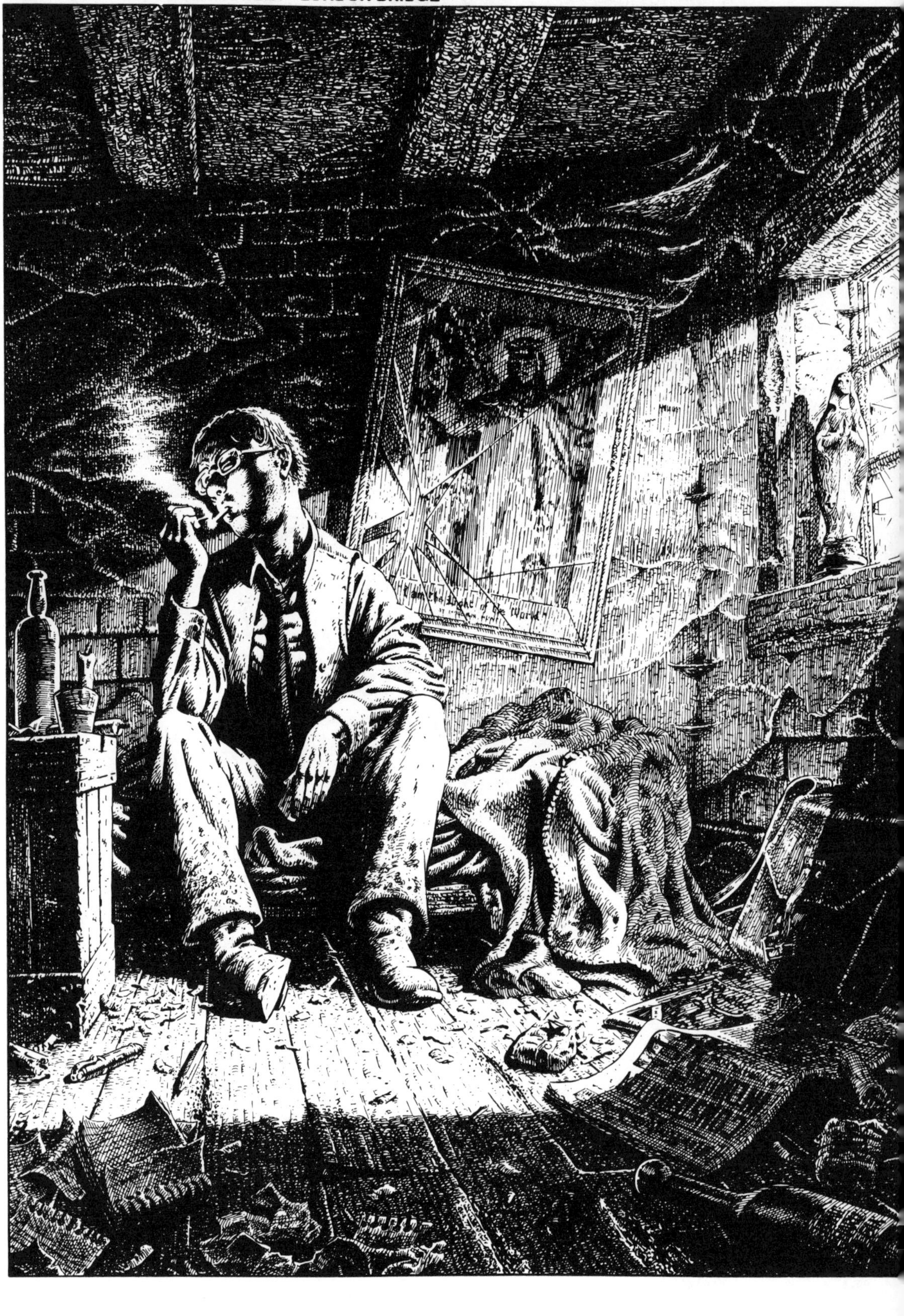

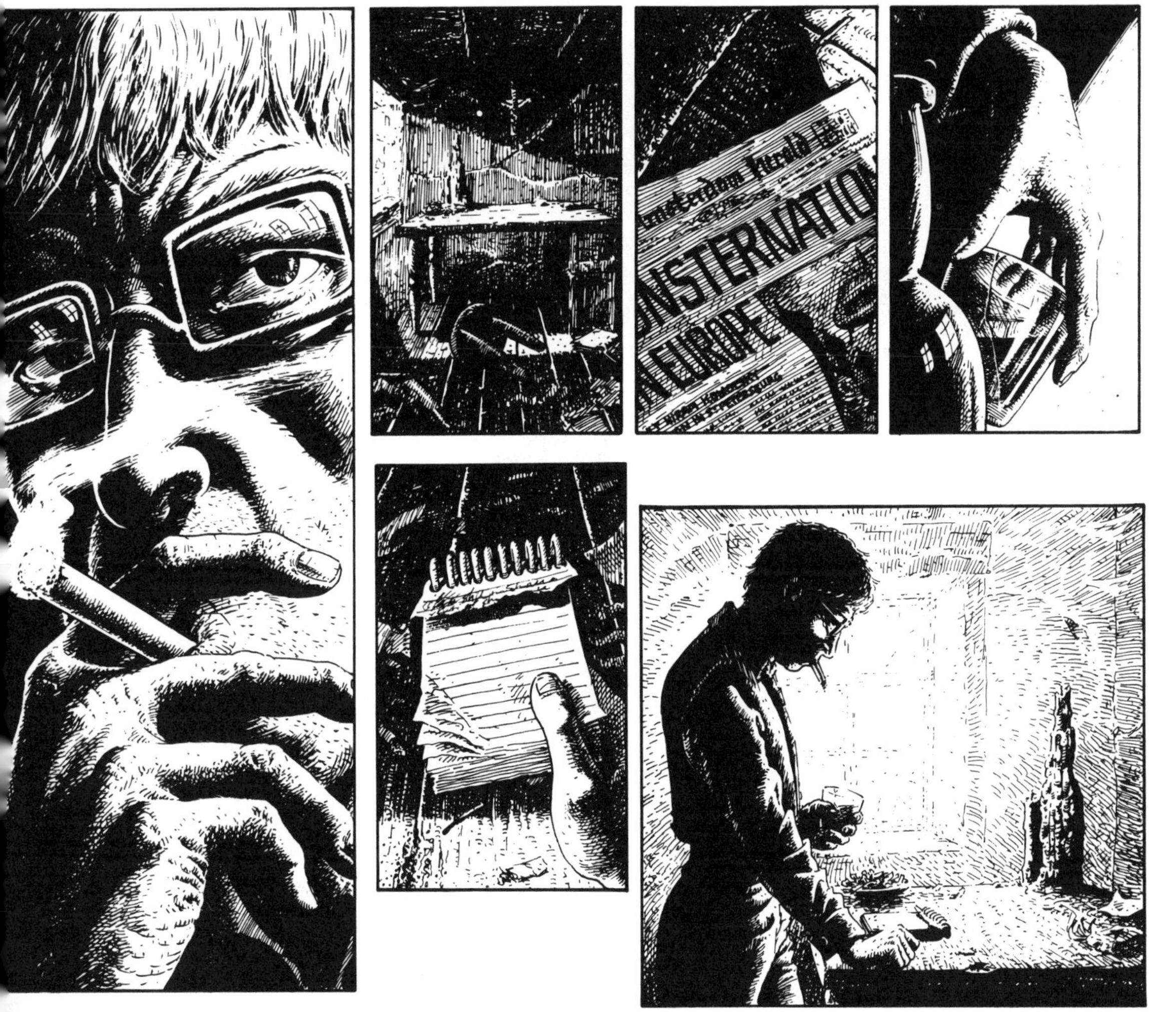

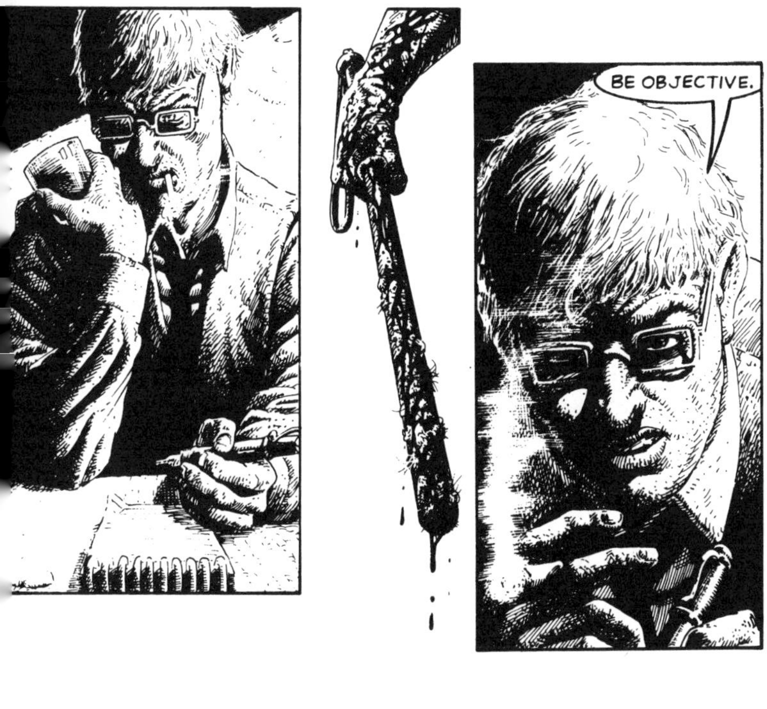

BE OBJECTIVE.

I can hardly believe that one week has passed since I reported the bloody massacre that occured on "Black Tuesday". Here, in England, it has been a week of fear and oppression. Of palpable terror, apprehension and anger. Of Parliamentarian severity and revolutionary fervour.

To you, readers of The New Amsterdam Herald, this week will have been dominated by the speeches, celebrations and street parties following the Gettysberg Declaration of Union between our nation and the estranged English colonies. And rightly so. As President Theodore J.F. Roosevelt has proclaimed; "The UCA is now the major power in North America ...and with power comes responsibility". We must end our isolationist stance and move into the world arena. Events now taking place in Europe demand our full attention. And London is the explosive centre of these events.

Since the regicide of "Charles III" and the slaughter of his followers in Whitechapel last week and the immediate declaration of a "State of Emergency" by the Cromwell regime, the situation has rapidly deteriorated into a spiral of violence and outrage.

Following the skirmish, the corpse of the Pretender King was removed from Whitechapel and taken to Westminster where it was beheaded in mock solemnity and the head thrown into the crowd. After Puritan citizens had used it as a football, it was capped with a paper crown and impaled on a spike over Westminster Gate where it now grins upon the city, summoning retribution.

The violence which followed the raid by the Supreme Puritan Guard on the Royalist Headquarters in the Maze, together with unconfirmed reports of armed resistance elsewhere in the country was all the justification Nathaniel Cromwell, head of the Church, State and Government, needed to introduce his new "Iron Fist" Emergency Powers. Chillingly, we see that the more frightened a Government gets, the more terror is employed to enforce the regime. Martial law has been norm here since "the Troubles" began in the seventeenth century, but seldom has it been so brutal or insidious.

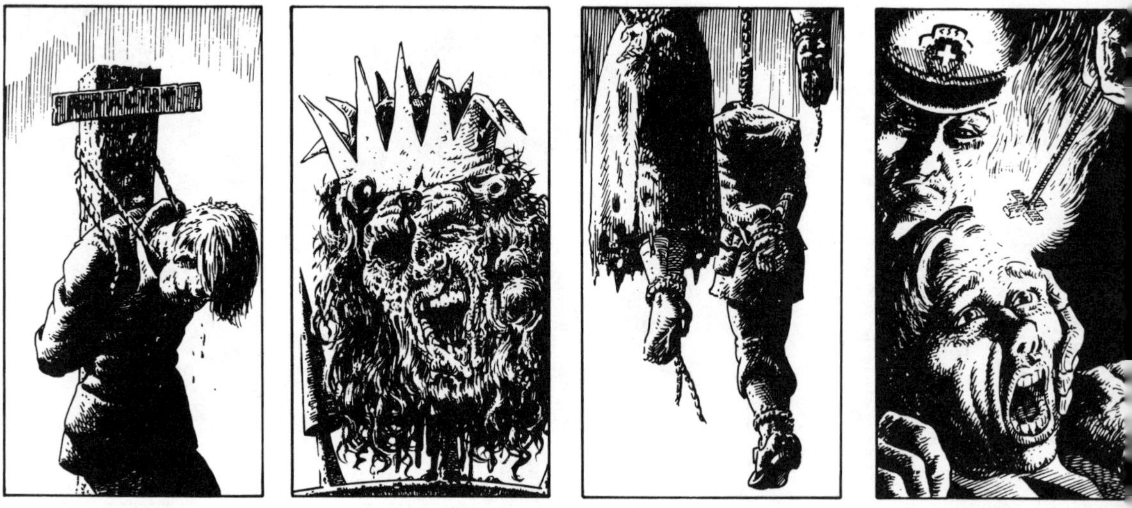

TUES 3 OCT 13.42 WHITECHAPEL

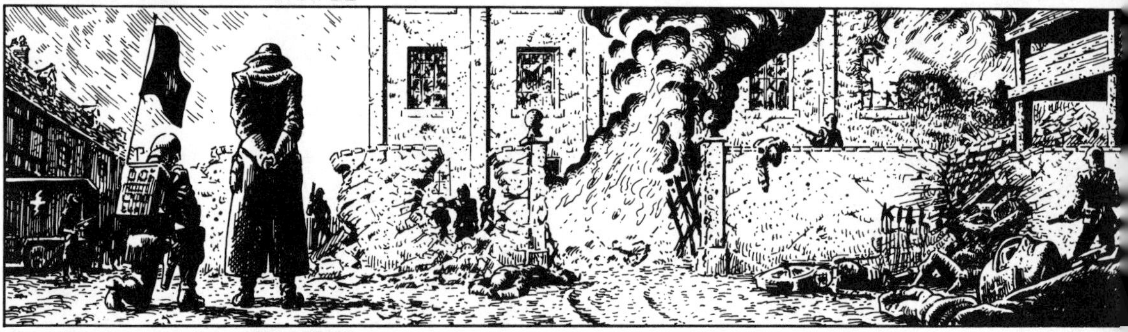
KILL

Solid facts are difficult to come by. Even the State-controlled press is under a news blackout, cannot report directly on controversial issues and is limited to the contents of handouts and occasional press conferences by the State Bureau of Information. Moreover, the leaving of empty columns in newspapers caused by government censorship has been labelled "subversive". In actuality, Puritan journals this week have all been preoccupied with tomorrow's forthcoming rally and march-past, expected to be an impressive show of strength by the Cromwell Dictatorship. However, through my contacts in Fleet Street and the grapevine here in the Maze, I can form a picture of a land torn by oppression and unrest, poised on the brink of open civil warfare.

Literally hundreds of people are missing, presumed gaoled by government forces. Imprisonment and torture without trial or formal charges are commonplace. The staccato rattle of firing squads frequently resounds across the city. Mere suspicion of being a Royalist sympathiser or secret Roman Catholic is enough to bring to the attention of the SPG or Cromwell's own "Committee of State Security"; the CCS.

The extremity of Government action is exemplified by the persecution of suspected rebels in West England (formerly Wales), this week. General Richard "Dirty Dick" Standish introduced his "Scorched Earth" policy, his SPG razing to the ground buildings and sometimes whole villages that have harboured suspects.

The activities of the CCS, under the direct command of Matthew Pennington, Head of Intelligence, are even more extreme. Responsible for organised beatings, on-the-spot street executions and suchlike, they are currently conducting a massive series of lightning raids on the homes of suspected dissidents, their relations and known associates. Those unfortunates who are caught by the "Holy Correction" squads are branded on the forehead with a red-hot cross, as a warning to others.

Alarm and dispair are spreading through the communities, both Puritan and Romanist. Royalist Direct Action Groups have begun to strike back. Terrorist reprisals are sweeping the ten Major-Generalships that constitute England. The fire-bombing of the houses of local Government officials and the "kneecapping" of parliamentarian supporters has been eclipsed by the horrific new instrument of vengeance, the "Puritan Collar". This is a rubber tyre, filled with benzin, that is placed around the necks of informers or captured militia and set alight. Responsibility for some of these incinerations has been claimed by the "Organization of Revolutionary Justice".

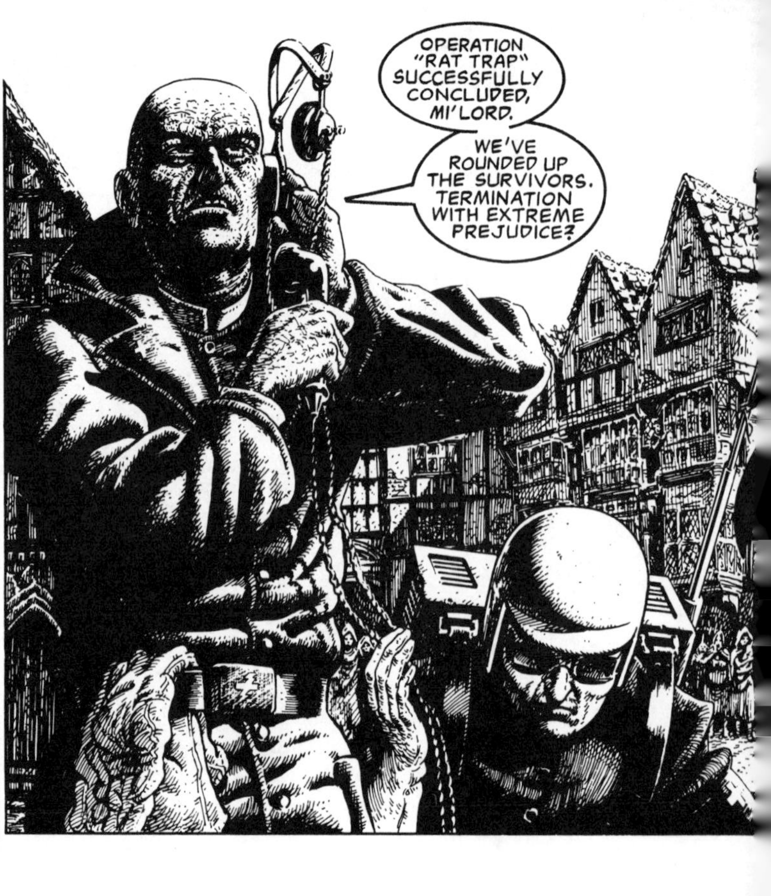
OPERATION "RAT TRAP" SUCCESSFULLY CONCLUDED, MI'LORD.
WE'VE ROUNDED UP THE SURVIVORS. TERMINATION WITH EXTREME PREJUDICE?

OVT. RADIO CENTRE; NASBY CIRCUS 13.42

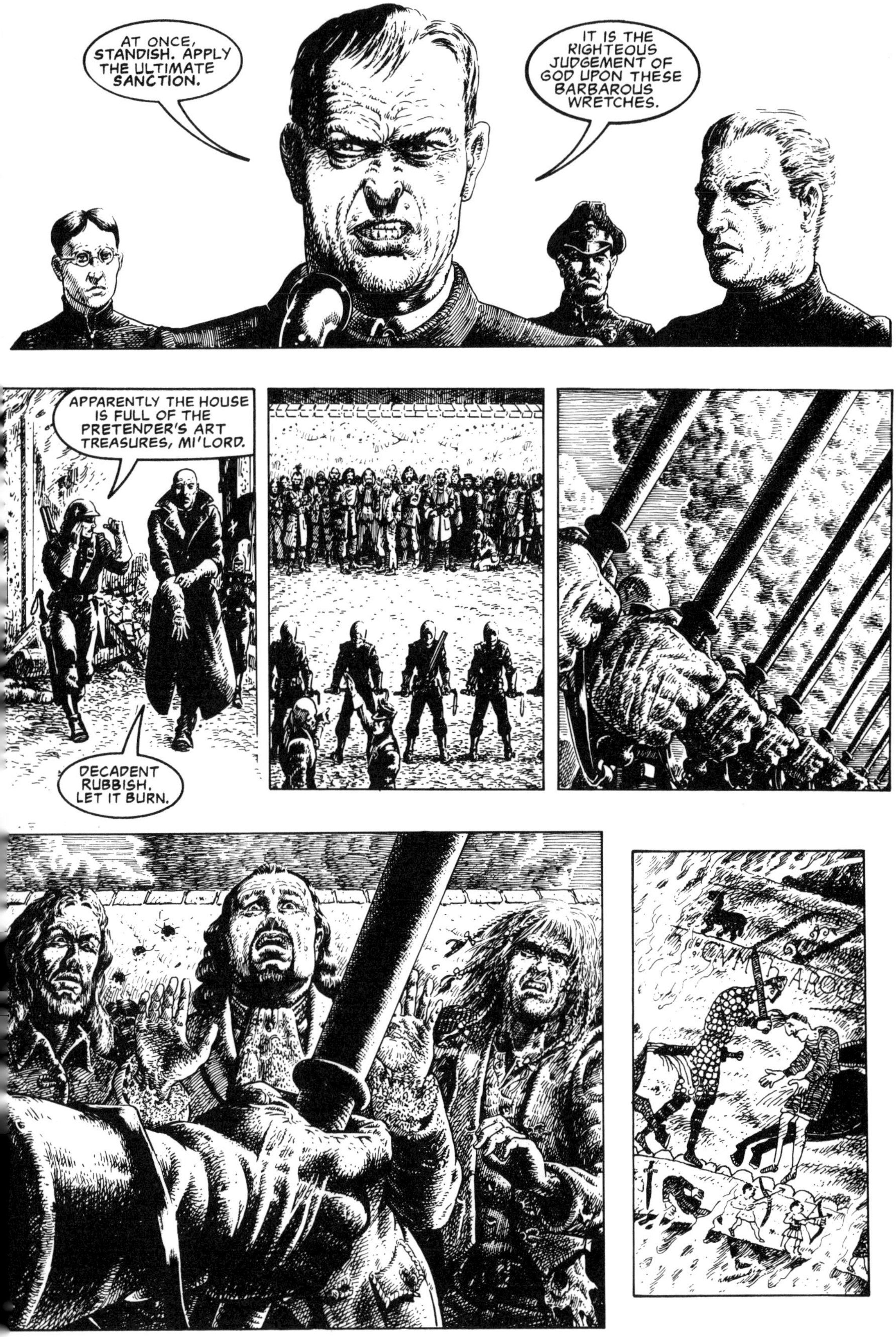
AT ONCE, STANDISH. APPLY THE ULTIMATE SANCTION.
IT IS THE RIGHTEOUS JUDGEMENT OF GOD UPON THESE BARBAROUS WRETCHES.
APPARENTLY THE HOUSE IS FULL OF THE PRETENDER'S ART TREASURES, MI'LORD.
DECADENT RUBBISH. LET IT BURN.

OH, CHRIST.
BASTARDS!

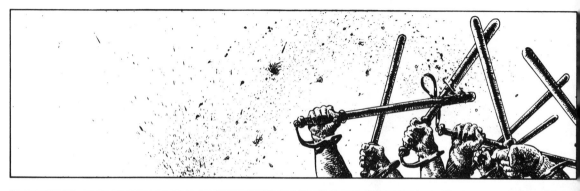

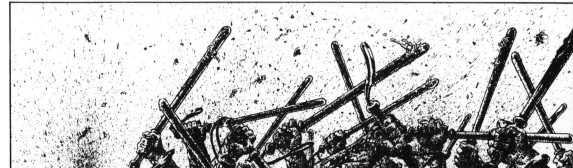

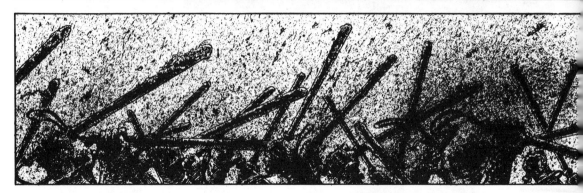

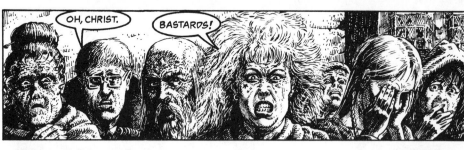

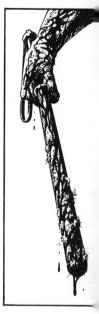

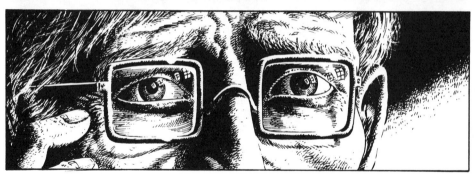

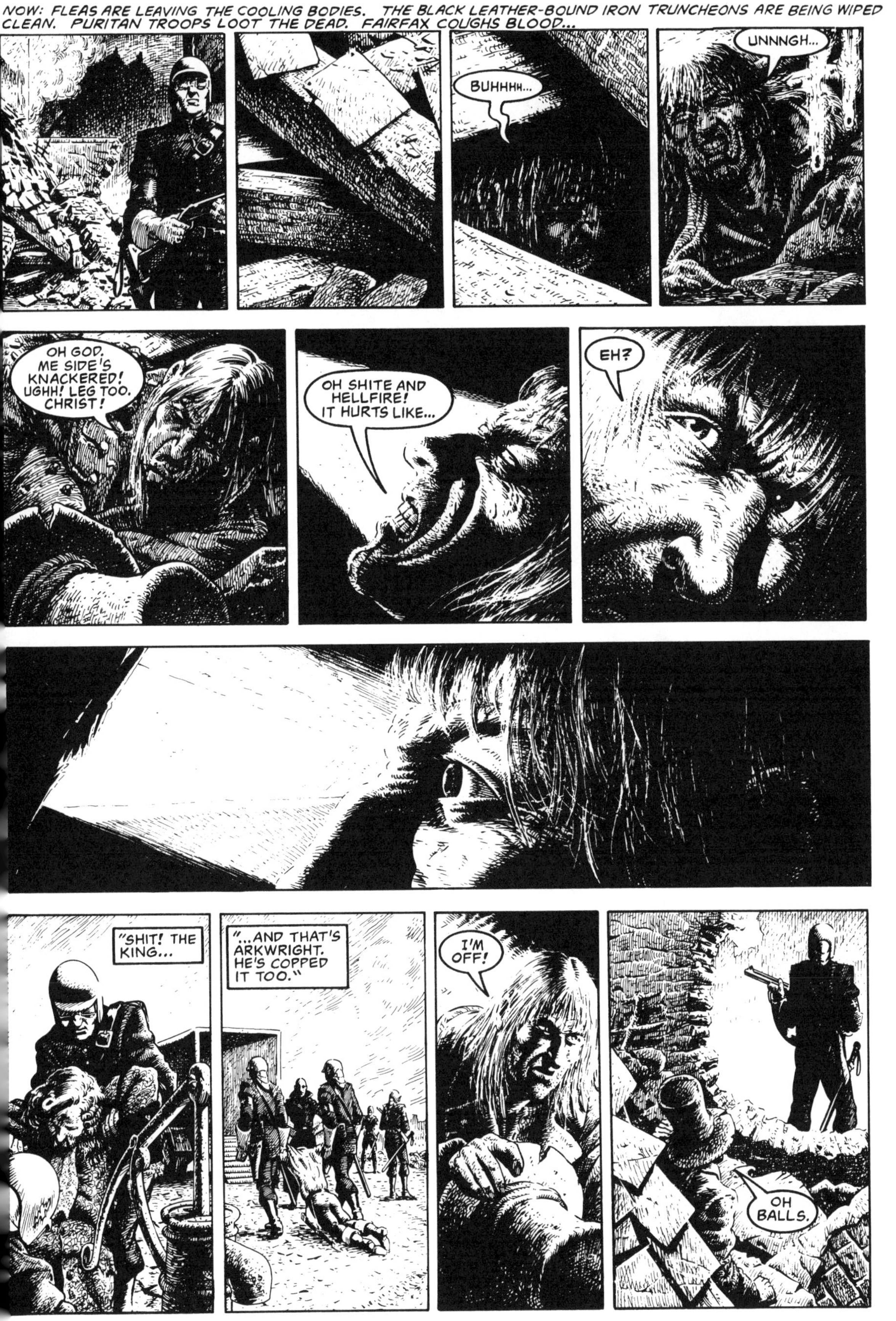
NOW: FLEAS ARE LEAVING THE COOLING BODIES. THE BLACK LEATHER-BOUND IRON TRUNCHEONS ARE BEING WIPED CLEAN. PURITAN TROOPS LOOT THE DEAD. FAIRFAX COUGHS BLOOD...
BUHHHH...
UNNNGH...
OH GOD. ME SIDE'S KNACKERED! UGHH! LEG TOO. CHRIST!
OH SHITE AND HELLFIRE! IT HURTS LIKE...
EH?
"SHIT! THE KING...
"...AND THAT'S ARKWRIGHT. HE'S COPPED IT TOO."
I'M OFF!
OH BALLS.

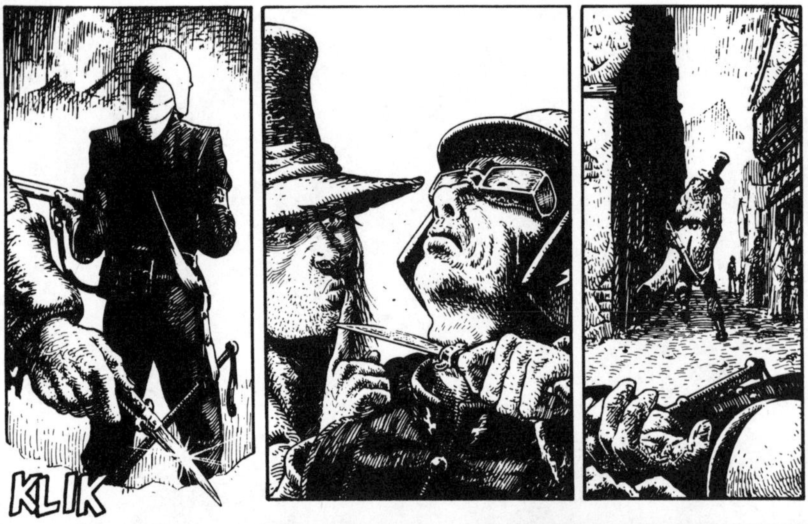
KLIK

It had been assumed after the demise of "King" Charles and his hereditary lords that the Royalists would be leaderless and disorganised. Obviously, this is not the case and speculation about the new leader of the revolutionaries is rife. This is apparently Charles' sister, the "Princess Royale", who has declared herself "Queen Anne I" of "Great Britain" in a speech broadcast by the illegal Royalist wireless station "The Voice of Liberty".

As for myself, I am still hiding in The Maze, the Royalist Sector behind the London Wall, following the expulsion of foreign press agents. The freak drought and unseasonably warm weather have made conditions in this centuries-old inner city slum unbearable. The stench from the rubbish and raw faecal filth that lines the streets, the disease and starvation have all increased to horrific levels. The growth in the number and size of the rats and fleas has reached biblical proportions. Also I'm running out of smokes. Cigarettes are prohibited in England and the rough blackmarket tobacco smoked in clay pipes turns my stomach.

I intend to leave this room, this safe haven in London Bridge, dodge the Thames Patrol boats and roundhead border guards and make my way to Aldershot--where the Royalist forces seem to be massing--to bring you first hand observations of their activities. It'll be dangerous. I don't even know if this dispatch will reach you, but wish me luck.

"Letter to America"
Hiram Kowolsky
Foreign Correspondent, New Amsterdam Herald

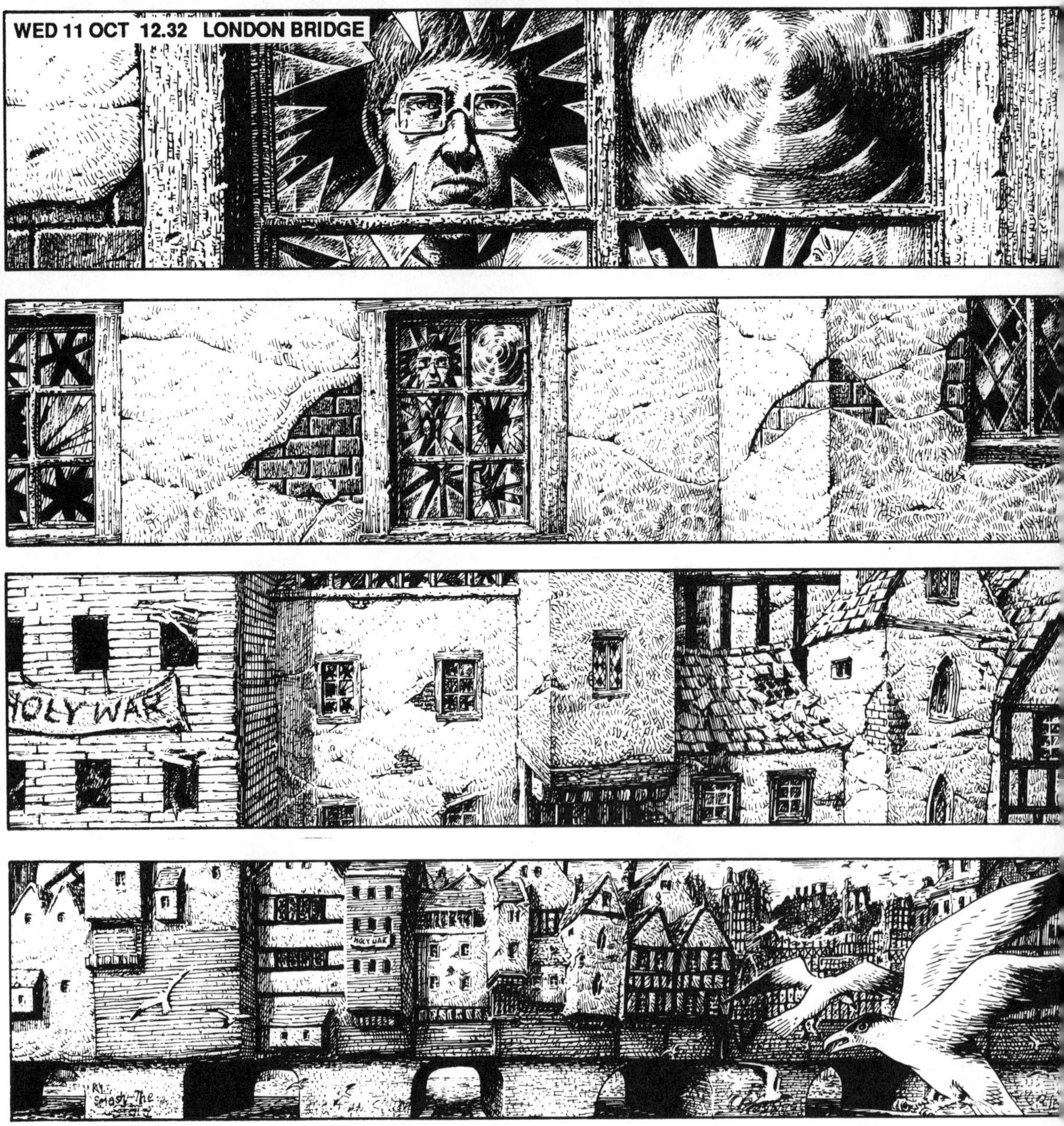
WED 11 OCT 12.32 LONDON BRIDGE
HOLY WAR
HOLY WAR

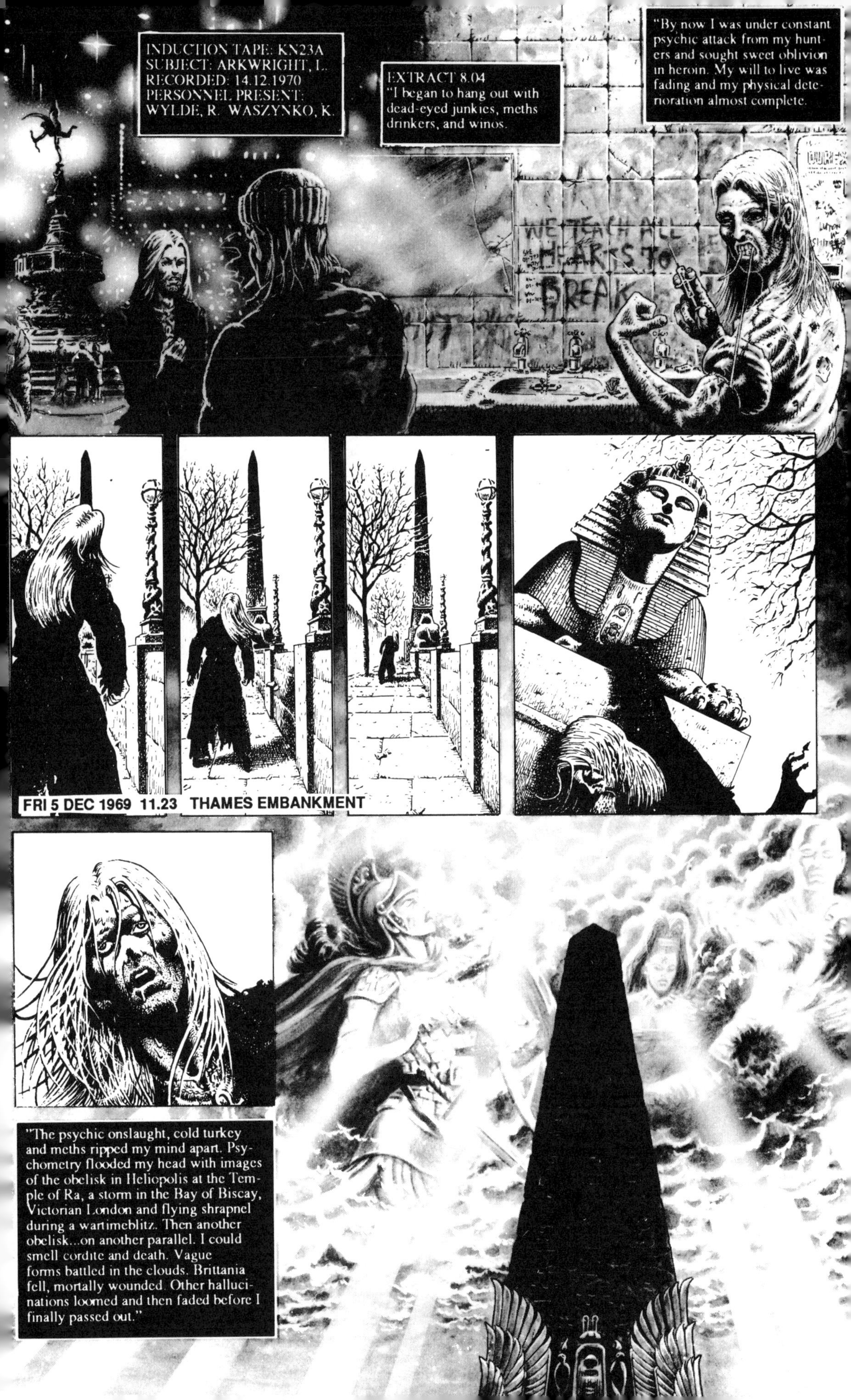
INDUCTION TAPE: KN23A
SUBJECT: ARKWRIGHT, L.
RECORDED: 14.12.1970
PERSONNEL PRESENT:
WYLDE, R. WASZYNKO, K.
EXTRACT 8.04
"I began to hang out with dead-eyed junkies, meths drinkers, and winos.
"By now I was under constant psychic attack from my hunters and sought sweet oblivion in heroin. My will to live was fading and my physical deterioration almost complete.
WE TEACH ALL HEARTS TO BREAK
FRI 5 DEC 1969 11.23 THAMES EMBANKMENT
"The psychic onslaught, cold turkey and meths ripped my mind apart. Psychometry flooded my head with images of the obelisk in Heliopolis at the Temple of Ra, a storm in the Bay of Biscay, Victorian London and flying shrapnel during a wartimeblitz. Then another obelisk...on another parallel. I could smell cordite and death. Vague forms battled in the clouds. Brittania fell, mortally wounded. Other hallucinations loomed and then faded before I finally passed out."

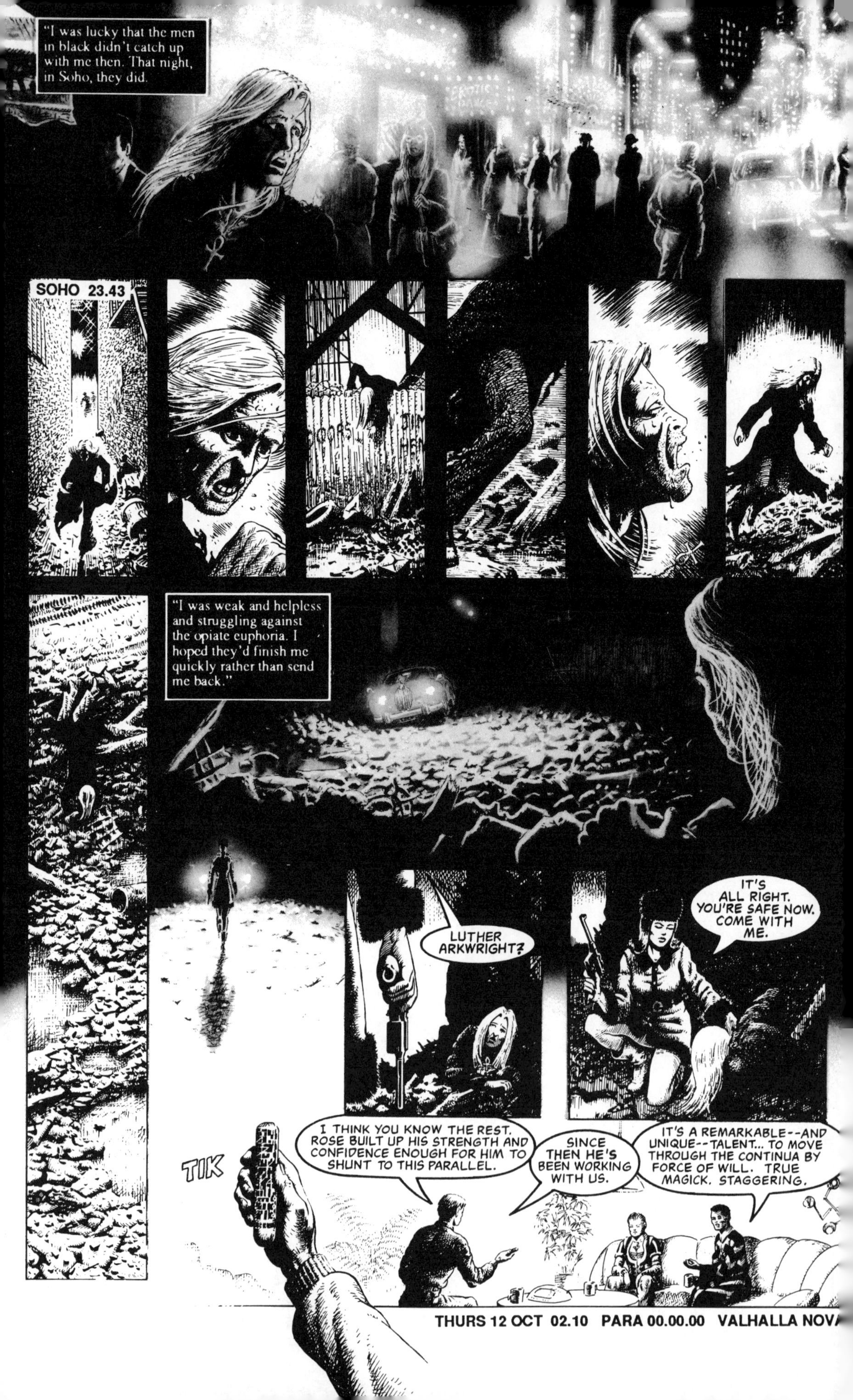
"I was lucky that the men in black didn't catch up with me then. That night, in Soho, they did.
SOHO 23.43
"I was weak and helpless and struggling against the opiate euphoria. I hoped they'd finish me quickly rather than send me back."
LUTHER ARKWRIGHT?
IT'S ALL RIGHT. YOU'RE SAFE NOW. COME WITH ME.
TIK
I THINK YOU KNOW THE REST. ROSE BUILT UP HIS STRENGTH AND CONFIDENCE ENOUGH FOR HIM TO SHUNT TO THIS PARALLEL.
SINCE THEN HE'S BEEN WORKING WITH US.
IT'S A REMARKABLE--AND UNIQUE--TALENT... TO MOVE THROUGH THE CONTINUA BY FORCE OF WILL. TRUE MAGICK. STAGGERING.
THURS 12 OCT 02.10 PARA 00.00.00 VALHALLA NOVA

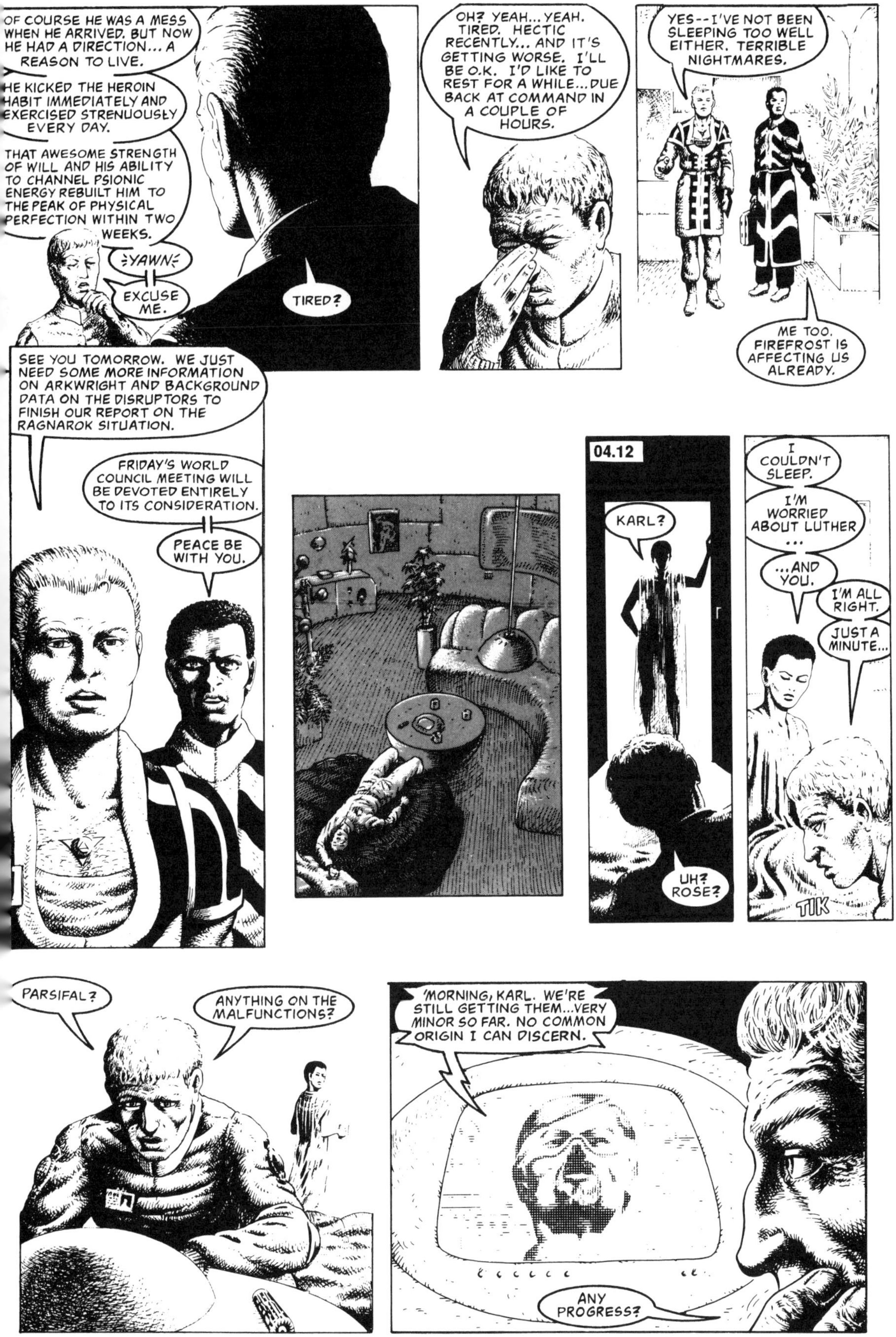
OF COURSE HE WAS A MESS WHEN HE ARRIVED. BUT NOW HE HAD A DIRECTION... A REASON TO LIVE.
HE KICKED THE HEROIN HABIT IMMEDIATELY AND EXERCISED STRENUOUSLY EVERY DAY.
THAT AWESOME STRENGTH OF WILL AND HIS ABILITY TO CHANNEL PSIONIC ENERGY REBUILT HIM TO THE PEAK OF PHYSICAL PERFECTION WITHIN TWO WEEKS.
YAWN
EXCUSE ME.
TIRED?
OH? YEAH... YEAH. TIRED. HECTIC RECENTLY... AND IT'S GETTING WORSE. I'LL BE O.K. I'D LIKE TO REST FOR A WHILE... DUE BACK AT COMMAND IN A COUPLE OF HOURS.
YES--I'VE NOT BEEN SLEEPING TOO WELL EITHER. TERRIBLE NIGHTMARES.
ME TOO. FIREFROST IS AFFECTING US ALREADY.
SEE YOU TOMORROW. WE JUST NEED SOME MORE INFORMATION ON ARKWRIGHT AND BACKGROUND DATA ON THE DISRUPTORS TO FINISH OUR REPORT ON THE RAGNAROK SITUATION.
FRIDAY'S WORLD COUNCIL MEETING WILL BE DEVOTED ENTIRELY TO ITS CONSIDERATION.
PEACE BE WITH YOU.
04.12
KARL?
UH? ROSE?
I COULDN'T SLEEP.
I'M WORRIED ABOUT LUTHER...
...AND YOU.
I'M ALL RIGHT.
JUST A MINUTE...
TIK
PARSIFAL?
ANYTHING ON THE MALFUNCTIONS?
'MORNING, KARL. WE'RE STILL GETTING THEM... VERY MINOR SO FAR. NO COMMON ORIGIN I CAN DISCERN.
ANY PROGRESS?

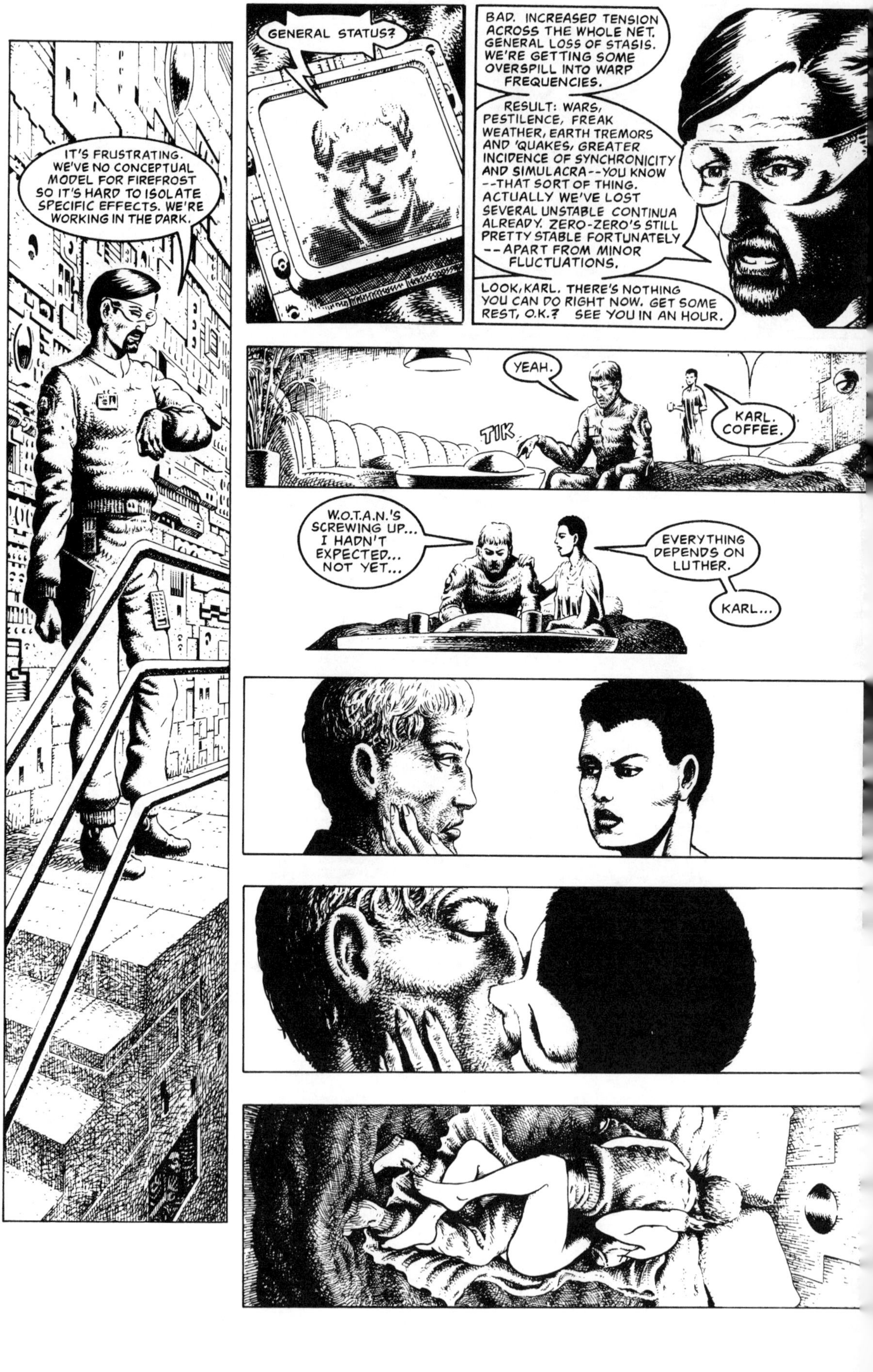
IT'S FRUSTRATING. WE'VE NO CONCEPTUAL MODEL FOR FIREFROST SO IT'S HARD TO ISOLATE SPECIFIC EFFECTS. WE'RE WORKING IN THE DARK.
GENERAL STATUS?
BAD. INCREASED TENSION ACROSS THE WHOLE NET. GENERAL LOSS OF STASIS. WE'RE GETTING SOME OVERSPILL INTO WARP FREQUENCIES.
RESULT: WARS, PESTILENCE, FREAK WEATHER, EARTH TREMORS AND 'QUAKES, GREATER INCIDENCE OF SYNCHRONICITY AND SIMULACRA--YOU KNOW --THAT SORT OF THING. ACTUALLY WE'VE LOST SEVERAL UNSTABLE CONTINUA ALREADY. ZERO-ZERO'S STILL PRETTY STABLE FORTUNATELY --APART FROM MINOR FLUCTUATIONS.
LOOK, KARL. THERE'S NOTHING YOU CAN DO RIGHT NOW. GET SOME REST, O.K.? SEE YOU IN AN HOUR.
YEAH.
TIK
KARL. COFFEE.
W.O.T.A.N.'S SCREWING UP... I HADN'T EXPECTED... NOT YET...
EVERYTHING DEPENDS ON LUTHER.
KARL...

HURS 12 OCT 12.00 WESTMINSTER SQUARE

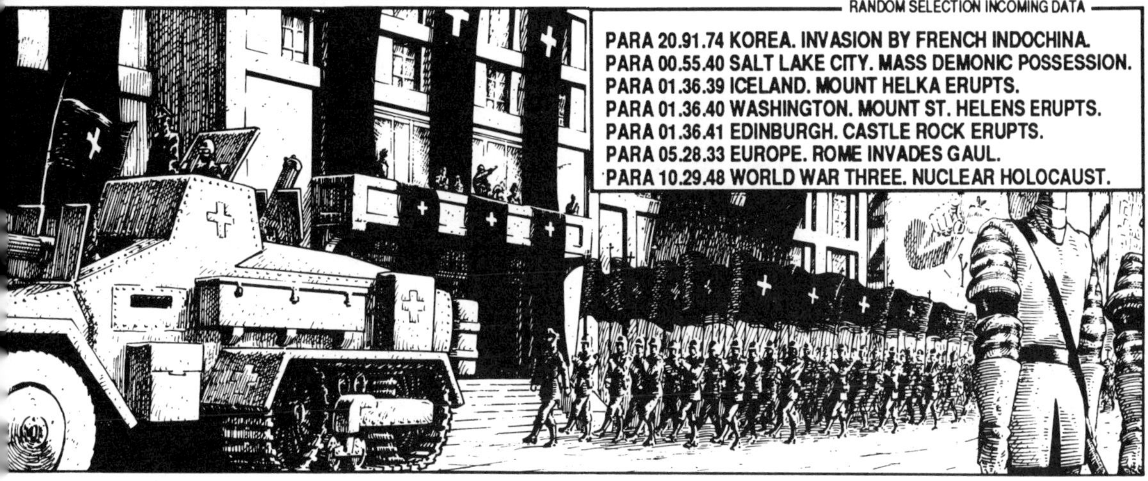
RANDOM SELECTION INCOMING DATA
PARA 20.91.74 KOREA. INVASION BY FRENCH INDOCHINA.
PARA 00.55.40 SALT LAKE CITY. MASS DEMONIC POSSESSION.
PARA 01.36.39 ICELAND. MOUNT HELKA ERUPTS.
PARA 01.36.40 WASHINGTON. MOUNT ST. HELENS ERUPTS.
PARA 01.36.41 EDINBURGH. CASTLE ROCK ERUPTS.
PARA 05.28.33 EUROPE. ROME INVADES GAUL.
PARA 10.29.48 WORLD WAR THREE. NUCLEAR HOLOCAUST.

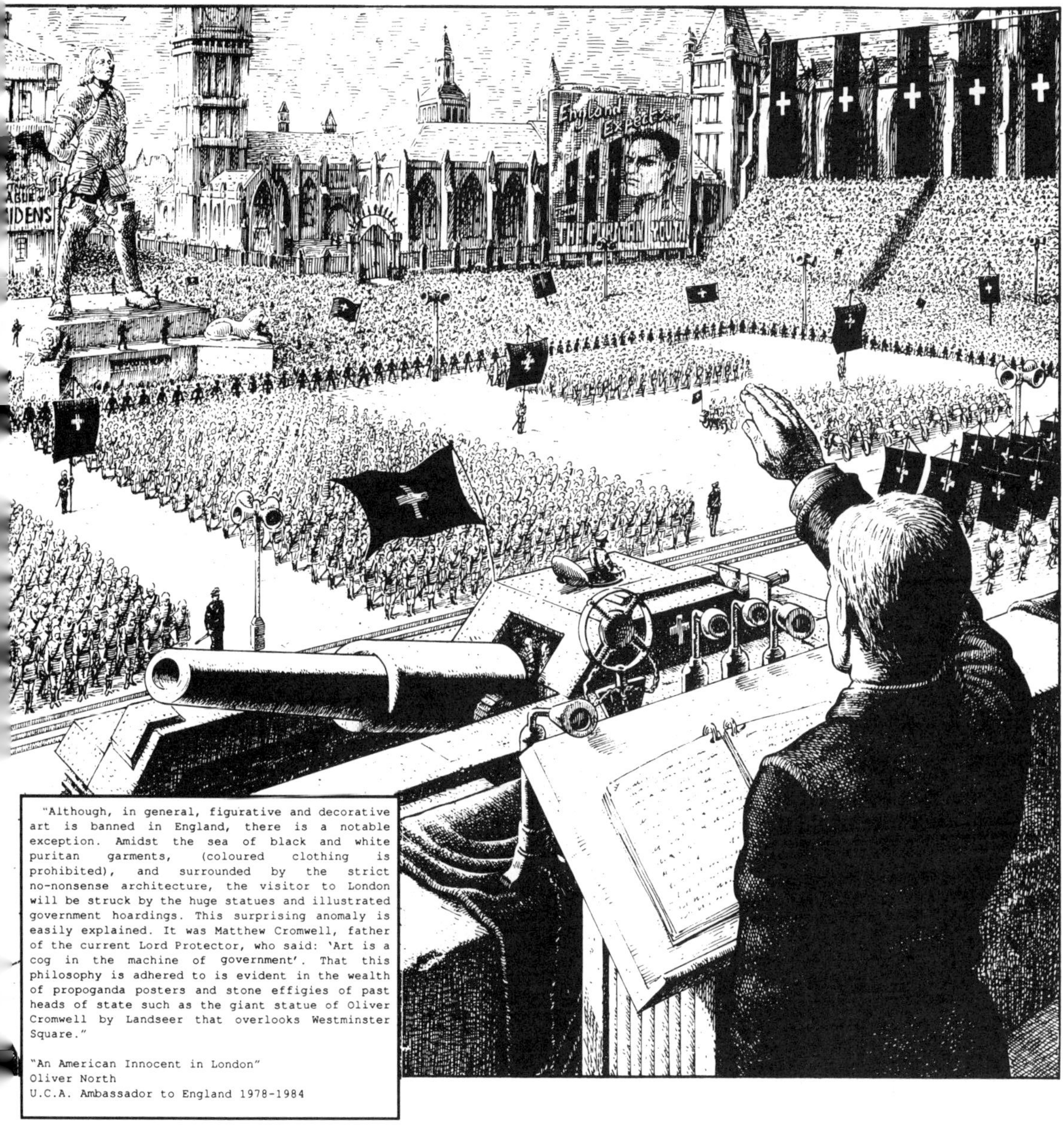
England Expects
"Although, in general, figurative and decorative art is banned in England, there is a notable exception. Amidst the sea of black and white puritan garments, (coloured clothing is prohibited), and surrounded by the strict no-nonsense architecture, the visitor to London will be struck by the huge statues and illustrated government hoardings. This surprising anomaly is easily explained. It was Matthew Cromwell, father of the current Lord Protector, who said: 'Art is a cog in the machine of government'. That this philosophy is adhered to is evident in the wealth of propoganda posters and stone effigies of past heads of state such as the giant statue of Oliver Cromwell by Landseer that overlooks Westminster Square."
"An American Innocent in London"
Oliver North
U.C.A. Ambassador to England 1978-1984

...AND LOUDSPEAKERS RINGING THE WHOLE OF WESTMINSTER, MI'LORD. WE'VE ALSO POSITIONED MICROPHONES SO AS TO RELAY BACK TO THE CROWD THEIR CRIES AND SHOUTS OF APPROVAL. IT'LL INCREASE THE VOLUME AND ENCOURAGE EVEN MORE RESPONSE...

OH, THEY'LL RESPOND ALL RIGHT ...

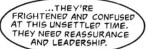

...THEY'RE FRIGHTENED AND CONFUSED AT THIS UNSETTLED TIME. THEY NEED REASSURANCE AND LEADERSHIP.

THE SHEEP NEED THEIR SHEPHERD.

I'VE PLANTED 500 UNUNIFORMED CSS IN AMONGST THEM. THEY'LL SINGLE OUT AND DEAL WITH ANY TROUBLEMAKERS AND LEAD THE CHANTING.

THE WHOLE NATION WILL BE LISTENING, MI'LORD. THE EBC WILL FILL THE WIRELESS WITH IT ALL WEEK. FLEET STREET HAS HAD ITS ORDERS. MAXIMUM PROPAGANDA WILL BE EFFECTED.

WELL? HAVE YOU REACHED A DECISION?

EXCELLENT.

YES, DAMN YOU. I AGREE. HE'S INSANE AND IMMORAL. WE MUST SIEZE POWER.

THESE... GIRLS. ARE YOU CERTAIN OF YOUR INFORMATION?

ABSOLUTELY.

PENNINGTON'S CSS SUPPLY HIM WITH ROYALIST WENCHES, PRESSGANGED FROM THE MAZE. HE HAS HIS UNSPEAKABLE PLEASURES WITH THEM. THEY DIE IN AGONY. THE CSS DISPOSE OF THE BODIES.

IF YOU NEED EVIDENCE LOOK AT THE VENEREAL SCABS ON HIS FACE.

GOD'S VENGEANCE! OH, INFAMY AND PERDITION!

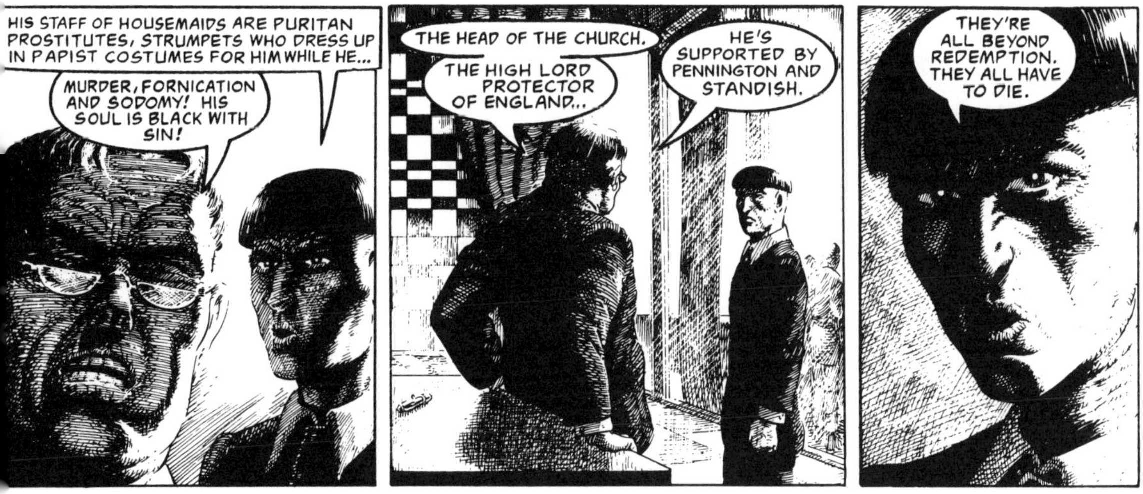
HIS STAFF OF HOUSEMAIDS ARE PURITAN PROSTITUTES, STRUMPETS WHO DRESS UP IN PAPIST COSTUMES FOR HIM WHILE HE...
MURDER, FORNICATION AND SODOMY! HIS SOUL IS BLACK WITH SIN!
THE HEAD OF THE CHURCH.
THE HIGH LORD PROTECTOR OF ENGLAND...
HE'S SUPPORTED BY PENNINGTON AND STANDISH.
THEY'RE ALL BEYOND REDEMPTION. THEY ALL HAVE TO DIE.

2.30

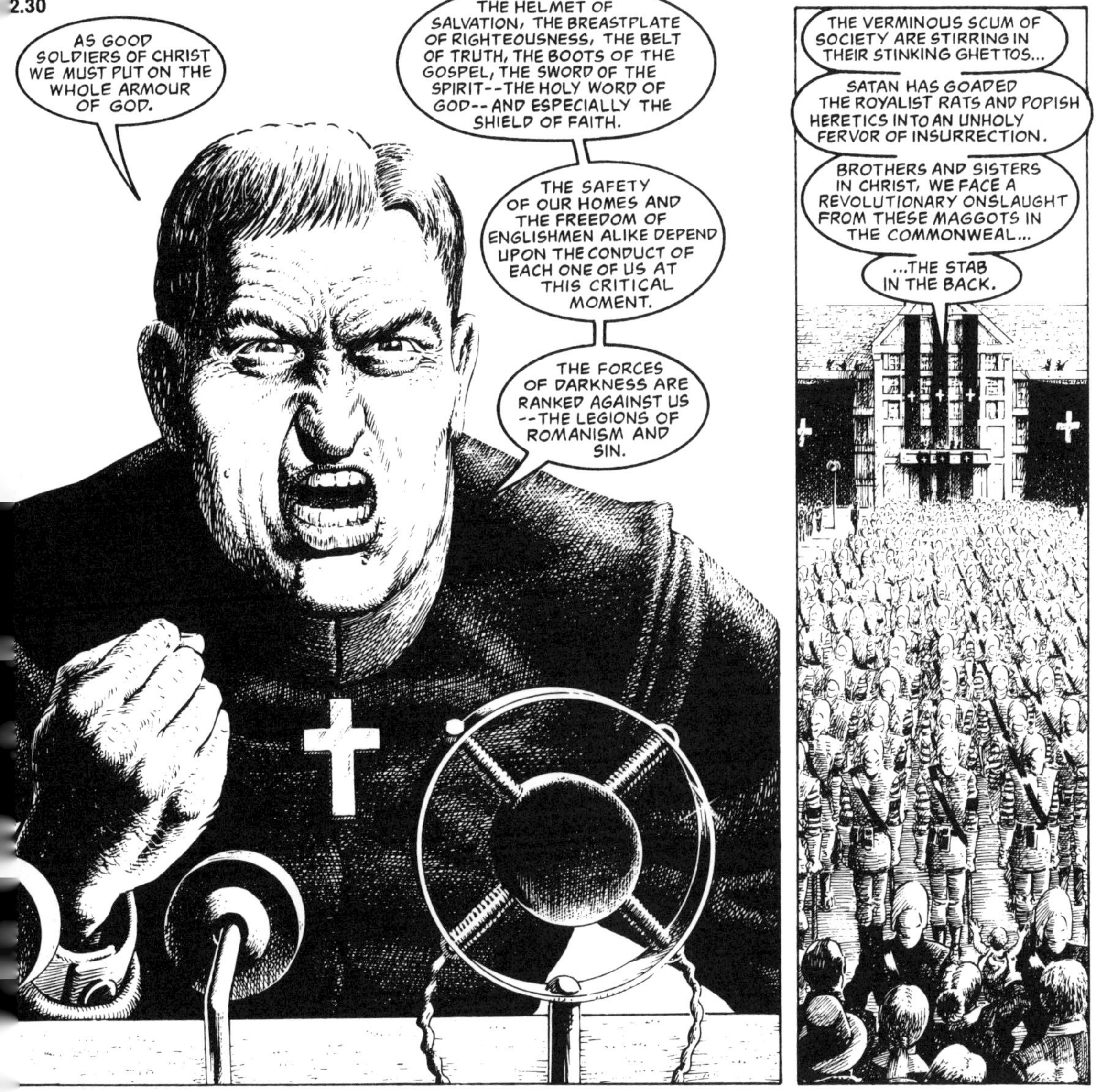
AS GOOD SOLDIERS OF CHRIST WE MUST PUT ON THE WHOLE ARMOUR OF GOD.
THE HELMET OF SALVATION, THE BREASTPLATE OF RIGHTEOUSNESS, THE BELT OF TRUTH, THE BOOTS OF THE GOSPEL, THE SWORD OF THE SPIRIT--THE HOLY WORD OF GOD--AND ESPECIALLY THE SHIELD OF FAITH.
THE SAFETY OF OUR HOMES AND THE FREEDOM OF ENGLISHMEN ALIKE DEPEND UPON THE CONDUCT OF EACH ONE OF US AT THIS CRITICAL MOMENT.
THE FORCES OF DARKNESS ARE RANKED AGAINST US --THE LEGIONS OF ROMANISM AND SIN.
THE VERMINOUS SCUM OF SOCIETY ARE STIRRING IN THEIR STINKING GHETTOS...
SATAN HAS GOADED THE ROYALIST RATS AND POPISH HERETICS INTO AN UNHOLY FERVOR OF INSURRECTION.
BROTHERS AND SISTERS IN CHRIST, WE FACE A REVOLUTIONARY ONSLAUGHT FROM THESE MAGGOTS IN THE COMMONWEAL...
...THE STAB IN THE BACK.

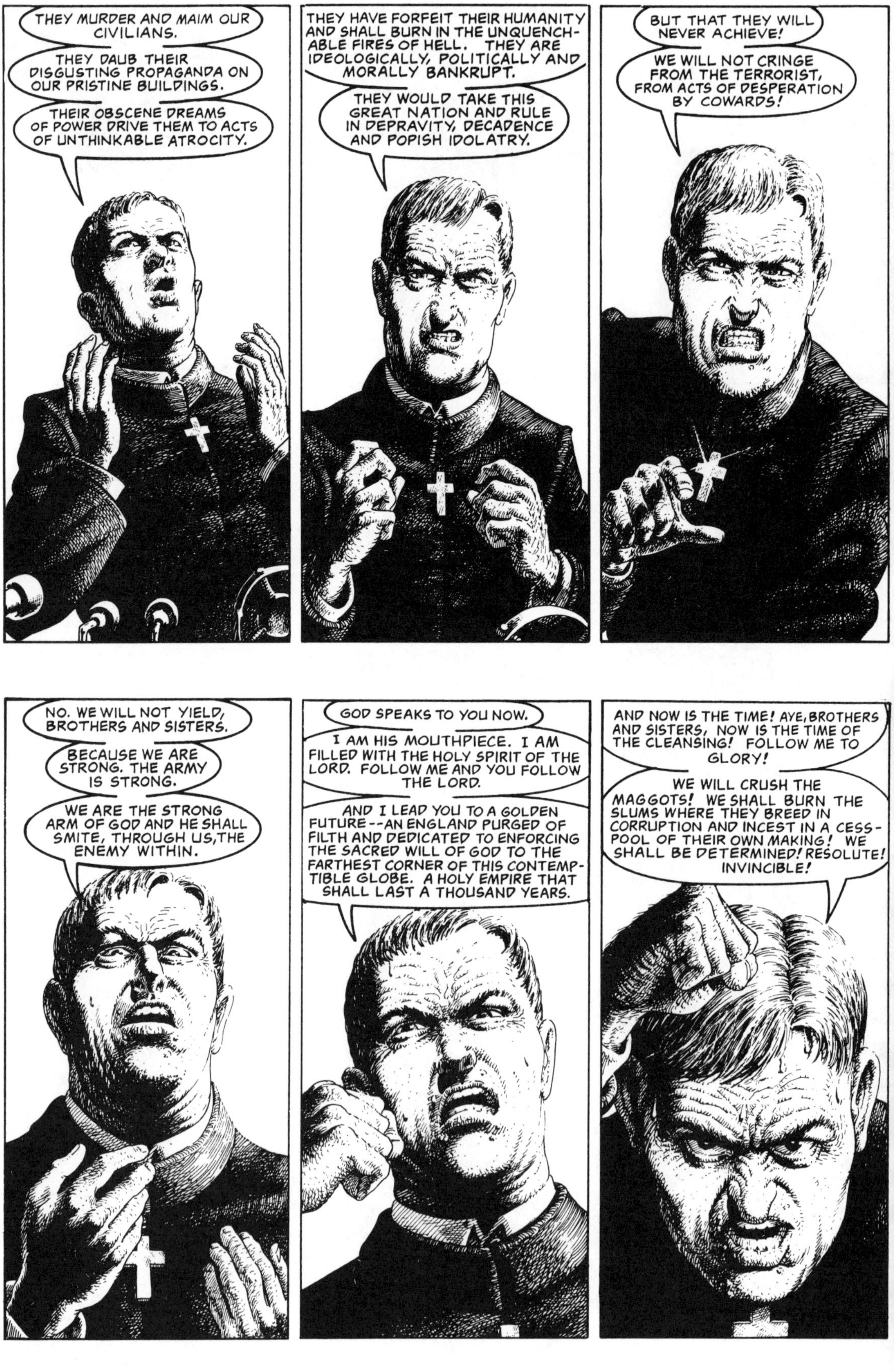
THEY MURDER AND MAIM OUR CIVILIANS.
THEY DAUB THEIR DISGUSTING PROPAGANDA ON OUR PRISTINE BUILDINGS.
THEIR OBSCENE DREAMS OF POWER DRIVE THEM TO ACTS OF UNTHINKABLE ATROCITY.
THEY HAVE FORFEIT THEIR HUMANITY AND SHALL BURN IN THE UNQUENCH-ABLE FIRES OF HELL. THEY ARE IDEOLOGICALLY, POLITICALLY AND MORALLY BANKRUPT.
THEY WOULD TAKE THIS GREAT NATION AND RULE IN DEPRAVITY, DECADENCE AND POPISH IDOLATRY.
BUT THAT THEY WILL NEVER ACHIEVE!
WE WILL NOT CRINGE FROM THE TERRORIST, FROM ACTS OF DESPERATION BY COWARDS!
NO. WE WILL NOT YIELD, BROTHERS AND SISTERS.
BECAUSE WE ARE STRONG. THE ARMY IS STRONG.
WE ARE THE STRONG ARM OF GOD AND HE SHALL SMITE, THROUGH US, THE ENEMY WITHIN.
GOD SPEAKS TO YOU NOW.
I AM HIS MOUTHPIECE. I AM FILLED WITH THE HOLY SPIRIT OF THE LORD. FOLLOW ME AND YOU FOLLOW THE LORD.
AND I LEAD YOU TO A GOLDEN FUTURE--AN ENGLAND PURGED OF FILTH AND DEDICATED TO ENFORCING THE SACRED WILL OF GOD TO THE FARTHEST CORNER OF THIS CONTEMP-TIBLE GLOBE. A HOLY EMPIRE THAT SHALL LAST A THOUSAND YEARS.
AND NOW IS THE TIME! AYE, BROTHERS AND SISTERS, NOW IS THE TIME OF THE CLEANSING! FOLLOW ME TO GLORY!
WE WILL CRUSH THE MAGGOTS! WE SHALL BURN THE SLUMS WHERE THEY BREED IN CORRUPTION AND INCEST IN A CESS-POOL OF THEIR OWN MAKING! WE SHALL BE DETERMINED! RESOLUTE! INVINCIBLE!

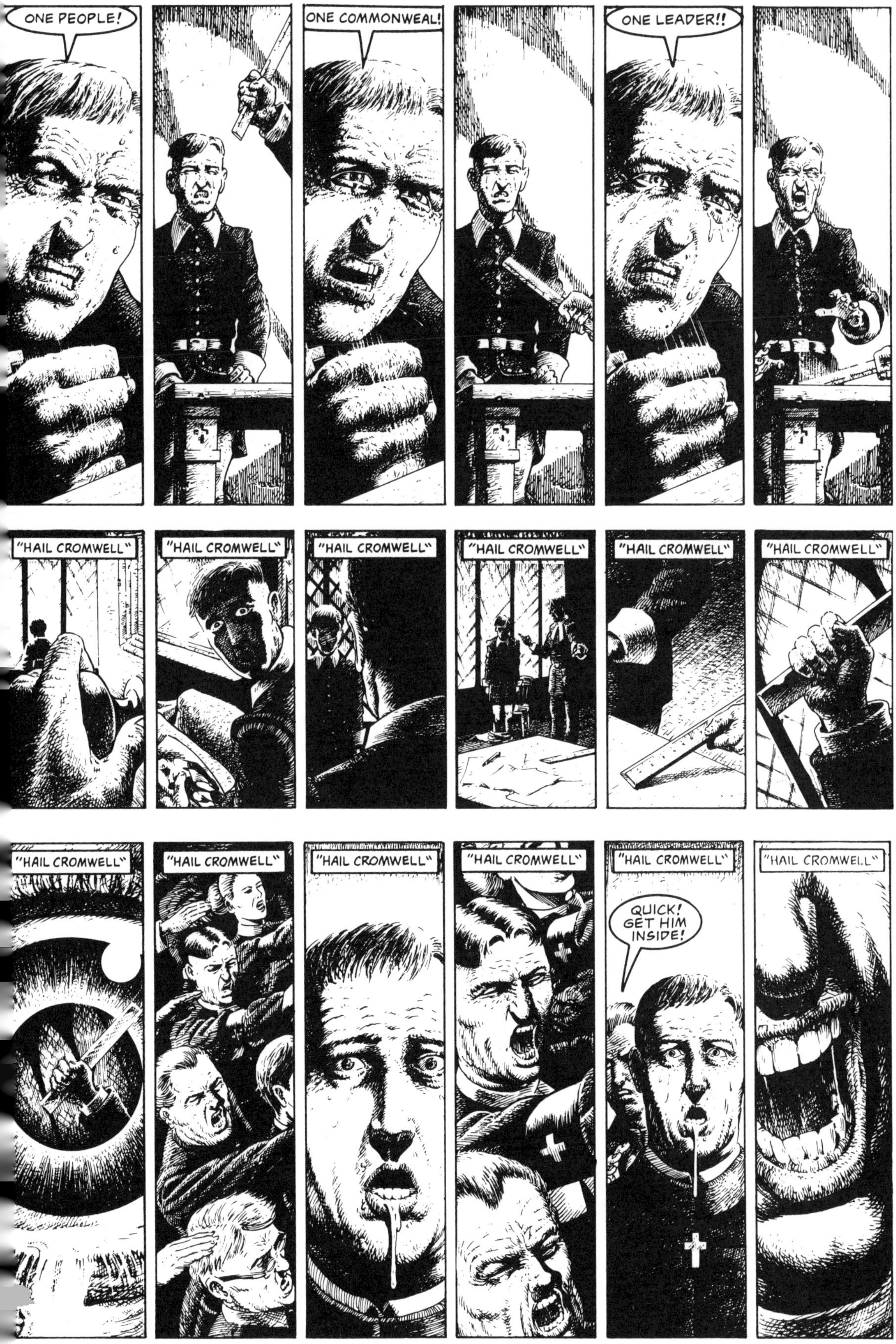
ONE PEOPLE!
ONE COMMONWEAL!
ONE LEADER!!
"HAIL CROMWELL"
"HAIL CROMWELL"
"HAIL CROMWELL"
"HAIL CROMWELL"
"HAIL CROMWELL"
"HAIL CROMWELL"
"HAIL CROMWELL"
"HAIL CROMWELL"
"HAIL CROMWELL"
"HAIL CROMWELL"
"HAIL CROMWELL"
QUICK! GET HIM INSIDE!
"HAIL CROMWELL"

THURS 12 OCT 09.22 PARA 00.00.00 VALHALLA NOVA

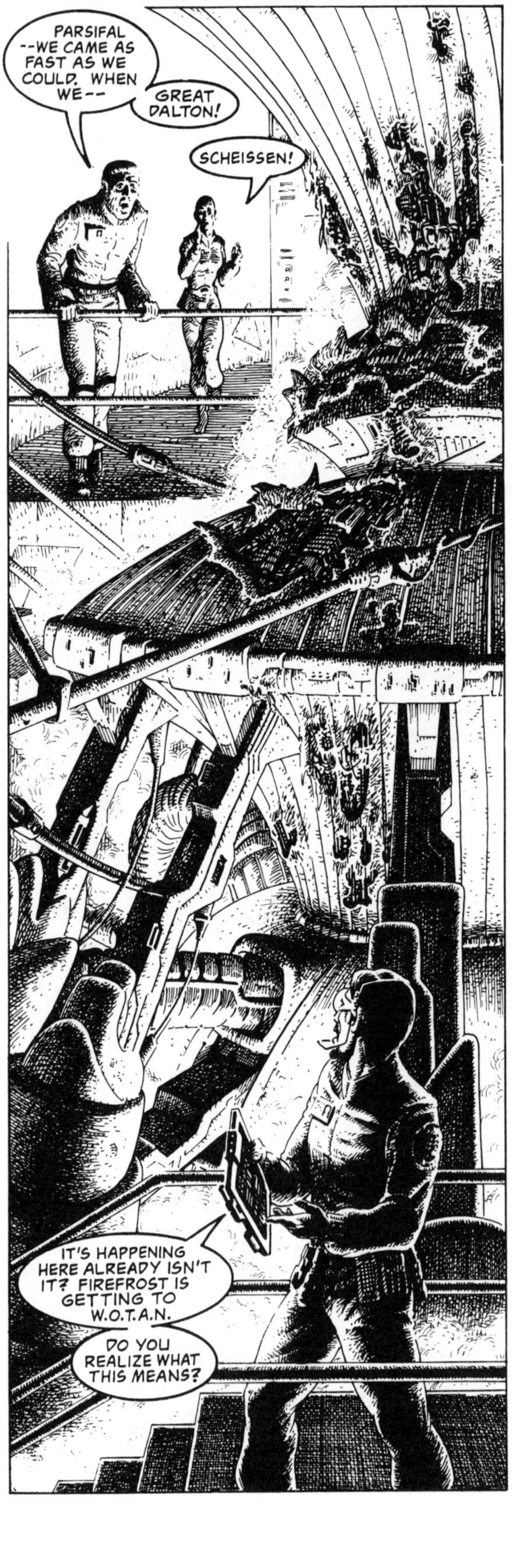

PARSIFAL --WE CAME AS FAST AS WE COULD. WHEN WE--
GREAT DALTON!
SCHEISSEN!
IT'S HAPPENING HERE ALREADY ISN'T IT? FIREFROST IS GETTING TO W.O.T.A.N.
DO YOU REALIZE WHAT THIS MEANS?

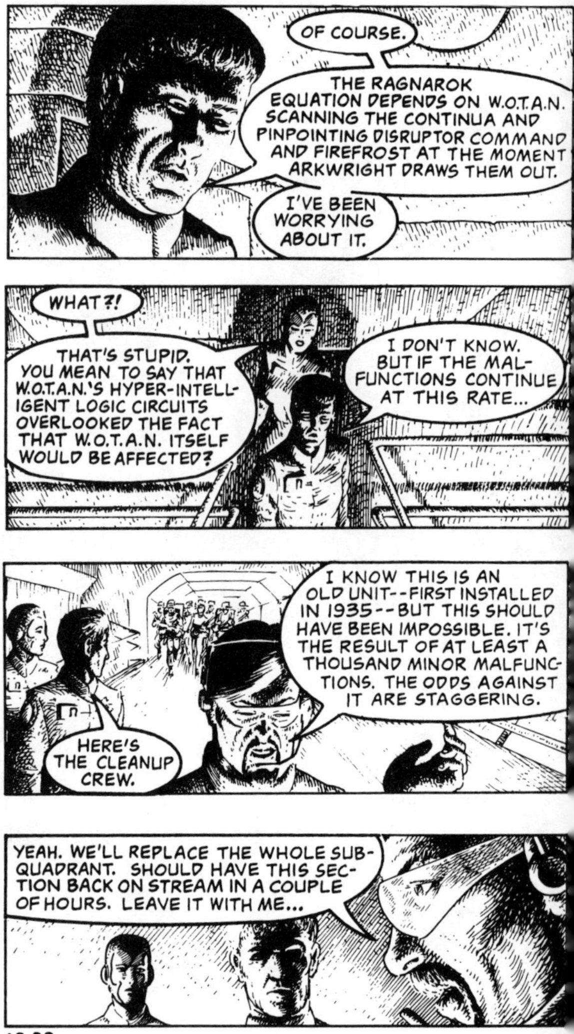

OF COURSE.
THE RAGNAROK EQUATION DEPENDS ON W.O.T.A.N. SCANNING THE CONTINUA AND PINPOINTING DISRUPTOR COMMAND AND FIREFROST AT THE MOMENT ARKWRIGHT DRAWS THEM OUT.
I'VE BEEN WORRYING ABOUT IT.
WHAT?!
THAT'S STUPID. YOU MEAN TO SAY THAT W.O.T.A.N.'S HYPER-INTELLIGENT LOGIC CIRCUITS OVERLOOKED THE FACT THAT W.O.T.A.N. ITSELF WOULD BE AFFECTED?
I DON'T KNOW. BUT IF THE MALFUNCTIONS CONTINUE AT THIS RATE...
HERE'S THE CLEANUP CREW.
I KNOW THIS IS AN OLD UNIT--FIRST INSTALLED IN 1935--BUT THIS SHOULD HAVE BEEN IMPOSSIBLE. IT'S THE RESULT OF AT LEAST A THOUSAND MINOR MALFUNCTIONS. THE ODDS AGAINST IT ARE STAGGERING.
YEAH. WE'LL REPLACE THE WHOLE SUB-QUADRANT. SHOULD HAVE THIS SECTION BACK ON STREAM IN A COUPLE OF HOURS. LEAVE IT WITH ME...

10.03

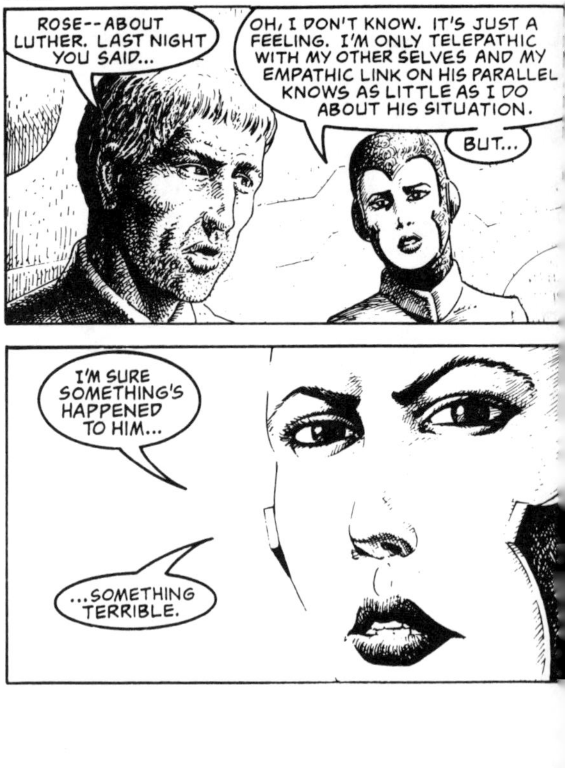

ROSE--ABOUT LUTHER. LAST NIGHT YOU SAID...
OH, I DON'T KNOW. IT'S JUST A FEELING. I'M ONLY TELEPATHIC WITH MY OTHER SELVES AND MY EMPATHIC LINK ON HIS PARALLEL KNOWS AS LITTLE AS I DO ABOUT HIS SITUATION.
BUT...
I'M SURE SOMETHING'S HAPPENED TO HIM...
...SOMETHING TERRIBLE.

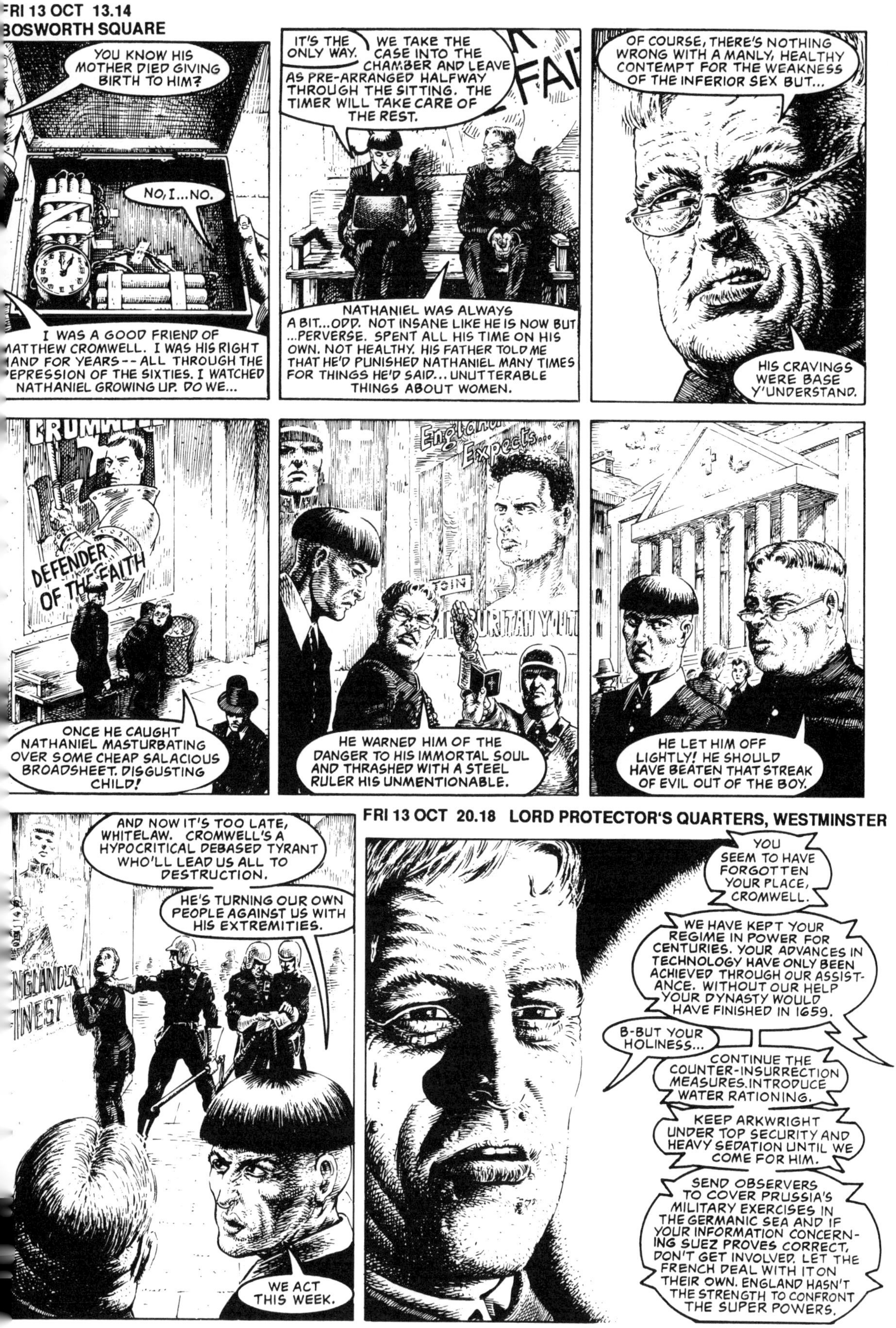
FRI 13 OCT 13.14
BOSWORTH SQUARE
YOU KNOW HIS MOTHER DIED GIVING BIRTH TO HIM?
NO, I...NO.
I WAS A GOOD FRIEND OF MATTHEW CROMWELL. I WAS HIS RIGHT HAND FOR YEARS -- ALL THROUGH THE DEPRESSION OF THE SIXTIES. I WATCHED NATHANIEL GROWING UP. DO WE...
IT'S THE ONLY WAY.
WE TAKE THE CASE INTO THE CHAMBER AND LEAVE AS PRE-ARRANGED HALFWAY THROUGH THE SITTING. THE TIMER WILL TAKE CARE OF THE REST.
NATHANIEL WAS ALWAYS A BIT...ODD. NOT INSANE LIKE HE IS NOW BUT ...PERVERSE. SPENT ALL HIS TIME ON HIS OWN. NOT HEALTHY. HIS FATHER TOLD ME THAT HE'D PUNISHED NATHANIEL MANY TIMES FOR THINGS HE'D SAID... UNUTTERABLE THINGS ABOUT WOMEN.
OF COURSE, THERE'S NOTHING WRONG WITH A MANLY, HEALTHY CONTEMPT FOR THE WEAKNESS OF THE INFERIOR SEX BUT...
HIS CRAVINGS WERE BASE Y'UNDERSTAND.
DEFENDER OF THE FAITH
ONCE HE CAUGHT NATHANIEL MASTURBATING OVER SOME CHEAP SALACIOUS BROADSHEET. DISGUSTING CHILD!
England Expects...
JOIN
PURITAN YOUT
HE WARNED HIM OF THE DANGER TO HIS IMMORTAL SOUL AND THRASHED WITH A STEEL RULER HIS UNMENTIONABLE.
HE LET HIM OFF LIGHTLY! HE SHOULD HAVE BEATEN THAT STREAK OF EVIL OUT OF THE BOY.
AND NOW IT'S TOO LATE, WHITELAW. CROMWELL'S A HYPOCRITICAL DEBASED TYRANT WHO'LL LEAD US ALL TO DESTRUCTION.
HE'S TURNING OUR OWN PEOPLE AGAINST US WITH HIS EXTREMITIES.
NGLAND'S INEST
WE ACT THIS WEEK.
FRI 13 OCT 20.18 LORD PROTECTOR'S QUARTERS, WESTMINSTER
YOU SEEM TO HAVE FORGOTTEN YOUR PLACE, CROMWELL.
WE HAVE KEPT YOUR REGIME IN POWER FOR CENTURIES. YOUR ADVANCES IN TECHNOLOGY HAVE ONLY BEEN ACHIEVED THROUGH OUR ASSISTANCE. WITHOUT OUR HELP YOUR DYNASTY WOULD HAVE FINISHED IN 1659.
B-BUT YOUR HOLINESS...
CONTINUE THE COUNTER-INSURRECTION MEASURES. INTRODUCE WATER RATIONING.
KEEP ARKWRIGHT UNDER TOP SECURITY AND HEAVY SEDATION UNTIL WE COME FOR HIM.
SEND OBSERVERS TO COVER PRUSSIA'S MILITARY EXERCISES IN THE GERMANIC SEA AND IF YOUR INFORMATION CONCERNING SUEZ PROVES CORRECT, DON'T GET INVOLVED. LET THE FRENCH DEAL WITH IT ON THEIR OWN. ENGLAND HASN'T THE STRENGTH TO CONFRONT THE SUPER POWERS.

AND AS FOR YOUR ERRANT COLONIES IN AMERICA, DEAL WITH THEM AFTER YOU'VE PUT DOWN YOUR REBELS AT HOME. IT'S ONLY A COUNTRY OF PEASANT FARMERS AND REFUGEES FROM THE PRUSSIAN EMPIRE. IT CAN WAIT.

THIS COMMUNICATION IS TERMINATED.

NO! WAIT!

WAIT!

DAMN DAMN DAMN!

UUGH! MY HEAD!

WHERE'S THAT QUACK'S PILLS?

20.21

MY COMFORT.

20.53

NOT FOR ORDINARY MEN ARE YOU?

THEY ARE WEAK.

THEY SIN.

GLUG GOD'S GLUG LIEUTENANT CAN GLUG COMMIT GLUG NO GLUG SIN GLUG

21.10

OH GOD. I'M BURNING, GOD. SATAN ATTACKS ME ONCE MORE.

I FEEL THE FIRE ETERNAL.

21.25

OH GOD ⁓BUURRP⁓

GOD CLEAVE MY DARKNESH WITH THY SHWORD.

OLY BIBLE

GOVERNMENT AUTHORISED

21.32

DON'T YOU LOOK AT ME LIKE THAT!

WHAT THE BLOODY HELL DO YOU MEAN?! WHY, YOU...

GO TO HELL, YOU SHMUG BASHTARD!

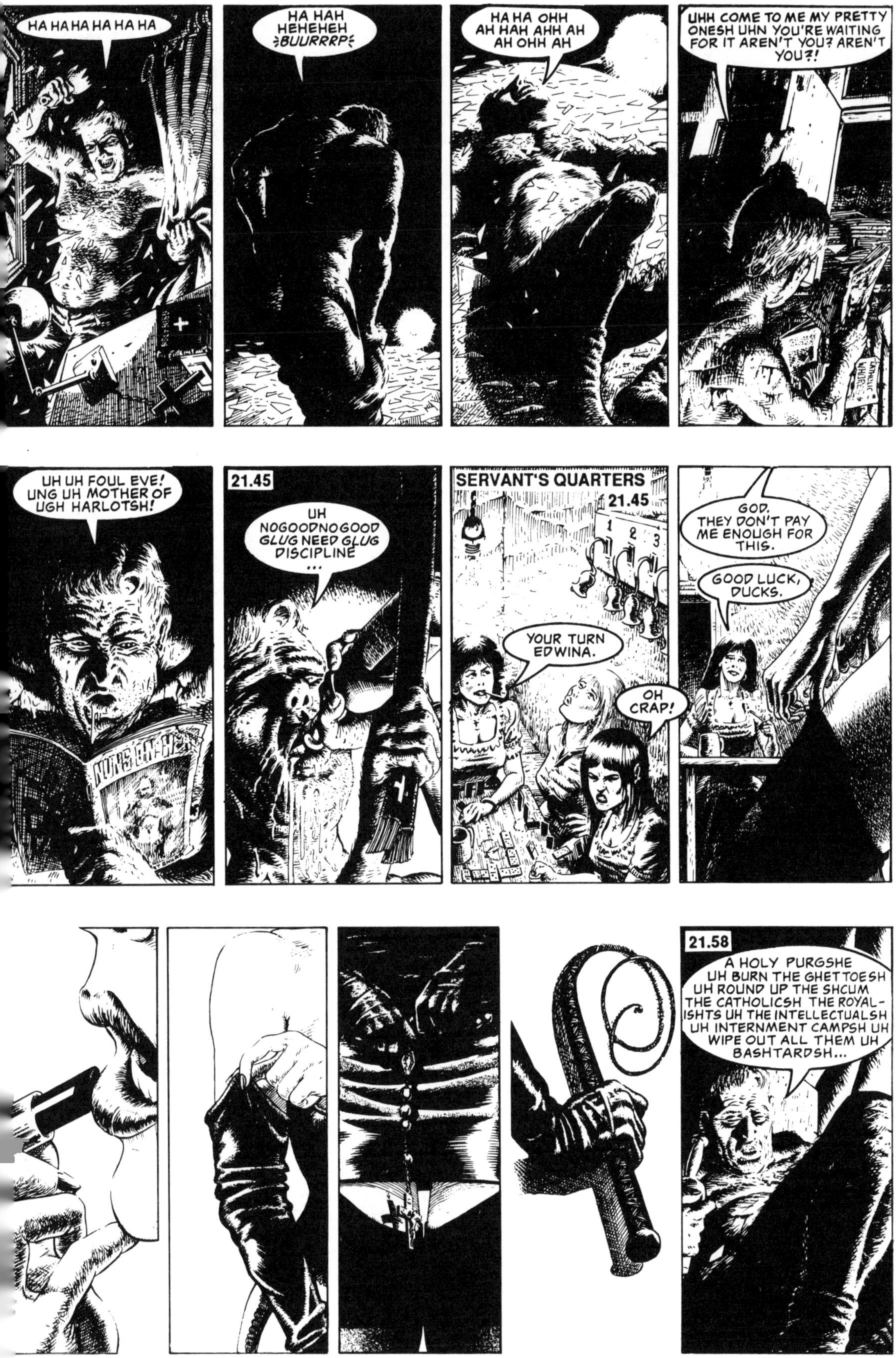
HA HA HA HA HA HA HA
HA HAH HEHEHEH BUURRRP
HA HA OHH AH HAH AHH AH AH OHH AH
UHH COME TO ME MY PRETTY ONESH UHN YOU'RE WAITING FOR IT AREN'T YOU? AREN'T YOU?!
UH UH FOUL EVE! UNG UH MOTHER OF UGH HARLOTSH!
21.45
UH NOGOODNOGOOD GLUG NEED GLUG DISCIPLINE ...
SERVANT'S QUARTERS
21.45
YOUR TURN EDWINA.
OH CRAP!
GOD. THEY DON'T PAY ME ENOUGH FOR THIS.
GOOD LUCK, DUCKS.
21.58
A HOLY PURGSHE UH BURN THE GHETTOESH UH ROUND UP THE SHCUM THE CATHOLICSH THE ROYAL-ISHTS UH THE INTELLECTUALSH UH INTERNMENT CAMPSH UH WIPE OUT ALL THEM UH BASHTARDSH...

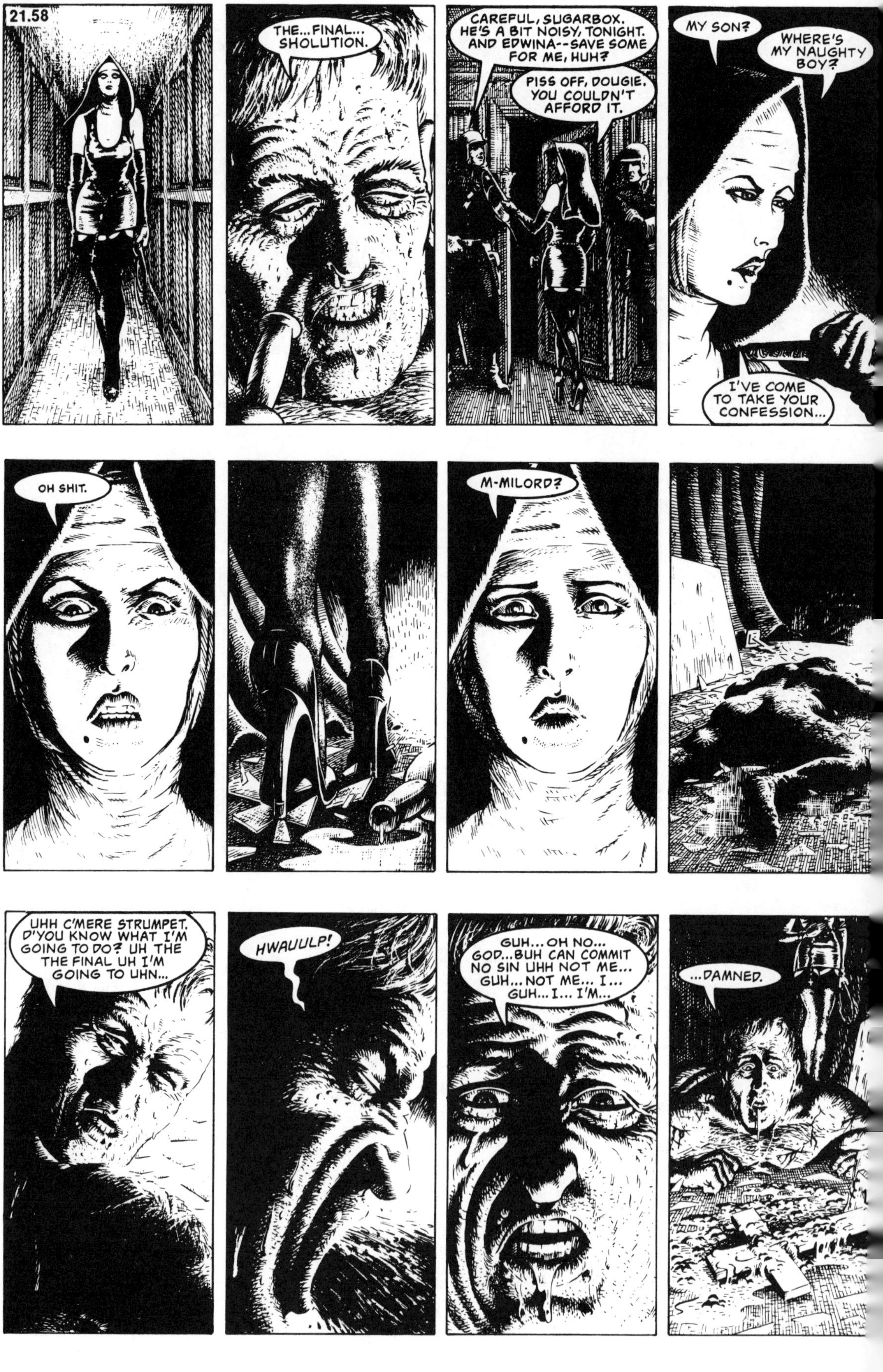
21.58
THE...FINAL...
SHOLUTION.
CAREFUL, SUGARBOX. HE'S A BIT NOISY, TONIGHT. AND EDWINA--SAVE SOME FOR ME, HUH?
PISS OFF, DOUGIE. YOU COULDN'T AFFORD IT.
MY SON?
WHERE'S MY NAUGHTY BOY?
I'VE COME TO TAKE YOUR CONFESSION...
OH SHIT.
M-MILORD?
UHH C'MERE STRUMPET. D'YOU KNOW WHAT I'M GOING TO DO? UH THE THE FINAL UH I'M GOING TO UHN...
HWAUULP!
GUH... OH NO... GOD...BUH CAN COMMIT NO SIN UHH NOT ME... GUH... NOT ME... I... GUH... I... I'M...
...DAMNED.

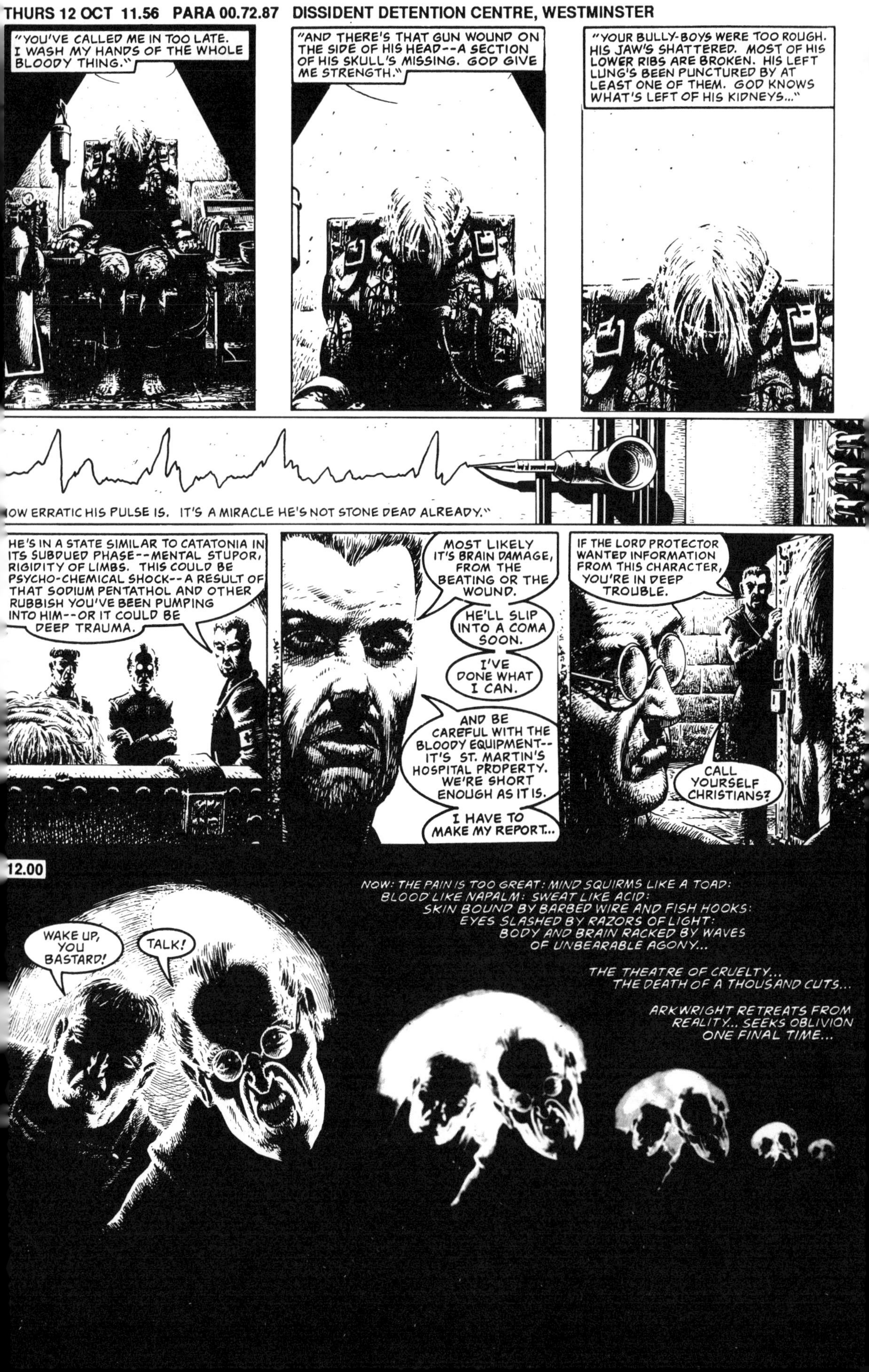
THURS 12 OCT 11.56 PARA 00.72.87 DISSIDENT DETENTION CENTRE, WESTMINSTER
"YOU'VE CALLED ME IN TOO LATE. I WASH MY HANDS OF THE WHOLE BLOODY THING."
"AND THERE'S THAT GUN WOUND ON THE SIDE OF HIS HEAD--A SECTION OF HIS SKULL'S MISSING. GOD GIVE ME STRENGTH."
"YOUR BULLY-BOYS WERE TOO ROUGH. HIS JAW'S SHATTERED. MOST OF HIS LOWER RIBS ARE BROKEN. HIS LEFT LUNG'S BEEN PUNCTURED BY AT LEAST ONE OF THEM. GOD KNOWS WHAT'S LEFT OF HIS KIDNEYS..."
OW ERRATIC HIS PULSE IS. IT'S A MIRACLE HE'S NOT STONE DEAD ALREADY."
HE'S IN A STATE SIMILAR TO CATATONIA IN ITS SUBDUED PHASE--MENTAL STUPOR, RIGIDITY OF LIMBS. THIS COULD BE PSYCHO-CHEMICAL SHOCK--A RESULT OF THAT SODIUM PENTATHOL AND OTHER RUBBISH YOU'VE BEEN PUMPING INTO HIM--OR IT COULD BE DEEP TRAUMA.
MOST LIKELY IT'S BRAIN DAMAGE, FROM THE BEATING OR THE WOUND.
HE'LL SLIP INTO A COMA SOON.
I'VE DONE WHAT I CAN.
AND BE CAREFUL WITH THE BLOODY EQUIPMENT--IT'S ST. MARTIN'S HOSPITAL PROPERTY. WE'RE SHORT ENOUGH AS IT IS.
I HAVE TO MAKE MY REPORT...
IF THE LORD PROTECTOR WANTED INFORMATION FROM THIS CHARACTER, YOU'RE IN DEEP TROUBLE.
CALL YOURSELF CHRISTIANS?
12.00
NOW: THE PAIN IS TOO GREAT: MIND SQUIRMS LIKE A TOAD: BLOOD LIKE NAPALM: SWEAT LIKE ACID: SKIN BOUND BY BARBED WIRE AND FISH HOOKS: EYES SLASHED BY RAZORS OF LIGHT: BODY AND BRAIN RACKED BY WAVES OF UNBEARABLE AGONY...
WAKE UP, YOU BASTARD!
TALK!
THE THEATRE OF CRUELTY... THE DEATH OF A THOUSAND CUTS...
ARKWRIGHT RETREATS FROM REALITY... SEEKS OBLIVION ONE FINAL TIME...

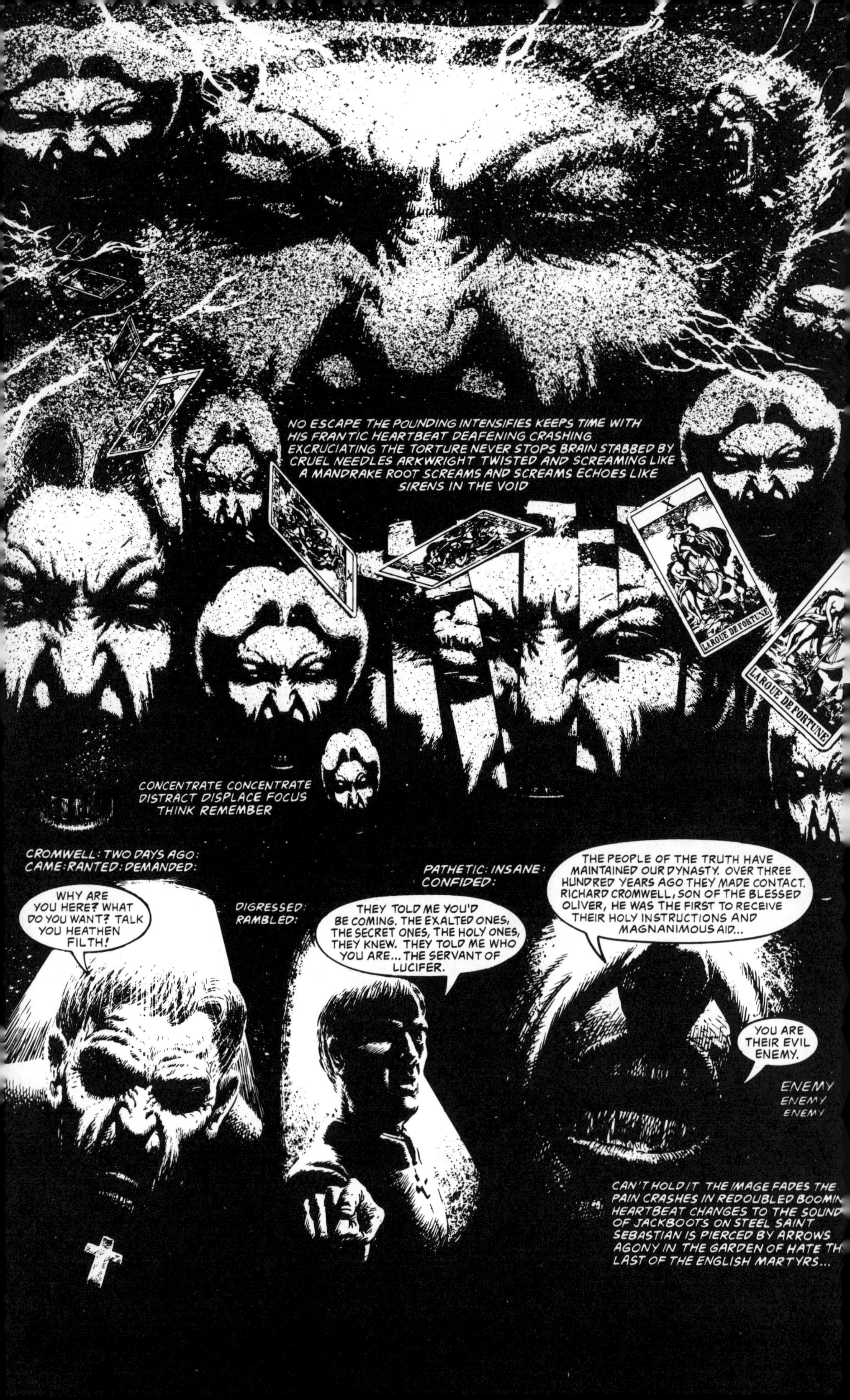
NO ESCAPE THE POUNDING INTENSIFIES KEEPS TIME WITH HIS FRANTIC HEARTBEAT DEAFENING CRASHING EXCRUCIATING THE TORTURE NEVER STOPS BRAIN STABBED BY CRUEL NEEDLES ARKWRIGHT TWISTED AND SCREAMING LIKE A MANDRAKE ROOT SCREAMS AND SCREAMS ECHOES LIKE SIRENS IN THE VOID
X
LA ROUE DE FORTUNE
LA ROUE DE FORTUNE
CONCENTRATE CONCENTRATE DISTRACT DISPLACE FOCUS THINK REMEMBER
CROMWELL: TWO DAYS AGO: CAME: RANTED: DEMANDED:
WHY ARE YOU HERE? WHAT DO YOU WANT? TALK YOU HEATHEN FILTH!
DIGRESSED: RAMBLED:
THEY TOLD ME YOU'D BE COMING. THE EXALTED ONES, THE SECRET ONES, THE HOLY ONES, THEY KNEW. THEY TOLD ME WHO YOU ARE... THE SERVANT OF LUCIFER.
PATHETIC: INSANE: CONFIDED:
THE PEOPLE OF THE TRUTH HAVE MAINTAINED OUR DYNASTY. OVER THREE HUNDRED YEARS AGO THEY MADE CONTACT. RICHARD CROMWELL, SON OF THE BLESSED OLIVER, HE WAS THE FIRST TO RECEIVE THEIR HOLY INSTRUCTIONS AND MAGNANIMOUS AID...
YOU ARE THEIR EVIL ENEMY.
ENEMY
ENEMY
ENEMY
CAN'T HOLD IT THE IMAGE FADES THE PAIN CRASHES IN REDOUBLED BOOMIN HEARTBEAT CHANGES TO THE SOUND OF JACKBOOTS ON STEEL SAINT SEBASTIAN IS PIERCED BY ARROWS AGONY IN THE GARDEN OF HATE TH LAST OF THE ENGLISH MARTYRS...

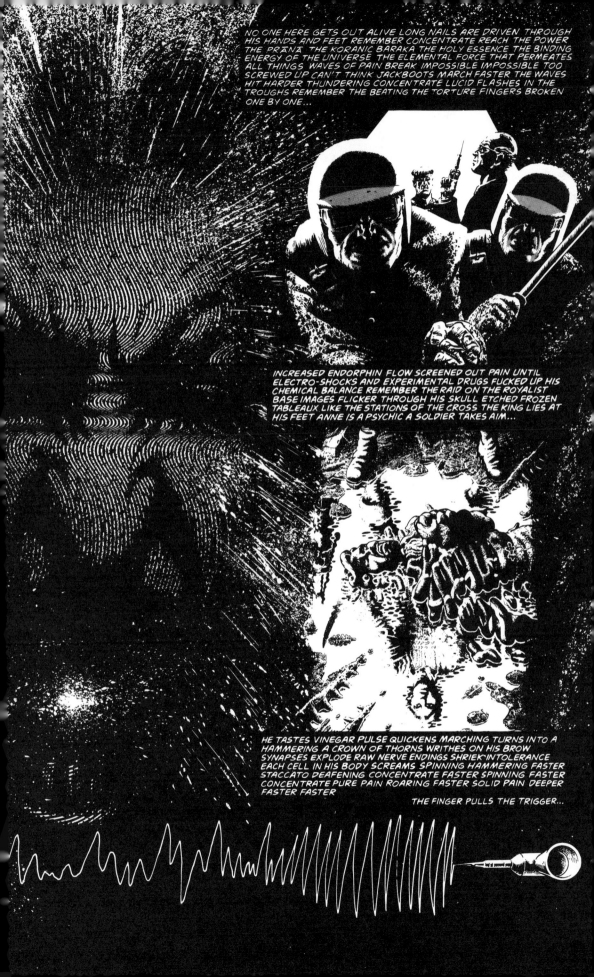

NO ONE HERE GETS OUT ALIVE LONG NAILS ARE DRIVEN THROUGH HIS HANDS AND FEET REMEMBER CONCENTRATE REACH THE POWER THE PRĀNA THE KORANIC BARAKA THE HOLY ESSENCE THE BINDING ENERGY OF THE UNIVERSE THE ELEMENTAL FORCE THAT PERMEATES ALL THINGS WAVES OF PAIN BREAK IMPOSSIBLE IMPOSSIBLE TOO SCREWED UP CAN'T THINK JACKBOOTS MARCH FASTER THE WAVES HIT HARDER THUNDERING CONCENTRATE LUCID FLASHES IN THE TROUGHS REMEMBER THE BEATING THE TORTURE FINGERS BROKEN ONE BY ONE...

INCREASED ENDORPHIN FLOW SCREENED OUT PAIN UNTIL ELECTRO-SHOCKS AND EXPERIMENTAL DRUGS FUCKED UP HIS CHEMICAL BALANCE REMEMBER THE RAID ON THE ROYALIST BASE IMAGES FLICKER THROUGH HIS SKULL ETCHED FROZEN TABLEAUX LIKE THE STATIONS OF THE CROSS THE KING LIES AT HIS FEET ANNE IS A PSYCHIC A SOLDIER TAKES AIM...

HE TASTES VINEGAR PULSE QUICKENS MARCHING TURNS INTO A HAMMERING A CROWN OF THORNS WRITHES ON HIS BROW SYNAPSES EXPLODE RAW NERVE ENDINGS SHRIEK INTOLERANCE EACH CELL IN HIS BODY SCREAMS SPINNING HAMMERING FASTER STACCATO DEAFENING CONCENTRATE FASTER SPINNING FASTER CONCENTRATE PURE PAIN ROARING FASTER SOLID PAIN DEEPER FASTER FASTER

THE FINGER PULLS THE TRIGGER...

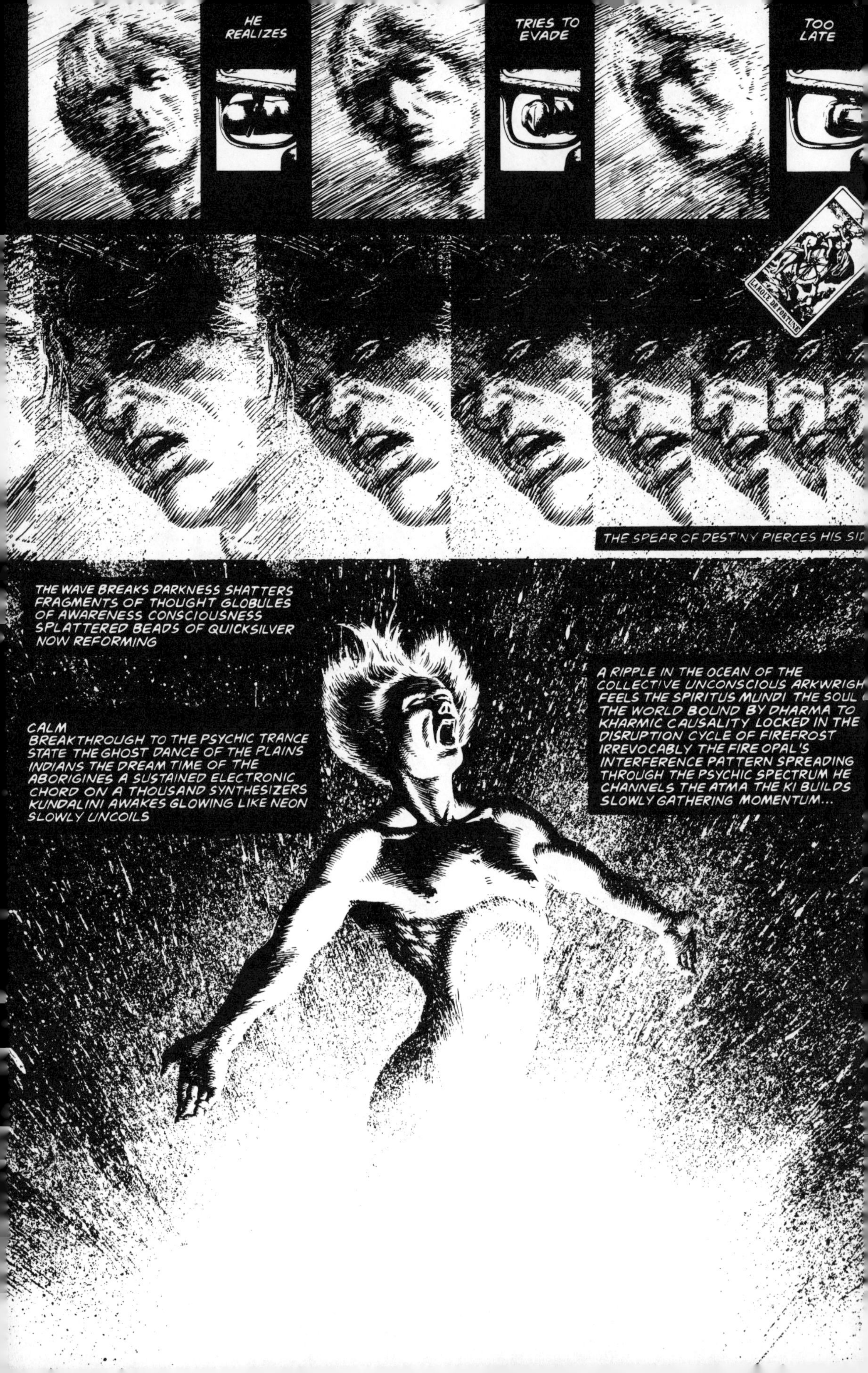
HE REALIZES
TRIES TO EVADE
TOO LATE
LA ROUE DE FORTUNE
THE SPEAR OF DESTINY PIERCES HIS SID
THE WAVE BREAKS DARKNESS SHATTERS FRAGMENTS OF THOUGHT GLOBULES OF AWARENESS CONSCIOUSNESS SPLATTERED BEADS OF QUICKSILVER NOW REFORMING
CALM
BREAKTHROUGH TO THE PSYCHIC TRANCE STATE THE GHOST DANCE OF THE PLAINS INDIANS THE DREAM TIME OF THE ABORIGINES A SUSTAINED ELECTRONIC CHORD ON A THOUSAND SYNTHESIZERS KUNDALINI AWAKES GLOWING LIKE NEON SLOWLY UNCOILS
A RIPPLE IN THE OCEAN OF THE COLLECTIVE UNCONSCIOUS ARKWRIGH FEELS THE SPIRITUS MUNDI THE SOUL THE WORLD BOUND BY DHARMA TO KHARMIC CAUSALITY LOCKED IN THE DISRUPTION CYCLE OF FIREFROST IRREVOCABLY THE FIRE OPAL'S INTERFERENCE PATTERN SPREADING THROUGH THE PSYCHIC SPECTRUM HE CHANNELS THE ATMA THE KI BUILDS SLOWLY GATHERING MOMENTUM...

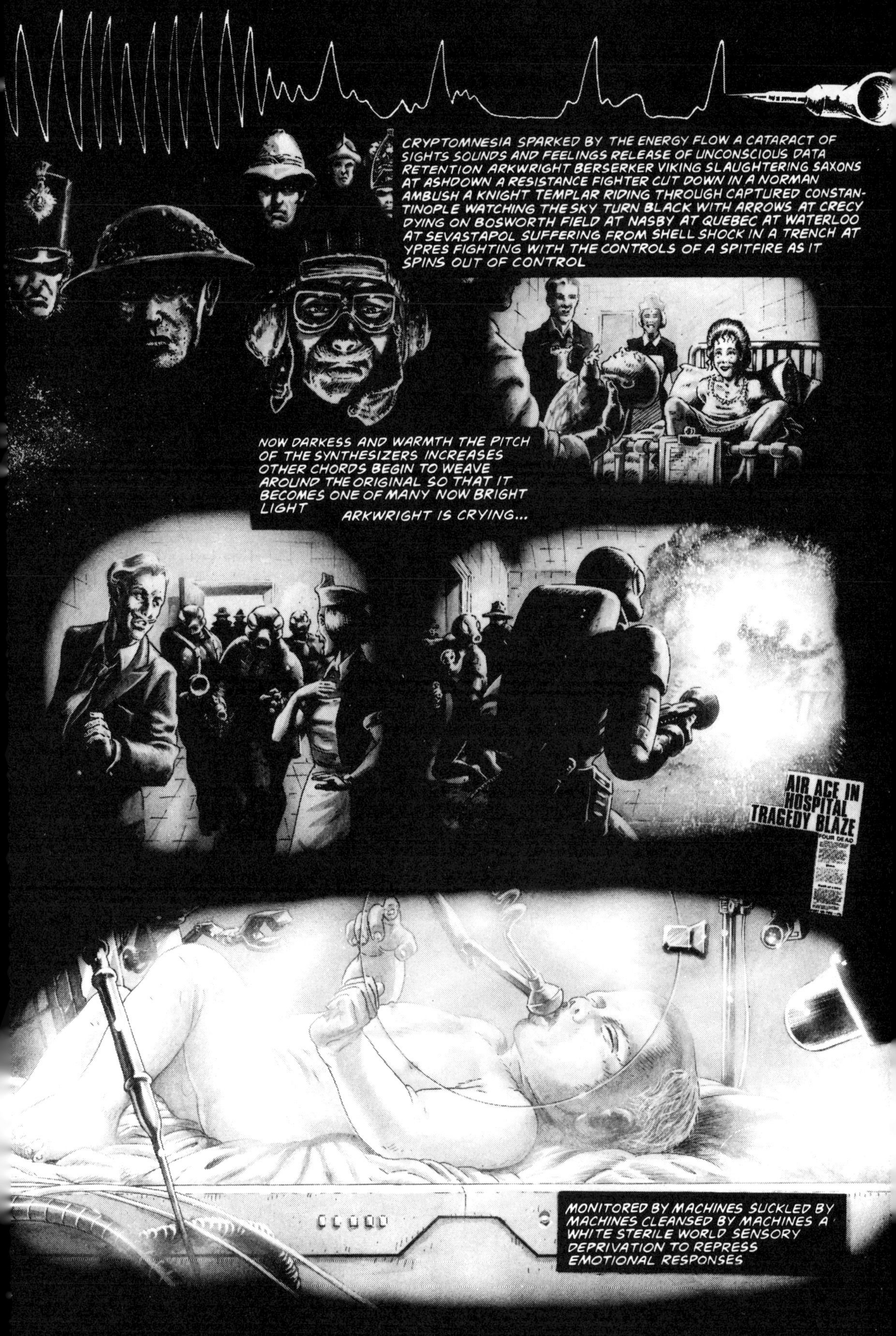
CRYPTOMNESIA SPARKED BY THE ENERGY FLOW A CATARACT OF SIGHTS SOUNDS AND FEELINGS RELEASE OF UNCONSCIOUS DATA RETENTION ARKWRIGHT BERSERKER VIKING SLAUGHTERING SAXONS AT ASHDOWN A RESISTANCE FIGHTER CUT DOWN IN A NORMAN AMBUSH A KNIGHT TEMPLAR RIDING THROUGH CAPTURED CONSTAN-TINOPLE WATCHING THE SKY TURN BLACK WITH ARROWS AT CRECY DYING ON BOSWORTH FIELD AT NASBY AT QUEBEC AT WATERLOO AT SEVASTAPOL SUFFERING FROM SHELL SHOCK IN A TRENCH AT YPRES FIGHTING WITH THE CONTROLS OF A SPITFIRE AS IT SPINS OUT OF CONTROL
NOW DARKESS AND WARMTH THE PITCH OF THE SYNTHESIZERS INCREASES OTHER CHORDS BEGIN TO WEAVE AROUND THE ORIGINAL SO THAT IT BECOMES ONE OF MANY NOW BRIGHT LIGHT
ARKWRIGHT IS CRYING...
AIR ACE IN HOSPITAL TRAGEDY BLAZE
FOUR DEAD
MONITORED BY MACHINES SUCKLED BY MACHINES CLEANSED BY MACHINES A WHITE STERILE WORLD SENSORY DEPRIVATION TO REPRESS EMOTIONAL RESPONSES

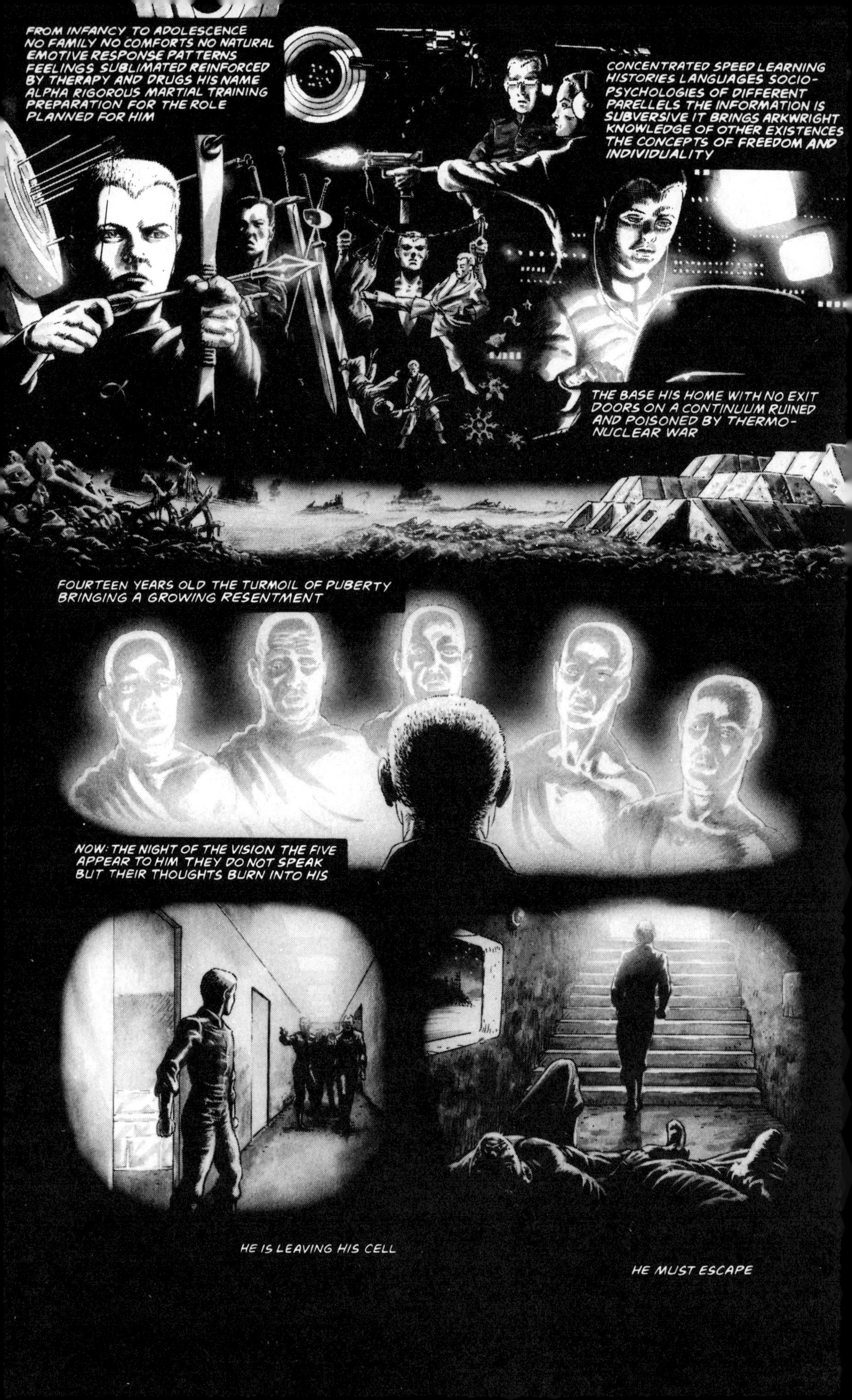
FROM INFANCY TO ADOLESCENCE NO FAMILY NO COMFORTS NO NATURAL EMOTIVE RESPONSE PATTERNS FEELINGS SUBLIMATED REINFORCED BY THERAPY AND DRUGS HIS NAME ALPHA RIGOROUS MARTIAL TRAINING PREPARATION FOR THE ROLE PLANNED FOR HIM
CONCENTRATED SPEED LEARNING HISTORIES LANGUAGES SOCIO-PSYCHOLOGIES OF DIFFERENT PARELLELS THE INFORMATION IS SUBVERSIVE IT BRINGS ARKWRIGHT KNOWLEDGE OF OTHER EXISTENCES THE CONCEPTS OF FREEDOM AND INDIVIDUALITY
THE BASE HIS HOME WITH NO EXIT DOORS ON A CONTINUUM RUINED AND POISONED BY THERMO-NUCLEAR WAR
FOURTEEN YEARS OLD THE TURMOIL OF PUBERTY BRINGING A GROWING RESENTMENT
NOW: THE NIGHT OF THE VISION THE FIVE APPEAR TO HIM THEY DO NOT SPEAK BUT THEIR THOUGHTS BURN INTO HIS
HE IS LEAVING HIS CELL
HE MUST ESCAPE

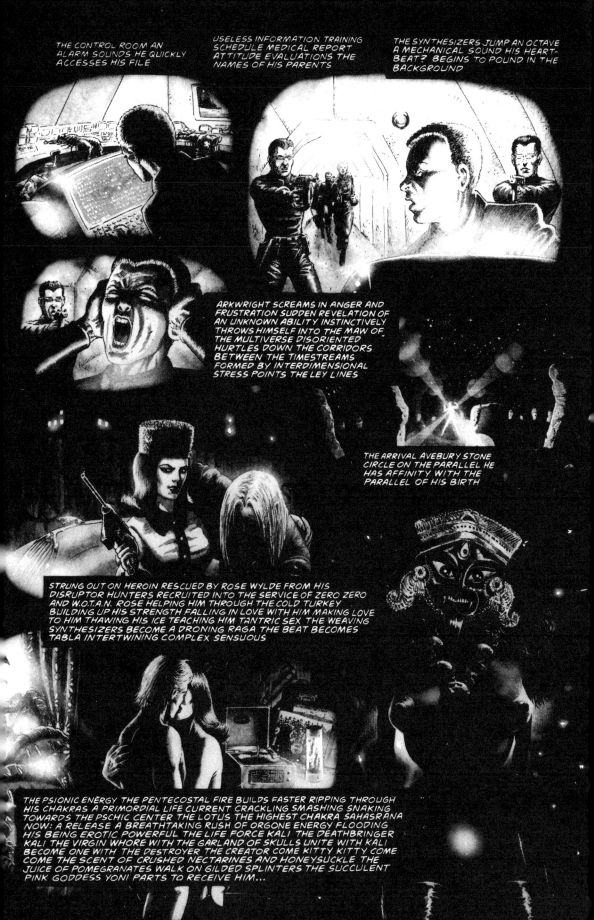

THE CONTROL ROOM AN ALARM SOUNDS HE QUICKLY ACCESSES HIS FILE

USELESS INFORMATION TRAINING SCHEDULE MEDICAL REPORT ATTITUDE EVALUATIONS THE NAMES OF HIS PARENTS

THE SYNTHESIZERS JUMP AN OCTAVE A MECHANICAL SOUND HIS HEART-BEAT? BEGINS TO POUND IN THE BACKGROUND

ARKWRIGHT SCREAMS IN ANGER AND FRUSTRATION SUDDEN REVELATION OF AN UNKNOWN ABILITY INSTINCTIVELY THROWS HIMSELF INTO THE MAW OF THE MULTIVERSE DISORIENTED HURTLES DOWN THE CORRIDORS BETWEEN THE TIMESTREAMS FORMED BY INTERDIMENSIONAL STRESS POINTS THE LEY LINES

THE ARRIVAL AVEBURY STONE CIRCLE ON THE PARALLEL HE HAS AFFINITY WITH THE PARALLEL OF HIS BIRTH

STRUNG OUT ON HEROIN RESCUED BY ROSE WYLDE FROM HIS DISRUPTOR HUNTERS RECRUITED INTO THE SERVICE OF ZERO ZERO AND W.O.T.A.N. ROSE HELPING HIM THROUGH THE COLD TURKEY BUILDING UP HIS STRENGTH FALLING IN LOVE WITH HIM MAKING LOVE TO HIM THAWING HIS ICE TEACHING HIM TANTRIC SEX THE WEAVING SYNTHESIZERS BECOME A DRONING RAGA THE BEAT BECOMES TABLA INTERTWINING COMPLEX SENSUOUS

THE PSIONIC ENERGY THE PENTECOSTAL FIRE BUILDS FASTER RIPPING THROUGH HIS CHAKRAS A PRIMORDIAL LIFE CURRENT CRACKLING SMASHING SNAKING TOWARDS THE PSCHIC CENTER THE LOTUS THE HIGHEST CHAKRA SAHASRANA NOW: A RELEASE A BREATHTAKING RUSH OF ORGONE ENERGY FLOODING HIS BEING EROTIC POWERFUL THE LIFE FORCE KALI THE DEATHBRINGER KALI THE VIRGIN WHORE WITH THE GARLAND OF SKULLS UNITE WITH KALI BECOME ONE WITH THE DESTROYER THE CREATOR COME KITTY KITTY COME COME THE SCENT OF CRUSHED NECTARINES AND HONEYSUCKLE THE JUICE OF POMEGRANATES WALK ON GILDED SPLINTERS THE SUCCULENT PINK GODDESS YONI PARTS TO RECEIVE HIM...

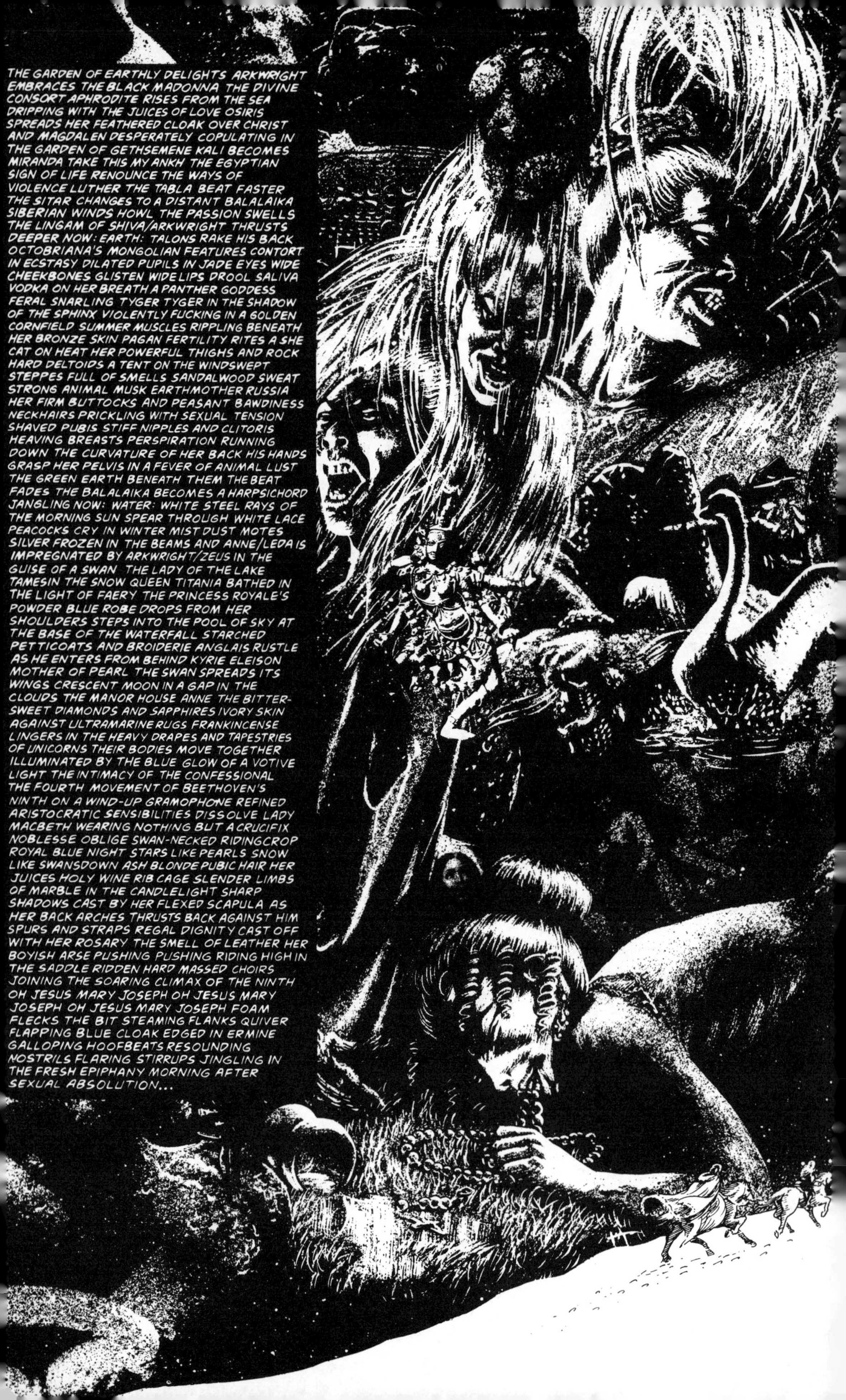
THE GARDEN OF EARTHLY DELIGHTS ARKWRIGHT EMBRACES THE BLACK MADONNA THE DIVINE CONSORT APHRODITE RISES FROM THE SEA DRIPPING WITH THE JUICES OF LOVE OSIRIS SPREADS HER FEATHERED CLOAK OVER CHRIST AND MAGDALEN DESPERATELY COPULATING IN THE GARDEN OF GETHSEMENE KALI BECOMES MIRANDA TAKE THIS MY ANKH THE EGYPTIAN SIGN OF LIFE RENOUNCE THE WAYS OF VIOLENCE LUTHER THE TABLA BEAT FASTER THE SITAR CHANGES TO A DISTANT BALALAIKA SIBERIAN WINDS HOWL THE PASSION SWELLS THE LINGAM OF SHIVA/ARKWRIGHT THRUSTS DEEPER NOW: EARTH: TALONS RAKE HIS BACK OCTOBRIANA'S MONGOLIAN FEATURES CONTORT IN ECSTASY DILATED PUPILS IN JADE EYES WIDE CHEEKBONES GLISTEN WIDE LIPS DROOL SALIVA VODKA ON HER BREATH A PANTHER GODDESS FERAL SNARLING TYGER TYGER IN THE SHADOW OF THE SPHINX VIOLENTLY FUCKING IN A GOLDEN CORNFIELD SUMMER MUSCLES RIPPLING BENEATH HER BRONZE SKIN PAGAN FERTILITY RITES A SHE CAT ON HEAT HER POWERFUL THIGHS AND ROCK HARD DELTOIDS A TENT ON THE WINDSWEPT STEPPES FULL OF SMELLS SANDALWOOD SWEAT STRONG ANIMAL MUSK EARTHMOTHER RUSSIA HER FIRM BUTTOCKS AND PEASANT BAWDINESS NECKHAIRS PRICKLING WITH SEXUAL TENSION SHAVED PUBIS STIFF NIPPLES AND CLITORIS HEAVING BREASTS PERSPIRATION RUNNING DOWN THE CURVATURE OF HER BACK HIS HANDS GRASP HER PELVIS IN A FEVER OF ANIMAL LUST THE GREEN EARTH BENEATH THEM THE BEAT FADES THE BALALAIKA BECOMES A HARPSICHORD JANGLING NOW: WATER: WHITE STEEL RAYS OF THE MORNING SUN SPEAR THROUGH WHITE LACE PEACOCKS CRY IN WINTER MIST DUST MOTES SILVER FROZEN IN THE BEAMS AND ANNE/LEDA IS IMPREGNATED BY ARKWRIGHT/ZEUS IN THE GUISE OF A SWAN THE LADY OF THE LAKE TAMESIN THE SNOW QUEEN TITANIA BATHED IN THE LIGHT OF FAERY THE PRINCESS ROYALE'S POWDER BLUE ROBE DROPS FROM HER SHOULDERS STEPS INTO THE POOL OF SKY AT THE BASE OF THE WATERFALL STARCHED PETTICOATS AND BROIDERIE ANGLAIS RUSTLE AS HE ENTERS FROM BEHIND KYRIE ELEISON MOTHER OF PEARL THE SWAN SPREADS ITS WINGS CRESCENT MOON IN A GAP IN THE CLOUDS THE MANOR HOUSE ANNE THE BITTER-SWEET DIAMONDS AND SAPPHIRES IVORY SKIN AGAINST ULTRAMARINE RUGS FRANKINCENSE LINGERS IN THE HEAVY DRAPES AND TAPESTRIES OF UNICORNS THEIR BODIES MOVE TOGETHER ILLUMINATED BY THE BLUE GLOW OF A VOTIVE LIGHT THE INTIMACY OF THE CONFESSIONAL THE FOURTH MOVEMENT OF BEETHOVEN'S NINTH ON A WIND-UP GRAMOPHONE REFINED ARISTOCRATIC SENSIBILITIES DISSOLVE LADY MACBETH WEARING NOTHING BUT A CRUCIFIX NOBLESSE OBLIGE SWAN-NECKED RIDINGCROP ROYAL BLUE NIGHT STARS LIKE PEARLS SNOW LIKE SWANSDOWN ASH BLONDE PUBIC HAIR HER JUICES HOLY WINE RIB CAGE SLENDER LIMBS OF MARBLE IN THE CANDLELIGHT SHARP SHADOWS CAST BY HER FLEXED SCAPULA AS HER BACK ARCHES THRUSTS BACK AGAINST HIM SPURS AND STRAPS REGAL DIGNITY CAST OFF WITH HER ROSARY THE SMELL OF LEATHER HER BOYISH ARSE PUSHING PUSHING RIDING HIGH IN THE SADDLE RIDDEN HARD MASSED CHOIRS JOINING THE SOARING CLIMAX OF THE NINTH OH JESUS MARY JOSEPH OH JESUS MARY JOSEPH OH JESUS MARY JOSEPH FOAM FLECKS THE BIT STEAMING FLANKS QUIVER FLAPPING BLUE CLOAK EDGED IN ERMINE GALLOPING HOOFBEATS RESOUNDING NOSTRILS FLARING STIRRUPS JINGLING IN THE FRESH EPIPHANY MORNING AFTER SEXUAL ABSOLUTION...

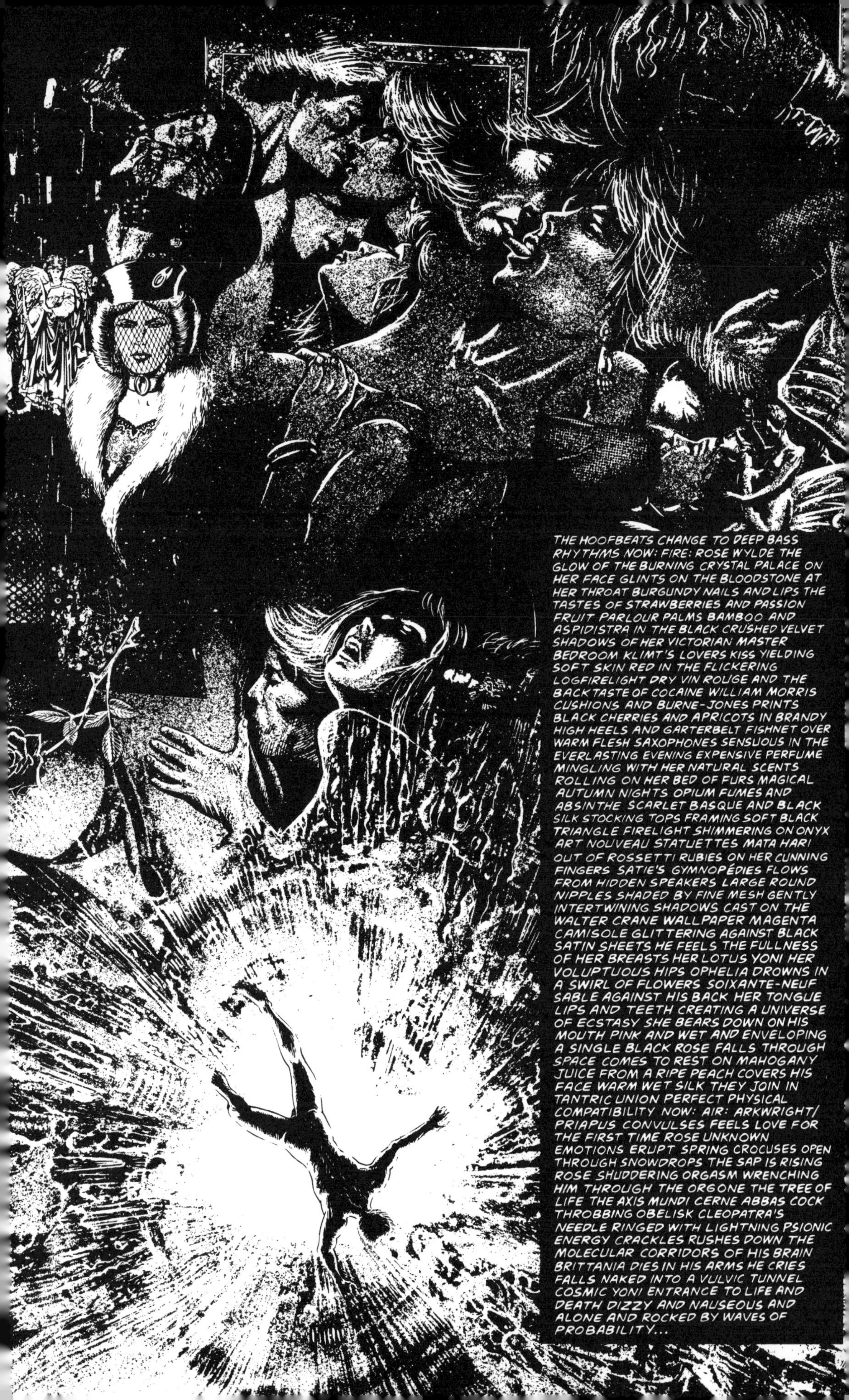
THE HOOFBEATS CHANGE TO DEEP BASS RHYTHMS NOW: FIRE: ROSE WYLDE THE GLOW OF THE BURNING CRYSTAL PALACE ON HER FACE GLINTS ON THE BLOODSTONE AT HER THROAT BURGUNDY NAILS AND LIPS THE TASTES OF STRAWBERRIES AND PASSION FRUIT PARLOUR PALMS BAMBOO AND ASPIDISTRA IN THE BLACK CRUSHED VELVET SHADOWS OF HER VICTORIAN MASTER BEDROOM KLIMT'S LOVERS KISS YIELDING SOFT SKIN RED IN THE FLICKERING LOGFIRELIGHT DRY VIN ROUGE AND THE BACKTASTE OF COCAINE WILLIAM MORRIS CUSHIONS AND BURNE-JONES PRINTS BLACK CHERRIES AND APRICOTS IN BRANDY HIGH HEELS AND GARTERBELT FISHNET OVER WARM FLESH SAXOPHONES SENSUOUS IN THE EVERLASTING EVENING EXPENSIVE PERFUME MINGLING WITH HER NATURAL SCENTS ROLLING ON HER BED OF FURS MAGICAL AUTUMN NIGHTS OPIUM FUMES AND ABSINTHE SCARLET BASQUE AND BLACK SILK STOCKING TOPS FRAMING SOFT BLACK TRIANGLE FIRELIGHT SHIMMERING ON ONYX ART NOUVEAU STATUETTES MATA HARI OUT OF ROSSETTI RUBIES ON HER CUNNING FINGERS SATIE'S GYMNOPÉDIES FLOWS FROM HIDDEN SPEAKERS LARGE ROUND NIPPLES SHADED BY FINE MESH GENTLY INTERTWINING SHADOWS CAST ON THE WALTER CRANE WALLPAPER MAGENTA CAMISOLE GLITTERING AGAINST BLACK SATIN SHEETS HE FEELS THE FULLNESS OF HER BREASTS HER LOTUS YONI HER VOLUPTUOUS HIPS OPHELIA DROWNS IN A SWIRL OF FLOWERS SOIXANTE-NEUF SABLE AGAINST HIS BACK HER TONGUE LIPS AND TEETH CREATING A UNIVERSE OF ECSTASY SHE BEARS DOWN ON HIS MOUTH PINK AND WET AND ENVELOPING A SINGLE BLACK ROSE FALLS THROUGH SPACE COMES TO REST ON MAHOGANY JUICE FROM A RIPE PEACH COVERS HIS FACE WARM WET SILK THEY JOIN IN TANTRIC UNION PERFECT PHYSICAL COMPATIBILITY NOW: AIR: ARKWRIGHT/ PRIAPUS CONVULSES FEELS LOVE FOR THE FIRST TIME ROSE UNKNOWN EMOTIONS ERUPT SPRING CROCUSES OPEN THROUGH SNOWDROPS THE SAP IS RISING ROSE SHUDDERING ORGASM WRENCHING HIM THROUGH THE ORGONE THE TREE OF LIFE THE AXIS MUNDI CERNE ABBAS COCK THROBBING OBELISK CLEOPATRA'S NEEDLE RINGED WITH LIGHTNING PSIONIC ENERGY CRACKLES RUSHES DOWN THE MOLECULAR CORRIDORS OF HIS BRAIN BRITTANIA DIES IN HIS ARMS HE CRIES FALLS NAKED INTO A VULVIC TUNNEL COSMIC YONI ENTRANCE TO LIFE AND DEATH DIZZY AND NAUSEOUS AND ALONE AND ROCKED BY WAVES OF PROBABILITY...

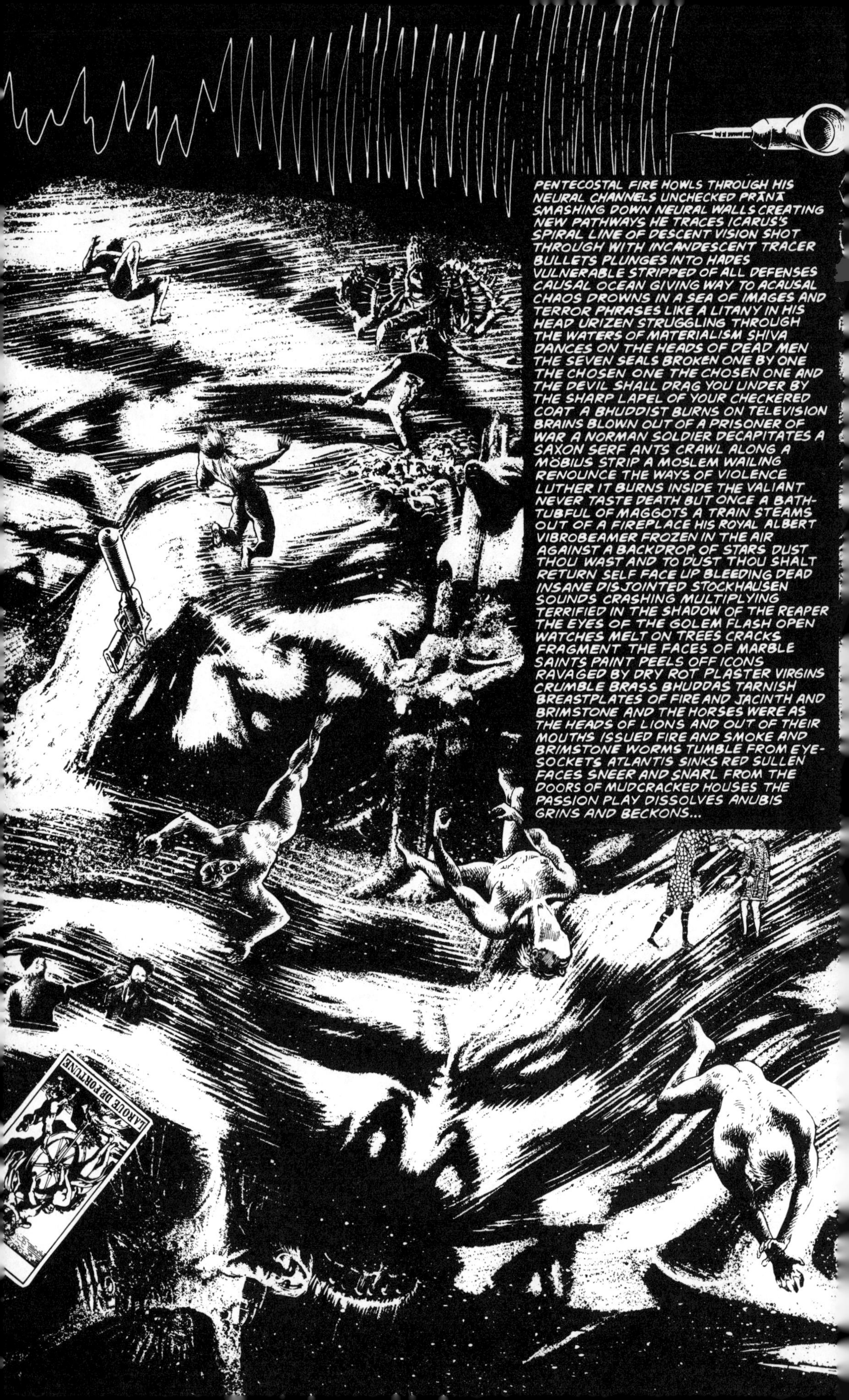
PENTECOSTAL FIRE HOWLS THROUGH HIS NEURAL CHANNELS UNCHECKED PRĀNĀ SMASHING DOWN NEURAL WALLS CREATING NEW PATHWAYS HE TRACES ICARUS'S SPIRAL LINE OF DESCENT VISION SHOT THROUGH WITH INCANDESCENT TRACER BULLETS PLUNGES INTO HADES VULNERABLE STRIPPED OF ALL DEFENSES CAUSAL OCEAN GIVING WAY TO ACAUSAL CHAOS DROWNS IN A SEA OF IMAGES AND TERROR PHRASES LIKE A LITANY IN HIS HEAD URIZEN STRUGGLING THROUGH THE WATERS OF MATERIALISM SHIVA DANCES ON THE HEADS OF DEAD MEN THE SEVEN SEALS BROKEN ONE BY ONE THE CHOSEN ONE THE CHOSEN ONE AND THE DEVIL SHALL DRAG YOU UNDER BY THE SHARP LAPEL OF YOUR CHECKERED COAT A BHUDDIST BURNS ON TELEVISION BRAINS BLOWN OUT OF A PRISONER OF WAR A NORMAN SOLDIER DECAPITATES A SAXON SERF ANTS CRAWL ALONG A MÖBIUS STRIP A MOSLEM WAILING RENOUNCE THE WAYS OF VIOLENCE LUTHER IT BURNS INSIDE THE VALIANT NEVER TASTE DEATH BUT ONCE A BATH-TUBFUL OF MAGGOTS A TRAIN STEAMS OUT OF A FIREPLACE HIS ROYAL ALBERT VIBROBEAMER FROZEN IN THE AIR AGAINST A BACKDROP OF STARS DUST THOU WAST AND TO DUST THOU SHALT RETURN SELF FACE UP BLEEDING DEAD INSANE DISJOINTED STOCKHAUSEN SOUNDS CRASHING MULTIPLYING TERRIFIED IN THE SHADOW OF THE REAPER THE EYES OF THE GOLEM FLASH OPEN WATCHES MELT ON TREES CRACKS FRAGMENT THE FACES OF MARBLE SAINTS PAINT PEELS OFF ICONS RAVAGED BY DRY ROT PLASTER VIRGINS CRUMBLE BRASS BHUDDAS TARNISH BREASTPLATES OF FIRE AND JACINTH AND BRIMSTONE AND THE HORSES WERE AS THE HEADS OF LIONS AND OUT OF THEIR MOUTHS ISSUED FIRE AND SMOKE AND BRIMSTONE WORMS TUMBLE FROM EYE-SOCKETS ATLANTIS SINKS RED SULLEN FACES SNEER AND SNARL FROM THE DOORS OF MUDCRACKED HOUSES THE PASSION PLAY DISSOLVES ANUBIS GRINS AND BECKONS...
LA ROUE DE FORTUNE

DEATH'S DARK VALE
NO ULTIMATE TRUTH NO MORAL ABSOLUTES
MYSTIC WHITE NOISE THE CURRENT HITS THE SAHASRANA CHAKRA
LA ROUE DE FORTUNE
BREAKDOWN OF EGO ILLUSION
DEATH.
XIII
LA MORT

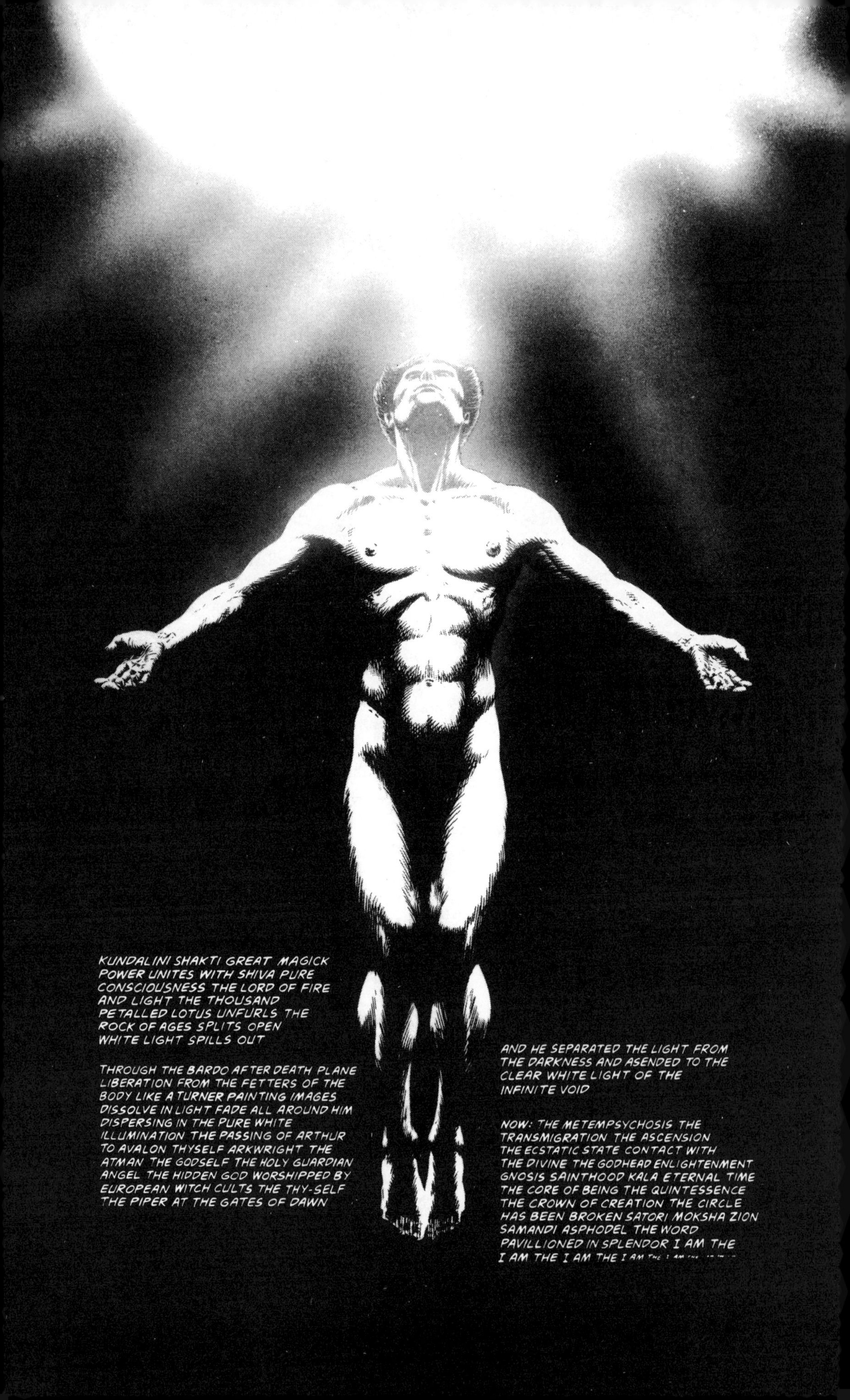
KUNDALINI SHAKTI GREAT MAGICK POWER UNITES WITH SHIVA PURE CONSCIOUSNESS THE LORD OF FIRE AND LIGHT THE THOUSAND PETALLED LOTUS UNFURLS THE ROCK OF AGES SPLITS OPEN WHITE LIGHT SPILLS OUT
THROUGH THE BARDO AFTER DEATH PLANE LIBERATION FROM THE FETTERS OF THE BODY LIKE A TURNER PAINTING IMAGES DISSOLVE IN LIGHT FADE ALL AROUND HIM DISPERSING IN THE PURE WHITE ILLUMINATION THE PASSING OF ARTHUR TO AVALON THYSELF ARKWRIGHT THE ATMAN THE GODSELF THE HOLY GUARDIAN ANGEL THE HIDDEN GOD WORSHIPPED BY EUROPEAN WITCH CULTS THE THY-SELF THE PIPER AT THE GATES OF DAWN
AND HE SEPARATED THE LIGHT FROM THE DARKNESS AND ASENDED TO THE CLEAR WHITE LIGHT OF THE INFINITE VOID
NOW: THE METEMPSYCHOSIS THE TRANSMIGRATION THE ASCENSION THE ECSTATIC STATE CONTACT WITH THE DIVINE THE GODHEAD ENLIGHTENMENT GNOSIS SAINTHOOD KALA ETERNAL TIME THE CORE OF BEING THE QUINTESSENCE THE CROWN OF CREATION THE CIRCLE HAS BEEN BROKEN SATORI MOKSHA ZION SAMANDI ASPHODEL THE WORD PAVILLIONED IN SPLENDOR I AM THE I AM THE I AM THE I AM

A TERRIBLE BEAUTY

RADIANT WHITE FIRE

PERFECT

PRISTINE

PURE

THE CELESTIAL ETHER

THE ASTRAL LIGHT

AKASHA

COSMIC AXIS CENTRAL POINT
OF TIME AND SPACE

UNION OF THE
INDIVIDUAL
AND THE INFINITE

DHARMA-KĀYA
NIRVANIC CONSCIOUSNESS

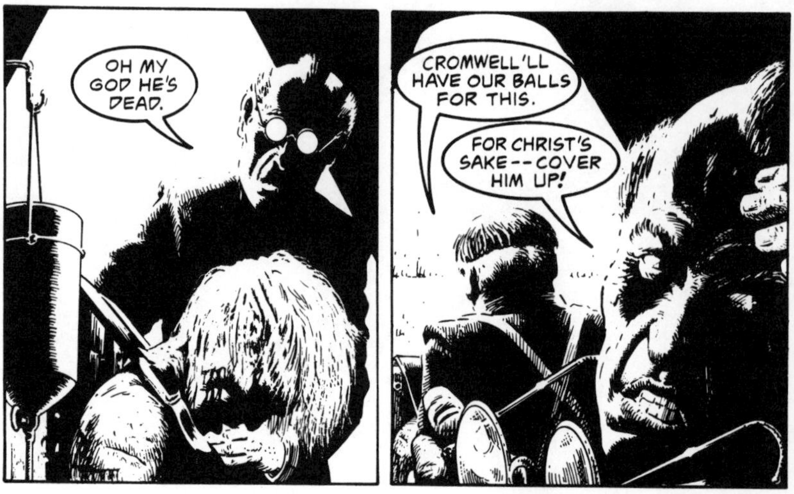
OH MY GOD HE'S DEAD.
CROMWELL'LL HAVE OUR BALLS FOR THIS.
FOR CHRIST'S SAKE--COVER HIM UP!
WHAT ARE WE GOING TO DO?
SIT DOWN. WE NEED TIME TO THINK.

PARA 10.97.32 LONDON. RAIN OF FROGS FOR TWO HOURS.
PARA 04.80.11 SOUTH AMERICA. EMPEROR TEOTIHUACAN ASSASSINATED.
PARA 20.14.78 MEXICO. EMPEROR WILHELM X ASSASSINATED IN BLOODY COUP.
PARA 02.17.50 MONGOLIA. KHAN THE MERCIFUL EMPEROR OF THE WORLD ASSASSINATED.
PARA 01.58.57 ZURICH. DAVID BOWIE ASSASSINATED IN TELEVISED CONCERT.
PARA 20.90.72 JAPAN. HUGE EARTHQUAKE LEVELS TOKYO.

THURS 12 OCT 08.12 TOXTETH, LIVERPOOL

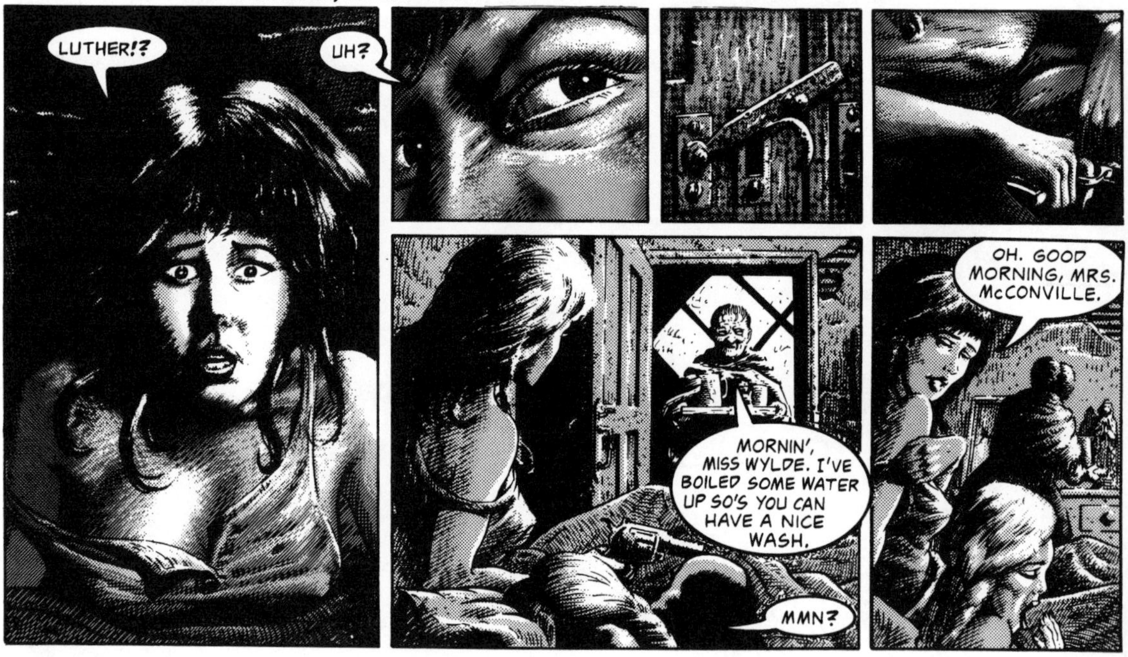
LUTHER!?
UH?
MORNIN', MISS WYLDE. I'VE BOILED SOME WATER UP SO'S YOU CAN HAVE A NICE WASH.
MMN?
OH. GOOD MORNING, MRS. McCONVILLE.

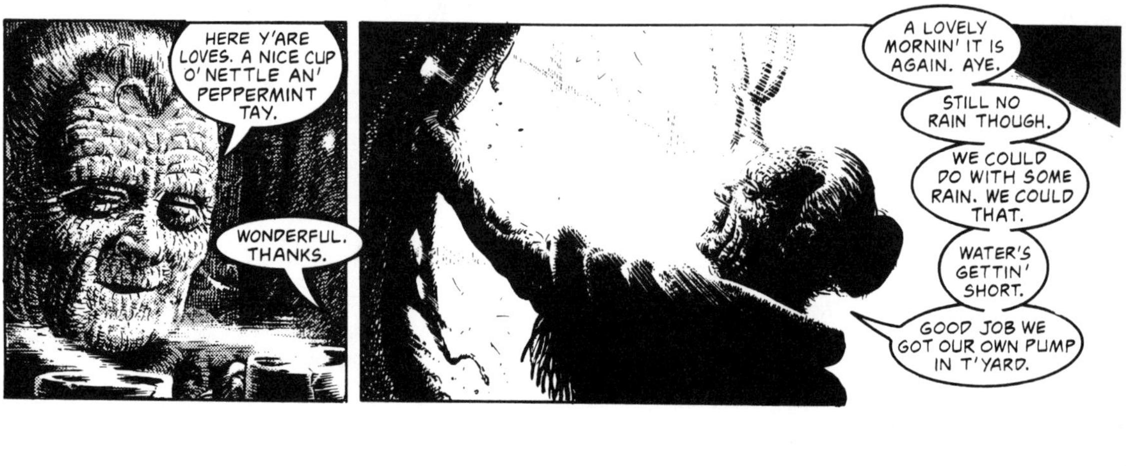
HERE Y'ARE LOVES. A NICE CUP O' NETTLE AN' PEPPERMINT TAY.
WONDERFUL. THANKS.
A LOVELY MORNIN' IT IS AGAIN. AYE.
STILL NO RAIN THOUGH.
WE COULD DO WITH SOME RAIN. WE COULD THAT.
WATER'S GETTIN' SHORT.
GOOD JOB WE GOT OUR OWN PUMP IN T'YARD.

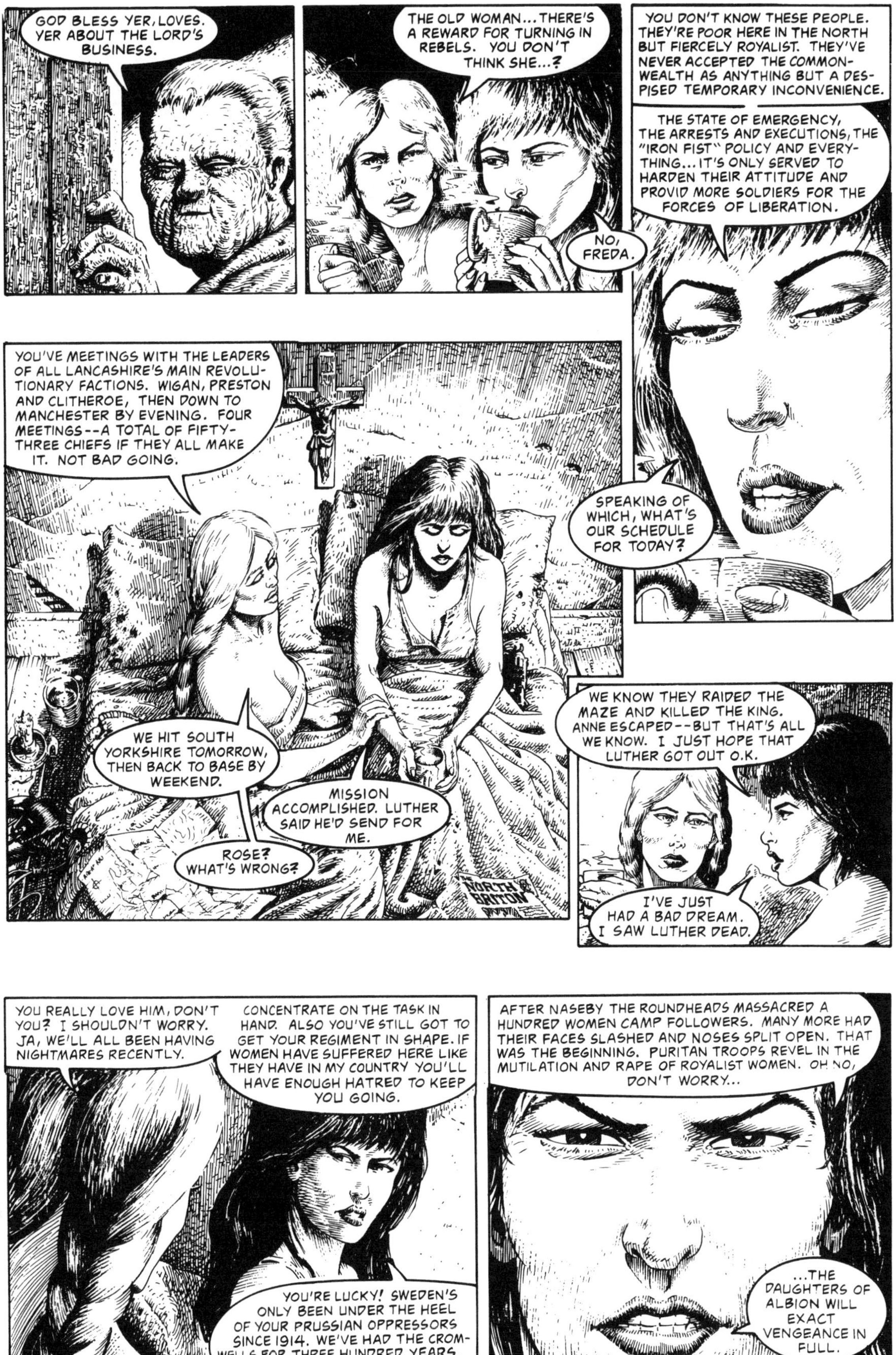
GOD BLESS YER, LOVES. YER ABOUT THE LORD'S BUSINESS.
THE OLD WOMAN... THERE'S A REWARD FOR TURNING IN REBELS. YOU DON'T THINK SHE...?
NO, FREDA.
YOU DON'T KNOW THESE PEOPLE. THEY'RE POOR HERE IN THE NORTH BUT FIERCELY ROYALIST. THEY'VE NEVER ACCEPTED THE COMMONWEALTH AS ANYTHING BUT A DESPISED TEMPORARY INCONVENIENCE.
THE STATE OF EMERGENCY, THE ARRESTS AND EXECUTIONS, THE "IRON FIST" POLICY AND EVERYTHING... IT'S ONLY SERVED TO HARDEN THEIR ATTITUDE AND PROVID MORE SOLDIERS FOR THE FORCES OF LIBERATION.
SPEAKING OF WHICH, WHAT'S OUR SCHEDULE FOR TODAY?
YOU'VE MEETINGS WITH THE LEADERS OF ALL LANCASHIRE'S MAIN REVOLUTIONARY FACTIONS. WIGAN, PRESTON AND CLITHEROE, THEN DOWN TO MANCHESTER BY EVENING. FOUR MEETINGS--A TOTAL OF FIFTY-THREE CHIEFS IF THEY ALL MAKE IT. NOT BAD GOING.
WE HIT SOUTH YORKSHIRE TOMORROW, THEN BACK TO BASE BY WEEKEND.
MISSION ACCOMPLISHED. LUTHER SAID HE'D SEND FOR ME.
ROSE? WHAT'S WRONG?
NORTH BRITON
I'VE JUST HAD A BAD DREAM. I SAW LUTHER DEAD.
WE KNOW THEY RAIDED THE MAZE AND KILLED THE KING. ANNE ESCAPED--BUT THAT'S ALL WE KNOW. I JUST HOPE THAT LUTHER GOT OUT O.K.
YOU REALLY LOVE HIM, DON'T YOU? I SHOULDN'T WORRY. JA, WE'LL ALL BEEN HAVING NIGHTMARES RECENTLY.
CONCENTRATE ON THE TASK IN HAND. ALSO YOU'VE STILL GOT TO GET YOUR REGIMENT IN SHAPE. IF WOMEN HAVE SUFFERED HERE LIKE THEY HAVE IN MY COUNTRY YOU'LL HAVE ENOUGH HATRED TO KEEP YOU GOING.
YOU'RE LUCKY! SWEDEN'S ONLY BEEN UNDER THE HEEL OF YOUR PRUSSIAN OPPRESSORS SINCE 1914. WE'VE HAD THE CROMWELLS FOR THREE HUNDRED YEARS.
AFTER NASEBY THE ROUNDHEADS MASSACRED A HUNDRED WOMEN CAMP FOLLOWERS. MANY MORE HAD THEIR FACES SLASHED AND NOSES SPLIT OPEN. THAT WAS THE BEGINNING. PURITAN TROOPS REVEL IN THE MUTILATION AND RAPE OF ROYALIST WOMEN. OH NO, DON'T WORRY...
...THE DAUGHTERS OF ALBION WILL EXACT VENGEANCE IN FULL.

FRI 13 OCT 22.00 GOVERNOR'S PALACE, DAM SQUARE, AMSTERDAM

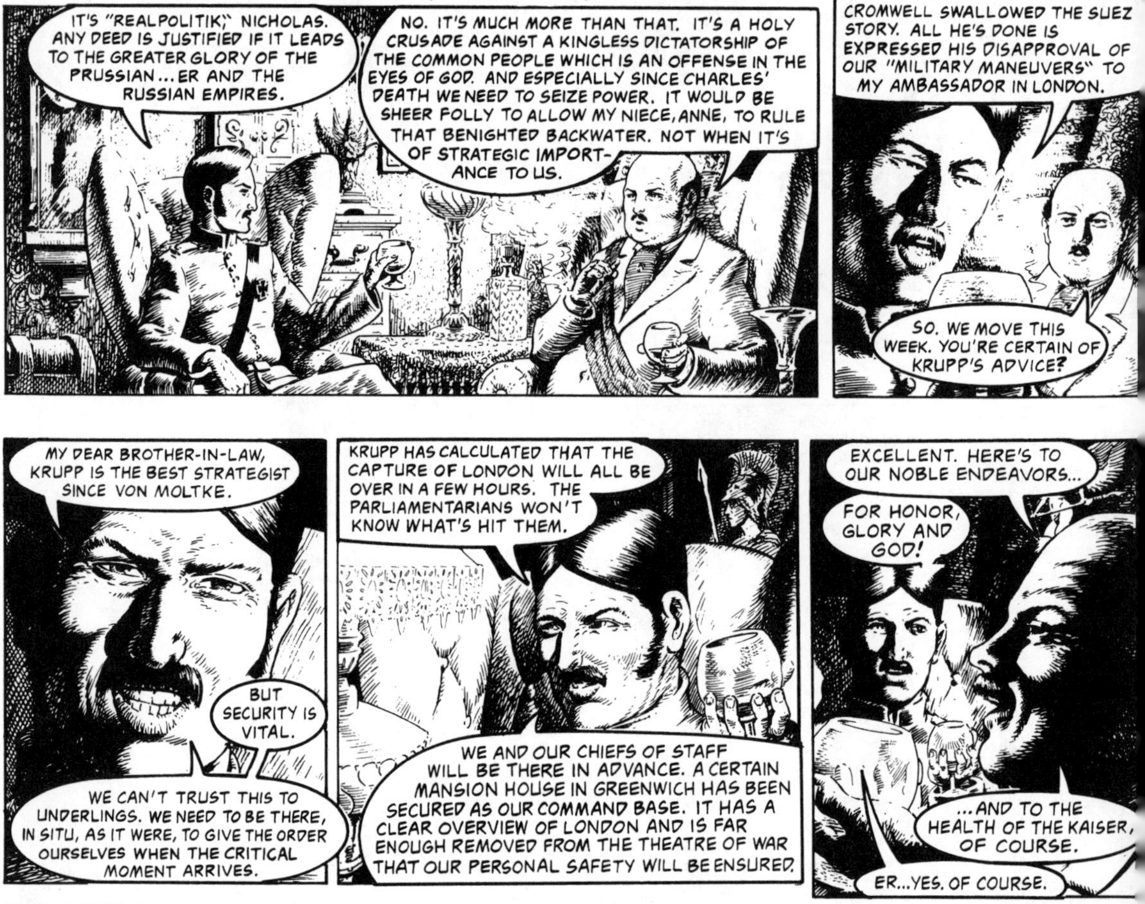
IT'S "REALPOLITIK," NICHOLAS. ANY DEED IS JUSTIFIED IF IT LEADS TO THE GREATER GLORY OF THE PRUSSIAN... ER AND THE RUSSIAN EMPIRES.
NO. IT'S MUCH MORE THAN THAT. IT'S A HOLY CRUSADE AGAINST A KINGLESS DICTATORSHIP OF THE COMMON PEOPLE WHICH IS AN OFFENSE IN THE EYES OF GOD. AND ESPECIALLY SINCE CHARLES' DEATH WE NEED TO SEIZE POWER. IT WOULD BE SHEER FOLLY TO ALLOW MY NIECE, ANNE, TO RULE THAT BENIGHTED BACKWATER. NOT WHEN IT'S OF STRATEGIC IMPORTANCE TO US.
CROMWELL SWALLOWED THE SUEZ STORY. ALL HE'S DONE IS EXPRESSED HIS DISAPPROVAL OF OUR "MILITARY MANEUVERS" TO MY AMBASSADOR IN LONDON.
SO. WE MOVE THIS WEEK. YOU'RE CERTAIN OF KRUPP'S ADVICE?
MY DEAR BROTHER-IN-LAW, KRUPP IS THE BEST STRATEGIST SINCE VON MOLTKE.
BUT SECURITY IS VITAL.
WE CAN'T TRUST THIS TO UNDERLINGS. WE NEED TO BE THERE, IN SITU, AS IT WERE, TO GIVE THE ORDER OURSELVES WHEN THE CRITICAL MOMENT ARRIVES.
KRUPP HAS CALCULATED THAT THE CAPTURE OF LONDON WILL ALL BE OVER IN A FEW HOURS. THE PARLIAMENTARIANS WON'T KNOW WHAT'S HIT THEM.
WE AND OUR CHIEFS OF STAFF WILL BE THERE IN ADVANCE. A CERTAIN MANSION HOUSE IN GREENWICH HAS BEEN SECURED AS OUR COMMAND BASE. IT HAS A CLEAR OVERVIEW OF LONDON AND IS FAR ENOUGH REMOVED FROM THE THEATRE OF WAR THAT OUR PERSONAL SAFETY WILL BE ENSURED.
EXCELLENT. HERE'S TO OUR NOBLE ENDEAVORS...
FOR HONOR, GLORY AND GOD!
...AND TO THE HEALTH OF THE KAISER, OF COURSE.
ER...YES. OF COURSE.

FRI 13 OCT 22.58 ILLICIT BAR, BLACKHORSE TEA ROOMS, PRESTON

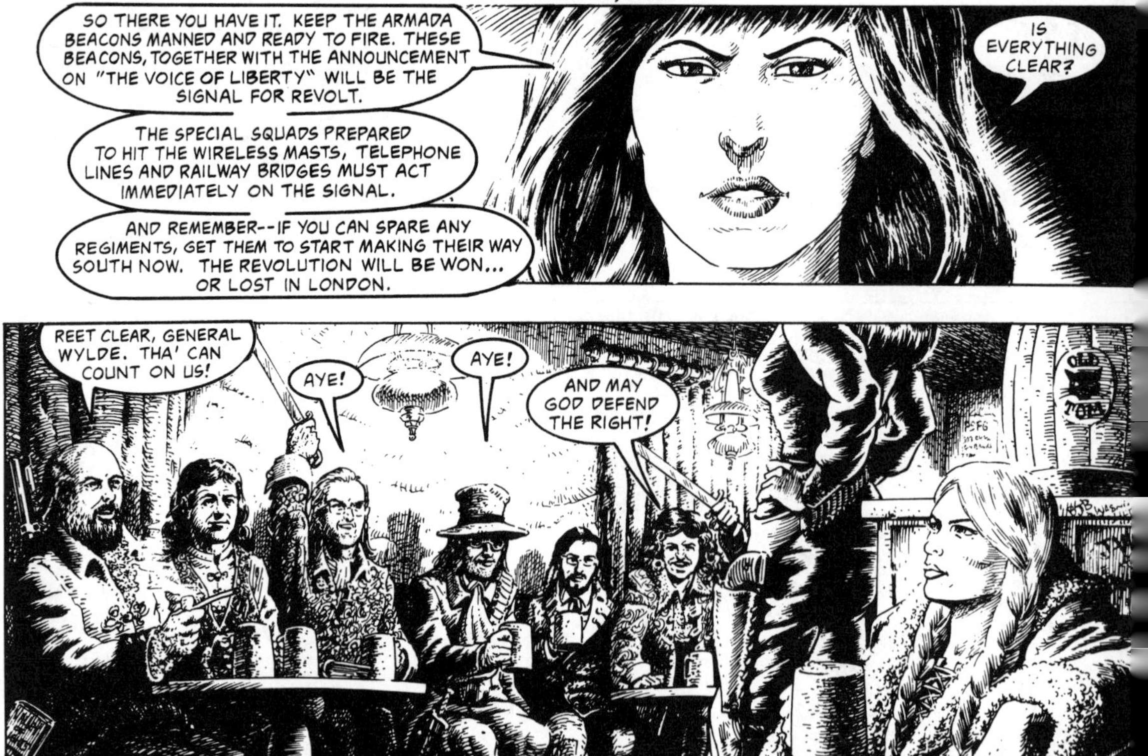
SO THERE YOU HAVE IT. KEEP THE ARMADA BEACONS MANNED AND READY TO FIRE. THESE BEACONS, TOGETHER WITH THE ANNOUNCEMENT ON "THE VOICE OF LIBERTY" WILL BE THE SIGNAL FOR REVOLT.
THE SPECIAL SQUADS PREPARED TO HIT THE WIRELESS MASTS, TELEPHONE LINES AND RAILWAY BRIDGES MUST ACT IMMEDIATELY ON THE SIGNAL.
AND REMEMBER--IF YOU CAN SPARE ANY REGIMENTS, GET THEM TO START MAKING THEIR WAY SOUTH NOW. THE REVOLUTION WILL BE WON... OR LOST IN LONDON.
IS EVERYTHING CLEAR?
REET CLEAR, GENERAL WYLDE. THA' CAN COUNT ON US!
AYE!
AYE!
AND MAY GOD DEFEND THE RIGHT!
OLD TOM

Now we must ask ourselves what a different being
ns. If we consider all the material we can find
t refers to this question, we find an assertion
t in becoming different beings, people aquire
y new qualities and powers which they do not
sess now. This is a common assertion which we
d in all kinds of systems admitting the idea of
chological or inner growth."

P.D. Ouspensky
The Psychology of Humanity's Possible Evolution"

The audio-visual-tactile-chemical range of the
ro-somatic circut controlling, integrating and
anising neuro-electric signals, manipulating the
ro-electricity of the brain, unencumbered by the
limitations of somatic or larval-survival
rints...an Alien Intellegence."

Dr. T. Leary

Tell of his might, O sing of his grace,
ose robe is the light, whose canopy space;
s chariots of wrath the deep thunder-clouds form,
dark is his path on the wings of the storm."

Robt. Grant 1779-1838

The Magician, The Magus, The Juggler: The shape made by his body and arm resembles the first Hebrew letter, Aleph. The card's number is one. The Magus is the child growing to adulthood. The figure one resembles an erect phallus and the horizontal figure 8, the leminiscate, represents the testes and stands for creative power; "In the beginning God created the heavens and the earth"; and he points with one hand to the sky and with the other to the ground, demonstrating the magical principle of "as above, so below." Positive and negative, spirit and matter, good and evil. Humanity made in the image of God potentially is God; God is humanity raised to its highest power.

The Magus' hand is raised to show the transmission from on high of the vital energy of the Godhead--the Divine White Brilliance of Kether. The leminiscate is the mathematical symbol for infinity and an emblem of eternal life. Eight in numerology stands for new life, a new beginning. Baptismal fonts are often octagonal and in Christian symbolism, 8 is the number of resurrection. This is echoed in the magician's belt, a snake devouring its own tail; an old gnostic symbol of ouroboros.

The card is linked to Mercury, Hermes and Thoth and the hermetic alchemical system of occultism in which the adept attempts to raise himself to the highest power and so become God. The magician who, according to Lévi, is "invested with a species of relative omnipotence and can operate in a manner which transcends the normal possibility of Man."

The Egyptian Thoth, the Ape, stood for intelligence and magical power. The ape has an evil connection for in Christian imagery it is linked to Satan who is "the ape of God." It, therefore, "unites the divine and diabolic," in Papus' phrase, the ape is to human as human is to God. It is to "below" of which man is the "above."

Mercury in alchemical symbolism stood for the spirit of vital energy of the divine concealed in matter. It had a double nature, combining opposites. Because the juggler unites the divine and diabolic, there are sinister possibilities in the card. The magician can be a black magician. Evil, as well as good, has its roots in the divine.

Dr. S. Heywood
"The Occult Tarot," 1914

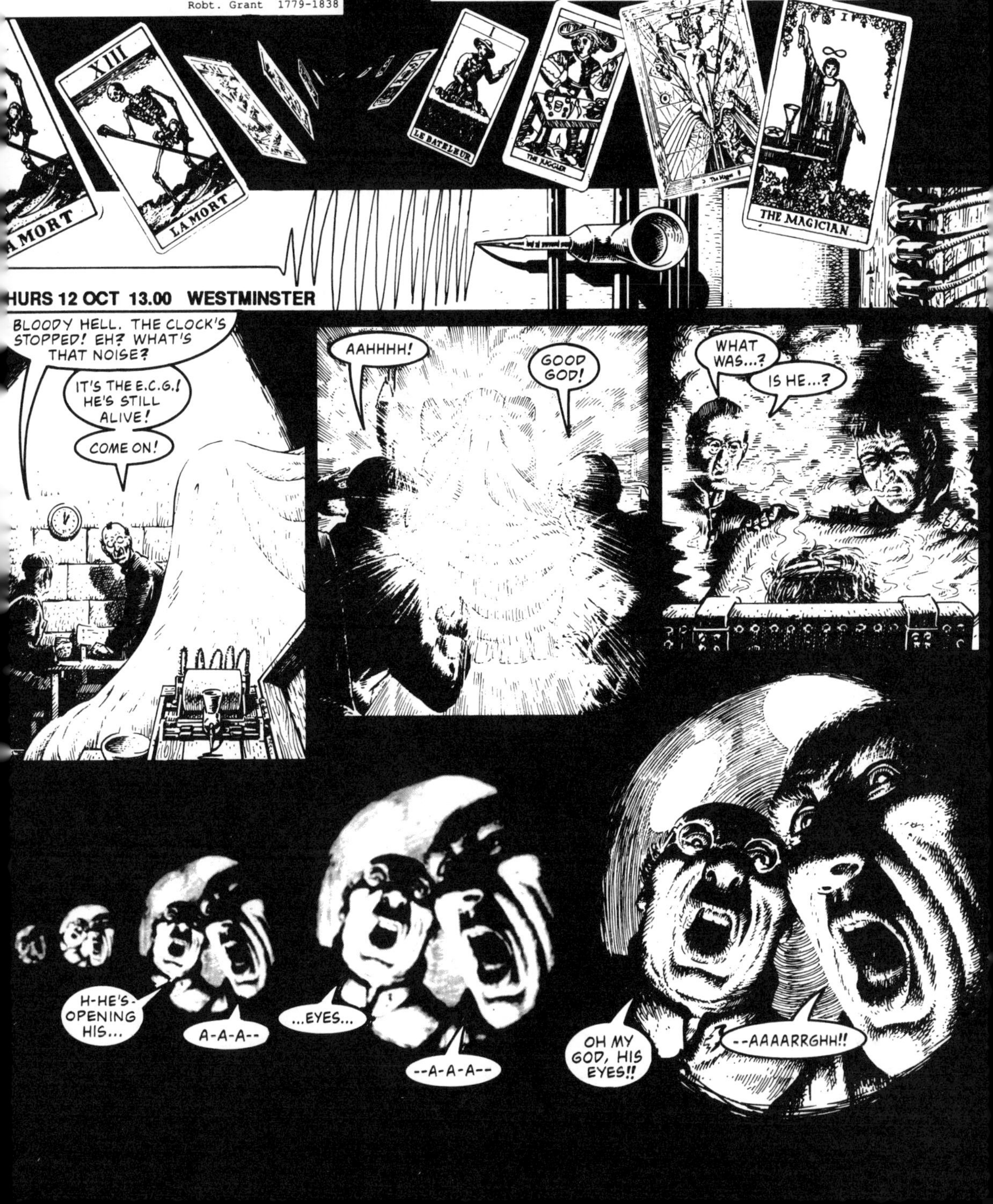

XIII
LA MORT
LA MORT
LE BATELEUR
THE JUGGLER
THE MAGICIAN.
HURS 12 OCT 13.00 WESTMINSTER
BLOODY HELL. THE CLOCK'S STOPPED! EH? WHAT'S THAT NOISE?
IT'S THE E.C.G.! HE'S STILL ALIVE!
COME ON!
AAHHHH!
GOOD GOD!
WHAT WAS...?
IS HE...?
H-HE'S-OPENING HIS...
A-A-A--
...EYES...
--A-A-A--
OH MY GOD, HIS EYES!!
--AAAARRGHH!!

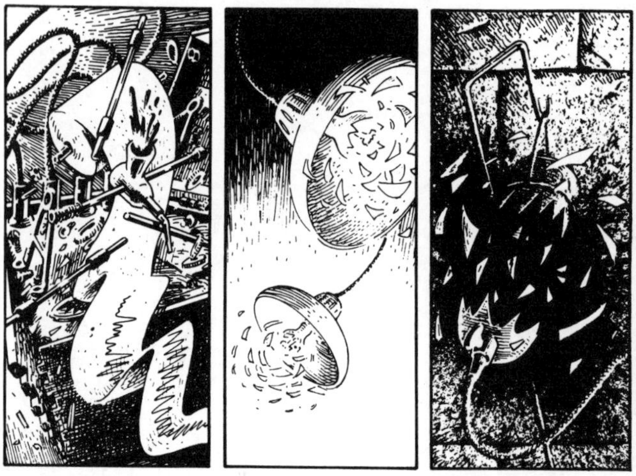

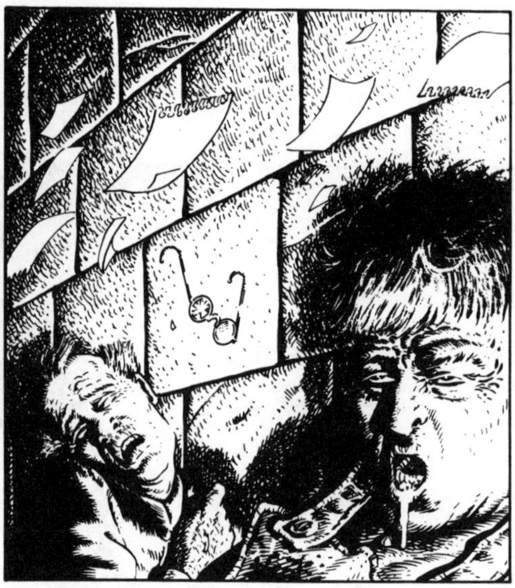

A HOWL LIKE THE RUSHING OF A MIGHTY WIND: THE AIR IS ELECTRIFIED BY WILD PSIONICS: HIS HALO/BIOSPHERE/AURA IS BLINDING: NOW: THE FLOODGATES OPEN: UNBLINKERED TOTAL AWARENESS: ABSOLUTE PERCEPTION: ARWRIGHT IS BOMBARDED BY SENSORY INPUT UNFILTERED BY PRECONDITIONED MENTAL SCREENS.

THE LEATHER RESTRAINING STRAPS ROT AND FALL AWAY...

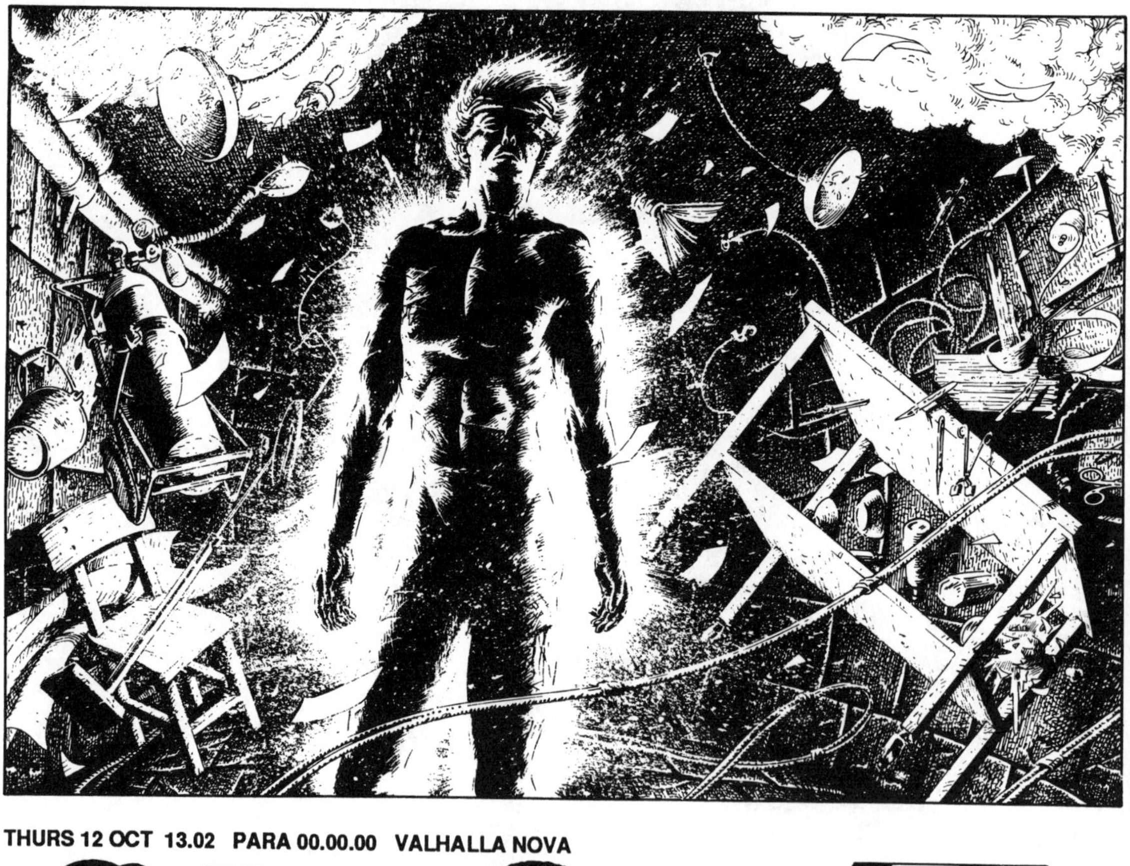

THURS 12 OCT 13.02 PARA 00.00.00 VALHALLA NOVA

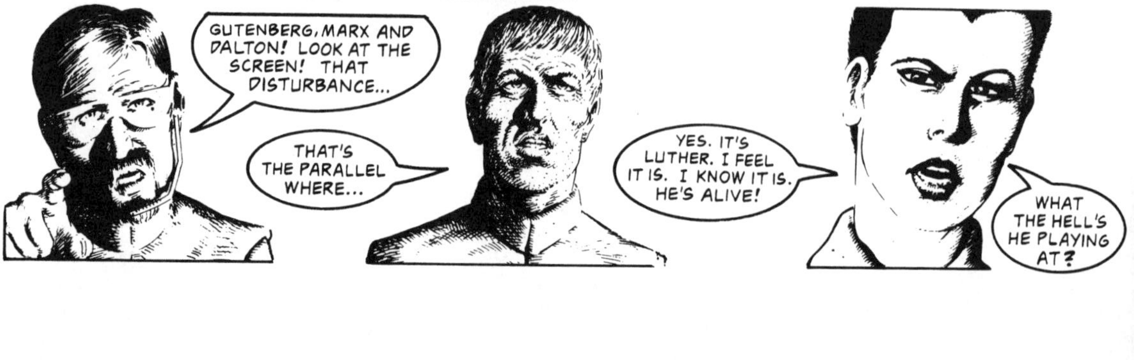
GUTENBERG, MARX AND DALTON! LOOK AT THE SCREEN! THAT DISTURBANCE...
THAT'S THE PARALLEL WHERE...
YES. IT'S LUTHER. I FEEL IT IS. I KNOW IT IS. HE'S ALIVE!
WHAT THE HELL'S HE PLAYING AT?

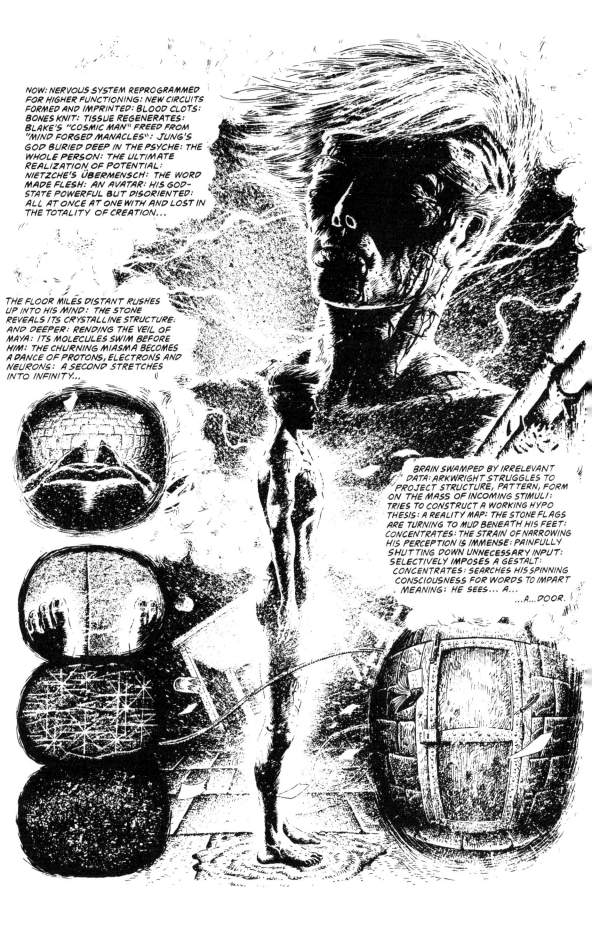

NOW: NERVOUS SYSTEM REPROGRAMMED FOR HIGHER FUNCTIONING: NEW CIRCUITS FORMED AND IMPRINTED: BLOOD CLOTS: BONES KNIT: TISSUE REGENERATES: BLAKE'S "COSMIC MAN" FREED FROM "MIND FORGED MANACLES": JUNG'S GOD BURIED DEEP IN THE PSYCHE: THE WHOLE PERSON: THE ULTIMATE REALIZATION OF POTENTIAL: NIETZCHE'S ÜBERMENSCH: THE WORD MADE FLESH: AN AVATAR: HIS GOD-STATE POWERFUL BUT DISORIENTED: ALL AT ONCE AT ONE WITH AND LOST IN THE TOTALITY OF CREATION...

THE FLOOR MILES DISTANT RUSHES UP INTO HIS MIND: THE STONE REVEALS ITS CRYSTALLINE STRUCTURE: AND DEEPER: RENDING THE VEIL OF MAYA: ITS MOLECULES SWIM BEFORE HIM: THE CHURNING MIASMA BECOMES A DANCE OF PROTONS, ELECTRONS AND NEURONS: A SECOND STRETCHES INTO INFINITY...

BRAIN SWAMPED BY IRRELEVANT DATA: ARKWRIGHT STRUGGLES TO PROJECT STRUCTURE, PATTERN, FORM ON THE MASS OF INCOMING STIMULI: TRIES TO CONSTRUCT A WORKING HYPO THESIS: A REALITY MAP: THE STONE FLAGS ARE TURNING TO MUD BENEATH HIS FEET: CONCENTRATES: THE STRAIN OF NARROWING HIS PERCEPTION IS IMMENSE: PAINFULLY SHUTTING DOWN UNNECESSARY INPUT: SELECTIVELY IMPOSES A GESTALT: CONCENTRATES: SEARCHES HIS SPINNING CONSCIOUSNESS FOR WORDS TO IMPART MEANING: HE SEES... A...

...A...DOOR.

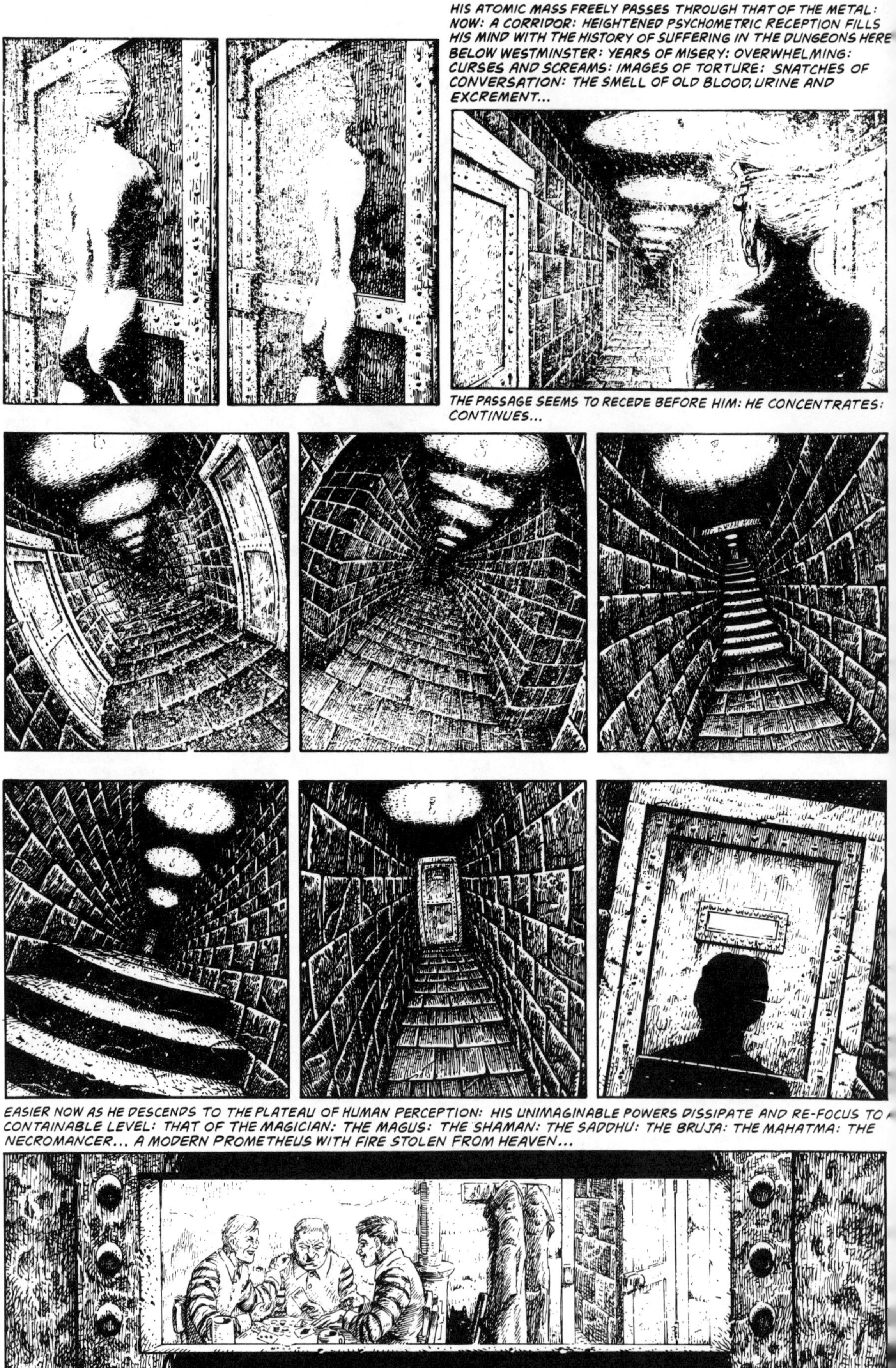
HIS ATOMIC MASS FREELY PASSES THROUGH THAT OF THE METAL: NOW: A CORRIDOR: HEIGHTENED PSYCHOMETRIC RECEPTION FILLS HIS MIND WITH THE HISTORY OF SUFFERING IN THE DUNGEONS HERE BELOW WESTMINSTER: YEARS OF MISERY: OVERWHELMING: CURSES AND SCREAMS: IMAGES OF TORTURE: SNATCHES OF CONVERSATION: THE SMELL OF OLD BLOOD, URINE AND EXCREMENT...
THE PASSAGE SEEMS TO RECEDE BEFORE HIM: HE CONCENTRATES: CONTINUES...
EASIER NOW AS HE DESCENDS TO THE PLATEAU OF HUMAN PERCEPTION: HIS UNIMAGINABLE POWERS DISSIPATE AND RE-FOCUS TO CONTAINABLE LEVEL: THAT OF THE MAGICIAN: THE MAGUS: THE SHAMAN: THE SADDHU: THE BRUJA: THE MAHATMA: THE NECROMANCER... A MODERN PROMETHEUS WITH FIRE STOLEN FROM HEAVEN...

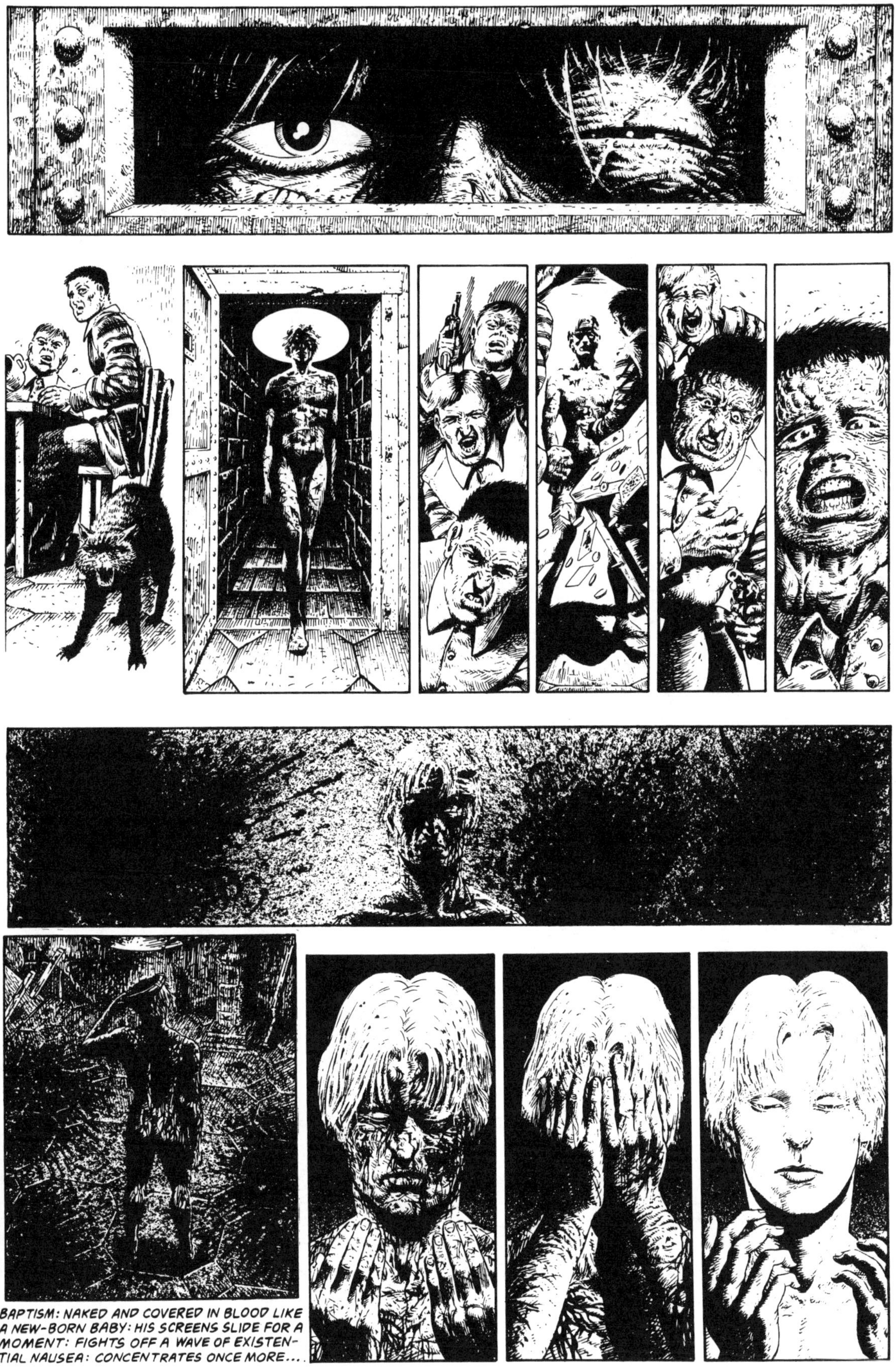
BAPTISM: NAKED AND COVERED IN BLOOD LIKE A NEW-BORN BABY: HIS SCREENS SLIDE FOR A MOMENT: FIGHTS OFF A WAVE OF EXISTENTIAL NAUSEA: CONCENTRATES ONCE MORE....

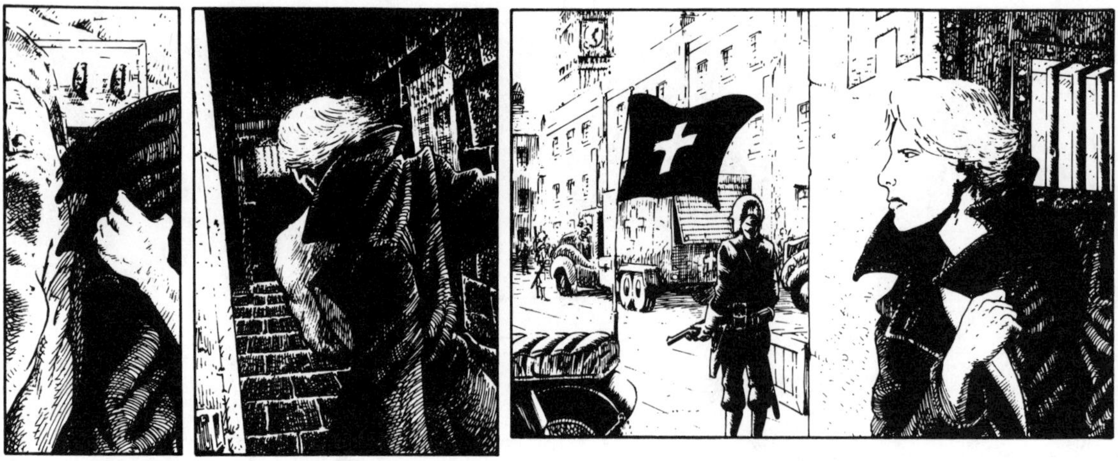

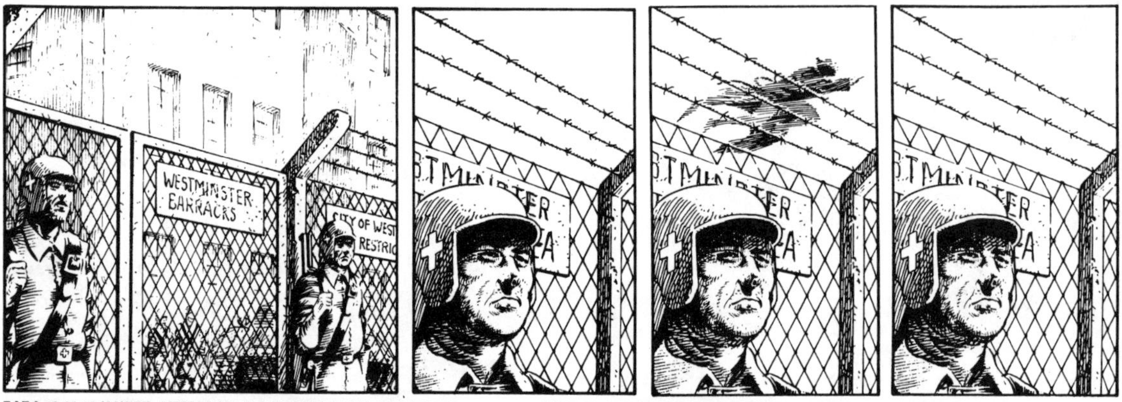
WESTMINSTER BARRACKS

PARA 10.30.62 HAWAII. AMERICAN 6th FLEET SUNK BY TIDAL WAVES.
PARA 02.43.42 MUNICH. ACID RAIN DOWNPOUR KILLS THOUSANDS.
PARA 00.81.55 GREENWICH. VIOLENT SUNSPOT ACTIVITY MONITORED.
PARA 02.18.58 NORMANDY CHANNEL. TANKER CONTAINING TOXIC WASTE STRUCK BY LIGHTNING, SPILLING CARGO.
PARA 01.58.03 EUROPE. BLACK DEATH SWEEPING OVER THE CONTINENT.
PARA 02.81.95 NOTTINGHAM. GOVERNOR K'ANG HSI DECLARES INDEPENDENCE FROM CHINA.

THURS 12 OCT 17.05 ALDERSHOT, HAMPSHIRE

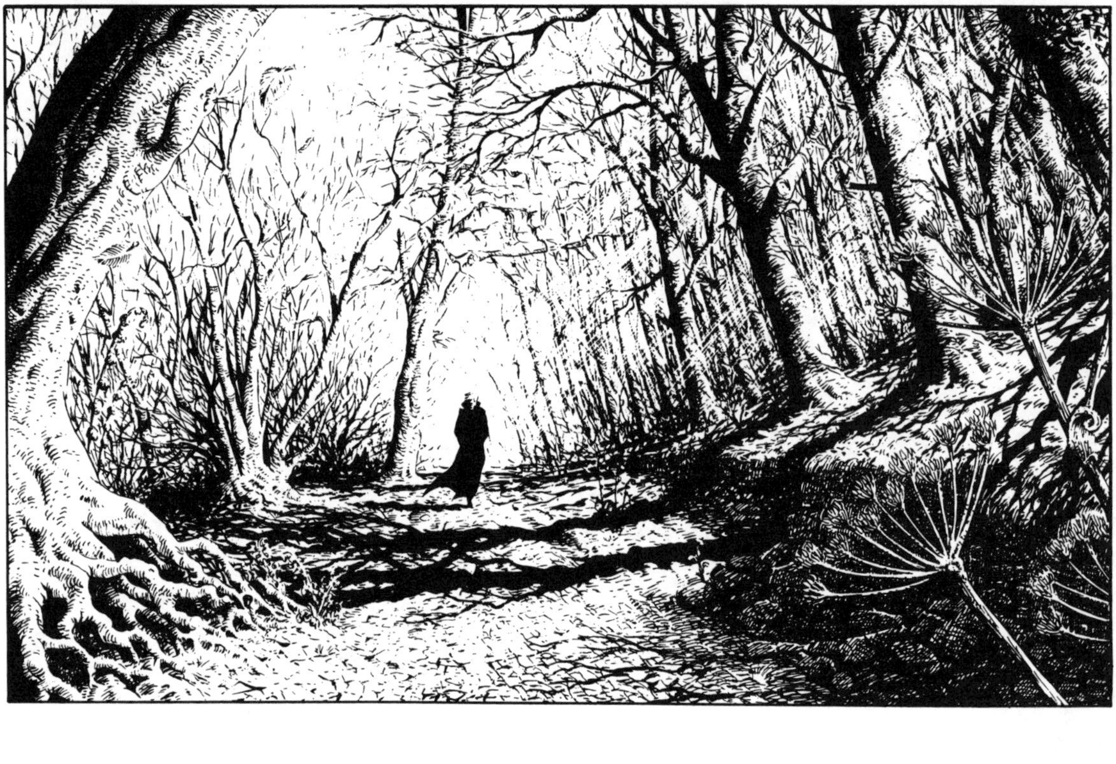

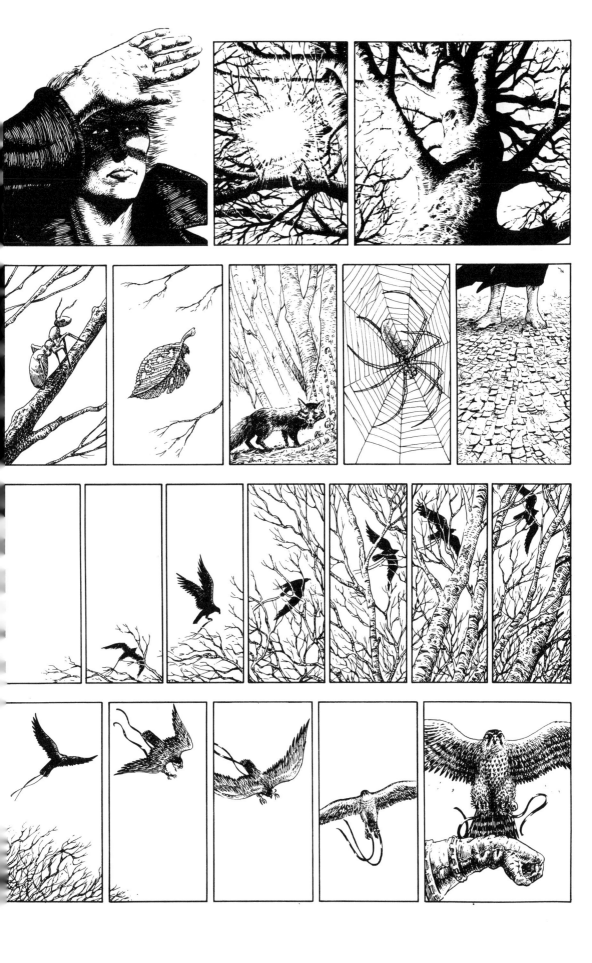

MY HOLY WARRIOR RETURNS.

I KNEW YOU WERE ALIVE. I COULD FEEL YOU APPROACH.

I'VE BEEN WAITING FOR YOU.

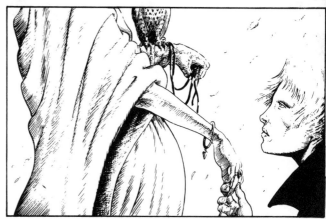

PSYCHOMETRY: ANNE: THE PRINCESS ROYALE GROWING UP IN IRELAND AWAY FROM CIVIL WAR TORN ENGLAND: SIX YEARS OLD: HER FATHER JAMES VII DIED OF T.B.: SHE CRIED: CHARLES LAUGHED: SEVEN YEARS OLD: BITTER: CHARLES FAVORED BEFORE HER: SPOILT: GROOMED FOR KINGSHIP: TEN YEARS: CONTINUALLY MOLESTED BY THE PRIEST IN THE CONFESSIONAL: A TEST SENT BY GOD: TWELVE: SHOUTING HAIL MARYS WHILST GALLOPING HER PONY UNTIL SHE WAS SORE BETWEEN HER LEGS: SIXTEEN: AS MARY MAGDALEN IN HER SEXUAL FANTASIES ABOUT JESUS: TWENTY: MARRIED AND WIDOWED WITHIN A YEAR: THE MISCARRIAGE: TWENTY EIGHT: LAST WINTER: MAKING LOVE WITH ARKWRIGHT: THE MANOR HOUSE ON THE ISLE OF MAN: LAST SPRING: THE MAZE: HER DESIRE FOR HIM: HER LUST: LAST WEEK: CHARLES' DEATH: FLEEING THE RAID THROUGH THE OLD TUNNELS...

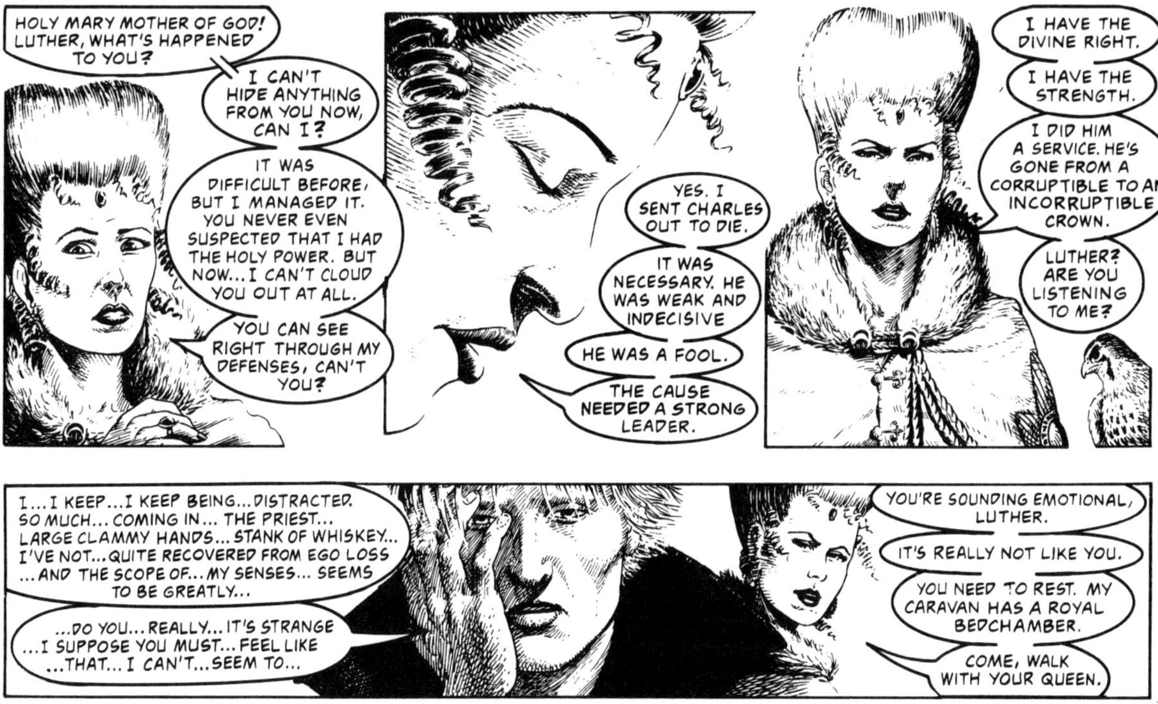
HOLY MARY MOTHER OF GOD! LUTHER, WHAT'S HAPPENED TO YOU?
I CAN'T HIDE ANYTHING FROM YOU NOW, CAN I?
IT WAS DIFFICULT BEFORE, BUT I MANAGED IT. YOU NEVER EVEN SUSPECTED THAT I HAD THE HOLY POWER. BUT NOW... I CAN'T CLOUD YOU OUT AT ALL.
YOU CAN SEE RIGHT THROUGH MY DEFENSES, CAN'T YOU?
YES. I SENT CHARLES OUT TO DIE.
IT WAS NECESSARY. HE WAS WEAK AND INDECISIVE
HE WAS A FOOL.
THE CAUSE NEEDED A STRONG LEADER.
I HAVE THE DIVINE RIGHT.
I HAVE THE STRENGTH.
I DID HIM A SERVICE. HE'S GONE FROM A CORRUPTIBLE TO AN INCORRUPTIBLE CROWN.
LUTHER? ARE YOU LISTENING TO ME?
I... I KEEP... I KEEP BEING... DISTRACTED. SO MUCH... COMING IN... THE PRIEST... LARGE CLAMMY HANDS... STANK OF WHISKEY... I'VE NOT... QUITE RECOVERED FROM EGO LOSS ...AND THE SCOPE OF... MY SENSES... SEEMS TO BE GREATLY...
...DO YOU... REALLY... IT'S STRANGE ...I SUPPOSE YOU MUST... FEEL LIKE ...THAT... I CAN'T... SEEM TO...
YOU'RE SOUNDING EMOTIONAL, LUTHER.
IT'S REALLY NOT LIKE YOU.
YOU NEED TO REST. MY CARAVAN HAS A ROYAL BEDCHAMBER.
COME, WALK WITH YOUR QUEEN.

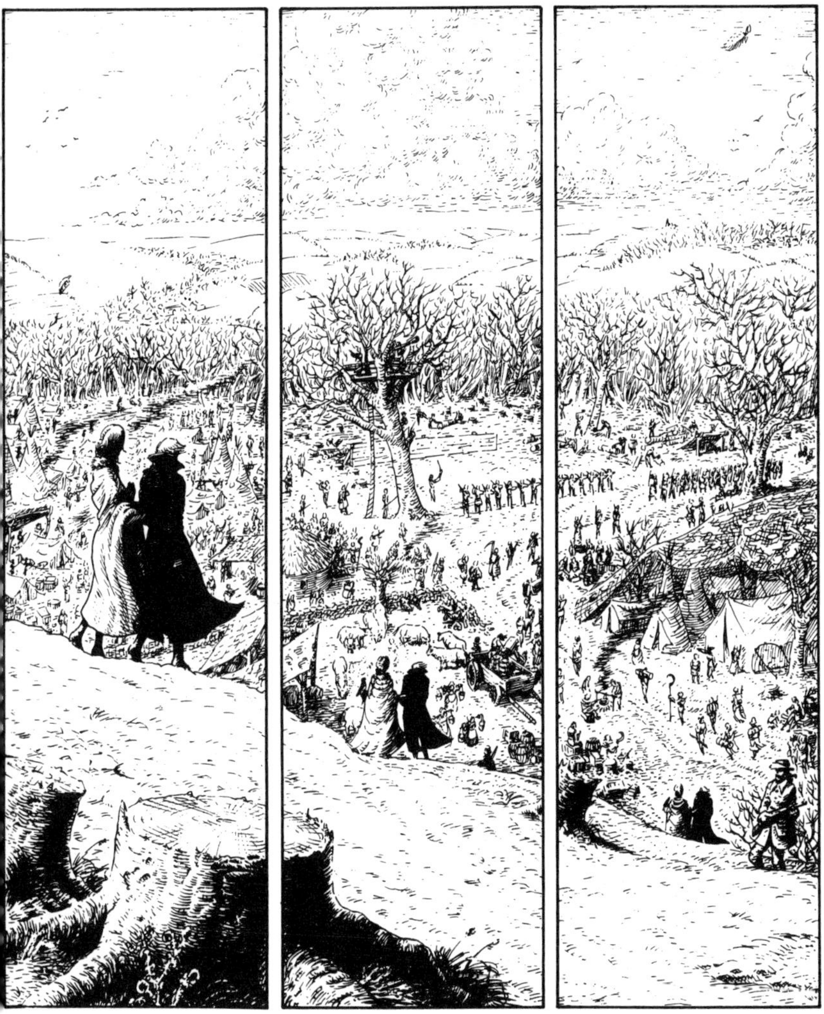

If you are reading this despatch it is a minor miracle of communications. It has had to be smuggled out of England, via the royalist underground network, and onto a ship bound for New Amsterdam. Right now, dear readers, I'll have to assume that it has reached you intact.

As in my last report, I'm still here in the Royalist encampment at Aldershot, Hampshire, observing the preparations for war. Drill, weapons training and combat practice go on all around me. Continuous is the noise of rounds being fired, gun barrels being ground and ploughshares being beaten into swords, metaphorically and literally.

Each day, hundreds arrive from all over the country and swell the revolutionary forces. These include factions as diverse as The Royalist Liberation Front, The Holy War Direct Action Group, The Sheet Lightning Club, The Soldiers of the Blessed Virgin, The Daughters of Albion, The Sealed Knot and The Sacred Heart Death Brigade. Mercian pikemen mingle with Jacobites and cavaliers. Here are Spanish mercenaries, Jesuits Against Subjugation and mohocks. Among these I've seen children as young as twelve bearing axes and shotguns.

Also present are members of the I.R.A.--the Irish Royalist Army--who comprise the personal guard of the youthful rebel leader, "Anne the First." The new, self-titled "Queen of Great Britain" has proved to be a force to be reckoned with. Even though she appears to be in full-term pregnancy, the vivacious 29-year old aristocrat is to be seen striding about the base issuing orders, supervising and co-ordinating activities and making impromptu speeches to boost morale and harden resolve. My next despatch will carry an exclusive interview with this revolutionary leader who many are calling "The Iron Lady."

Morale is actually quite high here already. Despite the drought, there have been sufficient local wells to ensure a regular water ration. Food is getting a little sparser, however, as more recruits arrive. This is despite the regular delivery of food and medical supplies from sympathisers both in England and the Prussian Empire. Also farms, stores and fields within a radius of twenty miles have been looted in order to feed the growing army. This is considered "fair game," as in England only Puritan men are allowed to own land (and vote--although few bother as Cromwell's puppet "Rump" parliament has long since been impotent). Buildings in the surrounding area have been commandeered by the rebels and, it is said, the owners and their families put to death.

The same fate has befallen many roundhead patrols that have ventured into the vicinity. In fact, one can only wonder why the Lord Protector has delayed in attacking this position. Rumour has it that he is nervous of the presence of the Prussian Fleet in the Germanic Sea, who have, during their course of manoeuvres, breached England's self-imposed "exclusion zone" several times and have even been within sight of the Thames estuary.

He may have delayed too long. Already the cry, whether on "The Voice of Liberty," by messenger pigeon, or on the people's lips, is for "The October Revolution."

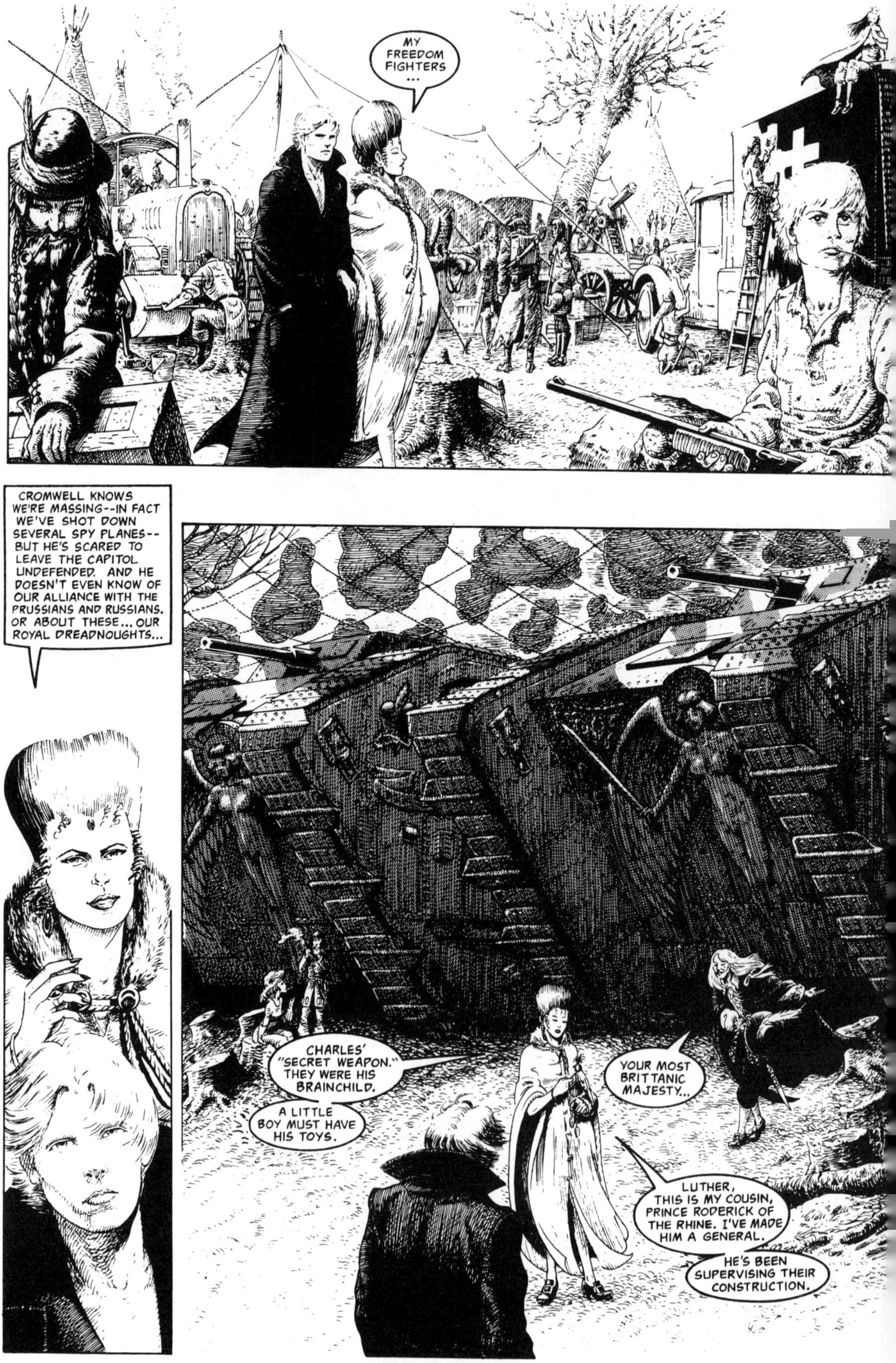
MY FREEDOM FIGHTERS ...
CROMWELL KNOWS WE'RE MASSING--IN FACT WE'VE SHOT DOWN SEVERAL SPY PLANES--BUT HE'S SCARED TO LEAVE THE CAPITOL UNDEFENDED. AND HE DOESN'T EVEN KNOW OF OUR ALLIANCE WITH THE PRUSSIANS AND RUSSIANS. OR ABOUT THESE... OUR ROYAL DREADNOUGHTS...
CHARLES' "SECRET WEAPON." THEY WERE HIS BRAINCHILD.
A LITTLE BOY MUST HAVE HIS TOYS.
YOUR MOST BRITTANIC MAJESTY...
LUTHER, THIS IS MY COUSIN, PRINCE RODERICK OF THE RHINE. I'VE MADE HIM A GENERAL.
HE'S BEEN SUPERVISING THEIR CONSTRUCTION.

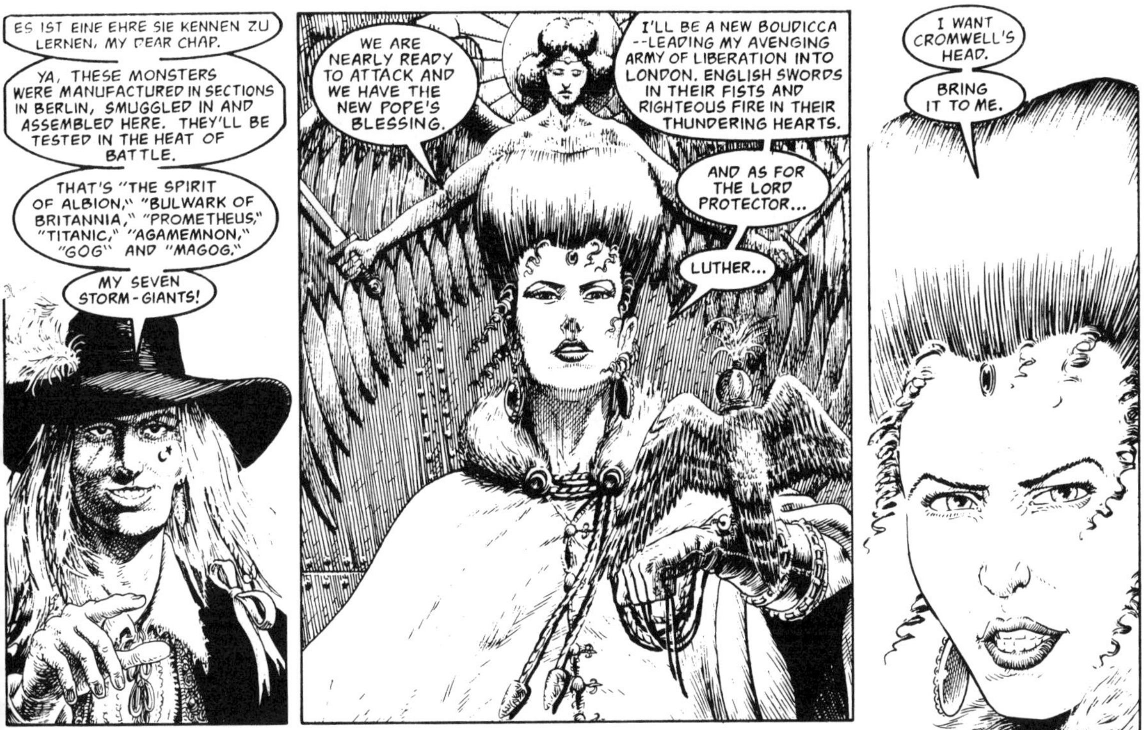
ES IST EINE EHRE SIE KENNEN ZU LERNEN, MY DEAR CHAP.
YA, THESE MONSTERS WERE MANUFACTURED IN SECTIONS IN BERLIN, SMUGGLED IN AND ASSEMBLED HERE. THEY'LL BE TESTED IN THE HEAT OF BATTLE.
THAT'S "THE SPIRIT OF ALBION," "BULWARK OF BRITANNIA," "PROMETHEUS," "TITANIC," "AGAMEMNON," "GOG" AND "MAGOG."
MY SEVEN STORM-GIANTS!
WE ARE NEARLY READY TO ATTACK AND WE HAVE THE NEW POPE'S BLESSING.
I'LL BE A NEW BOUDICCA --LEADING MY AVENGING ARMY OF LIBERATION INTO LONDON. ENGLISH SWORDS IN THEIR FISTS AND RIGHTEOUS FIRE IN THEIR THUNDERING HEARTS.
AND AS FOR THE LORD PROTECTOR...
LUTHER...
I WANT CROMWELL'S HEAD.
BRING IT TO ME.

PARA 01.22.23 MALVINAS. IMPERIAL AIRSHIP "BELGRANO" CRASHES IN PORT GALTIERI.
PARA 01.15.81 RUSSIA'S "TSAR WARS" ORBITAL DEFENCE SYSTEM DEVELOPS FAULT AND SHOOTS DOWN 3 U.S. PASSENGER AIRLINERS.
PARA 04.88.03 SCOTLAND. KING JAMES XXI DECLARES WAR ON AFGHANISTAN.
PARA 00.88.55 DUBLIN. SWARM OF ANTS COVERS CITY.
PARA 01.14.23 LONDON. CHARTISTS SEIZE POWER IN MILITARY COUP.
PARA 01.16.21 U.S.A. 250 MEMBERS OF ORANGE COUNTY JOHN BIRCH SOCIETY EXPERIENCE TERMINAL OCULOGYRIC CRISIS.

17.45

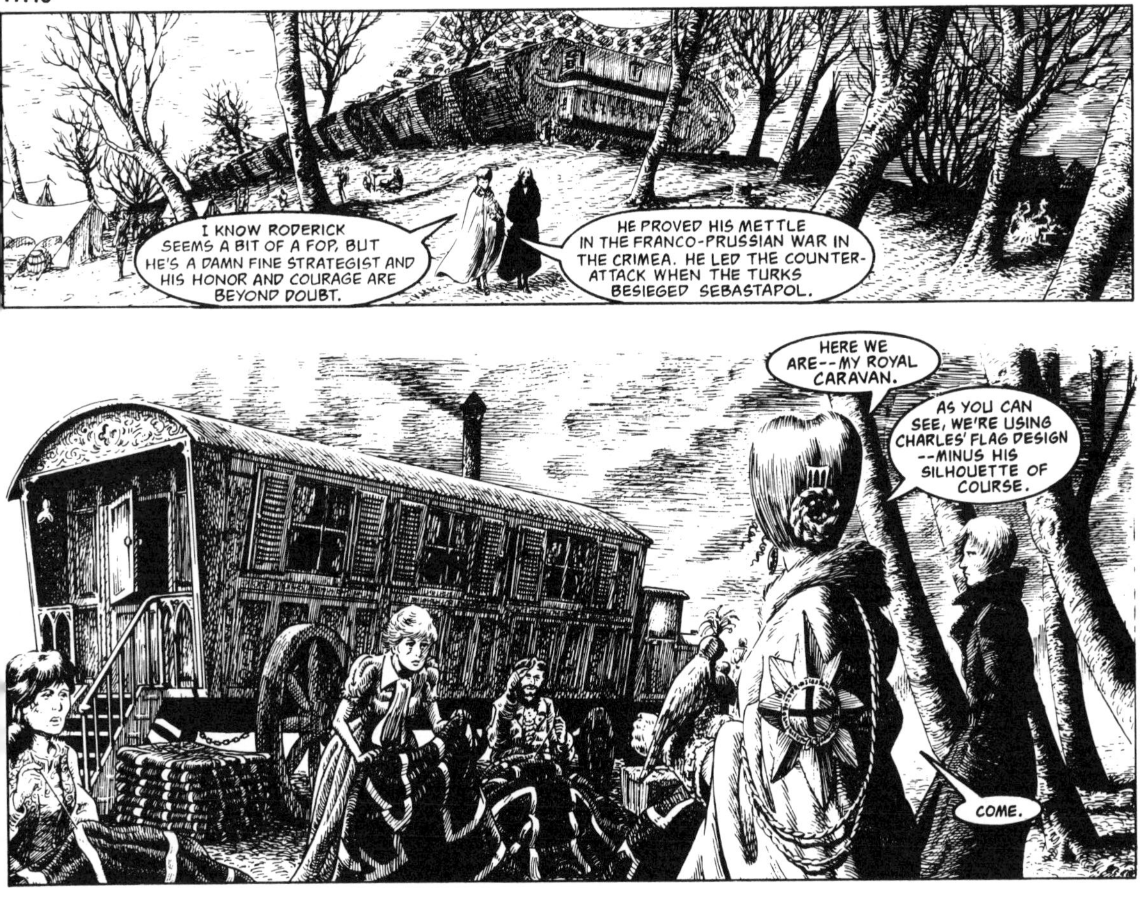
I KNOW RODERICK SEEMS A BIT OF A FOP, BUT HE'S A DAMN FINE STRATEGIST AND HIS HONOR AND COURAGE ARE BEYOND DOUBT.
HE PROVED HIS METTLE IN THE FRANCO-PRUSSIAN WAR IN THE CRIMEA. HE LED THE COUNTER-ATTACK WHEN THE TURKS BESIEGED SEBASTAPOL.
HERE WE ARE--MY ROYAL CARAVAN.
AS YOU CAN SEE, WE'RE USING CHARLES' FLAG DESIGN --MINUS HIS SILHOUETTE OF COURSE.
COME.

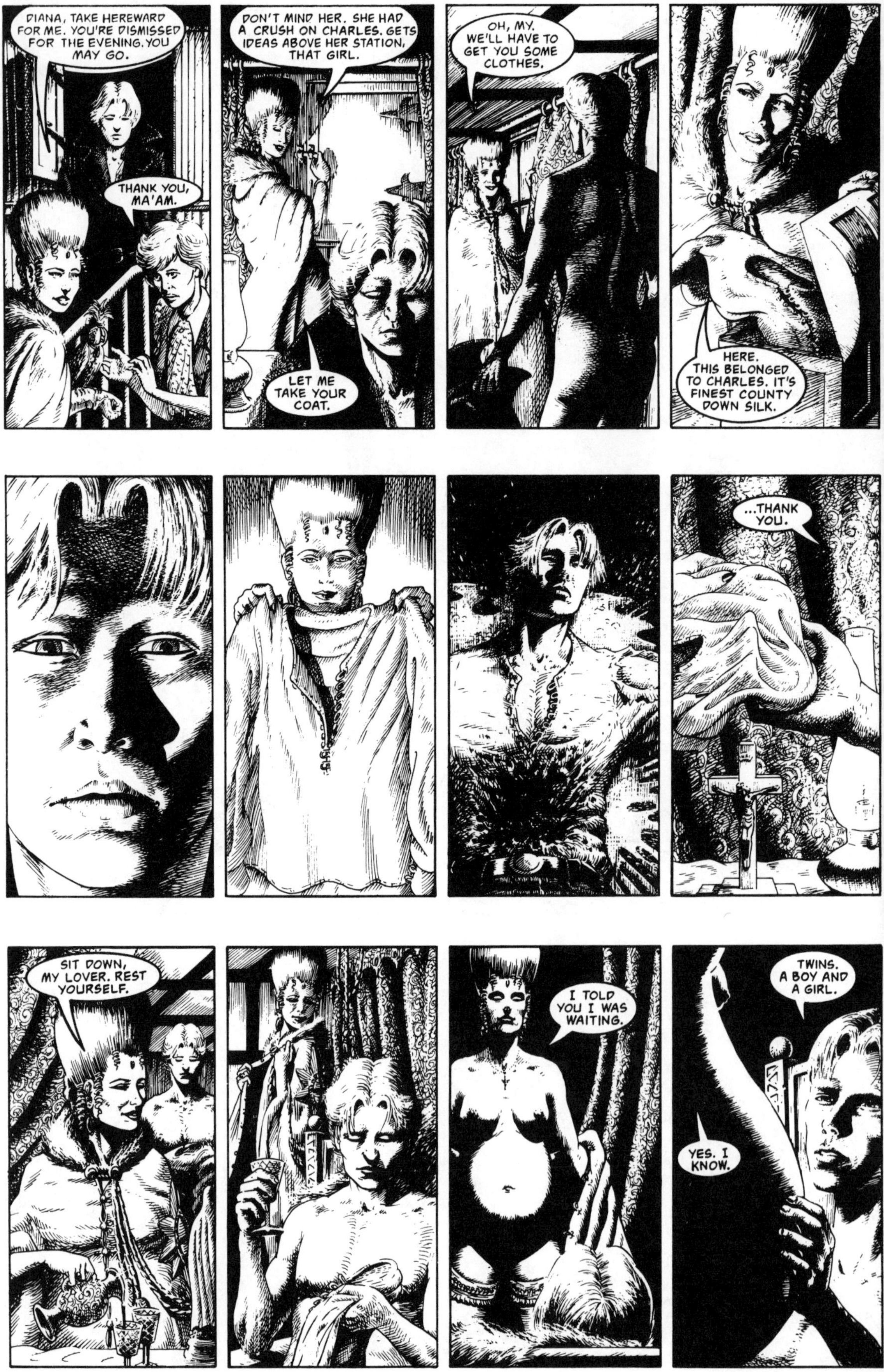
DIANA, TAKE HEREWARD FOR ME. YOU'RE DISMISSED FOR THE EVENING. YOU MAY GO.
THANK YOU, MA'AM.
DON'T MIND HER. SHE HAD A CRUSH ON CHARLES. GETS IDEAS ABOVE HER STATION, THAT GIRL.
LET ME TAKE YOUR COAT.
OH, MY. WE'LL HAVE TO GET YOU SOME CLOTHES.
HERE. THIS BELONGED TO CHARLES. IT'S FINEST COUNTY DOWN SILK.
...THANK YOU.
SIT DOWN, MY LOVER. REST YOURSELF.
I TOLD YOU I WAS WAITING.
TWINS. A BOY AND A GIRL.
YES. I KNOW.

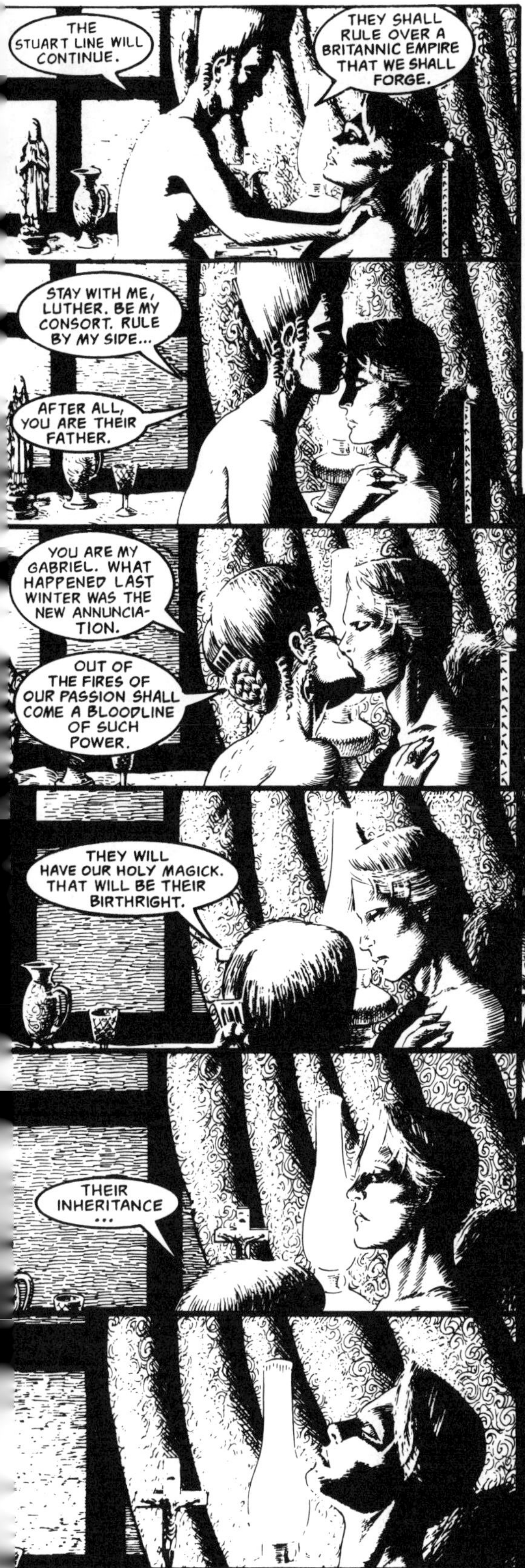
THE STUART LINE WILL CONTINUE.
THEY SHALL RULE OVER A BRITANNIC EMPIRE THAT WE SHALL FORGE.
STAY WITH ME, LUTHER. BE MY CONSORT. RULE BY MY SIDE...
AFTER ALL, YOU ARE THEIR FATHER.
YOU ARE MY GABRIEL. WHAT HAPPENED LAST WINTER WAS THE NEW ANNUNCIATION.
OUT OF THE FIRES OF OUR PASSION SHALL COME A BLOODLINE OF SUCH POWER.
THEY WILL HAVE OUR HOLY MAGICK. THAT WILL BE THEIR BIRTHRIGHT.
THEIR INHERITANCE ...

24.14

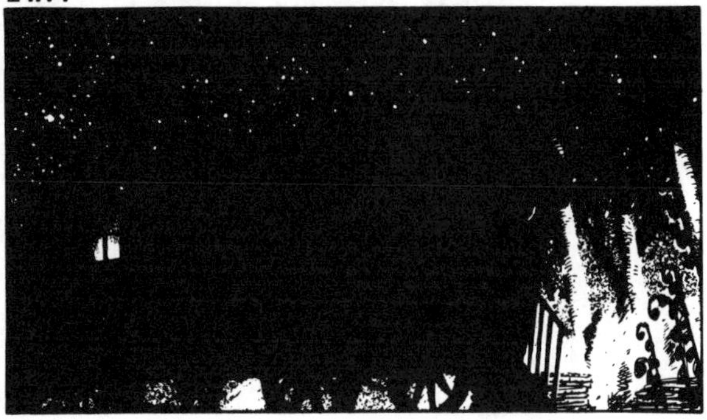

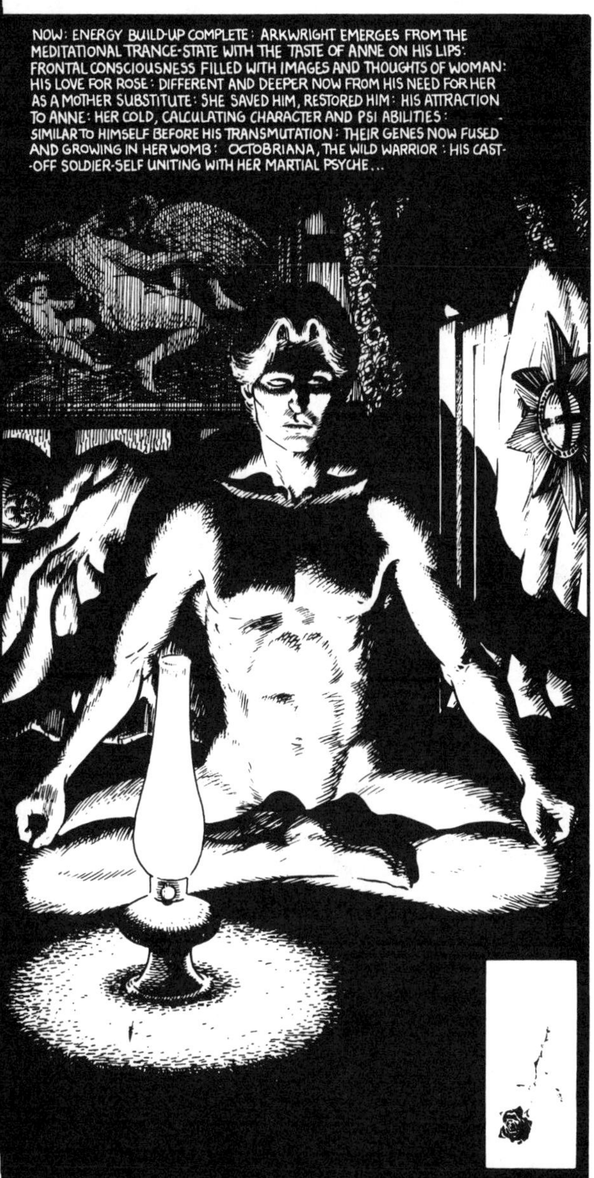
NOW: ENERGY BUILD-UP COMPLETE: ARKWRIGHT EMERGES FROM THE MEDITATIONAL TRANCE-STATE WITH THE TASTE OF ANNE ON HIS LIPS: FRONTAL CONSCIOUSNESS FILLED WITH IMAGES AND THOUGHTS OF WOMAN: HIS LOVE FOR ROSE: DIFFERENT AND DEEPER NOW FROM HIS NEED FOR HER AS A MOTHER SUBSTITUTE: SHE SAVED HIM, RESTORED HIM: HIS ATTRACTION TO ANNE: HER COLD, CALCULATING CHARACTER AND PSI ABILITIES: SIMILAR TO HIMSELF BEFORE HIS TRANSMUTATION: THEIR GENES NOW FUSED AND GROWING IN HER WOMB: OCTOBRIANA, THE WILD WARRIOR: HIS CAST-OFF SOLDIER-SELF UNITING WITH HER MARTIAL PSYCHE...
IN HIS WHOLE LIFE HE HAS ONLY BEEN CLOSE TO THREE PEOPLE: THREE LOVERS: THREE WOMEN: AND NOW HE KNOWS THAT ONLY ROSE MATTERS AND FIREFROST MUST BE STOPPED SO THAT ROSE SHALL LIVE.

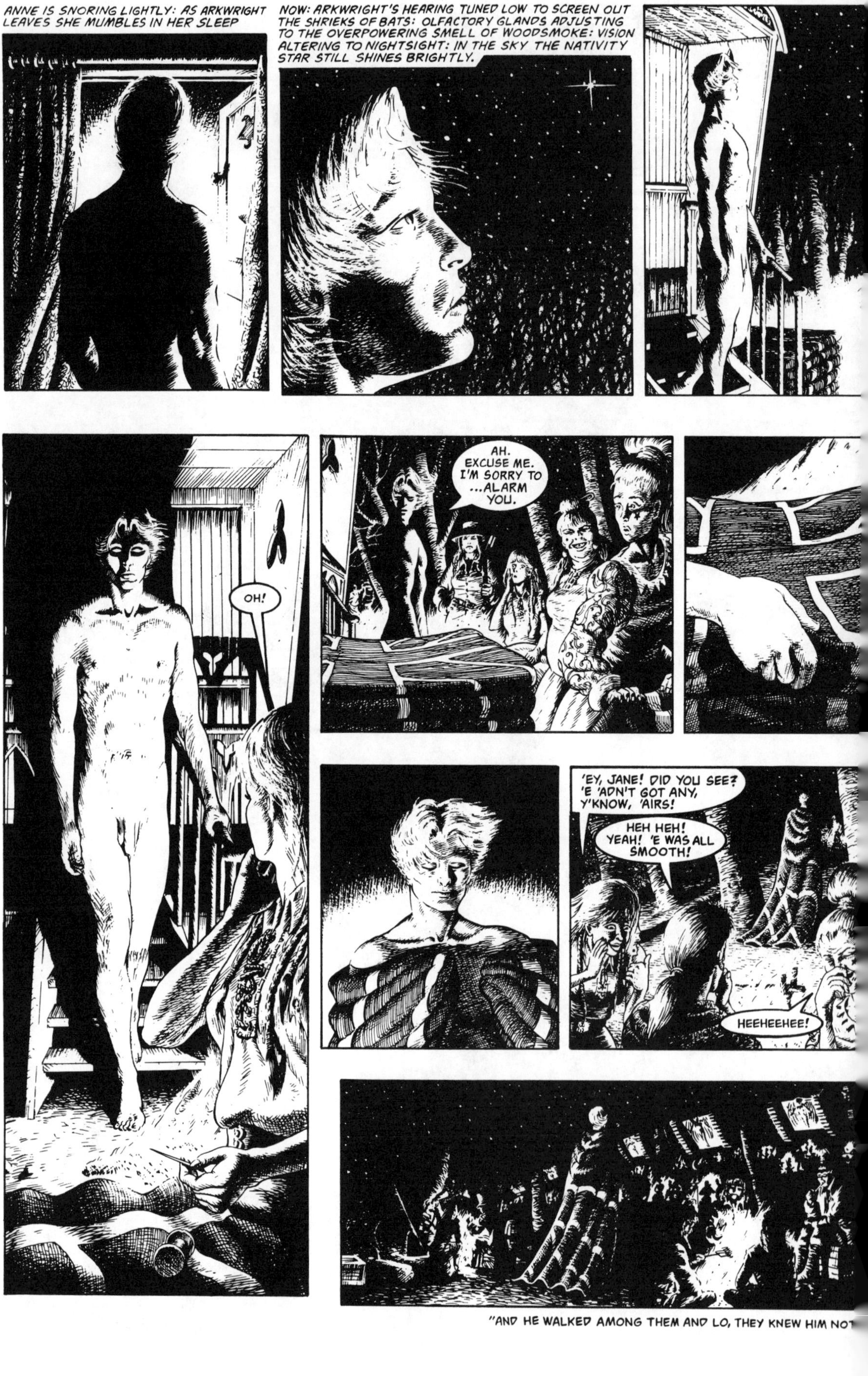
ANNE IS SNORING LIGHTLY: AS ARKWRIGHT LEAVES SHE MUMBLES IN HER SLEEP
NOW: ARKWRIGHT'S HEARING TUNED LOW TO SCREEN OUT THE SHRIEKS OF BATS: OLFACTORY GLANDS ADJUSTING TO THE OVERPOWERING SMELL OF WOODSMOKE: VISION ALTERING TO NIGHTSIGHT: IN THE SKY THE NATIVITY STAR STILL SHINES BRIGHTLY.
OH!
AH. EXCUSE ME. I'M SORRY TO ...ALARM YOU.
'EY, JANE! DID YOU SEE? 'E 'ADN'T GOT ANY, Y'KNOW, 'AIRS!
HEH HEH! YEAH! 'E WAS ALL SMOOTH!
HEEHEEHEE!
"AND HE WALKED AMONG THEM AND LO, THEY KNEW HIM NOT

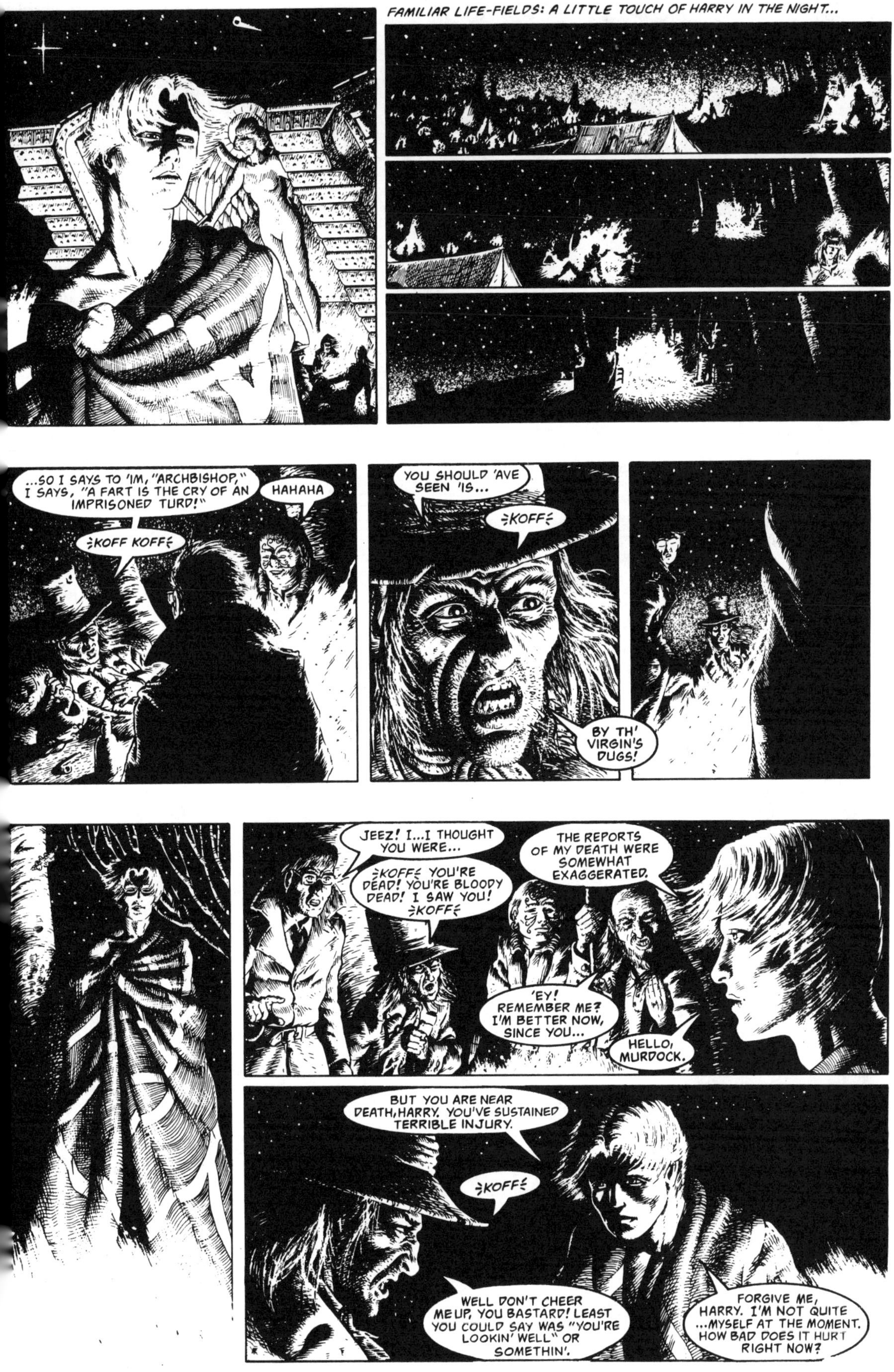
FAMILIAR LIFE-FIELDS: A LITTLE TOUCH OF HARRY IN THE NIGHT...
...SO I SAYS TO 'IM, "ARCHBISHOP," I SAYS, "A FART IS THE CRY OF AN IMPRISONED TURD!"
HAHAHA
KOFF KOFF
YOU SHOULD 'AVE SEEN 'IS...
KOFF
BY TH' VIRGIN'S DUGS!
JEEZ! I...I THOUGHT YOU WERE...
KOFF YOU'RE DEAD! YOU'RE BLOODY DEAD! I SAW YOU! KOFF
THE REPORTS OF MY DEATH WERE SOMEWHAT EXAGGERATED.
'EY! REMEMBER ME? I'M BETTER NOW, SINCE YOU...
HELLO, MURDOCK.
BUT YOU ARE NEAR DEATH, HARRY. YOU'VE SUSTAINED TERRIBLE INJURY.
KOFF
WELL DON'T CHEER ME UP, YOU BASTARD! LEAST YOU COULD SAY WAS "YOU'RE LOOKIN' WELL" OR SOMETHIN'.
FORGIVE ME, HARRY. I'M NOT QUITE ...MYSELF AT THE MOMENT. HOW BAD DOES IT HURT RIGHT NOW?

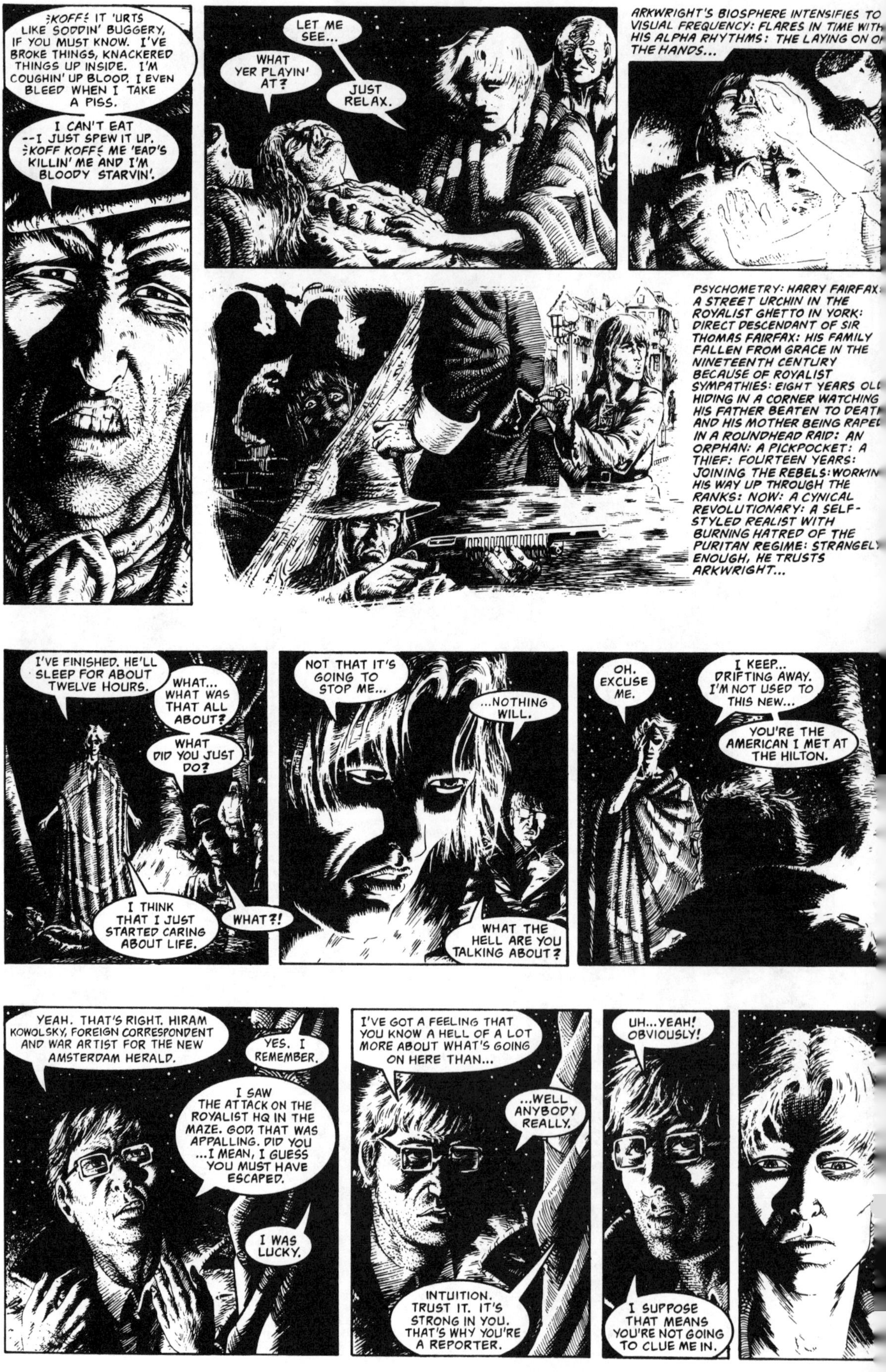

ƷKOFFƸ IT 'URTS LIKE SODDIN' BUGGERY, IF YOU MUST KNOW. I'VE BROKE THINGS, KNACKERED THINGS UP INSIDE. I'M COUGHIN' UP BLOOD. I EVEN BLEED WHEN I TAKE A PISS.
I CAN'T EAT --I JUST SPEW IT UP. ƷKOFF KOFFƸ ME 'EAD'S KILLIN' ME AND I'M BLOODY STARVIN'.
LET ME SEE...
WHAT YER PLAYIN' AT?
JUST RELAX.
ARKWRIGHT'S BIOSPHERE INTENSIFIES TO VISUAL FREQUENCY: FLARES IN TIME WITH HIS ALPHA RHYTHMS: THE LAYING ON OF THE HANDS...
PSYCHOMETRY: HARRY FAIRFAX: A STREET URCHIN IN THE ROYALIST GHETTO IN YORK: DIRECT DESCENDANT OF SIR THOMAS FAIRFAX: HIS FAMILY FALLEN FROM GRACE IN THE NINETEENTH CENTURY BECAUSE OF ROYALIST SYMPATHIES: EIGHT YEARS OLD HIDING IN A CORNER WATCHING HIS FATHER BEATEN TO DEATH AND HIS MOTHER BEING RAPED IN A ROUNDHEAD RAID: AN ORPHAN: A PICKPOCKET: A THIEF: FOURTEEN YEARS: JOINING THE REBELS: WORKING HIS WAY UP THROUGH THE RANKS: NOW: A CYNICAL REVOLUTIONARY: A SELF-STYLED REALIST WITH BURNING HATRED OF THE PURITAN REGIME: STRANGELY ENOUGH, HE TRUSTS ARKWRIGHT...
I'VE FINISHED. HE'LL SLEEP FOR ABOUT TWELVE HOURS.
WHAT... WHAT WAS THAT ALL ABOUT?
WHAT DID YOU JUST DO?
I THINK THAT I JUST STARTED CARING ABOUT LIFE.
WHAT?!
NOT THAT IT'S GOING TO STOP ME...
...NOTHING WILL.
WHAT THE HELL ARE YOU TALKING ABOUT?
OH. EXCUSE ME.
I KEEP... DRIFTING AWAY. I'M NOT USED TO THIS NEW...
YOU'RE THE AMERICAN I MET AT THE HILTON.
YEAH. THAT'S RIGHT. HIRAM KOWOLSKY, FOREIGN CORRESPONDENT AND WAR ARTIST FOR THE NEW AMSTERDAM HERALD.
YES. I REMEMBER.
I SAW THE ATTACK ON THE ROYALIST HQ IN THE MAZE. GOD, THAT WAS APPALLING. DID YOU ...I MEAN, I GUESS YOU MUST HAVE ESCAPED.
I WAS LUCKY.
I'VE GOT A FEELING THAT YOU KNOW A HELL OF A LOT MORE ABOUT WHAT'S GOING ON HERE THAN...
...WELL ANYBODY REALLY.
INTUITION. TRUST IT. IT'S STRONG IN YOU. THAT'S WHY YOU'RE A REPORTER.
UH...YEAH! OBVIOUSLY!
I SUPPOSE THAT MEANS YOU'RE NOT GOING TO CLUE ME IN.

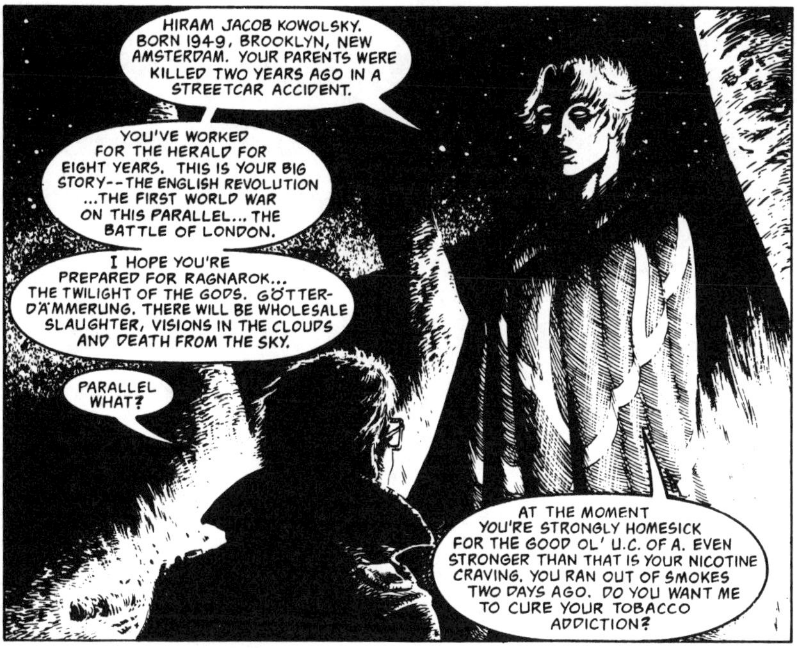
HIRAM JACOB KOWOLSKY. BORN 1949, BROOKLYN, NEW AMSTERDAM. YOUR PARENTS WERE KILLED TWO YEARS AGO IN A STREETCAR ACCIDENT.
YOU'VE WORKED FOR THE HERALD FOR EIGHT YEARS. THIS IS YOUR BIG STORY--THE ENGLISH REVOLUTION ...THE FIRST WORLD WAR ON THIS PARALLEL... THE BATTLE OF LONDON.
I HOPE YOU'RE PREPARED FOR RAGNAROK... THE TWILIGHT OF THE GODS. GÖTTER-DÄMMERUNG. THERE WILL BE WHOLESALE SLAUGHTER, VISIONS IN THE CLOUDS AND DEATH FROM THE SKY.
PARALLEL WHAT?
AT THE MOMENT YOU'RE STRONGLY HOMESICK FOR THE GOOD OL' U.C. OF A. EVEN STRONGER THAN THAT IS YOUR NICOTINE CRAVING. YOU RAN OUT OF SMOKES TWO DAYS AGO. DO YOU WANT ME TO CURE YOUR TOBACCO ADDICTION?

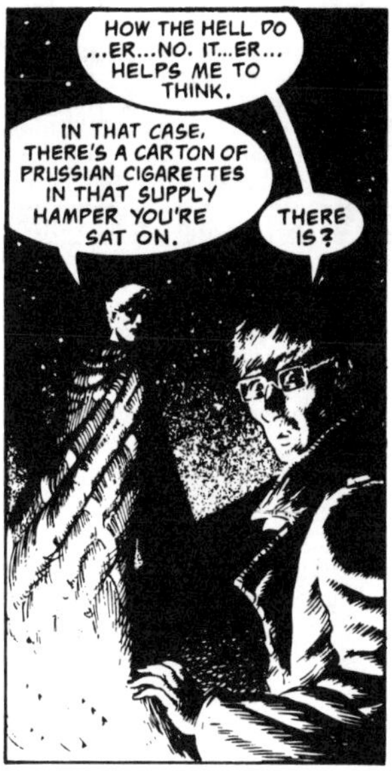
HOW THE HELL DO ...ER...NO. IT...ER... HELPS ME TO THINK.
IN THAT CASE, THERE'S A CARTON OF PRUSSIAN CIGARETTES IN THAT SUPPLY HAMPER YOU'RE SAT ON.
THERE IS?

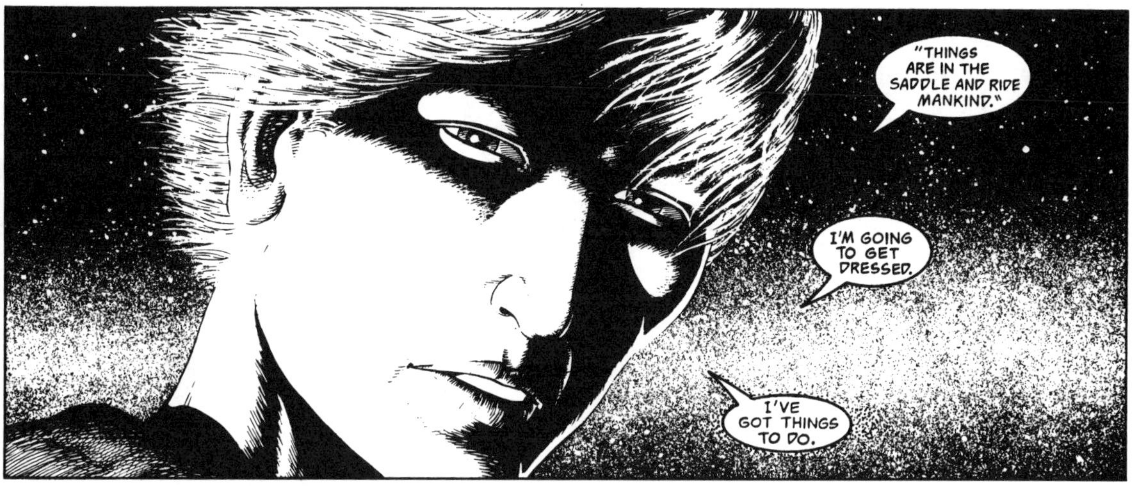
"THINGS ARE IN THE SADDLE AND RIDE MANKIND."
I'M GOING TO GET DRESSED.
I'VE GOT THINGS TO DO.

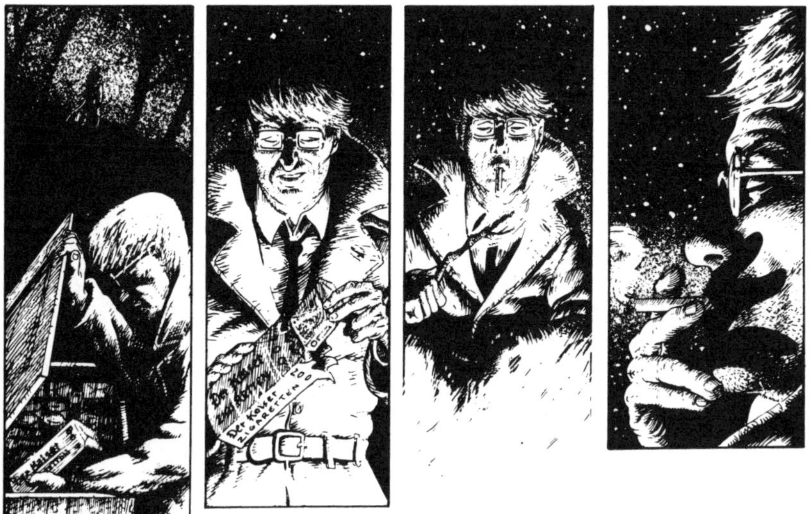

The atmosphere here is almost that of an open-air festival. A camaraderie has developed between the different groups. I've seen Lancastrians openly chatting with Yorkshiremen and Scotsmen getting drunk with Welshmen. Even the women revolutionaries are being acknowledged as equals by the men. This is being seen as something of a political statement, as is clothing.

Under Puritan laws, only functional black and white attire is permitted, the exception being certain army uniforms. The use of dress to convey anti-governmental beliefs is being taken by some to a new level. Besides the expected cavalier finery and Jacobite kilts, outlandish costume of all kinds can be observed. Unorthodox hairstyles and facial tattoos are becoming symbols of revolt. One group--"The Fundamentalists," an "Ancient Britain" faction--have taken to painting themselves in woad.

Meanwhile, the Puritan Purge goes on. Last night, we heard that SPG troops had torched the Maze. Survivors fleeing the inferno were captured and sent to the new internment camp in Islington. The situation is fast approaching breaking point.

"Letter to America"
Hiram Kowolsky
New Amsterdam Herald

PARA 02.53.21 NEW YORK. 45% OF KITTENS BEING BORN WITH TWO HEADS.
PARA 10.57.12 PERSIA. SPACE SHUTTLE EXPLODES ON TAKE OFF.
PARA 01.42.21 WORLD WAR THREE. NUCLEAR HOLOCAUST.
PARA 01.42.22 WORLD WAR THREE. NUCLEAR HOLOCAUST.
PARA 01.42.23 WORLD WAR THREE. NUCLEAR HOLOCAUST.
PARA 20.18.13 GENEVA. 32 HEADS OF STATE DIE IN TERRORIST ATTACK.
PARA 02.10.73 PRAGUE. SPONTANEOUS HUMAN COMBUSTION OUTBREAK.
PARA 04.59.32 MASSIVE FLUCTUATIONS IN EARTH'S MAGNETIC FIELD. WIDESPREAD DESTRUCTION.

Extracts: "The Collegiate Church of St. Peter in Westminster."

"The Abbey has been a sacred place for a thousand years or more. Even when Westminster was a marshy waste, men came here to pray and build shrines to their gods."

"The Temple of Apollo, built on this gravel peninsula in the Thames marshes by the Romans, was destroyed by an earthquake in 154 AD."

"One can only imagine what the building would have looked like today if it has not suffered from damnable puritan vandalism. After the Civil War the tombs and effigies of Kings and poets were torn out, the stained glass smashed and replaced by clear windows, the exquisite mediaeval pavement mutilated, the 13th century tapestries burned, the high altar and organ destroyed and all ornament hacked off and plastered over. And to complete the desecration, the whole place was cluttered up by pews for the common herd."

Cardinal T. Schmidt,
Westphalian Institute of Ecclesiastical Architecture.

MON 16 OCT 08.28 WESTMINSTER SQUARE

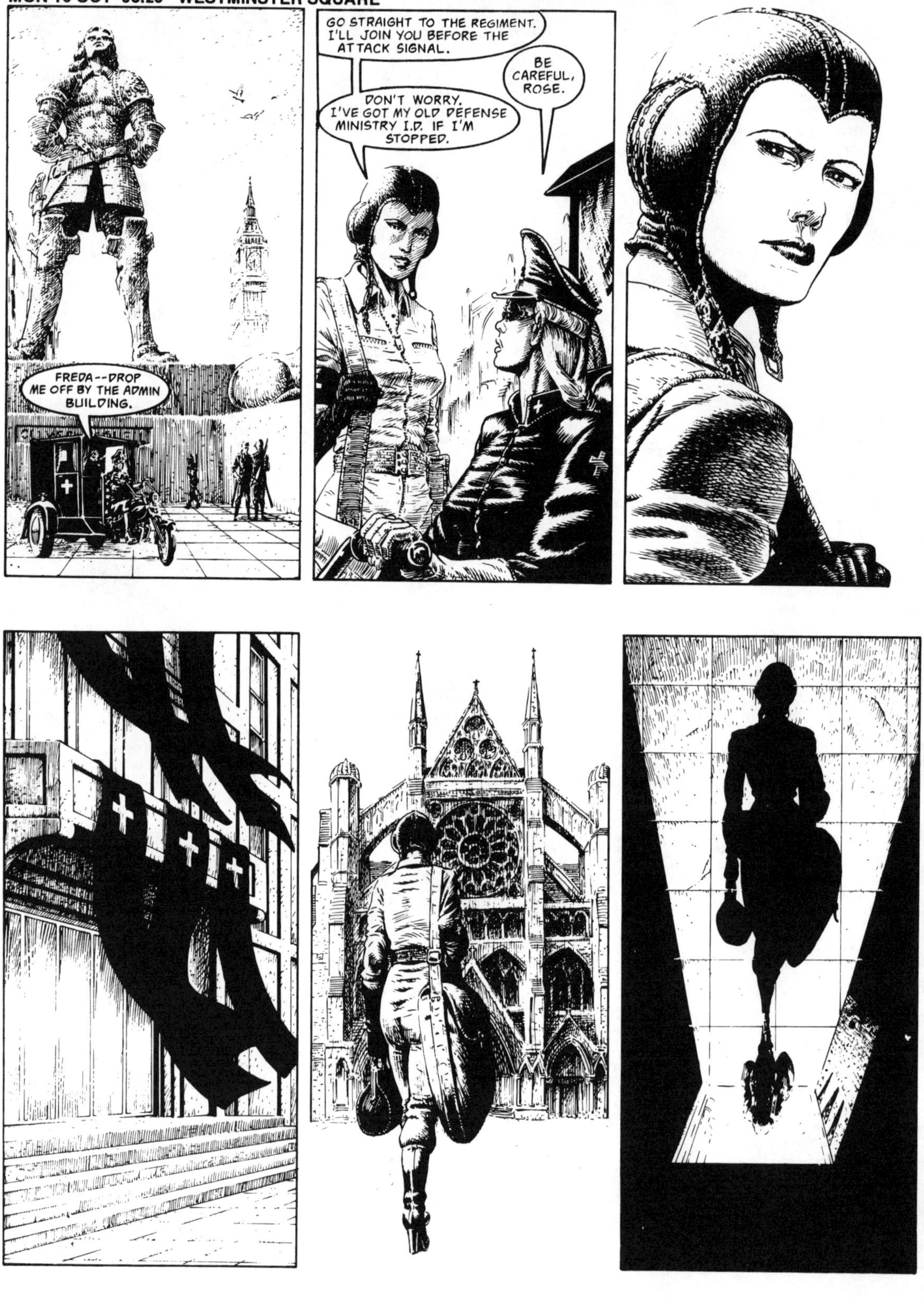
FREDA--DROP ME OFF BY THE ADMIN BUILDING.
GO STRAIGHT TO THE REGIMENT. I'LL JOIN YOU BEFORE THE ATTACK SIGNAL.
DON'T WORRY. I'VE GOT MY OLD DEFENSE MINISTRY I.D. IF I'M STOPPED.
BE CAREFUL, ROSE.

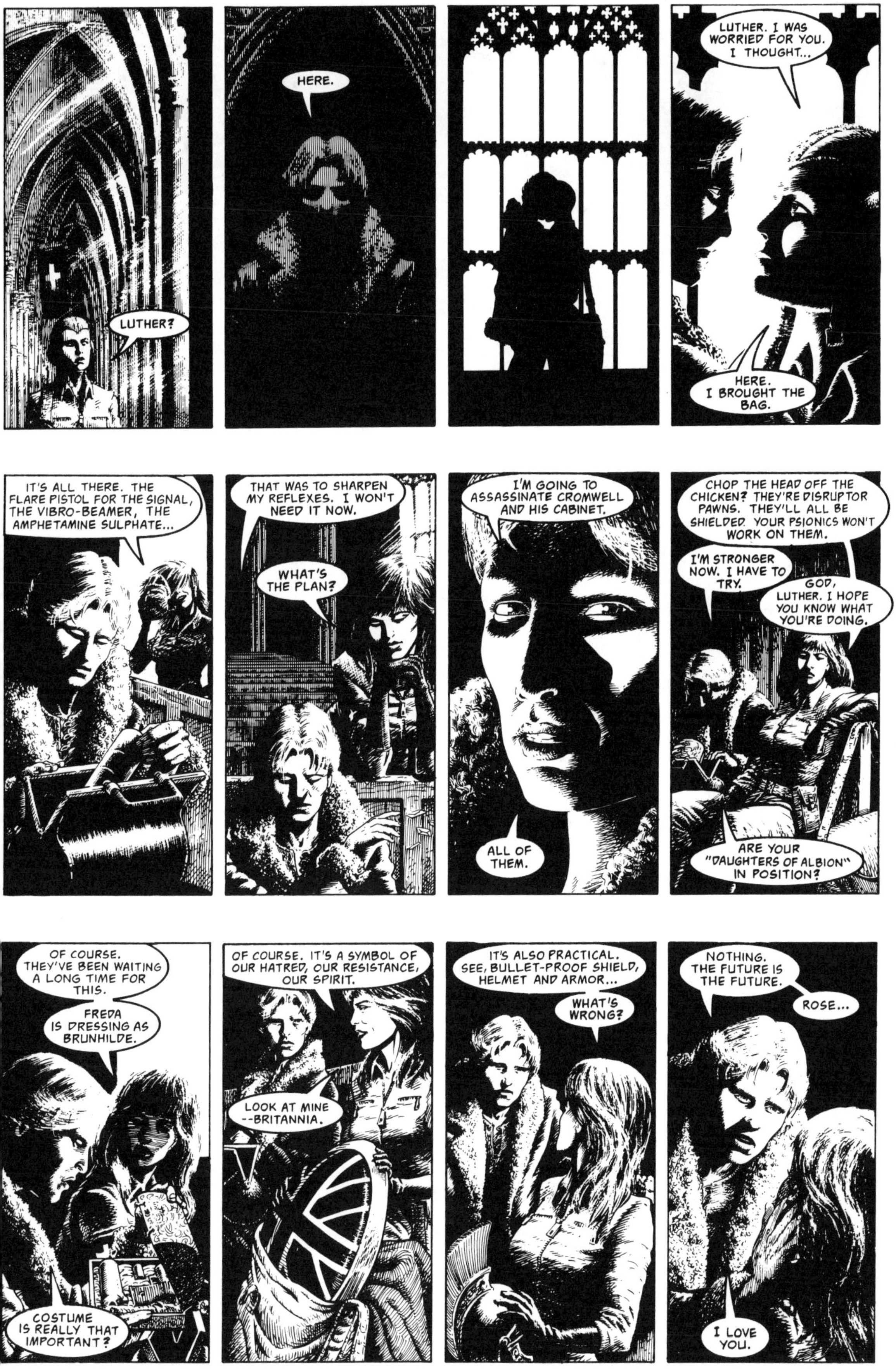
LUTHER?
HERE.
LUTHER. I WAS WORRIED FOR YOU. I THOUGHT...
HERE. I BROUGHT THE BAG.
IT'S ALL THERE. THE FLARE PISTOL FOR THE SIGNAL, THE VIBRO-BEAMER, THE AMPHETAMINE SULPHATE...
THAT WAS TO SHARPEN MY REFLEXES. I WON'T NEED IT NOW.
WHAT'S THE PLAN?
I'M GOING TO ASSASSINATE CROMWELL AND HIS CABINET.
ALL OF THEM.
CHOP THE HEAD OFF THE CHICKEN? THEY'RE DISRUPTOR PAWNS. THEY'LL ALL BE SHIELDED. YOUR PSIONICS WON'T WORK ON THEM.
I'M STRONGER NOW. I HAVE TO TRY.
GOD, LUTHER. I HOPE YOU KNOW WHAT YOU'RE DOING.
ARE YOUR "DAUGHTERS OF ALBION" IN POSITION?
OF COURSE. THEY'VE BEEN WAITING A LONG TIME FOR THIS.
FREDA IS DRESSING AS BRUNHILDE.
COSTUME IS REALLY THAT IMPORTANT?
OF COURSE. IT'S A SYMBOL OF OUR HATRED, OUR RESISTANCE, OUR SPIRIT.
LOOK AT MINE --BRITANNIA.
IT'S ALSO PRACTICAL. SEE, BULLET-PROOF SHIELD, HELMET AND ARMOR...
WHAT'S WRONG?
NOTHING. THE FUTURE IS THE FUTURE.
ROSE...
I LOVE YOU.

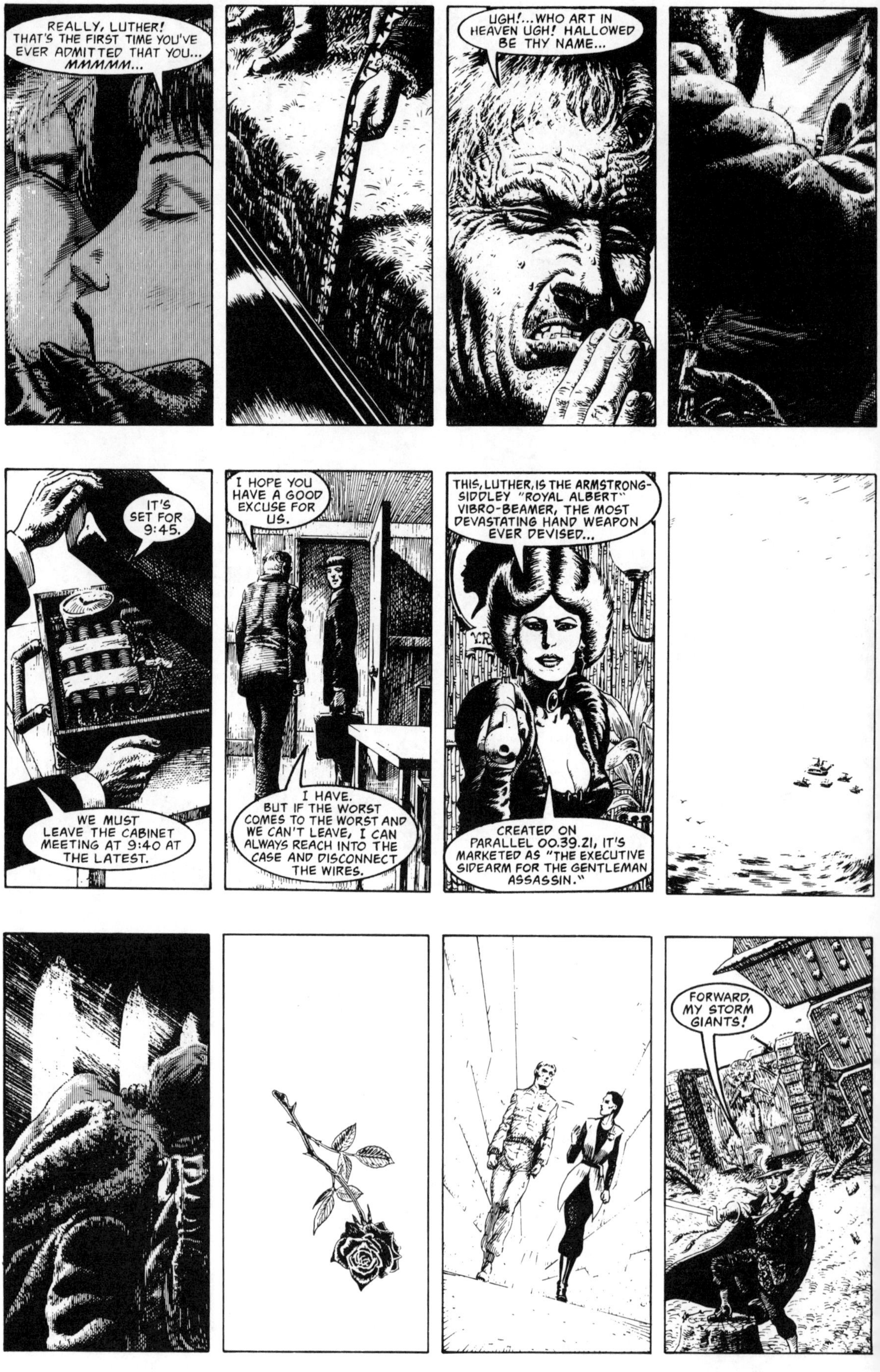
REALLY, LUTHER! THAT'S THE FIRST TIME YOU'VE EVER ADMITTED THAT YOU... MMMMMM...
UGH!...WHO ART IN HEAVEN UGH! HALLOWED BE THY NAME...
IT'S SET FOR 9:45.
WE MUST LEAVE THE CABINET MEETING AT 9:40 AT THE LATEST.
I HOPE YOU HAVE A GOOD EXCUSE FOR US.
I HAVE. BUT IF THE WORST COMES TO THE WORST AND WE CAN'T LEAVE, I CAN ALWAYS REACH INTO THE CASE AND DISCONNECT THE WIRES.
THIS, LUTHER, IS THE ARMSTRONG-SIDDLEY "ROYAL ALBERT" VIBRO-BEAMER, THE MOST DEVASTATING HAND WEAPON EVER DEVISED...
CREATED ON PARALLEL 00.39.21, IT'S MARKETED AS "THE EXECUTIVE SIDEARM FOR THE GENTLEMAN ASSASSIN."
FORWARD, MY STORM GIANTS!

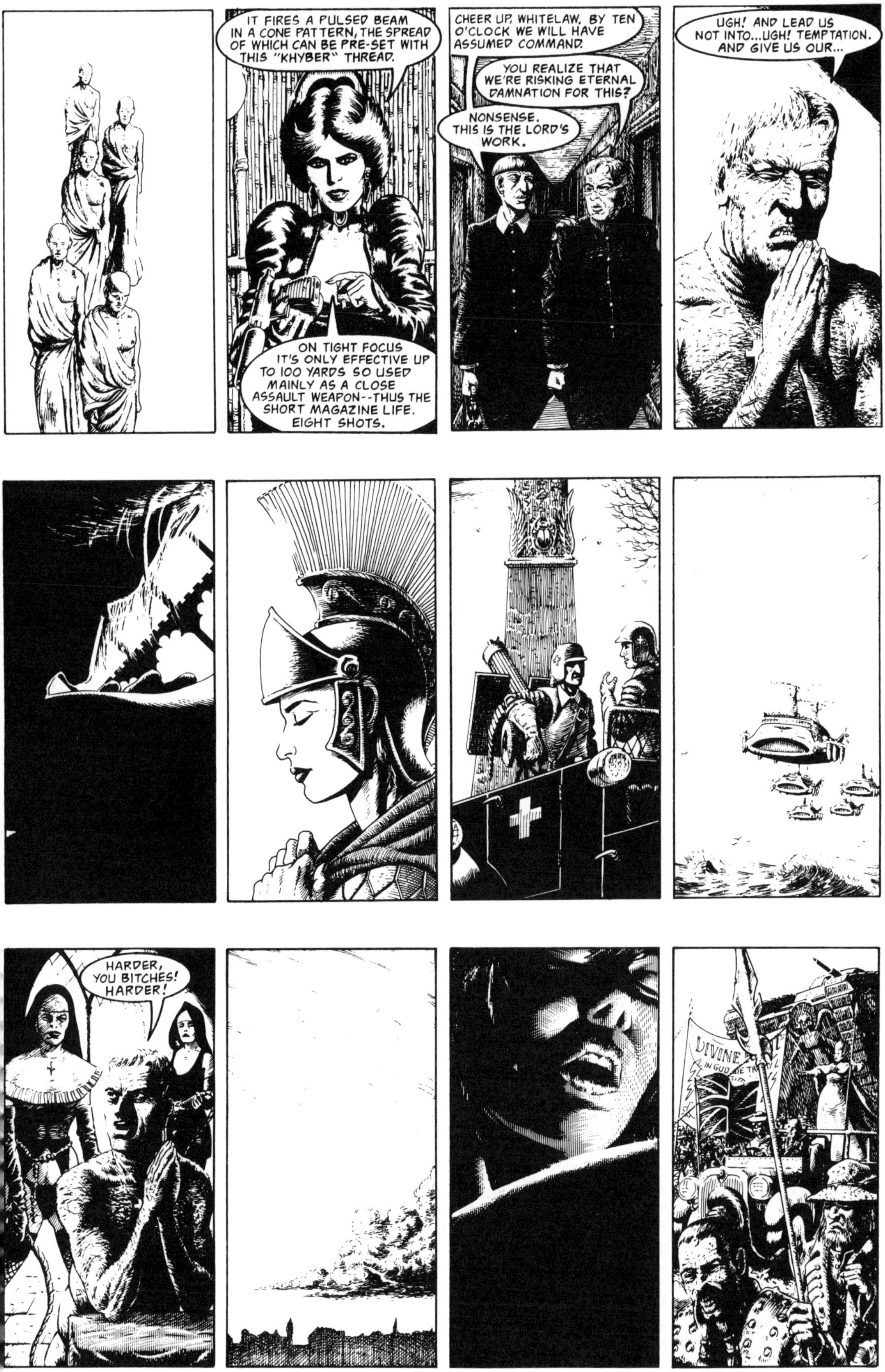
IT FIRES A PULSED BEAM IN A CONE PATTERN, THE SPREAD OF WHICH CAN BE PRE-SET WITH THIS "KHYBER" THREAD.
ON TIGHT FOCUS IT'S ONLY EFFECTIVE UP TO 100 YARDS SO USED MAINLY AS A CLOSE ASSAULT WEAPON--THUS THE SHORT MAGAZINE LIFE. EIGHT SHOTS.
CHEER UP, WHITELAW. BY TEN O'CLOCK WE WILL HAVE ASSUMED COMMAND.
YOU REALIZE THAT WE'RE RISKING ETERNAL DAMNATION FOR THIS?
NONSENSE. THIS IS THE LORD'S WORK.
UGH! AND LEAD US NOT INTO...UGH! TEMPTATION. AND GIVE US OUR...
HARDER, YOU BITCHES! HARDER!
DIVINE

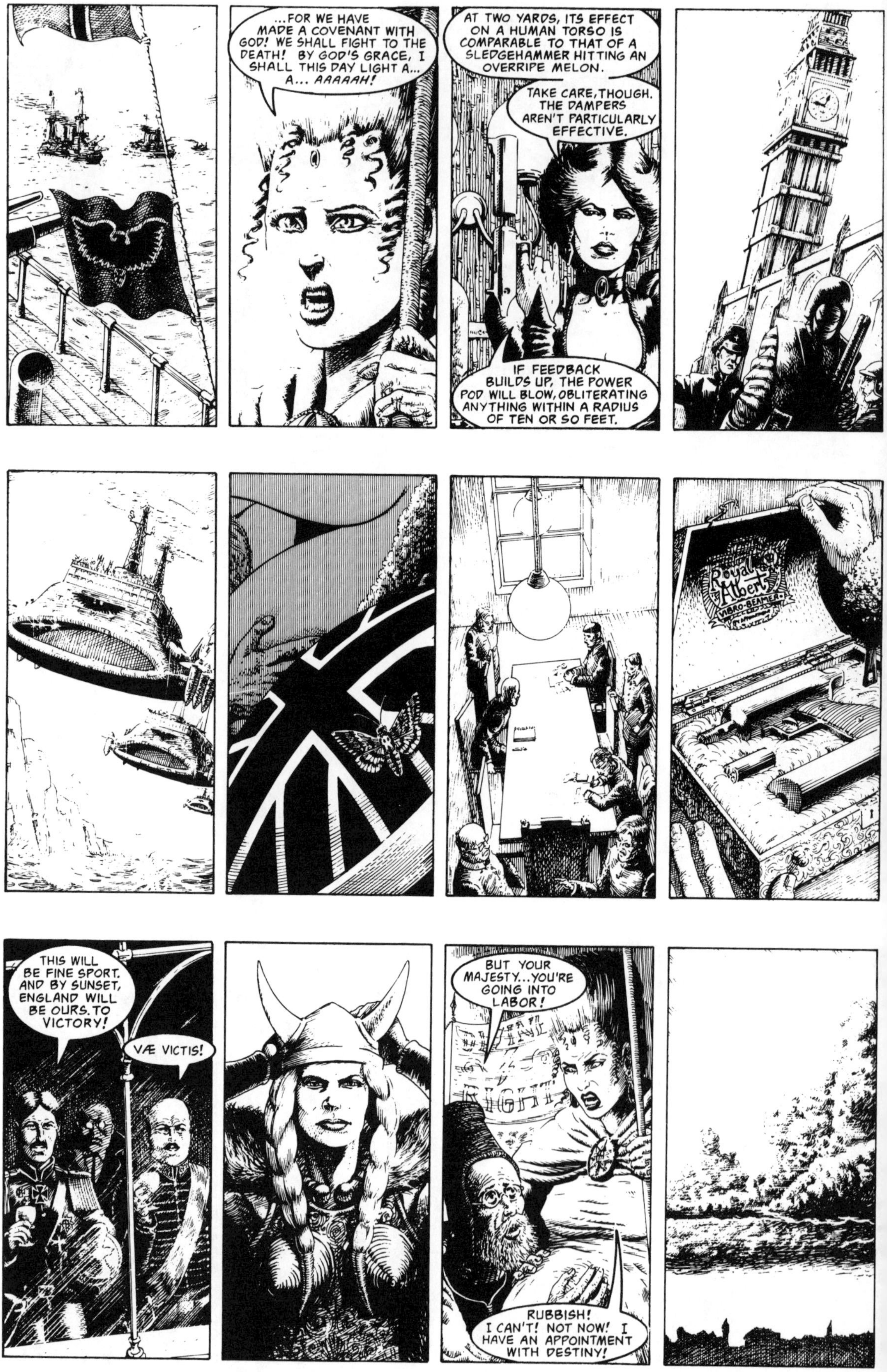
...FOR WE HAVE MADE A COVENANT WITH GOD! WE SHALL FIGHT TO THE DEATH! BY GOD'S GRACE, I SHALL THIS DAY LIGHT A... A... AAAAAAH!
AT TWO YARDS, ITS EFFECT ON A HUMAN TORSO IS COMPARABLE TO THAT OF A SLEDGEHAMMER HITTING AN OVERRIPE MELON.
TAKE CARE, THOUGH. THE DAMPERS AREN'T PARTICULARLY EFFECTIVE.
IF FEEDBACK BUILDS UP, THE POWER POD WILL BLOW, OBLITERATING ANYTHING WITHIN A RADIUS OF TEN OR SO FEET.
Royal Albert
VIBRO-BEAMER
THIS WILL BE FINE SPORT. AND BY SUNSET, ENGLAND WILL BE OURS. TO VICTORY!
VÆ VICTIS!
BUT YOUR MAJESTY... YOU'RE GOING INTO LABOR!
RUBBISH! I CAN'T! NOT NOW! I HAVE AN APPOINTMENT WITH DESTINY!

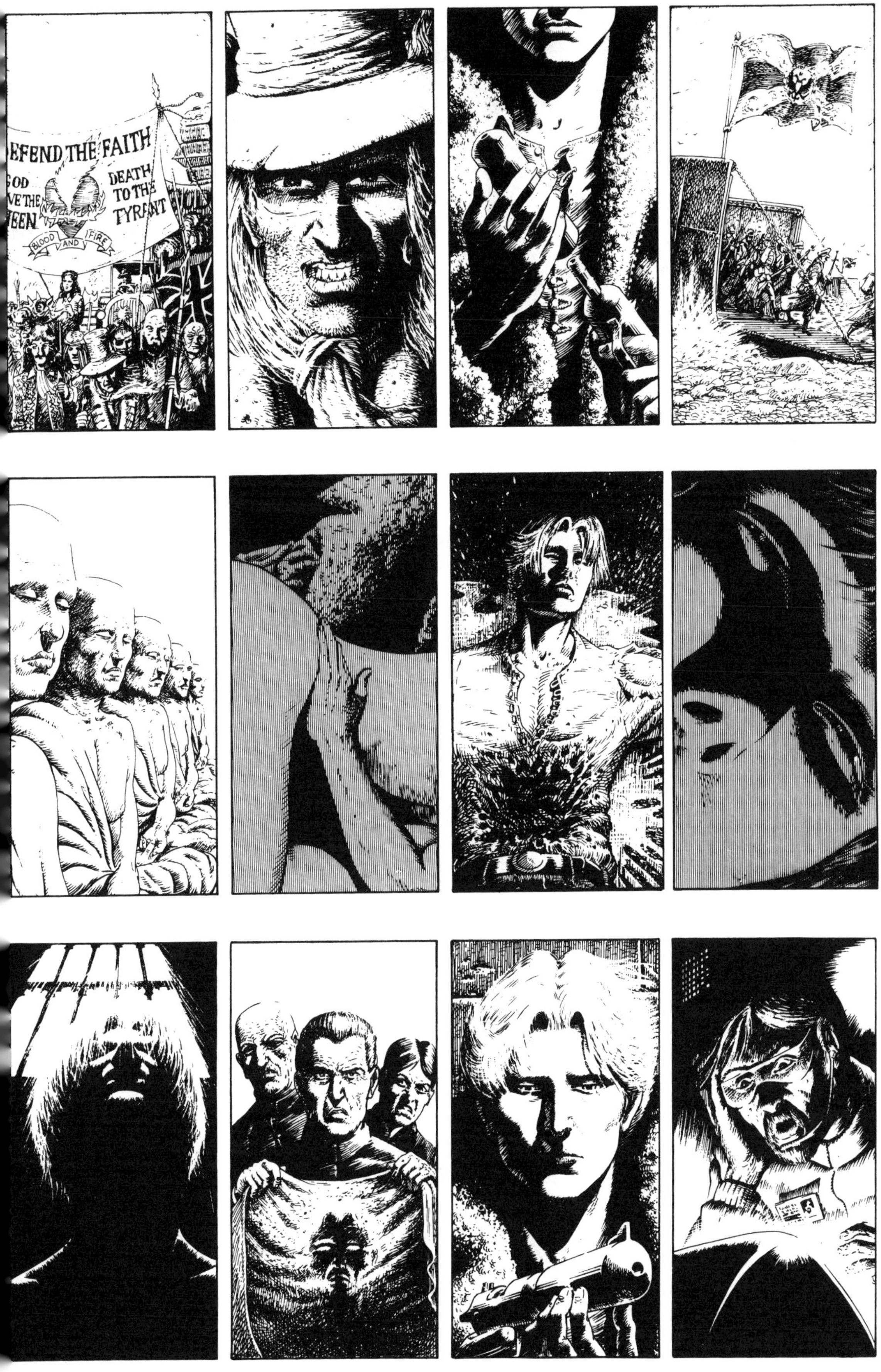
EFEND THE FAITH
OD
VE THE
EEN
DEATH
TO THE
TYRANT
BLOOD AND FIRE

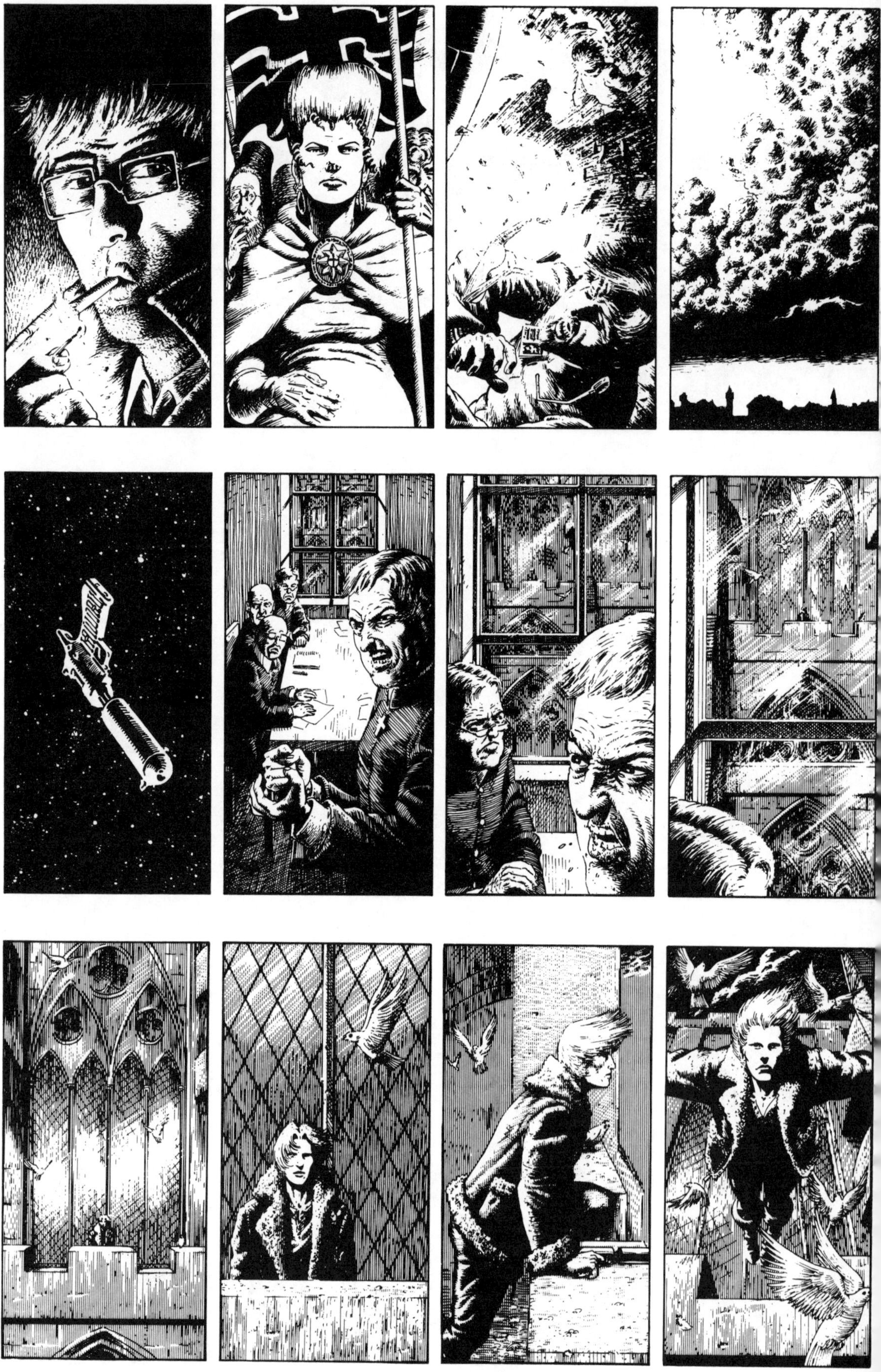

MON 16 OCT 09.25 PARA 00.00.00 LONDON WORLD CONGRESS TERMINAL

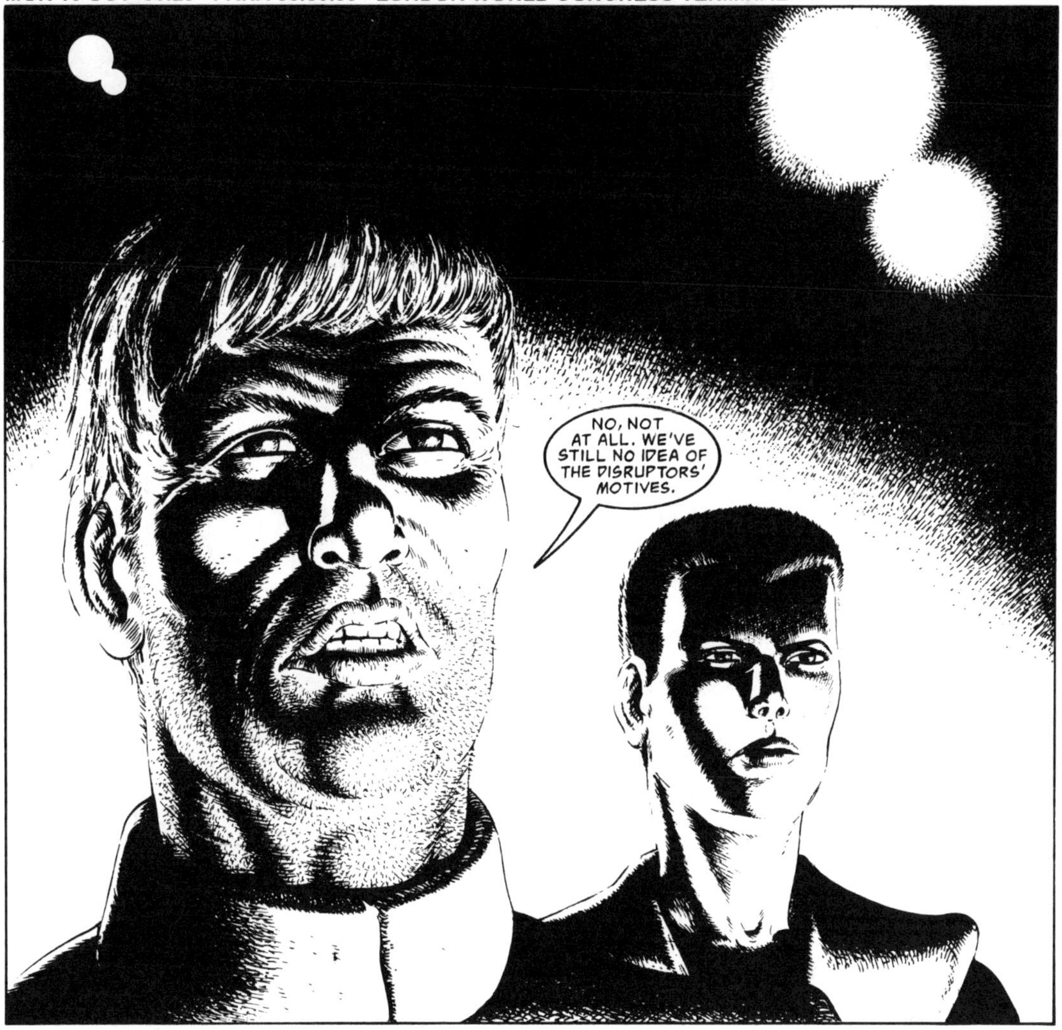
NO, NOT AT ALL. WE'VE STILL NO IDEA OF THE DISRUPTORS' MOTIVES.

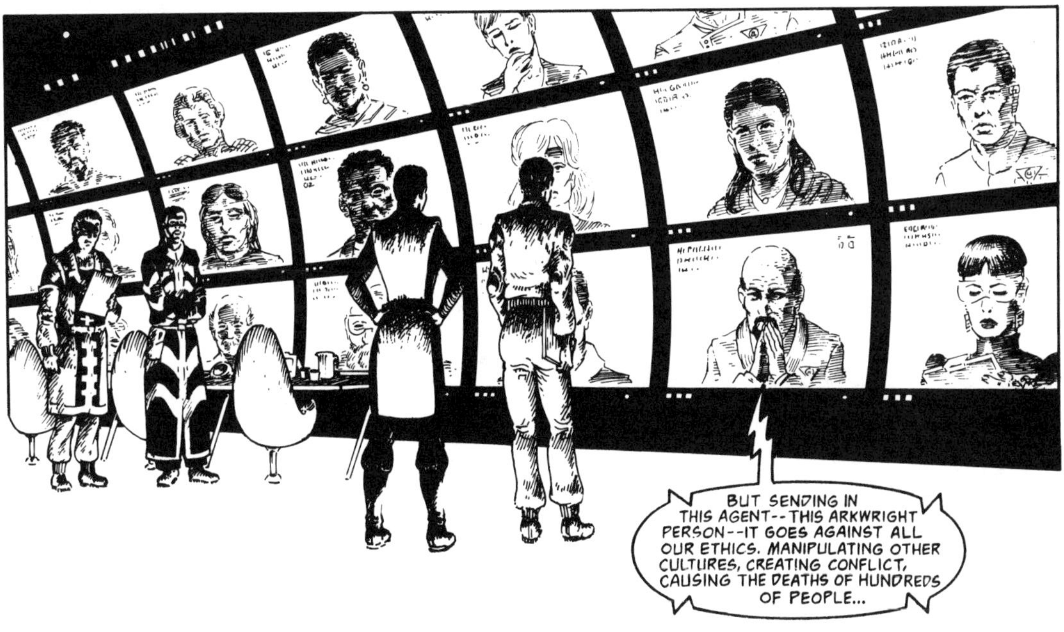
BUT SENDING IN THIS AGENT--THIS ARKWRIGHT PERSON--IT GOES AGAINST ALL OUR ETHICS. MANIPULATING OTHER CULTURES, CREATING CONFLICT, CAUSING THE DEATHS OF HUNDREDS OF PEOPLE...

PARA 00.72.87   RICHMOND, LONDON   09.31

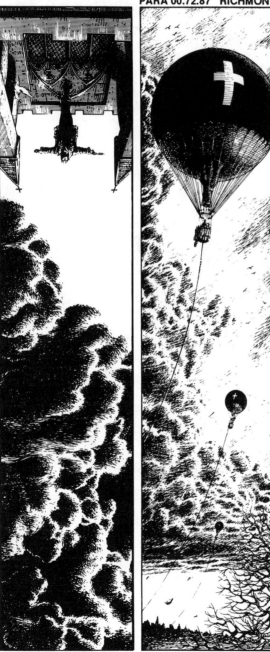

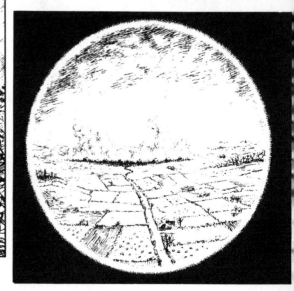

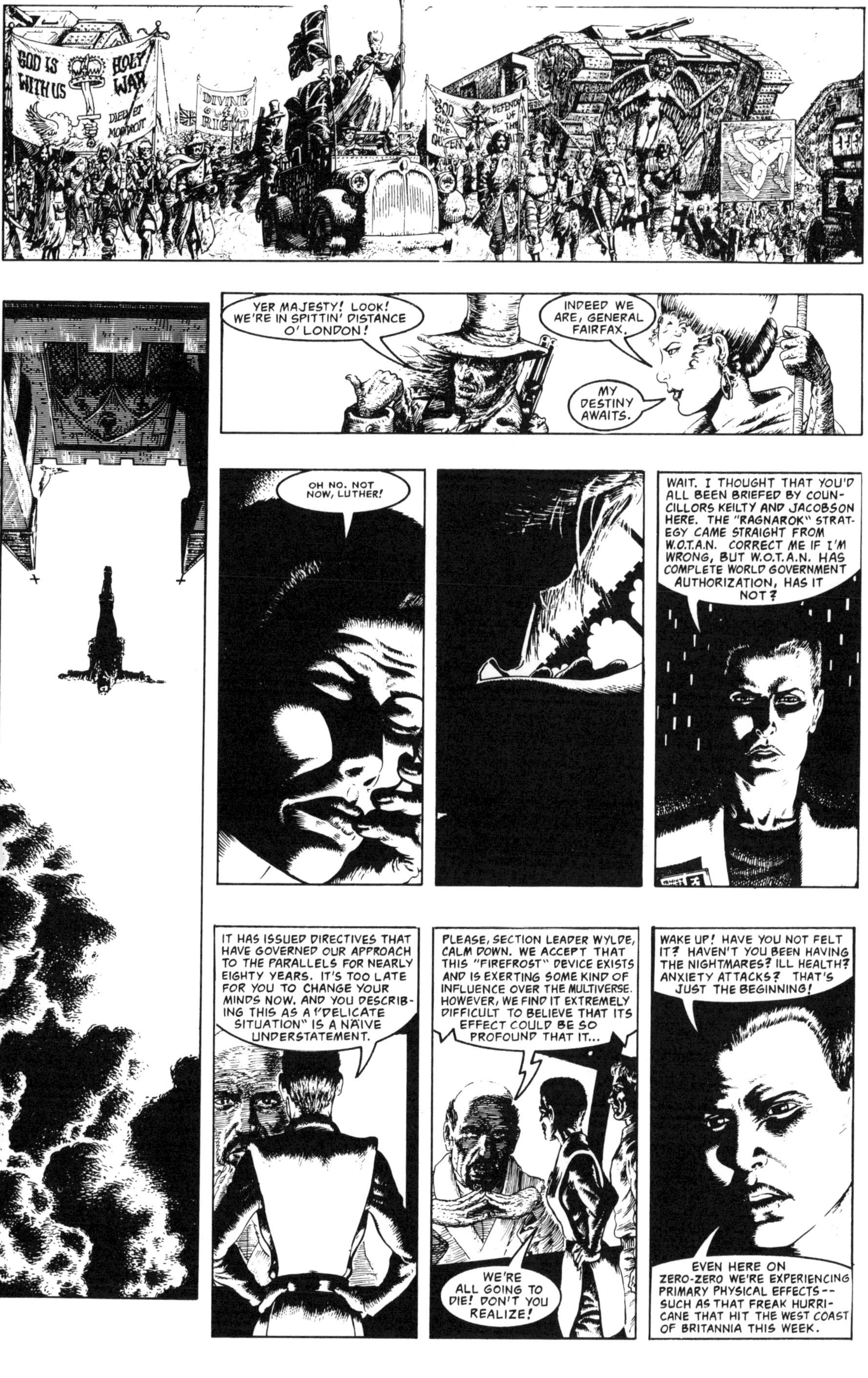
GOD IS WITH US
HOLY WAR
DIEU ET MON DROIT
DIVINE RIGHT
GOD SAVE THE QUEEN
DEFENDER OF THE
YER MAJESTY! LOOK! WE'RE IN SPITTIN' DISTANCE O' LONDON!
INDEED WE ARE, GENERAL FAIRFAX.
MY DESTINY AWAITS.
OH NO. NOT NOW, LUTHER!
WAIT. I THOUGHT THAT YOU'D ALL BEEN BRIEFED BY COUNCILLORS KEILTY AND JACOBSON HERE. THE "RAGNAROK" STRATEGY CAME STRAIGHT FROM W.O.T.A.N. CORRECT ME IF I'M WRONG, BUT W.O.T.A.N. HAS COMPLETE WORLD GOVERNMENT AUTHORIZATION, HAS IT NOT?
IT HAS ISSUED DIRECTIVES THAT HAVE GOVERNED OUR APPROACH TO THE PARALLELS FOR NEARLY EIGHTY YEARS. IT'S TOO LATE FOR YOU TO CHANGE YOUR MINDS NOW. AND YOU DESCRIBING THIS AS A "DELICATE SITUATION" IS A NAÏVE UNDERSTATEMENT.
PLEASE, SECTION LEADER WYLDE, CALM DOWN. WE ACCEPT THAT THIS "FIREFROST" DEVICE EXISTS AND IS EXERTING SOME KIND OF INFLUENCE OVER THE MULTIVERSE. HOWEVER, WE FIND IT EXTREMELY DIFFICULT TO BELIEVE THAT ITS EFFECT COULD BE SO PROFOUND THAT IT...
WE'RE ALL GOING TO DIE! DON'T YOU REALIZE!
WAKE UP! HAVE YOU NOT FELT IT? HAVEN'T YOU BEEN HAVING THE NIGHTMARES? ILL HEALTH? ANXIETY ATTACKS? THAT'S JUST THE BEGINNING!
EVEN HERE ON ZERO-ZERO WE'RE EXPERIENCING PRIMARY PHYSICAL EFFECTS -- SUCH AS THAT FREAK HURRICANE THAT HIT THE WEST COAST OF BRITANNIA THIS WEEK.

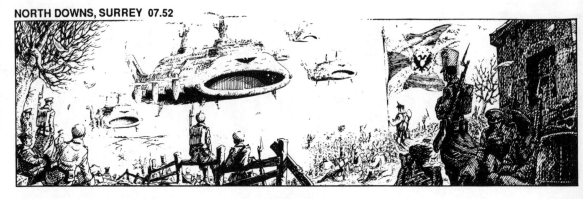

AND IT'S GETTING WORSE. THESE EFFECTS WILL ACCELERATE IN GEOMETRIC PROGRESSION UNTIL...

WE ARE AWARE OF THE THEORY, PR.WYLDE AND I REPEAT: CALM DOWN.

WE ARE NOT HERE TO BE LECTURED. WE ARE HERE TO DECIDE WHETHER THE RAGNAROK PROGRAM IS SUITABLE AND MORALLY...

SCHEISSEN!

W.O.T.A.N. IS EXPLICIT: OUR ONLY CHANCE OF FINDING FIRE-FROST IS TO CREATE A CRISIS SITUATION FOR THE DISRUPTORS SO THEY HAVE TO SEND IN THEIR ROOKS, THEIR SHOCK TROOPS, IN ORDER TO MAINTAIN THEIR POSITION ON THAT PARALLEL.

WHEN THIS OCCURS, W.O.T.A.N.'S SENSORY WEBS WILL PICK UP THE VORTEX FORMED BY THEIR ARRIVAL AND TRACE THEM BACK TO SOURCE.

ONCE WE HAVE THE LOCATION, ARKWRIGHT CAN BE DIRECTED THERE TO TRY AND SHUT THE FIRE OPAL DOWN, THOUGH MARX KNOWS HOW HE...

ENOUGH! PR.WYLDE, YOU HAVE SEVERELY TRIED THE PATIENCE OF THIS ASSEMBLY WITH YOUR OUTBURSTS...

TEAM LEADER WASZYNKO!

SPEAKING.

W.O.T.A.N.'S JUST BLOWN A SOLAR INTERFACE UNIT. SOME SORT OF SATELLITE MALFUNCTION.

PARSIFAL WAS CAUGHT IN THE BLAST.

O.K. VERONIQUE, WE'RE ON OUR WAY!

KARL! WAIT! YOU CAN'T JUST WALK OUT OF A WORLD GOVERNMENT CONGRESS!

CAN'T I? SCREW THIS CHARADE!

COME ON, ROSE.

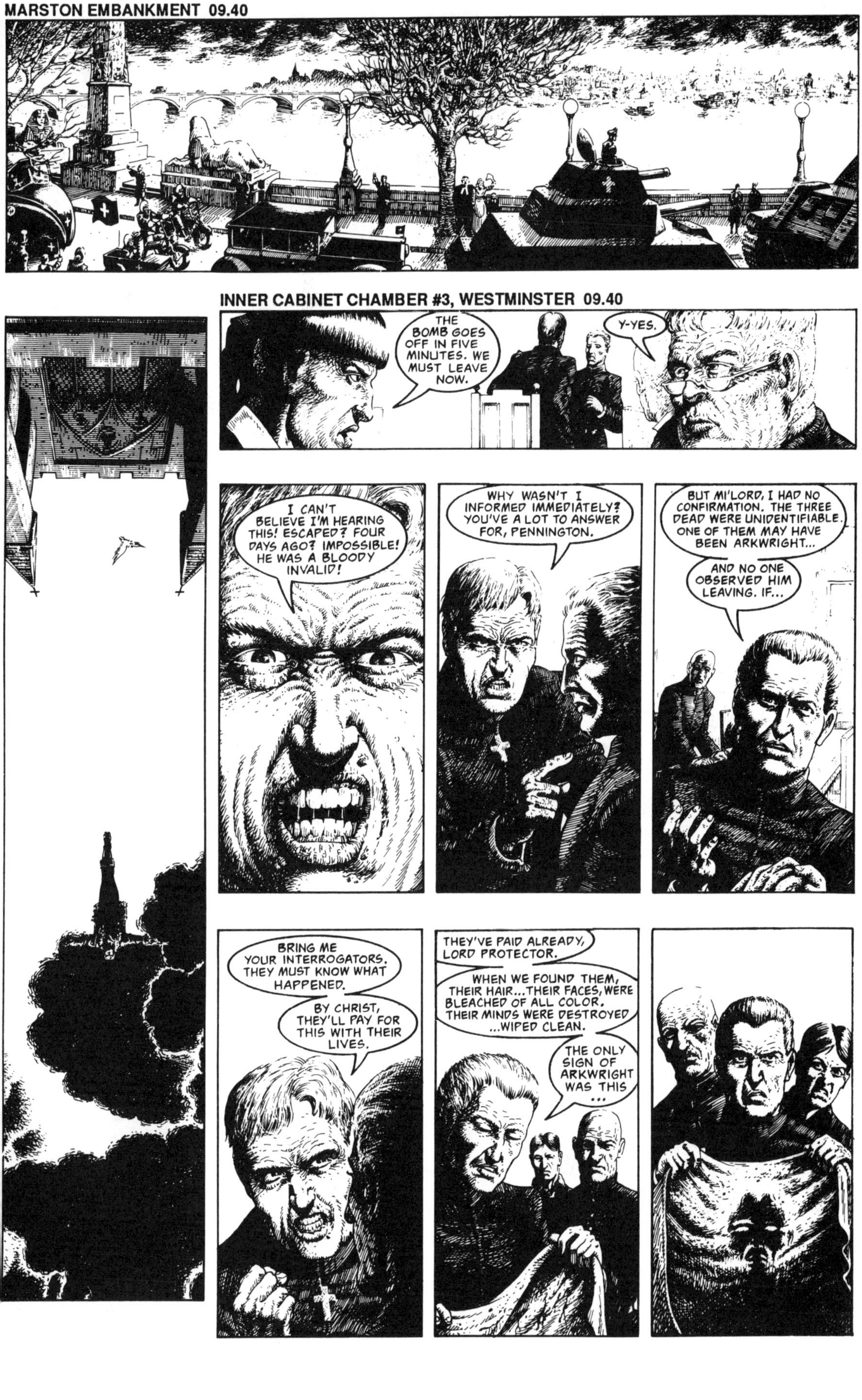
MARSTON EMBANKMENT 09.40
INNER CABINET CHAMBER #3, WESTMINSTER 09.40
THE BOMB GOES OFF IN FIVE MINUTES. WE MUST LEAVE NOW.
Y-YES.
I CAN'T BELIEVE I'M HEARING THIS! ESCAPED? FOUR DAYS AGO? IMPOSSIBLE! HE WAS A BLOODY INVALID!
WHY WASN'T I INFORMED IMMEDIATELY? YOU'VE A LOT TO ANSWER FOR, PENNINGTON.
BUT MI'LORD, I HAD NO CONFIRMATION. THE THREE DEAD WERE UNIDENTIFIABLE. ONE OF THEM MAY HAVE BEEN ARKWRIGHT...
AND NO ONE OBSERVED HIM LEAVING. IF...
BRING ME YOUR INTERROGATORS. THEY MUST KNOW WHAT HAPPENED.
BY CHRIST, THEY'LL PAY FOR THIS WITH THEIR LIVES.
THEY'VE PAID ALREADY, LORD PROTECTOR.
WHEN WE FOUND THEM, THEIR HAIR...THEIR FACES, WERE BLEACHED OF ALL COLOR. THEIR MINDS WERE DESTROYED ...WIPED CLEAN.
THE ONLY SIGN OF ARKWRIGHT WAS THIS ...

REPEAT: CALLING LONDON! PLEASE RESPOND!

THE FLEET IS DESTROYED! WE'RE OUTCLASSED! THERE'S NOTHING TO HOLD THE PRUSSIANS! THE ESTUARY IS WIDE OPEN! CAN YOU HEAR ME? PLEASE RESPOND! CALLING LONDON!

M-MY GOD! IT'S LIKE THAT SHROUD THEY WORSHIP AT THE VATICAN! WHAT DOES IT MEAN?

I KNOW NOW... ARKWRIGHT IS THE ANTICHRIST... MANTRIPLESIX! THE HOLY ONES WERE RIGHT...

UH? YES, MISS BRADSHAW?

URGENT DISPATCH, MI'LORD: PRIORITY ONE: CAPTAIN BRIDGE-MAN, 1ST CITY OUTER CIRCLE DEFENSE WATCH.

AT LAST! THE ENEMY'S MOVING ON LONDON! THEY'RE WITHIN SIGHT OF OUR BALLOON OBSERVERS. WE HAVE THEM NOW!

PUT THE CITY MARSHALS ON BATTLE STATUS: BLACK ALERT.

HAIL CROMWELL!

OH, MI'LORD-- THE FRENCH AMBASSADOR IS STILL DEMANDING AN AUDIENCE.

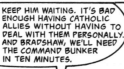

KEEP HIM WAITING. IT'S BAD ENOUGH HAVING CATHOLIC ALLIES WITHOUT HAVING TO DEAL WITH THEM PERSONALLY. AND BRADSHAW, WE'LL NEED THE COMMAND BUNKER IN TEN MINUTES.

HMM. IT SEEMS THAT THE TERRORISTS HAVE SOME SORT OF WAR MACHINES.

I'LL LEAVE NOW, MI'LORD. I WANT TO OVERSEE THE DEFENSE POSITIONS.

NO, STANDISH. SIT DOWN.

THIS IS HISTORY IN THE MAKING. WE WILL NOT BE INTIMIDATED.

LORD PROTECTOR, WHITELAW AND I MUST ALSO BEG LEAVE. IT IS IMPERATIVE THAT WE ARE AT...

ST. JAMES PARK 09.40

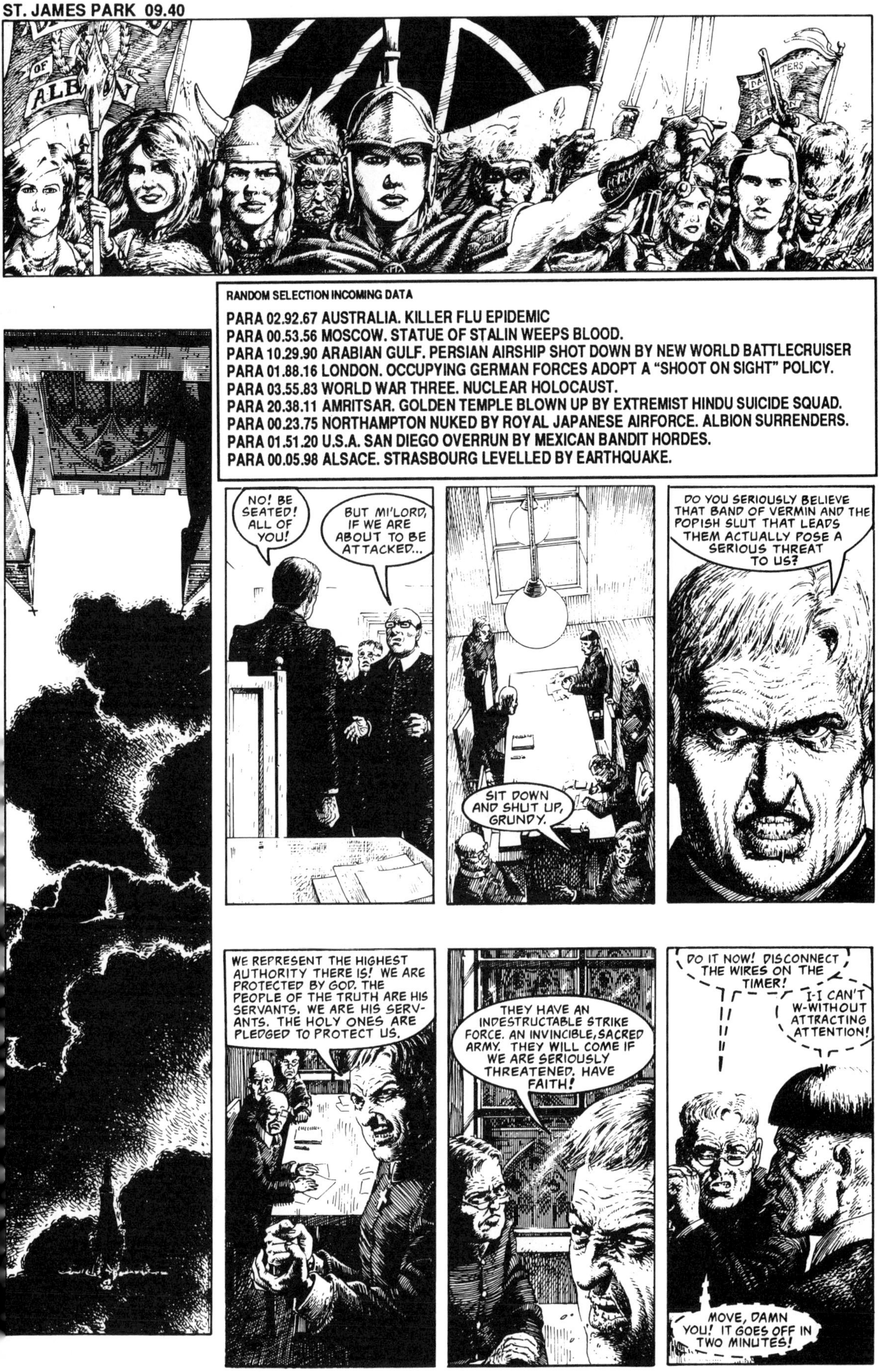

OF ALBION
DAUGHTERS OF ALBION
RANDOM SELECTION INCOMING DATA
PARA 02.92.67 AUSTRALIA. KILLER FLU EPIDEMIC
PARA 00.53.56 MOSCOW. STATUE OF STALIN WEEPS BLOOD.
PARA 10.29.90 ARABIAN GULF. PERSIAN AIRSHIP SHOT DOWN BY NEW WORLD BATTLECRUISER
PARA 01.88.16 LONDON. OCCUPYING GERMAN FORCES ADOPT A "SHOOT ON SIGHT" POLICY.
PARA 03.55.83 WORLD WAR THREE. NUCLEAR HOLOCAUST.
PARA 20.38.11 AMRITSAR. GOLDEN TEMPLE BLOWN UP BY EXTREMIST HINDU SUICIDE SQUAD.
PARA 00.23.75 NORTHAMPTON NUKED BY ROYAL JAPANESE AIRFORCE. ALBION SURRENDERS.
PARA 01.51.20 U.S.A. SAN DIEGO OVERRUN BY MEXICAN BANDIT HORDES.
PARA 00.05.98 ALSACE. STRASBOURG LEVELLED BY EARTHQUAKE.
NO! BE SEATED! ALL OF YOU!
BUT MI'LORD, IF WE ARE ABOUT TO BE ATTACKED...
SIT DOWN AND SHUT UP, GRUNDY.
DO YOU SERIOUSLY BELIEVE THAT BAND OF VERMIN AND THE POPISH SLUT THAT LEADS THEM ACTUALLY POSE A SERIOUS THREAT TO US?
WE REPRESENT THE HIGHEST AUTHORITY THERE IS! WE ARE PROTECTED BY GOD. THE PEOPLE OF THE TRUTH ARE HIS SERVANTS. WE ARE HIS SERVANTS. THE HOLY ONES ARE PLEDGED TO PROTECT US.
THEY HAVE AN INDESTRUCTABLE STRIKE FORCE. AN INVINCIBLE, SACRED ARMY. THEY WILL COME IF WE ARE SERIOUSLY THREATENED. HAVE FAITH!
DO IT NOW! DISCONNECT THE WIRES ON THE TIMER!
I-I CAN'T W-WITHOUT ATTRACTING ATTENTION!
MOVE, DAMN YOU! IT GOES OFF IN TWO MINUTES!

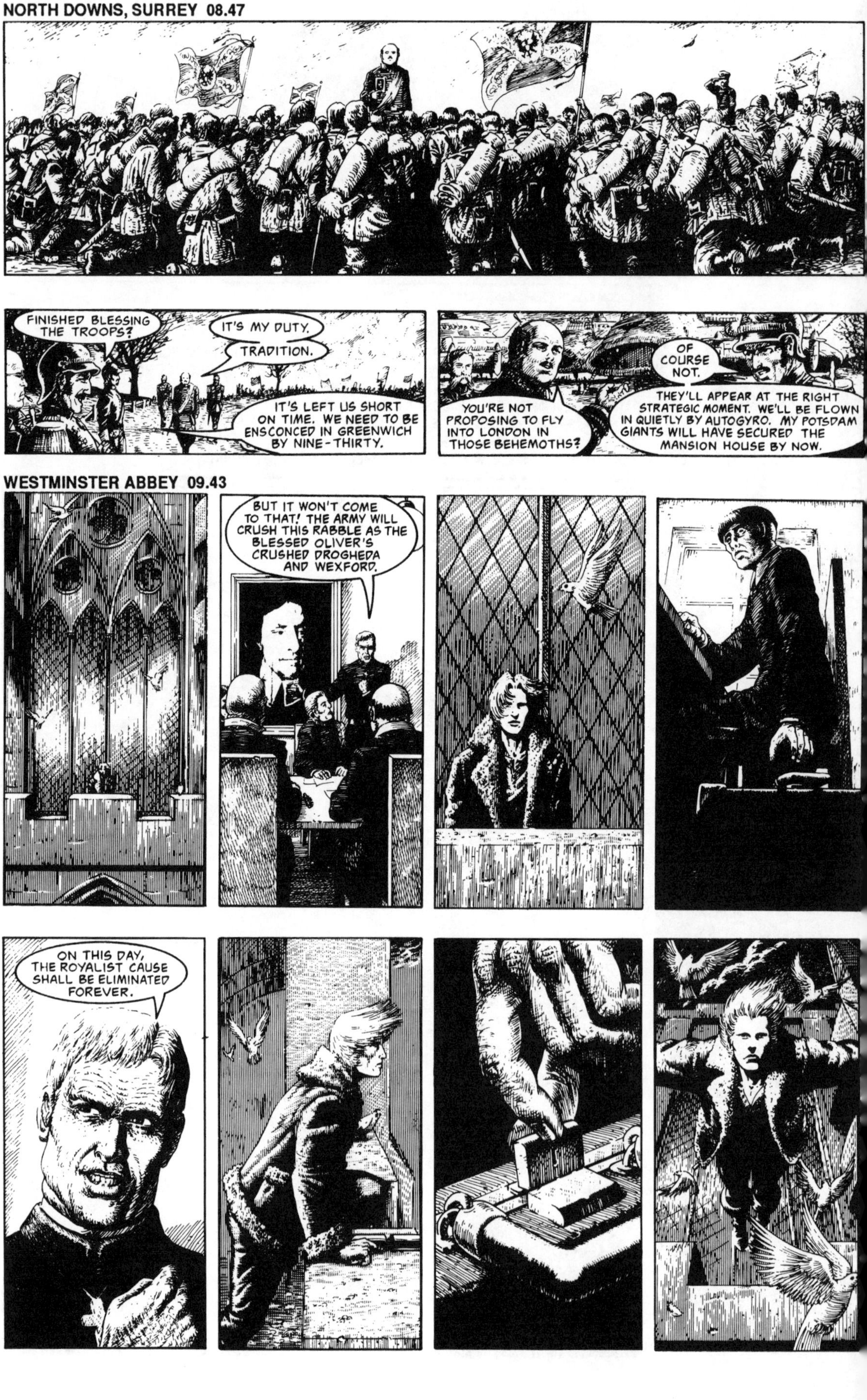
NORTH DOWNS, SURREY 08.47
FINISHED BLESSING THE TROOPS?
IT'S MY DUTY.
TRADITION.
IT'S LEFT US SHORT ON TIME. WE NEED TO BE ENSCONCED IN GREENWICH BY NINE-THIRTY.
YOU'RE NOT PROPOSING TO FLY INTO LONDON IN THOSE BEHEMOTHS?
OF COURSE NOT.
THEY'LL APPEAR AT THE RIGHT STRATEGIC MOMENT. WE'LL BE FLOWN IN QUIETLY BY AUTOGYRO. MY POTSDAM GIANTS WILL HAVE SECURED THE MANSION HOUSE BY NOW.
WESTMINSTER ABBEY 09.43
BUT IT WON'T COME TO THAT! THE ARMY WILL CRUSH THIS RABBLE AS THE BLESSED OLIVER'S CRUSHED DROGHEDA AND WEXFORD.
ON THIS DAY, THE ROYALIST CAUSE SHALL BE ELIMINATED FOREVER.

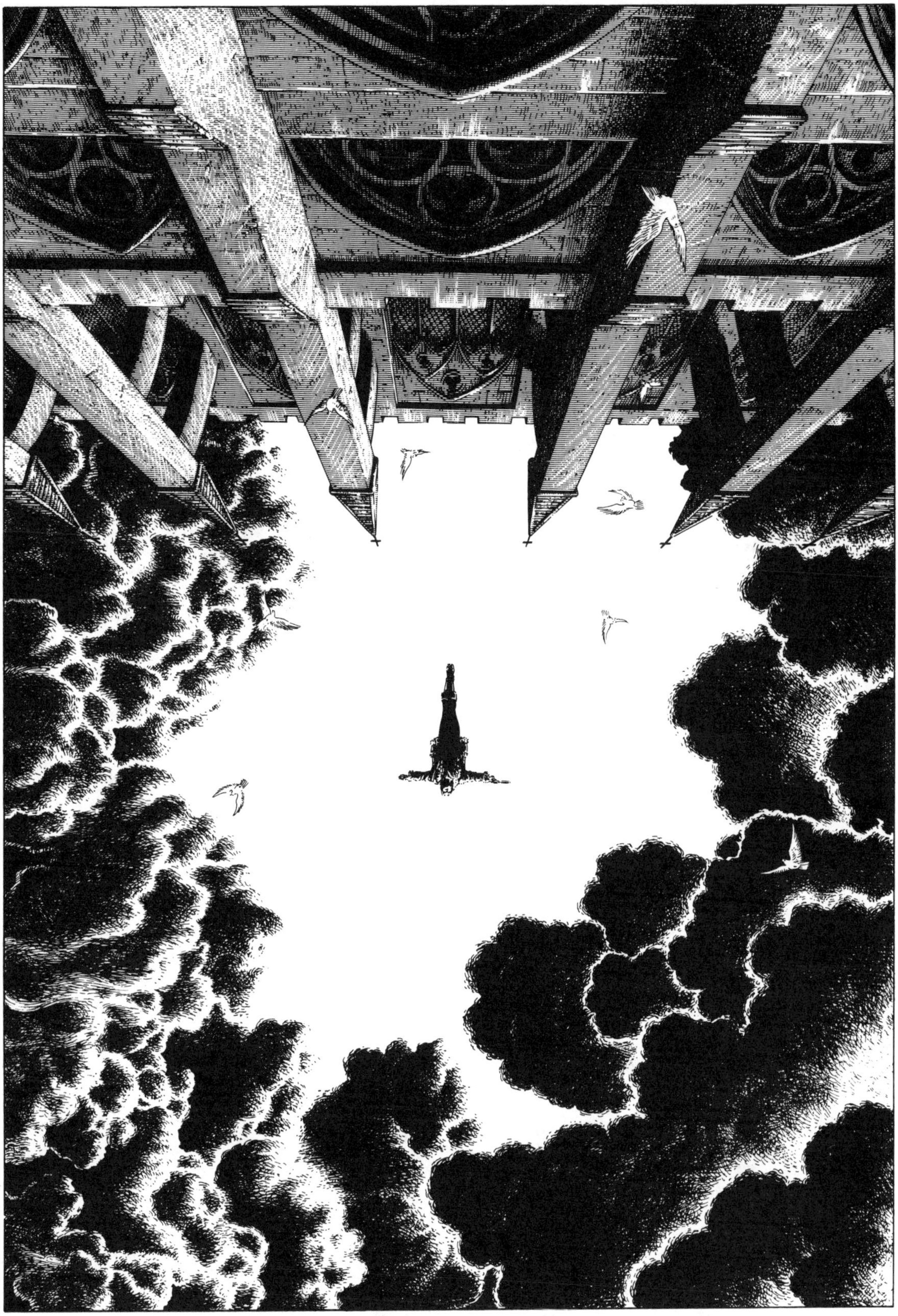

MON 16 OCT 09.43 PARA 00.72.87 WESTMINSTER

"As a 'newly forged man,' the shaman believes that he can overcome the material boundries of existence--that he can repeal the physical laws and reach into the very structure of the universe."

The Second Reality
Johannes von Buttlar Trans. Nicholas Fry

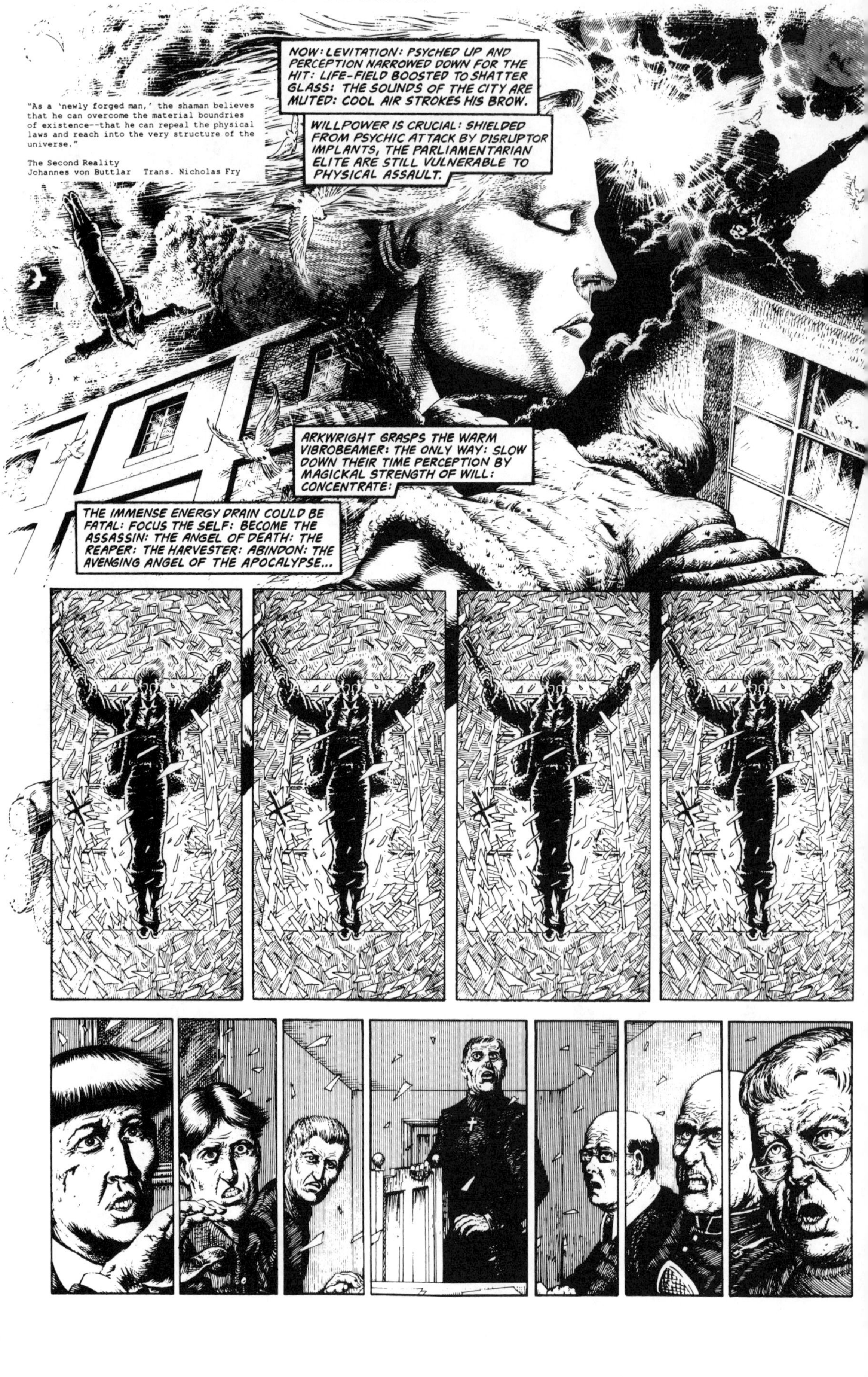
NOW: LEVITATION: PSYCHED UP AND PERCEPTION NARROWED DOWN FOR THE HIT: LIFE-FIELD BOOSTED TO SHATTER GLASS: THE SOUNDS OF THE CITY ARE MUTED: COOL AIR STROKES HIS BROW.
WILLPOWER IS CRUCIAL: SHIELDED FROM PSYCHIC ATTACK BY DISRUPTOR IMPLANTS, THE PARLIAMENTARIAN ELITE ARE STILL VULNERABLE TO PHYSICAL ASSAULT.
ARKWRIGHT GRASPS THE WARM VIBROBEAMER: THE ONLY WAY: SLOW DOWN THEIR TIME PERCEPTION BY MAGICKAL STRENGTH OF WILL: CONCENTRATE:
THE IMMENSE ENERGY DRAIN COULD BE FATAL: FOCUS THE SELF: BECOME THE ASSASSIN: THE ANGEL OF DEATH: THE REAPER: THE HARVESTER: ABINDON: THE AVENGING ANGEL OF THE APOCALYPSE...

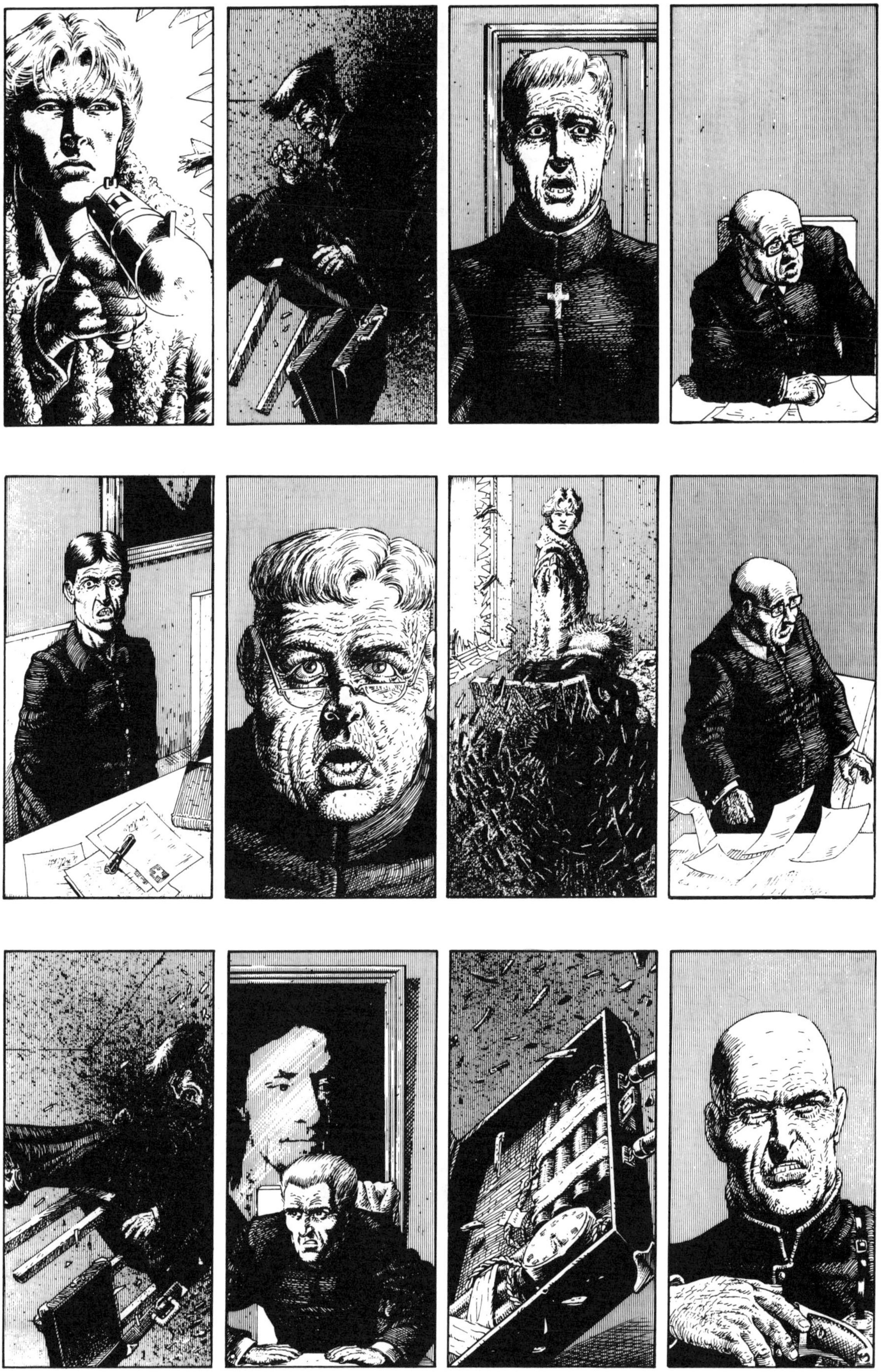

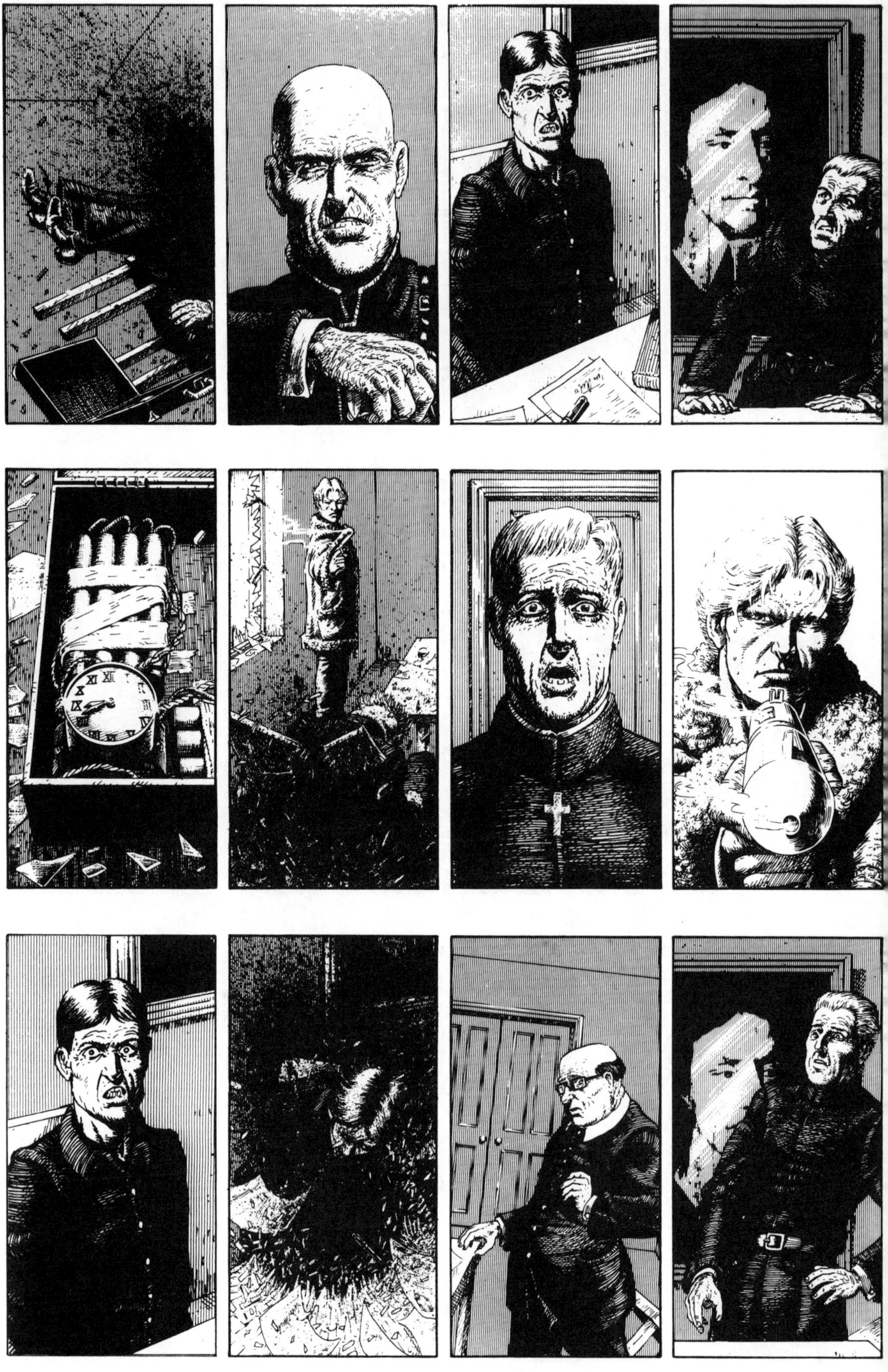

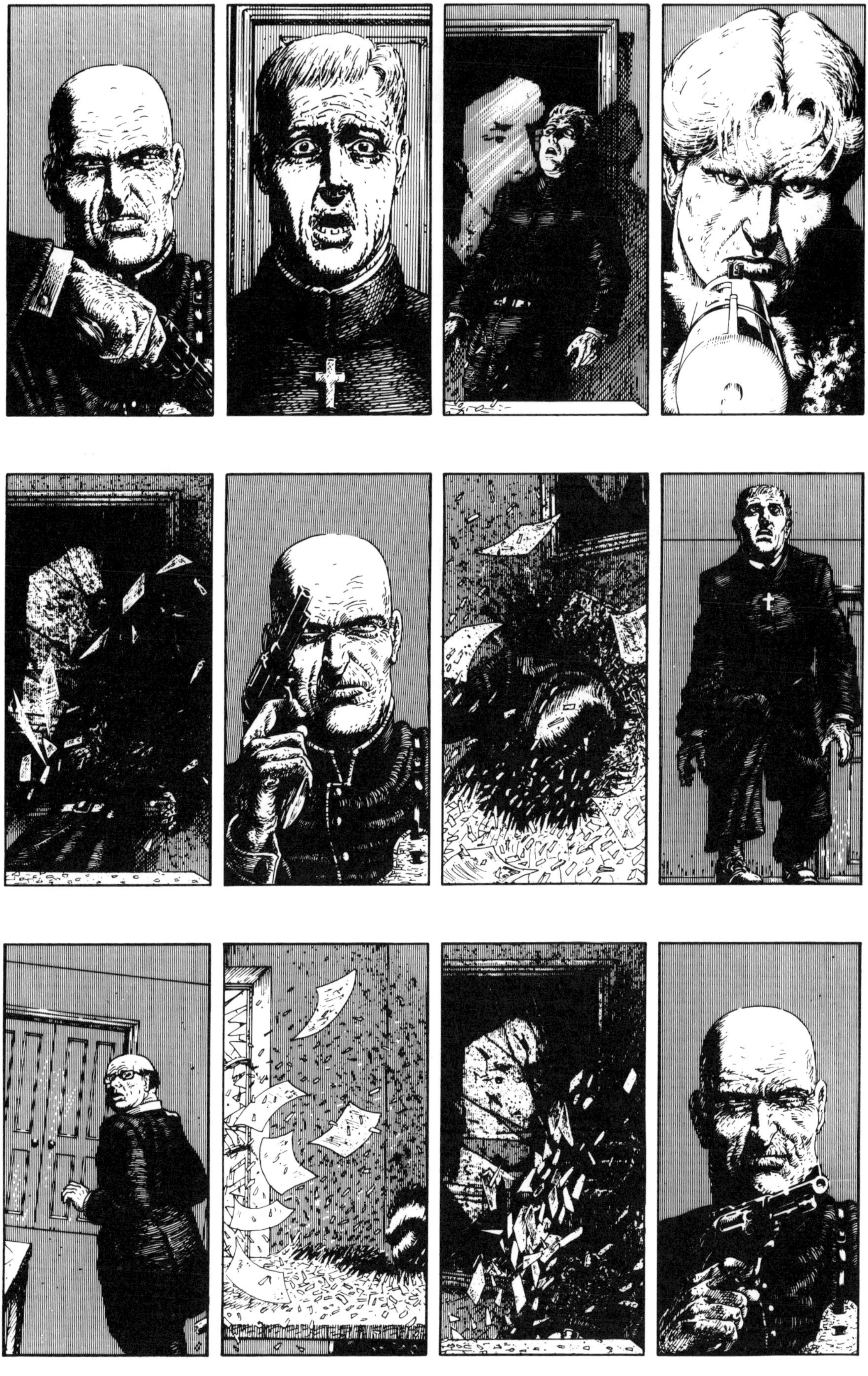

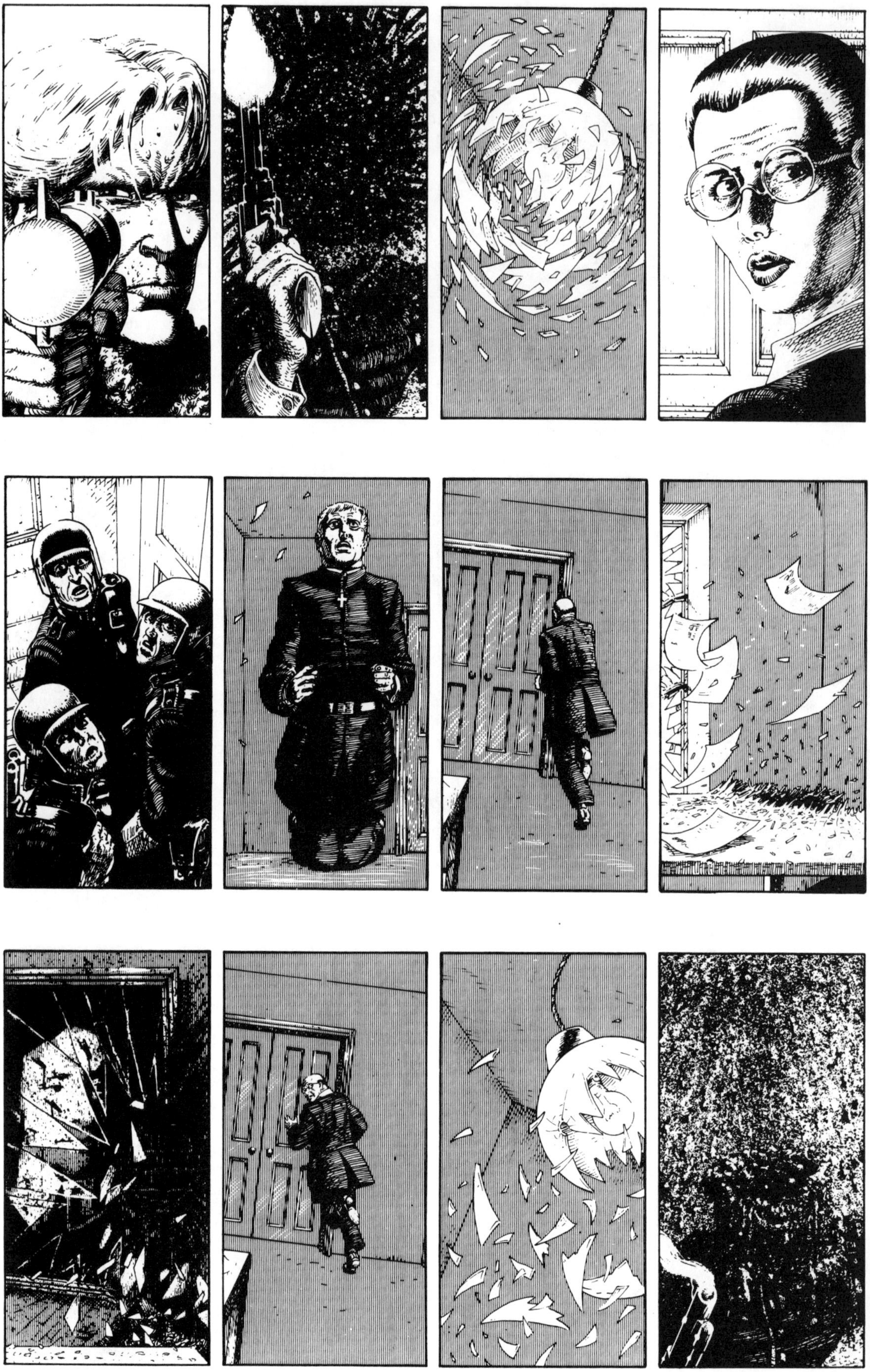

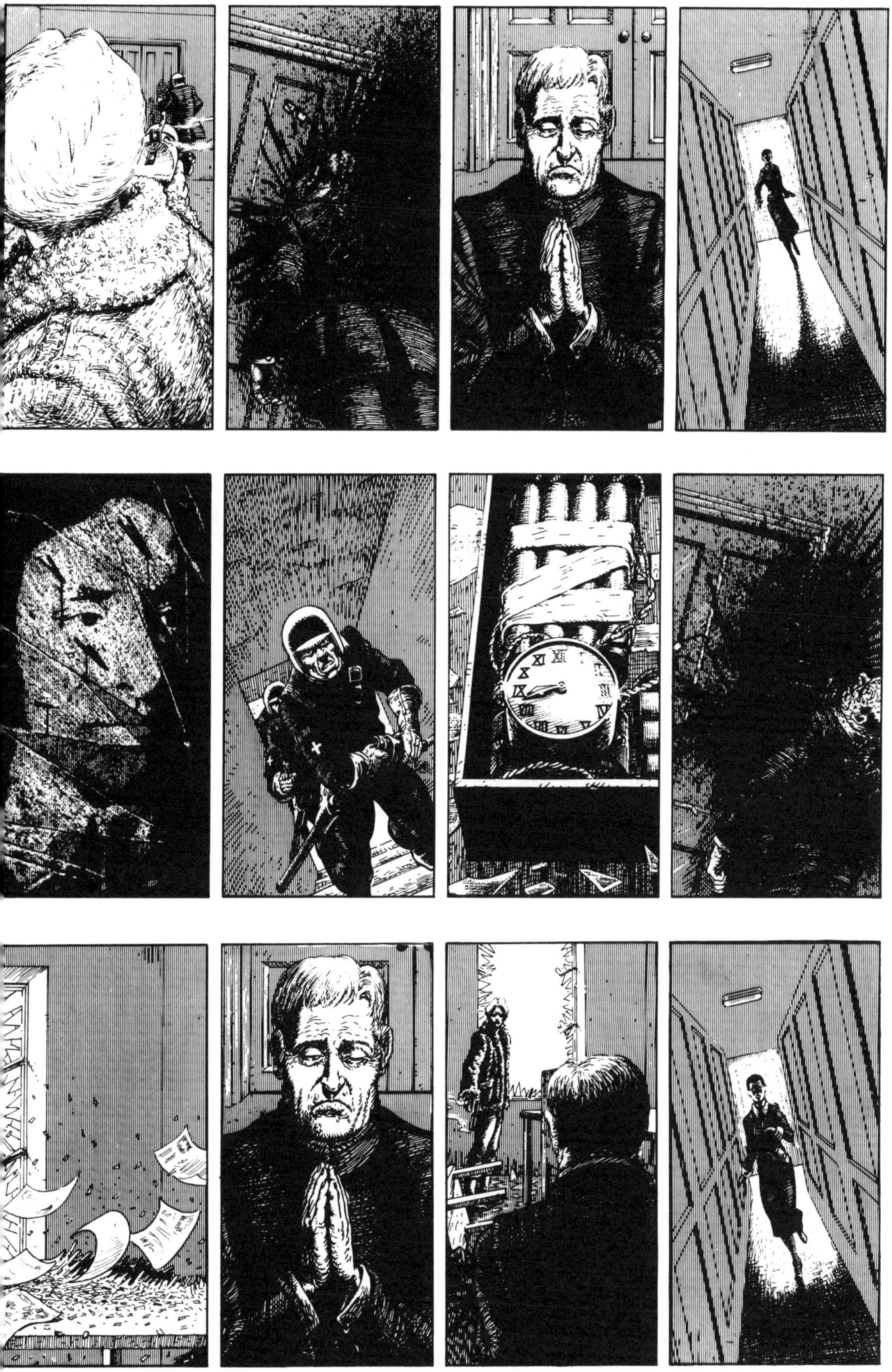

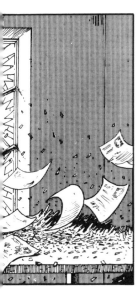

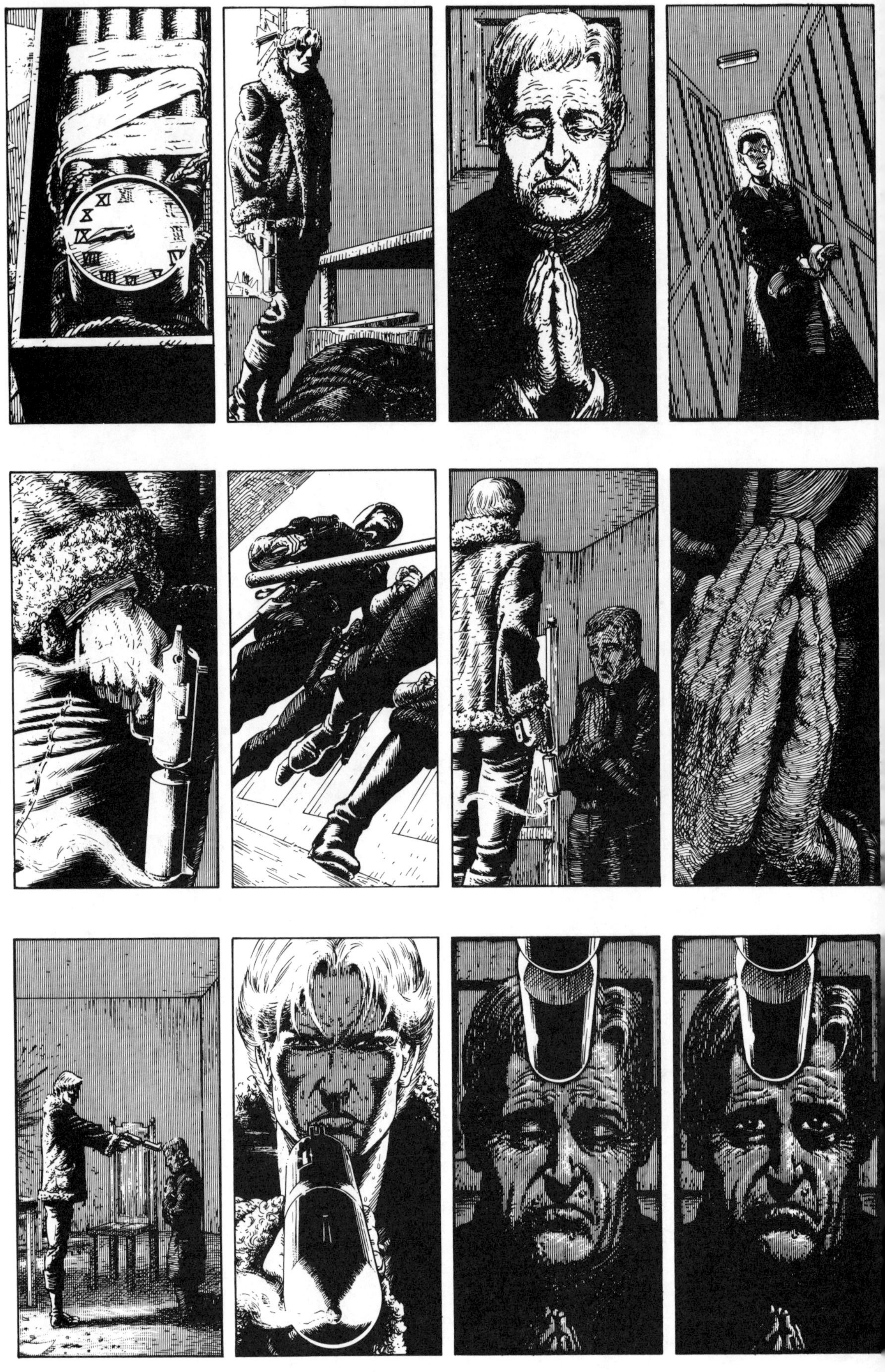

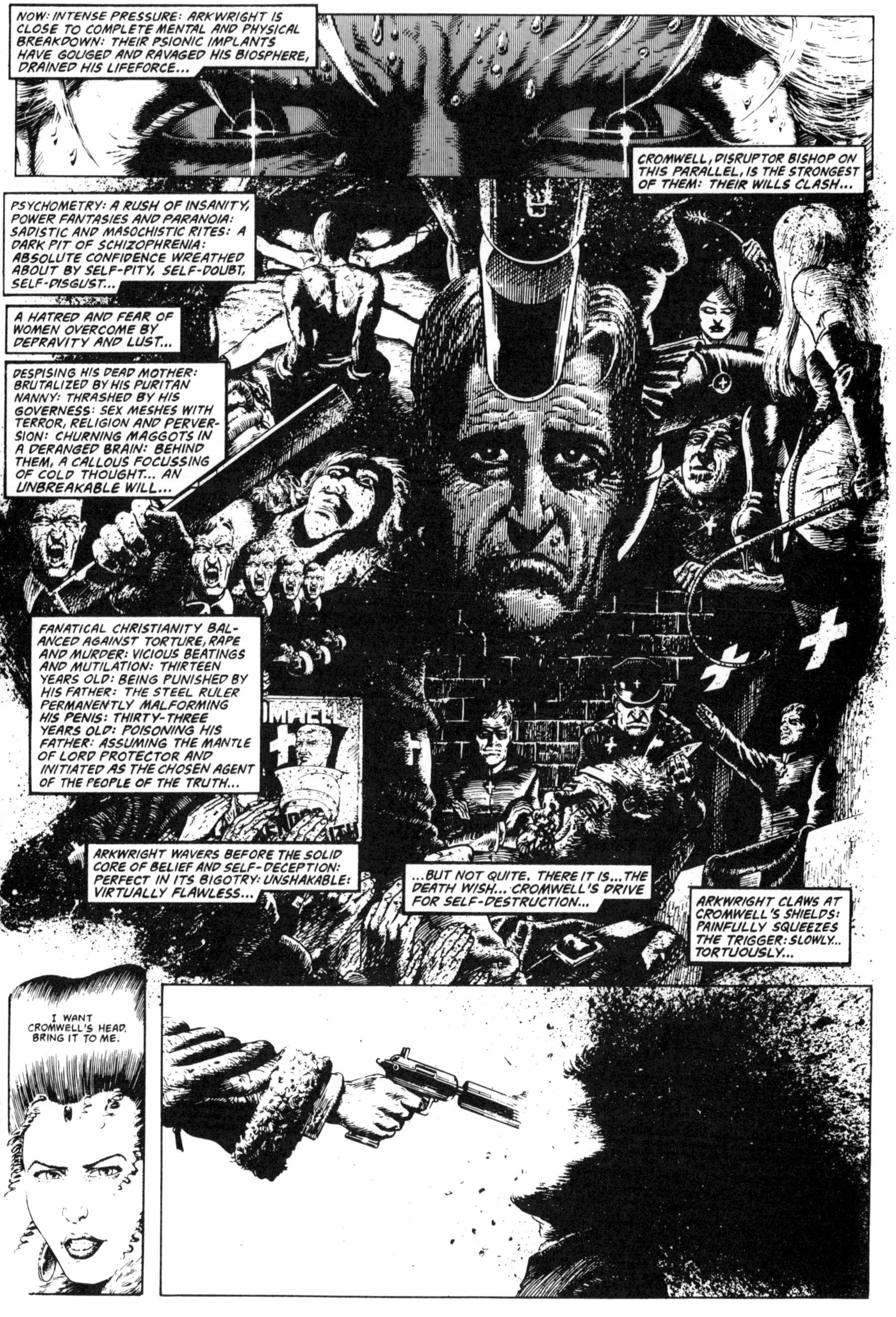
NOW: INTENSE PRESSURE: ARKWRIGHT IS CLOSE TO COMPLETE MENTAL AND PHYSICAL BREAKDOWN: THEIR PSIONIC IMPLANTS HAVE GOUGED AND RAVAGED HIS BIOSPHERE, DRAINED HIS LIFEFORCE...
CROMWELL, DISRUPTOR BISHOP ON THIS PARALLEL, IS THE STRONGEST OF THEM: THEIR WILLS CLASH...
PSYCHOMETRY: A RUSH OF INSANITY, POWER FANTASIES AND PARANOIA: SADISTIC AND MASOCHISTIC RITES: A DARK PIT OF SCHIZOPHRENIA: ABSOLUTE CONFIDENCE WREATHED ABOUT BY SELF-PITY, SELF-DOUBT, SELF-DISGUST...
A HATRED AND FEAR OF WOMEN OVERCOME BY DEPRAVITY AND LUST...
DESPISING HIS DEAD MOTHER: BRUTALIZED BY HIS PURITAN NANNY: THRASHED BY HIS GOVERNESS: SEX MESHES WITH TERROR, RELIGION AND PERVERSION: CHURNING MAGGOTS IN A DERANGED BRAIN: BEHIND THEM, A CALLOUS FOCUSSING OF COLD THOUGHT... AN UNBREAKABLE WILL...
FANATICAL CHRISTIANITY BALANCED AGAINST TORTURE, RAPE AND MURDER: VICIOUS BEATINGS AND MUTILATION: THIRTEEN YEARS OLD: BEING PUNISHED BY HIS FATHER: THE STEEL RULER PERMANENTLY MALFORMING HIS PENIS: THIRTY-THREE YEARS OLD: POISONING HIS FATHER: ASSUMING THE MANTLE OF LORD PROTECTOR AND INITIATED AS THE CHOSEN AGENT OF THE PEOPLE OF THE TRUTH...
ARKWRIGHT WAVERS BEFORE THE SOLID CORE OF BELIEF AND SELF-DECEPTION: PERFECT IN ITS BIGOTRY: UNSHAKABLE: VIRTUALLY FLAWLESS...
...BUT NOT QUITE. THERE IT IS... THE DEATH WISH... CROMWELL'S DRIVE FOR SELF-DESTRUCTION...
ARKWRIGHT CLAWS AT CROMWELL'S SHIELDS: PAINFULLY SQUEEZES THE TRIGGER: SLOWLY... TORTUOUSLY...
I WANT CROMWELL'S HEAD. BRING IT TO ME.

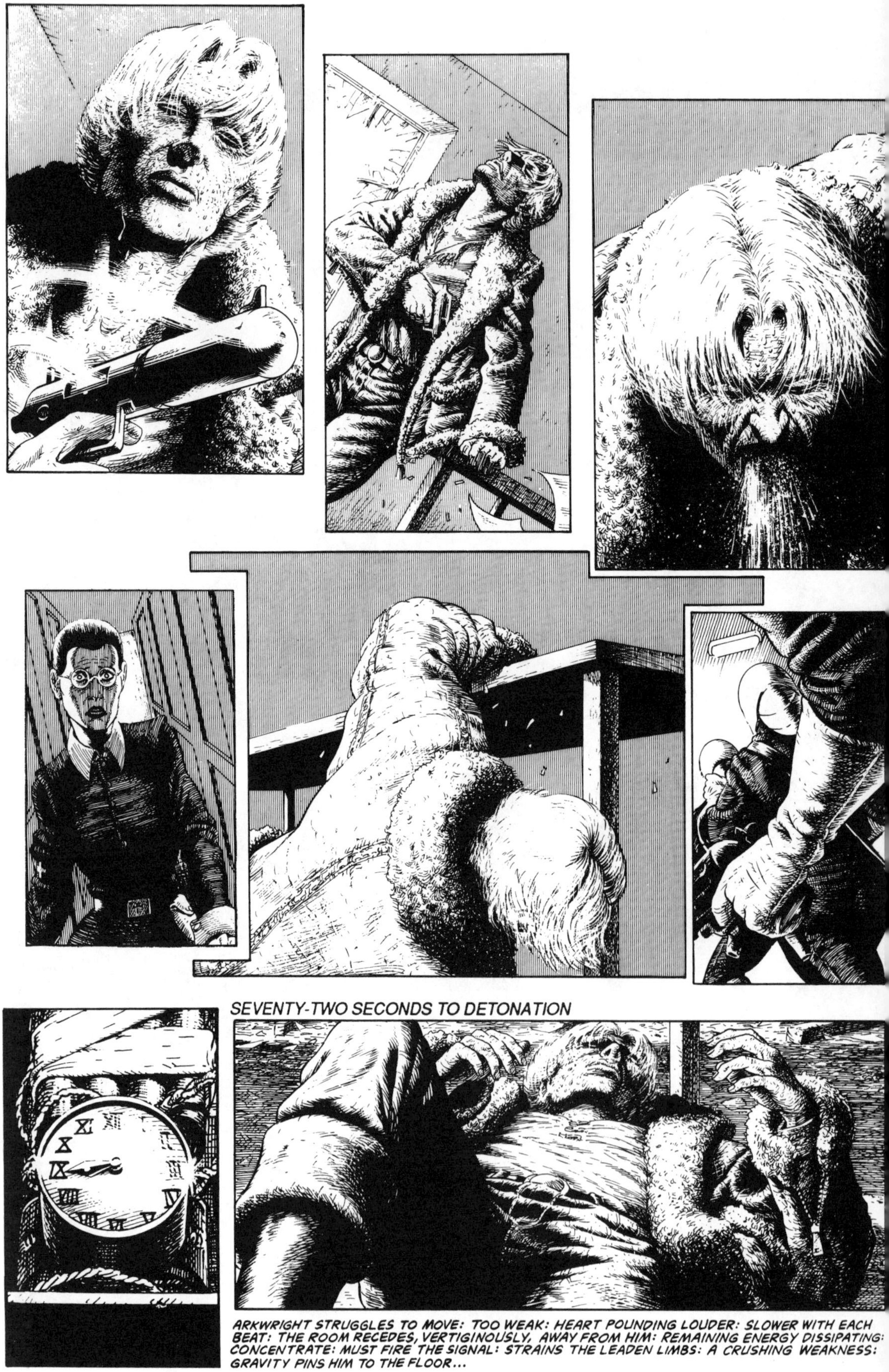
SEVENTY-TWO SECONDS TO DETONATION
ARKWRIGHT STRUGGLES TO MOVE: TOO WEAK: HEART POUNDING LOUDER: SLOWER WITH EACH BEAT: THE ROOM RECEDES, VERTIGINOUSLY, AWAY FROM HIM: REMAINING ENERGY DISSIPATING: CONCENTRATE: MUST FIRE THE SIGNAL: STRAINS THE LEADEN LIMBS: A CRUSHING WEAKNESS: GRAVITY PINS HIM TO THE FLOOR...
SEVENTY SECONDS TO DETONATIO

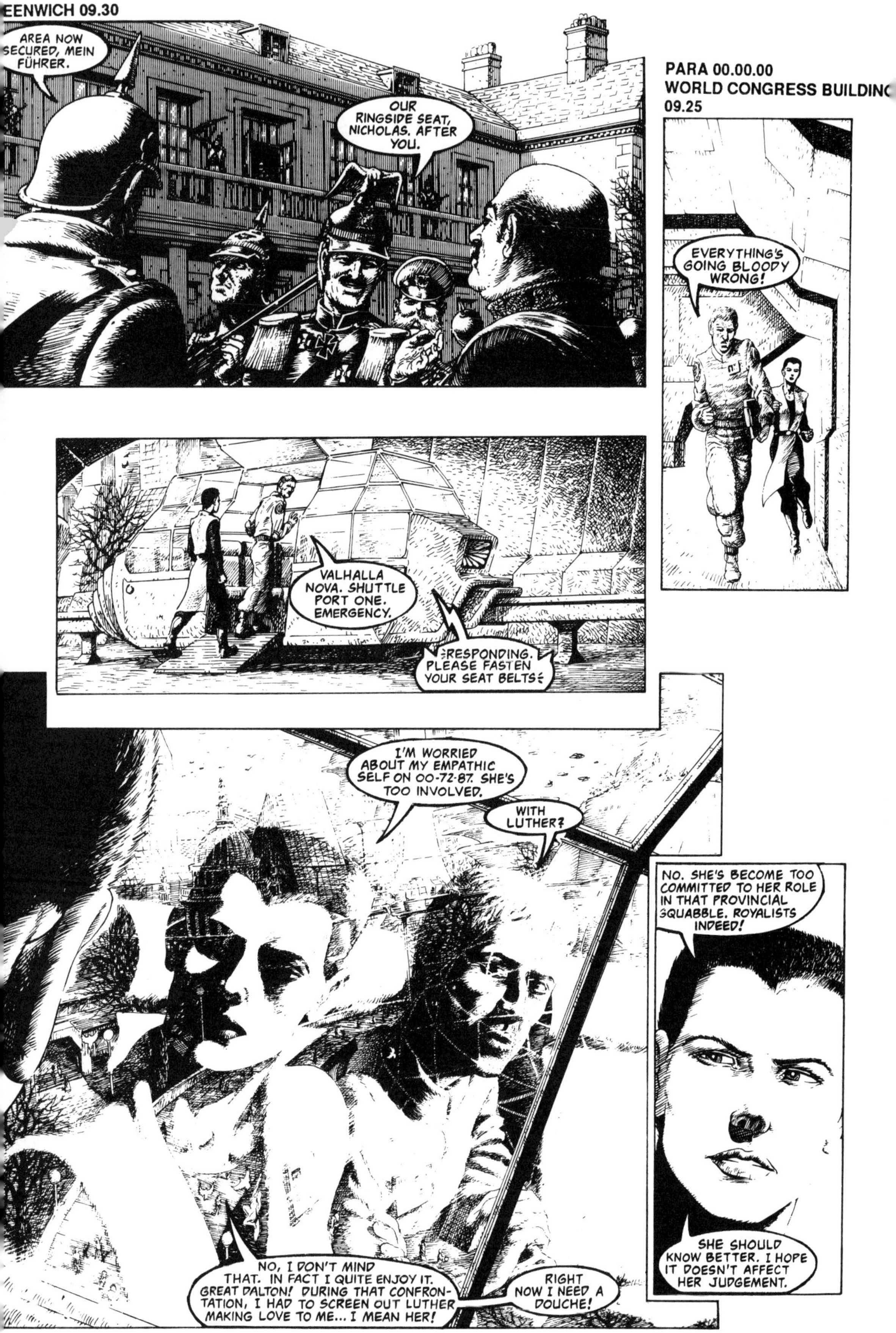
EENWICH 09.30
AREA NOW SECURED, MEIN FÜHRER.
OUR RINGSIDE SEAT, NICHOLAS. AFTER YOU.
PARA 00.00.00
WORLD CONGRESS BUILDIN
09.25
EVERYTHING'S GOING BLOODY WRONG!
VALHALLA NOVA. SHUTTLE PORT ONE. EMERGENCY.
RESPONDING. PLEASE FASTEN YOUR SEAT BELTS
I'M WORRIED ABOUT MY EMPATHIC SELF ON 00-72-87. SHE'S TOO INVOLVED.
WITH LUTHER?
NO. SHE'S BECOME TOO COMMITTED TO HER ROLE IN THAT PROVINCIAL SQUABBLE. ROYALISTS INDEED!
SHE SHOULD KNOW BETTER. I HOPE IT DOESN'T AFFECT HER JUDGEMENT.
NO, I DON'T MIND THAT. IN FACT I QUITE ENJOY IT. GREAT DALTON! DURING THAT CONFRONTATION, I HAD TO SCREEN OUT LUTHER MAKING LOVE TO ME... I MEAN HER!
RIGHT NOW I NEED A DOUCHE!

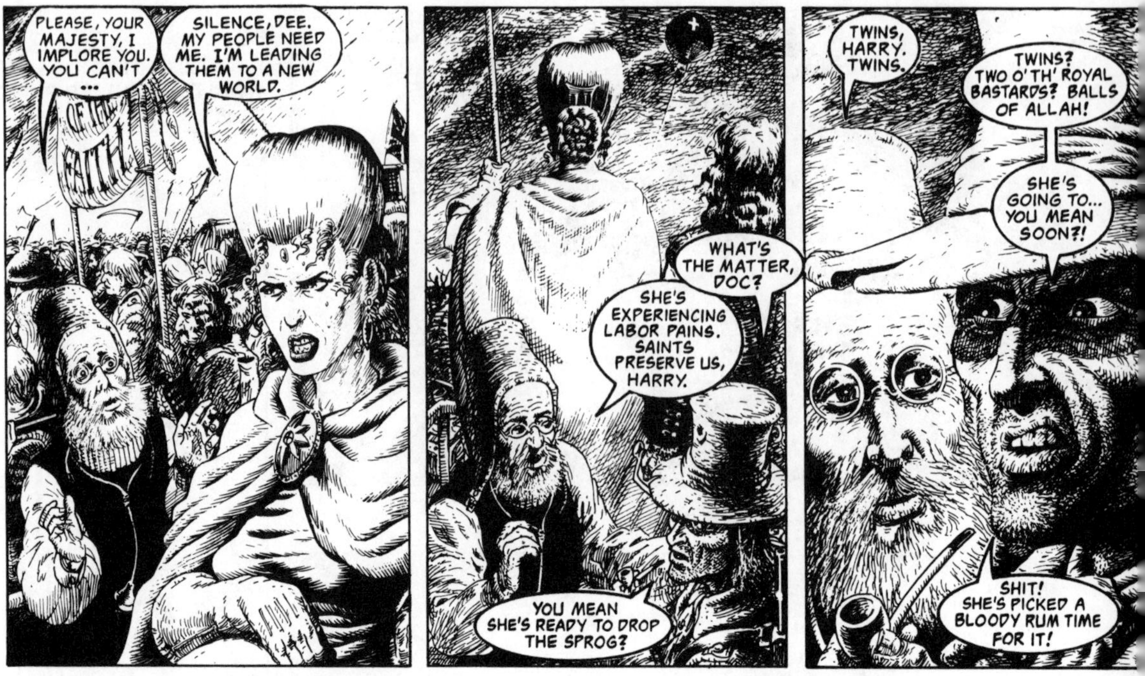
PLEASE, YOUR MAJESTY, I IMPLORE YOU. YOU CAN'T ...
SILENCE, DEE. MY PEOPLE NEED ME. I'M LEADING THEM TO A NEW WORLD.
WHAT'S THE MATTER, DOC?
SHE'S EXPERIENCING LABOR PAINS. SAINTS PRESERVE US, HARRY.
YOU MEAN SHE'S READY TO DROP THE SPROG?
TWINS, HARRY. TWINS.
TWINS? TWO O'TH' ROYAL BASTARDS? BALLS OF ALLAH!
SHE'S GOING TO... YOU MEAN SOON?!
SHIT! SHE'S PICKED A BLOODY RUM TIME FOR IT!

PARA 20.15.32 OZONE LAYER COLLAPSE. HOTHOUSE EFFECT
PARA 02.89.05 WASHINGTON. PLAGUE OF LOCUSTS.
PARA 03.59.51 SOLAR FLARES STERILIZE EARTH.
PARA 10.23.87 ROME. MASS DEMONIC POSSESSION.
PARA 01.08.91 WORLD WAR II DECLARED.
PARA 00.05.80 LONDON. TERRORIST NUCLEAR DEVICE EXPLODED.
PARA 20.09.16 PORT AU PRINCE. BABYDOC SPONTANEOUSLY MELT
PARA 01.55.42 ICELAND. MOUNT HELKA ERUPTS.
PARA 02.10.69 WORLD WAR I DECLARED.

12.30

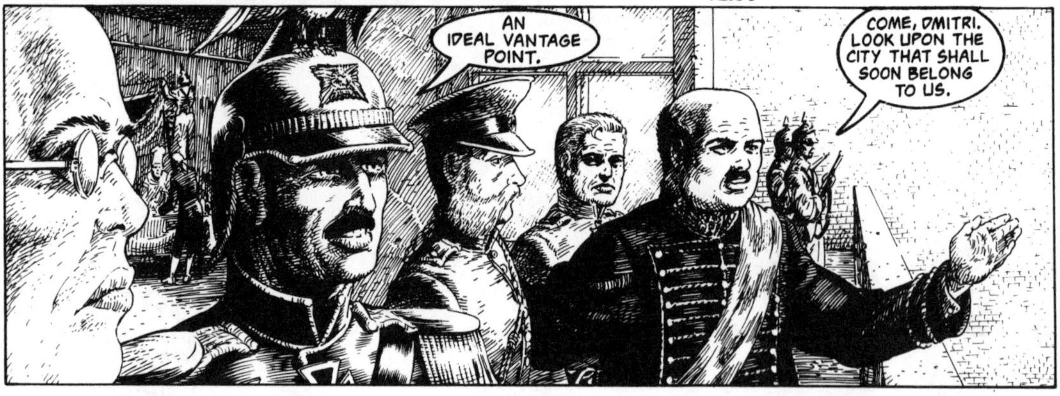
AN IDEAL VANTAGE POINT.
COME, DMITRI. LOOK UPON THE CITY THAT SHALL SOON BELONG TO US.

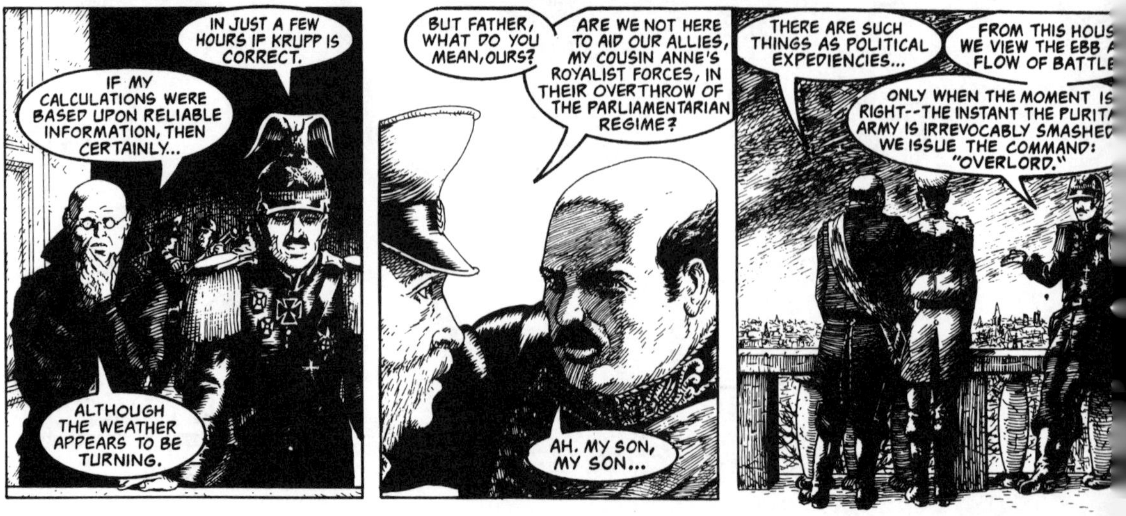
IN JUST A FEW HOURS IF KRUPP IS CORRECT.
IF MY CALCULATIONS WERE BASED UPON RELIABLE INFORMATION, THEN CERTAINLY...
ALTHOUGH THE WEATHER APPEARS TO BE TURNING.
BUT FATHER, WHAT DO YOU MEAN, OURS?
ARE WE NOT HERE TO AID OUR ALLIES, MY COUSIN ANNE'S ROYALIST FORCES, IN THEIR OVERTHROW OF THE PARLIAMENTARIAN REGIME?
AH. MY SON, MY SON...
THERE ARE SUCH THINGS AS POLITICAL EXPEDIENCIES...
FROM THIS HOUS WE VIEW THE EBB A FLOW OF BATTLE
ONLY WHEN THE MOMENT IS RIGHT--THE INSTANT THE PURITA ARMY IS IRREVOCABLY SMASHED WE ISSUE THE COMMAND: "OVERLORD."

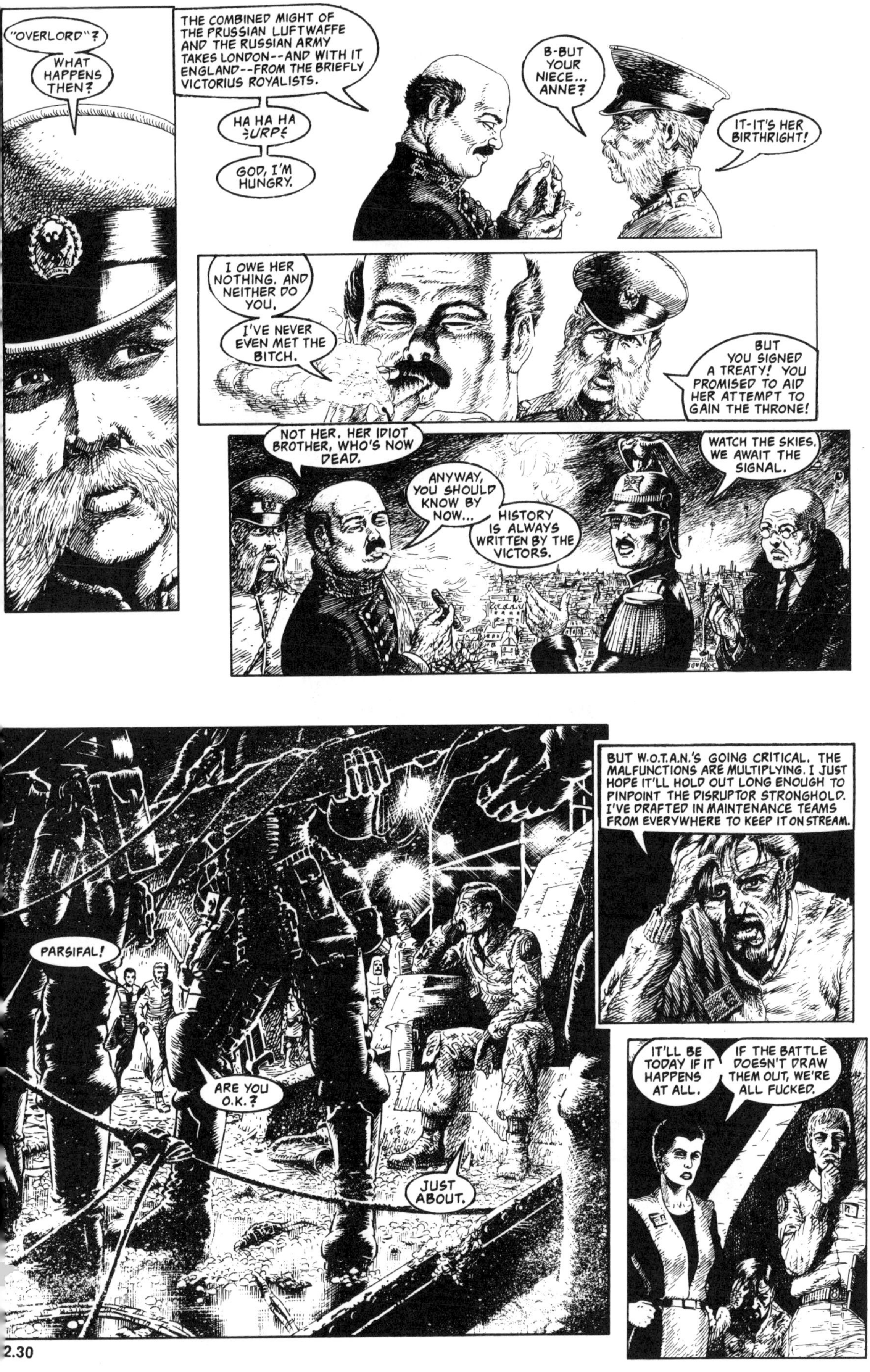
"OVERLORD"?
WHAT HAPPENS THEN?
THE COMBINED MIGHT OF THE PRUSSIAN LUFTWAFFE AND THE RUSSIAN ARMY TAKES LONDON--AND WITH IT ENGLAND--FROM THE BRIEFLY VICTORIUS ROYALISTS.
HA HA HA BURP
GOD, I'M HUNGRY.
B-BUT YOUR NIECE... ANNE?
IT-IT'S HER BIRTHRIGHT!
I OWE HER NOTHING. AND NEITHER DO YOU.
I'VE NEVER EVEN MET THE BITCH.
BUT YOU SIGNED A TREATY! YOU PROMISED TO AID HER ATTEMPT TO GAIN THE THRONE!
NOT HER. HER IDIOT BROTHER, WHO'S NOW DEAD.
ANYWAY, YOU SHOULD KNOW BY NOW...
HISTORY IS ALWAYS WRITTEN BY THE VICTORS.
WATCH THE SKIES. WE AWAIT THE SIGNAL.
PARSIFAL!
ARE YOU O.K.?
JUST ABOUT.
BUT W.O.T.A.N.'S GOING CRITICAL. THE MALFUNCTIONS ARE MULTIPLYING. I JUST HOPE IT'LL HOLD OUT LONG ENOUGH TO PINPOINT THE DISRUPTOR STRONGHOLD. I'VE DRAFTED IN MAINTENANCE TEAMS FROM EVERYWHERE TO KEEP IT ON STREAM.
IT'LL BE TODAY IF IT HAPPENS AT ALL.
IF THE BATTLE DOESN'T DRAW THEM OUT, WE'RE ALL FUCKED.

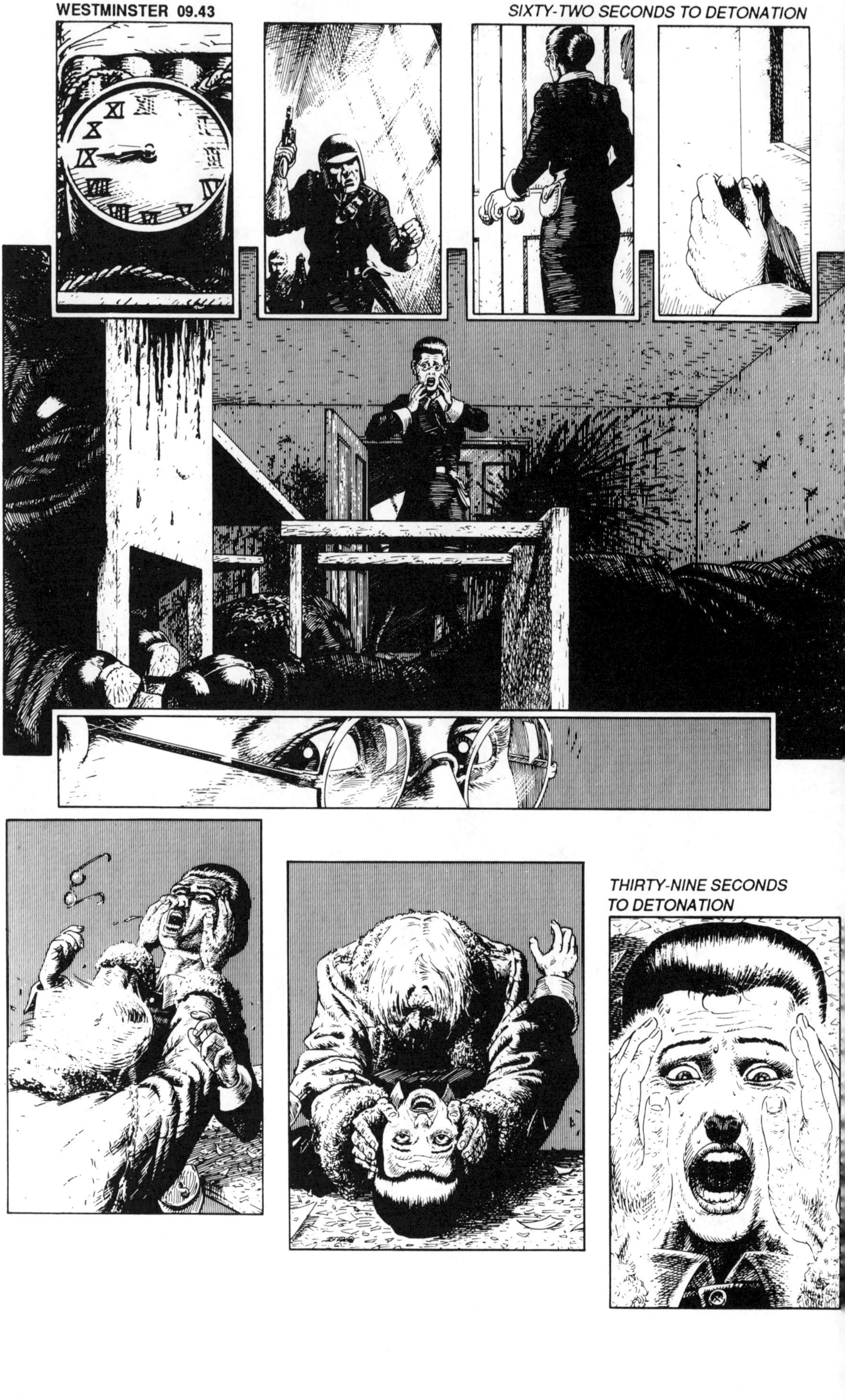
WESTMINSTER 09.43
SIXTY-TWO SECONDS TO DETONATION
THIRTY-NINE SECONDS TO DETONATION

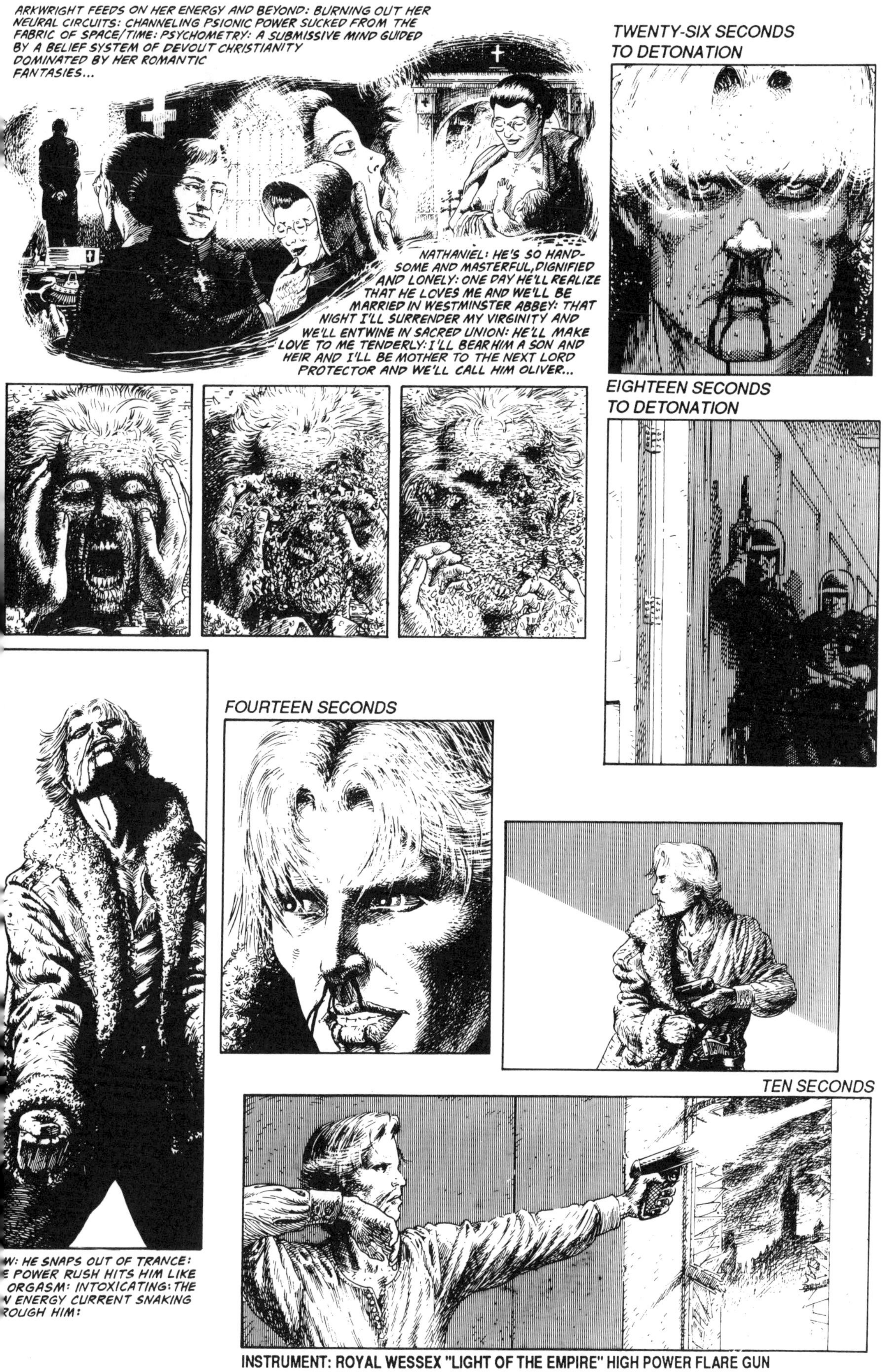
ARKWRIGHT FEEDS ON HER ENERGY AND BEYOND: BURNING OUT HER NEURAL CIRCUITS: CHANNELING PSIONIC POWER SUCKED FROM THE FABRIC OF SPACE/TIME: PSYCHOMETRY: A SUBMISSIVE MIND GUIDED BY A BELIEF SYSTEM OF DEVOUT CHRISTIANITY DOMINATED BY HER ROMANTIC FANTASIES...
NATHANIEL: HE'S SO HANDSOME AND MASTERFUL, DIGNIFIED AND LONELY: ONE DAY HE'LL REALIZE THAT HE LOVES ME AND WE'LL BE MARRIED IN WESTMINSTER ABBEY: THAT NIGHT I'LL SURRENDER MY VIRGINITY AND WE'LL ENTWINE IN SACRED UNION: HE'LL MAKE LOVE TO ME TENDERLY: I'LL BEAR HIM A SON AND HEIR AND I'LL BE MOTHER TO THE NEXT LORD PROTECTOR AND WE'LL CALL HIM OLIVER...
TWENTY-SIX SECONDS TO DETONATION
EIGHTEEN SECONDS TO DETONATION
FOURTEEN SECONDS
W: HE SNAPS OUT OF TRANCE: E POWER RUSH HITS HIM LIKE ORGASM: INTOXICATING: THE N ENERGY CURRENT SNAKING ROUGH HIM:
TEN SECONDS
INSTRUMENT: ROYAL WESSEX "LIGHT OF THE EMPIRE" HIGH POWER FLARE GUN

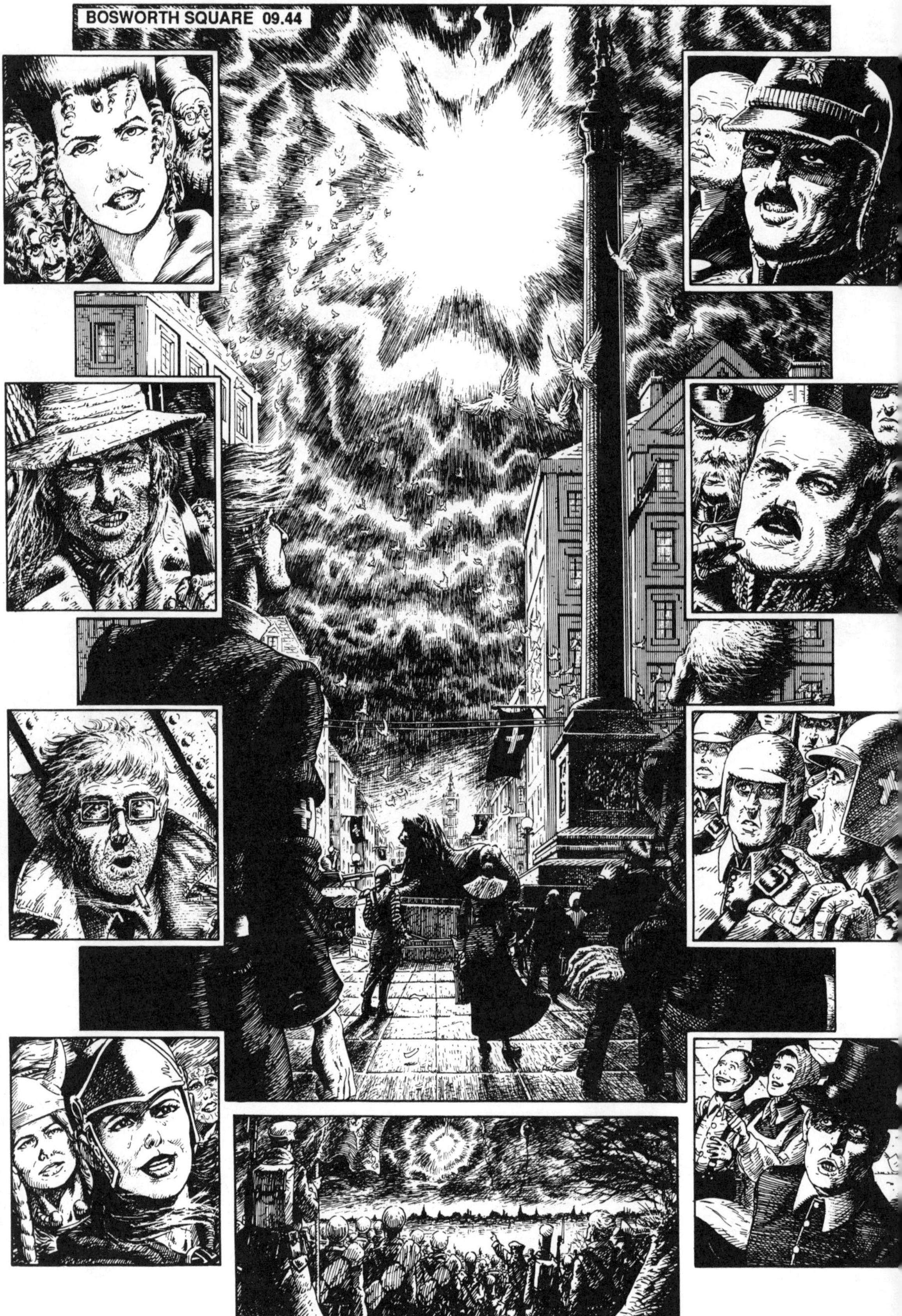
BOSWORTH SQUARE 09.44
WANDSWORTH 09.44

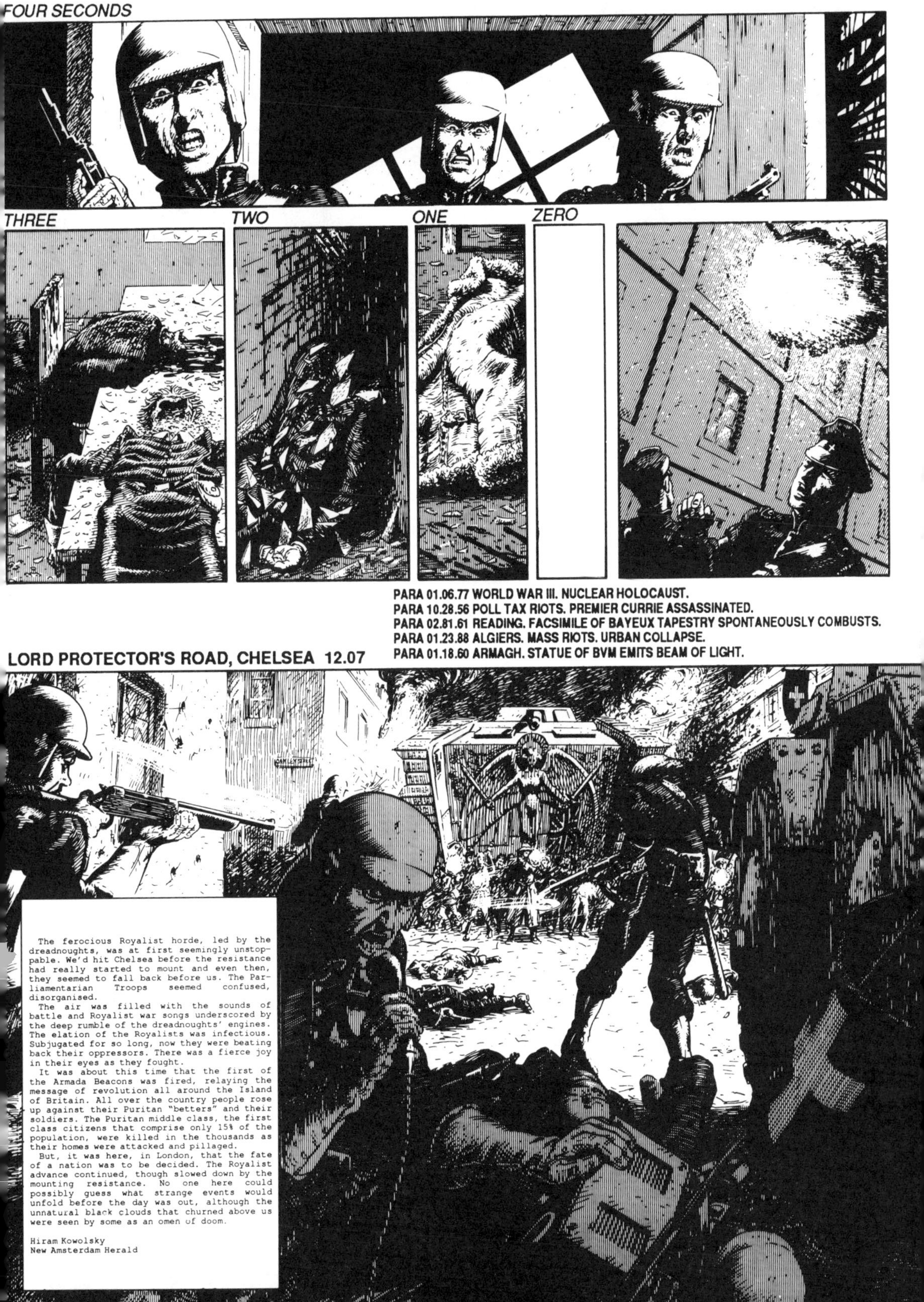
FOUR SECONDS
THREE
TWO
ONE
ZERO
PARA 01.06.77 WORLD WAR III. NUCLEAR HOLOCAUST.
PARA 10.28.56 POLL TAX RIOTS. PREMIER CURRIE ASSASSINATED.
PARA 02.81.61 READING. FACSIMILE OF BAYEUX TAPESTRY SPONTANEOUSLY COMBUSTS.
PARA 01.23.88 ALGIERS. MASS RIOTS. URBAN COLLAPSE.
PARA 01.18.60 ARMAGH. STATUE OF BVM EMITS BEAM OF LIGHT.
LORD PROTECTOR'S ROAD, CHELSEA 12.07
The ferocious Royalist horde, led by the dreadnoughts, was at first seemingly unstoppable. We'd hit Chelsea before the resistance had really started to mount and even then, they seemed to fall back before us. The Parliamentarian Troops seemed confused, disorganised.
The air was filled with the sounds of battle and Royalist war songs underscored by the deep rumble of the dreadnoughts' engines. The elation of the Royalists was infectious. Subjugated for so long, now they were beating back their oppressors. There was a fierce joy in their eyes as they fought.
It was about this time that the first of the Armada Beacons was fired, relaying the message of revolution all around the Island of Britain. All over the country people rose up against their Puritan "betters" and their soldiers. The Puritan middle class, the first class citizens that comprise only 15% of the population, were killed in the thousands as their homes were attacked and pillaged.
But, it was here, in London, that the fate of a nation was to be decided. The Royalist advance continued, though slowed down by the mounting resistance. No one here could possibly guess what strange events would unfold before the day was out, although the unnatural black clouds that churned above us were seen by some as an omen of doom.
Hiram Kowolsky
New Amsterdam Herald

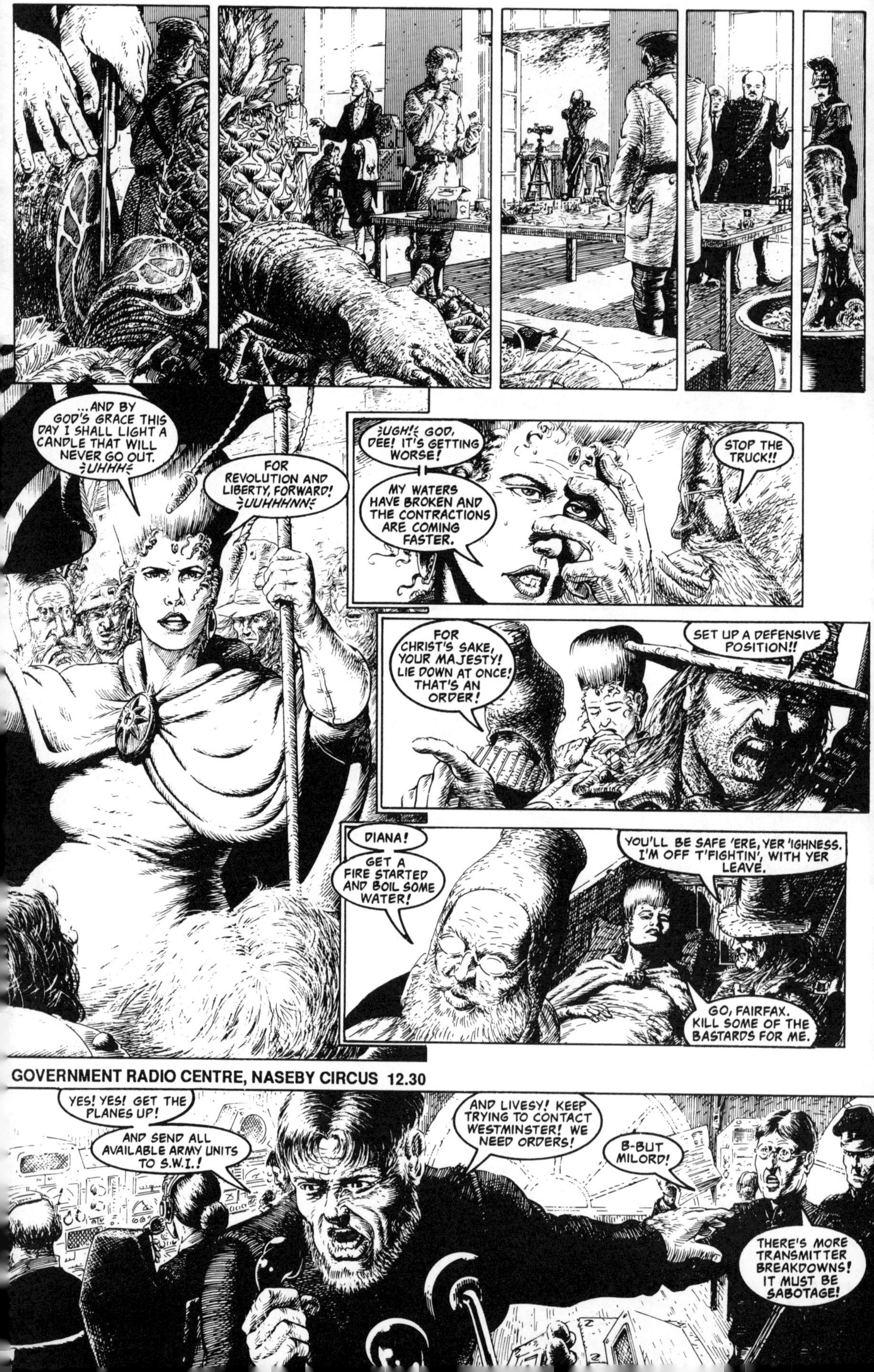
...AND BY GOD'S GRACE THIS DAY I SHALL LIGHT A CANDLE THAT WILL NEVER GO OUT. UHHH
FOR REVOLUTION AND LIBERTY, FORWARD! UUHHHHN
UGH! GOD, DEE! IT'S GETTING WORSE!
MY WATERS HAVE BROKEN AND THE CONTRACTIONS ARE COMING FASTER.
STOP THE TRUCK!!
FOR CHRIST'S SAKE, YOUR MAJESTY! LIE DOWN AT ONCE! THAT'S AN ORDER!
SET UP A DEFENSIVE POSITION!!
DIANA!
GET A FIRE STARTED AND BOIL SOME WATER!
YOU'LL BE SAFE 'ERE, YER 'IGHNESS. I'M OFF T'FIGHTIN', WITH YER LEAVE.
GO, FAIRFAX. KILL SOME OF THE BASTARDS FOR ME.
GOVERNMENT RADIO CENTRE, NASEBY CIRCUS 12.30
YES! YES! GET THE PLANES UP!
AND SEND ALL AVAILABLE ARMY UNITS TO S.W.I.!
AND LIVESY! KEEP TRYING TO CONTACT WESTMINSTER! WE NEED ORDERS!
B-BUT MILORD!
THERE'S MORE TRANSMITTER BREAKDOWNS! IT MUST BE SABOTAGE!

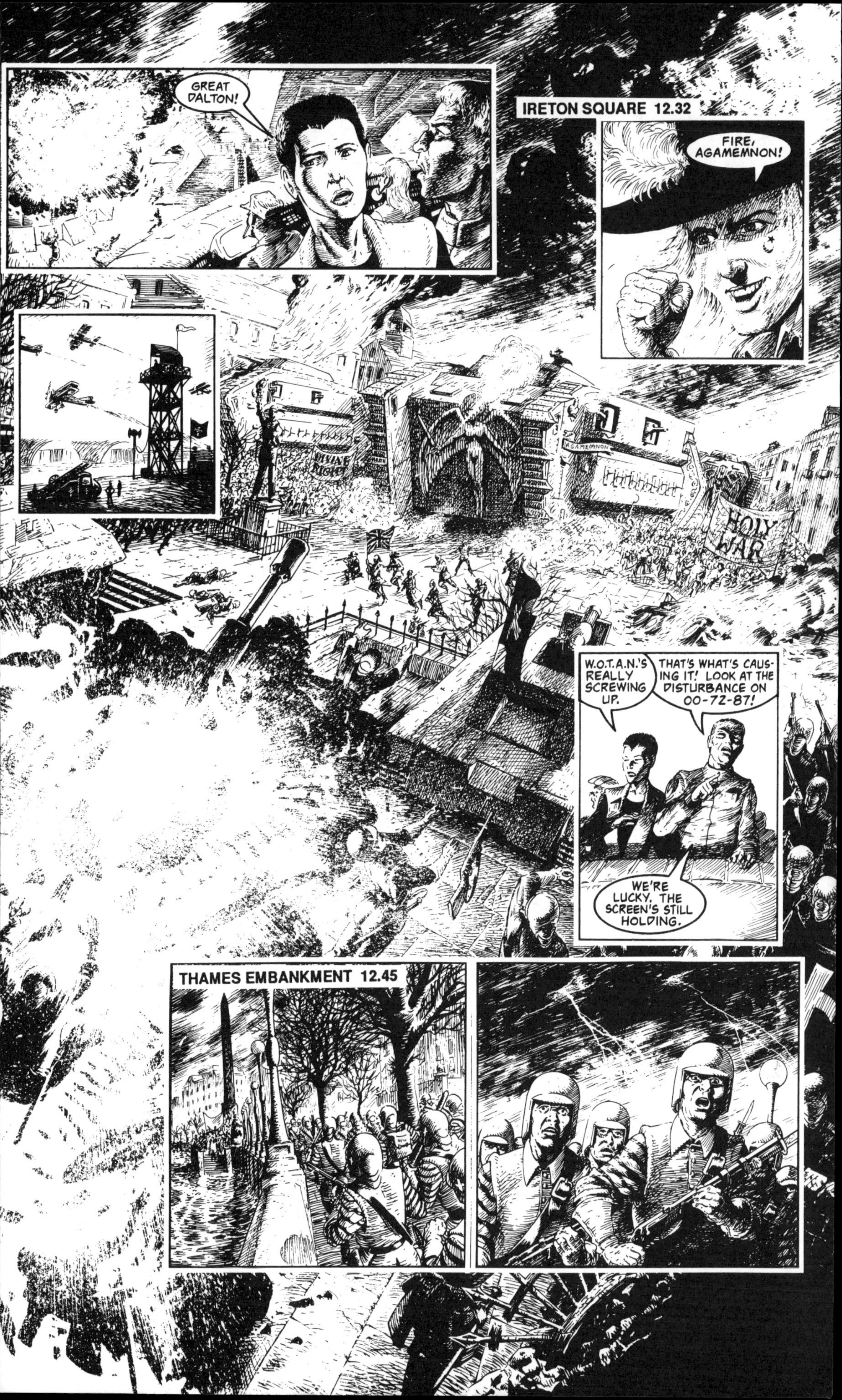
GREAT DALTON!
IRETON SQUARE 12.32
FIRE, AGAMEMNON!
DIVINE RIGHT
AGAMEMNON
HOLY WAR
W.O.T.A.N.'S REALLY SCREWING UP.
THAT'S WHAT'S CAUSING IT! LOOK AT THE DISTURBANCE ON 00-72-87!
WE'RE LUCKY. THE SCREEN'S STILL HOLDING.
THAMES EMBANKMENT 12.45

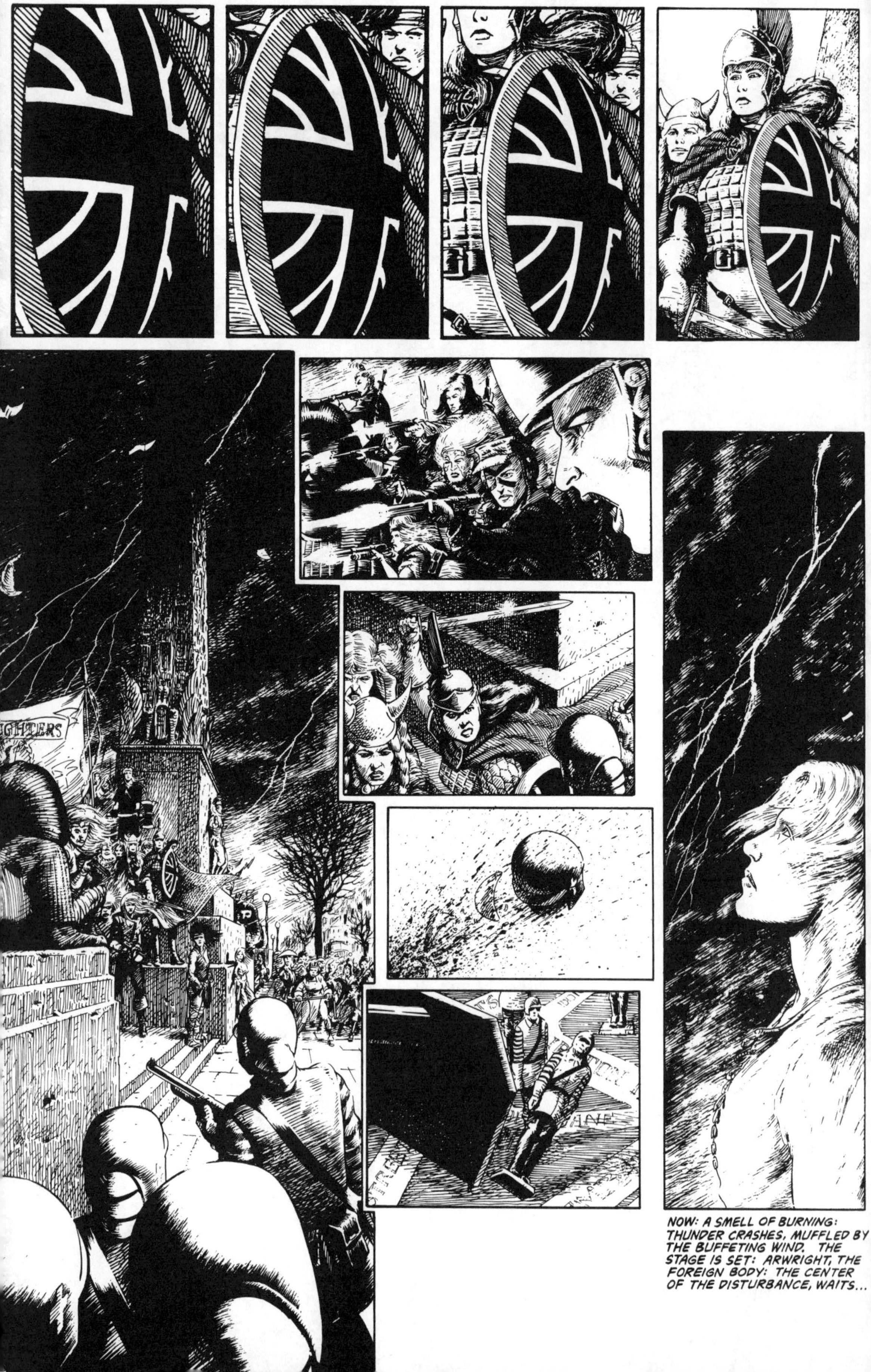
NOW: A SMELL OF BURNING: THUNDER CRASHES, MUFFLED BY THE BUFFETING WIND. THE STAGE IS SET: ARWRIGHT, THE FOREIGN BODY: THE CENTER OF THE DISTURBANCE, WAITS...

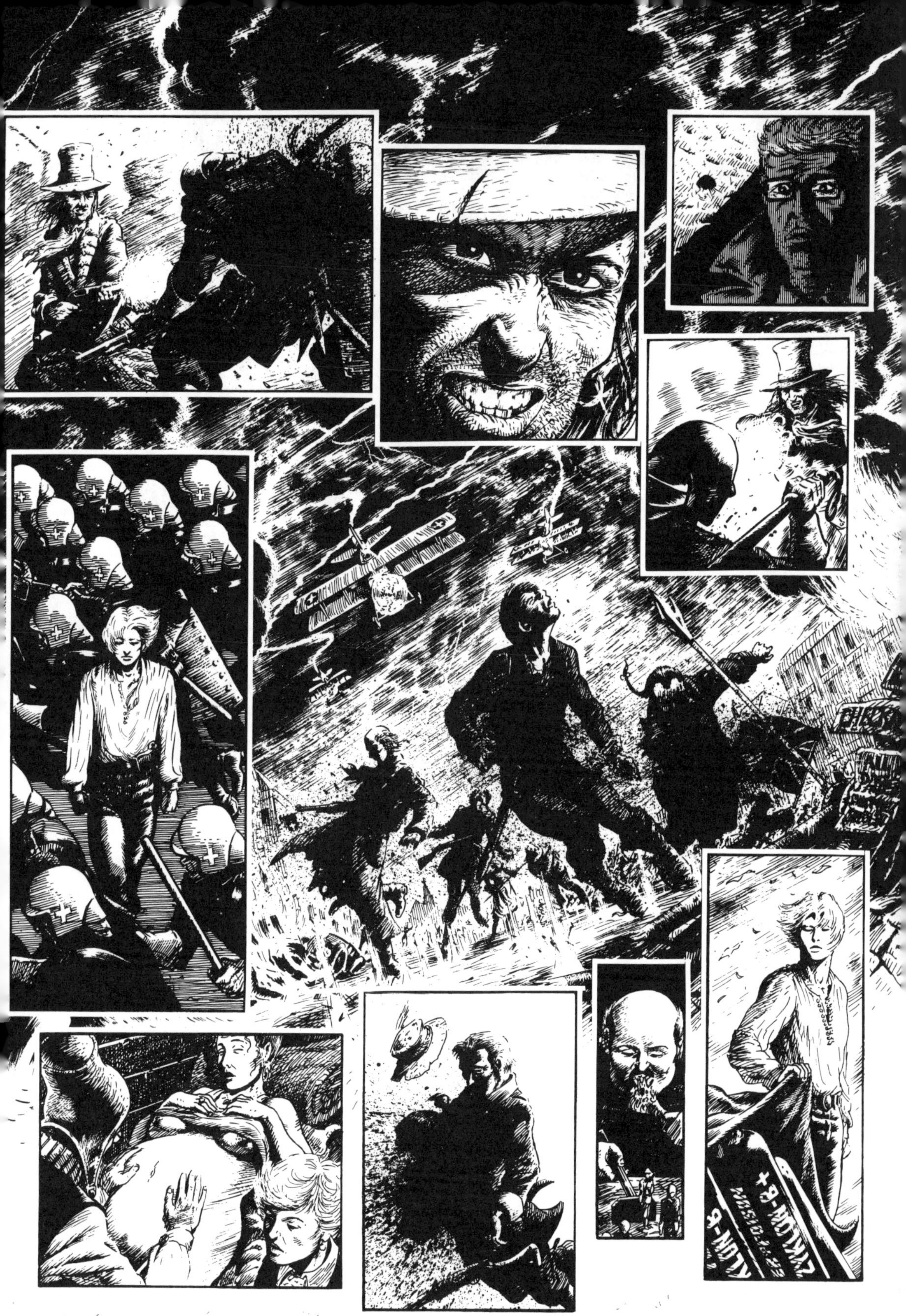

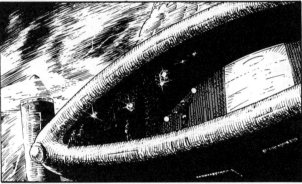

...AND THEY CAN'T USE THEIR HUGE FIELD GUNS IN A SITUATION LIKE THIS.

HA! ALL THAT EXPENSIVE IRONMONGERY-- USELESS! HA HA HA!

THEY'RE RESTRICTED TO SMALL TANKS, HALF-TRACKS AND THE LIKE.

HERE COME MY INFANTRY ...

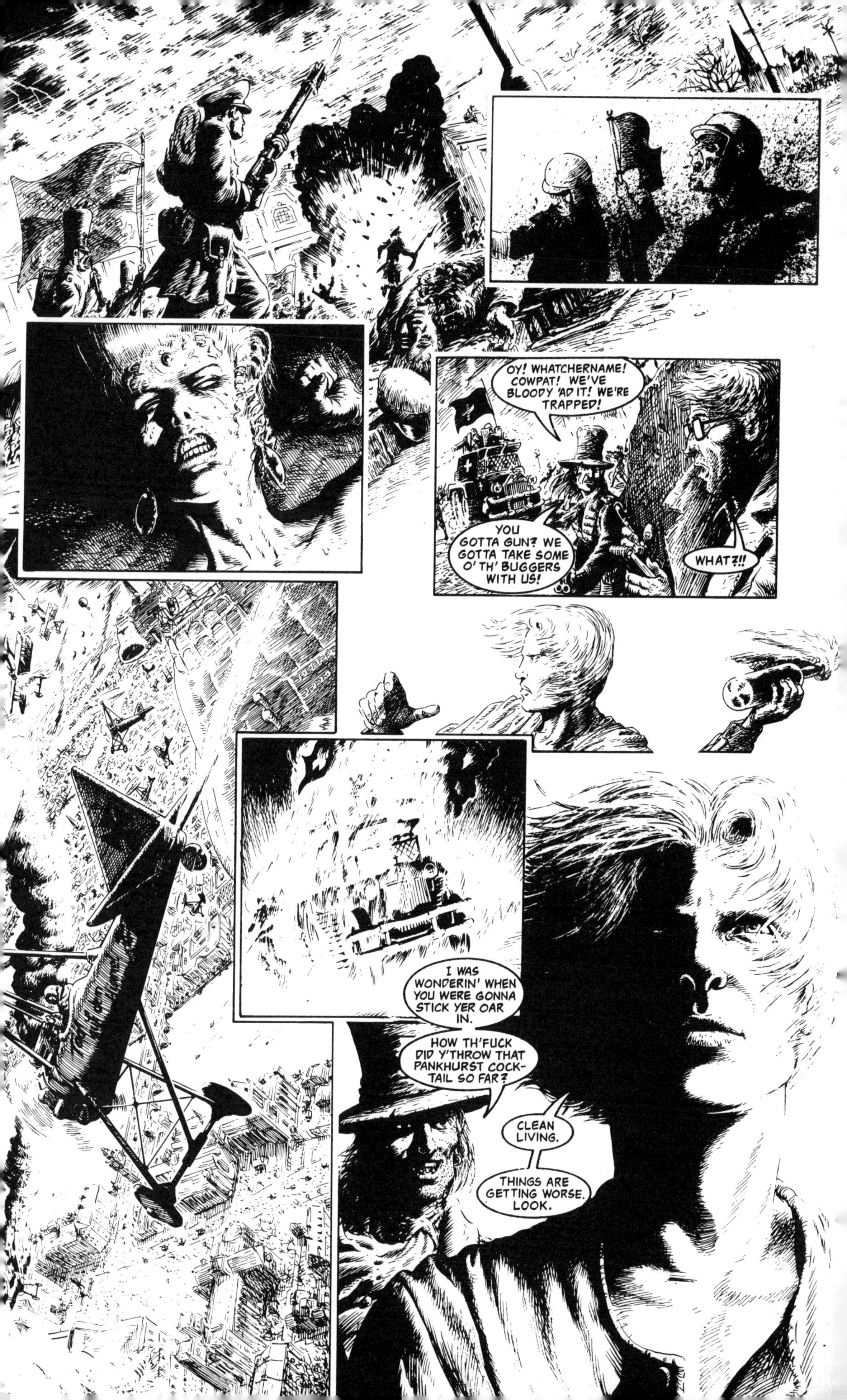
OY! WHATCHERNAME! COWPAT! WE'VE BLOODY 'AD IT! WE'RE TRAPPED!
YOU GOTTA GUN? WE GOTTA TAKE SOME O' TH' BUGGERS WITH US!
WHAT?!!
I WAS WONDERIN' WHEN YOU WERE GONNA STICK YER OAR IN.
HOW TH'FUCK DID Y'THROW THAT PANKHURST COCK-TAIL SO FAR?
CLEAN LIVING.
THINGS ARE GETTING WORSE. LOOK.

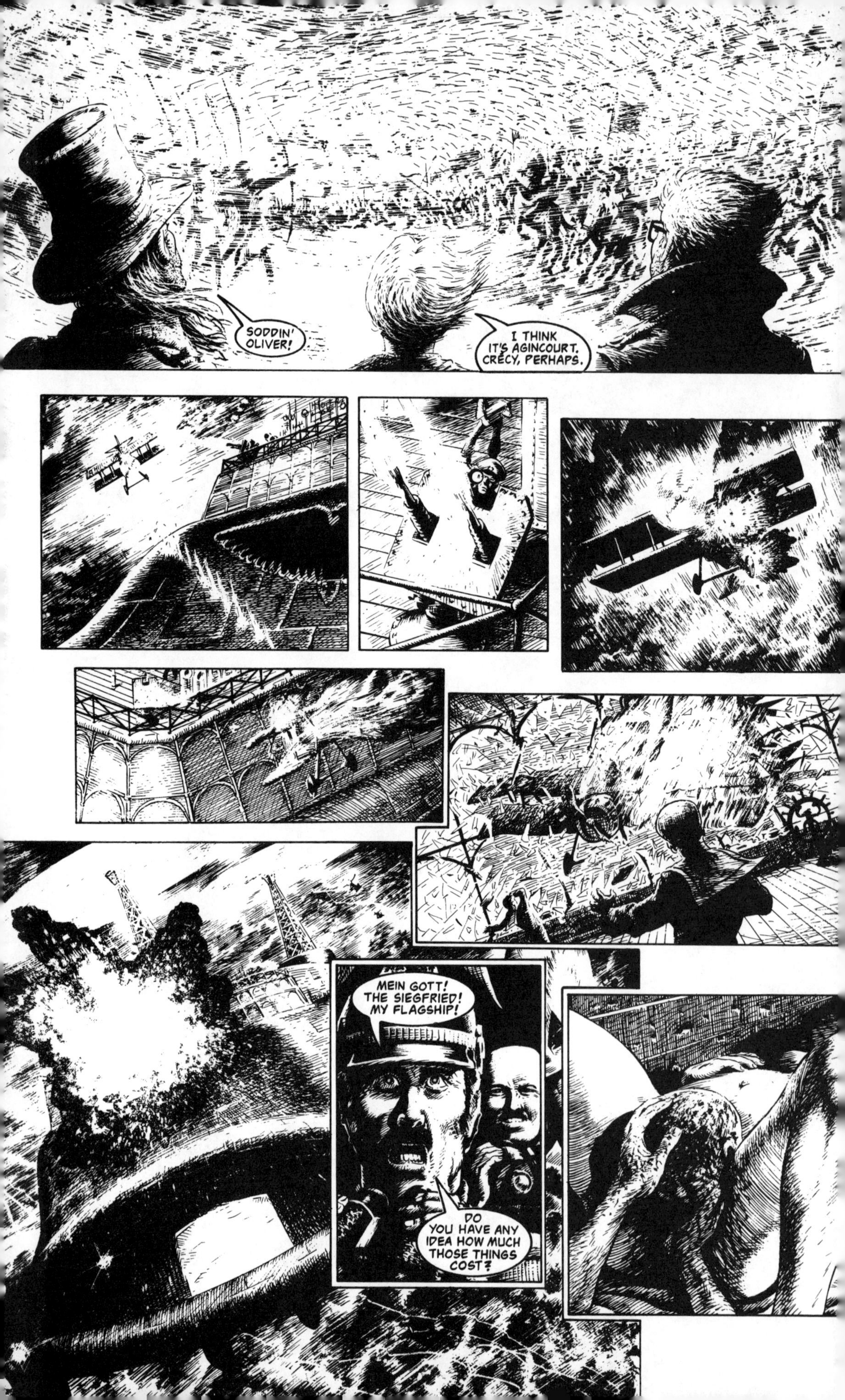
SODDIN' OLIVER!
I THINK IT'S AGINCOURT. CRÉCY, PERHAPS.
MEIN GOTT! THE SIEGFRIED! MY FLAGSHIP!
DO YOU HAVE ANY IDEA HOW MUCH THOSE THINGS COST?

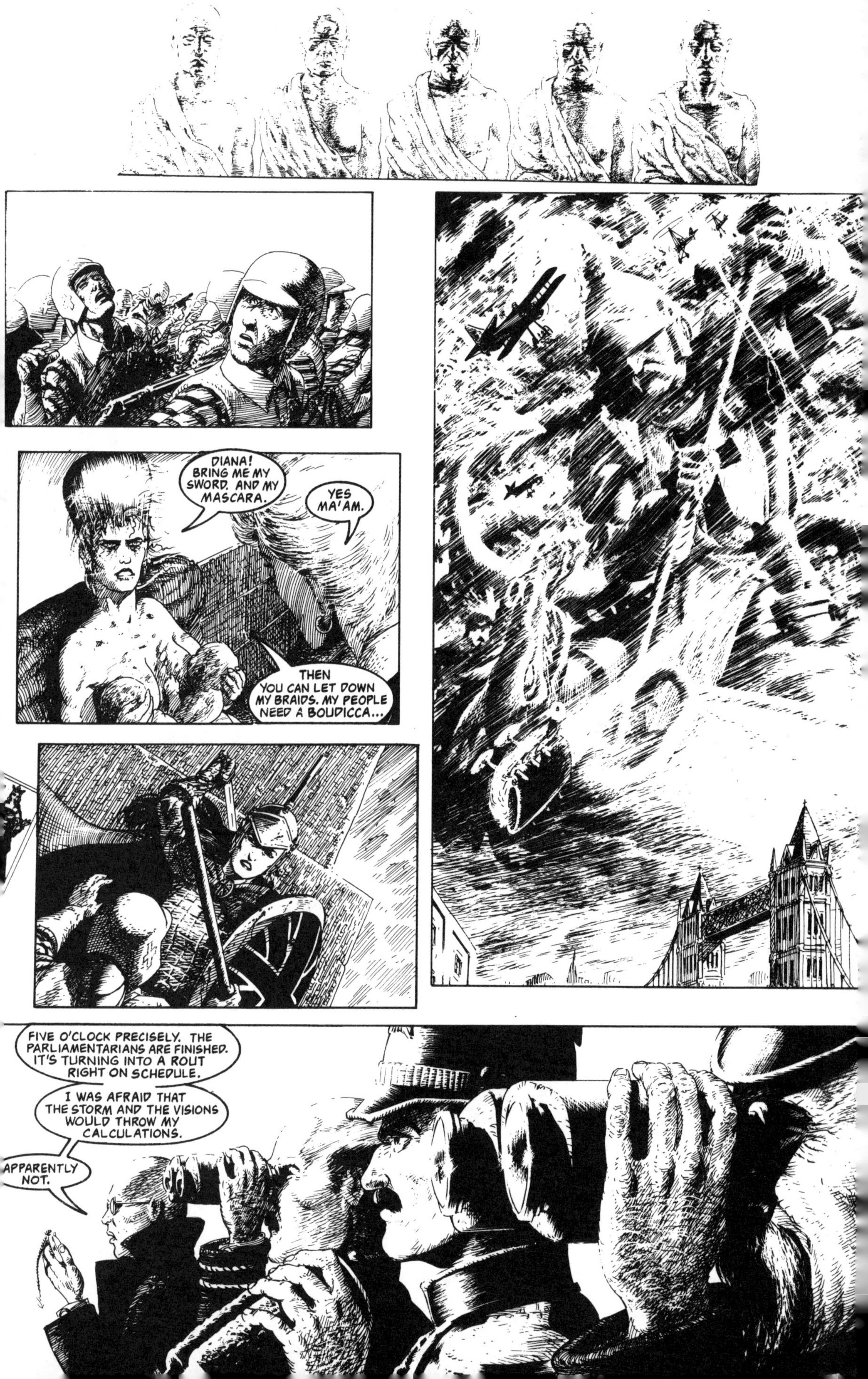
DIANA! BRING ME MY SWORD. AND MY MASCARA.
YES MA'AM.
THEN YOU CAN LET DOWN MY BRAIDS. MY PEOPLE NEED A BOUDICCA...
FIVE O'CLOCK PRECISELY. THE PARLIAMENTARIANS ARE FINISHED. IT'S TURNING INTO A ROUT RIGHT ON SCHEDULE.
I WAS AFRAID THAT THE STORM AND THE VISIONS WOULD THROW MY CALCULATIONS.
APPARENTLY NOT.

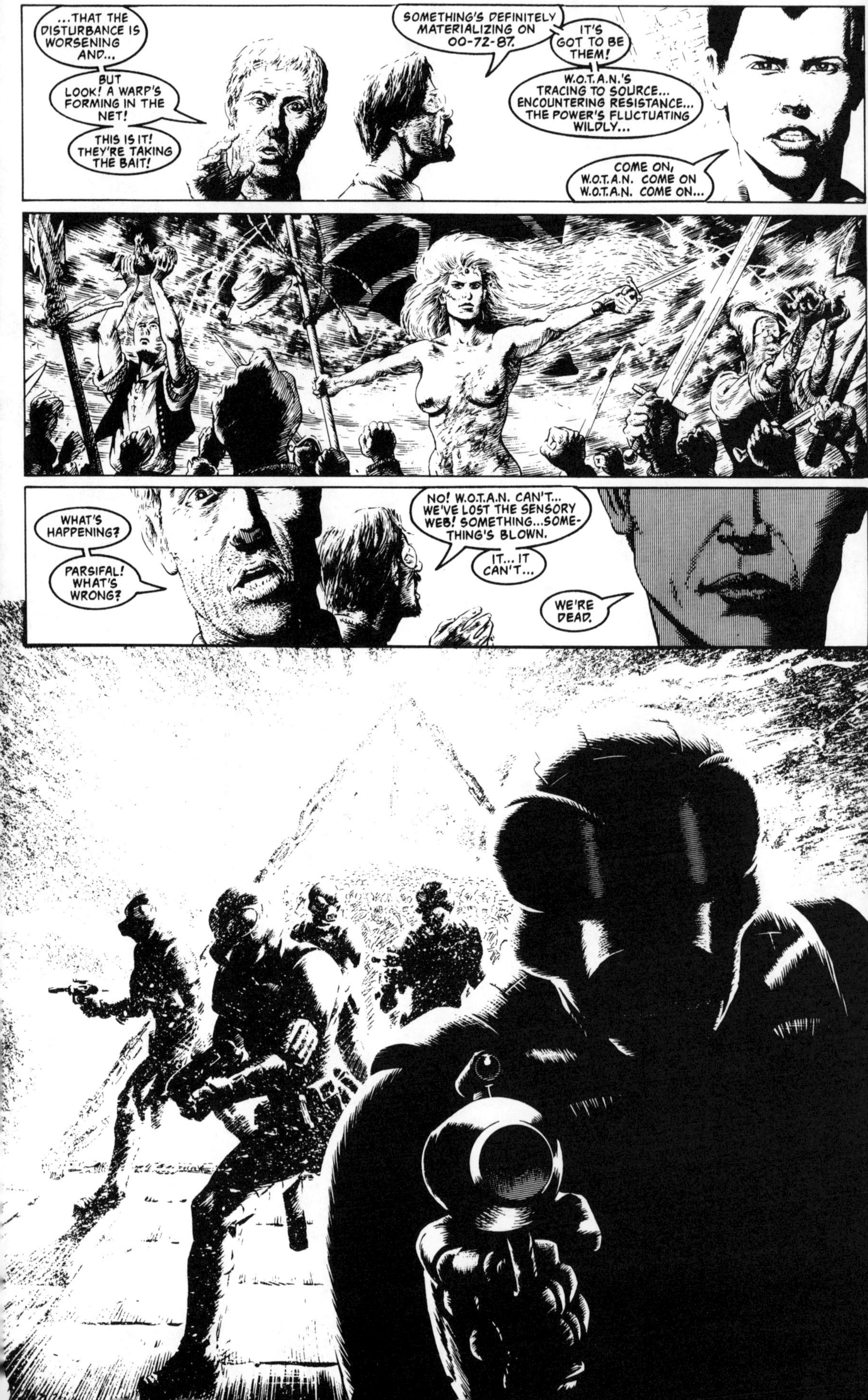
...THAT THE DISTURBANCE IS WORSENING AND...
BUT LOOK! A WARP'S FORMING IN THE NET!
THIS IS IT! THEY'RE TAKING THE BAIT!
SOMETHING'S DEFINITELY MATERIALIZING ON 00-72-87.
IT'S GOT TO BE THEM!
W.O.T.A.N.'S TRACING TO SOURCE... ENCOUNTERING RESISTANCE... THE POWER'S FLUCTUATING WILDLY...
COME ON, W.O.T.A.N. COME ON W.O.T.A.N. COME ON...
WHAT'S HAPPENING?
PARSIFAL! WHAT'S WRONG?
NO! W.O.T.A.N. CAN'T... WE'VE LOST THE SENSORY WEB! SOMETHING...SOMETHING'S BLOWN.
IT... IT CAN'T...
WE'RE DEAD.

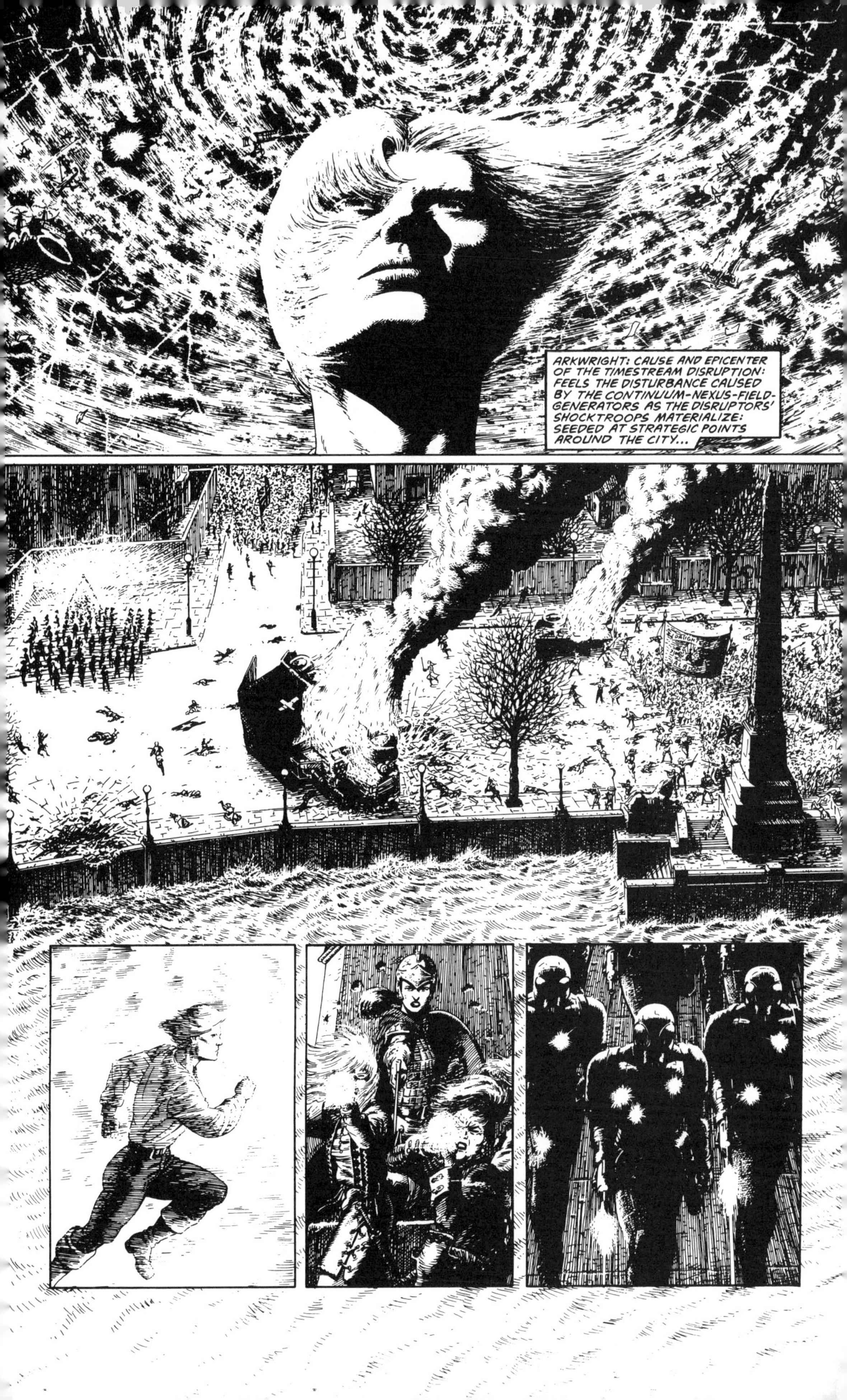
ARKWRIGHT: CAUSE AND EPICENTER OF THE TIMESTREAM DISRUPTION: FEELS THE DISTURBANCE CAUSED BY THE CONTINUUM-NEXUS-FIELD-GENERATORS AS THE DISRUPTORS' SHOCKTROOPS MATERIALIZE: SEEDED AT STRATEGIC POINTS AROUND THE CITY...

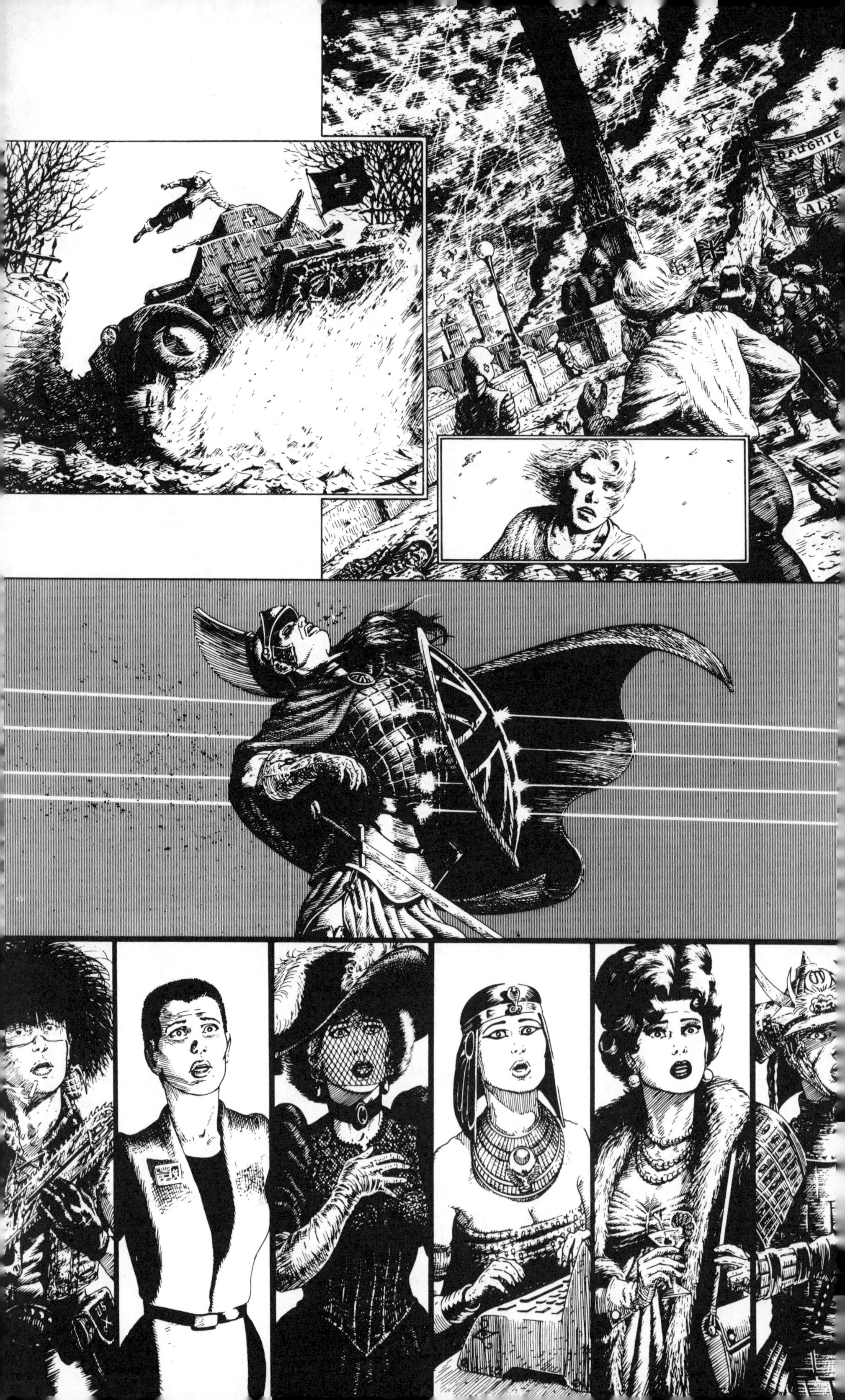

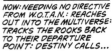

BE
SEEING
YOU.

NOW: NEEDING NO DIRECTIVE
FROM W.O.T.A.N.: REACHES
OUT INTO THE MULTIVERSE:
TRACKS THE ROOKS BACK
TO THEIR DEPARTURE
POINT: DESTINY CALLS...

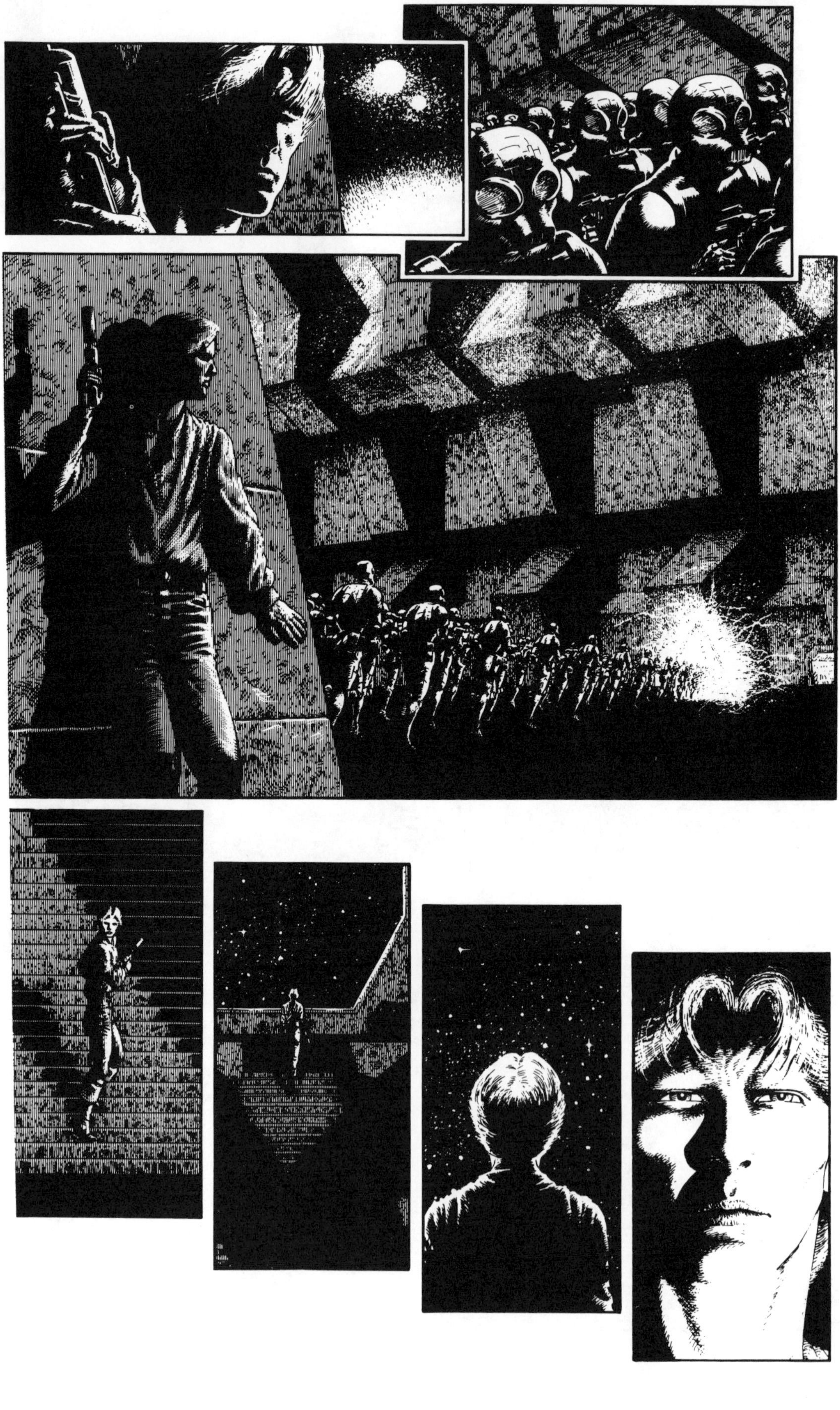

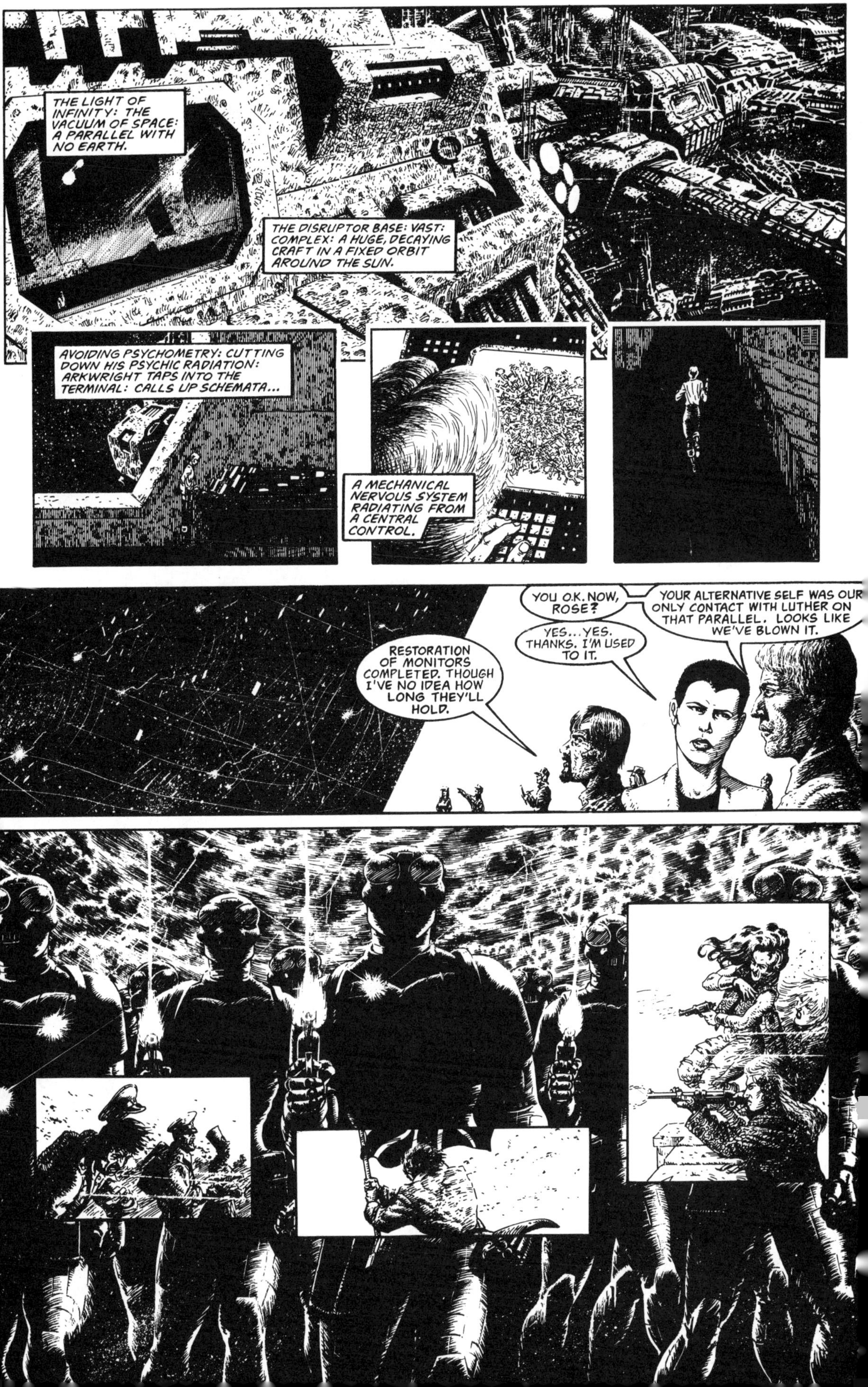
THE LIGHT OF INFINITY: THE VACUUM OF SPACE: A PARALLEL WITH NO EARTH.
THE DISRUPTOR BASE: VAST: COMPLEX: A HUGE, DECAYING CRAFT IN A FIXED ORBIT AROUND THE SUN.
AVOIDING PSYCHOMETRY: CUTTING DOWN HIS PSYCHIC RADIATION: ARKWRIGHT TAPS INTO THE TERMINAL: CALLS UP SCHEMATA...
A MECHANICAL NERVOUS SYSTEM RADIATING FROM A CENTRAL CONTROL.
RESTORATION OF MONITORS COMPLETED. THOUGH I'VE NO IDEA HOW LONG THEY'LL HOLD.
YOU O.K. NOW, ROSE?
YES... YES. THANKS. I'M USED TO IT.
YOUR ALTERNATIVE SELF WAS OUR ONLY CONTACT WITH LUTHER ON THAT PARALLEL. LOOKS LIKE WE'VE BLOWN IT.

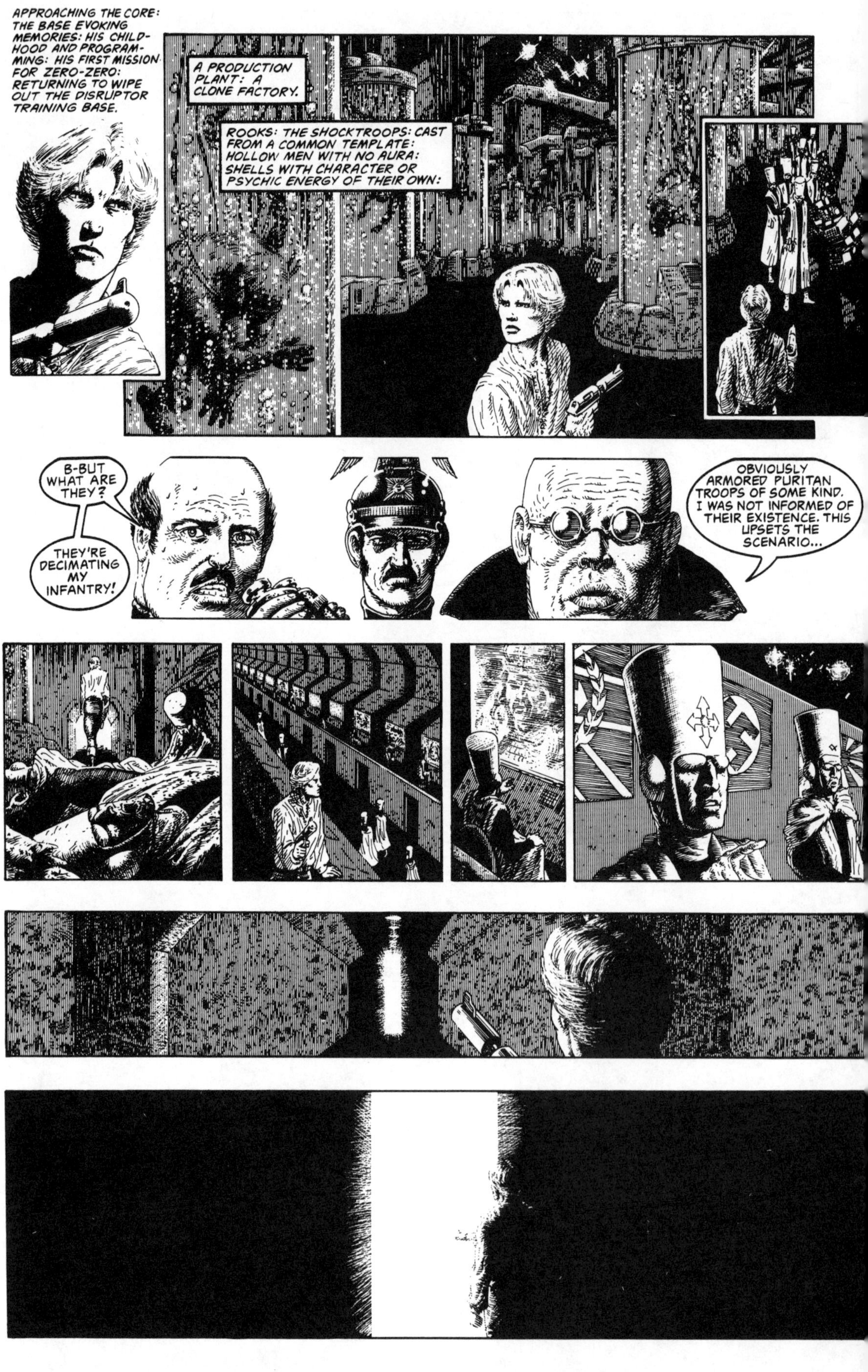
APPROACHING THE CORE: THE BASE EVOKING MEMORIES: HIS CHILDHOOD AND PROGRAMMING: HIS FIRST MISSION FOR ZERO-ZERO: RETURNING TO WIPE OUT THE DISRUPTOR TRAINING BASE.
A PRODUCTION PLANT: A CLONE FACTORY.
ROOKS: THE SHOCKTROOPS: CAST FROM A COMMON TEMPLATE: HOLLOW MEN WITH NO AURA: SHELLS WITH CHARACTER OR PSYCHIC ENERGY OF THEIR OWN:
B-BUT WHAT ARE THEY?
THEY'RE DECIMATING MY INFANTRY!
OBVIOUSLY ARMORED PURITAN TROOPS OF SOME KIND. I WAS NOT INFORMED OF THEIR EXISTENCE. THIS UPSETS THE SCENARIO...

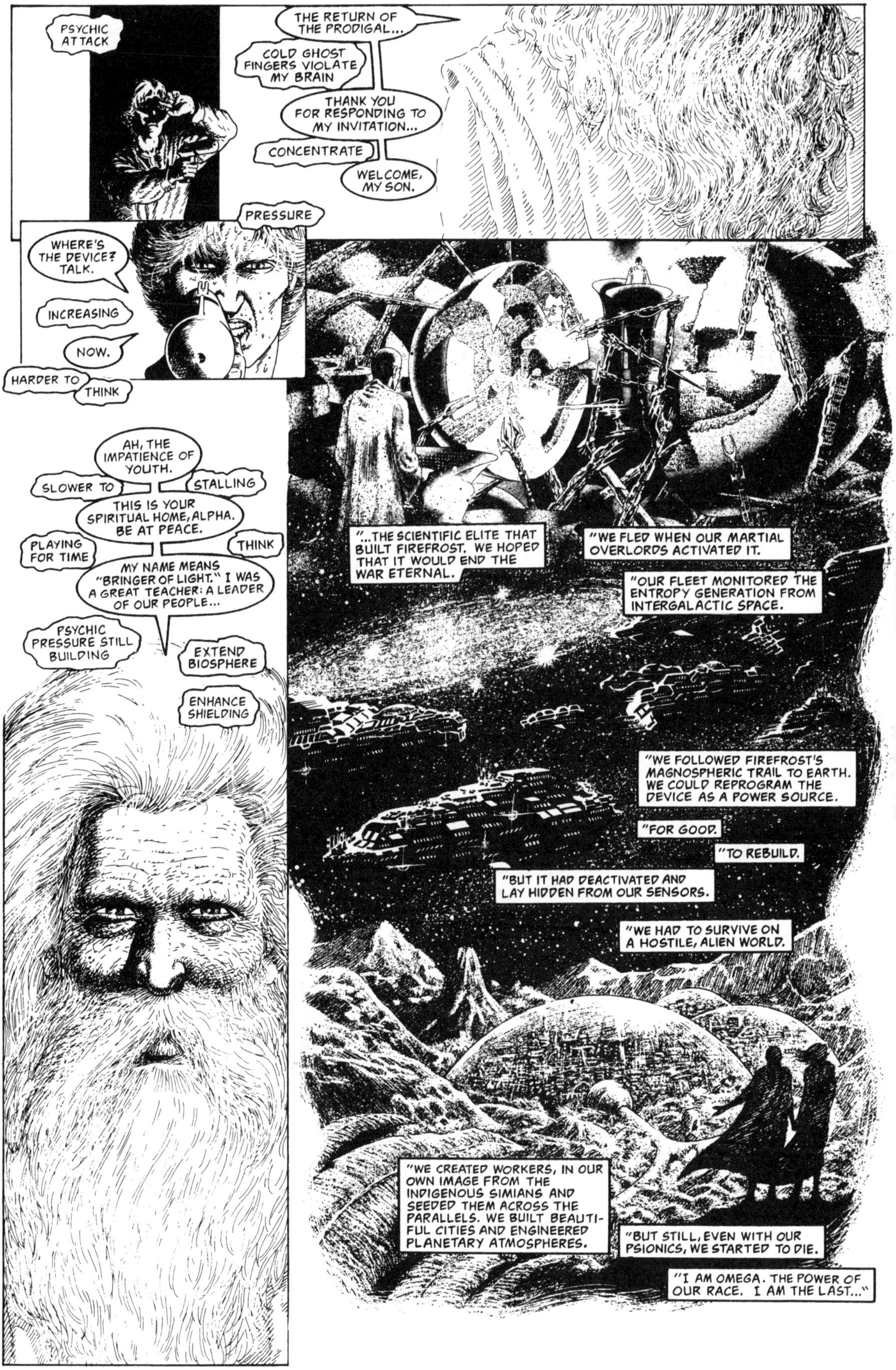
PSYCHIC ATTACK
THE RETURN OF THE PRODIGAL...
COLD GHOST FINGERS VIOLATE MY BRAIN
THANK YOU FOR RESPONDING TO MY INVITATION...
CONCENTRATE
WELCOME, MY SON.
PRESSURE
WHERE'S THE DEVICE? TALK.
INCREASING
NOW.
HARDER TO
THINK
AH, THE IMPATIENCE OF YOUTH.
SLOWER TO
STALLING
THIS IS YOUR SPIRITUAL HOME, ALPHA. BE AT PEACE.
PLAYING FOR TIME
THINK
MY NAME MEANS "BRINGER OF LIGHT." I WAS A GREAT TEACHER: A LEADER OF OUR PEOPLE...
PSYCHIC PRESSURE STILL BUILDING
EXTEND BIOSPHERE
ENHANCE SHIELDING
"...THE SCIENTIFIC ELITE THAT BUILT FIREFROST. WE HOPED THAT IT WOULD END THE WAR ETERNAL.
"WE FLED WHEN OUR MARTIAL OVERLORDS ACTIVATED IT.
"OUR FLEET MONITORED THE ENTROPY GENERATION FROM INTERGALACTIC SPACE.
"WE FOLLOWED FIREFROST'S MAGNOSPHERIC TRAIL TO EARTH. WE COULD REPROGRAM THE DEVICE AS A POWER SOURCE.
"FOR GOOD.
"TO REBUILD.
"BUT IT HAD DEACTIVATED AND LAY HIDDEN FROM OUR SENSORS.
"WE HAD TO SURVIVE ON A HOSTILE, ALIEN WORLD.
"WE CREATED WORKERS, IN OUR OWN IMAGE FROM THE INDIGENOUS SIMIANS AND SEEDED THEM ACROSS THE PARALLELS. WE BUILT BEAUTIFUL CITIES AND ENGINEERED PLANETARY ATMOSPHERES.
"BUT STILL, EVEN WITH OUR PSIONICS, WE STARTED TO DIE.
"I AM OMEGA. THE POWER OF OUR RACE. I AM THE LAST..."

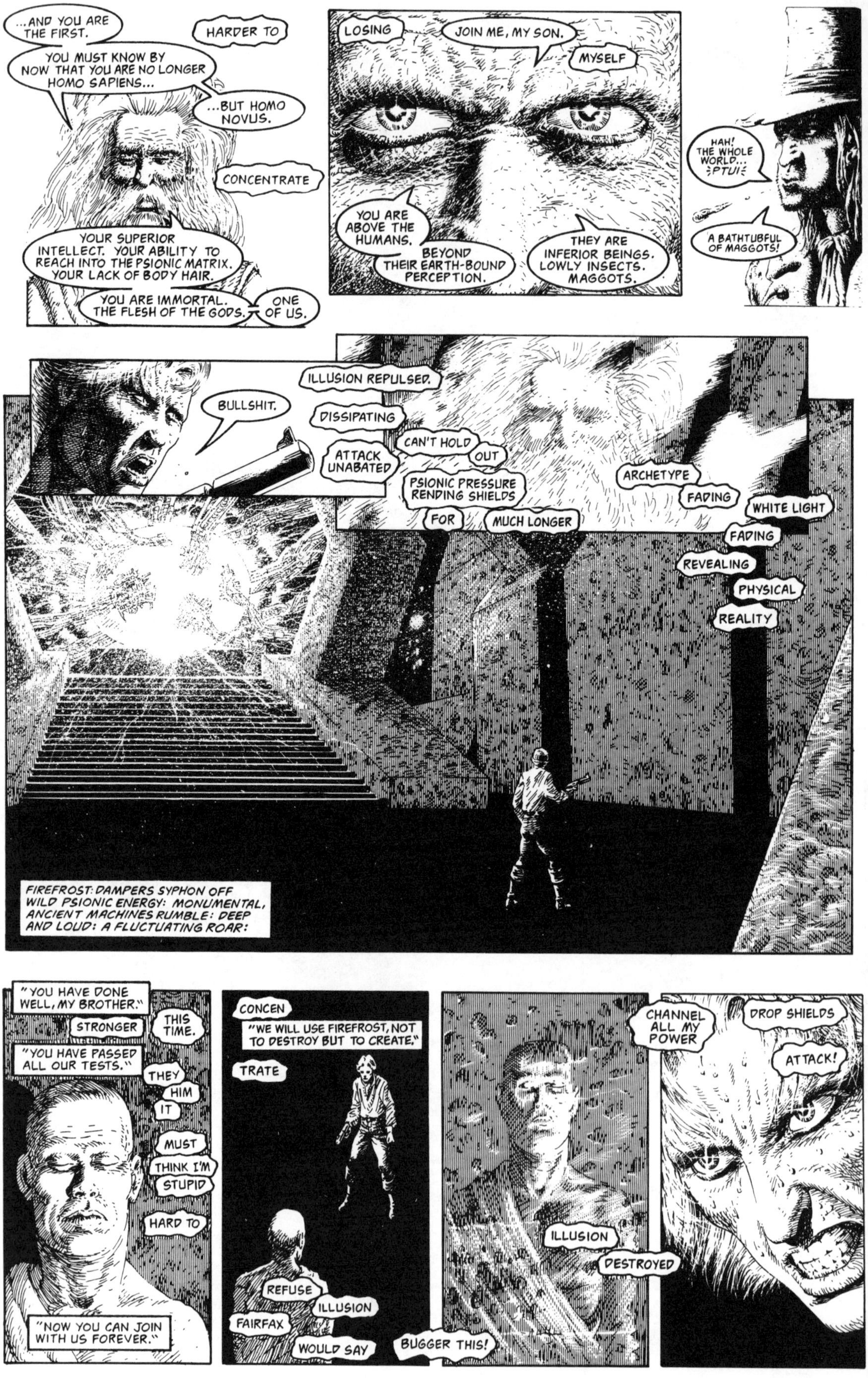
...AND YOU ARE THE FIRST.
YOU MUST KNOW BY NOW THAT YOU ARE NO LONGER HOMO SAPIENS...
...BUT HOMO NOVUS.
HARDER TO
CONCENTRATE
YOUR SUPERIOR INTELLECT. YOUR ABILITY TO REACH INTO THE PSIONIC MATRIX. YOUR LACK OF BODY HAIR.
YOU ARE IMMORTAL. THE FLESH OF THE GODS.
ONE OF US.
LOSING
JOIN ME, MY SON.
MYSELF
YOU ARE ABOVE THE HUMANS.
BEYOND THEIR EARTH-BOUND PERCEPTION.
THEY ARE INFERIOR BEINGS. LOWLY INSECTS. MAGGOTS.
HAH! THE WHOLE WORLD... PTUI
A BATHTUBFUL OF MAGGOTS!
BULLSHIT.
ILLUSION REPULSED.
DISSIPATING
ATTACK UNABATED
CAN'T HOLD
OUT
PSIONIC PRESSURE RENDING SHIELDS
FOR
MUCH LONGER
ARCHETYPE
FADING
WHITE LIGHT
FADING
REVEALING
PHYSICAL
REALITY
FIREFROST: DAMPERS SYPHON OFF WILD PSIONIC ENERGY: MONUMENTAL, ANCIENT MACHINES RUMBLE: DEEP AND LOUD: A FLUCTUATING ROAR:
"YOU HAVE DONE WELL, MY BROTHER."
STRONGER
THIS TIME.
"YOU HAVE PASSED ALL OUR TESTS."
THEY
HIM
IT
MUST
THINK I'M
STUPID
HARD TO
"NOW YOU CAN JOIN WITH US FOREVER."
CONCEN
"WE WILL USE FIREFROST, NOT TO DESTROY BUT TO CREATE."
TRATE
REFUSE
ILLUSION
FAIRFAX
WOULD SAY
BUGGER THIS!
ILLUSION
DESTROYED
CHANNEL ALL MY POWER
DROP SHIELDS
ATTACK!

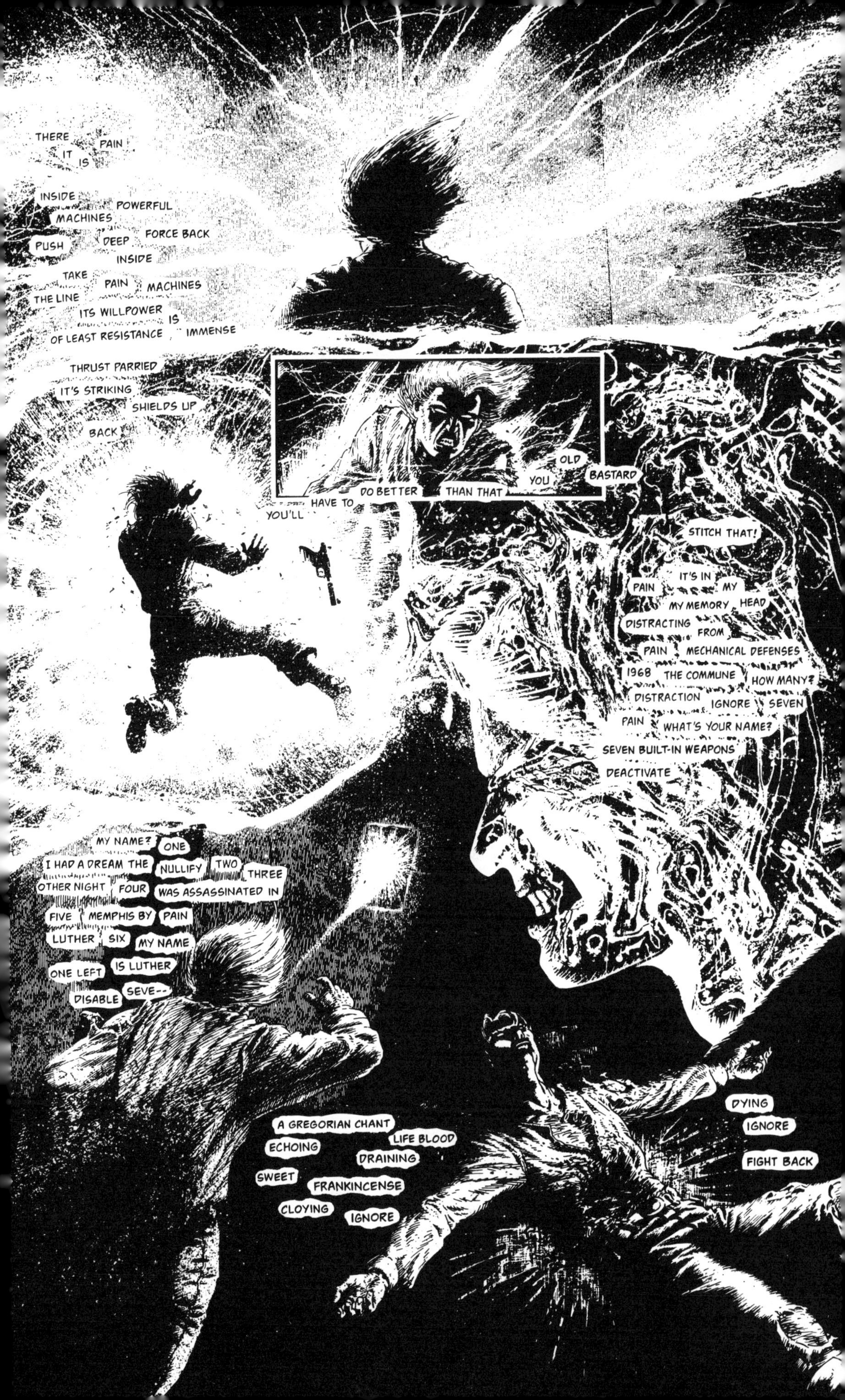
THERE
IT
IS
PAIN
INSIDE
POWERFUL
MACHINES
PUSH
DEEP
FORCE BACK
INSIDE
TAKE
THE LINE
PAIN
MACHINES
ITS WILLPOWER
IS
OF LEAST RESISTANCE
IMMENSE
THRUST PARRIED
IT'S STRIKING
SHIELDS UP
BACK
YOU'LL
HAVE TO
DO BETTER
THAN THAT
YOU
OLD
BASTARD
STITCH THAT!
PAIN
IT'S IN
MY
MY MEMORY
HEAD
DISTRACTING
FROM
PAIN
MECHANICAL DEFENSES
1968
THE COMMUNE
HOW MANY?
DISTRACTION
IGNORE
SEVEN
PAIN
WHAT'S YOUR NAME?
SEVEN BUILT-IN WEAPONS
DEACTIVATE
MY NAME?
ONE
I HAD A DREAM THE
NULLIFY
TWO
THREE
OTHER NIGHT
FOUR
WAS ASSASSINATED IN
FIVE
MEMPHIS BY
PAIN
LUTHER
SIX
MY NAME
ONE LEFT
IS LUTHER
DISABLE
SEVE--
A GREGORIAN CHANT
LIFE BLOOD
ECHOING
DRAINING
SWEET
FRANKINCENSE
CLOYING
IGNORE
DYING
IGNORE
FIGHT BACK

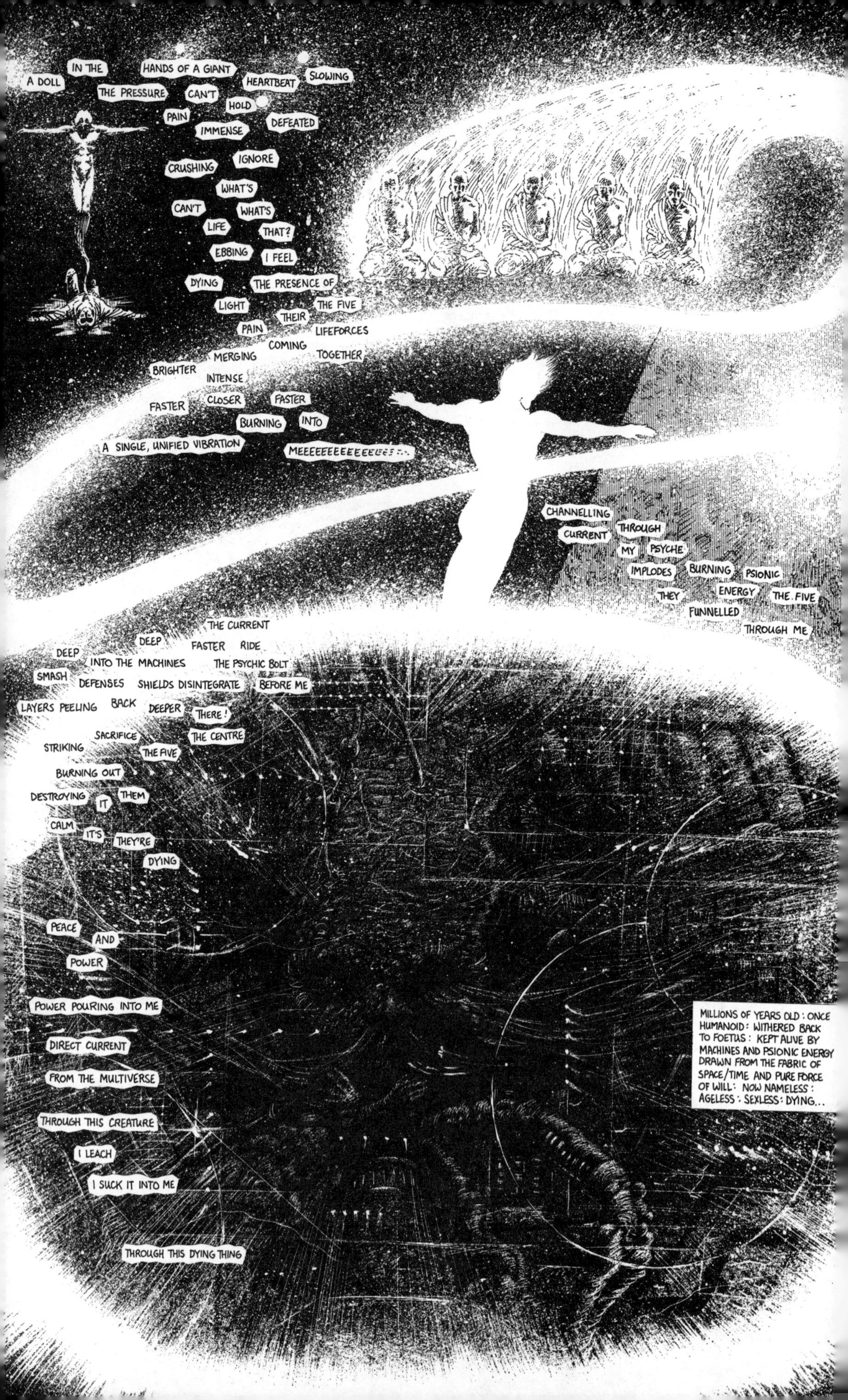
A DOLL
IN THE
HANDS OF A GIANT
HEARTBEAT
SLOWING
THE PRESSURE
CAN'T
HOLD
PAIN
IMMENSE
DEFEATED
CRUSHING
IGNORE
WHAT'S
CAN'T
WHAT'S
LIFE
THAT?
EBBING
I FEEL
DYING
THE PRESENCE OF
LIGHT
THEIR
THE FIVE
PAIN
LIFEFORCES
COMING
MERGING
TOGETHER
BRIGHTER
INTENSE
FASTER
CLOSER
FASTER
BURNING
INTO
A SINGLE, UNIFIED VIBRATION
MEEEEEEEEEEEEEEE...
CHANNELLING
CURRENT
THROUGH
MY
PSYCHE
IMPLODES
BURNING
PSIONIC
THEY
ENERGY
THE FIVE
FUNNELLED
THROUGH ME
THE CURRENT
DEEP
DEEP
FASTER
RIDE
INTO THE MACHINES
THE PSYCHIC BOLT
SMASH
DEFENSES
SHIELDS DISINTEGRATE
BEFORE ME
LAYERS PEELING
BACK
DEEPER
THERE!
SACRIFICE
THE CENTRE
STRIKING
THE FIVE
BURNING OUT
DESTROYING
IT
THEM
CALM
IT'S
THEY'RE
DYING
PEACE
AND
POWER
POWER POURING INTO ME
DIRECT CURRENT
FROM THE MULTIVERSE
THROUGH THIS CREATURE
I LEACH
I SUCK IT INTO ME
THROUGH THIS DYING THING
MILLIONS OF YEARS OLD: ONCE HUMANOID: WITHERED BACK TO FOETUS: KEPT ALIVE BY MACHINES AND PSIONIC ENERGY DRAWN FROM THE FABRIC OF SPACE/TIME AND PURE FORCE OF WILL: NOW NAMELESS: AGELESS: SEXLESS: DYING...

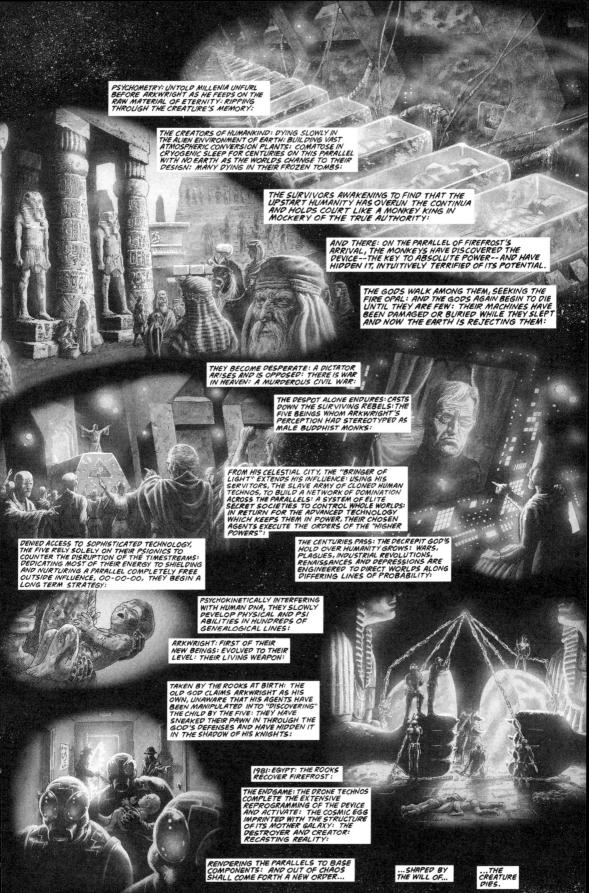

PSYCHOMETRY: UNTOLD MILLENIA UNFURL BEFORE ARKWRIGHT AS HE FEEDS ON THE RAW MATERIAL OF ETERNITY: RIPPING THROUGH THE CREATURE'S MEMORY:

THE CREATORS OF HUMANKIND: DYING SLOWLY IN THE ALIEN ENVIRONMENT OF EARTH: BUILDING VAST ATMOSPHERIC CONVERSION PLANTS: COMATOSE IN CRYOGENIC SLEEP FOR CENTURIES ON THIS PARALLEL WITH NO EARTH AS THE WORLDS CHANGE TO THEIR DESIGN: MANY DYING IN THEIR FROZEN TOMBS:

THE SURVIVORS AWAKENING TO FIND THAT THE UPSTART HUMANITY HAS OVERUN THE CONTINUA AND HOLDS COURT LIKE A MONKEY KING IN MOCKERY OF THE TRUE AUTHORITY:

AND THERE: ON THE PARALLEL OF FIREFROST'S ARRIVAL, THE MONKEYS HAVE DISCOVERED THE DEVICE—THE KEY TO ABSOLUTE POWER—AND HAVE HIDDEN IT, INTUITIVELY TERRIFIED OF ITS POTENTIAL.

THE GODS WALK AMONG THEM, SEEKING THE FIRE OPAL: AND THE GODS AGAIN BEGIN TO DIE UNTIL THEY ARE FEW: THEIR MACHINES HAVE BEEN DAMAGED OR BURIED WHILE THEY SLEPT AND NOW THE EARTH IS REJECTING THEM:

THEY BECOME DESPERATE: A DICTATOR ARISES AND IS OPPOSED: THERE IS WAR IN HEAVEN: A MURDEROUS CIVIL WAR:

THE DESPOT ALONE ENDURES: CASTS DOWN THE SURVIVING REBELS: THE FIVE BEINGS WHOM ARKWRIGHT'S PERCEPTION HAD STEREOTYPED AS MALE BUDDHIST MONKS:

FROM HIS CELESTIAL CITY, THE "BRINGER OF LIGHT" EXTENDS HIS INFLUENCE: USING HIS SERVITORS, THE SLAVE ARMY OF CLONED HUMAN TECHNOS, TO BUILD A NETWORK OF DOMINATION ACROSS THE PARALLELS: A SYSTEM OF ELITE SECRET SOCIETIES TO CONTROL WHOLE WORLDS: IN RETURN FOR THE ADVANCED TECHNOLOGY WHICH KEEPS THEM IN POWER, THEIR CHOSEN AGENTS EXECUTE THE ORDERS OF THE "HIGHER POWERS":

DENIED ACCESS TO SOPHISTICATED TECHNOLOGY, THE FIVE RELY SOLELY ON THEIR PSIONICS TO COUNTER THE DISRUPTION OF THE TIMESTREAMS: DEDICATING MOST OF THEIR ENERGY TO SHIELDING AND NURTURING A PARALLEL COMPLETELY FREE OUTSIDE INFLUENCE, OO-OO-OO, THEY BEGIN A LONG TERM STRATEGY:

THE CENTURIES PASS: THE DECREPIT GOD'S HOLD OVER HUMANITY GROWS: WARS, PLAGUES, INDUSTRIAL REVOLUTIONS, RENAISSANCES AND DEPRESSIONS ARE ENGINEERED TO DIRECT WORLDS ALONG DIFFERING LINES OF PROBABILITY:

PSYCHOKINETICALLY INTERFERING WITH HUMAN DNA, THEY SLOWLY DEVELOP PHYSICAL AND PSI ABILITIES IN HUNDREDS OF GENEALOGICAL LINES:

ARKWRIGHT: FIRST OF THEIR NEW BEINGS: EVOLVED TO THEIR LEVEL: THEIR LIVING WEAPON:

TAKEN BY THE ROOKS AT BIRTH: THE OLD GOD CLAIMS ARKWRIGHT AS HIS OWN, UNAWARE THAT HIS AGENTS HAVE BEEN MANIPULATED INTO "DISCOVERING" THE CHILD BY THE FIVE: THEY HAVE SNEAKED THEIR PAWN IN THROUGH THE GOD'S DEFENSES AND HAVE HIDDEN IT IN THE SHADOW OF HIS KNIGHTS:

1981: EGYPT: THE ROOKS RECOVER FIREFROST:

THE ENDGAME: THE DRONE TECHNOS COMPLETE THE EXTENSIVE REPROGRAMMING OF THE DEVICE AND ACTIVATE: THE COSMIC EGG IMPRINTED WITH THE STRUCTURE OF ITS MOTHER GALAXY: THE DESTROYER AND CREATOR: RECASTING REALITY:

RENDERING THE PARALLELS TO BASE COMPONENTS: AND OUT OF CHAOS SHALL COME FORTH A NEW ORDER...

...SHAPED BY THE WILL OF...

...THE CREATURE DIES.

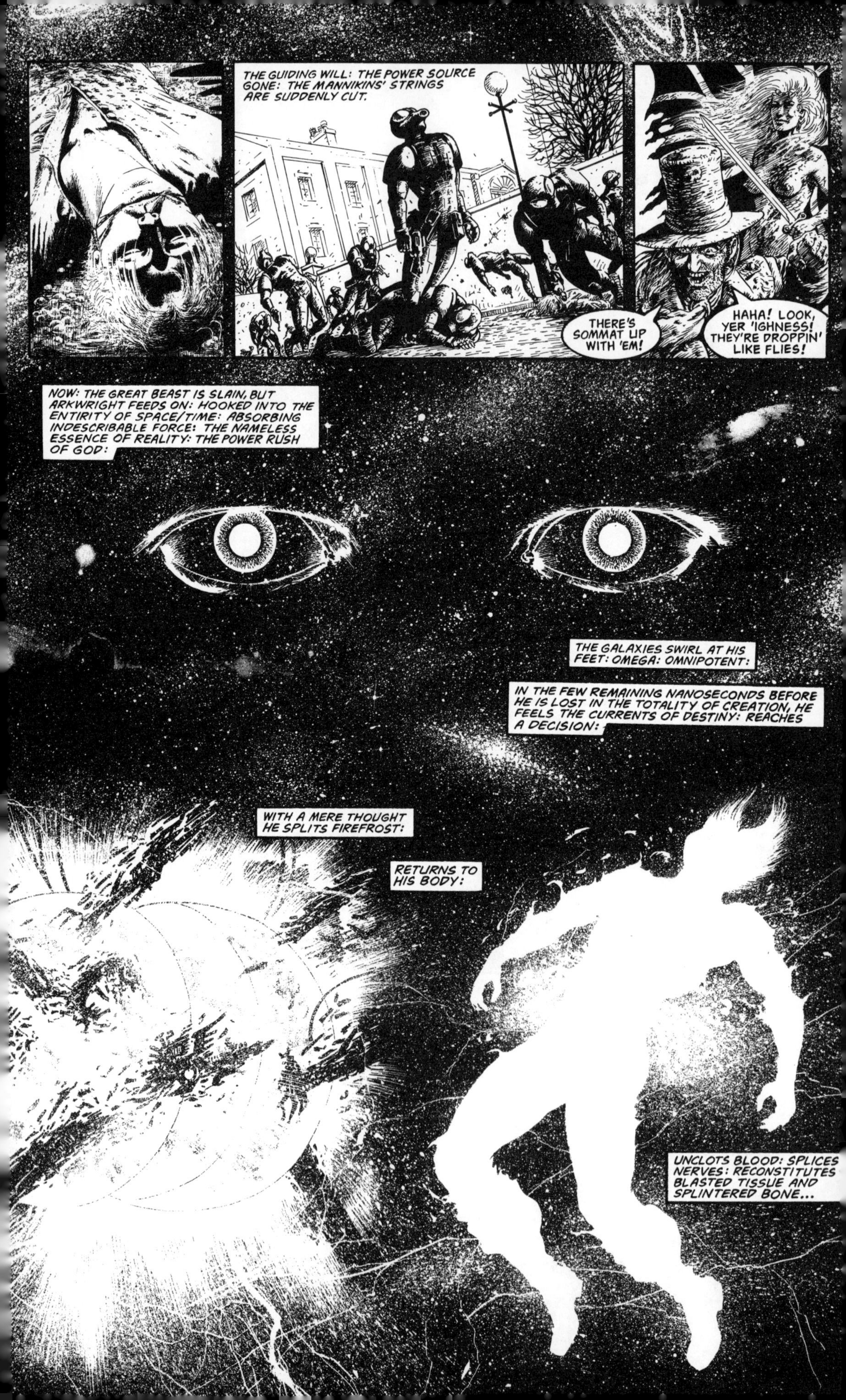
THE GUIDING WILL: THE POWER SOURCE GONE: THE MANNIKINS' STRINGS ARE SUDDENLY CUT.
HAHA! LOOK, YER 'IGHNESS! THEY'RE DROPPIN' LIKE FLIES!
THERE'S SOMMAT UP WITH 'EM!
NOW: THE GREAT BEAST IS SLAIN, BUT ARKWRIGHT FEEDS ON: HOOKED INTO THE ENTIRITY OF SPACE/TIME: ABSORBING INDESCRIBABLE FORCE: THE NAMELESS ESSENCE OF REALITY: THE POWER RUSH OF GOD:
THE GALAXIES SWIRL AT HIS FEET: OMEGA: OMNIPOTENT:
IN THE FEW REMAINING NANOSECONDS BEFORE HE IS LOST IN THE TOTALITY OF CREATION, HE FEELS THE CURRENTS OF DESTINY: REACHES A DECISION:
WITH A MERE THOUGHT HE SPLITS FIREFROST:
RETURNS TO HIS BODY:
UNCLOTS BLOOD: SPLICES NERVES: RECONSTITUTES BLASTED TISSUE AND SPLINTERED BONE...

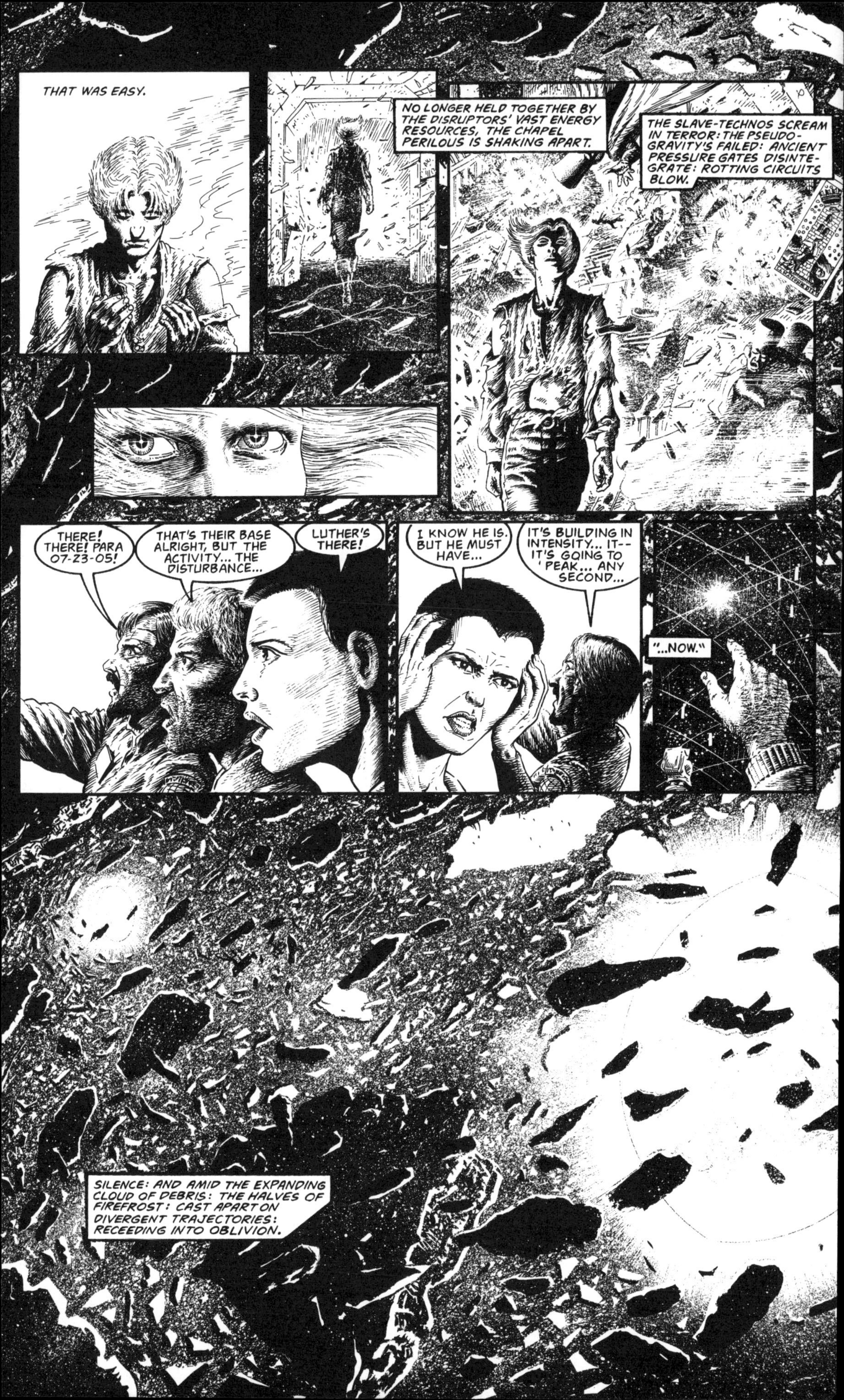
THAT WAS EASY.
NO LONGER HELD TOGETHER BY THE DISRUPTORS' VAST ENERGY RESOURCES, THE CHAPEL PERILOUS IS SHAKING APART.
THE SLAVE-TECHNOS SCREAM IN TERROR: THE PSEUDO-GRAVITY'S FAILED: ANCIENT PRESSURE GATES DISINTEGRATE: ROTTING CIRCUITS BLOW.
THERE! THERE! PARA 07-23-05!
THAT'S THEIR BASE ALRIGHT, BUT THE ACTIVITY... THE DISTURBANCE...
LUTHER'S THERE!
I KNOW HE IS. BUT HE MUST HAVE...
IT'S BUILDING IN INTENSITY... IT-- IT'S GOING TO PEAK... ANY SECOND...
"...NOW."
SILENCE: AND AMID THE EXPANDING CLOUD OF DEBRIS: THE HALVES OF FIREFROST: CAST APART ON DIVERGENT TRAJECTORIES: RECEEDING INTO OBLIVION.

MON 16 OCT 18.20 PARA 00.72.87 GREENWICH

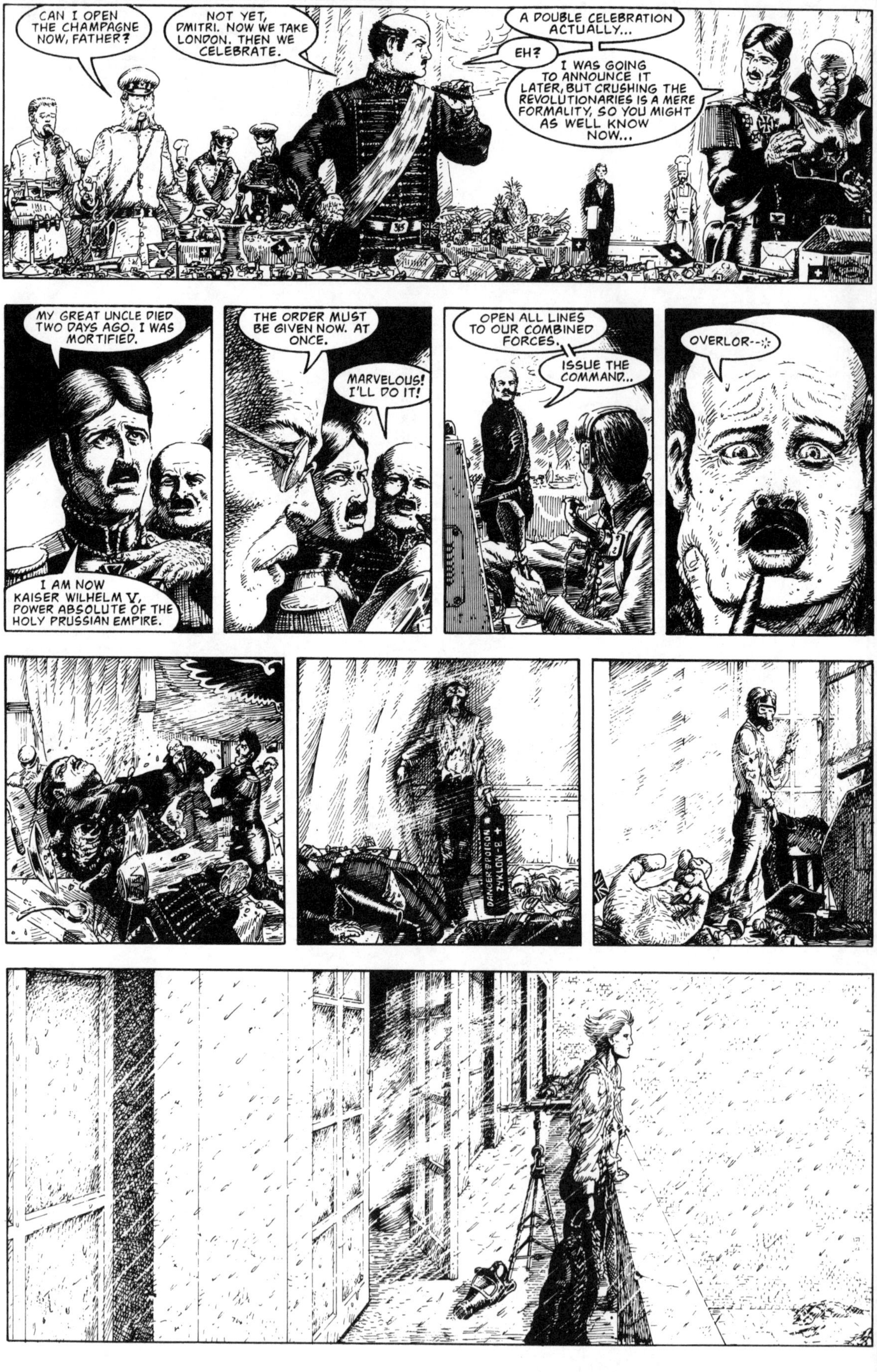
CAN I OPEN THE CHAMPAGNE NOW, FATHER?
NOT YET, DMITRI. NOW WE TAKE LONDON. THEN WE CELEBRATE.
A DOUBLE CELEBRATION ACTUALLY...
EH?
I WAS GOING TO ANNOUNCE IT LATER, BUT CRUSHING THE REVOLUTIONARIES IS A MERE FORMALITY, SO YOU MIGHT AS WELL KNOW NOW...
MY GREAT UNCLE DIED TWO DAYS AGO. I WAS MORTIFIED.
I AM NOW KAISER WILHELM V, POWER ABSOLUTE OF THE HOLY PRUSSIAN EMPIRE.
THE ORDER MUST BE GIVEN NOW. AT ONCE.
MARVELOUS! I'LL DO IT!
OPEN ALL LINES TO OUR COMBINED FORCES.
ISSUE THE COMMAND...
OVERLOR--
DANGER POISON ZYKLON-B

 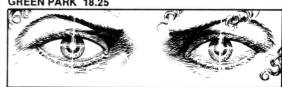

IT IS DONE!

DIANA!

ISSUE A STATEMENT TO OUR ALLIES...

"IT IS MY SAD DUTY TO INFORM YOU THAT YOUR NOBLE LEADERS HAVE BEEN KILLED IN A PARLIAMENTARIAN GAS ATTACK ON THEIR H.Q. GREAT BRITAIN SHALL ALWAYS HONOR THEIR GLORIOUS SACRIFICE. A.R."

FAIRFAX! BREAK OPEN THE CHAMPAGNE!

ST. PETERSBURG 18.41 GMT

ТЕЛЕГРАМ OCTOBRIANA STOP CZAR RETIRED STOP STORM THE WINTER PALACE AT YOUR LEISURE STOP LOVE STOP LUTHER

PARA 00.00.00 VALHALLA NOVA 18.45

YOU MEAN TO SAY THAT W.O.T.A.N. HAD PREDICTED EVERYTHING?

ITS OWN VULNERABILITY TO FIREFROST? LUTHER FINDING THE BASE WITHOUT HELP? DEACTIVATING THE OPAL?!

IT SEEMS SO. APPARENTLY WE WEREN'T INFORMED IN CASE IT AFFECTED THE OUTCOME OF THE RAGNAROK PROGRAM.

WHY, OF ALL THE...

RANDOM SELECTION INCOMING DATA

LUTHER MUST SURELY REALIZE THE TRUTH BY NOW.

THE TRUTH?

ABOUT HIMSELF. W.O.T.A.N. KNEW FROM THE BEGINNING...

INDICATES RESTORATION

...THAT HE'S NOT HUMAN. THAT HE IS THE NEXT STAGE OF HUMANITY'S EVOLUTION.

HE'S MORE THAN THAT, KARL.

OF EQUILIBRIUM

HE'S THE SAVIOR OF THE BLOODY MULTI-VERSE!

WESTMINSTER 18.45

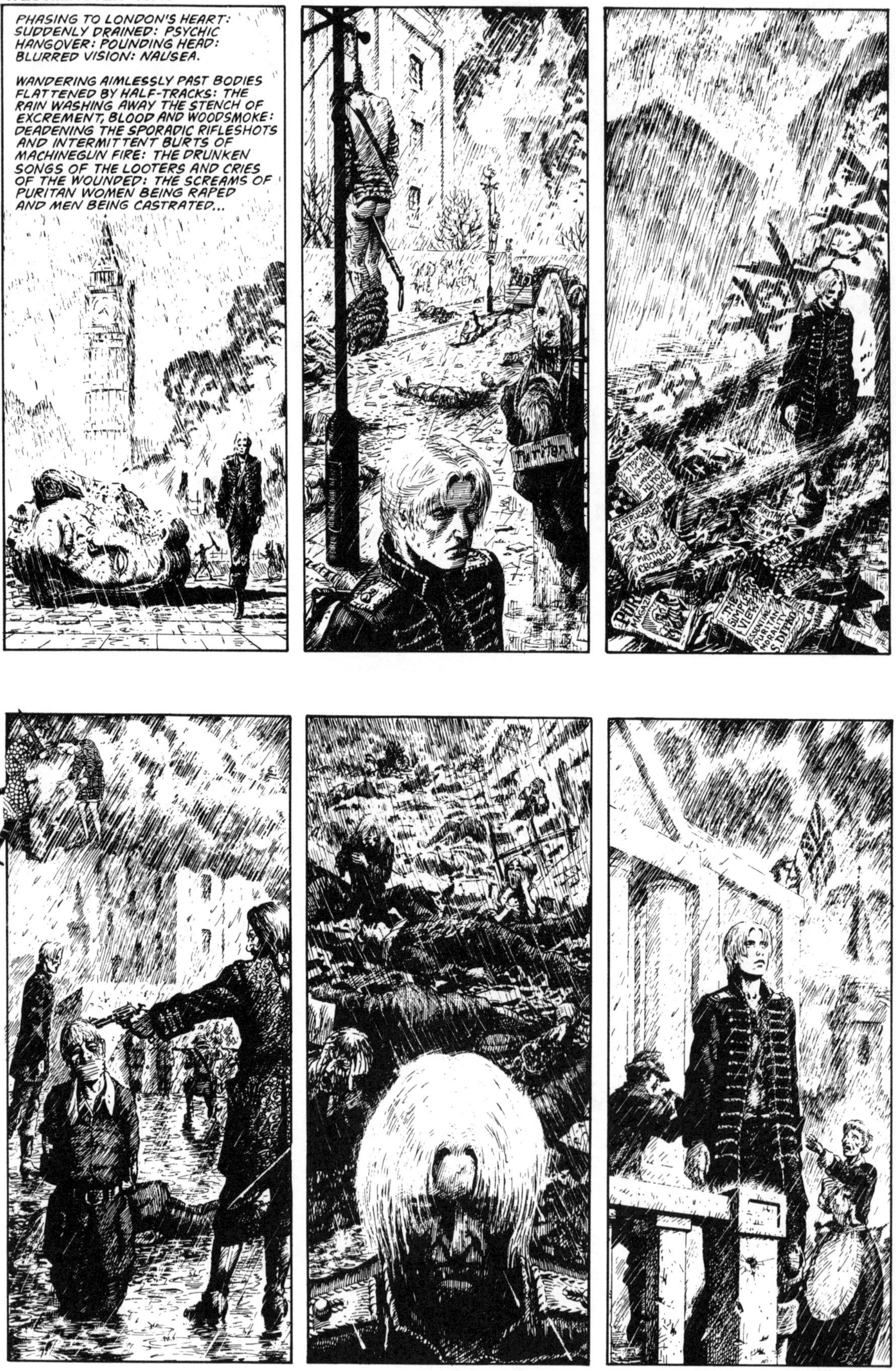
PHASING TO LONDON'S HEART: SUDDENLY DRAINED: PSYCHIC HANGOVER: POUNDING HEAD: BLURRED VISION: NAUSEA.
WANDERING AIMLESSLY PAST BODIES FLATTENED BY HALF-TRACKS: THE RAIN WASHING AWAY THE STENCH OF EXCREMENT, BLOOD AND WOODSMOKE: DEADENING THE SPORADIC RIFLESHOTS AND INTERMITTENT BURTS OF MACHINEGUN FIRE: THE DRUNKEN SONGS OF THE LOOTERS AND CRIES OF THE WOUNDED: THE SCREAMS OF PURITAN WOMEN BEING RAPED AND MEN BEING CASTRATED...
MY STRUGGLE
MATTHEW CROMWELL
THE PURITAN YOUTH MOVEMENT
THE SIMPLE VIEW
ESSENTIAL PURITAN MORALITY S. DIPPKO
BLACK WHITE

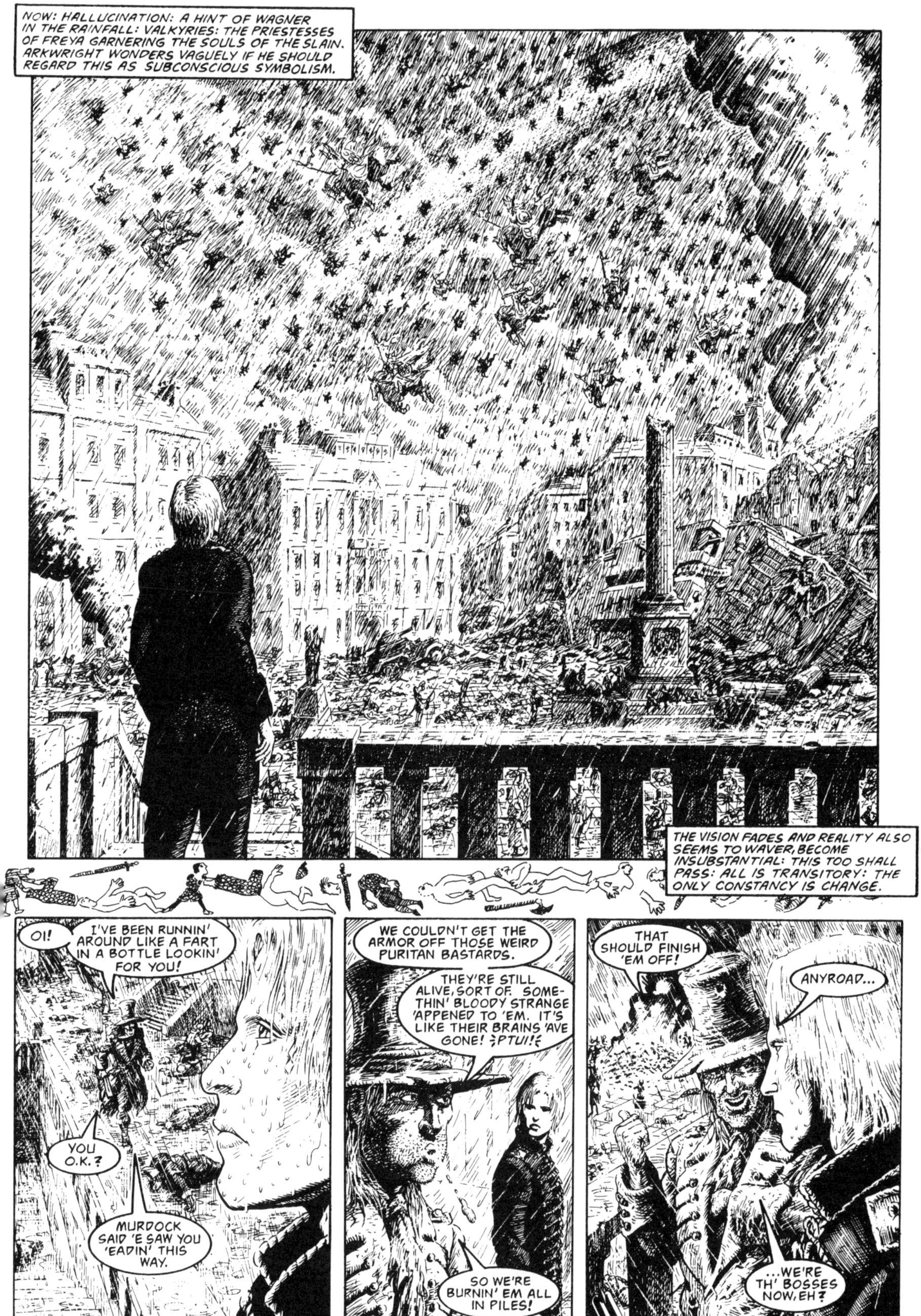
NOW: HALLUCINATION: A HINT OF WAGNER IN THE RAINFALL: VALKYRIES: THE PRIESTESSES OF FREYA GARNERING THE SOULS OF THE SLAIN. ARKWRIGHT WONDERS VAGUELY IF HE SHOULD REGARD THIS AS SUBCONSCIOUS SYMBOLISM.
THE VISION FADES AND REALITY ALSO SEEMS TO WAVER, BECOME INSUBSTANTIAL: THIS TOO SHALL PASS: ALL IS TRANSITORY: THE ONLY CONSTANCY IS CHANGE.
OI!
I'VE BEEN RUNNIN' AROUND LIKE A FART IN A BOTTLE LOOKIN' FOR YOU!
YOU O.K.?
MURDOCK SAID 'E SAW YOU 'EADIN' THIS WAY.
WE COULDN'T GET THE ARMOR OFF THOSE WEIRD PURITAN BASTARDS.
THEY'RE STILL ALIVE, SORT OF. SOMETHIN' BLOODY STRANGE 'APPENED TO 'EM. IT'S LIKE THEIR BRAINS 'AVE GONE! PTUI!
SO WE'RE BURNIN' EM ALL IN PILES!
THAT SHOULD FINISH 'EM OFF!
ANYROAD...
...WE'RE TH' BOSSES NOW, EH?

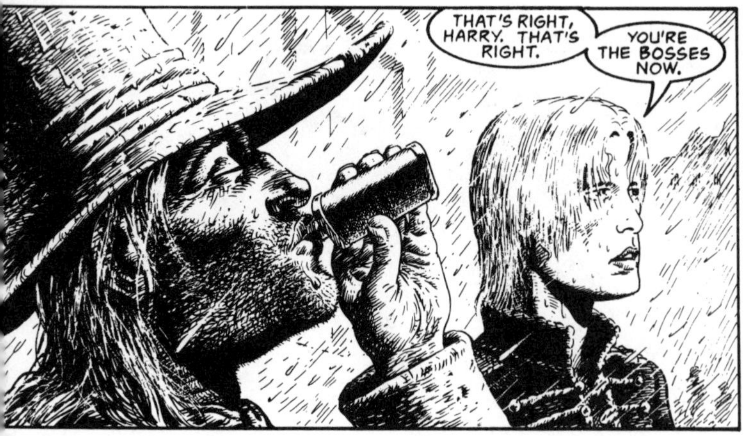
THAT'S RIGHT, HARRY. THAT'S RIGHT.
YOU'RE THE BOSSES NOW.

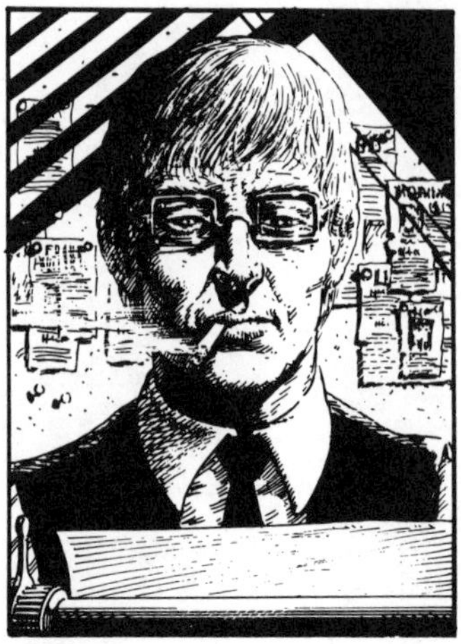

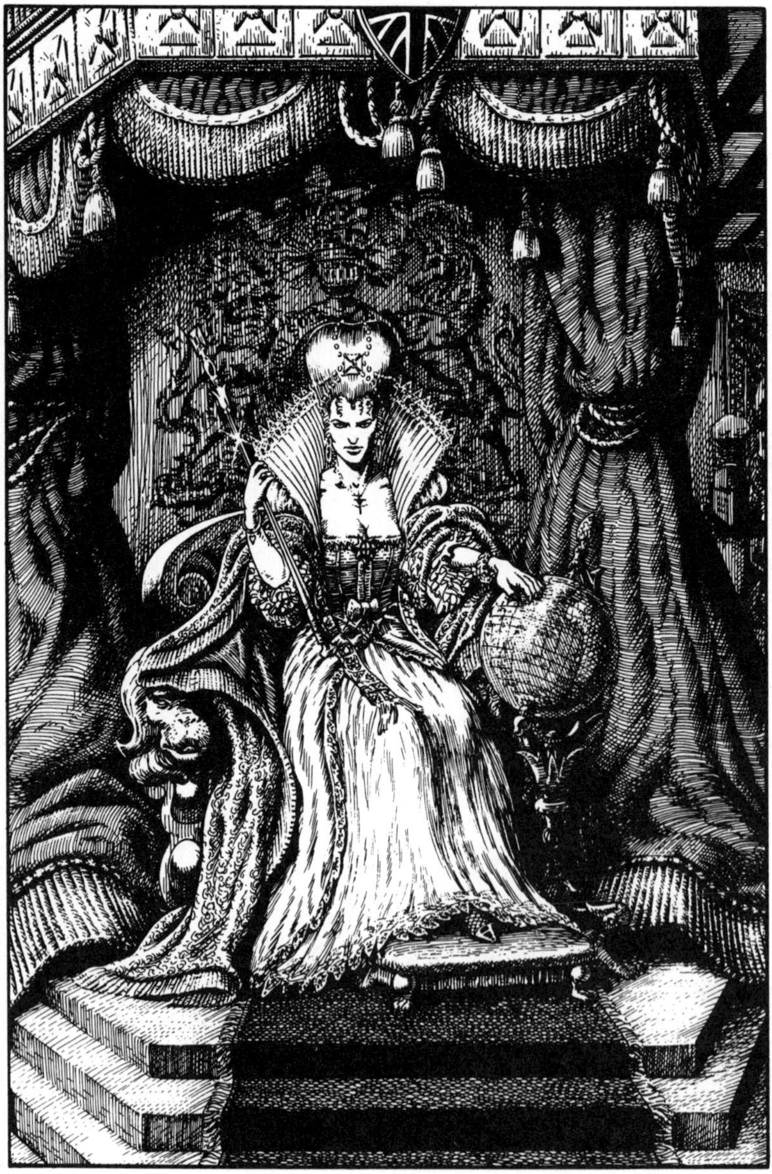

"And at this historic moment, as we see the victory firework display in the sky and hear the bells ringing all over London, we can only quote Saint Francis of Assisi:

'Where there is discord, may we bring harmony,
Where there is error, may we bring truth,
Where there is doubt, may we bring faith,
Where there is despair, may we bring hope.'

We shall have to learn again to be one nation, or one day we shall be no nation. We shall build here, on this precious stone set in the silver sea, a home fit for heroes."

Queen Anne I of Great Britain
Speech to the Nation

"The Terror," as it was called, lasted for about two weeks, although the street executions and mass hangings at the triple gallows at Tyburn went on for several months. The renamed "Royal Broadcasting Corporation" wireless channel relayed the show trials of Puritan generals and administrators to all the Nation. Bodies of the Cromwell dynasty were exhumed from Westminster Abbey and thrown to the mob for sport. History was already being rewritten in favor of the new regime.

I can see religious intolerance reaching another climax in the rigorous persecution of puritans who refuse to be amenable to the enactments of the proposed "Clarendon Code." Counter-insurgency Puritan liberation movements will spring up only to be crushed as Oliver Cromwell crushed the diggers and levellers in his time.

The popular image of the Restoration here in America, as a time of celebration and liberation was, nevertheless, more or less correct. The Parliamentarian Commonwealth was a joyless period in Britain's history and many ordinary citizens were genuinely glad that it was now over. The Restoration lifted a weight of oppression and people were eager to catch up on lost time.

People called it a "new Elizabethan Era" and the capital rejoiced. The church bells rang out and for the first time in years music other than that of the devotional kind was sung in public. Staunch puritans became outspoken royalists overnight. "Divine decadence" was the catchphrase at the myriad streetparties and parades. Fountains flowed with wine, and I actually saw fornicating couples on the sidewalks. The newly re-named streets were thronged with dancing celebrants, ballad-mongers, mummers and "refuseniks"-the Russian troops who declined returning to their post-revolutionary homeland and settled in Britain.

And colors! The monochrome city of Cromwell was painted rainbow hues and draped with bunting and flags, festooned with banners and patriotic posters featuring likenesses of the Queen. The new fashions too were outrageously flamboyant.

The whole had a dizzying effect and even I was swept along by the infectious mood. It was as I suffered from one of the many hangovers I incurred at that time that I first wondered what the future held for this country once the euphoria of the Restoration had worn off.

Over all the ceremonies and festivities loomed the benign presence of "the Iron Lady." Crowned by the new pope in Westminster Abbey, Queen Anne lost no time cementing the union between England, Scotland, Wales and Ireland and signing pacts of alliance with the U.C.A., France and the new communard rulers of Russia. You may remember the photographs of the treaty-signings that appeared in our newspapers, including the famous picture of Russian Premier Gorbachov hugging our vice-president, Mrs. Monroe.

The Queen utilized such publicity to present a positive image of herself to Britain and the world and made much use of her children, Prince Henry and Princess Mary, "Les Jumeaux Royaux," in this respect. Her appearances in public were numerous and always accompanied by an army of photographers and wireless reporters. She visited hospitals and unveiled monuments, such as the giant tableau in Greenwich honoring the heads of State of Britain's allies who perished in the treacherous gas attack by the desperate Puritans.

The most popular and most striking publicity image of the Queen, the famous "Hope and Glory" photograph, was taken during her speech at the lying-in-state of revolutionary General Rose Wylde, at Westminster. The dramatic pose, her face lit from beneath by the torches of the "Daughters of Albion" guard of honor, the tear curving down her cheek, combined into a moving and powerful icon.

But what do we really know of the Queen, voted "Woman of the Year" by our own "Picture Post" magazine only recently? Her speeches are stirring, true, but contain nothing of substance or intent. And now with Anne firmly ensconced on the Throne, these have become less and less frequent.

Her first act as Queen was to abolish the puppet "rump" parliament. This is one disturbing aspect. The distinction between Parliament, mother to our own, the democratic priciples which it represents and Cromwell's military dictatorship seems to have been blurred, purposefully erased, the ideals of the Commonwealth forgotten. Anne is now absolute monarch. She is now more powerful than Cromwell ever was.

And what of her resolution to build "a home fit for heroes?" An ostentacious show was made of the treasury funds made available for public works. The construction of new roads, bridges and railways were the physical manifestations of that investment. With the inception of "The Institute for the Diffusion of Knowledge," and its proposed scheme of school and university construction, the citizens had the promise of mass education for the first time. 60% of Britain is, at present, illiterate. Grants were made available to Artists and Theatricals. I can actually foresee a flowering of art and culture, a British renaissance that is long overdue.

This all sounds very rosy, but it seems to independent observers as if Anne is gearing the country up for something. The educational grants are biased towards science and engineering. The Tyneside dockbuilding project currently employing 80% of the Yorkshire laborforce seems far in excess of its requirement: to build a "merchant navy." How many ships does Britain need? It is already self-sufficient--a legacy of Puritan isolationism. Why the increasing number of armament factories?

With the Queen's abolition of Cromwell's No-Immigration policy, refugees from the once-proud Prussian Empire are flocking to Britain. The reason for Anne's much-publicised offer of sanctuary and funding to fleeing German scientists was dubious in the least, especially as they seem to have been allocated to defense-orientated projects.

The Super Powers are in decline. As Russia flounders in post-revolutionary turmoil and confusion, and Prussia is torn apart by civil war as each state champions its own pretender Kaiser, Britain builds in strength. And I remember.

I remember one day that fateful October. During the afternoon I heard Queen Anne rallying her freedom fighters with an impromtu speech. She ended with the phrase, "...and we shall build an Empire on which the sun will never set," ringing in the air. Later that night I encountered a remarkable man. He quoted Emerson to me: "Things are in the saddle and ride mankind."

Hiram Kowolsky
"The English Revolution"

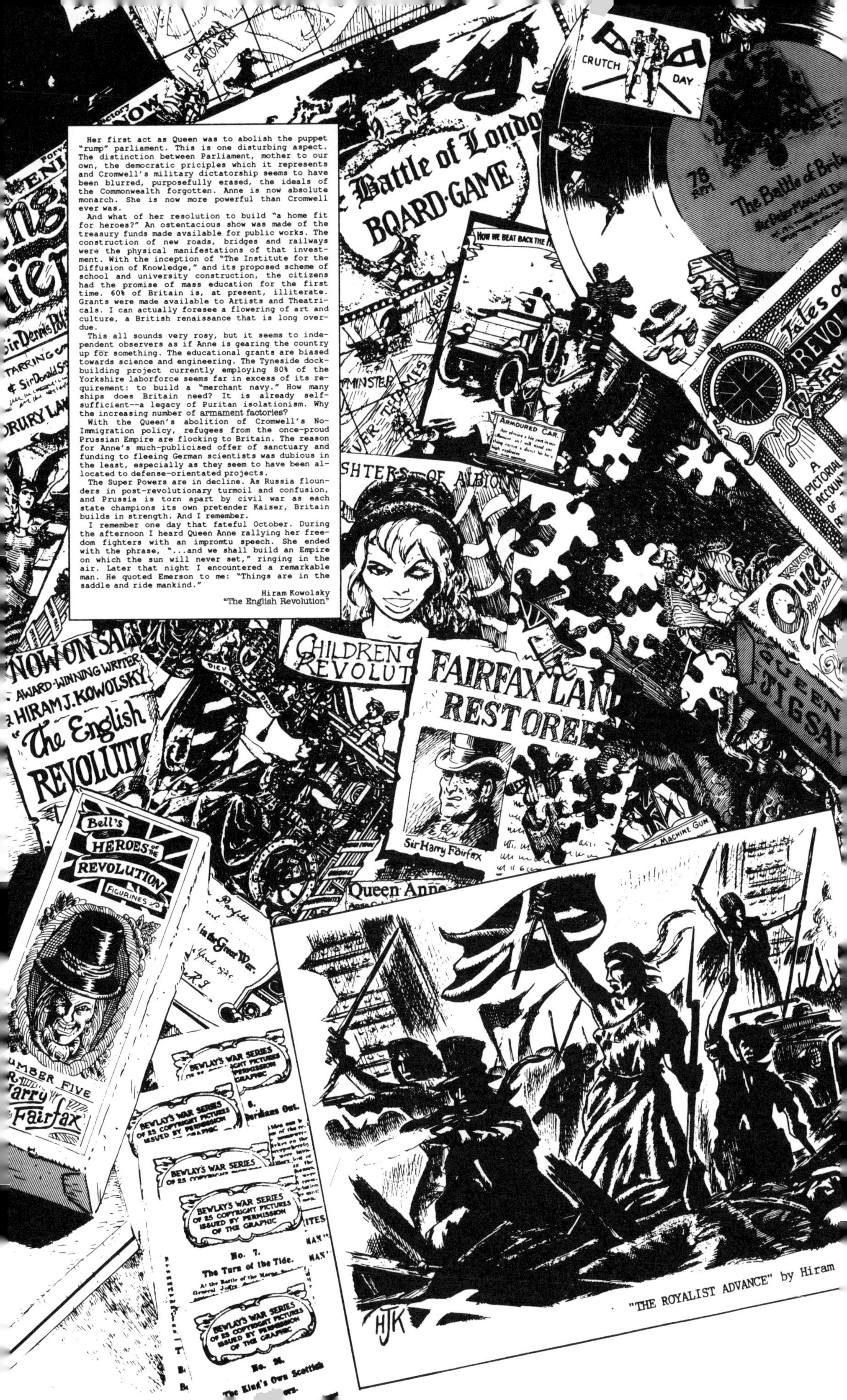

CRUTCH DAY
Battle of London
BOARD-GAME
78 RPM
ARMOURED CAR
CHILDREN OF REVOLUTION
FAIRFAX LAND RESTORED
Sir Harry Fairfax
MACHINE GUN
NOW ON SALE
AWARD-WINNING WRITER
HIRAM J. KOWOLSKY
The English REVOLUTION
Bell's HEROES OF THE REVOLUTION FIGURINES
NUMBER FIVE
Harry Fairfax
Queen Anne
BEWLAY'S WAR SERIES
OF 25 COPYRIGHT PICTURES ISSUED BY PERMISSION OF THE GRAPHIC
No. 7.
The Turn of the Tide.
No. 26.
HJK

"THE ROYALIST ADVANCE" by Hiram

TUES 31 OCT 18.45 HIGHGATE

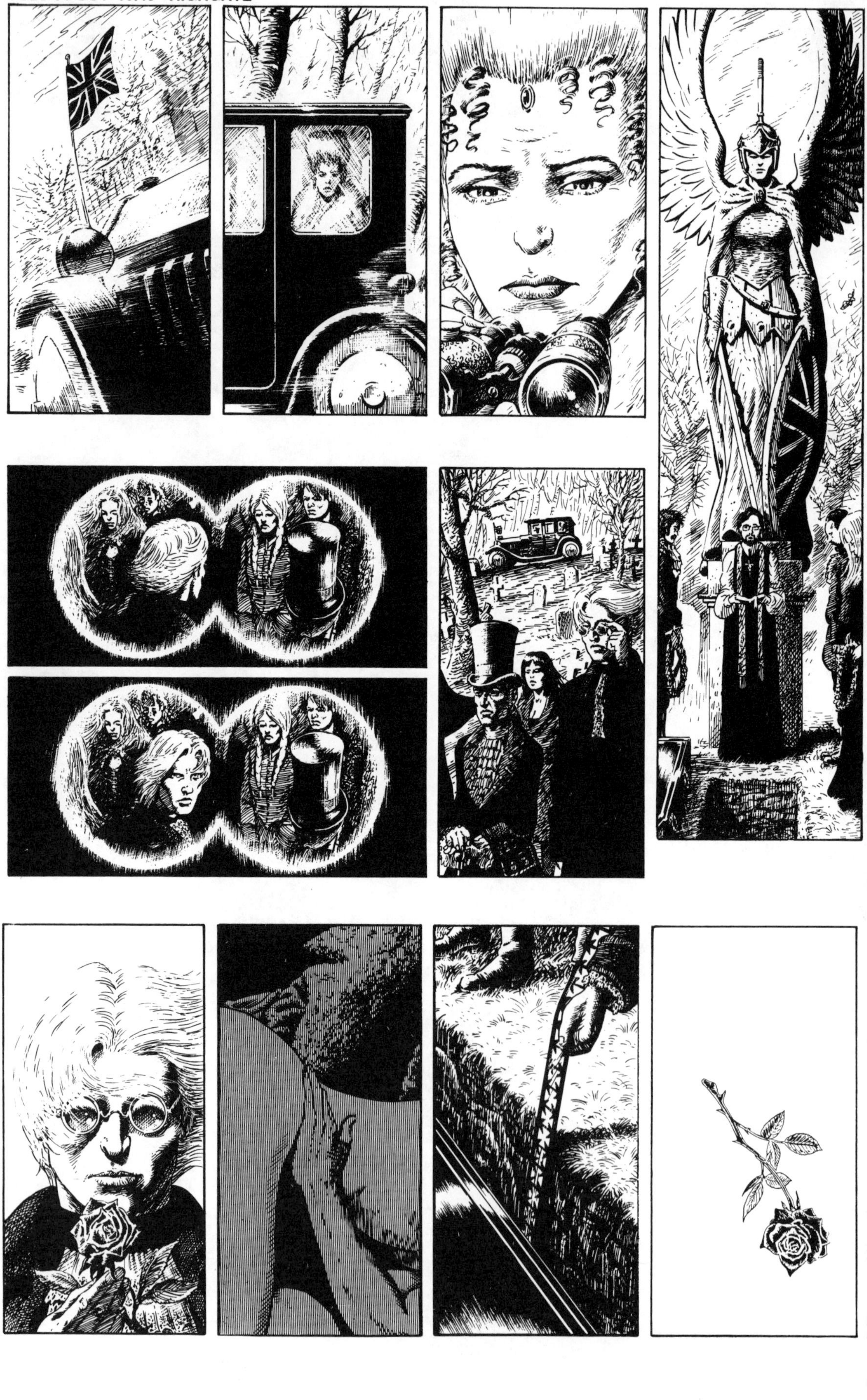

TUES 31 OCT 23.59 PARA 00.38.56 WHITBY

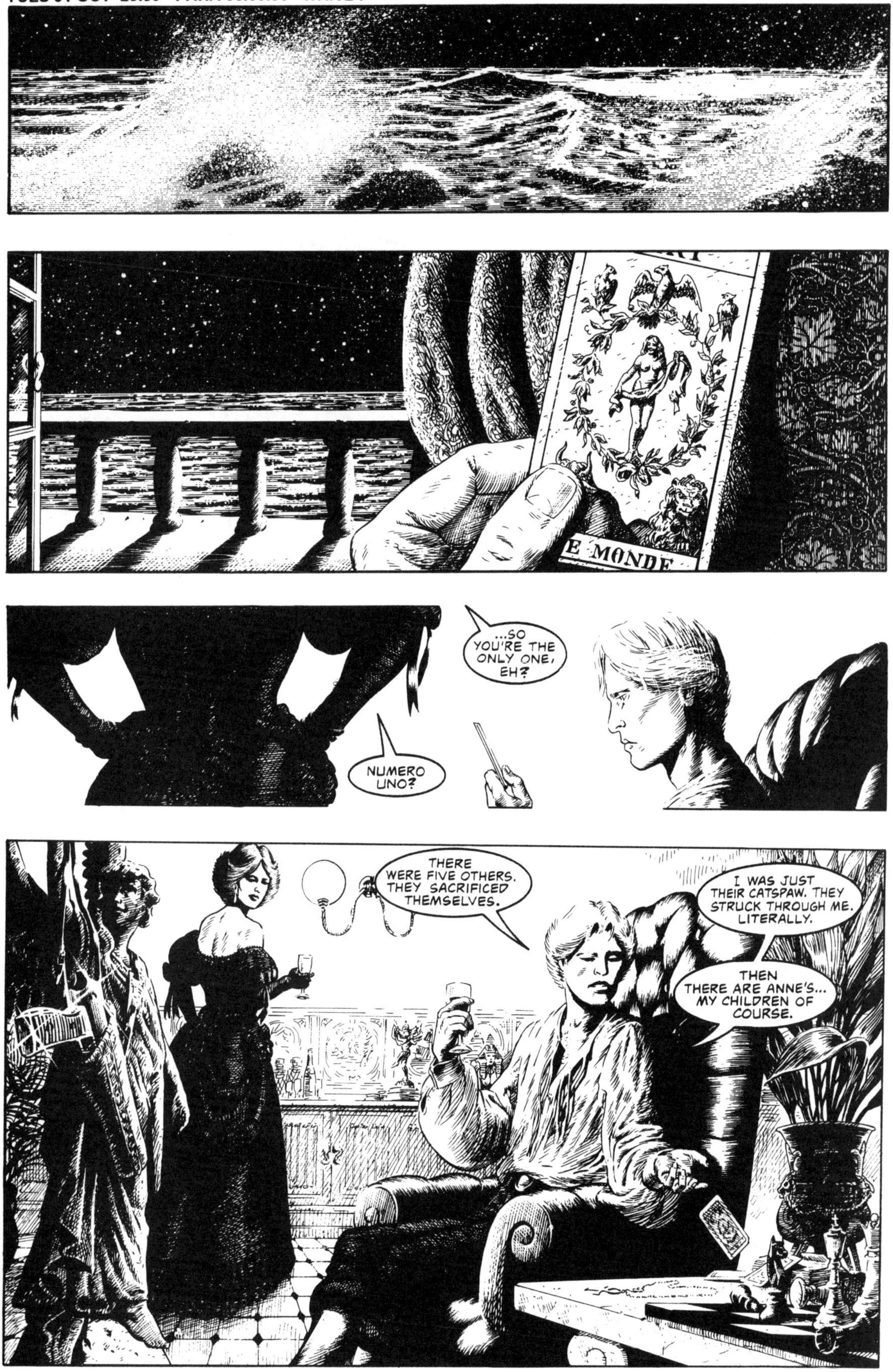
E MONDE
...SO YOU'RE THE ONLY ONE, EH?
NUMERO UNO?
THERE WERE FIVE OTHERS. THEY SACRIFICED THEMSELVES.
I WAS JUST THEIR CATSPAW. THEY STRUCK THROUGH ME. LITERALLY.
THEN THERE ARE ANNE'S... MY CHILDREN OF COURSE.

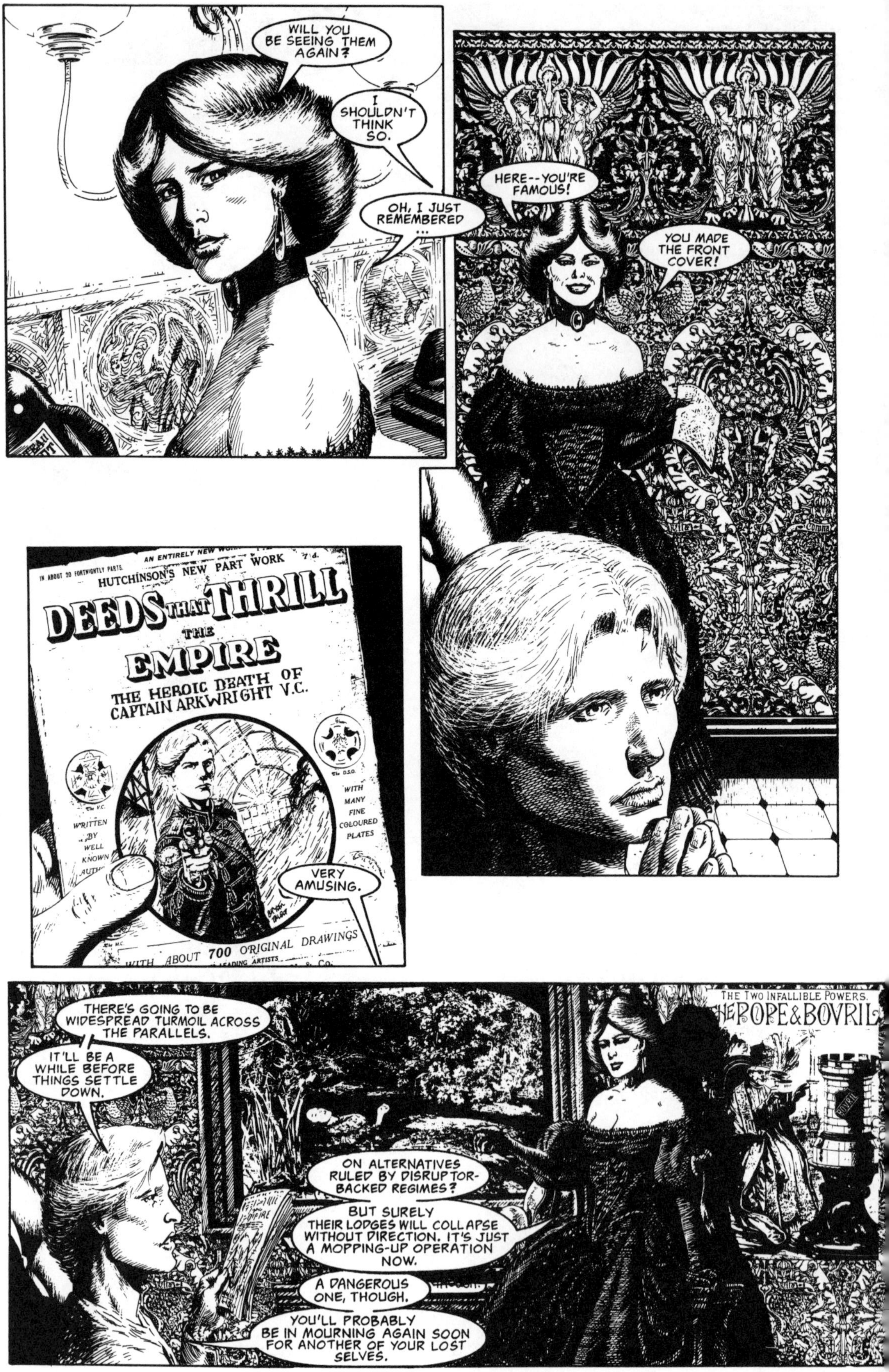
WILL YOU BE SEEING THEM AGAIN?
I SHOULDN'T THINK SO.
OH, I JUST REMEMBERED ...
HERE--YOU'RE FAMOUS!
YOU MADE THE FRONT COVER!
IN ABOUT 20 FORTNIGHTLY PARTS.
AN ENTIRELY NEW
HUTCHINSON'S NEW PART WORK
DEEDS THAT THRILL THE EMPIRE
THE HEROIC DEATH OF CAPTAIN ARKWRIGHT V.C.
The V.C.
The D.S.O.
WRITTEN BY WELL KNOWN
WITH MANY FINE COLOURED PLATES
WITH ABOUT 700 ORIGINAL DRAWINGS
VERY AMUSING.
THERE'S GOING TO BE WIDESPREAD TURMOIL ACROSS THE PARALLELS.
IT'LL BE A WHILE BEFORE THINGS SETTLE DOWN.
THE TWO INFALLIBLE POWERS.
THE POPE & BOVRIL
ON ALTERNATIVES RULED BY DISRUPTOR-BACKED REGIMES?
BUT SURELY THEIR LODGES WILL COLLAPSE WITHOUT DIRECTION. IT'S JUST A MOPPING-UP OPERATION NOW.
A DANGEROUS ONE, THOUGH.
YOU'LL PROBABLY BE IN MOURNING AGAIN SOON FOR ANOTHER OF YOUR LOST SELVES.

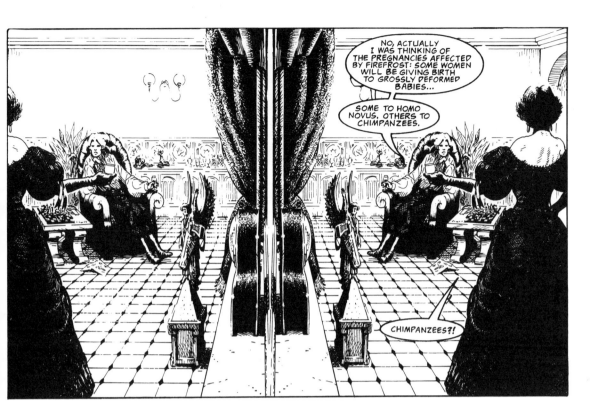

NO, ACTUALLY I WAS THINKING OF THE PREGNANCIES AFFECTED BY FIREFROST: SOME WOMEN WILL BE GIVING BIRTH TO GROSSLY DEFORMED BABIES...

SOME TO HOMO NOVUS, OTHERS TO CHIMPANZEES.

CHIMPANZEES?!

ONLY ONE PERCENT OF YOUR D.N.A., HUMAN D.N.A., DIFFERS FROM THAT OF THE CHIMPS. THE SAME AS THE DIFFERENCE BETWEEN YOURS AND MINE.

ARE YOU IMPLYING THAT YOU SEE ME AS A MONKEY?

NOT AT ALL. YOU'RE PSYCHIC. YOU'RE ONLY HALF AN APE.

WHY, YOU...

AS ABOVE, SO BELOW.

WELL, I CAN SEE THAT BEING GOD FOR A WHILE DIDN'T IMPROVE YOUR SENSE OF HUMOR.

I SUPPOSE THAT NOVUS WILL SUPERCEDE SAPIENS?

EVENTUALLY.

THIS IS AN IMPORTANT HISTORICAL STAGE--AN EON-SHIFT. WE'RE POISED ON THE DAWN OF A NEW AGE--HUMANITY FREED TO FOLLOW ITS OWN DESTINY.

AQUARIUS?

CHILDHOOD'S END.

MM. I'LL GET ANOTHER BOTTLE FROM THE CELLAR.

MIRANDA WAS RIGHT.

LUTHER?! WHAT ARE YOU DOING WITH THE...?

NO! I MEAN YOU SHOULDN'T...

THE...THE POWER POD WILL...

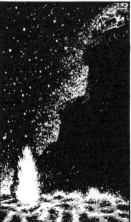

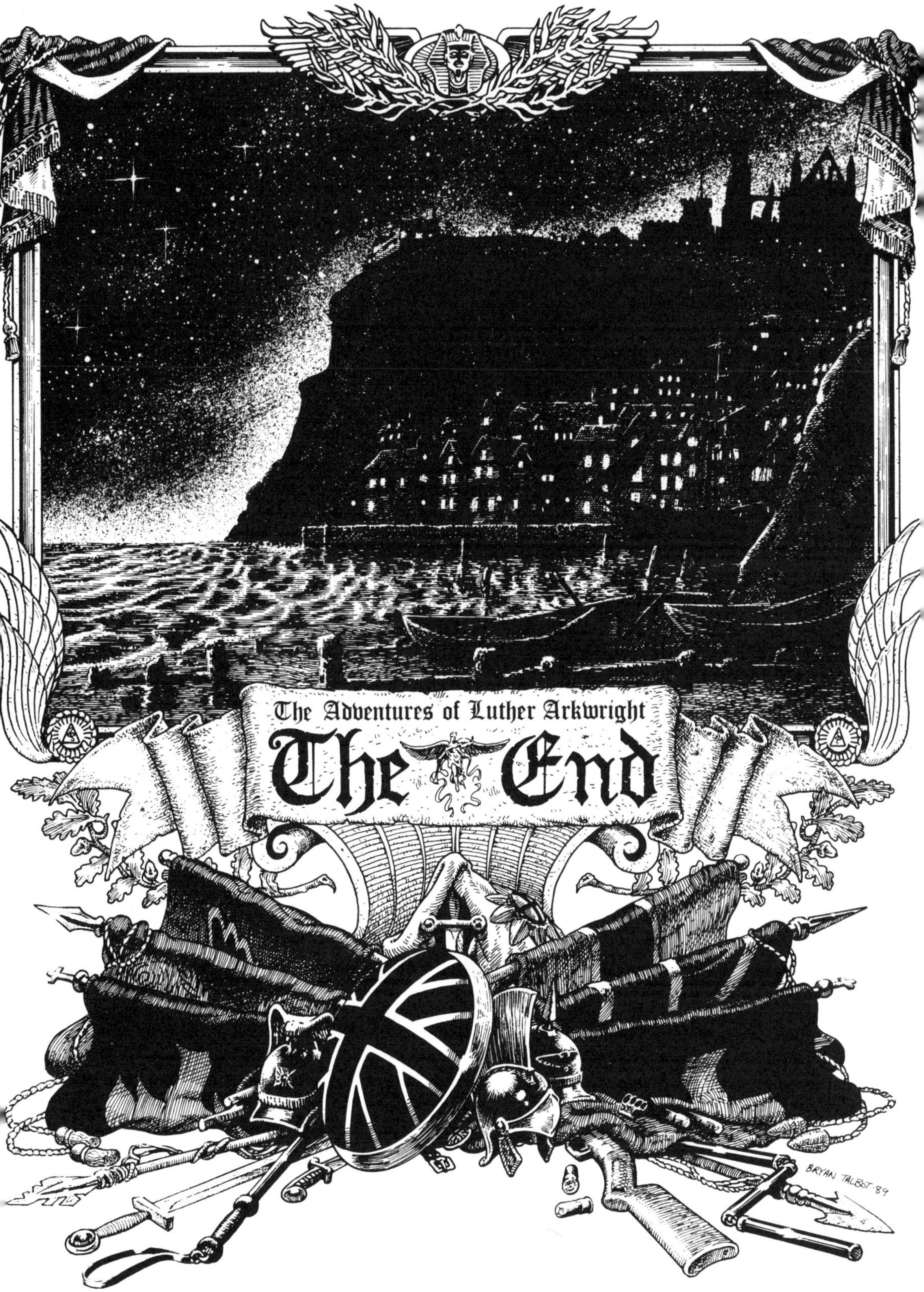
The Adventures of Luther Arkwright
The End
BRYAN TALBOT '89

"The activities of life are governed by the second law of thermodynamics. This says that the natural state of matter is chaos and that all things tend to run down and become random and disordered. Living systems consist of highly organised matter. They create order out of disorder, but it is a constant struggle against the process of disruption."

Lyall Watson

The Adventures of Luther Arkwright
is dedicated to Serge Boissevain, whose
enthusiasm and support made it possible.

Many thanks to the following artists
for contributing to the "ephemera" page:
John Coulthart, Fox, Dave Windett,
Chris Brindle.

Thanks also to Lawrence Dean for
proofreading, and to my family for putting
up with me for the duration of this work.

series editor & publisher Mike Richardson
collection editor Lynn Adair
collection designer Amy Arendts
collection design manager Brian Gogolin

executive vice president Neil Hankerson
vice president of publishing David Scroggy
vice president of sales & marketing Lou Bank
vice president of finance Andy Karabatsos
general counsel Mark Anderson
director of editorial adm. Meloney C. Chadwick
creative director Randy Stradley
director of production & design Cindy Marks
art director Mark Cox
computer graphics director Sean Tierney
director of sales & marketing Michael Martens
director of licensing Tod Borleske
director of m.i.s. Dale LaFountain
director of human resources Kim Haines

Published by
Dark Horse Comics, Inc.
10956 SE Main Street
Milwaukie, OR 97222

First edition: July 1997
ISBN: 1-56971-255-7

1 3 5 7 9 10 8 6 4 2
Printed in Canada

This book collects issues one through nine of the Dark Horse comic-book series *The Adventures of Luther Arkwright*™.